IN GOOD SOIL

Other seeds fell in good soil and produced their crop, some a hundredfold, some sixty, some thirty.

Matthew 13:8

IN GOOD SOIL

The Founding of

Saint Louis Priory and School

1954 – 1973

by

Timothy Horner OSB

Saint Louis Abbey Press

Library of Congress
Catalog Card Number 2001 126956
ISBN 0-9662104-1-7

Printed in the United States of America

CONTENTS

ILLUSTRATIONS (after p. 6)

PREFACE

WHEN I joined the Abbey of Ampleforth in northern England, one of the thoughts I had was, "Too bad I shall never see the United States". I need not have worried. In due course, Ampleforth Abbey made a foundation in Saint Louis, Missouri and I was sent to be one of the first three monks of the new monastery. Again in due course, Saint Louis Priory and Saint Louis Priory School came into existence and achieved a degree of maturity such that it seemed worth recording the stages of their growth. Early in 1995, Abbot Luke Rigby, abbot of what had by then become Saint Louis Abbey, suggested that one of the original three monks should undertake the task. As Father Columba Cary-Elwes, the first prior of the Priory, had died and as Father Luke, was already too busy, there was only one of the three left.

There was no shortage of material: Father Columba kept a diary, rather full for the early days, but became more sketchy as time went on. The group of our local supporters, which was incorporated as Catholic Preparatory School for Boys but soon became the Saint Louis Priory Society, kept good minutes of its meetings. I kept for each school year an Organization File, into which were put copies of all the documents considered to be important. There were the other files of monastery and school and the memories of the monks who had been here for all or part of the period 1954-73, which is the period covered here. 1973 marks the end of an era because in that year Saint Louis Priory became independent of the mother abbey.

This book is about a dream that became a reality. The principal characters are the original group of dreamers in Saint Louis, Missouri, and their successors; the monks of Ampleforth Abbey in Yorkshire, England; the men who, over the years, came from England to establish Saint Louis Priory and School and the men from the United States and Canada who joined them; and--a cast of thousands--the boys in the school and their families. There was also a much smaller group: the monks of Portsmouth Priory, Rhode Island and the faculty of their school, Portsmouth Priory School. That was the school attended by the sons of several of our dreamers, and its monks, especially Prior Aelred Graham, a monk of Ampleforth on loan to Portsmouth, were the essential link between the dreamers of Saint Louis and the Benedictine schoolmasters of Ampleforth. The book is also, to an extent that surprised the author, about Anglo-American interplay in character, mindset, language and humor, and much else, as will be seen. The monks were trained at Ampleforth, but never intended to simply duplicate Ampleforth's monastery or school

Following the example of Julius Caesar, I have referred to myself in the third person. It could hardly be otherwise. The style and spelling are intended to be American, except where we quote documents written by Englishmen, but no doubt some anglicisms have crept in. It was peculiarly difficult to write "skeptical". Another difficulty was that so many of the small incidents that I remember involved myself, which is why I remember them. Others have been asked to contribute their memories but little has been forthcoming. And yet anecdotes are revealing in a history such as this. In 1928 Jean Guiraud published his *Histoire Partiale, Histoire Vraie* (Biased history is true history) . We might adapt his title and say in a monastic context *Histoire Anecdotique, Histoire Vraie* (Anecdotal history is true history). A community comes alive in its folklore.

There is a difference of style between Part 1 and Part 2: the reader may find the former, which ends in 1960 with our first graduation, more attractive and the latter more informative. This is partly because most of our adventures occurred in the earlier days when everything was new to us. As we became more settled and experienced, our life took on a more even tenor. But Horace in his *Ars Poetica, 343,* writes, "*Omne tulit punctum qui miscuit utile dulci*", which by a slight stretch one might translate, "Everyone applauds one who mingles the attractive and the informative".

I must thank Abbot Luke, who gave me the task and set me off on it; Abbot Patrick Barry for improvements, especially typographical, Father Paul, who has supplied many facts, and fellow-monks for answering questions and checking data; Julie Constantino and the staff of the Development Office, who have given constant help, Brian Barry, Madeleine Rourke and Terri Wood for their expertise at the computer; Marty McCabe who arranged a memory-storming session with several faculty members of long standing; and all those who have made suggestions for this work's improvement.

Saint Louis, 24 August 2001 Timothy Horner OSB

Part One: Origins: 1954 - 1960

List of Abbreviations:

CCE	*Father Columba Cary-Elwes, O.S.B. (Father Columba)*
EBC	*English Benedictine Congregation*
INC	*Catholic Preparatory School for Boys, Incorporated*
JH	*Junior House*
JLR	*Father Jerome Luke Rigby, O.S.B. (Father Luke)*
JMTH	*Father John Michael Timothy Horner, O.S.B. (Father Timothy)*
LS	*In the Lord's Service*
OSB	*Order of Saint Benedict*
PS	*Priory School: the first name of the school's newspaper*
Record	*The Record, the school's newspaper*
Shield	*The Shield, the school's yearbook*
SLAJ	*Saint Louis Abbey Journal*
SLPJ	*Saint Louis Priory Journal*

APERITIF

SAINT Louis Priory School was due to open its doors for the first time on Thursday, 6 September 1956. Earlier that week, just as we were thinking that, although the boys' lockers had not yet arrived, at least the buildings were for the most part ready, a large snag appeared in the shape of a small man from the County Building Department. He met Father Timothy, the headmaster, outside the remodeled barn, in which the classrooms now were, and said "Where are the rest rooms?" Father Timothy pointed proudly to the converted equipment shed a few yards away, to which the boys would walk. "And what will they do if it rains?" "I suppose they will get wet." The small man then said it was contrary to the building code not to have an under-cover way from classrooms to rest rooms and that unless we provided one, he would close the school. As this was two days before we opened, Father Timothy did not take him seriously and said we would look into it. The man went away muttering threats and brandishing a red closure notice. Father Timothy did remember to tell Father Luke, our procurator, or business manager.

This covered way had been in the plans for the remodeling, but had been taken out for the time being to ensure that other more important items were ready for the opening of school. On the first day of classes the official came back, met Father Luke and asked how things were going. Father Luke thanked him and said everything was fine. "Oh no it's not" said the little man. "You have no occupancy permit for this building and you are breaking the law. You have three days to get that under-cover walkway, or I will close the school." Father Luke then called John O'Brien, our contractor for the remodeling, who said he would take care of the little man--those were not his exact words--whom he knew from of old, and who had at one time worked for him. Soon after, we constructed the covered way, which in due course became a home for bumble bees, which stung no boys, but should, in fairness, have stung the little man.

We had by now classrooms, a faculty and a schedule, textbooks and athletic equipment, a football field ready and tennis courts nearly ready, set lists and a letter indicating how the boys should dress. We had thirty students. The first five boys in alphabetical order were of Scandinavian, French, English, German and Irish origin respectively, which was typical except for the absence of Italian and Hispanic names.

What we did not have was desks. Father Luke had ordered them in plenty of time and delivery had been promised for August. Then it was "Next week, Father", then "Tomorrow morning, Father", then "This afternoon, Father". They did come in eighty cartons late in the afternoon of the day before school was to open. We had them put into one of the four classrooms in the barn, which had been converted into four classrooms. Father Columba, the Prior of Saint Louis Priory, was busy in the monastic library; Father Luke was down town doing our final shopping after having dealt with the boilerman, the electrician, the plumber, the builders and sundry others, including the little man; Father Ian, our fourth monk, who had arrived a month before school was due to open, and Father Timothy were making shelves for the sports store, when our sporting goods salesman came to ask if the football helmets had arrived. No? he would see they were here right away. Another truck arrived with an enormous man and two freezers. He disposed of them. Then, thinking "we had practically nothing left to do except to unpack the desks and chairs . . . arrange the classrooms, assemble the tables for the dining room and arrange that, sort out the recreation room, wax and polish all the floors, then sit down and compose a rousing harangue to deliver to the boys on the following morning,"[1] we decided to say Vespers, have supper and then unpack the desks.

After supper we opened the cartons, and discovered that the desks were not assembled but "KD", that is, knocked down, and that most of the pre-drilled holes for the screws had been drilled in the wrong places; and we had no power drill. That meant using a brace and bit. There were thirty desks and a few spares, and a number of holes for each desk. We had a night's work before us. Providentially just at that moment Mr. Charles F. Bealke, accompanied by his son Charlie, who was to start school with us the following day, came by to bring us a sack of potatoes. They made the mistake of asking how things were going. We told them, and they went home to get us a power drill, came back and stayed to help. By great good fortune we also had staying with us two Old Boys (alumni) from Ampleforth (our school in England), Randal Marlin and Frank van den Berg, otherwise we might still have been at work when the school bus arrived.

In the midst of our labors we had a completely unexpected excitement: there in the middle of the floor was a huge tarantula, of

---

[1] JMTH, Letter dated 11 September 1956, to the Prior of Ampleforth; and LS p.47.

the tropical not the Missouri variety, brightly colored with black, vivid blue, green, red and perhaps other colors on its body, and with long black legs. Its body was large and very deep, almost a cube, and its legs long enough that it would have covered a large plate. It was really more like a little octopus, and had one leg that seemed to oscillate independently of the others. Perhaps it had been damaged in transit. The desks must have been made somewhere where tarantulas are native, and the spider must have jumped into a carton and hibernated. It was quite lively and no doubt hungry when it emerged. It would have been a striking sight anywhere and at any time. On this rather tense occasion it was a godsend. There was a cry of "kill it", but Father Timothy put it on one of the desk tops and deposited it outside the barn. It occurred to him later that this humane act was not very wise. It would have been an ill omen if one of the boys had been bitten by a tarantula on the first day of school.

We were not well-practiced assemblers and so we did not finish until around midnight. Any hope of a good night's rest before our opening day had long vanished, but we did now have two classrooms full of desks. As we went wearily to bed someone said, quoting Stanley Holloway, "Let battle commence"; he was a prophet.

1. The Cloister Plan: architect's impression. *(see p. 52)*

2. At Ampleforth, Father Luke, Prior Columba, Fathers Timothy and Ian receive news from Saint Louis. *(see p. 42)*

3. Fred Switzer greets Fathers Luke and Timothy and Prior Columba at Union Station, Saint Louis, 19 October 1955. *(see p. 47)*

RESIDENCE OF MR. & MRS. ALBERT C. STANNARD, ST. LOUIS COUNTY, MISSOURI

4a. The Stannard House (now, the Switzer House) (see pp. 47-49)

4b. The Archway building and the Barn. (see p. 52)

5. *Fred Switzer addresses Inc.* *(see p. 12)*

6. Fathers Brendan and Thomas, Prior Columba, Fathers Ian, Luke, Timothy and Austin under the elms on the lawn behind the Stannard House. *(see p. 59)*

7. Our first Summer School, June - July 1956. *(see p. 95)*

8. Abbot Herbert Byrne blesses the foundation stone of the monastery with Cardinal Ritter, Prior Tunink of Pevely, Father Clarke, pastor of Saint Monica, Creve Coeur, Prior Columba and Father Timothy on 4 November 1957. (see pp. 160-61)

9a. Gymnasium (see p. 179)

9b. Church (1962) and Monastery (1958) with Science Wing (1959) in background. The high school was built in 1969-70 along the line of the road between the church and the science wing. (see pp. 226-34, 131-38 and 173-74)

10a. At our first graduation, Cardinal Ritter congratulates our National Merit finalists, George Hellmuth, Ed Boedeker and Fran Oates, June 1960. (see pp. 203-6)

10b. Graduation on the lawn of the Stannard House. (see p. 290)

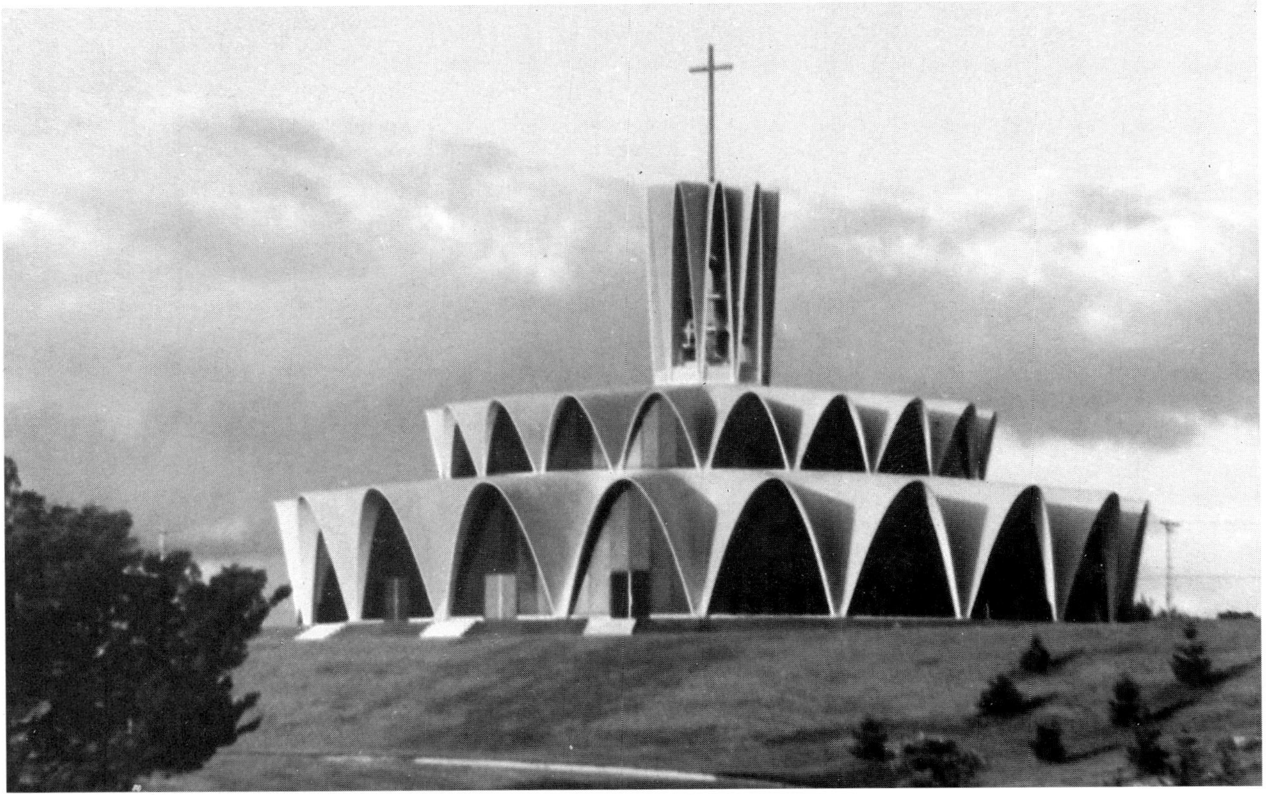

11. *The Church of Saint Louis Priory.* *(see pp. 226-34)*

12 a. The first quadrant of forms, with plywood in place for the initial pouring. (see p. 227)

b. The first form is finally extracted. (see p. 227

c. The Interior of the bays: with wooden laths for the plaster. (see p. 228)

d. The complete shell. (see p. 228

13. Father and Son dinner, 1962. Tom Tobin is at the right-end of the middle row. *(see p. 375)*

14a. Father Austin keeps his music students busy. *(see p. 360)*

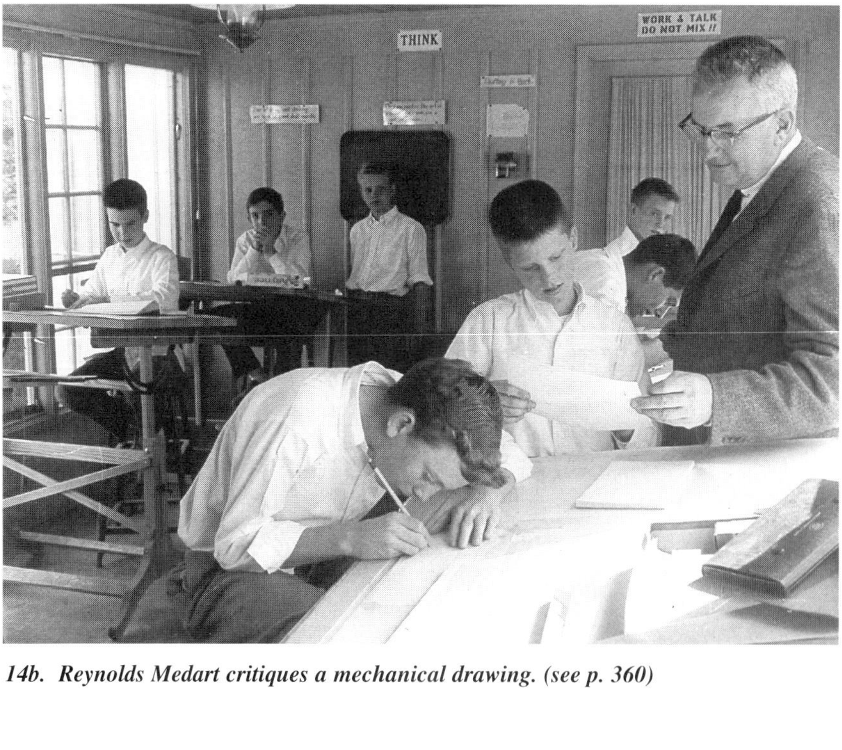

14b. Reynolds Medart critiques a mechanical drawing. *(see p. 360)*

15a. Bill Daake outreaches an opponent. *(see p. 349)*

15b. Priory's Jim Merenda finds running room. *(see p. 353)*

16. Father Timothy, Prior Columba, Abbot Luke, Abbot Patrick Barry of Ampleforth and Father Ian after Abbot Luke's elevation in 1989. Prior Columba, Abbot Patrick and Father Ian were visiting for the occasion. *(see pp. 416-17)*

CHAPTER 1

Background

IF such was the preparation, clearly this was to be no ordinary enterprise. What, then, were the events that led to this hectic preparation? They will be easier to follow if we recognize that there were three main groups involved in them: the first was the group of Catholic men in Saint Louis, who made the invitation; the second was the monks of the Benedictine Abbey of Ampleforth in England, who accepted the invitation; the third was the monks, and especially the prior of Portsmouth Priory (now Abbey) and School in Rhode Island, which was the vital connecting link.

We start in Saint Louis, a city on the Mississippi just below its junction with the Missouri, founded in 1764 by French traders from the South, and named for King Saint Louis IX of France. The early civic leaders were mostly Catholic but in the westward migration from the East, White Anglo-Saxon Protestants came to dominate. Even so, after World War II, the population was around 40% Catholic and Catholics were beginning to be influential again in the professions and in business. In this city, from soon after the end of World War II, a group of leading Catholics had been discussing the idea of a Catholic school which would offer something different from what was offered by the existing schools, good as those were.

As long ago as 1938 Archbishop, later Cardinal, John J. Glennon had, for this very purpose, commissioned his lawyer, Mr. Clifford Greve, to buy a property in Huntleigh Woods in West Saint Louis County, provided that all the residents of the area agreed. A meeting of the residents was held, eighteen of the twenty attended and agreed. The two absentees were Catholic. They were thought likely to agree, but in fact they did not, and the scheme fell through. So the sons of the leading Catholics in Saint Louis continued to attend the existing Catholic schools in Saint Louis, or schools such as Portsmouth Priory School in Rhode Island, a Benedictine boarding school but some fifteen hundred miles away, or Saint Louis Country Day School, an excellent local day school but not Catholic.

In 1946 Cardinal Glennon died and Archbishop, later Cardinal, Joseph E. Ritter succeeded him. The members of the group we have mentioned continued their discussions, and when they were not discussing, were involved in what much later became known as networking. As a result many influential people were made aware of the scheme, and in varying degrees were interested in it. Mr. William Garneau Weld was the chairman of the group, and members included Messrs. Clarkson Carpenter, Jr. and Samuel J. Mitchell, who made inquiries about real estate, and many prominent Catholic laymen.

Quite independently, Dr. J. Gerard Mudd, an alumnus of Canterbury School in Connecticut, a boys' college-preparatory school run by lay Catholics, and his friend Mr. Frank E. Brennan had been airing a similar idea and in 1953 wrote about it to the Archbishop. Frank was the salesman and Gerry contributed youth, enthusiasm, a keen interest in education and a natural talent for acting as a catalyst. The Archbishop replied favorably and suggested that they amalgamate with the first group, which they did. The group approached the Benedictines at Labadie, just outside Saint Louis. They were not interested, but Mr. Henry C. Hughes, a friend of these monks, was, and joined the group. Soon after this, Clarkson Carpenter introduced to the group a determined lawyer of Saint Louis, whose father had established a very successful licorice factory downtown. This was Mr. Fred M. Switzer, Jr. He proved to be the leader they had been seeking and to him in due course Bill Weld cheerfully yielded the leadership of the group. Fred saw that the group's hand would be greatly strengthened and their determination much more evident if they had some land.

We must now consider why the remote Abbey of Ampleforth, on the edge of the Yorkshire Moors in England, was interested in the invitation from Saint Louis, Missouri, a place virtually unknown at the time to the majority of the Yorkshire monks. Then we shall be in a better position to understand the growth of the monastery and school, and to contemplate the foundation's labor pains, its pangs of birth, its early struggles through infancy and adolescence, and to see it achieve in due course a measure of maturity.

But first we need to be able to refer to the new foundation. Its official name was to be the Priory of Saint Mary and Saint Louis. That was never an easy mouthful either for everyday conversation or for those on the sidelines who wished to encourage our various teams. It was soon shortened to Saint Louis Priory, and that in its turn to the Priory or just Priory; and those are the names we shall use here.

The Priory was to be a foundation from the Benedictine Abbey[2] of Ampleforth in Yorkshire, a county (now divided into three counties) in the north of England. The Ampleforth community is itself the lineal descendant of the royal abbey founded in the mists of early English history at Westminster, then on the Island of Thorney, in the marshes west of the small city of London.

There are legends of Westminster Abbey's foundation by King Lucius in A.D.184, well before the beginning of Christian monasticism, its restoration by King Sebert in 604, its miraculous consecration by Saint Peter at the same time, its endowment by a succession of kings and its nurture by a long line of Popes, but these stories are based on a collection of much later, and unreliable, charters. The date of its foundation is therefore obscure, but it is a matter of history that between 957 and 970 it was restored by Saint Dunstan, and again restored by King Edward the Confessor soon after 1042. It was a royal abbey then, and still treasures its personal connection with the monarch. All appointments to the Chapter of Westminster are still made by the monarch without intervention by the Prime Minister. The Abbey was also placed immediately under the protection of the Holy See of Rome. It was a privileged and richly endowed house, and saw the coronation of the kings and queens of England, as it still does.[3]

---

[2] Benedictines all over the world are often referred to as the Benedictine Order as though they were organized from the top down in a pyramidal structure. In reality, the effective unit is the abbey or priory. In 1215 Pope Innocent III instructed these units to group themselves together in Congregations by countries. By 1218 the English monasteries had complied, certainly the first and possibly the only Congregation to do so, and thus became the senior Benedictine Congregation. The English Benedictine Congregation (E.B.C.) later yielded pride of place to the Cassinese Congregation because Monte Cassino, whence the name "Cassinese", was Saint Benedict's own monastery. Each congregation is headed by an Abbot President. These congregations in turn are gathered into a loose Confederation or Order under the Abbot Primate, who resides in Rome. When a monk makes his vow of obedience, he makes it to the abbot of his abbey, not to the Abbot President, nor to the Abbot Primate. If either of the latter were to tell a monk to stop smoking, he would attach great weight to what they said, but if his own abbot told him, he would stop.

[3] Abbot Justin McCann, Dom Columba Cary-Elwes, edd. *Ampleforth and its Origins* (London: Burns Oates and Washbourne, 1952) chapters 3 and 4; and Edward Carpenter, ed. *A House of Kings* (London: John Baker, 1966)

King Henry VIII started in 1535 the dissolution of the monasteries in England, but Westminster was one of the last houses to be dissolved, signing only on 16 January 1540 the deed by which it surrendered into the king's hands the whole monastery and all its possessions "spontaneously and of our own free will" and "forever".[4]

Sixteen years later under the Catholic Queen Mary there was a brief restoration, but under Queen Elizabeth in 1559 the suppression became final. Some of the monks were imprisoned, some dispersed to various parts of England, some went abroad. One of those who was frequently and perhaps continuously in prison was Father Sigebert Buckley, who, in his late eighties, when he was the last surviving member of the English Benedictine Congregation and therefore had the legal power to do so, aggregated to the Congregation, which was himself, two young men who wished to be English Benedictine monks. This occurred in 1607, and Father Sigebert died in 1610. On this slender thread depends our continuity with the pre-Dissolution English Benedictines.[5]

After that, since monasteries had been made illegal in England, those who wished to become monks had to go abroad, but this too was soon made illegal. Nonetheless young Englishmen still slipped away across the Channel either to join existing monasteries abroad or to found new ones. The descendant of Westminster was established at Dieulouard in Eastern France. Starting there in 1608, the community, which included the two young monks aggregated by Father Sigebert, gradually built up both its numbers and its finances, the latter with the help of a school, a fishery and a brewery, but they never made the liqueur, Benedictine. There they stayed until the French Revolution forced them to seek a new home.

They left Dieulouard in 1793. Fortunately, by that time the English Penal Laws against Catholics had become in most respects a dead letter and these monks were able to settle again in their own country first in Lancashire and then, in 1802, at Ampleforth. There they

---

[4] McCann, *op.cit.* p.53

[5] That he had this power was one of the results of the effective compliance of the English Benedictines with the command of Pope Innocent III in 1215, as in note 2 above. Had they failed to comply, as most, and perhaps all, other Benedictines did fail, Father Sigebert would have been able to make the two men monks of Westminster but not of the English Benedictine Congregation, which would not have existed. The present expression of this power may be found in the 1983 Code of Canon Law, Canon 120, 2.

established a school for boys and at the same time continued to serve the parishes or "missions" which monks from Dieulouard had served, often at great risk, during the previous two centuries. They never brewed beer nor fished commercially.

In 1952 Ampleforth celebrated with some éclat its sesqui-centennial. The monastic community was observant and hard-working and by then numbered over one hundred and forty men and was attracting novices; their school's reputation was high (a few years later it was judged to be "the best buy in British education") the number of students, then about six hundred and fifty, was increasing and, to all appearances, likely to continue to do so; morale was high. Then on January 25 1954, Father Paul Nevill, headmaster for the previous thirty years, died. As it was he who had led the school to prominence, his death was felt to be the end of an era, and by the same token, an opportunity for new ventures.

It is not surprising that in these circumstances the monks had thoughts of making a foundation. What they had in mind at the time was not a monastery to run a school like Ampleforth, still less a foundation abroad, but rather a monastery in or near a city, preferably in the north of England, with a school serving needy families. The abbot had in fact for many years been receiving invitations and suggestions for ventures, educational and missionary, both in England and abroad, even as far away as Thailand. These were all investigated, but none of them won approval. Two were more attractive than the others and were the subject of earnest discussion: one was turned down for geographical, the other for financial reasons. The latter, for a Grammar School in Warrington, a city in the North-West of England and one where Ampleforth manned at that time four parishes, had seemed particularly attractive, and many monks both at Ampleforth and on Ampleforth's parishes had been deeply disappointed that it was financially impossible. There was, then, a strong but unsatisfied urge to "do something" and some frustration that money was so great an obstacle. This was good soil for seeds such as those soon to be brought from Saint Louis.

CHAPTER 2

Preparations in Saint Louis

FROM the time that Fred Switzer joined the group in Saint Louis, action predominated. This is not to imply that the original group had been inert. They had been in close touch both with the Archbishop and with one of his leading priests, Monsignor Charleville B. Faris, pastor of Annunziata Church in Ladue, at whose parish many of their meetings were held; they had made the project known to a large number of influential Catholic lay men and women; they had laid the groundwork for the organization which in due course became the Saint Louis Abbey Society; and no less important than this, their discussions had brought to the surface many of the significant issues. Although they had not reached decisions on all of them, they had clarified what decisions were needed. These were substantial achievements.

In pursuit of land, the group first looked at an eighteen acre property in Ladue called Trail's End Stables, most of which is now the Racquet Club West, and bought an option on it. Although the asking price ($300,000) of the Trail's End property was so high and its re-zoning evoked such strong opposition from the local residents that the idea had been dropped by May 1954, and although what we later acquired was far more suitable, this was the first step from dream toward reality. The group's first written record states that "a special meeting of Catholic men interested in the formation of a preparatory school for boys" was held at 8.00 p.m. on 13 May 1954 at Annunziata Parish.

Fifteen men were present. At the meeting, Bill Weld, still acting as chairman, outlined progress so far; the idea of buying Trail's End Stables was abandoned, and a motion for incorporation under the name *Catholic Preparatory School for Boys, Incorporated* was carried.

The group then elected Fred Switzer as President, Bill Weld as Vice-President and Henry Hughes as Secretary and Treasurer. These three served as the board of directors until incorporation. Monsignor Faris was named spiritual advisor and host. Finally Fred Switzer called a planning meeting of officers and committee heads for 1.00 p.m. on 17 May at the Noonday Club, a private club founded in 1893 primarily to provide lunch for professional men working downtown.

It was a pleasant venue where a fair amount of the group's business had been and was to be transacted.

Archbishop Ritter's original idea had been a school with a lay staff, like Canterbury School. Apart from Bill Weld, whose sons had attended Portsmouth Priory School and who had always had in mind a school staffed by religious, preferably monks, most of the group had thought the same as the archbishop. Fred Switzer, however, who, like Bill, had sons at Portsmouth, and had been a seminarian for a short time, agreed with Bill Weld and proposed looking for a religious community to undertake the task. The Jesuits were approached but averred that they could spare no men. The nearest Benedictine Abbeys said the same. One added that seminaries, not high schools, are the appropriate educational work for monks.

Unabashed, Bill Weld wrote to Father Aelred Wall, O.S.B., headmaster of Portsmouth Priory School, and here we come to the third group involved in the preparatory events. Father Wall showed the letter to his Prior, Father Aelred Graham, O.S.B., a monk of Ampleforth who had been seconded to Portsmouth to be their Prior, and asked him if he would consider the project. Prior Aelred then replied to Bill Weld that, though Portsmouth did not have the manpower, he thought that one of the Benedictine houses in England might be interested. This secured him an invitation to come to Saint Louis to meet the group, which he did at some time before 1 August 1954. He discussed the project at length, and viewed the proposed site, namely the Gallagher property of a little over fifty acres on Conway Road in West Saint Louis County.[6] Both sides were satisfied: the group invited Father Aelred to be their ambassador to the English Benedictines, and he agreed to go.

Before this Fred Switzer had made it clear that, if efforts to elicit widespread support for the project were to be successful, two further steps needed to be taken: the group must secure for itself some measure of public status; and it must compose a written statement of its aims.

Public status was secured by forming on 22 June 1954 a not-for-profit Missouri Corporation under the title of *Catholic Preparatory School for Boys, Incorporated*. This meant, among other things, that donations to the corporation would be tax-deductible. The names of those who signed the Articles of Incorporation are in Appendix A 1a.

In parenthesis it may be said that in England at that time public bodies wrote after their names "Limited" (abbreviated to "Ltd.") rather

---

[6] *See* p.19, *below*.

than "Incorporated", and made no attempt to pronounce it or even, except perhaps facetiously, to include it in conversation. The addition of “Incorporated” or "Inc." whenever Catholic Preparatory School for Boys was mentioned, being unfamiliar, struck the monks at Ampleforth as slightly humorous. As the whole name seemed rather ponderous, we started, among ourselves, referring to the organization as "Inc" plain and simple, and the usage gradually spread on both sides of the Atlantic. It started as a sign of gently jocular esteem and deepened into a term of real affection.

The composition of a written statement to be presented to those who might be asked to undertake the establishment of the school or to support it financially or both, was made far easier by the discussions that had been going on for so long; and because of them Fred Switzer and Mr. Lemoine Skinner, Jr., Inc's Director of Public Relations, were quickly able to produce a statement dated 21 June 1954 and revised on 26 October 1954. It was entitled *Catholic Preparatory School for Boys, Inc. Statement of Principles*, and was approved by Archbishop Ritter. A *Supplementary Statement* was written in November 1955 after the arrival of the first three monks. These are printed in Appendices B 1a and B 1b. In Appendix B 1c, for comparison, is printed the statement, *Philosophy and Objectives*, written for the school's evaluation in 1992. It is the most graceful tribute possible to the long-sighted wisdom of the founding laity that so much not only of the substance but even of the phrasing of the original document is still in force.

What did this original document say? The purpose was to establish and support a boys' school which would offer its students a Catholic, college-preparatory education of the highest excellence so as to enable them to enter the colleges, universities and technical schools of their choice and to thrive at them.

The school should start with grades nine through twelve, but should include grades five through eight as soon as practical. It was to have a strong Catholic flavor. The curriculum should be like that of Portsmouth Priory School; the faculty, too, should be excellent, well paid and as numerous as could be afforded; the standards should be related to those of such organizations as the College Entrance Examination Board; the classes should be small; athletics and extra-curricular activity should be encouraged but should not dominate; and "moral probity, intellectual development, physical well-being, good discipline and good manners" should have their appropriate place.

The buildings were to be "simple and adequate, but all ostentation and heavy investment in monumental edifices should be avoided"; and finally "the school should exemplify the Western Catholic tradition in the full intellectual and religious richness of that tradition through many centuries . . . " The monks who were to come to Saint Louis, except perhaps Father Columba, never saw this document until well after the die was cast, otherwise they might have been daunted by the prospect of living up to that last sentence.

We can read the statement today without much quickening of the heartbeat; but think back to Saint Louis of the mid-fifties. The Catholic Church in the United States had put vast effort and vast sums of money into developing its own educational system from the beginning of grade school through college, and Catholics were expected to support the system. Its backbone was the heroic Sisters, who, in those days before Sister Formation programs, had often received only the bare minimum of preparation; classrooms were full and over-full; and Monsignor John Tracy Ellis had not yet dropped his bombshell drawing attention to the plight of Catholic intellectual life.[7]

Monsignor Ellis wrote, "(American Catholics) have suffered from the timidity that characterizes minority groups, from the effects of a ghetto they have themselves fostered, and, too, from a sense of inferiority induced by their consciousness of the inadequacy of Catholic scholarship." And again, "The chief blame, I firmly believe, lies with the Catholics themselves. It lies in their frequently self-imposed ghetto mentality which prevents them from mingling as they should with their non-Catholic colleagues, and in their lack of industry and the habits of work, to which [Professor Robert M.] Hutchins alluded in 1937."[8]

The University of Notre Dame had a national reputation but primarily for football, and Georgetown was known for its teaching of foreign languages, but few if any other Catholic schools could claim a national reputation. In such a setting, Inc's principles were a revolutionary and exciting challenge, especially in their insistence on small classes and on preparing boys to enter the college of their choice.

---

[7] *American Catholics and the Intellectual Life* (Chicago: The Heritage Foundation, Inc. 1956) of which our library holds a copy autographed to Father Columba.

[8] *Ibid*, pp. 56 and 57.

Having achieved public status and having composed a written statement, the group took up again its pursuit of property and on 18 July 1954 signed a deed to purchase for $138,000 the 51.368 acres of the Gallagher property, to which we have already referred.[9] This was funded by Fred Switzer and his brothers.

[9] *See* p.13 *above.*

CHAPTER 3

Prior Aelred to Ampleforth

PRIOR Aelred Graham had by now consulted Abbot Herbert Byrne, who, besides being the Abbot of Ampleforth, Prior Aelred's own monastery, was also Abbot President of the English Benedictine Congregation.[10] With Abbot Herbert's consent and in accordance with the charge laid upon him by Inc, and armed with the first version of their *Statement of Principles*, Prior Aelred crossed the Atlantic in the summer of 1954 and, very properly, went first to Downside Abbey, the senior English Benedictine house. The monks there were cool to the proposal, and Prior Aelred headed then for Ampleforth, the next senior house. There, besides meeting with Abbot Herbert and his Council, he was able to lay the matter before a meeting open to the whole community.

This he did in a very fair manner, but we all realized that he had come as an advocate and not as an advisor. We listened attentively to all that he had to say and were skeptical on only two points: he said that the climate in Saint Louis was temperate, which seemed improbable, even though we did not know at that time that the British Consul in Saint Louis and his staff received tropical pay because of the climate--that is, until the Consular Service learnt about the availability of air-conditioning in Saint Louis.

The other point was more serious. It was said that the students would reach no more than a good School Certificate standard and that therefore the project would not demand any of Ampleforth's highest level teachers. The School Certificate was an English, nation-wide, public examination of a standard like or a little below that of the Achievement Tests of the College Board.

This was a very far-reaching consideration, affecting, as it did, the nature of the staff which Ampleforth would be required to send out, if it accepted the invitation. Prior Aelred may not have said in so many words that anyone could teach the boys of Saint Louis, but it was easy to make that inference from what he said.

We were skeptical of this too, both as a matter of fact and because bright boys are bright boys all over the world, and even if their level

---

[10] *See above*, p. 9, footnote 2

of knowledge were lower than that of bright boys at Ampleforth, they would still need to be taught by teachers at least as bright as themselves. On both counts our skepticism turned out to be well justified.

Beyond these doubts, there was also a group of monks, mostly those who were deeply involved in the school, who feared that the foundation would siphon off men who would be urgently needed at an expanding Ampleforth, where the school staff was already fully extended.

Nonetheless, Prior Aelred received a sympathetic hearing. The climate at Ampleforth was right, and the price, too, was right, as he was able to make promises of full financial and other support that made the project extremely attractive. He was empowered to say, in fact, that Catholic Preparatory School for Boys, Inc. would finance the buildings and guarantee support for the monks until the school was able to support itself. This was much more than was contained in any other proposal made to Ampleforth.

All this occurred after the annual Conventual Chapter, but led to much informal discussion, and the upshot was that Abbot Herbert, after consultation with his Council of Seniors, sent a cable to Fred Switzer inviting the Saint Louisans to send over a delegation to present their case, but making no promises about the outcome.[11] This may not have been all that they were hoping for, but at least it was enough not to squelch the plan.

Meanwhile the group had been busy. How busy was a mark of the faith and generosity of everyone concerned. They had signed the contract for the purchase of the Gallagher property; they had made contact with many of the Catholic lay leaders of Saint Louis; they had made contact also with leading educators in Saint Louis and at colleges outside Saint Louis, such as the University of Notre Dame, which had recently cooperated with the Ford Foundation in a study of the nature and methods of education in the liberal arts; and they had collected in cash a little over $27,000 for a school which at that point neither existed nor even had the promise of anybody to run it. After meetings of the members of the board, at which they appointed

[11] The Conventual Chapter is a meeting of all the solemnly professed (i.e. for life) monks of a monastery. There is a regular annual meeting, and extraordinary meetings may be called as needed. It is somewhat like the annual general meeting of a corporation. The abbot is also advised by a Council of Seniors, some of who are appointed by him and some elected by the Conventual Chapter.

Mercantile Trust Company as their bank and approved sundry expenses including Prior Aelred's travel, there was held at Annunziata Parish on 18 October 1954 the first meeting of the members of the new corporation. Thirty-seven important men were present, of whom twenty-three were later to have boys in the school.

After the approval of the purchase of the Gallagher property and of payment of the balance of the mortgage on it, thirty-eight men were nominated as directors and were unanimously elected. They are listed in Appendix A 1b. Father Aelred then gave an encouraging account of his visit to, and reception at, Ampleforth. Sixteen more directors were added on 14 March 1955 and are listed in Appendix A 1c.

CHAPTER 4

Atlantic Ambassadors

ON 26 October the new Board of Directors held its first meeting, also at Annunziata Parish, and elected as officers: President, Fred Switzer; Vice-Presidents, Bill Weld and Gerry Mudd; Treasurer, Mr. Dumont G. Dempsey; Secretary, Henry Hughes. These officers were then authorized to go to Ampleforth to invite the Abbot to found a monastery and school on the Gallagher property; and on 4 November they went. The party which set sail consisted of Messrs Switzer, Weld and Hughes and Dr. Mudd, Dr. Mudd's mother and the wives of all the men except Bill Weld. They were accompanied by the future Superintendent of Diocesan Schools, Father, later Monsignor, James T. Curtin, who represented the Archbishop. His presence was more important than may have been recognized, because Ampleforth had, soon after World War I, made an unsuccessful foundation in Calgary, Alberta, whose failure was due largely to lack of episcopal enthusiasm.

Several generations earlier, Fred Switzer's German ancestors had emigrated by way of Ireland to the United States. Fred did not go into the family business but studied law at Harvard rather than licorice in Saint Louis and became a prominent attorney in the city. He was a man of great wisdom who combined vision and action. To these qualities he added skill in negotiation and a deep faith. Without him the Priory and school would not have come into existence. Bill Weld, like Fred, had had two sons at Portsmouth Priory School. He was proud of his descent from the Welds of Lulworth in England and because of them took a keen interest in the history of the English Recusant Catholics.[12] Henry Hughes had French and Southern forebears with a special connection with Bardstown, Kentucky. He too was a lawyer, energetic and enthusiastic. Gerry Mudd was a doctor, who pioneered heart catheterization at Saint Louis University Hospital. His father was a partner of Mr. J. C. Penney. Father Curtin was to be the Archdiocesan Superintendent of Schools, a new office whose

---

[12] Shortly before coming to Saint Louis, Father Timothy had met one of the English Welds. As soon as he met Bill, he was struck by the facial resemblance, especially in their smiles. Yet their common ancestor must have been at least six generations back.

scope was still in process of definition. Of these men at that time, only Fred had sons who might benefit from the school; Gerry's son was born later.

Before the deputation sailed on the Queen Mary, the members met Prior Aelred in New York. He impressed on them that it was vital to the project to convince the monks of Ampleforth that this was a call to work for the church and to do God's will, a call which would probably go unanswered if Ampleforth did not accept. There was abundant need for educational activity in England; it was the apostolic aspect that would make Saint Louis distinctive. This argument from God's will may have started as a tactical ploy, but soon deepened into a conviction held and cherished by both parties.

Already Benedictine enough in spirit to recognize that idleness is the enemy of the soul, the deputation held a council of war on board and decided that only Fred Switzer should speak before the Council at Ampleforth, thereby ensuring at least that they would speak with only one voice. Not all their activity was solemn. From a lower deck a religious sister waved to them. She turned out to be Father Curtin's cousin and one of a group of Little Sisters of the Poor who were traveling to France. Fred invited them to a "tea party". When the champagne was uncorked, the Sisters protested that they might not drink wine until they reached France, where "it was the drink of the country". A friendly bishop on board rescued them from their quandary by claiming universal jurisdiction over all travelers on the high seas and giving them permission to imbibe. It was before Vatican II. In return the Sisters promised their prayers. Fred Switzer believed that this was why the embassy was successful.

On arrival, the group went to the Savoy, one of London's better known hotels. Leaving the women there, the men went north to Ampleforth. They were able to mingle freely with the monks and conversed with many of them. They were given the use of the monastic guest room for their headquarters. This was one of the few rooms that could be kept what Americans might call warm. It had a fire, on which they piled all available fuel. Unfortunately their idea of comfortable warmth and that of the guest room maid did not coincide. She would come in, find the room unbearably hot ("what a fug!", pronounced to rhyme with the first syllable of `sugar', were her words) and throw open all the windows. The deputation would return, close the windows and build up the fire again; the maid would come in . . . Neither side prevailed. It is not easy to overcome American know-how; it is not easy to defeat a Yorkshire lass.

They were not much like the general run of visitors to Ampleforth. No doubt the Queen Mary and the Savoy had their effect on us, not to mention transatlantic calls to their senators ("Oh sure, father, we can fix that") or calls from U.S.A. to the monastery at 2 a.m., and their consumption of bacon and marmalade in combination, which especially struck Father Columba. No doubt they did a bit of a "snow job" on us, and we were more impressed than we should have been by their self-assurance. Had we known more about American salesmanship and lack of understatement, we might have been more hesitant, but nobody could have failed to be impressed by them. They were clearly sincere and altruistic--only one of them at the time stood to gain by the school in the sense of sending a son there--and what they were offering was clearly substantial. They were confident that they could make good all that they were promising. Here is where we might have been more hesitant, but in the event we were not deceived.

The men were shown the upper school, Gilling's medieval and Tudor Castle, which serves as the grade school for Ampleforth, the ruins of the great Cistercian abbeys of Rievaulx and Byland, and other local beauty spots. Viola Switzer and Marjorie Hughes, who with the others had been "roughing it at the Savoy" as one of the party put it, came up to Ampleforth for an afternoon. But the high point and indeed the whole point of the visit was the meeting of the men with the abbot's council, which took place in the comfort of the school guest room.

Fred Switzer outlined the need of Catholics in Saint Louis for an education of the kind that Ampleforth was especially equipped to offer, and the service that this would be to the church not only in Saint Louis but in the whole of U.S.A. He repeated the promise that the group would buy the land, build the buildings and support the monks until they could support themselves, and pointed to the acquisition of fifty expensive acres as proof of serious intent. He added that religious vocations were plentiful in Saint Louis and that there was every prospect that eager young Saint Louisans would soon make the foundation self-supporting without further need of reinforcements from Ampleforth.[13] Surely the monks, if they accepted, would be responding to God's call.

In response to the observation that Ampleforth, if it accepted the invitation, would have to hire laymen to replace any monks who were sent to Saint Louis, Fred said that Inc would pay for them. This led to

[13] This was true at the time but was not how things turned out.

discussion years later since Fred thought he had set a limit of ten years for this payment, whereas Abbot Herbert did not remember any limit.

Fred, an accomplished lawyer, made a powerful presentation. Much of its effect could be foreseen, but he could not have known that financial stringency had caused other proposals to be turned down and that Inc's offer of full support would be so opportune.

Like the apostles, the men left the council glad, though for the opposite reason: they had not suffered humiliation but, rather, had been warmly received. The Council of Seniors recommended to Abbot Herbert that the invitation should be put before an extraordinary Conventual Chapter for discussion and a vote. The Council also advised the abbot to send a reconnaissance party to Saint Louis so that the professed monks would have information provided by some of themselves. Father Richard Wright and Father Robert Coverdale were chosen. Neither had shown any special enthusiasm for the scheme and both might be regarded as very English, and as men to whom Missouri's "show me" could well be said to apply.

The American deputation returned to Saint Louis both satisfied and anxious. Their mission had gone well, but the outcome was still uncertain. One result of the preparations for the mission and of the discussions at Ampleforth was a great increase in Inc's awareness that they were getting a monastery as well as a school, or more exactly that they were getting a monastery first of all, and that the monastery would establish the school. This change of focus was welcomed for its spiritual value. It also enlarged the scope of the project's appeal to include any who, though not particularly interested in the school, might still be excited at the thought of having a great abbey which could be to Saint Louis what Westminster Abbey had been to London.

Father Richard and Father Robert from Ampleforth reached Saint Louis on 7 December and stayed until 19 December. They were, naturally, shown every hospitality. This included seeing the property, meeting members of Inc, being introduced to the Archbishop and to local clergy, conferring with local educators both Catholic and not, and, especially, meeting local religious involved in education. Saint Louis was something of a stronghold of both Jesuits and Religious of the Sacred Heart. The former had a large high school for boys and a university, the latter a school for boys through the eighth grade as well as their schools and a college for girls. Their cordiality to the idea of another boys' school was therefore important. The scouts returned to Ampleforth convinced not only of the need for the school but also of the welcome it would receive from the Archbishop, from the Catholic educators in Saint Louis and from the Catholic laity.

It was something of a *tour de force* for the two monks to master in so short a time such a mass of strange material--strange to them, that is--and to digest it into a report of sixteen pages.[14] There are, to be sure, some minor errors of fact, and they do repeat the claim that no higher standard would be required than a "good School Certificate level", but as we read their report over forty years later, we still feel admiration for its broad sweep and agreement with its general thrust.

This report, they wrote, "is not an advocacy or a plea for rejection" although, as they admit, "it has not been too easy to maintain complete objectivity in the face of great kindness, consideration and generosity on the part of the Saint Louis group who were our hosts . . ." The main body of the report starts with a statement of the support of the Archbishop, who for some time "had been aware of the great need for an independent Preparatory School of high scholastic quality, and had given his full approval to this project because it was sponsored by laymen whom he knew to be solid and sound Catholics and substantial citizens." He looked for a canonical *domus formata* (established house) which would in due course become an abbey. He would give his approval "in the widest terms, binding his successor not to turn us out, but leaving us free to go." He believed that vocations would be plentiful.

The local clergy whom they met were no less cordial, and Father Paul C. Reinert S.J., then President of Saint Louis University, said that the need for such a school in Saint Louis was "desperate"; the repercussions of such a foundation would spread far beyond Saint Louis.

They also met a learned priest from San Francisco, who believed that "there was no better milieu than Saint Louis for us . . . The most stable and solid Catholics were to be found there. They had real Catholic traditions and would find liturgical Catholicism congenial." These opinions were later confirmed by the Apostolic Delegate, Archbishop Amleto Cicognani, whom the fathers visited in Washington, DC.

In the next few pages they outlined with accuracy and skill the layout of American education, and opined that the grading system was such that an American registrar would be needed, as the task "would probably be beyond the competence of an Englishman in the early years." Not so. Then they turned to finances: Inc would acquire the land with its buildings, bring the monks over, meet the school's operating deficit for the first few years, and "temporarily at least"

---

[14] The bulk of the report may be found in Appendix B 2.

compensate Ampleforth for the men hired to replace the monks coming to Saint Louis. "Details of how this compensation should be evaluated and paid were not discussed at the present stage".

In due course, more buildings would be needed. Inc would then cooperate fully in planning for them and in executing the plan. A sum of about $1 million was involved and there was adequate assurance of its availability, but Inc thought it wiser not to launch a drive for this until Ampleforth had accepted the invitation. When the monks came over, Inc would form a new corporation, to which all funds and title deeds would be transferred.[15]

The fathers then turned their attention to the staffing of the school. Reporting that Fred Switzer had said that since his visit to Ampleforth "he had come to realize much more that the heart of the school was the monastery," they added that American lay faculty would be an essential adjunct to the monks, and that they should be the best available; they might be difficult but not impossible to find. The lay faculty would include that important man, the athletic director. They foresaw the possibility of importing British lay faculty "but not of course from Ampleforth". Versatility was more important than specialist knowledge.

Next they reported on the site and its buildings, its location west of the city in an area of expected growth; they said they were advised not to have a formal parent-school association, on the grounds that "formal resolutions pushed through by an ambitious and loquacious parent can be embarrassing".

They concluded by stressing the high esteem for Portsmouth, the need for higher standards and more discipline in American and especially in American Catholic education, the urgency of offering Catholics an education at least equivalent to the best available in non-Catholic schools, the need for leaders and even the need for better Anglo-American relations.

Their last sentence, not fully in accord with their initial declaration of non-advocacy, is "[The offer] is made in the most generous terms possible, and if we may at this final point express a personal opinion, we would urge that if it is at all possible, the Community should go forward with this enterprise."[16]

It was a very persuasive report in favor of the project and impressed all who read it. After the fathers' visit to Saint Louis, Fred Switzer

---

[15] It did not happen quite as soon as that.

[16] Both men were by then very much in favor of the project.

wrote to Abbot Herbert on 3 January 1955 to comment on the impression they had made on Saint Louis. "I have never been connected with any project, either civic or religious, affecting the community [i.e. the people of Saint Louis] where the response has been so uniformly favorable. Even as to our non-Catholic friends the prospect seems to appeal to them . . ." and later "There is no question in my mind that the possibility of having a monastery in connection with the school has broadened and increased the interest in our project." And again "I wish to eliminate any implication or thought that we here are bargaining. We feel that we are rather cooperating in a great mission." He ended by inviting the abbot, if Ampleforth voted for the foundation, to visit Saint Louis as the guest of Inc.

The next weeks of anxious waiting cannot have been made easier for Inc by the arrival in early January of a cable from Abbot Herbert saying that owing to changed circumstances, it appeared that Ampleforth could not spare the nine monks thought necessary to form a monastery and would be able to spare only three monks with no assurance that more could be sent later. Would this be satisfactory to the Saint Louis group?[17]

Providentially Prior Aelred appeared in Saint Louis and diagnosed the cable as the result of the opposition of a small group of monks at Ampleforth who were apprehensive about the effect on the school there. This was, however, not the whole story--and, having been away from Ampleforth for so long he may well not have known the whole story -- but what he said served to smooth the ruffled feathers.[18] He knew too that Abbot Herbert was temperamentally more inclined to promise less and achieve more than to raise false hopes. Fred Switzer therefore cabled back that they had every confidence that, if the

---

[17] *LS* p.13. One lesson to be drawn from our experience is that three men are not enough for starting a new house. The three of us all agreed to that.

[18] With the increasing popularity of the school at Ampleforth had come a corresponding increase in the number of students, which in turn led to a need for more monks on the school staff. The extent of this need was becoming more apparent at about the same time as the request was being made from Saint Louis. Further, although the attitude towards lay faculty was changing, there was at that time little support among the monks at Ampleforth for the idea of placing lay men, let alone lay women, in key positions. Any foundation, if it was to be respectably staffed, was bound to draw off a certain number of monks capable of holding key positions.

Conventual Chapter accepted the invitation, Ampleforth would be able to carry out the decision as agreed.

CHAPTER 5

The Decision and its Sequel

THE awaited day arrived and the Chapter opened at Ampleforth on 17 January 1955. Abbot Herbert outlined the matter and said that there were excellent reasons to accept and excellent reasons to reject the invitation; the only stupid view would be that it was obvious which we should do; he saw it as important that we were being asked to do something quite altruistic; it would not benefit Ampleforth but would benefit the church in the United States. Fathers Richard and Robert spoke in favor, as did many others and as did Father Timothy, who thought he was not likely to be personally involved. The cardinal speech was from Father Sebastian, an older monk of accepted wisdom and deeply committed to the school at Ampleforth. His support of the proposal carried great weight. By the remarkable margin of four to one, the vote was in favor.

Abbot Herbert cabled Fred Switzer laconically and economically, "Ampleforth accepts gracious invitation to found Priory and school in your archdiocese. Byrne". Fred cabled back expansively and expensively, "We are all happy to receive the good news. It has inspired the strongest and most heartfelt enthusiasm among us. The Archbishop is most pleased. I unhesitatingly pledge you the strong support of our group and the warm welcome of our community. Our finance committee met today and inspired by your cable initiated a very fine program. We are most grateful. Awaiting your letter. Switzer."

The "very fine program" mentioned in Fred's cable was this: to round up one hundred people who would be the key supporters of the project; each of them would in turn find another three people who would work for the campaign; these four hundred workers would then each approach five prospects. At first their aim was to raise $500,000 immediately and $1 million later on, but this was soon revised to raising the whole $1.5 million in one fell swoop. Lemoine Skinner, a public relations expert, started by advising the campaign as a volunteer, but in March 1955 was hired at $750 a month to direct it. He was a graduate of Princeton University and was keenly interested in education. He was married to a Catholic, but was not Catholic himself. He was sympathetic especially to things monastic, became a good friend of the monks and their trusted advisor. Along with many another bright idea, he later devised the logo of the church, which is still on our letterhead. At this point he surveyed the information available on the prospects and slightly modified the original plan. He divided the prospects into three categories: those who would themselves work and would recruit three other workers; those who would themselves contribute and would approach five other prospects; those who would give or had given but would not work.

This was all unfamiliar ground to the men from Ampleforth. In England at that time schools were expected to support themselves out of tuition. Ampleforth had some other sources of revenue, and had always had generous benefactors, but their gifts were windfalls rather than part of the planning. In the United States it was very different. Tuition was not expected to cover all the costs of operation, let alone capital expenses. Fund-raising was, therefore, an accepted part of educational administration. The problem Inc had to solve was not how to set about the drive--there were numerous well-tested methods--but how to succeed in convincing people who had already been approached for many worthy causes that this new school was a particularly worthwhile project. In their favor were the accepted convention that "if I support your project, you are in honor bound to support mine" and the tradition of amazing generosity among the wealthy. Against them, those same wealthy were a well-harvested field.

When Fred Switzer informed the Archbishop of the good news from Ampleforth, he received this encouraging reply dated 18 February 1955:

> Dear Mr. Switzer:
>
> I am pleased to give my approval and recommendation to the proposed Catholic Preparatory School for Boys to be conducted by the Benedictine Monks of Ampleforth Abbey. I hope that the efforts of your Committee to obtain the necessary financial backing will meet with every success, and that you will receive generous and substantial contributions.
>
> It is hardly necessary to point out that such a school is needed and will be a valuable asset to the Catholic Educational Program in the Archdiocese of Saint Louis.
>
> Sincerely yours in Christ,
>
> Joseph E. Ritter

At Ampleforth, shortly after the Chapter, Abbot Herbert told Father Columba Cary-Elwes, then Prior of Ampleforth, that he wanted him to be Prior of the new Priory, but could not announce it before the abbatial election which was due in April. If the monks elected someone other than himself, the new abbot might choose a different Prior.

About the other members of the team rumors were rife inside and outside the monastery. Father Timothy was curate of a tiny parish at Oswaldkirk, two miles from the abbey. One of the parishioners said to him one day, "We hear you're going to America". "Oh no," he replied, "I haven't heard anything like that, and I'm sure the abbot would tell me before he told you," and thought no more of it. Not for the first time nor the last, the laity knew more than the clergy.

Meanwhile, Abbot Herbert was interviewing each monk in turn and asking if he would like to go to Saint Louis. He asked Father Luke whether if he were sent to Saint Louis he would find it intolerable, and Father Luke replied that he would not. In due course he came to Father Timothy and asked if he would like to go to Saint Louis. He said, "No". When asked why not, he said that he had joined the Ampleforth community because he wanted to be at Ampleforth, and that his family and friends were in England. When the abbot asked if he would go to Saint Louis if sent, he replied that he thought his vow of obedience left him no choice. Even when Father Abbot said that he was glad to hear that, Father Timothy thought the abbot was simply saying the abbatial equivalent of "What a good boy are you!" and took no fright.

At the election, Abbot Herbert was easily re-elected. He confirmed to Father Columba that he wanted him to go to Saint Louis as founding Prior, and on Good Friday he sent for Father Timothy and said, "Father, I think you had better sit down." Then Father Timothy knew. The next words were, "Father dear, I am going to uproot you". Father Luke was the last to receive his posting. Father Abbot went to his room after the summer term had started and again said ominously that Father Luke had better sit down. Then he too knew.

At the time, Father Columba was fifty-one, Father Luke thirty-two and Father Timothy thirty-four. All three had been boys in the school at Ampleforth. Father Columba had been in the wine business for three years and then joined the monastery. He spent three years reading Modern Languages at Saint Benet's Hall, the Ampleforth house of studies at Oxford. He then taught Religion, French and Spanish, and was a housemaster in the school and then Prior in the monastery. Father Luke went straight from the school into the monastery in 1941, and then also went to Saint Benet's Hall, where he read English and had as his tutor C. S. Lewis. On his return to Ampleforth, he taught English and religion and coached each season. He was also assigned to Saint Chad's parish in Kirkby Moorside, fifteen miles from Ampleforth, which entailed residing there for the weekend. His father was a banker, but that and keeping the parish accounts at Kirkby were all his experience of finance. Abbot Herbert, when he told Father Luke of his posting, added that dollars were different from pounds, and someone who had experience with pounds would have to unlearn it all in order to deal with dollars. Father Luke had the advantage of having had little experience with pounds. Father Timothy had two years at Christ Church, Oxford reading Classics and then six years serving in the Royal Artillery in England and Burma in World War II. He entered the novitiate in September 1946. He had two more years at Oxford, one going more deeply into ancient history and philosophy and one, with the Dominicans, starting theology. He taught Religion, Latin, Greek and English in the school and coached all seasons, with a special love for cricket. He was also school librarian and had the tiny parish of Saint Aidan, Oswaldkirk.

The men at Saint Louis, meanwhile had not been idle. Prior Aelred had indicated that the Gallagher property by itself was not enough, and the men of the embassy must have felt, as they learnt of and then viewed Ampleforth's two thousand acres, that the monks might feel a bit cramped on fifty-three. They cast their eyes at the adjacent properties, which belonged to the Nolands, the Stannards, the Singers and the Reasors and entered into negotiations. The Nolands would not sell then, and except for one acre, never did. Their property is now a sub-division. The Stannards agreed to sell their 32.307 acres for $150,000 and did so on 10 February 1955. Besides the acreage, there was a substantial brick and concrete house designed by Mr. Raymond E. Maritz in a pleasing neo-colonial style, and a barn and several free-standing frame buildings, which the English call outhouses and the Americans do not. This led to some wry comments, as when Father Luke was describing an architect's model to some of our friends and referred more than once to some of the buildings as outhouses. Before long he noticed that some of the group were asking what this building was or that one, and that his replies were causing some amusement. On another occasion we said we were planning to put the boys' locker rooms in one of the outhouses, and this too was misunderstood. Regardless, the Stannards left us a very useful amount of machinery and equipment in the aforesaid frame buildings.

As the overlap between the Gallagher and the Stannard properties was only a few yards at one corner, Inc persuaded the Nolands to sell for $3000 one acre at the junction to afford easier access between the two. They achieved this purchase on 31 March 1955, and then owned nearly eighty-five acres of expensive real estate.

CHAPTER 6

Countdown

THE custom of honoring founders and founders' kin is an ancient one in England, and descendants of the founders of some Oxford colleges are still able to attend those colleges without payment, if they qualify academically. Accordingly in April 1955 Abbot Herbert sent Fred Switzer an airletter which included the following paragraphs:

> We would wish that all who in any way, according to their means and opportunities, aid in the establishment of the house of prayer which we intend the Saint Louis Benedictine Monastery to be should have a share in the fruit of the Masses, prayers and good works of the monks for as long as that monastery lasts in this world, for they may truly be called the Founders of the monastery.
>
> Founders' kin likewise--that is to say, their immediate family and descendants--shall have the same privilege.
>
> When the monastery has been canonically established, it is our intention that henceforth a Mass be offered each week for the Benefactors of the House as is our custom here.

Our monastery, therefore, celebrates Mass every week for our original and all subsequent benefactors. The relevant paragraphs of Abbot Herbert's letter were incorporated in a letter sent by Bill Weld on 13 April to the men concerned, and on 18 April Fred Switzer was writing to the whole group:

> It is hard to overstate the grandeur and the challenge of the work we have undertaken here together. We are joined as founders of an institution that will exert an immeasurable spiritual and intellectual influence. We have a great privilege as founders. We have as well a great responsibility.

Note the order: "spiritual and intellectual". These letters seem to mark a turning point in the expression by the leaders of Inc of their understanding of what they were receiving. They had asked for a school, but were receiving instead a monastery which would run a school. They may have been surprised at first, but soon took eagerly to the idea; and it was not too long before they saw that it brought not only spiritual but also financial advantage. In November 1955 in their *Supplementary Statement of the Program*, after saying that the primary appeal must be to Catholics interested in seeing their sons go on to college, they wrote, "It must not be overlooked, however, that there is a great and broad appeal here to every person interested in being identified with the establishment of a great Benedictine monastery in our community."

On 11 May outdoors at the Gallagher House, Inc held a grand chicken barbecue for all potential workers on the fund-raising drive. It then turned its attention to the next notable event, the visit of Abbot Herbert and Prior Columba. Of this there is a record in a document to which both men contributed.[19]

The two monks started at Portsmouth Priory and attended Graduation there, and then, accompanied by Prior Aelred Graham, flew to Saint Louis, where they arrived in mid-afternoon on Thursday 16 June for a twelve-day visit, which was to be hectic by any standards. Although in many ways similar to that of Father Richard and Father Robert, it was rather more high-powered, because abbots and priors are rather more high-powered than simple monks. Each day had typically a meeting or visit in the morning, a luncheon with educators or other notables, a visit in the afternoon followed by a dinner. It must have been quite a trick for the monks to fit in their prayers.

Weary as they were on arrival, they could not resist the urge to walk round the property, and as they did so, Father Columba threw Benedictine medals onto any adjacent property that looked attractive.[20] It proved effective.

Because they were meeting many of the same people as Father Richard and Father Robert had met, many of the opinions expressed

[19] *Notes on an American Journey Made in June 1955 by Abbot Byrne and Fr. Columba Whose Chief Purpose was to Examine the Conditions for the Founding of Saint Louis Priory and School.* This may be found in our archives in the same file as Father Columba's Diary.

[20] In the hope of enlisting Saint Benedict's intercession in acquiring the property.

to them were the same and many of their conclusions were the same, but some new impressions also emerge, as quotations or paraphrases from their report will show: parents, they wrote, tend to regard education as functional, as preparation for a job and as leading to success, usually monetary, “but there is also a nebulous belief in Education with a capital E. No one, however, can define just what they mean by that.” They openly want English ideas of education, but we must leave them to say so; bright boys enter the professions or business rather than, as often in England, the upper levels of the Civil Service; scholars as such are less highly regarded than in Europe; discipline is maintained without the application of force, mostly; the honor system is widespread, the monitorial system of boys disciplining other boys is not; Saint Louisans were surprised that in the school library at Ampleforth boys would obey a simple sign reading SILENCE; a respected headmaster said that boys in Saint Louis felt it was "sissy" to be polite, and not worthy of a free citizen to show deference.

The representatives of Catholic colleges and universities with whom they spoke--and these included Notre Dame, which they visited after Saint Louis--urged that Catholic boys should attend Catholic schools; sixty per cent of Catholics at college are at non-Catholic colleges, and of those, they were told, seventy per cent lose their faith; the chaplains at non-Catholic universities are not so well treated as at Oxford and Cambridge, and are not always so wise. This was weighty even though not altogether unprejudiced advice on a topic whose importance we recognized even then and experienced very directly later on. The reader must remember that this advice was given in the mid-fifties to men for whom the issue had never yet been a real one, there being no Catholic colleges in England. There the aim was to make Catholic students firm enough in their faith to be able to thrive in the setting of a university, which would always be non-Catholic.

There were also occasions whose intellectual content was less heavy but which caused equal wear and tear. These were social events at private clubs such as the Missouri Athletic Club and the Deer Creek Club, or at the homes of individuals such as Mr. August A. Busch, Jr. at Grant's Farm or Mr. Joseph Desloge at Vouziers. At the dinners they were exposed to the custom of standing, talking and drinking for up to two hours and then sitting down to food without alcohol.[21]

---

[21] The word "exposed" is a good example of difference in nuance between English here and English there: In England one is exposed mostly to bad things like pneumonia; in US also to good things like Algebra. When we first heard

Another subject that was very much on Father Columba's mind was architecture and architects. One of our first tasks would be to choose an architect, and that could be done only on the basis of the architectural style of his buildings. Granite, Father Columba thought then, would be too expensive and modern functional architecture too impersonal. Brick was abundant in Saint Louis and could be used very attractively. The architect of the Stannard House, Mr. Raymond E. Maritz, was an exponent of the neo-colonial style, and the Stannard House was attractive but derivative. Nonetheless, in the architectural stakes he had the inside track as being the man on the spot, and as knowing the property. His architecture was not original but in the mid-fifties examples of original American architecture, apart from tepees and skyscrapers, were few.

On 27 June the pair, buffeted but still game, left Saint Louis for Notre Dame where they were entertained by Fathers Mathis and Sheedy. It was a cursory visit but left them wondering whether really good students in the liberal arts would be fully extended there. They went on to St. Anselm Priory in Washington, DC, and while there visited the Landon School, a well-known college-preparatory school, and then the British Ambassador, Sir Roger Makins, and the Papal Nuncio, Archbishop Amleto Cicognani, both of whom were gracious and welcoming and promised support. Their final stop was with Mr. and Mrs. Robert L. Hoguet in New York. They were long-standing friends of Portsmouth Priory and became good friends of ours too, providing a soft landing for monks coming from England by sea and a launching pad for those going the other way. Mr. Hoguet, a banker/lawyer, impressed upon Abbot Herbert and Prior Columba, and later upon Father Luke, the opinion that every self-respecting, progressive institution had to live in the red, and a priory which was not working on some great scheme for the future and planning new buildings for it was reactionary and moribund and not worth supporting. Father Columba notes that he was "humorously insistent, but still insistent."

Finally they comment on the overcrowding of classrooms in the Catholic system from the very beginning and even into college. Much later, we asked a Sister who had sixty Texan children in her classroom how she managed to teach them anything. She quipped, "Father, I

---

that boys of fourteen might well not have been exposed to Latin, Greek, French, Algebra or Geometry, both the fact and the way of expressing it seemed strange to us.

don't teach them; I just act as referee". Bearing in mind this background, we may quote in its entirety the last paragraph of their account:

> What is expected of us–in a small way–is to provide an education which aims at excellence in every way and not at quantity or mass production. The Jesuits are the first to welcome us. Small classes, personal relationships, discipline, high standards of scholarship, deep religious training, these are what they want, so that some Catholics can hold their own among the leaders of the country and be fine Catholics too.

During the rest of the summer there was much preparation and discussion on both sides of the Atlantic. Saint Louis was mainly concerned with practicalities like providing knives and forks and altar cloths and similar necessities, but there was also one very large concern: the acquisition of more land. The tale that Abbot Herbert exclaimed, "Do you expect us to establish a monastery and school on a pocket handkerchief?" is probably apocryphal, but those members of Inc who had visited Ampleforth had seen for themselves the spaciousness there and were coming to recognize that a monastery needs, for its own well-being, a certain amount of elbow room. The Gallagher and Stannard properties did not provide this and Inc started to look at our other neighbors, and to drop more Benedictine medals on their properties.

At Ampleforth, where the school year then did not end until late in July, the members of the new team had little time to spare from their duties in the monastery and school, but they did snatch the odd moment and met in the guest room that had been used by the American envoys. There they considered what to call the new foundation; should it be a day school or a boarding school; what could or should the curriculum be; at what level should we start; what sports should we offer; and similar matters. Sometimes they had simply to find a reply to queries raised in letters from Saint Louis.

The name chosen was *The Priory of Saint Mary and Saint Louis*, honoring Our Lady because she had been involved in the project from the beginning and including Saint Louis by a kind of pun as the name both of the city to which we were going and of its patron Saint.

Because Ampleforth is a boarding school, all our instincts were for a boarding school in Saint Louis, but that idea met with a strong contrary recommendation from Inc on the grounds that in Saint Louis, unlike either England or New England, most people had little esteem for boarding schools and regarded them as places to which the young were sent if they could not make the grade anywhere else. We did not want to begin with any strikes against us and decided at least to start with a day school. But we asked ourselves how we could fit the various clubs and activities and informal meetings with the boys into the schedule of a day school. It was and remains a good question. It was certainly in our minds at that time that we would in due course develop into a full boarding, or perhaps a five-day boarding, school.

We thought the curriculum would be much the same as at Ampleforth: Religion, Latin, French or Spanish, English, Mathematics, which we still abbreviated to Maths, History and Science, with suitable boys being able to opt, in Churchill's phrase, for Greek as a treat.[22]

The question of level was more complex. There was a strong, but not universal, feeling among our friends in Saint Louis that we should start at the fifth grade (age 10). This view was championed by Dr. Robert Dean Mattis, who later took care of the monks' eyes. There is much to be said for that in principle (Ampleforth's grade school started even earlier) and there was an additional local argument, that Saint Louis Country Day School, as it then was, started in the fifth grade. It was feared, justifiably, as we found to our cost, that boys might go there to get a good preparation for Priory and then, come the day of transfer, find that they liked the school, had made many good friends and did not want to leave. We felt too that although in their early years boys are as well or better taught by women than by men, somewhere along the line, and possibly around the fifth grade, they are better taught by men. Against this, none of us had taught boys of that tender age and it seemed foolish, when so many other things confronting us in a new country were bound to be unfamiliar, to add to them an unfamiliar age of boy. And so we decided to keep within the range of our experience and to start with the ninth grade, the regular beginning of high school, or in Ampleforth terms, upper school. In the event, for each of the first two years we accepted thirty boys, or two sets, into the ninth grade, and in the third year one set each into the seventh and eighth grades and again two sets into the ninth, to give us, theoretically, two grades of fifteen and three high school classes of thirty.

The standard choice of sports in Saint Louis was American football, basketball and baseball. Other possibilities were soccer, track, tennis,

---

[22] At that time "Math" seemed woefully truncated; now "Maths" seems hard to pronounce.

cross-country, swimming, boxing and wrestling, all of which, except wrestling, existed at Ampleforth. Rugby and, with great sorrow, cricket we excluded as there would be in Saint Louis no inter-school competition. American football we did not know, but were told that it was almost mandatory. Basketball is played in England mainly by girls and baseball we thought at the time to be a barely recognizable descendant of rounders. None of the standard American sports had made much impression across the Atlantic.[23]

We did not have to make a decision at once, so we decided to wait until we arrived. We were, however, concerned: we would not be able to coach any of the standard American sports, which was sad both because coaching is often good exercise and enjoyable and because it is a good way to get to know boys and to be known by them outside the classroom. We feared that we might be on the outside looking in on what would be an important, even though secondary, part of the school's life.

To counterbalance this we sketched--hardly more than an adumbration--the outlines of the idea of the Priory family, which gradually emerged as one of our most notable characteristics. It kept us in touch with the boys and their families not only while they were in school but also, in many cases, for life. It involved us in many a wedding, baptism and funeral. We tried actively to follow the careers of our alumni when they went on to college, and for several years starting in 1960 we held an annual Day of Recollection around Christmas at the end of which alumni told us how they were getting on in college and whether they thought their preparation had been adequate. It meant much more, too. One of our first African-American students, who had something like a two hour bus journey each way each day, eventually found that this was too much. He left us and went to another school. One evening he came back with a fellow-student from his new school, came into the headmaster's office and said, "Father, I wanted to come to tell you that I am doing well in my new school; and I have brought Mary along to show her the school, so I would like you to meet my beautiful date."

The members of Inc, the faculty and the students and their families were the most numerous members of the Priory family, but no less important were our secretaries, cooks, and maintenance men, architects, contractors and salesmen, and others, so many of whom

---

[23] Father Timothy attended a basketball game between Oxford University and Bristol University, at which he was one of perhaps ten spectators.

were to become and remain our friends. More will be said of them in the proper place. Upon arrival in Saint Louis we began to see how much closer than at Ampleforth was to be our relationship not only with parents but with all the members of Inc, and with others; and so the Priory family came to include all those who in whatever way advised, supported, helped and encouraged us.

In the 1950s Ampleforth was still rather remote. Telephone service was slow and uncertain and monastic answering of the telephone was equally slow and uncertain. There was a bus service from York to Ampleforth's door, a friendly, meandering and leisurely bus, whose driver knew that Mrs. X went shopping on Thursdays and would wait for her if she were not at the stop.

There was a train service to Gilling, a few miles from the abbey; and there were of course roads, but no motorways. Getting to Ampleforth by any means was sufficiently difficult to discourage casual or repeated visits. It was a great change to find that in Saint Louis the telephone service was prompt[24] (Mr. Stannard was president of Southwestern Bell Telephone Company and had an extension in almost every room of his house, from which we benefitted for over a year after he moved out and before Bell caught up with us. Bell fought to get Father Luke to pay for these extensions, but that was a losing battle from the start) and driving out from downtown, even though only parts of Highway 40 were then completed, was comparatively expeditious. Our clientele was on our doorstep in a way unthinkable at Ampleforth then or even now. This easy accessibility by telephone was desirable in many ways but was to prove no unmixed blessing. Soon after our arrival, Father Timothy had to call Washington. He dialed the number and sat back to think what he wanted to say. He was still unprepared two or three seconds later when his party answered. Moreover, just as our friends were accessible to us, so were we to them, and not only to them but to anyone who discovered our number. Thus Father Timothy was working at his desk one evening and counting on not being interrupted, when the phone rang. It was a man wanting to sell him, for $5400, an acre of land near Cape Canaveral. His engaging interlocutor went into his sales pitch, which was very well done, and then said, "How would it be if you called me 'Sol' and I called you

[24] There were drawbacks too: one year in one of the telephone directories the entry immediately before "Saint Louis Priory School" was "Saint Louis Obedience Training school for dogs". That led to some interesting telephone calls: "We have a candidate for your school." "Oh! How many legs has he?"

'Tim'?" Father Timothy replied that he did not think that would be at all well. Undeterred, the man went on for fifty minutes and Father Timothy, then unpracticed, could find no way to shake him off. At last he said, "I think there is something you should know: my disposable annual income is $120." With hardly a pause, the man said, "Well, good night, father," [25] and Father Timothy was left thinking, "Why did I not think of that forty minutes sooner?"

Letters from Saint Louis to us in England raised a variety of problems: where should we site the running track? (we declined to do this simply from air photographs) Could we design a coat of arms? Would we accept the offer of a wooden statue of Saint George and his dragon to be made by a Swiss carver? How should the women's auxiliary attach the antependia to the altars they were preparing for us? It fell mostly to Father Columba to solve these conundrums.

Then there were the more personal aspects of preparation: the whole complicated process of immigration occupied an undue amount of our time, even though we were neither criminals nor communists. Because Father Timothy had been born in what is now Pakistan, the American Consulate in Liverpool tried to put him on the Pakistani list, with its small quota of permitted immigrants. But after much struggle and puff and intervention by Senators and Congressmen, we eventually received our papers. We equipped ourselves with caps and gowns and M.A.'s hoods against future graduations, though in fact we never wore them, both because it was not the custom and because our lay faculty had no comparable garments, even though they had comparable degrees.

Our worst ordeal was the photograph. Not unnaturally, our supporters in Saint Louis wanted to see what they were getting. As none of us had had a formal portrait photograph taken since joining the monastery, we had nothing on file, and so were steered to an unknown studio in York. When we walked in, there was in a sylvan setting a rustic bench with a painted stream trying to flow behind it,

---

[25] Like most monasteries, we had problems with phone messages. Brother Antony Hookham spent much time on this tedious job and was very good-natured but also hard of hearing. Father Timothy called one day from the airport to ask for someone to pick him up. T. Hullo Brother Antony. This is Father Timothy. A. He's not here. T. No, this is Father Timothy. A. You can't speak to him; he's out of town. And so on. Father Timothy hung up and tried again: T. I'm at the airport. Could someone come and pick me up? A. Of course. Who is this? T. Father Timothy. A. Oh, that's funny, there was a call for you just a minute ago.

and opposite it the maestro with an Edwardian-looking plate camera on an enormous stand and with an ample black veil to cover the actual moment of photography, almost as though it were an improper intrusion into our privacy. We ought to have left at once, but we knew of nowhere else to go. The results were lugubrious, as might have been expected, and can have been little help to Inc's fund-raising. Fortunately another picture became available through the English press. It showed the three first monks walking outside the abbey at Ampleforth with Father Ian Petit, our first reinforcement. There must have been a real, not painted, breeze blowing and the scene is happier and more natural. (*See* plate 2)

Father Columba and Father Timothy also attended in August a Fulbright Conference, held at University College, Oxford, at which lectures were given by a variety of American experts on a variety of American subjects. It was enjoyable and somewhat informative, but the scope was so general that it hardly dented the carapace of our ignorance. Perhaps its most useful contribution was to remind us that the Americans and the British are indeed "divided by a common language" and that Saint Louis was likely to seem to us no less foreign than Salamanca.

Many other people gave us advice; indeed, few could resist. Among the most useful was a discourse by Sir Herbert Read[26] on American attitudes towards earned wealth and inherited wealth, and a warning from an experienced uncle that, tot for tot, alcohol is stronger in U.S.A. than in the British Isles, or else the tots more generous.

---

[26] He was a distinguished English author and art critic. He and Lady Read were good friends of Father Austin and of many of the monks at Ampleforth.

CHAPTER 7

Lift-off

ON 3 October 1955, with the monks standing around to wish them well, Fathers Columba, Luke and Timothy left Ampleforth to say brief farewells to family and friends; and then the day came. On 6 October the three of us, after our last vacation in England for a while, met at Victoria Station in London to take the train to Southampton. This is the station from which countless small boys used to depart for their boarding grade schools in the sunny south, and it was with somewhat similar feelings of excitement and apprehension that we, waving goodbye like those small boys to our nearest and dearest, or such of them as came to see us off, departed for Southampton and the Queen Elizabeth, on which we were to cross the Atlantic. We duly boarded, found our cabins, greeted our steward and stretched our legs. It was an anti-climax that we were delayed for a day by high winds, and a source of chagrin that we saw the *United States* set out nonetheless, she having, we were told, a more favorable berth. Next day, 7 October, the wind abated and at 1.00 p.m. we sailed or, more accurately, were nuzzled out into position by a swarm of tugs. And so, accompanied by a flurry of telegrams from family, friends, well-wishers and, which especially heartened us, from Ampleforth monks serving on our various parishes around the country, we left our homeland. Then at our first dinner a bottle of champagne arrived at the table. We thought it was either a mistake or possibly just the normal procedure on such a ship. It was in fact from one of Ampleforth's most loyal Old Boys (alumni), Mr. A. F. M. (Fred) Wright, brother of one monk at Ampleforth and uncle of three others. We drank his health. That was not the only delight of the table, for we found that we had sitting with us two scholarly Jesuits, one of whom was Father Walter J. Burghardt, who became famous for *Preaching the Just Word*, and the other Father Edgar Smothers, both returning from a European conference on Patristics.

The trip was uneventful, though once or twice there was enough movement for the Queen to put out her stabilizing fins. We said Mass each day under the aegis of an Irish Senior Steward, of whom it was said that he once mistook a High Church Anglican divine for a Catholic priest, assigned him a time to say Mass, and arranged to serve the Mass himself. The Roman Mass then was still in Latin, but the

Anglican started off "In the name of the Father and of the Son and of the Holy Ghost. Amen. I will go unto the altar of God", to which his server replied "Not in my ship you won't", and that was the end of that. He ruled with a firm hand, and it may have been his experience with the Anglican that made him rather sticky with us when he asked for our *celebrets*[27] and found that we had none. This was, in those days, a considerable error on our part, but eventually Father Columba's transparent honesty convinced him.

We were invited for cocktails to the cabin of Commodore Sir Ivan Thompson, the Captain, and introduced as men going to found another public school, this one in the United States. This was almost exactly what we were not intending to do. At no time did we aim to turn the unsuspecting boys of Saint Louis into young English gentlemen. But it did, sadly, focus attention on us, and almost inevitably brought up the question of corporal punishment. We were surprised then, and not for the last time, at the prominence of corporal punishment in the image that both Americans and British had of the British public school. We were also invited to tour the engine room, from which Father Luke remembers the enormous propeller shafts and Father Timothy the enormous pistons.

With great excitement we stood on deck as we came into the narrows and waited for our first view of New York's famous skyline, known to every European from countless movies. Father Columba had been there before, and so when the first bumps appeared on the horizon, "There it is," he cried. They turned out to be oversize storage tanks for natural gas. Father Columba's reputation for local expertise suffered, but after all, every bump on the horizon resembles every other. The real thing, however, soon followed and was indeed a spectacle, surreal had it not been real.

We were met by Mr. Hoguet and Prior Aelred Graham, which was just as well because the longshoremen were celebrating Columbus Day, 12 October, and we had motley bags, trunks and tea chests, twenty-three pieces in all, and all rather shabby compared with the other elegant matched sets on the quay. While we stood by feeling rather helpless, Mr. Hoguet arranged for their dispatch to Saint Louis, and we saw no more of them for a while. The Hoguets entertained us at their brownstone house on Ninety-Second Street, and between meals drove us round New York to Times Square, Wall Street,

---

[27] A *celebret* was a document, signed by the appropriate abbot or bishop, authorizing a Catholic priest to celebrate Mass in places where he was not known--something like an ecclesiastical passport.

Broadway, Fifth Avenue and J. P. Morgan's front door. The Empire State Building was veiled in mist, so we did not then see the panorama of New York from its top. One highlight was a visit to the Frick Museum with its famous Holbein of Saint Thomas More. We were startled then that the guards were wearing side-arms. We were startled also to see a large sign reading NO PARKING ON THE PAVEMENT. As "pavement" to us meant "sidewalk" we naturally wondered what kind of people needed to be told not to park there. New Yorkers had implied, somewhat in jest, that we should look out for arrows and tomahawks in Saint Louis, but it appeared to us at that moment that New York was not much different. Both ideas were, of course, false.

Another highlight was a visit to the United Nations building when the Council was in session. We were shown around by Father de Souza, S.J., the Indian delegate, listened to part of a debate, were introduced to Sir Pierson Dixon, head of the British delegation, and shown the Secretary General's office and the meditation room. The only religious statue we saw seemed to be of Zeus. At dinner that evening, Mr. Hoguet repeated his view that no enterprising organization should ever operate other than in the red, and one of his daughters launched into a diatribe against corporal punishment.

On 15 October we left by train for our next stop, Saint Anselm Priory (now Abbey) in Washington, DC. Saint Anselm and Portsmouth Priories were then the two American houses of the English Benedictine Congregation and we were to be the third. It was good to return to monastic life after so much gallivanting. Their community welcomed us with warmth and showed us, partly with the help of Patrick O'Donovan, an Old Amplefordian, (alumnus of Ampleforth) who was the Washington correspondent for the London *Observer*, attractions that included the Library of Congress, the Capitol, the National Gallery and Mount Vernon.

There was less bustle in Washington than in New York and the layout seemed more gracious. It was here that the three of us met and explicitly agreed that our priority was the monastery, and that the timetable should as far as possible be arranged in such a way that all the monks could attend all the monastic duties. This could not be so at Ampleforth, but we believed that it should be possible to make it so in a day school. The other two were pleased and perhaps a little surprised that the headmaster was as keen on this as they.

On the evening of 18 October we boarded the night train, took possession of our couchettes, and headed for Covington, Kentucky, where we were to say Mass the next morning. After Mass at the Cathedral we set out on the final leg of our journey rather slowly along rather wobbly rails. We crossed the Mississippi, but the water was disappointingly low and muddy. It looked more like the Limpopo River though without the fever trees.

CHAPTER 8

Arrival and Early Days

WE reached Saint Louis at 3.50 p.m. on the sunny afternoon of Wednesday 19 October, the feast-day both of the North American Martyrs and of Saint Frideswide, the patron saint of Oxford. It was probably no hotter than the low eighties, but this was warm for our thick, English, woolen suits. Although we were all eagerness to see our new home, that was not the immediate plan for us. The leaders of Inc and many others were awaiting us. We greeted them, were photographed again and again, perhaps in the hope of getting something better than what we had sent them, and then whisked off to a reception at the house of Mrs. Charles M. Huttig. She was president of the women's arm of the fund-raising and had a number of her helpers there to greet us. With them was Monsignor William F. Mullally, who had been in Burma in World War II and would, they hoped, have something in common with Father Timothy; but Burma is a large country and the Americans and British were at opposite ends of it. Our chief memory of the reception was that the amazingly high volume of sound made conversation very conjectural, as we often missed much of what the other person was saying. It was like the three deaf men on the London underground: "Is this Wembley?" "No, Thursday." "So am I; let's go and have a drink." There was certainly plenty to drink at the reception.

Fred Switzer then drove us out from the reception to our property. On the way he said he hoped that we would not be disappointed in the house as it was rather old. It flashed through our European heads that a substantial house could not have been built this far out from the city before 1800 and probably much later than that, so the house could not be that old, when Fred continued, "Yes, it was built in the late thirties, just before World War II." Words like "old" and "big" are comparative terms, and we were to find again and again that our standards of comparison were quite different from those current in Saint Louis. Our "old" tended to be much older and our "big" much smaller.

At about 7.00 p.m. we finally drove down Mason Road at dusk. There is a little valley between the road and the Stannard House, which was to be our first home on the property. All its lights had been turned on and the house seemed to float on its ridge like an enchanted palace. It was a notable arrival.

Again there was a crowd waiting for us, and for their dinner, but Father Columba insisted that the monks' first act should be to say Vespers and Compline, which we did in the chapel beautifully arranged for us by the Ladies' group, headed by Fred Switzer's wife, Viola and Clarkson Carpenter's wife Dorothy Jane, or DJ. At the end the three of us sang, if that is the right word, the *Salve, Regina*[28] to Our Lady. That done, we sat down to our first meal in our new foundation. In due course our guests departed, but not before Dewey Dempsey, Inc's treasurer, slipped into Father Luke's hand an envelope and said "That should make things easier for you". The envelope contained a check for $10,000, more money than Father Luke or any of us had ever held in his hand in his life. And so, immensely wealthy, we went to bed, Father Columba in one of two small rooms at the north end of the house, which had been the servants' quarters, Father Luke in what was to be his office at the top of the stairs, and Father Timothy in the reception room opposite the top of the stairs. We all slept well.

The Stannard House, which was to be our home for three years, was a two-story house, solidly built of brick, stone and concrete and neo-colonial in style.[29] The brick was painted white but its natural color was, very fashionably, starting to show through, and the shutters were of a green so dark as to appear black. The main entrance was through a gracefully rounded porch with columns, with a similarly rounded balcony above. In the hall there were leaded glass fan-lights over the doors and a fine curved staircase leading up to the second floor. On this floor were our bedrooms and no fewer than five bathroom suites. We must have been the only religious house in the world that had more bathrooms than monks, but the *Guinness Book of Records* has so far ignored us. The windows were fitted in winter with an inner storm-window, and in summer with a screen to keep out insects. That meant that you could not at any time of the year put your head out of the window, which felt surprisingly restrictive to those fresh from England. We had not recognized that putting one's head out of the window was so much of a national pastime. The house was also, after

---

[28] Hail, Queen.

[29] We have kept in the text the name which the house had for the whole period covered by this history. On 8 December 1997, it was officially renamed the Switzer House, in honor of Fred Switzer, who was present at the ceremony.

Ampleforth, suffocating, so we had some of the storm windows replaced with screens. We breathed more easily, but our help froze, or so they claimed.

Initially the choir, where we recited our prayers, was in the sun room on ground level, and the first chapel, where we celebrated Mass, was upstairs in the room above the sun room. The chapel soon moved downstairs to the drawing room, next to the choir, which was still in the sunroom. Meals were in the breakfast room and our library in the dining room. The rathskeller was the calefactory, or monks' common room, except for state occasions such as the banquet for Dr. and Mrs. Mario Salvador, when we turned it into a banqueting hall. Mario was the organist at the Cathedral.

Next morning at 7.30 we said Mass for the success of the whole venture. A sizeable congregation was present, all men. We later came to attribute this high rate of Mass-attendance by men to the success of the Jesuits in getting the Catholic men of Saint Louis into the habit of making an annual Retreat at the Jesuits' White House, built in a commanding spot overlooking a beautiful reach of the Mississippi.

On 21 October we recited the Divine Office in choir for the first time. We rose at 5.00 a.m. and said Matins and Lauds, starting at 5.20. One of us then said Mass (this was long before concelebration) while the other meditated, then vice versa, then we had Prime, Conventual Mass, celebrated by the third of us, and either one or two of the Little Hours depending on the day. This took us to about 7.45 and breakfast. Lunch was at 1.00 p.m., with the remaining Little Hour or Hours, Vespers at 6.15, supper at 6.30 and Compline at 9.00. Our sole venture into song was again the *Salve, Regina* at the end of Compline. We put out our lights at 10.00 p.m. This regime was generally reasonable, but could on occasion be quite demanding.

On 1 November we attended a meeting of the Men's Club at Our Lady of Lourdes Parish, got back to Priory about 11.00 p.m., said the Office of the Dead for All Souls,[30] and rose next morning at 5.00 to say our three Masses each, nine in all, for the faithful departed. We had planned to say the Office for the Dead before going to the meeting but had been delayed by having to lay the carpet in the chapel, which, like so many other tasks, took our inexperience longer than expected.

We were kept busy for the first few days: we met Archbishop Ritter and other clergy, we visited Saint Louis Country Day School and

[30] All Souls was on 2 November, but we were then still on occasion saying Matins (anticipated) the previous evening.

many other schools, and many hospitals and churches; had meals at a country club and at restaurants, at one of which a “small” steak was nearly a foot long, attended a football game and were startled both by the defensive armor worn by the players and by the antics and gender of the cheerleaders--Father Timothy asked one of them if she enjoyed football and was told she did not; she just came to watch the boys--and on 25 October attended at Annunziata parish our first meeting of Inc and delivered our first speeches. After the speeches we came to the real purpose of the meeting, to distribute to the captains of the fund-raising teams some twelve hundred cards each bearing the name of a prospective donor. The whole meeting lasted a little less than two hours, a tribute to Fred Switzer's sense of urgency.

We were also taken on excursions into the countryside, well wooded to the South, and were impressed by the beauty of the Fall leaves and by the limestone Ozarks with their red granite core. Then, when we had time to catch our breath, we recognized three pressing problems: subsistence, driving and architecture.

Subsistence meant that we had to shop, and none of us had had much recent practice at that. Fortunately there were some men and many women eager to help us, that is mainly to help Father Luke, to learn. Not that they were always the best advisors for monks. One of them recommended Straub's. When Father Luke suggested that it might be a bit beyond our style, she replied, "Oh no! It's much cheaper in the long run." How long the run had to be we never found out. Fortunately for monastic frugality, Father Luke soon ferreted out less expensive sources such as Cherrick's Railway salvage operation and Holstein's second-hand furniture store. Father Columba and Father Timothy accompanied Father Luke on some of the earlier shopping expeditions, but soon had seen all they needed to see, and Father Luke bore the brunt of the shopping thereafter.

There were, however, special expeditions on which Father Luke did not go alone. One such was to Cherrick's. Goaded by jibes about dented cans and battered cartons, Father Luke invited Father Timothy to come and see Cherrick's for himself. We set off. As we approached the warehouse a strange buzzing became audible. Father Luke brushed off some suggestions about its source, but when we arrived, every fly in Saint Louis, and perhaps some from East Saint Louis, was present. A forty-gallon drum of molasses had fallen from the loading dock and burst. It was a hot summer's day, and for Father Luke a long one.

We also all three visited Holstein's and acquired a supply of scratched or dented furniture quite suitable for the monks' rooms.

Much of it is still in use over forty years later. Mr. Holstein was much amused by our constant use of "fortnight" and referred to Father Luke as Father Fortnight. He also had an interesting conversation by phone with Father Columba. Father Columba called, wanting to make some enquiry, and started rather formally, "This is Father Columba Cary-Elwes, Prior of Saint Louis Priory". He was startled to receive the response, "Oh no it's not." Father Columba said that indeed he was Father Columba, only to be told again that he was not and that Mr. Holstein knew who he really was. It took several minutes to establish that Father Columba really was who he said, at the end of which he asked, naturally, what was going on. Mr. Holstein replied that he had an impish friend who delighted in saying on the phone that he was the Mayor of New York, or the Archbishop of Sioux City, or whatever high-falutin name came into his head. This time Mr. Holstein thought he had spotted him and was not going to be fooled again.

The next pressing problem was to get our driving licences. We each had an English driving licence, but with a difference. Father Luke had taken and passed the English driving test; Father Timothy had, after several letters, persuaded the English authorities to grant him a licence on the grounds that he had been a driving instructor in the Army in World War II; but Father Columba had acquired his licence in 1921 before the days of testing, when all you had to do was to pay half-a-crown and receive your licence. Since then, wisely, he had hardly driven at all.

In the three-car garage, when we arrived, was an aging Cadillac of considerable length and with a control panel that could have served as an organ console, a forest of knobs. We were told that there was a police district that might look more favorably than most on Catholic priests, and were advised to go there. On the day of the test, therefore, Father Luke drove us to our appointment. We all took and passed the written part of the test, and then our officer for the driving test met us and said respectfully, "OK, which of you reverend gentlemen is going first?" Father Columba, with characteristic fearlessness, said, "I am the prior; I will go first." He got into the car and the officer asked him to put on the lights. Now Father Columba had previously taken the car out for a trial spin, but it was by daylight and he had not needed the lights. Confident that the answer must lie in one of the forest of knobs, he pulled the first, and the hood shot up. The officer gravely put it down again, and Father Columba pulled the next knob, which started the windshield-wipers; and the next, which produced a squirt of detergent. The officer came to the car, found the right knob and tested the lights. They set off and returned and Father Columba had passed, but the officer wrote at the bottom of the test report "general control poor". It is fair to record here that Father Columba and his guardian angel never had a serious accident and that they managed to do a U turn on Lindbergh Boulevard, which at the time was probably the busiest four-lane highway in Saint Louis. Neither of the other two monks ever achieved that.

The final problem, architecture, was our largest. It was now October 1955 and the school was due to open in September 1956. We had by then to have somewhere to teach. Should we build new buildings, or adapt the existing buildings, or try to incorporate the existing buildings into a new layout? Our friends exerted some pressure on us, as they had already done on Abbot Herbert and Father Columba in June, to use the architect of the Stannard House, Ray Maritz. He was familiar with the house, the other buildings and the grounds; he had shown that he could give us a very pleasing ensemble, even though in a derivative style; we were assured that such buildings would be thought to be very suitable for a school like ours. Indeed our supporters assumed at this stage of our acquaintance that we would choose a traditional style for a traditional school, even though we ourselves were far from convinced of that. In addition, Maritz seemed willing to produce a plan at the drop of a hat, so, with the warm support of our lay advisors, we decided to let him drop his hat.

He had already drawn an outline in the shape of a cloister or quadrangle, incorporating the large barn in the middle of one end and the small but elegant archway building in the middle of the other, with the Stannard House behind it. The equipment shed was to become part of the East side of the cloister. New buildings were to fill in the gaps and present a continuous façade. The barn was to become the chapel for both school and monastery, the West side of the quadrangle classrooms and other school rooms, the East side quarters for the monks. (*See* plate 1)

He came out on 27 October to discuss the plan with us. It had real charm, and cloisters are congenial to Benedictines. It made good use of the existing buildings and would have served the needs of monks and school for a number of years. It was also to be economical, as Maritz thought the bids should come in at around $60,000. And yet we did not feel fully comfortable. We had not in our minds reached a decision about the style of building that we wanted and felt hesitant about starting on a scale that would commit us to continue in the same way. One small thing set off warning-signals in our minds: whenever we questioned the looks of a feature, Maritz tended to reply, "Oh, we'll put some wisteria there"--a cosmetic rather than an architectural answer. After lengthy discussion with Maritz, with Inc, with our *ad hoc* building committee and among ourselves, we decided to go ahead and asked Maritz to produce the necessary drawings and specifications, a task which would take several weeks. The plan was eventually put out for bids on 24 January 1956, and we thought that we had solved one of our most pressing problems.[31]

To revert to our first weeks, we had also to find some staff. Fred Deal, the Stannards' yard man, had stayed on, and he was joined by Erwin Sellenriek, a local farmer, who was to come in by the hour, when he could, to look after the estate. Each in his own way was a gem. After various people had cooked various meals for us, Viola Switzer had found Genevieve, but she had been used to cooking for the upper crust and to having footmen and butlers to help her. We were not upper crust, there were no footmen, and she was expected to do the washing up. She gave notice, and before long Father Luke was able to hire Ellen Koebel, who served us well for several years. Not only did she both cook and do dishes, but when we started to get young men coming to stay with us to see if they wanted to become monks, she provided an American ear to listen to their musings about the strange ways of the English. You might call her our first, and last, Associate Novice Mistress. Much of the work indoors was done by Howard Casey. He was an interesting and thoughtful man, who gave Father Columba many copies of *Ebony Magazine*. Without being bitter, he had much to say about the difficulties of being black in America. He was a lesson in another way too; to us he looked just African-American, but he was in fact part Chinese and part Indian as well. Sadly, he was killed on 15 January 1956 when he got out of a car in a snow storm and was hit by another car. After Howard's death, Henry Hughes introduced to us his brother Joe Casey, who worked for us for a number of years in various capacities. He was notable not least because he held a second and sometimes a third job, so that he could put his five children through medical school. Finally, Maggie Hamilton came in once a week to do laundry.

We had two other tasks, public relations and property, no less important but less immediate than the first three. We needed to make ourselves known and we needed more land. On each we spent much thought and time.

Because there had been so much publicity and net-working before our arrival, what people now wanted was to see what they were getting,

---

[31] Letter of 11 February 1997 from Mr. Raymond E. Maritz, Jr.

and that meant us. Inc therefore planned with us a series of meetings of greater or less formality. They all had two things in common: speeches and refreshments. Father Columba spoke of the spiritual aspects of the Priory, Father Luke of the logistics and practical arrangements and Father Timothy of the school. Fred Switzer then added the essential facts about the fund-raising drive. In general, Father Columba emphasized that what was coming to Saint Louis was a monastery. The monks would run the school, but they were monks before they were schoolmasters, and that would affect the schedule; the monastery would be the spiritual center of a family. He also praised American generosity and the way in which Americans followed Bacon's dictum, "Money is like muck: it is meant to be spread." Father Luke promised to pursue good stewardship and to avoid extravagance, and often described the immediate needs. Father Timothy promised a school to challenge good but not necessarily brilliant students; there would be small classes and personal attention; we would provide abundant information but not indoctrination; we would aim to teach the boys to think for themselves. He tried to indicate diplomatically that boys would be accepted on their own merits and not because of the generosity of their parents, but few believed him then.

Our audiences were admittedly partial to us and were there because they were deeply interested, but even so, we were impressed by their attentiveness and good will. Making these speeches brought home to us again how much of our common language we do not in fact share. Vocabulary, metaphor, idiom, even pronunciation, all spread out traps for the unwary, and into many of them we fell. We noted that some metaphors long dead in England were brand new in Saint Louis, and vice versa. When Father Columba said that some action would really set the cat among the pigeons, a routine English metaphor, many people came up afterwards and complimented him on the brilliance of his imagery. Conversely, when Saint Louisans spoke routinely of a traffic snarl, we pictured cars curling up the ends of their chrome lips and baring their chrome teeth at one another like angry dogs.

We noted also that impromptu remarks were warmly received. At one Father and Son dinner much later the room was becoming stuffy and Judge James F. Nangle, who was sitting by a large sash window, opened it. The resulting fresh air made the heavy curtain swell out in the breeze. Father Timothy was at the microphone and said, "What are you doing, Judge, setting sail?"--a very mild sally, one might have thought--but had there been aisles in the dining room, the audience would have rolled in them. And then there was the matter of accent.

We were taken to a reception at Maryville College, which was then an all-women college staffed almost entirely by Religious of the Sacred Heart. A group of young women surrounded us and we talked. Every now and then one of them would turn her back to us and we could see her shoulders shaking. Eventually one of them said, "Fathers, do go on talking. It doesn't matter what you say; just go on talking." It was ironical to us that the speaker was a Southerner, and we might just as well have said the same to her.

Overall there was a refreshing immediacy of response that may well have been like that of audiences in ancient Athens.[32] But it also made us realize, in the literal sense of making real to ourselves, that we were a long way from home. Another event reinforced that feeling. Mr. David King, an Old Boy, or alumnus, of Ampleforth, visited us. Now there are English accents and English accents and his was *very* English. Each of us was surprised at how much we had enjoyed his visit and hearing him talk, and surprised again at the wrench when he left.

We got to know one another's speeches fairly well and even found ourselves insensibly poaching on one another's preserves. We met in parish halls or at the Priory; some meetings included dinners at restaurants or at the expensively simple quarters of the Deer Creek Club, a private dining club in Ladue built like a luxurious log cabin. These dinners were a startling reminder of another difference between American and English customs. In England a sherry-party or cocktail-party and a dinner were different kinds of entertainment. At the former there would be an abundance of sherry or cocktails with finger-food. The guests stood, circulated, conversed with ever-increasing liveliness and then departed. At a dinner there would be sherry or some other aperitif to open the guests' digestion, followed by the dinner, with a flow of wine and conversation. Food, alcohol and conversation were closely linked. In Saint Louis food and alcohol seemed to be much less closely combined, and there might be a two-hour alcoholic cocktail party and then dinner, at which the drink might be coffee or iced tea. This had the advantage over the English style of dinner-party that there was much longer to circulate and to meet many more people, and the disadvantage that by mealtime many people's powers of conversation were sadly diminished.

---

[32] Demosthenes once told his Athenian hearers that he had made the danger of war pass by *hōsper nephos*, like a cloud. They were so moved by the simile that they burst into tears.

Sometimes we entertained at the Priory. On 4 November we had Mass for the Ladies' Group, to be followed by breakfast. Half way through the Mass, Father Luke observed that the caterer had not arrived. When he went to telephone, the line was dead. Mrs. Dunstan and Barbara Chrisler set to and prepared coffee and someone had left a huge cake in the kitchen, so all was well.

In a less ordinary form of hospitality we provided a stirrup-cup for a meet of the Bridlespur Hunt. They assembled in front of the Stannard House in all their splendor and in due course moved off. Around mid-afternoon some of them returned. We asked one of them whether they had killed. "Oh yes." "Was it a good run?" There was a pause while the man looked at his boots and shuffled a bit. "Not really." "Oh, what happened?" "Well, er, well, one of the horses trod on the fox." The fox had sought refuge in a culvert, stayed there and emerged only when it thought the coast was clear. Unfortunately there was this horse crossing the little stream at just that moment.

All this activity came under the heading of Public Relations; property was a concern of a quite different sort. Every school needs space for buildings, playing fields and, nowadays, parking lots. If all boys are to take part in athletics, the school needs even more space for playing fields. But our property was also the home of the monks, and they needed not only living space but also elbow room to allow for a certain *quies monastica*.

From the very beginning monks have felt the pull both of the cenobitic, or community, life and of the eremitical, or solitary, life. Community life calls for a certain space to call its own and needs that space, if it is to thrive; the solitary life calls for a certain seclusion, a *fuga mundi* or flight from the world. The earliest monks went to the desert, where the acreage was unlimited. We knew that acres in our area were expensive and tried to restrict our wishes, but we had come from Ampleforth, where one could walk for a long way without leaving the property. So, although we admired the achievement of the men who had acquired our land, we did feel the need for more; and they graciously agreed.

At the beginning of 1956 we owned nearly eighty-five acres, a little over fifty of the Gallagher property and a little over thirty of the Stannard. The owner to our northwest was not interested in selling, except for the one acre for access between our two properties. The two owners to our east were open to discussion. Mr. Frank A. Singer, who owned the larger property, was the first to come to terms. On 20 March 1956 Inc bought from him a tract of 28 acres for $100,000. This included the sturdy frame building which for ten years was to house Father Ian and the seventh and eighth grades. Nearly two years later we acquired for $69,187.50 the rest of the Singer property, a tract of 27.675 acres marching with Highway 40. This was because Mr. Joseph Desloge believed we could not have too much land and so gave us this property mainly as an investment. How wise he was!

Mr. Charles H. Reasor held out for longer. On 28 July 1955 Inc negotiated an option to buy his 11.279 acres, and on 15 December of that year the Reasors acknowledged receipt of written notice of exercising the option and of the payments agreed to by that date. The payments would be put in escrow, and were to continue until January 1960 when the Reasors would move out. We at least half hoped that when they were surrounded by the activity and noise of the school they would move out earlier and perhaps less expensively, but neither hope was realized. The property included a sizeable and substantial house and two or three barns.[33] The price was $100,000. Later we agreed that they should stay on until 31 March and that is when they finally moved out. This property brought our estate to just over one hundred and fifty acres.

[33] We later discovered what seems to have been a still on their property, but that did not enter into the negotiations.

CHAPTER 9

Preparation

MUCH else filled the last two and a half months of 1955. There was a constant flow of visitors, many of whom were prospective parents. Although we could not show them the school, we could outline to them the plans we had in mind, and could show them the Stannard House itself, which would be a substantial part of those plans. As both Benedictines and Englishmen were something of a rarity in Saint Louis, and the combination unique, they may have come partly to see that, but come they certainly did.

There was conversation and discussion: conversation with visitors and discussion with Inc and among ourselves. Looking back one can see that it was our most spacious living, though we seemed at the time to be busy enough. We had to make room both for reflection on the experiences of each day and for planning ahead. In those early days we talked at meals instead of having a book read to us, and our talk seemed constructive, so we were startled to find, when a guest concealed a microphone in the bunch of flowers on the table, that three articulate and polite Englishmen, as we thought, completed only two sentences in the course of the whole meal. All the rest were either left unfinished or were interrupted. Our meals were in the breakfast room of the Stannard House, a pleasant oval-shaped room which just managed to hold all of us until the school library moved out of the dining room next door, and the monks could move in. As our numbers grew, we introduced reading at the evening meal, and monastic reading always has its lighter moments. Father Bede will long be remembered for misreading the Potawatomi Indians as "Watapotomi" and then commenting on the oddness of their name.[34] Fortunately for the sanity of monks, monastic meals themselves may also be a source of innocent merriment, as when Father Columba, who was not mechanically adept, handed to Father Thomas, who was, an aerosol container of whipped cream and explained how to use it. Father Thomas aimed at his dessert and pressed firmly. The jet of

---

[34] It is said that at Ampleforth, when they were plowing through the many volumes of Pastor's *The Lives of the Popes*, the reader, in order to speed the plow, read only the left-hand pages; it is also said that nobody noticed.

whipped cream struck his dessert a glancing blow at high speed and ricocheted off all over the table. Another incident showed Father Columba more in character: he suffered a pain in his biceps, and seeing a bottle labeled "mucilage" and concluding that it might help the muscle, applied some to his biceps. Its only effect was to glue his tee-shirt to his arm. What was even more typical of him was that he eagerly told us about it.

Sometimes the merriment came from the food itself. Much of the food was unfamiliar to us, so a single example will have to stand for all. Soon after our arrival, we were given a large jar--a quart or two--of apple butter. To us it looked like apple fool, a common English dessert, so the three of us finished it off for supper one night. It seemed, perhaps, a little rich, but not unduly strange. Not long afterwards we met the donors, who asked how the apple butter was going. We said we had enjoyed it for supper last night. They then told us it was intended to last us a month.

In the evening, we were able to sit out after dinner under the noble elms and continue our conversations without feeling guiltily that we should either be somewhere else or be doing something else. The setting was audio-visually relaxing: the visual element came from the lawn and the elms. The lawn was smooth and well-mown but to our eyes the grass seemed rather long. We soon learnt that if you shaved it in the English manner, the summer sun immediately scorched it. The beauty of the lawn was enhanced by beds of colorful iris down either side, and on the north, two rows of vines, balanced by a small orchard on the south. The audio element came from the cicadas on the elms. They filled the air with their noise, winding themselves up to a crescendo and then winding down again. It was so much part of the ambience as to be soothing, and anyway we were not trying to go to sleep. If cicadas appear on a thirteen year-cycle, this was certainly their year. On the other side of the house, facing West, we had a grandstand view in the fall of a series of spectacular sunsets from brilliant to brooding, and for a short space, and greatly to our surprise, the Aurora Borealis, or Northern Lights, which we have never seen since.

On feast-days we would have coffee and candy or even B. and B. if the feast were big enough. Unfailingly on such feast-days our cat, Corry, born on Coronation Day, who never noticed us on ordinary days, would come to claim her saucer of milk. She was a descendant of the half-wild cats which, when we first arrived, inhabited the loft of the barn. When kittens were due, they were born at ground level. Then the mother would seize them by the scruff of their neck and carry them to the loft up a crude ladder whose rungs were over a foot apart, just about as much of a stretch as she could manage. The kittens would hiss and spit at you even before their eyes were open. We decided to try to domesticate them, and brought one of the kittens into the kitchen. When it started to mew, the mother heard it and approached but would not at first come in. Eventually maternal feeling overcame her wildness and she came in and we shut the door. The mother went berserk, jumped onto the table and then raced round the kitchen at that level, scattering pots and pans and dishes all over. Finally from the floor she jumped straight on to the top of a half-open closet door and stayed there, ready to take a swipe at anyone who approached her. One of her relatives was the occasion of a linguistic contretemps. He was called Red, and he disappeared. Fred Deal, our yard man, was fond of Red and was upset by his disappearance. We used to ask Fred for news, but there was none. Then one day Fred came by in great excitement saying "Red done came back". Father Timothy thought he was saying that Red doesn't come back and commiserated with him. Fred repeated his statement with even greater excitement and Father Timothy said he was sure Red would come back soon, and not to worry. This went on for several exchanges and then fortunately Red himself appeared. Father Timothy said "Why look, Fred, there he is", to which Fred replied "That's just what I done been telling you."

We never had, until nearly forty years later, a resident monastic dog, because, whereas half-wild cats are independent and can look after themselves, dogs need human companionship and care. A new monastic dog, unless he has an individual monk who is responsible for him, is overfed and spoilt for a month or two, and then tends to be neglected. But that does not mean that we were deprived of canine company. When we first arrived we had a surprisingly constant supply of dogs dumped on our property. We would feed them and entertain them, and then after a week or two they would sense the direction of home and disappear. We had also the dogs of families living on our grounds or nearby. The first of these was an Airedale, whose size enabled him to rest his fore-paws on the outer sill of the windows of the classrooms in the barn and look in. He looked in on a Latin class, rested for a minute or so, gave a twelve inch Airedale yawn and disappeared. Buckshot was a basset, who belonged to a friendly neighbor and regarded our grounds as an extension of his backyard. When we had cross-country races, he would hear the cheering, join in for the last few hundred yards and usually finish first. He never made the mistake of running the whole course. There was also, belonging to an early faculty member, a dog who despite bans kept reappearing in the faculty room. Its training had never been satisfactorily completed. There was also a German Shepherd who barked at a parent who had a heart condition. Then there was Sophie, a black Labrador, also the dog of a faculty man. She would have retained her elegant figure had the monastic cook been able to resist her constant requests to be fed. As it was, she became more and more swaybacked and at the end could hardly walk without sweeping the ground beneath her. And then there was Shadow, a female standard French Poodle, who was always a blithe spirit with her springy lope around the campus. Finally there was Natasha of mixed extraction, who did have a single master, Brother Symeon.

Besides these animals of varying degrees of domestication, there was also, especially in these early days, an abundance of wild life. The birds were the most striking. There were svelte and sweetly-singing wrens nesting in the boxes on the elms, sparrows that were much smarter and cleaner than their London counterparts, juncos, the occasional bluebird, oriole or bunting, and other small birds. In the summer, when the right flowers were blooming, we had humming birds of brilliant colors. The cardinal was here all year round, and to see a male on the top branch of a tree in the morning facing the sun and silhouetted against a clear blue sky made one stop and marvel. The blue jays were vulgar and raucous, but gorgeous in flight and useful as nature's alarm system; hawks and windhovers were often seen and there was many a woodpecker, including occasionally the large pileated woodpecker, which flies almost like a small heron. High overhead in the migrating season were hundreds of geese, honking as they flew in their wedges. There were rabbits and deer in profusion, squirrels, a few resident groundhogs, the occasional red fox, a very occasional wild turkey, chipmunks sometimes, a snake or two, and twice we saw a badger. Skunks we smelt from time to time. In our ponds were some fish and some snapping turtles. The fish could coexist with the turtles but ducks could not because the turtles snapped at their dangling feet and dragged them down below the surface. There were also many kinds of frogs with many kinds of voices, another of the memorable noises of Priory.

There were also insects, some, like the luna moth and the monarch butterfly, wonderfully beautiful; some, like the praying mantis and stick insect, odd and entirely harmless; some, like the hornets, painful; some like the black widow and brown recluse spiders, dangerous. When we came, there was an outdoor bell near the garage. Hornets nested in it and hated to be disturbed by its ringing. Maybe they resented the competition, but certainly they tried to sting the ringer, and sometimes succeeded. One black widow lived on the flagpole just where the rope was tied but never bit the flag-raiser. No brown recluses bit either monks or boys, but one did bite one of our parents at her home and, as the bite putrefies the flesh, left her with a hole in her leg that took many weeks to heal.

In November we attended Mass at Holy Cross church in North Saint Louis, the parish of Monsignor Martin B. Hellriegel, the leading liturgist in Saint Louis and friend of the French Benedictine liturgist, Dom Ermin Vitry. Nearly a decade before the second Vatican Council, Monsignor Hellriegel succeeded in making the liturgy truly the work of the people,[35] with a large choir and vigorous responses by the people. He introduced us at the Mass and made us stand to be greeted with applause. We were fresh enough from England to be embarrassed, but we became good friends with him nonetheless. On the way home, we were being driven by Mr. John Brod (Jack) Peters, a young man who was showing interest in becoming a monk. Without warning he pulled off the road and stopped suddenly, with a shower of gravel from the shoulder of the road, saying he felt faint from the idea that if he had an accident, he might wipe out the whole community. We took the wheel with alacrity.

We were also engaged in getting to know the local educators. Father Curtin had been to Ampleforth, where we had all seen him, and Father Columba had met most of the leading educators on his visit in the summer, but the other two monks had to start from scratch. We visited schools and attended meetings and social gatherings and were received graciously; but what pleased us most of all was the warm hospitality shown us by the Jesuits. They, with their University and their high school for boys, were the dominant Catholic educators in Saint Louis, and their high school was the Catholic school most likely to be affected by our arrival. It was a real relief to us when they declared that there were plenty of boys for both of us, and made us most welcome. We spent many of the greater feasts enjoying their hospitality, starting with Thanksgiving Day on 24 November.[36] The truth of their statement that there were boys to spare was shown when

[35] That is the meaning of the Greek roots of the word "liturgy".

[36] Against this background of hospitality we may recall that Father Columba went to visit Father Reinert at the university and parked as instructed in Father Reinert's reserved parking place. When they came out afterwards, they found that the campus police had covered Father Columba's windshield with opaque sticky paper for parking in this sacred spot.

in 1967 they opened De Smet Jesuit High School within two miles of us, and our two schools have coexisted since. The mention of Thanksgiving brings back the memory that for every Thanksgiving since then, Mr. and Mrs. William T. Dooley, Jr., with porterage by their children and relatives, have brought out to us a complete dinner of turkey and all the trappings and trimmings, solid and liquid, and all we have had to do was to heat and eat them. We were not surprised by American generosity, but it took us longer to recognize how thoughtful it so often was.

We attended a football game between arch-rivals Saint Louis University High School, run by the Jesuits, and Christian Brothers College, visited our neighbors at Chaminade, run by the Marianist Brothers, and the girls' school, Saint Joseph's Academy, for the sake of its architecture. Several of our key supporters were graduates of Saint Louis Country Day School, so we had been taken there very early on. We were now shown the new campus planned for The Principia, a Christian Science school just across the highway from us, and saw how much space students' cars absorb. They had skillfully laid out a series of terraces shielded by trees to accommodate a mass of cars without their being an eyesore. From the road one sees simply a green slope.

Monday 21 November was one of the most important of those early days, for on it we launched our fund-raising drive, THE DRIVE, with capital letters. There was intense planning for it, at which we were told that although in our previous speeches we had no doubt spoken well, we had also confirmed all the stereotypes about British understatement, and did we think we could pull out all the stops on this occasion? The Archbishop would be there with top brass from his Archdiocesan School Office, other notable clergy and about five hundred laity, drivers and driven. The meeting was held at Annunziata, Monsignor Faris' parish.[37] Father Curtin opened the meeting with appropriate prayer, Fred Switzer introduced each of us with hyperbole, we each spoke, Archbishop Ritter wondered why such a school had not been started sooner and gave us a warm endorsement and his blessing. Then Fred said what we really needed in the way of money. In our speeches we may not have achieved a diapason but it was certainly more than a tremolo, and the leaders of Inc were well pleased, though they foresaw that it would be "tough sledding from here on out". The meeting brought out the curious ambivalence in the American mind when it looks to the future: there is both

---

[37] Father Columba in his diary places the meeting at Immacolata Parish, but our memory is of Annunziata, and he often confused the two.

aggressive optimism and what may be called the Bud Wilkinson approach, which sees next Saturday's game as an almost insurmountable challenge against an unusually strong opponent.

We had by now sold the aging Cadillac and acquired a six-cylinder, 1955 Chevrolet in two tones of light green, and were on the track of a Ford station wagon with a Thunderbird engine. This greatly expanded our horizons, and Father Columba sent Father Luke and Father Timothy off to Atchison to visit the Benedictine abbey there, in its beautiful position on the bluffs over the Missouri River. They had a college and a prep school, both predominantly boarding. By now we knew that this meant a college-preparatory school and not, as in England, a grade school. We took special note of their boarding arrangements, as the idea of our running a boarding school was not dead, and Fred Switzer had been approached by a number of friends from all over the Middle West expressing interest in our school.

In Kansas City, on the way to Atchison, we visited first the "Fish" Church by Barry Byrne[38], a disciple of Frank Lloyd Wright, and then the delightful Rockhill Nelson Art Gallery. As we left, we missed the way and went into a shop to ask how to get onto the road for Atchison. When we found it hard to understand the reply--it was already dawning on us that there was not just one American accent but many--a friendly man standing in line behind us said "Follow me" and led us for several miles until we were on the right road.

At Atchison we studied the architecture of the abbey church, for which Barry Byrne was again the architect, admired the murals in the church, picked the brains of the prior, procurator, president of the college and headmaster of the Preparatory School, and renewed our acquaintance with Father Brendan Downey, who had been at Ampleforth's house of studies in Oxford. We sat in on one of his classes when he was lecturing on the English romantic poets and discussing one of Shelley's less satisfactory poems. When he had finished, he turned to Father Luke, the ex-pupil of C. S. Lewis, who added illuminating and laudatory comments. He then out of politeness asked Father Timothy what he thought. Father Timothy said he thought the poem was soft in the center and fuzzy round the edges. "Give examples". He did, and there ensued a lively discussion. After class one of the students said to Father Timothy "That was wonderful; I had no idea we were allowed to disagree with Father Brendan."

---

[38] Father Columba and Father Timothy visited the church again the following summer. Of the three of us, Father Columba was the most impressed.

Father Brendan took us to see his brother, a fellow monk, who was pastor of the Catholic church in the town. Being offered a seat in an over-stuffed chair, Father Timothy took it, saying as he sat down that he liked these chairs because the first time he had sat in one he reached down by the side of the cushion and pulled out a dollar bill. With that he reached down by the side of the cushion and pulled out a dollar bill.

Next day we went off to visit Conception Abbey, a Benedictine abbey in Northwest Missouri and not too far from Atchison, but arrived late because when Father Brendan said "Turn right" that might mean either right or left, and the driver did not tumble to this at once. When we left the main road, the side roads were dirt or gravel, some of which had been recently oiled. As at Atchison, we were amazed at the sheer amount of buildings at Conception, and we admired the abbey's Printery. Thence we drove to the abbey of Benedictine nuns at Clyde nearby, where they had perpetual adoration of the Blessed Sacrament. Their quiet devotion was impressive.

It had turned quite cold while we were at Atchison, well below zero Fahrenheit, but all the buildings were kept at over 70°, and we found the choir stifling. We had a wretched drive back to Saint Louis, and when we were still a hundred miles away, we came into freezing rain, our first experience of driving in it. We telephoned to say that we would be back in about three hours, whereupon Fred Switzer urged us to spend the night in a motel. We were young enough to ignore this sage counsel, but were grateful when our neighbor, Frank Singer, drove out to meet us and escort us home. A day or two before this, Frank Singer had remonstrated with Father Columba after our men had, to make entry easier, cut down a small tree at the gateway of his easement. Singer was right and Father Columba apologized, greatly to Singer's surprise. That was the beginning of a good friendship. Later, in making our tennis courts, we unwittingly encroached on his property before we owned it, and again he was gracious.

On 30 November while we were away at Atchison, the first work of construction for the school had begun. Oscar Sellenriek, Erwin's cousin, arrived with men and bulldozers to start levelling our playing field. It was just south of the Stannard House, and the work entailed, to our sorrow, taking the first bite out of the apple orchard. We lost as few trees as we could. The same day, while Father Columba was walking round the property with Mr. Joseph H. Vatterott, the latter suggested forming a building committee, on which he would be glad to serve. This seems to have been the first surfacing of the idea that our lay friends should help us in practical ways according to their specific expertise, and we did in fact seek the advice of such groups both for the "Cloister plan" and for our first major buildings. They were *ad hoc* rather than standing committees, and supplemented the already strong liaison between the monks and the leaders of Inc. Nearly forty years later the same idea led us to form the group now known as The Advisors.

CHAPTER 10

Christmas in the East

THE Maritz drawings for the Cloister plan were now nearing completion, and perhaps, had we been staying in Saint Louis a little longer, would have been put out for bids before Christmas. We were, however, planning to spend Christmas on the East Coast, taking advantage of the hospitable invitation of Prior Aelred to spend the time at Portsmouth Priory, Rhode Island. On 10 December Father Timothy left in the two-tone Chevrolet for an extensive tour of schools to the East of us, punctuated by the visit to Portsmouth. Father Columba left by train on the sixteenth and Father Luke arrived at Portsmouth a day or two before Christmas. The first major event at Portsmouth was the celebration of the feast. Solemnly sung Matins started at 10.30 p.m. and were followed by the Mass of midnight, after which we sang Lauds, solemnly again, and then each of us said the three Masses then prescribed for Christmas Day. We reached our beds about 3.30 a.m. utterly exhausted. It was not easy to be duly festive on the day itself.

While we were there, we had long discussions with the monks involved in the school and with Father Peter, the procurator or business manager. We met also with Mr. Jack Acheson, the associate headmaster, and this was especially fruitful as he had been a laymaster at Ampleforth before crossing the Atlantic and coming to Portsmouth, so he had already experienced much that was still in the future for us. The results of these discussions will be included in the summary which will be given of Father Timothy's trip.

Father Columba returned to Saint Louis by air on 28 December, bequeathing to Father Luke an engagement to speak in the Cathedral at Providence, Rhode Island on Unity and the Church of England. Father Luke and Father Timothy stayed on at Portsmouth, making a foray to Providence to visit Brown University and the Providence Public Library. As we were driving through Providence, we needed to find the way, and so were both studying the map. Without noticing it we rolled at snail's pace through a stop light. There seemed to be police on all four corners of the intersection, and all four blew their whistles. The nearest bore down on us with Hibernian ferocity. We had our coats buttoned up against the cold, but instinctively unbuttoned them to receive our visitor, thus revealing our clerical collars. When the officer saw them, his look became a gracious smile and he said in a brogue, "Oh father, I'm so sorry; can I help you?" We were grateful, but both felt more humbled than if he had given us a reprimand or even a ticket.

On New Year's Day 1956 we made a longer journey to visit first the Jesuit Prep School at Cranwell, then Canterbury School, of which Gerry Mudd was an alumnus, and finally Wesleyan University in Middletown, Connecticut. At one point in our drive, we were surprised to look up and see a wheel passing over the car about twenty feet up in the air. The car in front of us stopped and a truck coming towards us kept coming and sped by. The wheel had come off the truck, hit and shattered the hood and windshield of the car in front of us, and ricocheted off them and over us to land on the road behind.

When we reached Cranwell in its wonderful setting in the Berkshire Hills, we were embarrassed. We had inquired when the Jesuits were likely to celebrate the New Year and had been told that it would be either on New Year's Eve or at lunch on the day, so we had planned to arrive in the evening when it was all over. With a mixture of chagrin and delight we found that their gala dinner was in the evening. Their place had been a country club and had been given to them for the school. The dinner might have been a country club feast. When the estate was offered to the Jesuits, the donor first asked a nominal $50,000 for the property. The Jesuits replied that if he was going to give it to them for as little as that, he might as well give it to them for nothing. He agreed. To make the visit respectable Father Luke had a long consultation with the business manager, clearly an expert in public relations and finances, and Father Timothy one with the headmaster, and then we enjoyed our oysters and champagne with a clear conscience.

Next day we visited Canterbury School, and then Wesleyan University, where we met a professor whose personality and home were just like those to be found in North Oxford.[39] And so we returned to Portsmouth. A few days later we made a day trip to Boston to visit Harvard and especially its library, the National Association of Independent Schools, and in Milton the Secondary Education Board. On 8 January, Father Timothy started on the second leg of his trip, leaving Father Luke to deliver his ecumenical homily, teach for several weeks at Portsmouth and then return to Saint Louis.

---

[39] Many of Oxford University's professors live in North Oxford. Their homes are comfortable, middle-aged residences suitable for tweedy, pipe-smoking men in baggy-kneed pants.

Long journeys by car were prominent in our early days. There was this trip by Father Timothy; there was a trip to the West Coast by Father Columba and Father Timothy in the summer of 1956, whose purpose was partly vacation and partly to get a feel of the country. This will be described in due course. There were trips made by Father Timothy mostly in the summers to visit colleges. There were "auto-driveaway" trips, when a family wanted to have their car with them on vacation, but did not want the chore of the long drive, so one of the monks did the driving. It seems worthwhile, therefore, to give a fairly detailed account of two such journeys, and from them you can imagine Father Luke, suitably attired, setting off for the West Coast in a scarlet "drive-away" Corvette, and many other such trips.

What was the purpose of the trip we are about to describe? Father Timothy had learnt from his experience in the army that good information is the essential basis of good planning.[40] The first aim therefore was to gather information about the expectations of American universities and the methods of American high schools; next, to gather information about American students and to observe them in action; then to find out how welcome Catholic students were at non-Catholic colleges and what arrangements were made for them; finally, to make our school and its aims known to a selection of American Universities.

Father Timothy, then, as we mentioned above, left Saint Louis on 10 December 1955 and returned on 15 January 1956 having covered some five thousand miles at an average of twenty miles to the gallon and a cost in gas of a little over sixty dollars.[41] The second half of the trip was made with several hundredweights of books in the trunk. As the only sources for this trip are Father Timothy's *Diary of a Journey* and his memory, it may be smoothest to paraphrase his account and to use the first person for a few pages.

My first stop was to be in Cincinnati at the Sacred Heart Convent in Clifton. Route 50 was the most direct and the most beautiful but far from the fastest way to go, so I arrived very late at the convent, and in the dark mistakenly knocked at the door of the girls' dormitory and asked if I might spend the night there. When the giggles had subsided and the truth had been revealed, I was sent to the convent, where the Sisters received me warmly and asked me to give a one-day Retreat

---

[40] Cicero says, "Not to know what happened before you were born is to remain always a boy." (Or. 34.120)

[41] Gas at that time was between twenty and thirty cents a gallon, usually in the low twenties, and occasionally, during gas wars, dipping into the teens.

the next day. This was not possible, because I had a schedule to keep, so after some bargaining we settled for Mass, a sermon and an informal meeting with the community.

In the morning I did this and, as a result, set off much later than planned, still on beautiful US 50. I was delayed still more by snow and ice on the mountains of West Virginia. Eventually, around 11.00 p.m. I found a narrow and deserted grassy lane up in the mountains, pulled off onto it, unrolled my sleeping bag and was half way into it when headlights shone in my face and someone wanted to go by. After that I resumed my place stretched out on the back seat and slept fitfully because of the cold. In the morning the steering wheel was, until the car warmed up, too cold to hold for long. During the night a bottle (of medicine) in the car froze and burst.

Next day I reached Saint Anselm Priory in Washington, DC, met the headmaster and had a pleasant evening's discussion, but instead of trying to summarize what I learnt at each school, I shall give a general summary at the end.

From Washington I went to Lawrenceville in New Jersey, travelling part of the way on the Turnpike, a new experience, as this was long before the network of Interstate highways existed. It made planning much easier, as my average speed and maximum speed were virtually the same, and I enjoyed it except that while I was waiting at a toll booth someone rammed me from behind. The driver was a pleasant and cultured man, but the police took him in charge nonetheless.

Lawrenceville is on a beautiful campus of 400 acres, and the boys live in small houses scattered among the trees. The other most striking feature was a gigantic field house, with an indoor track and a 100 yards straightaway, basketball courts, a swimming pool and an ice-hockey rink all under one roof. This multi-million dollar building was the gift of an alumnus, and the administration seemed almost embarrassed at the largesse. We entered, and as we walked past the track, there was a boy exerting hardly even the bare minimum of effort. I was about to remark on him but thought better of it; and just as well, because my guide called the boy over and said, "I'd like you to meet our English exchange student."

I left and found another unused farm track and spent the night there, warmer this time and undisturbed. Next morning I said Mass at a parish in Princeton and was invited back to the Rectory for breakfast and a wash, but missed the way. A friendly housewife saw me at a loss in the street and invited me in, introduced me to the family and fed me. Unfortunately, in the excitement I locked the keys in the car and had to break the small, triangular side window and then get a glazier to repair it. The Dean of Admissions at Princeton was most friendly and talked especially about the position of Catholics, indicating that they were very welcome, as was true of the other Ivy League universities. This was interesting, as Princeton was at the time in the middle of a considerable row with its Catholic chaplain.

That afternoon I tracked down an alumnus of Ampleforth, who was at Princeton. After a tour of the campus, in the course of which the alumnus found his way round the library only with difficulty, we fetched up in the Nassau Tavern, adorned with oak beams, panelling and an open fire to resemble an English pub. We asked, consequently, for two pints of beer; the bartender did not know what pints were and had no means of measuring them. Or perhaps he had difficulty understanding me.

The next stop was at the Hotchkiss School in Lakeville, Connecticut, beautifully situated above the lake. By now it was 15 December and the boys had gone home for Christmas, but the headmaster was out skating on the lake. He appeared in a bright orange wind-cheater, jeans and skating boots. He was a big man and a big patch of color. Here, as at most of the schools visited, there are more than a few Catholic boys. They are expected to attend the school chapel.

Next day, the headmaster and faculty of Kent School all being in New York for a dinner for alumni, I went on to Canterbury, the Catholic boarding school run by laymen, at which Gerry Mudd had been a pupil. Again, most of the faculty were in New York, but the chaplain and one of the faculty and I had a long and instructive discussion against a background of music too good to be just a background, which was consequently a distraction. In my room I found and read a copy of the play *Tea and Sympathy*,[42] which deals with a New England boarding school, but from a perspective notably different from that of a headmaster.

At Choate next day, they explained their technique of interviewing boys: it was as much an interview of the parents as of the boy. As we would find out later at our own interviews, parents often expected to sit in on the interview. I then continued to New Haven, where I was to spend some time with friends from Oxford.

In the morning, I said Mass with the Dominicans, who managed to find a Roman Missal (the Dominican rite is somewhat different) along with a server with no idea of the Roman rite. They parked us in a

[42] Robert Anderson: *Tea and Sympathy* in *New Voices in the American Theatre* (New York: Modern Library 1955) pp.377-463.

corner of the back sacristy to fight it out. After breakfast, my friends and I drove over by way of Poughkeepsie, whose pronunciation is about as self-revealing as Cholmondeley[43], and after a picnic on the bluffs overlooking the Hudson River, which deserves all the compliments paid it by Mr. Churchill, reached West Point to visit the Military Academy and to learn from the chaplain about its rigorous code of discipline. Every offense was foreseen and given its place in the scale of punishment. It seemed to work for them, but would not suit our school. They were preparing for a dance, for which young ladies were being imported from a Catholic college nearby.

At Yale there was great enthusiasm about our plans. The description of Priory that seemed to say the most in the fewest words to them and to other East Coast colleges was that it would be a school along the same lines as Portsmouth Priory School, whose reputation with them was very high. By now snow was falling and the streets were becoming slick, so I saw little of the campus and remember only a glimpse of the Gothic gymnasium as I slid on toward Millbrook, where the headmaster, who had founded the school in 1931, welcomed me. Its distinctive characteristic was a community service program in which every boy contributed to the running of the school as astronomy assistant, clock curator, member of the milk bar committee, or in some similar position. The service was to the school community rather than outside, and worked very well.

Leaving there, I headed for Boston, and by 8.30 p.m. reached a motel not too far from the city and decided to sample for the first time that kind of accommodation. The price ($5.50) seemed high for 1955, but the convenience of parking on the doorstep was great. I went in, said Compline, our night prayer, and unwisely let my head touch the pillow before writing a few letters. I awoke fully dressed at 2.00 a.m., quickly got to bed and set the alarm, which I slept through with no bother at all and awoke again at 9.00 a.m. After finding at the nearest church nobody except workmen hammering together a crib, I drove on to Boston to visit the Massachusetts Institute of Technology. There, besides learning that M.I.T. believes that its scientists should have a reasonable grasp of the liberal arts--it was possible to major in a non-scientific subject--I saw two interesting modern buildings, one a thin-shell concrete auditorium in the shape of a triangle with sides curving upwards and touching the ground only at the apexes. The walls were of glass hung from the concrete. The other was a

---

[43] In England, pronounced "Chumly" to rhyme with glumly.

cylindrical brick inter-denominational chapel. The former I admired very much.

After a brief visit with the Catholic chaplain for M.I.T., I went to visit the Harvard chaplain, who was also chaplain of a then little-known Secular Institute called *Opus Dei*. After Mass and dinner with *Opus Dei*, I was dispatched to a hotel for the night. It had been zero degrees Fahrenheit at midday and by now was 10° to 15° below, and one car, which must have been out of anti- freeze, came to a noisy and grinding halt as it was going down the street. One expected to see a cascade of ice cubes from the radiator. The hotel room cost $6.25, so these two nights were my major item of expense. There was much to be said for sleeping in the car despite the head shaking of some sages.

At Harvard next morning I had one of the most satisfactory visits of all with Mr. David Henry, who was later joined by Dean Bender, with whom Father Richard and Father Robert had also spoken. We seemed to cover most of the important aspects of American education in both high school and college. They too would actively welcome well-prepared Catholic boys and believed that the Newman chaplaincies at Harvard and at most schools were thriving. Harvard was interested in a diversified student body and was ready to achieve that with scholarships and grants, loans and jobs. This was true in varying degrees all over. After that pleasant talk, I left for Portsmouth, where we all spent Christmas, as has already been described.

On Sunday 8 January 1956 I left Portsmouth for Groton. All was well until the car started to oscillate as though a rear tire were flat. I stopped, got out and almost fell on my nose. It was freezing rain again, which there they called silver rain. It was, if anything, more lethal than in Missouri, and made any speed over 25 m.p.h. as dangerous as Russian roulette. I arrived a little late for lunch and spent the rest of the day at Groton. It was one of very few schools that had not succumbed to the passion for brand new equipment. Many of the desks and closets had a well-used look rather like those at Ampleforth. They had just introduced a new system of counseling whereby each member of the faculty took a close interest in a small group of boys.

Next day I visited both Phillips Andover and Phillips Exeter. They are large schools--750 boys or so--in large colonial-style buildings, each on a spacious campus. At Andover boys and faculty ate at separate tables; at Groton they were all mixed in with one another. I spent the night with a Catholic laymaster and his family. He had lodgings in one of the dormitories and was what in an English school would be called a housemaster.

In the morning, after Mass and breakfast and reading a few stories to their young son, Tom, I drove to Saint Paul's, a church school which had retained a real connection with its church. As at many of the other schools, I sat in on a class. I was asked who Saint Benedict was, how a monk differs from a priest, who pays for the Pope's shoes. I ought to have said "Peter's pence" but did not think of it in time. The session was held in the school chapel. I was standing at the back as the boys went out. The first one shook my hand and said politely how much he had enjoyed it, whereupon the other forty-nine did the same. I felt like royalty at a soccer match. I spent a restful night in the "prophet's chamber", which is approached by a stone spiral stair and overlooks what would have been a mill-race, had there been a mill. Next day, the Vice-Rector was having a high-level discussion class with a group of seniors on the nature and aims of education. Their text was Newman's *The Idea of a University*. It was so interesting that I was late leaving for Dartmouth, which, like Brown, is one of the smaller Ivy League schools. Its campus has something of the atmosphere of a village green. They have a fine library and two frescoes, one by the Mexican painter Orozco depicting "Aspects of American Civilization", often savagely satirical and always short on optimism--a Graham Greene novel in paint; the other is in the cafeteria and redresses the balance with a bacchanalian representation of the gladdening of the heart of man.

Leaving Dartmouth after lunch, I paid a rapid visit to Mount Hermon School, which had been recommended as having school buildings which overcame the rectilinear angularity of so much modern architecture, and the monotony which can so easily accompany a long range of one-story buildings. They used the slope so that one side of the buildings was one story high, the other two. They also used expanses of glass so as to give a view right through the building at the hallway and main staircase, whose treads were supported at the sides without risers, giving a very airy feel.

I had been looking forward to the next part of the drive, which was across the upper Hudson to Cornell, but in fact it was snowy or foggy en route, and sometimes both, and, as I was running late, it was almost dark by the time I reached the Hudson Valley. I decided to drive on through the night and to pause from time to time for a snooze, which lasted until the car became too cold; then I drove on.

It took me that night and most of the next day to reach Ithaca, where I was to stay at the Newman chaplaincy. I arrived just after dark, found the house and pressed the door-bell, whereupon the lights went out all over Ithaca. Who can say whether it was coincidence or whether

I was the last straw that induced the power cut. Soon two shadowy figures appeared carrying candles and peering out into the falling snow. They took me in. There was a famous Jesuit there from the New York water-front, who fascinated us with tales of his parishioners. In the morning I met the President and the Dean of Admissions. Amongst other things they stressed the importance of training seniors in note-taking. The low point of the trip came now. I set off gingerly from Cornell over a road of packed snow. When after nearly an hour I had seen none of the names I expected, I stopped and looked at the map. I was on the right road but going in the wrong direction. There was no sun and I had arrived after dark the day before, but that hardly lessened my chagrin. I retraced my steps grinding both teeth and gears and was four hours late reaching Saint Vincent's Archabbey in Latrobe, Pennsylvania. They were Benedictinely hospitable nonetheless, showed me next day their college and seminary and, at what I still thought of as tea-time, introduced me to a monastic custom I had not met before, the *haustus*: the monks gathered in the calefactory and a lay-brother, a very persistent Ganymede, made the rounds with a seemingly bottomless pitcher of beer. Father Columba was informed, but never adopted the custom.

That afternoon, before the *haustus*, I had visited Shady Side Academy, near Pittsburgh, whose main interest to us was that it was a flourishing example of the five-day boarding school. The boys left after school on Friday and reappeared for a two-hour study hall on Sunday evening. There were also fairly numerous day-boys and a few full boarders. The attractions were that there was time for a wide range of activities and for interaction between faculty and students; the disadvantage, that the boys returned tired and distracted from their weekend. The study hall was almost fiercely administered in order to counteract this dissipation of mind. The staff felt that the system worked well for a school just outside a large city such as theirs or ours.

On Sunday, driving as hard as the law and the snow allowed, I covered the 650 miles back home in about fourteen hours.

This concludes our summary of Father Timothy's trip to the East Coast. Later, when he was doing his stint of teaching at Saint Anselm in Washington, DC, he visited Georgetown University and Catholic University, Georgetown Prep School and the Landon School. These visits, however, confirmed what he had already learnt rather than adding new information.

The data collected during all this visiting and the conclusions drawn from them were reported to Inc and fully discussed among ourselves.

Combined with what Father Luke learnt from his weeks of teaching at Portsmouth and Father Timothy from his in Washington, they gave us the basic information for adapting the methods we had grown up with to the needs of Midwestern boys.

What were our impressions and conclusions? The first impression was of the overwhelming generosity of the schools and colleges we visited in giving time, information, hospitality and welcome. This was universal, and neither of us can remember ever having been rebuffed or treated with anything except great friendliness.

Colleges certainly expected sixteen high school credits and looked for four years of English and preferred four of Mathematics as well. They hoped for some years of a foreign language, some history and some science. They did not seem to require more than what we were planning to provide; if anything, rather less. Naturally enough, they regarded performance in high school as the best predictor of performance in college and so regarded the high school transcript as an essential piece of evidence. They also recognized that it needed careful interpretation, and so were anxious to get to know the schools as well as they could. What the headmaster said about the boy was no less important, especially when they knew the headmaster or when his reports had in the past proved accurate.

State universities had to accept any graduate of an accredited high school in their state, but both they and the independent universities and colleges paid attention to the results from the tests of the College Entrance Examination Board, usually known as the College Board or C-E-E-B. A boy's performance in the Verbal and Mathematical Aptitude Tests of the College Board seemed to be used as a rule of thumb for forming a first impression of him. Some colleges, especially in the Midwest, preferred the American College Testing Program, or A-C-T, and some colleges accepted either.

Independent schools on the East Coast were very sensitive to charges of being elitist enclaves for the children of affluent inhabitants of New England, and were eager for diversity. At that time the Midwest was diversity, and that was to our advantage. These colleges were also aware that they were expensive, and therefore had generous scholarship programs, which were based more on need than on ability, unless it were athletic ability. They combined grants with student loans and jobs. In contrast with Oxford's assumption that you would do during the summer most of the bulk reading required by your course of studies, it was assumed here that most students would hold a summer job.

Accreditation was often the first topic addressed by the high schools we visited. In New England most independent schools were accredited, in the Midwest most were not. In New England the independent schools were far more numerous, and normally were older than the public (state-financed) schools. They were an integral and essential part of the system. Not so in the Midwest, where independent schools are mostly late-comers. Consequently the outlook of the New England Association was quite different from that of the North Central, with whom we would have to deal.

Most schools used an entrance examination of their own, consisting of an aptitude test and papers in English, Mathematics and possibly a language. In the classroom there was more emphasis on visual aids and projects, and, as Father Timothy wrote, "Contemporary theory emphasizes enthusiasm rather than industry, but many of the good schools are pleasantly old-fashioned in this". Grading periods and reports were more frequent than in England, seldom fewer than six a year. Much of a boy's motivation seemed to come from them. Letter grades were more common than numerical. Most schools had six or seven periods each day and full courses met four or five times a week. Classes were uniformly small, fifteen or fewer. Round-table discussion was common in the upper years, and often took place literally at round tables. Homogeneous grouping, that is clever boys taught together and less clever together, was normal, though not universal, and not always for all subjects. The ratio of faculty to students was one to ten, or fewer. Although neither this ratio nor this class size was regarded as magical, both were treated as norms which should not lightly be disregarded.

Very few schools had anything like a monitorial system of routine authority exercised by one boy over others in minor matters. Even where there were monitors or prefects, they had no power of summary punishment but referred the matter to the student court or to designated faculty. Consequently the ways of dealing with minor infringements seemed cumbersome, but we were assured that American boys were much more responsive than English boys to verbal reproach, especially from a priest.

Many of the schools visited had fine libraries, almost all on the Dewey Decimal System. The same was also true at that time of most of the colleges we visited. We followed them and later on had to spend countless hours converting to the Library of Congress system.[44] Many

[44] We embarked on this conversion in the late seventies with the notable help of Mr. Paul Falcey, who thereby earned the status of confrater.

of the schools, aware of the danger of creeping athleticism, emphasized intra-mural over inter-scholastic competition. Their extra-curricular activities included usually a flourishing glee club, drama, debate, and hobby clubs. Art and music were often built into the curriculum, but not usually for credit.

Faculty were hard to come by, but once acquired often developed great loyalty to the school. They seldom taught more than twenty hours a week and a new man might be paid $1800-2500 plus board and lodging, which then seemed high to us. They often had considerable say in the running of the school, and, in alliance with the Trustees, could make the headmaster's position unenviable.

American boys seemed, at least on the surface, very comparable to English boys. That impression, derived from admittedly brief contacts in the classroom and from casual conversation, was confirmed by Father Luke's and Father Timothy's experience of teaching American boys. The impression was correct enough as far as it went, but it misled us because we did not allow for one difference: the boys we met on the East Coast were part of a complete school and were in an environment whose traditions had been established over decades. The boys coming to our school would be freshmen in a brand new environment with no superstructure of upperclassmen or tradition to quell them; and that, as we soon found out, made all the difference.

That we had arrived at a very favorable moment for well-prepared Catholics who wanted to go to non-Catholic colleges is clear from what has already been said. One reason why such colleges wanted undergraduates of various faiths was that they were being charged with being almost exclusively White, Anglo-Saxon and Protestant (WASP). They wanted to show that they were not. But because of the situation described by Monsignor John Tracy Ellis,[45] there was no great supply of well-prepared Catholics, so the colleges were doubly interested in us as a possible source of such. They were also reassuring about the quality of the Newman Chaplaincies and sometimes the college even gave credit for courses taken at the chaplaincy.

How far we were successful in making ourselves known to the colleges we visited only they can say. They did, however, include our school on their lists of schools to be visited by their admission officers, and they did in due course accept a fair number of our applicants.

By and large, although the trip was exhausting and time-consuming, it was successful and well worth both the effort and the

---

[45] See p.15, *above*

time. As we go on, it will be seen that the conclusions drawn from the data collected on the trip affected all that we did in the school; not that we always acted according to them, but almost always they formed the basis of our discussions, even when we decided to act otherwise.

CHAPTER 11

Boys and Buildings

MEANWHILE, Father Columba, who had flown back from Portsmouth on 28 December, was confirming the affection and admiration that the leading members of Inc had for him, and was wrestling with the growing problems of Raymond Maritz' "cloister" plan. These were of two kinds: architectural and financial.

We had not decided in our own minds what style of architecture we wanted to adopt for the campus as a whole; at that time we would not even have referred to it as a campus. We were therefore anxious to keep construction at this stage to a minimum for fear of compromising or preempting our future choice of style. Although our thoughts had not crystallized, and although we would not then have used the word "image", our instincts were telling us that a neo-colonial campus would not project the image of the monastery and school that we wanted.

Many of the members of Inc, on the other hand, would have been very content with a neo-colonial campus in the style of the Stannard House. They saw the cloister plan as the nucleus of such a campus and therefore were not unduly concerned when it started to expand. In support of their vision they could point to several existing and highly presentable schools built in this style, models to which no one could object and for which we could not then produce any rival. We could only have a feeling of vague and unspecifiable discomfort. Lurking beneath the surface of our discussions with Inc and not then fully recognized by either party was a difference of expectation of what we and the school were to be like. Paradoxically, Inc expected the school to be much more English than we did, whereas we were fully determined not to try to turn Missouri boys into Little Lord Fauntleroys. This difference never grew into dissension; rather each side moved gently towards the other, and the school emerged as a rather odd and certainly unique Anglo-Missourian blend.

Finance was another matter. Maritz' original estimate at the end of October was $60,000. Father Columba's diary for 30 December mentions revised estimates of $181,000. From then on there is a flurry of references to discussions and meetings, including telephone calls to Father Luke and Father Timothy at Portsmouth. The building committee suggested by Joe Vatterott met for the first time on 4 January and again on the tenth. It was an *ad hoc*, not a standing committee, and included Fred Switzer and Raymond Maritz, Joe Vatterott and his friend Norman George, Don Musick and Ed Walsh. Many suggestions for reductions were made, but it was evident that there was no way of coming close to the original estimate of $60,000, and Father Columba warned Maritz that at this new price we might not be able to go ahead. Maritz graciously accepted the point.

Our original doubts about the plan had been assuaged by the belief, which in all probability was correct, that the value of what we believed we were getting for our $60,000 more than outweighed our doubts. If the price were to be that much higher, then our original doubts regained much of their validity.

Nor was this increase of price the only fly in the ointment. Father Curtin, who had already had wide experience in building schools and had been associated with us from the beginning, disagreed with our plans both in general and in detail. He believed that what we were building would determine future plans and that anyway some of the items were in the wrong place. We came to the conclusion that his experience was of schools radically different from ours and that his doubts were similar to our initial doubts, which we had considered in October and had overcome. One or two other friends, including Prior Aelred and Father Hilary Martin, both of Portsmouth Priory, were doubtful too. We paid special attention to Father Hilary's opinion both because he held it so strongly and because he had trained and practiced as an architect before becoming a monk. But one of the dormitories at Portsmouth was built in the style that he advocated, and we were dubious about its success. Most of the members of Inc, on the other hand, supported the cloister plan. Forty years later one may conclude that, had the price been near the original $60,000, we would probably have been right to go ahead, and the interference with later plans would, as it has turned out, have been minimal. And so, hoping that in some wonderful way the price would be right, we went ahead, and on 24 January 1956 the specifications were put out for bids. We waited anxiously.

This would have been enough to keep us busy, but there was much going on besides. Father Timothy had hired our first school secretary, Miss Christine M. Little, who stayed with us for three years and gave us a fine start in the organization of the school office and files. One could often tell the state of her mind from the sound of her footsteps on the parquet floors, and if the radio mentioned even the possibility of a tornado warning, she was off down the stairs two at a time.

In addition we had, in our English innocence, suggested an afternoon tea-party as a good way of getting to know people. After we had explained what that meant, the idea, rather to our alarm, was hailed as cute or even quaint, and Inc set as the date Friday 27 January. We, or rather Father Luke and the ladies, prepared what would be normal for such an occasion in England: sandwiches, bread and butter and jam, scones, cakes and tea. As the day approached and as we had more experience of the amount of alcohol that Saint Louisans associated with entertainment, we began to get cold feet. Would conversation flow with reasonable ease? None of the three of us was an Oscar Wilde.

The hour arrived, so did two hundred and fifty guests, and the party was a huge success. We even felt that we had struck a small blow for non-alcoholic hospitality. It was not until some months later that we discovered that many of our guests too had had cold feet, and had taken the precaution of assembling an hour or so ahead of time at Busch's Grove, a popular restaurant and bar, where they fortified themselves against the abstemiousness of the tea-party.

Of even greater significance were the preparations for our first entrance examination. Father Curtin had very kindly allowed us to use DuBourg High School on Saturday 4 February 1956 for the tests. The facilities were splendid, but there was some incongruity between the size of a school designed for three thousand students and our search for a class of thirty. No fewer than sixty-six boys turned up at the appointed place and time. Learning from our experiences at the schools we had visited, we secured an Intelligence Test, of which we were somewhat skeptical, and we prepared papers in English and Arithmetic. These took place in the morning and all the candidates had to take them. We also prepared optional papers in Algebra, Geometry, Latin, Greek, French, Spanish, German and Italian because, despite all the contrary evidence, we still could not believe that boys ready to enter the ninth grade could have avoided studying at least one or two of these subjects. In the event, two boys took the French paper, and that was it; and they did so only because their school had heard what we were planning and had given them a list of French words to memorize. The two boys handed in answer sheets which were entirely blank except where they recognized a French word from their list.

All these papers took a long time to prepare, but at least they did not take long to correct. In addition, as a result of having only the one test after lunch, we were able to leave Jack Peters, the young man who had shown interest in monastic life, to look after the two boys while the rest of us started on the interviews. We completed these the following day at Priory, and were then ready to correct and select. It should be noted that the boys wrote on their papers not their name but a number. In that way we did not know as we corrected each paper, whose paper we were correcting nor, consequently, did we know who the parents were. Our purpose was to eliminate any partiality on our part and any suspicion on the part of the parents that the degree of their generosity to us might affect our grading, and in both we were successful.

We had decided to award three scholarships with a nominal value of $100 each--the tuition was to be $750--which could be increased according to need, even up to full tuition. In this way a scholar, however wealthy his parents, would receive honor and a small tangible reward for his brilliance, and a needy boy could have his full need met. The primary criterion for these scholarships was the boy's academic ability, but we did also require of them and of all the candidates an interview, which we regarded as important input into the process of selection, especially when the boy was less strong academically. It often gave us a valuable impression of the boy's interests and strength of character or lack thereof. We also tried to get the boy's record from his grade school. We did not always succeed, and even when we did, it was not a sure guide until we came to know the individual schools. Fresh as we were from England, we saw athletic ability as an optional, though certainly desirable, extra and the idea of athletic scholarships never crossed our minds. Our athletic results for the early years confirm this.

Now and for some years afterwards, we had difficulty in explaining to Ampleforth the need for the amount of financial aid that we thought was necessary. The root of the difficulty was that the expenses of the kind of education we were offering were comparable to those of Saint Louis Country Day School and other similar independent schools, whose fees were higher than ours, whereas most of our parents were in reality choosing not between us and Country Day but between us and Saint Louis University High School and other similar Catholic schools, whose tuition was about one third of ours. Ampleforth saw that our fees were already lower than those of the schools which they perceived to be our competition, so why did we need to give more? We saw that without a strong program of financial aid, we would lose good boys to our real competition, the other Catholic schools. It was only when this was, after several years, discussed face to face rather than by letter that the misunderstanding was rooted out.

As we look back, it seems strange that we were unable to communicate more effectively. This inability was due partly to lack of time for lengthy correspondence, partly to the difficulty of trans-Atlantic telephoning, and mainly to the unfamiliarity to most of the community at Ampleforth of the whole scene in Saint Louis. It is clearer now than it was then that the burden of clarification rested with us, who knew both Ampleforth and Saint Louis, rather than with Ampleforth.

For our first class all the applicants were Catholic, but we soon had to decide whether to accept non-Catholic boys. The answer back then was not a foregone conclusion, and we decided to accept them but within limits.[46] We were after all a Catholic school and supported by Catholics, but a certain amount of diversity might be good for all concerned. Father Timothy always warned parents of non-Catholic boys that, although we would make no attempt to proselytize, it could happen that the boy would want to become a Catholic. If they would regard that as a mishap, they should not send us the boy.

A little later we had to decide about non-Christian boys. The wife of a prominent Jewish businessman asked Father Columba what we would do if there were two exactly equally qualified candidates for the last available place in a class, and one was Jewish and one Catholic. His reply is lost, but must have been that we would use the same procedure as if both boys were Catholic. In all probability, we would have accepted both, but the case never arose, as the few Jewish boys who applied were clearly acceptable.

The general outline of this process of admission has endured, though it has been much refined over the years. By and large it has served us well: some boys, of course, have turned out better than we expected and some worse, but on the whole we have been well pleased. What we can never know is how many mistakes we made with the boys we did not accept. Perhaps some would have done better than some that we did accept.

Be that as it may, we harvested from this first entrance examination and from the subsequent interviews a strong class of thirty, led by three scholars: Ed Boedeker, Fran Oates and John Rice. This first class still has a unique place in the hearts of the monks who were here to teach them.[47]

---

[46] The initial limit set by Abbot Herbert was 4%.

[47] Their names and those of the schools from which they came are listed in Appendix B 4.

Almost as important as the acquisition of a class for us to start with were two unplanned by-products of the examination. We turned down the son of parents who could have been major contributors to the school. It would not have been a kindness to the boy to have done otherwise. We had always said that this would be our policy, but few believed us. When we did what we said we would do, many people revised their opinion about "these monks". Providentially we achieved a major coup in public relations.

The other event concerned a boy whom we judged to be academically acceptable, but who seemed unlikely to make the most of his opportunity, and so the school did not want to accept him. This led to a contretemps with Inc, which the school lost. But when term started, it soon became clear that the school had been right. Thereafter Inc placed much greater trust in the school's judgement. This was one step, again unplanned, in the development of a very special relationship between Inc and the monks: Inc would advise and discuss and argue with us but its members never again imposed their view, which was all the more remarkable in that they were raising and often personally contributing the money that enabled us to carry on. They were paying the piper but refrained from calling the tune. No wonder the monks were convinced that God was taking special care of them.

In the hectic aftermath of the entrance examination, while we were correcting the papers, tabulating the results, making our decisions and mailing them to the parents, we also waited anxiously for the bids on the cloister plan to come in, our first such experience. The grand opening of the bids was on 9 February 1956 at 4.00 p.m. in the presence of all the contractors except one, who sent in a bid by phone. The social atmosphere was sultry, conversation among the contractors sparse, and the monks were trying to remain cheerful and optimistic. Our hopes and spirits were soon dashed: the lowest bid ($173,980) realized our worst fears, being nearly three times the original estimate of $60,000. We were no longer expecting $60,000 but did hope for a bid perhaps as low as $110,000. We sat there in stunned silence, and then Father Columba announced that we needed time to think about what to do next, so the contractors were downcast too. It was a moment of sorrow. By now none of us was strongly enthusiastic about the Cloister plan, but we had put much effort into it and developed a certain affection for it. We were disappointed that it had failed. After several days of intense lobbying by contractors and of daily discussion with Inc and among ourselves, and after much prayer, we decided to start afresh in another way, a decision which Ray Maritz accepted with great good grace. It was a little like a spouse calling off the wedding at the altar, and was a discouraging beginning. Only later were we able to look back and see it as a great mercy, and one that deepened our belief that God really was guiding us, and Our Lady, our patron, supporting us. In addition to avoiding what might have been a great mistake, we had clarified our thoughts and had acquired experience in planning and negotiating, which helped us greatly in future dealings with architects and contractors. What happened with the bids turned our lurking uneasiness into certainty and we decided that instead of building anything in any style before we were fully ready to make a considered decision about style, we would at once plan to adapt the existing buildings to cover our needs for the first two years, and then make a decision about style after proper deliberation. We judged that this adaptation would be possible. After considering the use of the Gallagher house for the monastery and rejecting the idea, we determined on using the Stannard House, the barn and the equipment shed for both monastery and school. In due course, and largely on Father Curtin's recommendation, we chose John O'Brien as our contractor for this remodeling. At the same time we intensified our search for an architect or architectural firm with the capacity, that is the staff, the originality of design and the mental flexibility, to cooperate with us and where necessary to guide us in the development of the monastery and school. We would look everywhere, but, other things being equal, we would prefer someone from Saint Louis both for his feel for the local scene and for ease of communication.

Father Columba wrote on this in the first issue of *The Saint Louis Priory Journal*: "We sought someone with whom we could work easily, who would be open to new ideas, who would have a high sense of the importance and spiritual significance of the project . . . neither ultra-modern nor sunk irretrievably in the past. We sought masterly competence, spiritual vision and friendliness."[48]

This search had been in our minds from the beginning and had already involved us in numerous visits to churches, schools, airports and buildings of all kinds in Saint Louis and on our travels elsewhere. When we went to Portsmouth Priory, to Saint Benedict's Abbey in Atchison, Kansas, to Saint John's Abbey in Collegeville, Minnesota we took great interest in their buildings and especially in their plans to build. We saw one fascinating new building at the Massachusetts Institute of Technology. We continued the search now and added to it consultation with many architects local, national and sometimes international. They were amazingly generous with their time. Mr.

[48] *SLPJ* I. 1, p.4.

Felix Candela from Mexico came to see us. He had built a number of exciting buildings, but we were concerned about their engineering. We had read in the papers of an Italian high-rise building which had fallen on its face. When we asked Mr. Candela how he calculated whether his buildings would stand up, he replied, in jest maybe, "We put them up, and if they stay up, we know we did the engineering right; if they fall down, we know we made a mistake." We doubted if we could afford that much excitement.

At this point, in the middle of February, Father Timothy left for Washington, DC to teach for a few weeks at St. Anselm, a monastery, like Portsmouth, of the English Benedictine Congregation. While he was away, Father Columba and Father Luke stepped up their program of visits to churches and schools, in the course of which they went to a church whose reredos Father Columba, by an interesting Freudian misprint, describes as “eroteric”. They received many visits from architects, mostly from Saint Louis but including Barry Byrne from out of town, and between visits and with all proper respect, they ran the American flag up our new eighty foot flag-pole for the first time on 22 February. Father Timothy returned from Washington early on 19 March. On 21 March, the Solemnity of Saint Benedict, the three monks held a formal meeting to choose our architect. By that time we had spoken with and studied the work of at least ten local architects, plus those who had come in from out of town. We had been impressed especially by the design of the then-new Saint Louis airport terminal[49] and by the versatility of the firm, and so we chose Hellmuth, Obata and Leinweber of Saint Louis. They soon became Hellmuth, Obata and Kassabaum, and were known as H-O-K. We came to know very well many members of their staff and to count them among our friends, and we came to believe that in Gyo Obata we had found a designer of genius. The next evening Mr. George F. Hellmuth came over and Father Columba invited him to be our architect. He accepted with joy.

Having chosen them we then asked them to go ahead with plans for the remodeling of the existing buildings. After considering several other possibilities, we settled on what had been Father Curtin's original suggestion for the barn--he was a wise advisor in those early days--and went ahead with John O'Brien as the contractor. We would turn the barn into four classrooms, with flexible dividers between them,

---

[49] The terminal was designed by Yamasaki, who soon afterwards left the firm, but we thought Obata was in the same tradition.

convert the equipment shed into rest rooms, showers, locker room and drying room, plus the boiler, and make room in the Stannard House for everything else. We thought this would serve well enough for the first two years and we prayed fervently that we would be able to complete by September 1958 the building which we hoped would house both monks and boys for a while. Further down the line, when the boys moved out into their new high school, it was to become exclusively the monastery. Our prayers were not heard.

In the Stannard House on the upper floor, Father Columba and Father Luke were to remain where they were, Father Columba in one of the two rooms at the north end and Father Luke in his office. Father Ian, when he came, would move into the cedar closet at the north end; the two larger rooms in the middle would be the monks' library-cum-calefactory (or common room) and the business office, and the "boudoir" at the top of the stairs would be the reception room. At the south end, what had been the master bedroom with his and her bathrooms and dressing rooms would become the headmaster's office, with his bed behind the bookcase, and his secretary's office in "her" dressing-room. Downstairs, the garage, next door to and north of the kitchen, would be the boys' dining room, and the small breakfast room south of the kitchen the monks dining room. The room next to that would be the school library (we had tried putting the books in the Rathskeller but they soon developed mildew), the drawing room remained the chapel and the sun room the monks' choir. The Rathskeller became the boys' common room as they were never still for long enough to grow mildew.

This makeshift scheme worked remarkably well, with one major exception: we were keen that the monastery should not only be the prime component of our lives but also be seen to be so. In this scheme it was not. Monastic spaces and school spaces were intermingled. That meant that the monastery building had to be the next one built. Since the siting of the monastery was linked to the siting of both church and school, that in turn meant that we had to decide all three sites rather sooner than we really wanted, since it was now our aim to do at any one stage as little as we could that would pre-determine what was done at later stages.

CHAPTER 12

The Last Months of Boylessness

DURING the month of March 1956 two public events affected our status: on 1 March, a rescript from Rome constituted us as a *domus formata* or established house. That gave us formal recognition of our existence and brought with it the obligation to recite the Divine Office in choir, which we had been doing all the time. Then on 19 March the Priory of Saint Mary and Saint Louis was incorporated by a pro forma decree of the State of Missouri. We were thus both religiously and civilly legitimated.[50]

Easter this year fell on 1 April. The week before Easter is called Holy Week, and its last days, Maundy Thursday, Good Friday, Holy Saturday and, as a culmination, Easter Sunday are for all Christian churches the high point of the liturgical year. They are also a time when the resources of a large monastery are fully deployed and are seen at their best. Our last Easter had been celebrated at Ampleforth, where nearly one hundred monks lived in the monastery, the others being on parishes away from the monastery. Here we were three, and though not unmusical, we were not front line canaries either. It strained us, therefore, to our limits to cope with the amount of singing in Holy Week, which is considerable today and was even more so in 1956. There was also much sacristy work to be done and though we had great help from the laity, we still had to do much ourselves. For the Vigil on Holy Saturday night, each of us thought that one of the others was preparing the fire, and when at the last moment we made that ready, no one could find the grains of incense for the Paschal candle. It made us more aware of the contribution that good preparation makes to prayerful liturgy. It made us miss Ampleforth.

Easter was followed by a succession of events some connected with our preparations for the opening of the school, others not. They indicate how we spent the balance of our ten months of preparation.

We spent much of Easter week collecting books from the Public Library downtown. These were their duplicates and mostly standard works, not very exciting, but extremely useful to us in building up the core of our library.

---

[50] *SLPJ* XIX. 1, p.72.

On 22 April Archbishop Fulton J. Sheen came to Saint Louis to promote the Pope's invitation to dioceses in the United States to send priests to South America, and in the case of Saint Louis to Bolivia. We went to hear him, as he was already famous for his appearances on television, and a good orator is always worth listening to. Father Columba in his diary described him as "Human, amusing, dramatic, clear, pictorial, sincere. He has a beautifully modulated voice, perfect sense of timing, an actor's gestures, controlled, graceful, fitting." We noticed especially the way in which he dealt with humor. He started with three jokes and then said the first half of what he wanted to say. Then, as people were becoming a little drowsy, he told three more jokes followed by the rest of his speech. The jokes were not connected with the subject-matter of his speech. An English speaker of similar caliber would probably have told no jokes as such but would have woven a thread of humor throughout the speech. That might have been more literary but perhaps Sheen was more in tune with American expectations. Anyway the upshot was that our archdiocese was the first in the United States to respond to the Pope's call.

After the speech in Kiel Auditorium there was a reception at the Chase/Park Plaza Hotel. Father Timothy was roped in for escorting the visitors up by the elevator to the proper room. To a priest in the first group he said, "Hello, Father, I'm Father Timothy" and received the reply, "I'm Archbishop X". To a priest in the next group he said the same and was told, "I'm Archabbot Y". To a priest in the third group he said more cautiously, "Are you an archbishop or an archabbot?" His reply was, "No, I'm an Archimandrite."

Two days later we attended a performance of a very different character, namely a benefit movie for Villa Duchesne, a girls' school run by Religious of the Sacred Heart. It was held at the Fox Theater, an exuberant building opened in 1929 and looking like Cecil B. de Mille's idea of Nebuchadnezzar's palace, but with a Wurlitzer organ added. The benefit started with a fashion show, with mothers of girls at Villa modeling the latest styles to the accompaniment of a rather tasteless commentary. In those days the Sisters were not allowed to attend such shows and so were saved embarrassment.

We had decided that for the moment, in the interest of public relations, we would accept invitations to dinner. This ceased when school started. On one such occasion, we were trying to find our hosts' house. Father Timothy went to what he thought was the right house and rang the bell. When the lady of the house came to the door and saw a clerical collar, her jaw dropped. She seemed relieved when all he did was to ask directions. We found our hosts and thought no more of it. Some months later we discovered that the reason for the dropped jaw was that the lady was hosting a meeting of the Planned Parenthood Association and thought that we were the clergy coming to break it up. Another time we were driven out to a farm in the country and at the end of a hot day spent a happy evening in their pool. When we finished dinner, Father Columba was asked to say the grace after meals. He ended, "May the souls of the faithful departed through the mercy of God rest in peace" and our host added, "And God rest the Irish who rotted in English jails." We had already agreed to take his son, and stood by our word. On yet another occasion, Father Timothy was invited to a barbecue with prospective parents. When they asked him what he drank he replied jokingly that he never drank anything except champagne. In due course he turned up for the barbecue. They had cocktails, moved to the barbecue pit for the main course and then, with loaded plates, went to the table, on which there was a large bottle of expensive champagne on ice. Having forgotten the remark he had made some weeks earlier, Father Timothy asked what they were celebrating. "But Father, you said you never drank anything except champagne." Father Timothy felt like a worm, but the wife saved the day by rounding on her husband and saying, "There you are, dear; I told you he was joking." There were also serious moments, as when our hosts said, “We are so eagerly looking forward to September, when we hand our son over to you and wash our hands of him.” All three of us exclaimed that this was not at all how it was; that the family remained the major element in the son's education.

We were entertained at Grant's Farm by Mr. August A. (Gussie) Busch, Jr. and his wife Trudy. They were most gracious, promised support and in due course sent us three sons. A little later Mr. Busch took us to dinner and then to his box at Sportsman's Park to watch his Cardinals play baseball. We saw but did not understand an exciting game. In the bottom of the ninth the Cardinals were a run behind but had the bases loaded with one out. The batter hit what looked to our cricketing eyes like a sizzling off-drive that should have scored the winning runs. The expert next to us snorted with disgust and left. The sizzling off-drive turned out to be a routine 4-6-3 double-play.

On our own account we hosted, at Inc's behest, a series of dinners at Priory for small groups of prospects. These dinners gave us a chance to get to know individuals who were not the top brass of Inc, and gave them a chance to meet us informally. We had guests to lunch more often than not. Some were for friendship, some for business, many for both. Doctor Robert J. Snyder, superintendent of the Parkway School District, in which we are, came and kindly allowed us to use the Mason

Ridge School's gym for our basketball season. Mr. Bud Harper, headmaster of Country Day School, came and invited Father Columba to join in a ceremony for the laying of the foundation stone of their new campus. In those days anything resembling a joint religious service with other denominations was forbidden. This was not to be such and was cleared with the archdiocese, but unfortunately the newspaper report made it appear to have been such and Father Columba had to explain to the Chancellor of the Archdiocese what had really happened. On another occasion, an Anglican Canon from Yorkshire came to visit. Father Columba took him and his wife and friends around the campus and ended with a prayer in the chapel, where they asked for his blessing. He felt constrained not to ask for a blessing in return even though ecumenically he was quite advanced. How remote that seems now!

We visited the Thomas Jefferson School, whose headmaster, Mr. Robin McCoy, was a mathematician. The school reflected that. He laid down his first principles and deduced the school from them. At the time of our visit, their last graduating class was that of 1955. 70% of that class went to Harvard, a most remarkable achievement. And yet, while we admired the logic of the concept of the school, we felt uneasy about its application. We wondered, for example, whether to teach Greek but not Latin was a wise choice.[51]

This was the most extreme case of a difference between the ways in which the American mind and the English mind instinctively work, a difference which kept coming to the surface. As Mr. Churchill observed at one of the meetings of the Joint Chiefs of Staff during World War II, the American instinct is to lay down a principle and then deduce action from it, the a priori approach. The English instinct is to start with what is there and to see what happens if we do this or that, the a posteriori approach.[52] The successes of the former way can be glorious, but if the principle is at all flawed, the deductions tend to magnify the flaws. The latter way usually eliminates egregious error, but easily leads to muddling through. It comes naturally to an American to ask "What is your philosophy of . . . ?" and the English are often at a loss for an answer. Imagine going into an English pub,

---

[51] The school has made many changes since then.

[52] Roughly, a priori reasoning is deductive, from known or assumed principles down to their consequences, and a posteriori reasoning is inductive, from experience back to its cause. The reasoning of syllogisms (all men are mortal; all monks are men; therefore all monks are mortal) is a priori; scientific reasoning is normally a posteriori.

walking towards the dart-board and asking one of the players "What is your philosophy of playing darts"?

Young Jesuits used to drop in on their way from the city to their house in the country, and one day we entertained some young men from their high school, one of whom later on was a postulant for a while. Much of this was the doing of Jack Peters, who was a postulant here, taught for a year, and then, as Brother Gregory, went over to Ampleforth for the novitiate and part of the juniorate before deciding that he was not called to be a monk for life. Vocations were very much on our minds, and the forecasts made to us before we came were apparently being justified. Charlie Rush was another visitor who later tried his vocation and nearly went all the way.

All these visits to us and by us punctuated our four ongoing activities: planning the future of the campus, i.e. monastery, church, school and related buildings; preparing for the opening of school in September; fund-raising; and seeking vocations.

The first involved us in numerous meetings with HOK and with Inc, and presupposed extensive discussions among ourselves. We had already met with HOK on the modifications to existing buildings. Now we started on 7 May a series of meetings about the overall plan. It will be tidier to describe these later on, but the reader should bear in mind here that a substantial amount of our time was already being taken up with architectural planning for the future. Some of our thinking for this we had done already and recorded in a document which, like a fair number of our earliest records, is undated. It was intended to be given to any architect interested in our project. It is three pages long and is printed, who can say why, in green. It is entitled, "*Basic Ideas for the Architect When Planning the Building of Saint Louis Priory and School.*"[53]

At the end of May, Father Columba had an opportunity at the Graduation at Webster College to ask Archbishop Ritter about the possibility of our getting a small parish near the monastery. "He showed interest and willingness," Father Columba thought, but also mentioned the danger of monks placing on the parish men for whom they could not find a job elsewhere, and of the parish becoming a place for society weddings. On 29 May Father Columba wrote to the Archbishop clarifying that we could not take this on at the moment, but would like it to be considered in due course,[54] and assuring him that we would never put in anyone poor at the job. In April 1957,

[53] *See* p.132 *below*. It is printed in Appendix B 3.

[54] See file "Ritter, Abp".

when asking permission to build a church, Father Columba repeated his interest in a parish, and Archbishop Ritter, in his reply of 15 April 1957 gave permission for the church and added, “When the time comes, I will arrange to have a parish associated with the monastery in accordance with your wishes.” And there the matter rested until 1966, except that when we built our church, we made a rule that we would not allow weddings there, with the exception of members of the family who gave us the church. The reason was partly what the Archbishop had said and partly the uneasiness of pastors, who felt that weddings should be in the bride's parish church.[55]

At the beginning of May we produced the first number of *The Priory Journal.* It starts, "This unpretentious little journal . . ." It covers 6 1/2 pages; the pages are half-size; it takes seven minutes to read. For all these reasons it was immensely popular. It contained an editorial mostly about the prayer of the monks, the latest information about Father Ian, who was to join us in July, a note from the school about the entrance examination and the summer school, an article on the choice of architects and, of course, a page about The Drive. Countless people told us they read every word. Subsequent issues grew longer. The longer they grew, the more impressive they were and the fewer were the readers of every word.

We were also in the process of assuming a coat of arms. In this, Father Columba enlisted the expertise of Father Wilfrid Bayne of Portsmouth Priory. The lower half was taken over from Westminster Abbey's coat and represents the river, for them the Thames, for us the Mississippi, and dry land. Above are the white rose for Our Lady, and more remotely for Yorkshire, and the fleur de lys for King Saint Louis. It appears on the second and all subsequent numbers of the Journal. The motto was *Laus Tibi Domine* (Praise to You, O Lord).[56]

Preparations for the opening of the school were simplified by not having to look for faculty. In the first year the monks did all the teaching except that Jack Peters took one set of History. We did, however, need to find a head coach and a part time music teacher. These were Mr. Ervin T Leimer and Mr. Kenneth J. Scheibal, both of whom laid solid foundations. We also had to find someone to supervise the feeding of the boys. For this purpose Mr. H. King

---

[55] When we became a parish and the parish came to use the abbey church, parishioners had the right to be married in the abbey church, because it was also their parish church.

[56] There is a description in plain English in *SLPJ* I. 2, p.5 and a technical description in XIX. 1, p.4.

Carter, already a friend of Father Luke, lent us for six months Mr. Charles Dattilo, who stayed for the next thirty-four years. We spent time choosing and acquiring school furniture both for the summer school and for the real thing in September. Mother Hildegarde Hellmuth, R.S.C.J., was a mentor to Father Luke in the art of acquisition at low or no cost.

More interesting was the acquisition of athletic equipment. Soccer and track were no problem, but football, and, in turn, basketball and baseball were territory unknown to us. We had the help of Erv Leimer, and he had the help, for football and soccer, of Mr. John L. Gilmore, the father of a boy accepted into our first class, but we must mention especially our salesman, Mr. George Thompson. He could have urged us to spend far beyond our needs and our means; instead he gave us wise advice for many years about what was quite adequate for our successive stages of growth. A notable example was a set of heavy capes cast off by the Saint Louis Knights, a semi-professional team. These capes at $10 each kept our bench-warmers warm for many a year.

Preparation for the Summer School was the most interesting part of our preparations because it would bring us into contact for the first time with our principal clients. Again we did not have to look for faculty since Father Columba was to teach Geography as the basis of History, Father Luke English with Penmanship, Father Timothy Greek and Mathematics, which were two separate courses. The school ran for five weeks starting on Monday 11 June. It taught the boys a certain amount, but more importantly gave them an introduction to the monks, to their teaching methods and to their accents. Equally importantly it gave us an introduction to the boys, and started to open our eyes to the difference, already alluded to, between a school with all the upper grades and all its traditions in place and a new school without them. Classes were held in the Rathskeller, which had a rather old floor of disintegrating vinyl tile. Father Luke came down the stairs into the rathskeller the first day to find the boys throwing pieces of the floor at one another. No one could have blamed him if he had asked to return to England or asked the boys to return home. Our difficulty was that we did not want to be so fierce as to scare the boys away from returning in September; nor did we want them to think that this was acceptable behavior. We erred, probably, on the side of leniency, and they did all come back in September.

Soon after the start of summer school, John O'Brien and his men began work on the remodeling. At the beginning of July, we paid off the debt on the Stannard property, which then became ours. The significance of this was mainly symbolic: we were here to stay.

Wednesday 4 July was a holiday for the summer school. We celebrated by walking over after Vespers to the Duffys, who lived over the ridge to our west. He was the British Consul in Saint Louis and also had a talk show on the radio. In late October 1958 commenting on the election of Pope John XXIII, which came soon after an atomic trial on Bikini Atoll, he said it was an open question which puff of smoke was of greater significance. He and his wife entertained us regally and introduced us to a deceptive drink called a Mint Julep. We had two and then walked home. Our difficulty in keeping to the path was not due solely to the dusk. A learning experience.

The following Wednesday was a feast of a different kind, the Solemnity of Saint Benedict. We held a grand evening Mass outside on the lawn behind the Stannard House. For this, in those days, we had to get archiepiscopal permission. Monks and nuns and some two hundred laity came to strengthen our singing, and Mass was celebrated with as much solemnity as we could manage. Monsignor Hellriegel came in the Benedictine habit indicating that he was a Benedictine oblate, and preached. It may not have been much compared with the Pontifical High Masses of Ampleforth, but it was prayerful and joyful and fostered the unity of Inc in a different way from dinners at the Deer Creek Club or fund-raising meetings.

As July wore on, Father Columba and Father Timothy spoke to a variety of groups ranging from the Serra Club to the Classics department at Saint Louis University. Father Columba agreed to give a theological lecture each week for a year to the religious at Villa Duchesne. Father Luke, who had been busy supervising the construction, left by car on 13 July for New York, where he was to pick up Father Ian from the *Queen Mary* and bring him back by way of Portsmouth, Niagara Falls and the Mudds' summer residence on Walloon Lake, Michigan. And then, to our delight, Paul Bryant, a very bright student of Professor William A. Barker at Saint Louis University, who was one of several young men who showed interest in monastic life, told us he planned to come as a postulant next year in September after his graduation.

On 1 August at about 8.30 p.m. Father Luke completed the last leg of his journey, the six hundred miles from Walloon. He brought with him our fourth member, Father Ian Petit, O.S.B. We gave them a few minutes to wash and then went to the chapel and with hearts truly full of gratitude sang the *Te Deum* (we praise you as God). Father Ian had been ordained priest at Ampleforth on 21 March, the main feast of

Saint Benedict, and had then gone to a monastery in France to brush up his French. While he was there, he was introduced both to the French language and to French customs. At breakfast the monks drank scalding coffee served in mugs without handles. The French monks, who wore leather belts, simply wrapped their belts around the mugs and so drank their coffee. Father Ian had only his English-style cloth belt, which was neither heat-resistant, nor strong enough to use in that way, and so he went thirsty, until he could borrow a local belt. He now had one month to settle in before the opening of school.

The monastic timetable at this point was[57]:

a.m.	4.40	rise
	5.00	Matins and Lauds
		Two rounds of Masses
		Prime and Terce
		Breakfast
	8.45	Sext, Conventual Mass
p.m.	12.30	Lunch, followed by None
	6.00	(or 6.15) Vespers, followed by
	6.30	Supper
	8.30	Compline
	9.40	Lights out

Father Columba and Father Timothy had for some time been thinking of making a trip toward the West, possibly even all the way to the West Coast. Now seemed to be the time, so on 9 August they set out in the Ford station wagon, of which Father Columba remarked later in the trip, "This car just wants to go eighty". Their destination was San Francisco and their purpose to get a feel for the country while at the same time taking a vacation. As this feel for the country was an important part of their settling down in the United States--so far they had seen only the eastern parts and had little awareness of either the sheer size or the diversity of the country--and as the trip included its fair share of adventures, we give an extended account of it here, based on the diary Father Columba providently kept.

Although there were only two of us, we took the station wagon thinking that we could sleep in it. We took out the back seat and padded the floor with cushions. As it turned out, we slept in it only

[57] *SLPJ* I. 2, p.1. For an explanation of the services, *see* p.217, footnote 154, *below*.

once, but that was a memorable once, and the chief usefulness of having a big car was to bring books home in it.

We left early on 9 August and by evening reached Cheyenne Wells, nearly 700 miles away. Most of our roads were two-lane then. We stayed with Father Keefer, a French missionary priest, who had founded all the churches between there and Denver, and told us wonderful tales of the pioneering days when he was a very young priest and Indians used to raid the city. He himself, against the advice of the few local Catholics, who said he would be risking his life, had staged a public debate with a hostile Protestant missionary and had done so well that it was the latter who had to jump off the back of the stage and flee. Next day, we had our first sight of the Rocky Mountains. We were disappointed by their unrockiness, and saw their real grandeur only when we reached the Tetons, but the colors on the mountains, especially at dawn and dusk, were varied and beautiful. It is a measure of how much we needed this trip that Father Timothy, and maybe Father Columba too, was surprised that we had reached the mountains so soon. He thought we would go up and over and then down to the Pacific. Instead we found that the mountains extended for several hundred miles, then came several hundred miles of desert, then another range of mountains and then finally the Pacific. We had seen all this on the American Automobile Association's Triptyk, but it had not sunk in.

We followed US 40 past Denver and over the Berthoud Pass, and then turned North into the Rocky Mountain National Park, following the Trail Ridge Road, which for a while is over 12,000 feet up. At one point, there were by the road some dirty gray banks. We looked at one another and said, "Surely not snow in August?" But it was. Soon after that we noticed that the gas gauge was at zero, which meant that we had to coast down the hairpin bends to Estes Park. Fortunately our brakes were good, but the driver did not have much chance to enjoy the splendid vistas, whereas the passenger had every opportunity to take in the precipitous drops. In Estes Park, Ellen (Mrs. Robert C.) Corley, one of our supporters, soothed our nerves and then we hastened on to a motel in Laramie.

After breakfast, we traversed the wide-open spaces of Wyoming and made for Yellowstone. By great good luck, we approached on US 287 from the east over a series of ridges until, reaching the top of the last ridge, we found spread out in front of us Jackson Lake and the Tetons. They are not enormous mountains but they are rocky, and the combination of the clear blue lake, the snow and the dark, sometimes chocolate, rocks all in the afternoon sun took our breath away.

In Yellowstone, we did our duty by Old Faithful and other old geysers, made arrangements at the Lodge to say Mass in the morning --the chaplain was a visiting Benedictine monk from Atchison, Kansas--and found a little loop road, off which there were prepared areas for pitching a tent or parking a car. We did the latter and prepared to sleep in the car. Father Columba was in the back with the tailgate down and his toes, inside his sleeping bag, emerging. Father Timothy in his sleeping bag was to sleep across the front seat. He was saying Compline, the monastic night prayer, under a street lamp on the loop road and had just finished, when out of the forest padded a big bear. Thinking that if he ran, that might encourage the animal to run after him, he walked as nonchalantly as he could to the car, jumped in at the front and shut the door. The bear went round to the back. Father Timothy turned to Father Columba, who was half asleep, and said, again as nonchalantly as he could, "Father, I think there's a bear sniffing at your toes." Father Columba thought it was not the bear but Timothy who was pulling his leg and said, "Timothy, you're just trying to frighten me." " No, there really is a bear." Father Columba raised himself up a little, saw the bear's snout and gave a bit of a yelp, but one sniff was enough for the bear and it loped off back into the forest. Father Columba slept well the rest of the night with the tailgate still down.

Next evening we were due at the Holy Cross Hospital in Salt Lake City to stay with Bishop Hunt. We arrived and a priest who looked little like a bishop met us. As he was showing us to our room, he opened the door of another room and said "This is the Episcopal Palace". "Oh" said Father Timothy, "and where is the episcopal ring?" "Here" he said, and held out his hand and on it the ring, which in embarrassment Father Timothy kissed. The bishop was very kind, and next day arranged for us a full tour of the Mormon Tabernacle. Both the city and the Mormons in it were very clean. We stayed there another night and then set off through the desert for Reno. West of the Great Salt Lake we passed the entrance to the Bonneville flats, and Father Timothy remembered that a boy at Ampleforth with him had an uncle who sometimes raced there, Captain G.E.T. Eyston. We stopped and saw a man driving out. We asked him whether by any chance Captain Eyston was around. He said "I am he". We reminisced for a while and then he invited us to a meal, but he was going back to Salt Lake City and we were going the opposite way.

Many people tried to sell us fly screens, water bottles and all kinds of gimmicks to ease our desert crossing, but we had stocked up with water and felt fully equipped. We reached Reno safely and spent the night in a hospital run by Dominican Sisters. We had hoped to spend the next night with Mr. and Mrs. William G. Weld, Jr., but they were away and had not received our letter, so we pushed on to San Francisco, hoping it would be cooler, and it was. We explored much more of their one-way system than we intended and always came back to Van Ness Avenue, but finally we got to the Franciscan Monastery, where we were warmly received. From then on we were guided by Mr. Paul Ryan, an architect and brother-in-law of our supporter, Bob Mattis. He showed us the Presidio, Chinatown, the Golden Gate and the other bridges, Fisherman's Wharf, the street cars and so on. It was the most European city we had visited, in the sense of having a past and being aware of it; and the weather was a relief after the desert.

We arrived in San Francisco on Tuesday 14 August and left on Friday 17 August heading south by way of the giant Sequoias to Carmel. There we made a pilgrimage to the Mission of San Carlos, where Fra Junipero Serra is buried. The Mission compound is still striking and well kept up. By evening we reached Bakersfield, one of the hottest places in the country, and spent the night in a Catholic hospital. It had been damaged in an earthquake in 1952, so the sisters were building one twice as big.

From there we drove to Boulder to visit the Hoover Dam. Neither of us was much inclined towards engineering, but we agreed that this must be one of the engineering wonders of the world. It controls the Colorado River after the river has passed through the Grand Canyon, and has created a vast pleasure park above the dam. We took the tour and noted the ghoulish fact that when, as did happen more than once, a man fell into the newly poured concrete, they had to dig out his corpse before continuing, because the human body is much weaker than concrete. We passed through Las Vegas, where it was 116° F. in the shade, and where there was one of the highest concentrations in the country of Catholic women religious. We drove down The Strip but did not stop.

Next day was the Day of the Canyons. Someone must have advised us to start with the Little Colorado Canyon, and we did so. It was almost deserted. We parked at the edge facing towards the Canyon with the front wheels against a railroad tie to prevent us falling in. It is on a far smaller scale than the Grand Canyon, but the drop of about six hundred feet is almost vertical. When we had gaped and gazed enough, Father Columba took the wheel, put the stick shift into second gear, said "This is reverse, isn't it?" and was about to let in the clutch. Father Timothy yelped "NO!" and knocked the gear lever into neutral; and so we survived to drive on to the Grand Canyon.

There was an early wide-screen movie about the Canyon, which we had both seen, but no matter how much you have seen or read, the real thing is still a unique experience. Its depth, its width, the strata, the colors of the strata and their variety at different times of day are ever-memorable. We were told that many types of rock are visible and that the lowest stratum is so old that it has lost all distinguishing characteristics and is just rock; but then what guides tell the visitor may be more poetry than truth. As we were standing at one of the view-points, a young man dressed as an American but looking like an Englishman came up to us. He was Frank van den Berg, who had been a student at Ampleforth when we were teaching there. We invited him to stop by in Saint Louis, which he did. Meeting him and Captain Eyston would have been surprising in New York and was astounding in the wide open spaces of the West.

It was hard to leave. We passed by the Painted Desert, which, were it by itself, would be another marvel, but seemed pale after the Canyon, and came to Holbrook, where we looked for the Catholic church. It was in the center of town and so was a Carnival with rides and roundabouts and a little Ferriss-wheel. On a platform a man with a colorful T-shirt and an ample beer-belly was announcing the votes in a beauty competition. Father Columba said, "How the priest must suffer from all that noise." Father Timothy said, "What will you bet that the priest is the man in the T-shirt?". Father Timothy won. We met the owner of the Carnival, a Catholic, who went round the area offering to set up his show for the local churches, which then shared in the profits. We were taken with the idea, but Father Luke, whom we told on our return, was not.

Next morning, we were having a cup of coffee in a cafe when four seedy men looked in, bought nothing and went out. When we drove off we heard an ominous noise, stopped and found a long screw in our tire. Having changed the wheel, we drove to the Petrified Forest, where trees, which had been lying on the ocean floor millennia before, became impregnated with silica. When the ocean receded, the trees dried out and by then were mineral with the texture of wood. After that, the Painted Cliffs, brilliant pinks and brown, yellow and off-white, and through more desert to Santa Fe, where Mr. and Mrs. Henry Stuart Castle, friends of Henry Hughes, took care of us. They arranged for us to stay at the Cathedral, and by day they showed us all the sights and sites in and around Santa Fe, including the old church of San Miguel. Just as England has more than one “Oldest Inn” so the United States has more than one “Oldest Church”. This is one.

We were also shown, in the Loretto chapel, a remarkable staircase, reputedly built by Saint Joseph in the guise of a beggar.

Our road next day ran along the eastern edge of the Sangre de Cristo Range. When we reached Raton, we ran into a hail storm unlike anything we had ever experienced. The hailstones were, as always, the size of golf balls or larger and soon formed a layer several inches deep on the road. It was like driving on a pebble beach. There was no shelter; we could not get out; we were afraid the windshield might be shattered. We proceeded at thirty miles an hour for what seemed like half an hour until we ran out of the storm. Then we did stop and inspected the car, which seemed to have nothing more than a few dents in the roof. Invigorated by the storm and our escape from it, we hurtled on to Cañon City where we were to stay two nights with the Benedictines at Holy Cross Abbey. They had eighty monks, a school, a summer camp and some parishes. From government surplus, they acquired lathes, drill presses and much fine equipment for their metal- and wood-working shops. The chain of military installations in Colorado frequently replaced this kind of machinery and the monks could buy it almost new and for little more than the cost of transportation. They took us to the Royal Gorge with its bridge one thousand feet above the Arkansas River, and on the last night showed us their skyline drive along a single-lane knife edge with hairpin bends. It had a precipice on each side. We took it at breakneck speed and only at the end did our driver reveal to us that it was a one-way road. In the dusk the mountain views were breath-taking and the lights of the city were beautiful from above. The monks' last kindness to us was the gift of several hundred duplicate books from their library. These we loaded into the unslept-in back of the station wagon. That made the back so low that when we put on our lights on low beam, oncoming traffic thought we were on high beam and flashed their lights at us, only to be truly dazzled when we put our lights on high. No accidents resulted but there may have been a near miss or two, and a near cuss or two.

It had been good to be back in Benedictine surroundings again, and we left them with sorrow, but knew that we were not far from home. We had planned to reach Junction City, but made such good time that we were able to push on to Topeka, where we stayed at a parish which had taken on an obligation for a very large number of sung Masses for the dead. Each day the celebrant sang parts of the Mass, even if he and the server were the only people there, and even if the celebrant were no singer. No wonder they were glad to see us, and we duly sang for our breakfast.

Finally, on 24 August we hastened home so as to be in time for first Vespers of Saint Louis, only to find that Father Luke and Father Ian expected us later and had gone swimming. Not altogether reluctantly we pursued them to the pool and dived in. After a happy reunion we returned from the Pfeffers' pool and, for the first time, sang Vespers of our patron, Saint Louis.

We covered about 5100 miles in sixteen days and burnt 337 gallons of gas costing about $110, so the mileage was very close to that of Father Timothy's eastern tour, the gas consumption higher because the station wagon was a bigger and heavier car, and gas was more expensive in the West in the summer than in the East in the winter. Each trip brought back a quantity of books. We were very conscious of our lack of and need for a library.

Our first impression, as Father Timothy's had been of his tour, was of the generous hospitality given both by those who were expecting us and by those who were not. Part of the reason for this may have been that a Catholic priest in, say, Holbrook, Arizona, does not have much priestly company, but the kindness went far beyond that and struck us as one of the most pleasing of American characteristics.

We were impressed too by the scale of the country. In England at that time, if you started almost anywhere and drove for fifty miles, it took a long time, and in addition you would expect to end in countryside quite different from that in which you started. We set out across the rolling plains of Kansas. We found them much less dull than we had been led to expect, but, like Old Man River, they certainly did keep on rolling. Likewise, mountains and deserts would go on for hundreds of miles. The phrase from the song, "The prairie sky is wide and high" had been nonsensical to us until we drove through not Texas but Wyoming. Again by contrast with England's green and pleasant land, the diversity of the country was astonishing to us. There was dense forest and open desert, there were flat plains and lumpy mountains, dry tracts and mighty rivers. We thought of Hopkins' poem, "The world is charged with the grandeur of God".[58] Very true that is of the United States; and over it all man had toiled, sometimes enhancing the grandeur, sometimes smudging it. The trails had become highways, some rivers had been dammed and their lakes

---

[58] W.H.Gardner, ed., *Poems and Prose of Gerard Manley Hopkins* (Harmondsworth: Penguin Books 1953) p.27.

had become sources of electricity and places of recreation, fishing villages had become asphalt jungles.[59]

The trip also brought into focus some of our observations about the climate. It was violent: the hailstorm proved that. We were no longer in a small island, no longer closely surrounded by water. We were in the middle of an enormous mass of land, where the veering of the wind brought completely different weather. Not only was the range of temperature--from over 100° F. in the summer to 15° below zero in the winter--far greater than in England, but the changes of temperature were far more rapid. We could have 70° on Christmas Day and freezing rain on New Year's Day; indeed, it could be 80° in the morning and 20° before midnight. So, if you put on summer dress in the morning, you were miserably cold later in the day. We had to get used to the sartorial habit of layering. Although we were not afflicted by hurricanes, no year passed without at least a tornado watch.[60] The weather was also unpredictable. That was no novelty for Englishmen, but, as we gradually came to accept, it affected both planning ahead and building. Nobody could guarantee that a day chosen for a picnic would be a nice day; nobody could guarantee that the weather would allow us to complete the walls and roof of a building before winter. In due course, we had some English visitors, and were able to take them out in Saint Louis on 1 December for a picnic in sunny, 80° weather.

---

[59] When we read a history of the Archdiocese of Saint Louis, we learnt that in the late 1830s a priest who had been sent from Saint Louis to minister to two or three hundred Catholics on the south-western shore of Lake Michigan, had written back to his archbishop to ask if a second priest could be sent, as he thought the place would grow. The place is now Chicago.

[60] A tornado touched down about two miles away, the closest through 1999.

CHAPTER 13

The First School Year

IT was as well that we returned from the trip refreshed and with a great admiration for our new country. In the next few weeks we would draw deeply on those reserves of energy and admiration, for it was now less than a fortnight to the opening of school.

While we had been away, the remodeling, which had started on 19 June, had, despite threats of a steel strike, which did not in the end affect us, gone well and the monks, including us when we returned, had, with much help from Henry Hughes and two Old Boys (alumni) from Ampleforth, who happened to come to stay with us, done a vast amount of manual labor. The cost of the remodeling was around $40,000.

On 2 September our public relations campaign received an unexpected boost. We had been invited to send four boys arrayed as Benedictine monks to take part in the Catholic Pageant of the Mid-America Jubilee by portraying the arrival of the Benedictines in Saint Louis. That meant simply walking across the stage in monastic dress. Later in the month we were again included in a similar program for the pageant, so quite a large number of people saw the Benedictine habit and a large banner of PRIORY.

We have already related what happened in the hours immediately before the opening of school: the little man who threatened to close the school, the late arrival of the desks and the welcome distraction of the tarantula.[61] After these interesting events, the opening of the school on Thursday 6 September was almost dull, and no one complained about that. The boys were due by 8.30 a.m. The first to arrive, long before that, was Michael Fox, one of only two boys who lived west of the school. Father Luke rode the school bus, which arrived so much ahead of schedule that the official photographer was not there, nor was anyone else with a camera, so this historic moment is without pictorial record.

The first event of the school year was the monks' Conventual Mass, celebrated in the drawing room of the Stannard House with the boys participating. This was followed by an Assembly and a guided tour, which cannot have taken very long. Then there was a milk break--we

---

[61] *See above*, pp. 4-5.

noticed that American boys lapped up milk, whereas English boys would have been reluctant--the issue of textbooks, a serving practice for the Mass on Sunday and then family style lunch and a visit to the Blessed Sacrament. In the afternoon, those boys who did not have equipment for sports were given it, there was a short sports practice, and the bus left at 4.00 p.m. On Friday, after the Conventual Mass, there were two classes in the morning followed by a choir practice, for the Mass on Sunday, and lunch; an audition to uncover latent singing talent, and then athletics and departure.

On Sunday 9 September we celebrated our Inaugural Mass at 10.00 a.m. on the lawn behind the Stannard House.[62] Archbishop Ritter came to join the celebration of the monks, the boys, their parents and many friends and supporters. Doctor Mario Salvador, the cathedral organist, came to play our Hammond organ and made it sound as if it had many pipes. Father Columba was the celebrant, Father Gerald Sheahan, S.J., principal of Saint Louis University High School and Father Louis Blume, S.M., principal of Chaminade College Preparatory School were Deacon and Sub-Deacon respectively. Fellow Benedictines from the monastery of Saint Pius X at Pevely came over and helped to lead the singing, and some of our boys served. At the end, the Archbishop "spoke in glowing terms about the future of the school which he said he had desired so long" [63] and stressed that everyone, monks, boys, parents and supporters, must have as their motive and aim the glory of God. He then made a quick tour and left.

On Monday 10 September 1956, school began in earnest with the regular daily schedule that is shown in the left-hand column. The right-hand column shows, for comparison, the schedule for Mondays in 1997-98.[64]

---

[62] *SLPJ* I. 2, p.1.

[63] *Ibid.* p.2.

[64] File: *Organization, September 1956* . . . undated document. The schedule for 1997-98 was the same for Monday, Tuesday and Wednesday, On Thursday there was a Faculty Meeting until 9.00 a.m. and classes were reduced to forty minutes. On Friday there was Mass at 8.15 a.m. in church for the whole school and period 1 was omitted. The X period was reserved for Advisory meetings, free time, tutoring and club meetings. In 1956 one period could follow directly after another, as the boys usually remained in the same classroom; by 1997 this was not so.

1956-57		1997-98	
a.m.		a.m.	
8.40	Students arrive	8.10 - 8.28	Assembly in church
8.45	Conventual Mass	8.32 - 9.16	1st period
9.15	Assembly	9.20 - 10.04	2nd period
9.20 - 10.05	1st period	10.08 - 10.52	3rd period
10.05 - 10.50	2nd period	10.56 - 11.40	4th period
10.50 - 11.00	break	11.44 - 12.08	X period
11.00 - 11.45	3rd period		
11.45 - 12.30	4th period		
p.m.		p.m.	
12.35	Lunch and visit to the Blessed Sacrament	12.08 - 12.32	Lunch
		12.36 - 1.20	5th period
1.10 - 1.50	5th period	1.24 - 2.08	6th period
1.50 - 2.35	6th period	2.12 - 2.56	7th period
2.35 - 3.15	7th period	3.16 - 4.48	JV sports
3.20 - 4.45	Athletics	- 5.16	V sports
5.00	Bus departs		

In 1956 there was daily Mass for the school, and some scheduled prayer at other times. The subjects, with the number of periods a week for each, were Religious Instruction(3), Latin(5), French or Spanish(5), English(4), History(4), Mathematics(5), and, as an option, Greek(5). During Greek classes the greekless had a study hall. There was also one period apiece for General Knowledge, General Music, Art, and Choir, four periods in all. Father Columba taught R.I., History and Spanish; Father Luke taught both sets of English; Father Ian taught R.I. and both sets of Mathematics; Father Timothy taught Greek and both sets of Latin. For most subjects there were two sets, A and B, with the boys divided according to what we thought was their ability. For Greek there was one set for the eighteen boys who opted for it, and one set each for French (14) and Spanish (16).

There were two sets for Art (which had to fit in with Greek) and one set each for General Knowledge, Music and Choir. Mr. Walker started the Art class until Mrs. Singer took over from him, and Mr. Scheibal taught Music. We all shared in the General Knowledge, and Father

Columba and Father Ian directed the choir. The classes where all thirty boys were together and for which there were no grades were those that most taxed the ingenuity of the teachers.

There were three units of homework a night Monday through Friday, and five for the weekend. Each unit was to take 45 minutes, and masters were to be "careful not to set too much homework, bearing in mind the weaker members of sets, but should demand prompt, complete and satisfactory execution of the tasks".[65]

There were initially two Retreats[66] each year for the whole school, at each of which two complete days were set aside for spiritual matters. A Retreat-giver was brought in, if it was not one of the monks, and gave four conferences each day. There was time for Confession, reflection, prayer, counseling and reading, along with choir practice and preparation for any special ceremonies. The first Retreat was on 30-31 October, and was given by Father Columba. The second, on 19-20 April in Holy Week, was given by Father John M. Martin, a Maryknoll father stationed in Saint Louis.

A few boys were driven to school by their parents but most rode the bus. This was an experience and, in some ways, an education in itself. One of our alumni wrote about it twenty years after his graduation: "The bus was never quiet. In varied volumes and pitches, some of us talked incessantly, most of us often, a few only when necessary. We joked, boasted, jibed, hoped, challenged, cursed, predicted, mocked, shared hard-won practical knowledge (especially on Mondays), exerted power, defended privacy, completed homework in the mornings and discussed sports, teachers, girls, music and cars in the evenings. It wasn't easy to drive the bus."[67]

Before we go on to describe what actually happened in the early years, it is appropriate to outline what our intentions were; appropriate but rather difficult, because our original intentions were modified by subsequent experience and so it is hard to be sure what is original and what is modification. In 1980 for our publication, *In the Lord's Service*, Father Timothy attempted such an outline, and we draw on it here.

---

[65] File: *Organization, September 1956* . . . document dated 10 September 1956.

[66] A Retreat is a time set aside from one's ordinary pursuits and devoted to religious exercises. Ampleforth had two Retreats for the school each year. We were impressed by the strength of the custom in Saint Louis, and especially by the Jesuits' Retreats at their White House, which contributed so much to the piety of laymen in Saint Louis. When we came, they were for men only.

[67] *LS* p.56.

Basic was the primacy of the monastery and the consequent precedence of the monastic schedule over that of the school. School activities were not scheduled at the same time as the monks' prayer, and so in the early years it was possible for all of us to attend all the Divine Office in choir. That was impossible at Ampleforth, and this impossibility was another reason for our never becoming a boarding school nor even adding a boarding element. There were, of course, occasional exceptions to universal attendance, but it was our norm. We desired this schedule for our own sake, but we also hoped that fidelity to it would be a good example to the boys, and reinforce what they learnt in religion classes and from their own experience of the liturgy. Monastic influence was also dominant in the classroom as all the solid subjects were taught by monks except the B set of History.

To understand the principles on which the school was established one must go far back into history. In the beginning there were no schools, and bringing up children was the natural corollary of producing them. The two formed a continuum and were, both equally, seen as the right and duty of parents. So strong was this view that in civilizations where Wisdom Literature existed--Egypt, Mesopotamia and Israel, for example--the life-molding words of wisdom were often cast in the form of a father's instruction to his child, "Listen, my son . . ." When, much later, Christian monasticism started in the Egyptian and other deserts, the venerated elder who could produce the words to set others on the right path was called *abba* (father) or sometimes *amma* (mother). The former accounts for our use of the title "abbot". As the knowledge and skills needed for civilized life became more specialized, parents found they had neither the time nor the ability to impart these skills to their children and hired others to do so. Thus, gradually, schools were born.

From this it is clear that the phrase *in loco parentis*, though rightly unpopular when invoked in defense of paternalism, contains much truth. Parents are the natural educators of their children and schoolmasters are their delegates. This idea, in which is contained the concept of the "Priory Family", was the basis of our relationship with our students and with their families, and this too led us away from the idea of a boarding school, since many of the parents of boarders would be so far away.

It is also clear that although schools provide a service to parents and although they are staffed by teachers, what they are about is the boys (or girls). Parents are needed because without them there would be no boys; teachers are useful because without them there would be no teaching, though there could be other means of instruction; but boys are the purpose and consequently the focus of the school. Without them there would be no school. The school is primarily for their good. This does not mean that they always know what is best for them. If teachers, who are professionals, do not, as a rule, know better than the boys what is good for the boys, they probably should not be teaching. It is the same with doctors, lawyers and other professionals.

The point is an important one. Many people: parents, grandparents, teachers, coaches, architects, manufacturers, suppliers, salesmen and others, may benefit from the existence of schools, but schools are run for the sake of the boys and not for the sake of anyone else. If one takes simply and solely this educational point of view, the reason for consulting the interests of the faculty is that a good and stable faculty is a benefit to the boys. Similarly the educational reason for trying to establish a good relationship with the boys' families is that harmony between the home and the school is a help to the boy, especially if anything goes wrong. Fortunately there are many other reasons, Christian, humanitarian, professional, social and even economic, for being nice to faculty and parents, but the basic concern is always the good of the boys.

Our aim in the school was to lay solid, simple and strong foundations, half-expecting, or perhaps less than half, that in five to ten years, as Abbot Herbert and others had suggested, eager young Americans would be snatching it out of our hands. We therefore offered what seemed to us the obvious subjects as listed above and intended to add Science for the last three years, as indeed we did. We hoped that the boys would reach in all these subjects "at least the level below which we thought one could not be regarded as having had a good education."[68]

The school was to be in the English tradition but was unequivocally for American boys and in an American setting. Therefore, although our first reaction to football and baseball was disappointment,[69] and although each of us in his heart of hearts greatly preferred rugger and cricket, we opted for the standard American sports, and likewise activities. In other words, there was nothing especially startling or innovative about what we planned to do, but we did hope to do it well,

---

[68] *LS* p.51.

[69] One letter to England described football as "a slow, poor game played in full armour." We have since revised our opinion of it. An Englishman seeing football for the first time naturally compares it with rugger and is irritated by the frequency of the stoppages. We were helped by a friend who suggested that we view football as animated chess.

to challenge even the brightest boys, and to teach them to think. That last expression, "to teach them to think", occurred frequently in our early publicity, but you cannot do it in a vacuum. You have to teach a subject in a thought-provoking way. Memory is essential, especially for younger boys and in the earlier stages of a subject, but is not where education takes place. If a boy memorized what the teacher had said and regurgitated it, he was to be given a bare pass. He could hardly be failed for repeating the teacher's undoubted truths, but he could hardly be praised for doing no thinking of his own. Along the same lines and to encourage independent research, we were keen, as will have been apparent, to collect a good library and to encourage the boys to use it.

It was not hard to foresee that the process of adjusting English ways to American boys and parents would call for a multitude of decisions. We therefore agreed, from the beginning, to adopt and adapt the meetings that at Ampleforth were called "housemasters' meetings". These were weekly meetings of the top officials in the school. In the early days here we were all top officials, so these were weekly meetings of all the monks. The members of the lay faculty were brought in gradually. This gave us a routine and reasonably expeditious way of dealing with the ordinary problems that were bound to arise, but we recognized that emergencies would need treatment immediately.

We then turned our thoughts to discipline and leadership, which were much harder. Before school started we had to publish a dress code. It stated that besides an Oxford gray suit for special occasions, "for every-day wear they should have a sober sports jacket, white convertible shirt with button-down cuffs," and a navy blue wool tie. "Pants may be gray flannel (`wash and wear' flannel pants are available), Nylodene, `pleatless', or other form of dress pants. Khakis will be acceptable only in hot weather, and jeans never."[70] We believed that dress affects behavior, but if any of us thought that the boys, if well-dressed, would automatically be well-behaved, he was soon disabused of that opinion.

The phrase we liked in connection with behavior was "ordered liberty",[71] with more order in the lower grades and more liberty in the upper. But we were starting with only the lowest grade of high school, and we soon found that the first task was to establish any sort of order

---

[70] File: Organization, September 1956.

[71] A favorite phrase of Father Paul Nevill, the headmaster of Ampleforth to whom we referred on p.11 *above*.

at all. There was no need to grant liberty: the boys initially took all they needed, and more.

Then the liberties they took generated a need for a system of discipline. The penances we had used at Ampleforth were not wholly applicable, and anyway Father Ian had had little experience of administering them. By the Wednesday of the first week of school we had written out a standard scheme: *lines* to be written out so many times--in these early days, they were usually lists of Latin, French or Spanish words in the hope of being somewhat educational; *checks*, five of which automatically enrolled a boy in *Detention Class*, which was held on Saturday morning and was awarded also for bad work or for bad discipline leading to bad work; and finally *Demerits*, a very severe reprimand awarded only by the headmaster and recorded on the boy's school record. If these proved inefficacious, there was left *suspension*, during which the boy did not attend school, but had to keep abreast of the classwork and homework that he was missing. Checks, demerits and suspension were not part of Ampleforth's system but came from Father Timothy's tour. We did not in the beginning use corporal punishment, but did introduce it later. We kept it for a number of years until it fell into desuetude. The occasion of its introduction was an instance of cheating, a vice we particularly wanted to prevent.

Leadership, too, is hard for a ninth grader, still part of the herd and not quite ready for the discipline of aloneness that is part of leadership. But we did start even then to provide some small scope for it. It is one of the greatest advantages of a boarding school that it can more easily provide such scope, especially for boys who, though not born leaders, deserve some practice in acquiring this difficult art.

The object of all this was to encourage each boy in his progress towards holiness, wisdom, maturity and knowledge and, in the process, to help him to see that privilege brings with it responsibility.

But now, since in educational theory as in many other theories it is easier to talk a good game than to play one, we must look at what actually happened and acknowledge that we often fell far short of these noble ideals.

Discipline in the classroom was not a major problem, although there was a certain amount of wear and tear of the faculty's nerves and one monk was heard to remark, some six weeks into term, that this was the first day on which he had not lost his temper. Father Columba told his diary, "The habit of work is not there." The classes were small, and although we had been anxious about the efficacy of the dividers between the classrooms in the barn, they turned out better than we had feared. If the master next door yelled, that was audible, but on the whole there was little distraction.

Lunch in the converted garage, which now had bright yellow walls and a blue ceiling, was family style, with the boys sitting at tables of about eight, each with a monk. As time went on we had a faculty member, monastic or lay, at each table and arranged a "faculty steeplechase" whereby the faculty, except Fathers Ian and Timothy, moved up one table each week. One of the boys was the waiter for the week and brought to the table the communal dishes from which each boy helped himself.

It soon became evident that American table manners were different from English even in matters such as holding a knife, and this made it harder for us to know what was normal at table and what should be discouraged. After two years of experience we gave the faculty some guidelines for boys' behavior in the refectory. As rules reflect what has been happening or not happening in the past, we print a selection here:

> Ties to be worn and correctly tied. “No tie, no lunch.”
> Coats to be worn, not sweaters, nor topcoats
> Utensils to be used in the normal manner.
> No selling of food.
> No foraging.
> No throwing of food, napkins, etc.
> No chewing with mouth open.
> No elbows on table.
> They should make some attempt at civilized conversation.
> etc. (see Emily Post)[72]

The main problem in those first days was the break after lunch. There was a group of boys who already knew one another from their previous school, where their surplus energy had been released on a playground with fairly narrow limits; at Priory there was much more space and therefore much more scope for roving or rushing around. This group was the rushing nucleus and the rest soon joined in. Father Columba was overheard to refer to this phenomenon as "mass hysteria", and the phrase caught on. "Let's have some mass hysteria" the boys said, and so released their surplus energy, but in a way which, although it could hardly be said to break any explicit rule, was

[72] File: *Organization, Sept. '58-June '59, Notes for the Faculty*, 10 April 59.

incompatible with either monastic or academic serenity. Behavior of this sort led also to damage, some accidental and some not. One boy removed a fuse from the locker-room boiler in such a way that a serviceman had to come out to fix it and for three days the boys had no hot water for their showers after football practice. They saw there was little future in that. Maybe we ought to have been as strict outside the classroom as in it, but using a loose rein did have one advantage: we soon saw who were the ringleaders and were able to act accordingly. Gradually limits were set and calm was restored, but it took both effort and time. This experience led us to try out an embryonic monitorial system by forming a committee of six "with very vague powers to help maintain law and order and a healthy spirit."[73] The monitorial system is normal in England but very rare in American schools, or at least in those Father Timothy visited. This Headmaster's Committee, which at first was partly advisory and partly disciplinary, developed its advisory branch quite satisfactorily, while the disciplinary branch withered and eventually, when a separate group of monitors was formed, dropped off.

And so the school had come into being. When we had time to reflect, our reflections depended on how imaginative and how optimistic each of us was. The more optimistic and less imaginative were quite confident about our survival, but others had their doubts. One even felt that life would be impossible. Since there had been a wave of teenage crime in Saint Louis, which had, at about the time of our arrival, been much publicized by the media, and since we heard later that at one local school a teacher had been tied up with rope, stowed away under his desk and not found until six hours later, such a feeling was not entirely unrealistic. A rabbit was released in one class, but that was about as far as rowdiness went in the classroom. To be sure, we could all see that there were one or two boys who were unlikely to be with us for very long, but there was also a nucleus of fine characters and good students around whom to build a strong class, and that was the aim to which we devoted ourselves.

The first school year was to have three terms: 6 September – 19 December; 3 January – 17 April; 23 April – 7 June. Following the American custom, we scheduled three grading periods in each of the first two terms. We very soon arrived at the first of these on 3 – 5 October, and duly set and corrected tests, and wrote reports. There was not a great deal to go on, but we felt that it was important to give the parents as soon as possible an impression of how their sons were

---

[73] JMTH, letter to Abbot Herbert, 8 October 1956.

faring, especially as this was their first experience of our system. They must have been shocked and confused to see that the passing grade varied by set and subject from 40 to 60 out of 100, and that the grades scored ranged from 12 to 95. We soon amended this madly confusing system making the passing grade the same, 60, in all sets and subjects, but we still heard often that "my son has never before had a grade below 90."

Our idea was that a grade of 80 meant that the boy had mastered 80% of the subject matter, and so on, an idea which, although it seemed logical enough to us, was unfamiliar to the parents. When we started sending transcripts to colleges, we indicated that a grade of 80 to 100 was our equivalent of A, 70-79 of B and 60-69 of C. Numerical grading, the system to which we were accustomed, allows at least the appearance of considerably more precision than letter grades, and we believed that with experienced teachers the greater precision was not simply an appearance, but was an accurate reflection of the progress the boy was making. After these first reports reached the homes, there were many ruffled feathers to be smoothed, and we had our first experience of the need for and difficulty of communication and cooperation between school and home. After a while, we had parents' evenings linked with the grading periods, especially with the first one, but that seemingly obvious idea would have been quite novel to us in the early days. Ampleforth had no meetings of that kind.

The first meeting which in any way resembled what we now have was on the evening of 14 October 1957, the second year of the school, and its purpose was not primarily for parents and faculty to meet one another but more for the parents of the tenth graders to meet those of the ninth. The monks were there, and they were most of the faculty. No doubt there was an address or two to the parents, and no doubt some of the conversation was about their sons, but the focus of the evening was quite different. But not even a simple operation of this sort was free from pitfalls. Father Columba was not especially good at remembering parents' names, so it was with joy in his eye that he saw a rather mature mother and recalled her name. He addressed her by it and was pleased by the answering joy in her eye. Then he spoilt it all by continuing, "I am so glad to see you; I have your grandson in class."

In athletics, twenty-four valiants had signed up for football and six for other sports. Perhaps the six were really no less valiant considering the pressure of public opinion to sign up for football. The twenty-four practiced hard and played five games as a C team. For quite a while in the school's history the pattern of all our games tended to be that we would do well for two or three quarters and perhaps even for part of the fourth, but gradually our small squad would become exhausted, many of our players having to play all the time, and would give up points at the end. Nonetheless we did have two glorious football victories, the first (26-7) on 13 October in our first home game, over Lutheran,[74] who came onto the field with FAITH printed on their uniforms. Inevitably our theological wits commented "they had faith and we gave them the works." The second victory (14-13) was over Lindbergh High School, which had started a C team program the same year as we had. Late in the fourth quarter, Lindbergh was leading 13-6 but we scored on almost the last play of the game and completed a pass for the two-point conversion and victory. Father Ian traveled back on the bus with the team on what was then an hour's drive. All the way back without any pause the boys chanted "two, four, six, eight, who do we appreciate? Priory, that's who". Father Ian was too battered even to say "shouldn't the first *who* be *whom*?" The game was memorable also because one of our players threw his helmet on the ground in disgust and was benched in disgrace. We ended our first season 2-3. The exploits of the six boys in other sports are not recorded, but there was some non-competitive tennis once the courts were ready.

In November we switched to basketball and soccer. For soccer we had the football field, which served just as well for soccer, except that it had a pronounced camber, for drainage, and so the ball rolled off the edges too easily. For basketball we had no gym, but Dr. Robert J. Snyder, superintendent of the Parkway School District, which had its headquarters then at Mason Ridge Elementary School just across the highway from us, very kindly allowed us to use the Mason Ridge gym and later the gym at Fern Ridge for this season. Mason Ridge was a little more than a quarter of a mile from us. Come the first day of basketball, Father Timothy was surprised to find the squad standing around outside the Stannard House. When asked what they were waiting for, they replied in all seriousness "transportation", and in their turn seemed surprised when they were told that there two ways of getting there, to walk or to run. Most of them ran, and after a while came to enjoy this novel experience. It was before the days of jogging. Their record was 2-11, the 2 being Lutheran and Country Day. In Soccer we started by beating Country Day 2-0, such a daunting start, apparently, that no one else would play us except our own faculty.

---

[74] There was only one Lutheran high school then in Saint Louis.

At the initiative of the Headmaster's Committee and despite the surprise of the monks that such a thing should be suggested for boys of so tender an age, the first school dance was held on 20 November at the school. It was followed by a rummage sale to pay off its outstanding bills. As the library picked up a copy of the new edition of the Liddell-Scott-Jones *Greek Lexicon* for fifty cents, Father Timothy was mollified. On 20 December we held our first Father and Son Dinner, squeezing all the boys and all their fathers and the monks into the unexpanded garage. Father Columba gave out eighteen "letters" for football.

Then came the end of the term with examinations and reports. We attached much importance to the examinations, on the grounds that they should reflect how much had really entered a boy's mind, while grades for homework were more a measure of conscientious application. The grade in the examination had, therefore, to be at least 50% of the final grade, the rest coming from homework, class work and the results of the two previous grading periods. Each master, besides recording the grades, wrote a brief comment on each of his pupils in each subject. The headmaster added a general report, and the package was dispatched. The examinations were on Monday and Tuesday, 17 and 18 December. Grades were to be handed in on 19 December and reports on 20 December. They were mailed at the weekend, and some must have arrived on Monday, 24 December, because on Christmas morning Father Timothy was horrified to receive a phone call from a distraught mother demanding an interview that very day. Of course she had her way, but the reports were never again mailed before Christmas. For those who failed any subject there were make-up examinations on 3 and 4 January.

We attached great importance to these reports, too, and spent on them much time and effort, believing that the combined wisdom of several professional educators should be helpful to the parents. On the whole it was, but here too we ran into unexpected problems with language. In many of the early reports we wrote that the boy had done quite good work but could do much better if he really exerted himself. This seemed illogical to the parents but sensible to us, because the word "quite" means "completely" to an American but "moderately" to an Englishman. There was also wide variation in the way families treated the reports: some took them very seriously and grounded their son if the reports were bad; others read them out to the whole family at the breakfast table and had a good laugh; one parent called and said she had enjoyed the reports so much that she had waited until everyone was asleep and then had crept downstairs, opened her husband's desk and re-read them. Then she too had a good laugh. The report said that her son was as obstinate as a Missouri mule. "You might have been writing about my husband," she said.

The monks, and no doubt the boys too, were glad of the Christmas break, even though it was, by English standards, brief. The term had been a strain especially on Father Luke, whom we have mentioned only seldom. Besides all the work of administration, he had also been teaching two classes of English, and to crown it all, his secretary had been taken from him to help with the fund-raising. From all of this he developed a carbuncle, which put him in hospital with the threat of surgery. Fortunately it burst just in time, but two months later he developed another. Despite these difficulties, he had achieved wonders in equipping and supplying monastery and school. We have already mentioned Cherrick's railroad salvage depot and Holstein's furniture store. The various outlets for government surplus materials were also among Father Luke's haunts.

The government surplus warehouse in Jefferson City made available to educational and charitable institutions a wide variety of items from hammers and nails and paint to desks and filing cabinets, and going up even to trucks and bulldozers. In due course Father Luke picked up both a truck and a bulldozer for $50 and $40 respectively, not to mention desks, filing cabinets, chairs etc. galore. The bulldozer, having graded a playing field, demolished a house and performed many less exacting tasks, nearly turned out to be a collectible. It was one of a rather small number built during World War II to construct airfields in the Pacific. When, in semi-retirement, it was abiding our call, a friend of the Abbey identified it as a rarity, and had we been able to get it to start, he would have bought it for much more than its original price. We were not able, and so, after more than thirty years of service, it was gently put down.

It is not surprising, then, that when we needed posts to support the wire mesh round the tennis courts, Father Luke went to government surplus in Jefferson City in the station wagon and loaded the posts into it. It was a slow journey back with that load on a poor road, and we were getting worried as it grew later and there was no sign of him. Around 9.00 p.m., we were relieved to hear a metallic clanking approaching along our easement, and the station wagon heavily laden hove into sight. As we had found previously with the load of books, the poles in the back had the effect of raising the beam of the headlights enough to dazzle and anger oncoming traffic, but at that time road rage was still unknown. That metallic clanking still sticks in the mind, along with the cicadas, the frogs and the song of the cardinals as one of the memorable sounds of those early days.

Also from government surplus came a thirty-hundredweight truck, driven for only 18000 miles, and mostly at low speed because it had been carrying ammunition. It was just what we needed and the price was $50. It says much for our economical outlook that Father Luke was quite exercised in mind whether we should take the risk of buying this pig in a poke.

But not all his dealings were with government surplus. We bought two steers. It fell to Father Luke to supervise their grazing, and in due course their slaughter. Then they had to be cut up. That was done in our kitchen with the help of an expert from a meat-packing company, and the meat was stored partly in our deep-freeze and partly in rented freezers. It was all rather like the late-Victorian stories of young men being sent abroad to the outposts of Empire and finding themselves having to do surgery in a remote village with the aid only of a boy scout's pocket-knife and their reserves of improvisation and bravado. Sometimes Father Luke had to risk his own life and limbs. A man appeared on our campus. Father Columba gave him some money for his train fare and asked Father Luke to take him to the station. On the way the man asked Father Luke if he could keep a secret and, on being assured that he could, said, "That's good. I was in a military hospital, and they tried to keep me in long after I thought I needed it, so I walked out. At the door there was a car with the engine running; I jumped in and drove off. When the guard at the gate tried to stop me, I had to run him down. They caught me and put me in jail for manslaughter. I just got out, and I'm on my way to visit my family." Not a comfortable errand.

Into all this managerial activity he also fitted some teaching, and he and Father Columba were much in demand for Days of Recollection and Retreats in the metropolitan area and further afield. The Jesuits had dominated this work for many years, so perhaps a different approach was welcome, but it has to be admitted that some came to hear their "just darling" accent. Other monks got into the act later on.

After our initial term of what Father Columba called "groping our way", the new term started on 3 January, and the remainder of the school year was much plainer sailing. We again had three grading periods, one each at the end of January, February and March, and again sent out grades and reports. The classrooms were becoming places of learning; homework was being done with respectable regularity and conscientiousness; the artists and musicians were beginning to show what they could do; and Father Ian and Father

Timothy, by way of musical appreciation, played the boys some of their favorite pieces of light classical music, of which the boys enjoyed *l'Apprenti Sorcier* and could not make head nor tail of Gilbert and Sullivan: the patter was far too rapid. In January and again in March, we sent the whole school to attend concerts by the Saint Louis Symphony at a neighboring public school. The boys behaved badly at the first but, after an invigorating harangue, better at the second. The cost, including the bus, was $2 a head.

There were occasional visiting speakers: one was Father Thomas W. Curry S.J. from Saint Louis University High School on the importance of public speaking. As a result of his talk several boys joined the debate team. A second was the British Consul, Mr. James Duffy, who spoke on British policy in the Near East. Finally Mr. Paul Bryant, later a novice with us, spoke about the atom.

We also took the whole school in a fleet of parents' station wagons to the Art Museum, where a young docent, who later worked with the distinguished classicist, Professor George E. Mylonas, took us on tour. In the course of the tour she sat us down in the room of the Impressionists to look around. When she asked what we saw, one of the boys, who had already staked his claim to a rank at the lower end of the class, said, "Color and light." Who could give a better description in three words? That is the kind of ability that does not show up in the results of College Board tests nor in class grades, but can be commented on in written reports from the school to the parents or from the school to colleges.

But we were still learning. There was a very cold spell in January and our pond froze over. At Ampleforth, when the lake froze, a monk was sent over to see if the ice would bear the whole school, and if it would, we declared a holiday and boys and faculty, skates in hand, set off for the lake. After declaring a holiday here and laying down strict safety precautions--there must always be a ladder and rope etc., by the pond when anyone was skating--we soon found that if we had a holiday every time the ice would bear the whole school, we would not do much teaching. Then it thawed and rained and the playing-fields were too soggy for practice, so Father Luke took the boys for a run. This novel event dismayed motorists and, at first, the boys. The latter came to enjoy it, but Father Luke was so stiff after the first run that he organized but did not participate in subsequent runs.

On Saturday 2 February we held our entrance examination for candidates for the ninth grade in 1957, this time at Priory. Seventy-seven candidates appeared. Learning from experience, we set papers in English and Arithmetic, used a standard IQ test, and had optional papers in languages and Algebra, to be used mainly for placement, but, as our flier to the grade schools stated, "good work done in them will be included in the evidence on which we shall judge scholarship candidates". The interviews, held in the breakfast room in the Stannard House, remained an important part of the test, and this was the year when one of the mothers appeared for the interview--without her son. The ingenious son had told his mother that the interview was for her. There was a subsidiary test on 23 March, and this proved later to be a bone of contention between us and the Archdiocese. A satisfactory lunch was available for fifty cents. From all this we reaped a class of thirty, of whom six, owing to the generosity of men who gave us funds earmarked for scholarships, received full or partial aid.

On 16 and 17 April, the Tuesday and Wednesday of Holy Week, we had our second Retreat for the school. The program was of an intensity which few would design today:

Tuesday 16 April

9.00	Mass
9.30	Milk and doughnuts
9.40	Assembly
9.55	First Conference
10.30	Singing practice (in classroom)
11.00	Milk break
11.15	Second Conference
11.50	Reading
12.20	Visit to the Blessed Sacrament
12.30	Lunch
1.10	Holy Week Ceremonies (in classroom)
1.35	Third Conference, followed by Confessions & reading
2.20	Stations of the Cross (in chapel)
3.00	Reading (in classroom)
3.30	Fourth Conference
4.10	Bus departs

Wednesday's program was very similar, but had Benediction instead of Stations of the Cross. Some of the boys and some of their parents came back for the Liturgies of Holy Week which, considering how few we were, went well except that Fran Oates, who was serving, stood so near a candle that his nylon surplice caught fire with spectacular instantaneity. He was promptly smothered in a rug and so was more startled than hurt. Father Peter Sidler from Portsmouth Priory was with us in exchange for Father Columba, who was giving the school Retreat at Portsmouth. Also with us was an Ampleforth alumnus, who was on his way back from Borneo to England. As he had bright and abundant red hair and an equally bright and abundant red beard, everyone called him the Wild Man from Borneo.

Each year Saint Louis holds a major book fair, at the end of which the leftovers are given to some charity on condition that they are removed at once. We were chosen as this year's charity. The fair closed at 10.00 p.m. on Sunday and the hall was needed for use on Monday morning. The monks took Father Luke's $50 truck, now given a beautiful new body by McCabe-Powers, and another truck, along with some volunteers both boys and men, packed some ten thousand books into cartons and piled them on the trucks. The boys climbed up on top of the cartons and, in the middle of the night, we careered several times through the deserted city and out into the county, where we unloaded the cartons and returned for more. We finished at 2.00 a.m. The boys enjoyed the lark, the library acquired some books and the school some workbooks, but we have never done it again.

Of far greater significance was a letter that went out on 27 March inviting the mothers of the ninth-graders to a meeting to discuss the formation of a Mothers' Club. "Innocuous refreshments" were promised and the phrase caught their fancy. Attendance was high. This notable organization certainly deserves its capital letters, but it has to be said that the idea was completely unfamiliar to the Ampleforth monks and was viewed by them with a hesitancy that verged on suspicion. We had, in fact, in the course of our various visits been warned more than once against the dangers of such parent organizations, and so had our scouts, when they came over in 1954. Nothing of the kind existed at Ampleforth, so we had no previous experience to guide us.[75]

The dangers were evident to us: the club might interfere in the running of the school and so make the life of the school authorities more difficult than necessary; it might even cause dissension and division in the very group that we needed to unite. Further, we had not yet become accustomed to the idea that in the United States the education of children came under the mother rather than under the father, nor, at that time, did we think it was a very good idea. On the other hand, the formation of some kind of group for parents was very much in line with our general policy of involvement and liaison with

[75] *See* Appendix B 2, *Relation of Parents to the School*

our lay supporters and of open communication with them. None of us foresaw the stunning extent of the contributions that the mothers would make to the school. At the meeting the mothers were predictably persuasive, and the minutes of the meeting[76] started with the sentence, "On Wednesday 24 April 1957, Father Timothy reluctantly acquiesced in the formation of the Mothers' Club," or words to that effect. Their achievements shall be chronicled in due course; suffice it here to say that life without them is now inconceivable.

Athletics in the spring included both Baseball and Track. In the former we played Lutheran twice and lost each time. In the latter we had more success. Father Ian was a sprinter of note and so coached most of the running; someone must have coached the shot-put; Father Timothy coached the hurdles,[77] about which he knew something, and the discus, about which he knew nothing. Having studied the appropriate book to discover from what part of the hand the discus was intended to emerge, he tried to pass on this fresh learning to our young discoboli, one of whom, to everyone's amazement, won the event in our first inter-scholastic track meet, at Brentwood. The scoring was confused but our arithmetic satisfied us that we had won. A meet against Chaminade was rained out, and we concluded the season with an intra-mural meet.[78]

Grading started in May on two new playing-fields, but bad weather prevented them from being ready for seeding until July, so they could not be used as early as we had hoped; Father Luke acquired a secretary/book-keeper, Miss Mary Bennace, who was to be with him for many a year; and then most unexpectedly, Father Luke and Father Timothy were invited to play cricket for the Missouri Cricket Association. The other players ranged all the way from the equivalent of major-leaguers to sand-lot. A matting pitch was ready in Forest Park, and the outfield grass was long. We played for a year or two and managed to represent Saint Louis against Chicago, but then had, very reluctantly, to give it up for lack of time. Had we persevered, we would both have been able to call ourselves Test Match Cricketers, as there was, a year or two later, a Test Match between U.S.A. and Canada,

---

[76] The original Minutes Book seems to have perished.

[77] The hurdles themselves were surplus hurdles wheedled from Brother Ralph of Chaminade by Dan Richardson ('60), who had attended Chaminade before coming to us for the ninth grade.

[78] The details may be found in the first issue of *P.S.*, the school newspaper.

played in Saint Louis. The standard of the team representing U.S.A. was such that we would both have been eligible to play.[79]

And so our first year drew to a close. The end-of-year examinations started on Wednesday 29 May. Thursday was a holiday for Memorial Day and Friday for our patronal feast, Our Lady, Mediatrix of Grace, which we celebrated with a Solemn High Mass in the morning. On Saturday 1 June in the afternoon we held the finals of our intra-mural track meet, and these were followed by our first Father and Son softball game. Father Ian and Father Timothy, ignorant of the rules and the skills, took part but the Fathers won nonetheless. On Monday, the examinations were concluded, there was a general tidying up and the bus departed at 4.00 p.m. On Tuesday evening we distributed prizes, which included two for Handwriting. All that remained was to grade papers, calculate the grade for the year, which had to take into account both the final examination and the grades for the other grading periods, write reports and send them out, and announce, where necessary, the ways of making up failures.[80] And then Priory's first year was history.

Did the year meet our expectations? That is hard to answer since we hardly knew what to expect. Were we inclined to say with Harry Hotspur, "Out of this nettle, danger, we pluck this flower, safety"? That would have been far too melodramatic. In retrospect, we might say that the biggest mistake, even though it was unavoidable, was to reduce from nine to three the number of monks initially sent out, but no-one remembers that we felt that at the time. Our two most positive feelings were, first, that this foundation was what God wanted, and if he wanted it, he would presumably watch over it; the second was of ever-increasing trust and confidence in Inc. Such minor uneasiness as we had originally felt was not so much over Inc's intention to carry out what they had promised as over their ability to do so. They had, after all, promised an amount of financial support that far exceeded both our experience and our wildest dreams; but they had kept their promise. According to Brining and Co.'s audit of 19 September 1956,

---

[79] The first Test Matches were between England and Australia. Other countries joined in later. The Missouri Cricket Association was the M.C.A., but when Father Timothy met in London a member of the Marylebone Cricket Club (M.C.C.), the doyen of all cricket clubs, he could not resist saying that he had been playing for the M.C.C. in Saint Louis. His reward was a harrumph to end all harrumphs.

[80] The highest grade in any subject was 92, the lowest, palindromically, 29; the latter led to the boy's repeating the year.

Inc had, by 31 July 1956, raised $611,995.44 in cash and pledges. We felt, in addition, some initial anxiety that he who paid the piper might also wish to call the tune. It strengthened our hand enormously that in the one instance where Inc did interfere in a school decision, our judgement was soon clearly vindicated.

About the school itself we felt that the past year might have been much worse, and were cautiously optimistic about the future. We inevitably judged the boys out of our background at Ampleforth and found them to be more open and friendly than the boys at Ampleforth. In native ability they were similar: some were very bright, some were not very bright, and most were in between; but in preparation they were far behind boys entering high school at Ampleforth, who would have studied Algebra and Geometry for sure, probably Latin and French as well, and possibly Greek. This was one fact which pushed us towards starting in the seventh grade.

In Art, Music and Speech, the results were not spectacular, nor was it to be expected that they would be, but three boys had pictures hung at the Catholic Art Center's exhibit; the orchestra played at Fontbonne's Music Festival; two boys won medals in a Speech Meet at Saint Louis University High School.[81]

In discipline, whether in the sense of behaving civilly in class and respecting rules outside class, or in the sense of being organized in their work, able to concentrate on it and to produce it neatly, they were very weak, apparently for lack of practice. There was a wide gap here between our expectations and theirs. It seemed to us, also, that instead of naturally respecting a teacher unless he proved himself unworthy of respect, they put the teacher on trial and made him earn their respect. That is a matter of attitude and probably reflected a feeling about teachers which was widespread among adults and on which many others have commented.

This was distressing but not altogether a surprise. Something of the kind was a reasonable inference from the eagerness with which we had been summoned to Missouri. What was a surprise was this: if one corrected or punished a boy at Ampleforth, he tended to resolve never to do that again, or at least never to be caught doing it, or would say to himself "I'll show him". Many boys here, when punished, tended to withdraw and say "Father X does not like me." Whereas much of the rest of their behavior was not unlike that of the frontier days, this seemed quite alien from those robust times. These are generalizations,

---

[81] *P.S.* I. 1.

certainly, and there were many exceptions; but they represent some of our thinking at the time. Did we think that on the whole the foundation stones had been laid in the right places? Yes, we did. Did we think that the boys, or most of them, would make the grade? Yes, we did.

CHAPTER 14

What Did We Do with the Rest of Our Time?

IDLENESS is the enemy of the soul, as Saint Benedict quotes,[82] and so it may seem that all the activity of the school's first year must have been immensely friendly to our souls. No doubt it was, but in fact the operation of the school was very far from being the whole story. Our primary task as monks was our full and, with numbers so small, more tiring round of monastic duties, but we had also three other principal and time-consuming areas of activity: Inc and fund-raising, vocations, and architectural planning. To these we had been giving much thought and energy at the same time as we were first preparing for and then operating the school; and of them we must now give a more thorough account.

From before our arrival in Saint Louis it was clear that our relationship with Inc would be far closer than that of Ampleforth with any lay group, and this for several reasons. Inc had been deeply involved in our plans from the beginning and we would have been, to say the least, both ungracious and imprudent to try to exclude them now, nor did we have any wish to do so. But even apart from that, we felt that an enterprise like ours needed the full co-operation of the lay men and women affected, and that if we asked for their co-operation, then in fairness we should not limit ourselves to keeping them informed of our proposals but should include them in our planning and listen to their views. Being in a foreign country we wished to draw on as much local wisdom as we could, and anyway we were financially dependent on Inc.

There is also a deeper reason for a close liaison between monks and laity, namely that monks, considered strictly as monks, are more lay than clerical. There is no evidence that Saint Benedict was a priest, and certainly his *Rule* assumed that most of the monks would not be. The preponderance of priests in the English Benedictine Congregation is due to history--the need in the seventeenth and eighteenth centuries for monks in exile from England to return and bring Mass and Sacraments to their countrymen--and not to the essence of monasticism. The monastic instinct, therefore, even for monks who are priests, is to see laity as their kith and kin.

---

[82] *Rule* 48,1.

It is a great tribute to Father Columba and to Fred Switzer that men of the stature of Inc's members were ready to express themselves with great freedom in our discussions, and then to abide by our decision; and on our part, we listened to them carefully and disagreed with them, when we did, only with caution and reluctance. Most often we were able to reach a British compromise with which everyone was content but in which no one got all they wanted. In this, oddly, being of different nationalities was at least as much help as hindrance. *Omne ignotum pro magnifico*[83] (if it's unknown, it must be wonderful), and we may well have both given and been given credit for greater wisdom than was actually present. If a member of Inc made some snap judgement, we were more likely to think it commendable decisiveness than rash impetuosity; and if we dithered, they would take it for admirable British caution.

Much of the communication between Inc and ourselves was by phone between Father Columba and Fred Switzer, and their harmonious relationship was one of our great strengths. But that still left a certain amount of liaison for the rest of us--Father Timothy recalls a fifty-minute phone call with Henry Hughes--and there were still numbers of meetings and dinners. Many of the latter were for The Drive, and again required each of us to make a speech; but now we could point to other people and to concrete things rather than to ourselves and to our abstract ideas. That it was productive is evident from the occasion when one of us sat down after his speech, and Joe Desloge turned to him and said "Splendid report, Father. I'll give you another $10,000," and did so.

There were certainly times when we would much rather have gone to bed than to a dinner at the Deer Creek Club, but we recognized nonetheless that, quite apart from fund-raising, there was also the matter of "friend-raising". And this was no chore because the friends to be raised were so friendly, and an evening spent with them might be tiring at the end of a busy day but was always enjoyable.

One Inc event deserves special mention. It occurred on the evening of Wednesday 29 May the first day of the end-of-year examinations. It had been planned for the previous Thursday, which would have been far more convenient, but a deluge of tropical rain during the previous night washed it out. Undaunted by this and by many prophecies of doom, the chairman, Bill Weld and his co-chairmen, (this was long before inclusive language) Mina (Mrs. William H.) Harrison and DJ (Mrs. Clarkson) Carpenter, carried on. We should

---

[83] Tacitus, *Agricola* 30

have known that if Mina and DJ put their heads together, the result would be both fantastic and on a grand scale. Their plan was to model the party on what they thought a royal garden party at Buckingham Palace would be like. Everyone was to come in their ultimate finery; there was to be a state coach; there were to be Beefeaters in full uniform acting as butlers; we were to serve everything from cucumber sandwiches to champagne. Little of this got past the censors. Wednesday came and rain was forecast, but we had 224 cars, over 500 children and nearly as many adults, and a beautiful sunny evening. The children played and ate from 5.00 until 8.00 p.m. and then had movies in a huge tent. The adults had cocktails from 5.00 to 7.00 p.m., then dinner on the lawn behind the Stannard House, followed by addresses from Father Columba on our building program, Father Timothy on our religious and educational aims, Father Reinert, president of Saint Louis University, on the importance of secondary education, and finally a recorded message of support from Archbishop Ritter, who could not be present on the altered date. Mr. Fristoe Mullins, chairman of The Drive, was M.C.[84] It was a gala, and one more instance of Inc's wonderful achievement, a wonder due to the energy and wisdom of its leaders and members and of many other workers, who made phone calls and visits, ate lunches and dinners, drank drinks and arranged events, all on our behalf.

Then there was the matter of vocations. Despite Abbot Herbert's suggestion about eager young Americans snatching the monastery and school out of our hands, none of us really planned on being in Saint Louis for only five to ten years. Although we were confident that Ampleforth would continue for some time to send us additional monks, we saw clearly that the future well-being of the monastery and school depended on our attracting to the monastery some of these eager young Americans who were reportedly so numerous in Saint Louis. We, and especially Father Columba, lost no opportunity of looking around for potential monks, and of doing more than just looking.

Our first candidate, who started as a postulant on 10 February 1957,[85] has already been mentioned: Jack Peters. He approached us at one of our earliest public meetings and soon became a familiar face on campus. He assured us that Advent wreaths were a very normal

---

[84] He took over in the spring at a time when the stock market was falling and there was a certain amount of alarm. JLR Letter of 16 March 1957.
[85] *Ibid.* 9 February 1957.

local custom (they were not so in England) and came out and made some for us. Without ever becoming our sacristan, he gave us much help in liturgical and para-liturgical matters, often in areas where we would not ourselves have expended much energy, as with the Advent wreaths, and so filled in many of the small gaps between local and English liturgical customs. He also brought out a number of his friends, some of whom, like Charlie Rush, tried their vocation with us, and others, like Messrs. Brent J. Williams, Edward J. Presti and George Hickenlooper, taught for us. At the beginning of March 1956 he corralled four undergraduates of Saint Louis University, including Charlie Rush, to make a Friday-through-Sunday Retreat here under Father Columba, and then brought out some singers to join them for a high Mass on the Sunday. He brought out miscellaneous singers on any number of occasions; sometimes they were quite miscellaneous. In Holy Week he was really in his element, and a great help. In Easter week we took the whole group out for a day in the country at Cuivre River State Park. In May, Jack organized a lunch for five young men from Saint Louis University High School. Father Columba loaded them with literature, and in due course one came for a Retreat here and later became a postulant.

On 16 March 1956, Father Columba was invited to Saint Louis University High School to speak, along with an Alexian Brother, a Marianist and a Redemptorist, on a panel on vocations--in those days the word was routinely used to mean religious vocations--and was pleased to find that he could communicate no less well with American boys than with English boys. The Archdiocese also had a program whereby priests and brothers were invited to speak at grade and high schools. On one later occasion one of the monks spoke to a group of over one hundred and, at the end, handed out reply cards for anyone interested. The Sister in charge must have urged them to be interested, as we received over one hundred responses. Father Columba, who had to reply to them, was less enthusiastic about that result than the monk. Vocations were very much on our minds, and the forecasts of their abundance, made to us before we came, were apparently being justified.

As we have already mentioned,[86] we were also on the route used by the Jesuit Scholastics from downtown to walk, on their day off, to their place in the country. On the way these young men used to look in on us for lunch or some refreshment. We encouraged them, but perhaps we encouraged them too much as they were soon instructed that it was

---

[86] *See* p.93 *above*.

proper to appear before the monks in clerical garb rather than in jeans, and that led to their ceasing to come at all.

Jack Peters was not the only source of applicants. In July, Dr. William A. Barker, a prospective parent and a professor of Physics at Saint Louis University, introduced to us Mr. Paul Bryant, one of his Ph.D. students, who, besides helping to develop the wrap-around windshield for cars and being a devotee of the Indianapolis 500, wanted to try his vocation with us. He came in September, and entered the novitiate at Ampleforth, but to our sorrow found it was not for him.

There were indeed, as we had been told and as this account shows, more than a few young men thinking about a religious vocation, and we did all we could to encourage them. The Journal for November 1956 reports "three possible candidates for the novitiate next year", and the issue for May 1957 says "A number of young men of Saint Louis will be going across the sea in the next few months to Ampleforth to join the novitiate there so as to become in due time the first American monks of St. Louis Priory." A list of our novices is given in Appendix A 2b.

Our third area of non-academic activity was architectural planning, in which we were all neophytes. We inevitably drew especially on our knowledge of Ampleforth, usually following their example, but sometimes resolving to do the opposite; for example, we rejected Ampleforth's "laymasters' common room" and called it the faculty room, to encourage monks to frequent it and to stress the unity of laity and monks on the faculty. To this knowledge we could add what we had picked up from our own visits in the United States, and here Father Timothy's tour of the eastern states was invaluable.

Having also acquired precious experience as a by-product of planning, bidding and rejecting the Cloister plan, and having remodeled the existing buildings in a way that would see us through the next two years, that is through June 1958, we now had to make plans for the monastery and school from 1958 on. This did not give us much time, a little over two years in all. It was, consequently, alarming to hear that The Principia, a Christian Science school and our neighbor across Highway 40, had taken ten years over planning their campus.

We had from the very beginning started to think about planning of this kind, and had recognized that we must first make an overall or master plan and then realize it piece by piece. The pieces might be whole buildings or parts of buildings, but if we built part of a building, then we had to be sure that we left room for the rest of it.

This turned out to apply both to the monastery, to which additions could be made at either end, and to the library, which could be extended southward. At the same time we wanted, especially in the early stages, to avoid building anything which would predetermine later buildings. We mentioned above[87] the American instinct for an a priori approach to planning and the English instinct for an a posteriori approach. Subconsciously we were trying to have the best of both these worlds: to have a master plan (a priori) but to keep it flexible and to allow for trial and error (a posteriori). A general plan of some sort would help to keep us from constructing a formless mess, and it would be up to us to stop it becoming a strait-jacket.

Our first document is called "*Provisional Forecast of Accommodations Required*" and is dated 23 November 1955, five weeks after our arrival. Although some of our thinking later turned out to have been wishful thinking, it was at least a start. It lists what we thought we would require for September 1955-56, 1956-57, 1957-58 and 1958-59 and includes, besides most of the spaces that we did provide, a bedroom and dining room for school guests, a gas tank for the procurator and other items that we did not get until much later.

Late in 1955 or very early in 1956 we produced, as we mentioned above,[88] a more detailed document: *Basic Ideas for the Architect When Planning the Buildings of Saint Louis Priory and School.* It presupposes that the Cloister Plan will be completed, so it cannot be after January 1956 even though the remarks about style do suggest a slightly later date. It may well have been composed over some length of time.

Some of the highlights are given here to show the state of our collective thought at the time: after observing that the plan must have a certain spaciousness and elasticity from the start, that we will not build all the buildings at once, that some of them will probably be enlarged later and therefore will need some elbow room, and that the cost will be related to the success of The Drive, we ask the architect "to use contemporary methods and style and yet keep in mind the traditional character of a monastic foundation. The family spirit needs to be emphasized in both monastery and school. The materials should be lasting but not lavish."

The church was to be geographically and psychologically central to the campus, and the altar to the church. The church might ultimately need thirty-five side altars. The monastery, which must be away from

---

[87] p.92

[88] p.93. For the document itself, *see* Appendix B 3.

the highway, "should ultimately be able to house one hundred monks or more" and should, besides the other necessities, include guest rooms and sick rooms. The church, the cloister, the monks' refectory, calefactory and library should be on the same level. Here we were thinking more of the aged than of the handicapped, whose needs were not conspicuous in architectural planning of that time; one library could possibly serve both monks and boys; we might have ten to twenty laybrothers.

The high school might grow to four hundred, which might include fifty boarders; its classrooms should be close together but the science laboratories could be a little bit away (this was a concession to Father Columba's keen sense of smell); there should be an administration building central to the school with offices for the headmaster and secretariat, deans of admission, studies etc., and for the procurator, or business manager, who "should be near his stores . . . and these should be near the refectories"; he should be accessible both to the monastery and to outside.

Besides basketball courts, the gym might include squash courts and rooms for wrestling and boxing; its outside walls might be shared with other buildings. We called for an auditorium, arts and crafts rooms, music rooms, carpentry shop, dark rooms, playing fields and car parks. And then there was to be a Junior School for probably not more than a hundred and twenty boys.

Not all of this came true. We have never had laybrothers, and now the distinction between laybrothers and choir monks has been abolished; the coming of concelebration has reduced the need for side altars to a minimum; and the central administration building does not include the procurator; we have never had boxing. Otherwise the contents of the campus today bear a surprisingly strong resemblance to what was projected in the beginning.

This very preliminary document was given to local architects and to those from farther away who either visited us or expressed interest in our project. When we finally chose HOK, we had already had extensive discussions among ourselves and with Inc; and HOK had, from *Basic Ideas*, some impression of our needs. We had also met with them to plan the remodeling of the buildings around the Stannard House, so we were not complete strangers.

In addition to *Basic Ideas*, we produced for HOK a document dealing mainly with the school. It changed the forecast for the junior school by calling for either two grades (7 & 8) or four (5, 6, 7 & 8) of fifty each, giving totals of either one hundred or two hundred. As guiding principles we laid down that:

1. It is virtually impossible to predict the exact form of the school in even as little as ten years' time. We can only suggest possible developments. This means that planning and construction must at the same time meet the needs of the moment and leave room for expansion. How this is done will vary: it probably entails rooms such as the auditorium being built much larger than is necessary immediately, but for ranges of rooms such as classrooms it will be enough to have space for additions. The point is that future developments will affect the initial plan. . . .

2. A school is amongst other things a home and should look like a home rather than an institution. It must have a style and a feeling quite different from that of a factory or a block of flats--or a multiple store. I [that is, Father Timothy] am at present open to argument on the merits of single-storeyed or multi-storeyed buildings.

3. Money is very much an object, but buildings and equipment should be sound and durable. I see no reason for discarding buildings after a mere 100 years of use.It may well be economical in the long run to use materials that cost more initially. Economy ought perhaps to be directed rather to economy of circulation and other non-operational space and to architectural ingenuities."[89]

The point made in #3 about durability proved to be very relevant. In the course of later discussion we were shown drawings of buildings that looked quite insubstantial. When we were assured that they were permanent, we skeptically asked how long "permanent" meant, and were told fifty years or so. This would not be permanent in Europe.

We now started, on 7 May 1956, a series of meetings with HOK about the overall plan. In these meetings we were greatly helped by a building committee consisting of Mr. Joseph Desloge, Mr. Joseph Gander, J. Gerard Mudd, M.D., Mr. Edward J. Walsh, Jr., and Mr. David Q. Wells.

---

[89] Document headed, "*General Introduction*" in Father Timothy's file: *Planning*.

It turned out to be an advantage that none of the monks, none of the committee and none of HOK's staff had ever planned a monastic campus before. We all had to start from scratch, which included defining such basic monastic terms as calefactory and enclosure, cloister and cell. In order to do this we had to think what these terms really meant to us in Saint Louis, which was not necessarily quite what they had meant to us at Ampleforth, and then to make sure that HOK understood our thinking. This was tedious, perhaps, but also beneficial. We were reminded of the belief about Imperial Chemical Industries in England, that they preferred applicants with university degrees in Latin and Greek to those with degrees in Chemistry on the grounds that neither group knew anything useful to I.C.I. but only the classicists recognized this. Similarly, an architect who had no idea what a calefactory is would have to absorb our ideas. In this way, while they were teaching us much about architecture, we were teaching them much about monasteries and monastic schools. It became a very fruitful partnership.

As we went on, the monastery of one hundred monks became one of eighty, and much later we came to think that thirty-five was not only a more attainable number but also more desirable; but this was after the Second Vatican Council. Initially, we kept the idea of an ultimate upper school with four hundred in grades nine through twelve and of a junior school either of two hundred in grades five through eight, or of one hundred in grades seven and eight. We thought then that we would double the class size in the ninth grade. We did not see the need to plan a dormitory building, as there was plenty of room on the campus for it, should we ever decide to take in boarders, and its position was not closely tied to any other building, so we did not need to leave room for it.

In 1956 it seemed reasonable to expect to attract one hundred monks in comparatively few years, and likewise with the projected number of boys. Neither expectation has been fully realized: not only did the number of vocations drop markedly after Vatican II but also our attitude towards large monasteries changed; and in the school, once we had started to take boys into the seventh grade, experience led us to abandon a large, regular entry into the ninth grade. Classes in the upper school were therefore the same size as, or, with attrition, a little smaller than those in the junior school. This meant that over the years classes in the junior school have become larger than the original plan, and those in the upper school smaller. Fortunately, as we were simply planning the general layout and never had any intention of building all the buildings at once, the reduction of numbers merely meant that there was some open ground where there might have been buildings.

At the meeting on 7 May, whose minutes cover fifteen pages, we were asked first of all what buildings we wanted and what would be in them. Gyo Obata said, "We would like to work with you in establishing a program which would put down in words all your requirements, requirements of each of the buildings. Then once the program is established, we will go into the study of each building, come up with rough space requirements and then we will meet with you and see if they are correct. Then gradually, after the space requirements are established, we will go into the design."[90]

Our discussion started with the monastery and its contents, and soon meandered, because when we mentioned rooms such as refectory, calefactory, cell and so on, we had to stop and explain their use; and when we mentioned numbers, whether of monks (100) or of books in the library (50,000), or dimensions of rooms, this usually led to discussion among ourselves and between us and HOK. Almost at once we asked for a covered way from the monastery to the church, so, although we did not build it for nearly thirty years, perhaps the little man from County planning did us a service after all. We called for a novitiate, lecture rooms, infirmary, guest rooms, kitchen. We discussed the size of the monks' cells (15 feet x 20 or 12 x 16) and whether to have showers in each room. We told HOK that we wanted to live frugally and settled for a central core of showers, toilets etc.

Then we were side-tracked once more. This time it was into a discussion of numbers in the school. When we got back on track, we turned to the church and repeated our two basic stipulations: that the church should be central to the campus, and that the altar should be central to the church. As so often at the beginning, but less and less as we went on, our thought was influenced by the corresponding layout at Ampleforth, where the monks were in a retro-choir on one side of the altar and the boys in the nave on the other. But, recognizing that in a day school the boys' families were likely to attend services more often than at Ampleforth, we wanted to plan for a larger number of worshippers other than boys. Father Columba mentioned one thousand as the maximum number that we might wish to squeeze in.

---

[90] We must have brought to the meeting lists of rooms required, but they have not survived. A list which may derive from them is printed in Appendix B 6.

We talked of stained glass, bells and three confessionals, on which George Hellmuth asked whether three would be enough "with all those boys and monks going to Confession at once," a pleasing picture. We then went on to a discussion of the business area. Father Luke was thinking of two offices plus one for the secretaries and one for the accountant, a caterer's office, housekeeper's room and bedroom and accommodation for live-in staff. There would be store-rooms, closets, strong-room and garages. Outside, there would be equipment sheds and tanks for oil and gas. Much of this would be needed only in a boarding school, so again we were drawing on our memories of Ampleforth.

Then we came back to the school. We repeated that we were thinking of a junior school of two grades (7-8) or four (5-8) with fifty boys to a grade; we were still thinking of a boarding element; we called for sightly parking lots; Father Timothy had been impressed by the possibility of wedge-shaped classrooms in some sort of circular arrangement like a pie; we were open to one story or two, and Gyo thought the slope of the ground might lend itself to two on one side of the building and one on the other, as at Mount Hermon School.

Among other ideas canvassed were a multi-purpose room for auditorium, band or choir practice (near the gym so that the noises would cancel out) and for concerts; a swimming pool with windows below the waterline, for the coaches to observe underwater techniques; a PA system into all classrooms, and finally a thirty-yard shooting range.

As the discussion progressed, there emerged some of the relationships among the buildings. The church should be central, with the monastery close to it on one side and the school, probably, on the other. The procurator, or business manager, served and should be close to both monastery and school, and his department needed to be accessible to delivery vans. And so on. It also emerged gradually that instead of trying to build half the monastery and half the school, we would build the monastery, and so have a building to point to as the monastery, and use half of it for monks and half for boys.

In due course, we naturally asked for a rough estimate of the cost and were told that we might think in terms of $400,000 for the church, $500,000 for the monastery and $1,000,000 for the school. The members of Inc, when they heard, were not dismayed.

This meeting has been reported at some length because it was typical of the many that we held. There was plenty of give and take; we made our proposals, which were then modified both by ourselves and by HOK; HOK listened carefully to our needs and clarified them by their questions. The discussions could no doubt have been both tidier and briefer, but their somewhat rambling nature often allowed submerged ideas to emerge. When they emerged more than once, as with the centrality of the church on the campus and of the altar in the church, we recognized that these really were important. At these meetings everyone was a facilitator.

The dominant feature of the terrain available for our buildings was a broad ridge running north and south and rising towards the south. It went on rising beyond our property until it dropped off to highway 40. East and slightly north of the northern end of the ridge was a knoll, now shared by the Science Wing and the Parish Center. The Stannard House was on the main ridge, slightly south of its center. West of the ridge was a valley, whose western side rose to Mason Road and went on rising on the other side of the road. The rest of the property sloped, for the most part gently, away from the ridge and the knoll. The ridge and the knoll seemed both to HOK and to us to be the obvious sites for our main buildings.

We were startled when HOK suggested demolishing the Stannard House to make way for the monastery and church. This was not irrational, as we would then be able to put the church, which we wanted to make the most important feature of the campus, on the dominant site; but to us, who were not used to the idea of serial demolition, it did seem unreasonable, as it meant doing away with a sturdy and handsome house, which was serving a useful purpose at the time and was likely so to continue. We vetoed the suggestion, and gradually a general layout began to take shape. The Stannard House and the Barn classrooms would remain. North of them and on a lower level but still dominant would be a large quadrangle, with the church in the center and the monastic buildings surrounding it on three sides, leaving open a view and approach from the west. The school would occupy the knoll north-east of the quadrangle, the gym would be south-east of the school and the playing fields south and south-east of the gym.

CHAPTER 15

Public Relations, Architecture and Our Church

WE were now able, towards the end of the school year 1956-57, to produce a booklet, *To Praise God and Serve Man*, which marked the coming together of two of our non-educational areas of activity: fund-raising and planning. It starts with a generous introduction by Archbishop Ritter, which we quote in full to show the warmth of his support for us:

> The establishment in this community of a Benedictine Priory and boys' preparatory school is of the greatest significance to the educational work and religious life of our Archdiocese. The establishment of such an institution has been my earnest desire for many years.
>
> The Saint Louis Priory and School stands in the great tradition of Catholic worship, scholarship and teaching. The devoted effort and generosity which have already accomplished the substantial task of bringing the institution into being; the splendid student body now enrolled; the excellent faculty nucleus all testify to the vitality of the establishment. It is an example of the fruits of Catholic Action which cannot fail to be felt throughout the Diocese.
>
> The scope and significance of the Priory and School reach far beyond the mere addition of another institution to the Archdiocesan educational facilities, important as that would be. The school itself will be more than a high school; a college preparatory institution, it will rigorously maintain the highest possible standards of educational excellence and call forth the very best efforts of our most promising boys. It will also be a monastery, devoted to the worship of God, to scholarship and to the education of young men to teach in the great Benedictine tradition. Together, the influence of the Priory and the School will spread from the institution itself throughout the community, the Archdiocese and indeed ultimately through the whole nation. It will be a guide and beacon to Catholic education everywhere.

An undertaking of this magnitude will continue to call forth from our people a like measure of devotion and sacrifice. It is my hope that the faithful of the Archdiocese, especially those able to contribute substantially to the Priory's physical needs, will respond to this appeal for funds. It is an appeal of special merit. It is an opportunity to help provide leadership and discipleship to represent Christ and His church in our community and in our world.

Sincerely yours in Christ,

Most Reverend Joseph E. Ritter
Archbishop of Saint Louis

That glowing introduction was in marked contrast with the local Bishop's attitude towards Ampleforth's attempted foundation in Calgary, Alberta just after World War I, but only Father Columba had any firsthand memory of that.

The booklet goes on to portray with a diagram (*See* p. *157*) and then to describe a five-year plan of buildings, roadways and playing fields to cost $2.5 million. The plan, stated to have been "the subject of months of intensive and prudent effort by the monks and their architects and lay advisors," was a very respectable start. The Monastery, the church, the gym, the junior school and many of the roadways are now just where they were planned then. The playing fields are in the same general area as planned except that the "Priory Bowl" has moved from the attractive and bowl-shaped area south of the junior school to an area at the east end of our property, where in the late Fall the turning leaves on the trees nearby may catch the sun and lift the spirit.

The high school has changed most. The original intention was a building in the form of a biplane. Two pairs of wings were to contain the classrooms and the laboratories, a central fuselage the administration, an auditorium for six hundred and common rooms for faculty and seniors. The library was to be the propeller, and rooms for art, music and shop the tail-plane. Only the library, the science wing and one classroom wing were to be built at this time, and as not all the classrooms would be needed for teaching, the others would be used as temporary quarters for administration and other needs. Of the library Father Timothy wrote,

> This is the intellectual center of the school. Here the boys exploit and expand, on their own, the interests aroused in their formal studies; here they venture into new fields of knowledge, or more deeply into the old; here the older boys start to acquire the familiarity with books and works of reference that they will call on so often in college; here some will simply sit and read for pleasure. A library is no hatchery for eggheads, but a quarry of necessary information and of pleasure for every boy. At Ampleforth, when the school library was re-organized, and its use promoted, the number of scholarships won to the universities was greatly increased, and the standard of studies was transformed throughout the school.[91]

In reality, only one of the four wings of the biplane, the science wing, was ever built, and as its roof has leaked persistently, it is as well that we did not have four such buildings. By the time we were ready to plan the high school, it had become clear that the space set aside for the monastic buildings was much more than we either needed or wanted, so the school took over the eastern side of the monastic quadrangle. This had the advantage of bringing it closer to both monastery and church, but left the science wing and its scientific smells out on their own. The gym was in an attractive spot to the east, down in the trees, and was made architecturally pleasing by a one hundred foot triangular truss running the length of the building to support the roof and to provide daylight. This truss was a bone of contention with the building committee, who then and on other occasions expressed their opinions with considerable vehemence, as did Father Timothy on the probability that the skylights over the locker room would leak. Both may have had the effect of putting HOK on their best "We'll show 'em" mettle.

In the booklet, Father Columba then reiterated the aims of the monastery and Father Timothy those of the school. Father Columba wrote in part:

> Saint Louis Priory, therefore, has a two-fold life; the one depending on the other. In the first place the monks worship God by singing the Divine Office in choir and offer Holy Mass daily. In the second, in those spaces of time between, they are occupied in the education of youth, leading them to the fullness of life, which is

---

[91] *SLPJ* II. 1, p.6.

the knowledge of Christ, the keeping of God's commands and the development of their personalities . . .

. . . It is inevitable and right that the life of a monastery should influence by its very being the thoughts and the desires of the boys passing through the school. They will reverence the liturgy of the Church. They will have an appreciation of the three vows, which will teach them restraint, whether they become priest, monk, or as more probable, layman in the world. They will acquire that taste for scholarship which is typical of most monasteries, and a sense of order, a love of peace and a humble submission to God in all things and service of their fellow men such as can be found both in the Rule and displayed in the lives of those who practise it.

Also in part, Father Timothy wrote:

. . . A truly Christian education aims at producing a man well-grounded in his faith and well-grounded too in secular studies and other pursuits. There is no contradiction between true Christianity and true scholarship, and the student should in fact be all the better Christian for being a better scholar, and all the better scholar for being a better Christian. This alone would lead us to strive for the highest possible scholastic standards and to include in our program a generous measure of the other valuable activities of schools such as athletics, the arts and crafts, and so on . . .

. . . The over-crowding of most colleges and the bulge in the school population are ceasing to be news, but that does not mean that their consequences are ceasing to be formidable. Not only does entrance demand greater and greater preparation, but even after entrance students cannot meet the ever more exacting demands of their courses, unless they have solidly mastered their high school work. The plight of the man who spends his years in college chasing the time wasted in high school is wretched indeed.

These high school years, then, are perhaps the most important in a student's formation, not because the matter covered in them is the most important that he tackles, but because, if he masters what he has to learn then, he is soundly and securely equipped to enter and survive his college courses . . .

> . . . We hope, also, in our pursuit of the highest standards, to join hands with the many educators across the nation who have similar ideals, so that besides learning from them, we too may make a worthy contribution to the advancement of education.

The booklet now gets down to business with instructions for making gifts and a list of over sixty suggestions of memorial items from $300,000 down to $500. It is pleasing to note that the two cheapest memorials are various items of athletic equipment on the one hand and, on the other, the frugal furnishings for a "small and plain but not prison-like" monk's cell. The last page lists the campaign chairman and nine co-chairmen (one is a woman), and twenty-seven Counselors of the Priory, who had met for the first time on 21 January 1957 at Fred Switzer's home. Their names may be found in Appendix A 1d.

There certainly had been “months of intensive . . . effort”, and the effort had been as prudent as we could make it, and yet none of us was entirely happy with the plan. This was due partly to our inexperience and consequent uneasiness about committing ourselves to a plan on this scale, partly to our increasing awareness that the build-up of monks from Ampleforth was likely to be slower than we had hoped, partly to our recognition, as the monastery building began to take shape, that unless we increased the size of the school, the present buildings would be adequate for a while. The number of monks was important because, as well as our faculty ratio of ten to one, we still aimed at a ratio of boys to monks of about fifteen to one. We thought we could expect to have about ten monks by 1960, which would mean a school of 150, which was what seventh and eighth grades of fifteen each, and upper school grades of thirty each would give us. Inc too was uneasy about raising $2.5 million, and, when we raised the possibility of staying at our present size of both school and plant, and digesting what we had, was not at all averse from reducing our goal from $2.5 million to $1.1 million. This new sum was to cover the monastery and gymnasium, which were by then under construction, the Science Wing, which would be new, along with money for classrooms, library, dining-room and heating plant. Our Journal for April 1958[92] expresses it thus:

> [These] building needs . . . represent a revision of the program and make it desirable to alter the plans for raising funds.

---

[92] *SLPJ* II,1,5.

> Instead of a continuous building program amounting to $2,500,000 over a period of five or more years, we now have a program amounting to $1,100,000 for buildings which should be provided over the next year or two. There will then be a substantial period of eight to ten years before additional school facilities will be required for an expanded student body and faculty.

Everyone then breathed more freely.

While all this was going on, we were continuing our talks with the Mudd family, who wanted to give us the church. There seemed to be enough support due to come from them over the next few years to justify us in going ahead and planning the church even though we would not be able to build it immediately. This turned out to be the most interesting part of our planning, because we were dealing not only with the most important building on the campus but also with, as we hoped, the most exciting piece of architecture.

In 1956 it was still the custom for the priest to celebrate Mass with his back to the people, but if, as at Ampleforth, the monks were on one side of the altar and the boys or other congregation on the other, a priest with his back to one would be facing the other. There might be on the altar a substantial tabernacle obscuring the view, but we were already thinking of putting this either on a side altar or even suspended above the high altar. Once more we reaffirmed to HOK our desire that the church be both geographically and architecturally the dominant building on the campus and that the altar be dominant and central in the church. It should be as close and as visible to everyone as possible. The whole design of the interior should encourage participation over spectatorship. It should have enough height to be dignified, but at the same time, if possible, should be economical in the same way as the other buildings. We added that we believed that stone, being the most durable, would also be the most suitable material for the church. We wanted the fittings in the church to be boy-proof.[93]

Having considered all this, HOK came up with the idea of a cruciform church with all four arms of the cross of equal length. This had the advantage that the back rows would be closer to the altar than in a long, rectangular church with the altar in the middle. Father Bede soon suggested that we should turn the Greek cross into an octagon. This would reduce the total length of wall and at the same time enclose more space and seat more people. This suggestion was

---

[93] This was why, when acoustics became a problem, we opposed the idea of putting speakers on the back of the pews.

adopted and was a notable step in the evolution of the final design. The next event was a notable shock: we were told that the estimated cost of our church, if we built it in stone, would be about four times our budget, so we abandoned stone and gave the architects *carte blanche* to choose a material and to make their recommendation. They chose concrete, as we had expected, and we agreed. Neither their recommendation nor our agreement was a surprise since by that time our own feeling about the style of our campus was moving from traditional towards modern, and although a stone church could have blended pleasantly enough with the brick buildings we were planning for monastery and school, a concrete church would be no less and perhaps much more pleasing. It also enlarged the range of possible designs.

Very early in January 1957 or perhaps even a little before,[94] HOK showed us two models of the church. Each was about one foot in diameter. The first was basically a polygonal glass wall with occasional bearing members and a corrugated roof of concrete. It was somewhat like a ruff in a portrait by Van Dyke. It was light and airy, spacious and attractive, and somehow soothing. It also seemed static. The second, also polygonal, was harder to describe. It was pyramidal, with a bottom row of triangular arches. Above that and slightly set back was a second row, and above that a third. One seemed to be looking at a concrete pinecone or artichoke. The concrete was to be covered by a copper sheath. It looked prickly; it was the more difficult but also the more interesting of the two designs, if only because it did not reveal all its charms at once. Some felt this was because it had none. It was certainly modern, but as we looked longer at it and overcame our first shock, we could see that there was some resemblance to the very traditional three-tiered Gothic arrangement of arcade, triforium and clerestory.

After a long discussion in which words like "honest", "organic", "sincere", "monstrous" and others were bandied about, we were asked to vote. There were four monks present. No one acquainted with monks will be surprised that the vote was 2-2, nor that those who voted against the pyramid later became its most ardent champions. Gyo Obata had the casting vote and voted for the pyramidal artichoke. Either now or later, George Hellmuth convinced the Mudd family that

[94] CCE *Diary*, January 1957.

the pyramid would become something beautiful and worthwhile, and he was not mistaken.[95]

Our next task was to win over the building committee, and after them Inc as a whole. The design was uncompromisingly modern and some members of Inc were, if not uncompromisingly, at least strongly traditional. Father Columba records, "As Father Timothy is sold on the scheme, he will try to sell it." He did this at the meeting on 7 January 1957 of the building committee, the architects and the monks. It was a great help that Joe Gander, president of Bank Building Corporation, was strongly in favor of the scheme and promised his technical support. The upshot of the meeting was that the plans and models for the church, monastery and gym were approved.

That was satisfactory, but by then a financial problem had arisen. It seemed that the Mudd family was likely to be able to find around $300,000 and the church was likely to cost around $500,000. What were we to do about the gap of $200,000? We felt we could hardly ask others to pay for a church which was to be named for one family; nor could we build the church without finding from somewhere the missing $200,000. Our tentative solution was that the bare structure of the church was estimated at about $300,000 and this seemed enough to justify the naming. Therefore we could go ahead and use funds given by others to make up the balance. As it turned out, by the time the church was built, the Mudd family was able and willing to foot the whole bill.[96]

On 21 January at Fred Switzer's home, there was a meeting of the Counselors. There is no record of the agenda, but the building plans must have been one, and probably the chief, item. There is no record of any general meeting of Inc between 11 July 1956 and 19 May 1958 so more widespread discussion of the plans must have been informal.

By mid-March it was clear that there was considerable opposition to the church. Some did not like the design, others the size and expense, and others again thought it would not stand up to the climate of Saint Louis. The monks at Ampleforth, whose opinion we sought, were not

---

[95] Fathers Columba and Luke voted for the ruff, Fathers Ian and Timothy for the pinecone. Over the years most of the votes in our community have been either unanimous or evenly divided.

[96] At this rather tense moment there is a gap in Father Columba's diary, which has no entry between 22 January and 19 March, on which date there is a summary of what had been happening in the interval.

attuned to architecture of this sort, and almost all of them thought it quite unsuitable, as it would have been, had it been built in their valley. Even the monks here were wavering, and Father Columba had actually written to HOK that as it stood the design was unacceptable.

As so often, the building, which has since won considerable acclaim, almost was never built, but in the nick of time HOK was able to make contact with Pier Luigi Nervi, the Italian architect/engineer who specialized in architectural, almost sculptural, concrete. He was judging a competition in Chicago and agreed to come to Saint Louis to confer with HOK on 21 March, the Feast of Saint Benedict--surely no coincidence. When Obata and Nervi and the others met and talked, the outcome was that the octagonal base became round and the arches changed, as Father Ian had suggested earlier, from being triangular to being parabolic. The diameter of the church and the height of the arches were reduced, but the copper sheath for the exterior remained.

There was still much work to be done on the interior and on the furnishings--we had had in March a visit from Frederick Cole, an English maker of stained glass and had been impressed[97]--but the structure of the building was now decided. Criticism, the brunt of which was courageously borne by Father Columba, continued but we stuck to our guns, and planning continued too.

Father Columba in our *Journal* for May 1957 invoked the authority of Cardinal Lercaro, whom he described as the most important promoter of modern churches: "Why not modern? The church must always be of today. 'Jesus Christ, yesterday and today, and the same for ever.' The church has always used the style of the times, Early Christian, Romanesque, Gothic, Renaissance, Baroque; always the architecture of the day. It is not possible to ask a modern architect to build today in any of the ancient styles."[98]

Perhaps the author of the *Letter to the Hebrews* would be surprised to find himself quoted in support of parabolic concrete, but the Cardinal's point is surely valid, and one of the reasons why we had chosen HOK was their talent for the modern idiom, in which they had produced the distinguished new building at the Saint Louis airport. At this point, as the funds promised were not yet available and as there was no immediate necessity for the church, we put the plans into cold storage, to be brought out when appropriate.

---

[97] JLR Letter of 3 March 1957.

[98] *SLPJ* I. 3, p.5.

While all this was going on, we had also been planning the monastery and the gym. The daughters of the late Birch Oliver Mahaffey: Adelaide Schlafly, Betsy Mullins, Dorothy Jane (DJ) Carpenter and Katherine Walsh, had undertaken to provide at least a large part of the money needed for the monastery and so we felt able to proceed. We approved the preliminary plans in February 1957 and in March HOK went ahead with the working drawings for the monastery and, a few days later, with those for the gym.[99] Then, what with our inexperience and the arrival of summer when we were seldom all in residence at the same time, we did not break ground until 29 September.

This was the state of our planning when *Architectural Forum* magazine gave prominence to a well-illustrated article on *A School in Praise of God*. The article was published in the issue for November 1957 but we had already had three meetings with the editor before the middle of September.[100] The writer refers to our project as "one that could become one of the most remarkable contemporary achievements in US religious and educational design". The church was to "rise from its high plaza in ruffles of thin concrete . . . The monastery elaborates on the traditional hollow rectangle . . ."; for the classrooms "the monks wanted neither bleak modern cells, nor an environment that would distract from intellectual concentration." The issue was dedicated to secondary schools and we were given pride of place.

---

[99] JLR letter of 16 March 1957.

[100] *Ibid.* 15 September 1957.

CHAPTER 16

Our Summers

FOR vacations the summer of 1956 had been exceptional, as we were in the throes of last minute preparations for the opening of school and had each simply snatched a vacation when we could. The summer of 1957 was the first summer of a regular pattern defined at its beginning by the end of one school year and at its end by the beginning of the next. Later in our history, those not directly involved in the school could take vacations at other times, but in 1957 we needed to establish some principles. The first few days of the summer were taken up with grades and reports and the last two weeks with the monks' Retreat and with meetings of the faculty. We decided to hold again a brief summer school, 10-21 June, for the incoming ninth graders, and twenty-two out of thirty attended it. The offerings were almost the same as the previous year's. How were we to manage the rest of the time?

There was never any shortage of work for the part of the summer that we were here, so the problem was how to fit in a vacation for each monk, what he should do during it and how he should pay for it. At Ampleforth, where the period between school years was a month shorter, most monks went to visit their family, and when we started having American monks, they did the same. It was, however, too expensive for each of the English monks to return to England every summer, so we established a four-year rotation. It started with Father Columba going to England this summer.

Part of the benefit of a vacation was to get away from the heat of Saint Louis, but that meant going some hundreds of miles, with the consequent expense. We investigated travel by bus and found that, with the help of clergy discount coupons, we could go long distances at low cost. There were snags, especially if one wore a clerical suit. At any stop, the suit was a magnet for bums; and besides this, on one occasion one of us had found an empty row at the back, only to have an inoffensive woman join him. After fifty miles or so, she turned to him and said, "Father, do I look normal?" How can one reply except to agree? She continued, "I'm glad to hear that; I just escaped this morning from an asylum. I'm a homicidal maniac." What does the well-mannered monk say next? She got off the bus at the next stop.

We have already mentioned the organization, Auto-Driveaway, which undertook to arrange for a reliable driver to deliver a car to a destination, and monks seemed as reliable as one could expect. Sometimes the car's destination and that of the monk were some distance apart, but one time the owners wanted the car driven to the TWA terminal at Boston and the monk wanted to fly TWA from Boston to England. He had to walk some twenty yards from the monastery to the car, and another twenty yards at Boston; otherwise he had his own wheels all the way.

This was the summer when Father Luke set off for the West Coast in his scarlet Corvette from Auto-Driveaway. He later claimed that it could reach 130 m.p.h., but how did he know? On the way he encountered in Oklahoma a Wild West pageant, in Santa Fe an Irish touring group from Dublin's Abbey Theatre, in Arizona the Painted Desert, the Petrified Forest and the Grand Canyon. He delivered the car in Fresno and caught the bus to Los Angeles to stay with friends. He supplemented his small amount of holiday money by filling in for the pastor at Carmel and giving, with the help of a doll called Sally, two Retreats at Sacramento to girls aged seven to thirteen. After a final day in San Francisco, he flew back to Saint Louis, where he was recognized as our expert on the West.

For the most part our holidays followed a pattern similar to the above: we did a number of "supplies" at parishes while the pastor went on vacation; we gave Retreats; we stayed with hospitable friends, and especially with the Mudds at Walloon. Later on, Father Timothy spent many summers visiting colleges and saw parts of all the forty-eight contiguous states. This was invaluable both in recommending colleges to boys and in getting them into college. It helped to prepare colleges to interpret our untypical grading system.

This particular summer he broke the mold in another way. Fred Switzer thought his son Fred would benefit from a vacation in a monk's company and offered Father Timothy the chance to go with his son wherever they decided. After rejecting West Africa as being the white man's grave, they decided on Mexico, Panama and Peru. In Peru they were royally entertained by an alumnus of Ampleforth, who had been Father Timothy's classmate. They watched a bull-fight in Mexico, inspected the Panama Canal and some small Caribbean islands, and in Peru climbed nearly to the top of Machu Picchu, paddled their own canoe, a dugout, on the Amazon, and saw dolphins near Iquitos, a thousand miles from the mouth of the river. That evening they were describing how, in the heat of the day, they had found a spot made shady by overhanging branches and had snoozed there. The local experts remarked that it was on just such branches that anacondas lie in wait for their prey.

Despite all our vacations, Father Luke signed on 17 July the final specifications for the new buildings and bids were sought that same week. When the bids came back at the beginning of August, they were about what HOK had predicted. We could not complain at that but we had been hoping that they would be lower, and so we spent several weeks discussing with HOK, our building committee and the contractors ways in which we could reduce the cost. In this we were greatly helped by the expertise of Mr. Joe Campagna, a developer, and Mr. David Q. Wells, a future parent, who met with us informally and with our building committee. We were helped also by the contractors, who were Paulus (general), Murphy (heating and plumbing) and Koenemann (electrical). As a result, we saved Inc something like $35,000, and were ready at the end of September to break ground and in mid-October to start construction.

That summer, Father Columba was due to give a Retreat to the Benedictine monks at Atchison, Kansas. He set off but at the end of our driveway recalled that he had an unbreakable engagement in Saint Louis, so Father Ian was sent instead. He had never driven any long distance before, but he managed both the three hundred miles each way and the Retreat itself with aplomb.

Another day Father Luke and Father Timothy drove about forty miles to Washington, a town of ten thousand on the banks of the Missouri, to pick up the Priory Journal, which had been printed by the Miller Press there. They took a picnic lunch, bought a bottle of Missouri wine at Augusta and found the field of a friendly farmer in which to picnic. It was a hot day, the wine was more than friendly, and the heat and the wine were soporific. We may have been a little late reaching Washington.

Also during the summer Mr. Buchholz, the father of the Davis Cup player, offered tennis instruction on our courts, and we joined the Inter-school Parents' Committee, which drew up a social code to guide parents and strengthen their hand against the teenage blackmail, "Everyone else's Mom lets them . . ."

The two most important events of the summer both involved transatlantic travel. Our monastic reinforcements, Father Bede Burge and Father Thomas Loughlin reached New York in mid-July, spent some time there, went on to Portsmouth Priory in Rhode Island and Saint Anselm Priory in Washington, DC, and arrived here at the end of the month.

Father Bede was a mathematician and an athlete, a large and gentle man, who had never been outside England except for one trip to the Isle of Man, a small island a few miles off the English coast. After being taken round New York, whose architecture at that date was largely derivative, and being asked what he thought, he replied that the only original contribution of the United States to architecture appeared to be the wigwam. He had a very keen analytical mind, which he applied not only to Mathematics but also to matters as diverse as football tactics and the most economical shape for a milk carton. He tried to devise a form of football as a board game like Monopoly, and tried to convince our dairy that they would save cardboard if they adopted his carton. The dairy agreed but thought his carton would be less stable. He was a most agreeable addition to our monastic community and the boys, too, liked him, but he developed or aggravated a heart problem, partly because he found the boys' idea of discipline unsatisfactory, so after a year we sadly saw him return to England. He did not really enjoy being in Saint Louis, but when he returned to Ampleforth and was involved in any discussion, his contribution was usually, "of course, in Saint Louis we used to do thus and so."

As Father Bede was a top-flight mathematician, so Father Thomas was a top-flight chemist. He had received his Ph.D. before joining the monastic community at Ampleforth, but had had little teaching experience and had worked instead in the business office. He had, however, kept up his reading of the Chemical magazines and so, although his teaching technique was rusty, his knowledge was not. He was also a keen and expert player and coach of Soccer. As is true of many Lancastrians, his *yes* was yes and his *no* was no. If you asked him to organize the Science department and he said yes, that is what he would do. If you asked him at the age of fifty-five to coach Soccer for one more year and he said no, there was no point in trying to twist his arm. The arrival of these two men was a joy for all of us, and Father Timothy was delighted to have two key departments in such expert hands, especially at a time when industry was courting those who were adept in Math and Science.

Hardly less of a joy was the other transatlantic journey, in the opposite direction, of three young Americans due to start their novitiate at Ampleforth on 14 September. These were Jack Peters, Paul Bryant and Joe Hanon. Jack Peters lived in the monastery and taught a course in the school for our first year. Paul Bryant was from Kansas City and by now had his Ph.D. in Physics from Saint Louis University. Joe Hanon, like Jack, was from Saint Louis. He came to know Father

Luke through a non-Catholic salesman at Lombardo's on Produce Row, who heard Joe saying he was interested in being a priest. Father Luke was the only priest the salesman knew and so it was to Father Luke that he referred Joe.

Since it was not considered feasible to send us from Ampleforth a monk to be novice master, Abbot Herbert decided, with some misgivings, that we should send our novices to Ampleforth, because this seemed preferable to the other options, namely, to keep them here for their novitiate or to send them to another monastery in the United States such as Portsmouth or Saint Meinrad. To keep them here would have been an enormous burden for Father Columba, who would have had to be their novice master, and to send them to another monastery ran the risk of bringing them up in a spirit other than our own, whereas Ampleforth was of our own monastic flesh and blood.

Our novices were to be accepted as being officially novices of Ampleforth. They were assured, however, that, when trained, they would return to our Priory unless education or ill-health required otherwise; and that, if the Priory ceased to exist, they would be free to join another American monastery, should they wish.

In hindsight, sending them to Ampleforth may have been one of our greatest mistakes. We certainly underestimated both the probable homesickness of young Americans and the differences between Saint Louis and Ampleforth. The former underestimation was pardonable. Young Englishmen who had grown up with the British Empire, or even with the British Commonwealth of Nations, were more accustomed to the idea of leaving home in late teens or early twenties. Father Columba had at that age spent eighteen months in France, and Father Timothy three years in India, Burma, Thailand and Malaya (as they then were) without undue discombobulation.

The latter underestimation was less excusable. We had already picked up many linguistic differences and had experienced the confusion and even embarrassment that these could cause, but it took us longer to see that there were two kinds of linguistic difference. The first was when a word meant one thing in England and another in the United States, as pavement means the roadway here and the sidewalk there. That could be confusing and even embarrassing, but was essentially straightforward. The second, which was more subtle, was when a word had different nuances in the two countries or, worse still, concealed a complex difference of ideals, behavior and mores. "Urchin", as we discovered from the indignant reaction of the parents of a boy so described, is a much more serious criticism in Saint Louis than in England; and "aggressive" which would hardly ever be used as a compliment in England was, at least in certain contexts, routinely so used here. It was this last kind of difference that caused not only confusion, but even misunderstanding and distrust both for us here and for our novices at Ampleforth.

Besides linguistics, the discomfort felt by the men we sent to Ampleforth was due to the different level of central heating--our novices would have called it a lack of central heating--the differences in food, sense of humor, ideas of politeness and discipline and so on. The sense of humor may have come as close to the heart of the matter as anything, because, like linguistic usage, it presupposes and depends on a whole range of assumptions about what is acceptable in many parts of life and what is not. So when the Ampleforth monks said, as they often did, that our novices were very good and nice but had no sense of humor, and when our novices said, as they often did, that the Ampleforth monks were very good and nice but had no sense of humor, they were commenting on a deep divergence. The novitiate is indeed a time of testing and probation; the tragedy was that these men were tested in many ways that were quite appropriate for Ampleforth monks but had little relevance to the real question for our men, whether God was calling them to be monks of Saint Louis Priory. Jack Peters, who made his Simple Profession at Ampleforth on 23 September 1958, the first Saint Louisan to do so, lasted longest, but none of the three became a monk for life, although all remained good friends with us.

We ourselves had difficulties in our relationship with Ampleforth, partly because we were in what was for Benedictines an abnormal situation. For us, the essential unit is the individual monastery, and the essential authority is our abbot. This has strengths and weaknesses, but it does mean that decisions about life on the spot are made on the spot. There do exist an Abbot President of the Congregation and an Abbot Primate of the whole Benedictine Confederation, but they exercise little ordinary authority in a particular monastery. A Benedictine does not relate to them in at all the same way as a Jesuit relates to his Provincial or to his General,. but he does relate very closely to his abbot. Consequently, if the abbot is far distant, that distance introduces something abnormal into the life of the monk. We were a dependent Priory, which meant that each monk was still fully under the Abbot of Ampleforth and that all our major decisions had to be approved by him and sometimes by his Council too. Yet we were several thousand miles away; some of the Council could have little or no idea of our needs and difficulties, and even the abbot could not keep in touch with the day-to-day situation, whether of our community as a whole or of each individual monk, in the same way as he would have done had we been at Ampleforth.

Communication was far slower and far less reliable then. Airmail took about two weeks for the round trip and surface mail might take months; cables were costly and faxes and E-mail were unknown; a telephone call went through any number of small exchanges and took a long time, if indeed one got through at all; and in any event, Abbot Herbert did not like to make important decisions over the phone. This is not the Benedictine way.

But there was more to it than either our juridical status or the physical difficulty of making contact with Ampleforth. When we left England we were as Amplefordian as any of the Ampleforth monks, but as time went on and because we never intended to establish a replica of Ampleforth, we made adjustments to American ways first in the school and later, because American monks arrived later than American boys, in the monastery. These adjustments in turn affected our own outlook so that, although we remained substantially Amplefordian, we adopted an ever-increasing number of American points of view and therefore became less in sympathy with corresponding points of view coming from Ampleforth. To take two examples: had Ampleforth monks ever said, which they did not, that cricket is a better game than baseball and therefore we ought to play cricket, we might have agreed with the statement but denied the conclusion drawn from it--and as time went on, some might also have denied the statement. When Ampleforth monks said, as they did, that our plans for the church were quite unsuitable and therefore we should not build it, we agreed that our plans would have been quite unsuitable for them but felt that fact to be irrelevant to our decision. All this led to our spending a disproportionate amount of time and energy explaining how the differences in our situation here necessitated ways of coping that differed from Ampleforth's ways. In general, though, Ampleforth was very tolerant in accepting our judgements even when that must have been for them a considerable act of faith.

There were also difficulties on this side of the Atlantic. We had been brought to Saint Louis at least partly because we were not American and therefore had something different and distinctive to offer, but we could not simply transplant English ways. We were English but were not in England. We were dealing with American boys and parents but did not have any deep grounding in American culture. We loved Ampleforth but could not be always talking of Ampleforth nor saying that at Ampleforth we would have done this or that. In deference to American sensitivities it became a custom and almost a policy not to talk about Ampleforth. Such deference had its good side, especially for the boys and for the lay faculty, but it brought with it some losses in the monastery for both American and English members. Much of the spirit of a community is transmitted from generation to generation in its folklore and its anecdotes. For many years these were taboo. That was a loss for the young Americans. In the English monks it engendered a kind of rootlessness and consequent nostalgia, which may have been part of the reason why a number of our members returned to England.[101]

Another custom, also almost a policy, arose and again it had its good and its bad side. Our friends were most generous in inviting us to the Symphony or to a ball game or to lunch, and often suggested that we bring along another monk. We were all busy and a time that one monk could manage might be very inconvenient for another, and yet the other might feel some pressure to accept the invitation of a fellow monk. We tended therefore not to share these invitations in order not to create the pressure. That was considerate, but it also led us not to seek our recreation together, and that was a loss to our communal life.

By now we were preparing for the new school year. It started with the Archdiocesan Educational Conference, at which Father Timothy gave a workshop on the education of bright students. In our early days here, these formidable gatherings consisted of several thousand religious Sisters, some lay teachers and some priests and brothers. At the first one he attended Father Timothy was twice discomforted. After one of the intervals he went to sit in a place other than the one he had occupied before. He became aware of a substantial sister looming over him, sprang to his feet and, using a common English idiom, said, "Sister, I'm so sorry; did I pinch your seat?" It was only when she blushed vividly that he was aware of how she had taken it. Soon after that, he was talking to another Sister, who asked him who he was and what he did. He explained. "And what do you have your Ph.D. in?" When he said that he did not have a Ph.D., she turned and walked away.

Another year he was asked to fill in on the platform for an absentee by introducing the ex-Mayor of Saint Louis, who would in turn introduce the Governor of Missouri. Father Timothy did so, although he had never before met the ex-Mayor. The Governor, after his talk,

---

[101] This was brought home to us by the television program, *Roots,* which dealt with the African roots of African-Americans.

returned the microphone to his good friend, the ex-Mayor, who thanked the Governor for his inspirational message and then returned the microphone to his good friend, Father um er, Father um er . . .

Figure 1: Five year plan, 1957. *See* p. 140

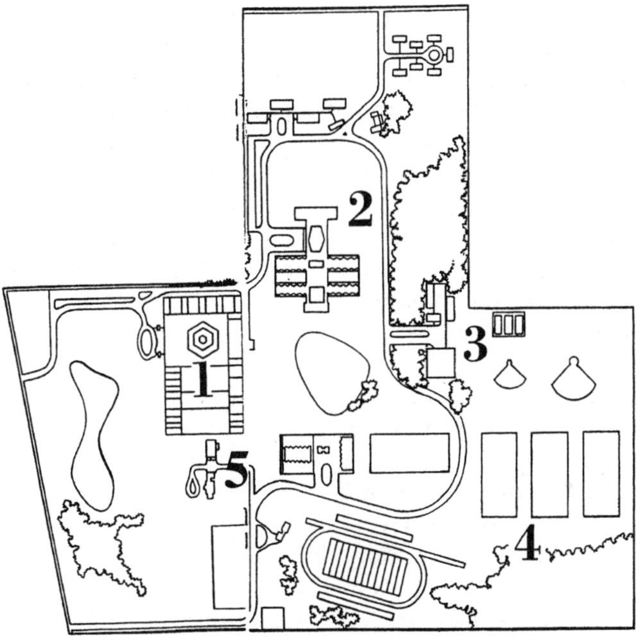

1 THE MONASTIC AREA

Library, chapel, classroom unit
Monk's living quarters
Administrative wing
Refectory

2 THE SCHOOL

Auditorium
General classroom wing
Multi-purpose area
Library
Art, music and shops wing

3 THE GYMNASIUM

4 PLAYING FIELDS

5 THE STANNARD (SWITZER) HOUSE

CHAPTER 17

The Second School Year

A school can have its first year of existence only once, and we did not shed any tears over that. But we had learnt from our experience in the first year, and fully intended to apply that learning when the boys returned. In addition, we prognosticated that the sophomores would react well to the responsibility of having a class of freshmen under them, and in that prognosis we were proved correct. In the conclusion of their editorial in the first issue of the school newspaper, which was then called P.S., standing for Priory School, they addressed the freshmen, "We have had a wonderful first year and we know that you will profit by our experiences. Glad to have you in the family." This was dated 10 September, so the new school year opened in an atmosphere of optimism.[102]

On 6 September we held make-up examinations for last year's delinquents and then started classes on 9 September. From the previous year's faculty we lost Jack Peters to the novitiate at Ampleforth, and Father Luke was reduced to one class of Calligraphy a week. This, however, was not the only blow he struck for beautiful handwriting. Touring the United States was an exhibition of Italic Handwriting which he managed to book for the Saint Louis Public Library. Ampleforth and Priory were both represented in it. Father Bede and Father Thomas taught primarily Math and Science, and two new lay faculty joined us: Dr. Edward Sarmiento for Modern Languages and Mr. Brent J. Williams for History. It says much for their versatility that they taught several other subjects as well. Mr. Daniel G. Croghan succeeded Erv Leimer as head coach and Mr. Larry Miller coached Tennis.

The program for the spiritual life of the school was slightly altered. All boys served Mass in rotation and in pairs, a sophomore with a freshman; by mid-October the time of Mass had changed to 11.50 a.m. so that boys could have a full breakfast at home[103] and still receive Holy Communion--the eucharistic fast was by then for three

---

[102] The name *P.S.* lasted for only one issue, after which the paper became and so far has remained *The Record.*

[103] We also offered milk, cereal and donuts before the first class, paid for by cash or ticket.

hours, not from midnight; everyone made a visit to the Blessed Sacrament after lunch and recited a decade of the Rosary; Confession was available each day at 4.45 p.m. The primacy of prayer in the life of the monks was shown when we invited the parents to a social evening on 14 October at 7.15 p.m. and then observed that the monks had to depart at 8.30 to say Compline. We did the same for Friday night basketball games: the monks could either be there for the first few minutes of a home game at 8.00 p.m., or could see the last few minutes when Compline was over. The reason for this was explained to the coaches and to the boys. Who can say how deeply they were impressed?

The boys' activities were now Art, Music, Carpentry, Mechanical Drawing and the school paper. Mrs. Edwin Taylor taught Art, Ken Scheibal continued with Music and Brent Williams moderated the paper. For Carpentry and Mechanical Drawing Ruth Pfeffer, first president of the Mothers' Club, recommended Mr. J. Reynolds Medart. He was competent to instruct in carpentry, mechanical drawing and photography, and at various times and in various places did so in all three. What was remarkable about him was that he was deaf, and when he spoke it was hard to understand him. Father Timothy was dubious, but an interview reassured him, and for many years Reynolds did wonderful work for us. This year, 1957-58, he started with carpentry and mechanical drawing with six boys on Saturday morning. The boys loved him and never took advantage of him. One summer he spent many days in the basement of the Singer House, which by then was home to the seventh and eighth grades, setting up a darkroom with several printers, enlargers and developing tanks, for which he provided running water, only to have the Fire Marshall come and condemn the whole layout. Father Timothy told Reynolds and waited for expostulation. Instead Reynolds said quietly, "Well, where do we go instead?" It is not often that one wants to use the word "sweet" of a man, but Reynolds was sweet, in the literal sense of being the complete opposite of sour.

Three changes affecting the subjects taught may be noted here: Science, which, in the sophomore year only, took the place of History, was to be taught in the barn, the Stannard rathskeller and then in the enlarged kitchen of the newly acquired Singer House. This was the first of many tests of Father Thomas' ingenuity. In the kitchen there were basins and running water and plenty of space for storage, but there the resemblance of a kitchen to a science laboratory ends. Exhaust pipes were run out through the windows and other necessary adaptations were made, and in the end Father Thomas had made a space where he could and did teach Chemistry. We were planning to build up a program of science no less strong than our program in languages and the humanities, and just as well, because on 4 October 1957 the Russians launched Sputnik I, and that in its turn launched a campaign across the country for more science in the schools.

The second change was the introduction of periodical tests of General Knowledge. These often included local knowledge and entailed visits to the Historical Society or the Art Museum. We blithely imagined that these institutions would welcome this exposure to the young but telephone calls from them indicated that they had not regarded the descent on them of a swarm of vociferous teenagers as an unmixed blessing.

The third change was the introduction of Latin Grammar Tests. These were an idea we brought from Ampleforth, but had tried for the first year to do without. Experience seemed to show that their absence was worse than their presence. They made a considerable impression on the boys and as the pass mark out of 200 was 180 for A sets and 170 for B sets, the boys' knowledge of Latin grammar was transformed. At first the tests were based on the American textbook, Bennett's *Latin Grammar*, but before long we reverted to the tried and true *Latin Grammar* produced in Victorian England by Dr. Kennedy, whose doctorate, typically for those days, was in Divinity. Lest that reversion seem chauvinist, we note that Kennedy's *Grammar* was itself based on the work of a learned German, and that too was typical. This small incident was repeated in a number of subjects because of a basic difference between American and British textbooks. In deference to our new surroundings we had started for the most part with American textbooks, but soon found that many of them provided much material that we felt should come from the teacher, who would adapt it to the particular class that he was teaching. American textbooks then were larger, more cumbersome and much more expensive than those from England, even after adding the cost of postage, so for a while our deliveries from Blackwell's bookshop in Oxford became larger each year.

As the school year got under way, so did the building program. On Sunday 29 September 1957 before three or four hundred of our friends, Bishop Leo C. Byrne broke ground for the new monastery. It was a beautiful autumn day, and the bishop "spoke with genuine enthusiasm of the work being done."[104] Then on Monday 4 November Abbot Herbert Byrne of Ampleforth--he and the bishop were not

---

[104] *SLPJ* I. 4, p.1.

related--before Archbishop Ritter and again a crowd of about four hundred, blessed the foundation stone. It was a gray day this time, but the Archbishop said he was glad we were here and commended the progress made so far. Abbot Herbert added that it was right to start by building the monastery, since it was here that young monks, the hope of this "young but virile institution," would be trained. Father Columba announced that the monastery would be named for Birch Oliver Mahaffey, the father of “the Mahaffey girls”, as Fred Switzer called them.

In the same issue of the *Journal*, Father Columba wrote that "on Monday 14 October, three men armed with a few bits of wood, surveying instruments and some string, arrived at the Priory. Work on the center section of the monastery and on the gymnasium had begun . . . The string and bits of wood soon gave way to an imposing array of excavators, bulldozers and scrapers, which have been coming and going with bewildering rapidity." The rapidity was particularly welcome as the building was to contain classrooms needed for the school year starting in September 1958. The forecast was for a severe winter, so we fell to praying that it would be wrong.

We started now to turn our attention to the schools from which we might expect to draw students, especially to the independent grade schools and to the parochial schools closest to us. We invited their principals to come out for a visit to the campus and an explanation of our aims. To help them get here we described our driveway as being 1082 feet down Mason Road from the highway, and Father Timothy claimed to have paced it off. The date was 22 September and the time 3.00 p.m. It is a tribute to their devotion to education that so many of them were willing to come in the middle of a Saturday afternoon. This was a more economical use of our time than inviting them one by one, and we were able to repeat it for a few years, but after a while the principals felt they knew us and our campus well enough. We also visited their schools, sometimes, as mentioned above, to talk about vocations. Over the years we have invited students from these schools to come out for spelling bees, Math contests and basketball and soccer tournaments and sometimes for a combination of these. We have hosted Catholic Youth Council (CYC) football and basketball leagues and track meets. All of these have been both a benefit to the boys concerned and a means of getting ourselves known to them in ways other than the annual Archdiocesan Open House day for all Catholic high schools.

Our second school year progressed in ways similar to the first except that mass hysteria was a thing of the past, even though there were twice as many boys and they could have been twice as hysterical. In the Barn, all four classrooms were occupied all the time; in the Singer kitchen, the sophomores were studying the table of elements along with eight pages of scientific terms derived from Greek and Latin, with a commentary by Father Thomas on each one. This was typical of Father Thomas' insistence that scientists must have a broad view of education and not a blinkered gaze at test tubes. They also did as many chemical experiments as the space allowed.

On the playing fields both B and C football teams had games with other schools--the B team went 2-4 and the C team 0-5. In soccer the Allcomers team of faculty and friends defeated the school; in fact the closest either B or C soccer team came to glory was one tie in five games. In basketball, we practiced on a court rented from the Farmers' Club of Creve Coeur. Our B and C teams were 2-5 and 1-6 respectively. In baseball we achieved a triple play but no victories, but in tennis we defeated John Burroughs, Saint Louis University High School twice, Parkway and Maplewood, and were tied with Country Day when darkness stopped play. Our track team won over Chaminade, won a triangular meet with C.B.C and DuBourg but was beaten by Parkway. Our tennis was brilliant, our track very good and our other sports modest, but the real achievement of the athletic program--and this remained true even when our results improved--was that it offered virtually every boy who wanted it a chance of playing his sport against another school. The coaches were, then and later, good at giving the benchwarmers their fair share of playing time. Figures that happen to survive for the school year 1966-67 show that 111 of 124 boys in the upper school and 55 of 58 in the Junior House represented the school against another school in at least one sport.

Towards the end of the school year, we were completely taken by surprise to find that we had fallen foul of an organization of which we had never even heard, the Missouri State High Schools Activities Association or MSHSAA.[105] At Ampleforth, if we wanted to play any sport against another school, we simply went ahead and arranged it, and so it never entered our heads that in the land of the free things would be otherwise. We were, however, reported to the MSHSAA for playing against MSHSAA member schools without MSHSAA

---

[105] Another example of the unexpected was our discovery that many schools charged admission to their sporting events. Hesitantly we followed suit and sold season passes at $2.50 for students and $4.00 for adults. After a few years this practice ceased.

permission. They rebuked us, asked for a list of schools against whom we had competed and required an assurance that we were not giving scholarships for athletics, another idea that had not entered our heads. We pleaded ignorance, truthfully, sent them the list and joined the Association. Father Ian, as Athletic Director, wrote a letter to all the schools on the list, apologizing for embroiling them with the MSHSAA and for not telling them that we were not a member of this organization. It was one more peril of running a school in a foreign land. The following fall, full of self-conscious virtue, we wrote to the MSHSAA for permission to arrange some contests in Rugby Football. The reply came back that the MSHSAA did not concern itself with Rugby Football and we could do whatever we pleased.

We had our two Retreats again, one at the end of October given by Father Luke and the other at the end of March by Father Mike Owens of the Archdiocese. We frayed some more of Father Ian's nerves by sending the boys to three more concerts given by the Saint Louis Symphony. The Mothers' Club formed a telephone committee, which was invaluable, for example, on days when a heavy snowfall at 5.00 a.m. made school impossible. We could make one call and in due course all our school families would be informed.

We were reluctant to use it on days when driving might be difficult but not impossible and we still planned to have school. It was long before answering devices were on the market, nor did the radio and television stations yet make announcements about schools opening or closing. On such days, the phone would start ringing soon after 5.00 a.m., too early for the telephone committee, and Father Timothy had to answer again and again the question, "Is there school today?" To save time, he took to picking up the phone and saying, "Yes there is", hardly listening to the question, until one ingenious youth asked, "Is there a school holiday today?" and was delighted to receive the reply, "Yes there is." His triumph was sweet but short-lived. We recognized his voice and called him back.

The Father and Son dinner was held on 17 December at the Bath and Tennis Club at a price, over which we agonized, of $7 a couple. The focus was again on sports. In the course of the speeches Father Columba remarked biblically that you can tell a school by its fruits, which showed that we were still not immune from messy linguistic pitfalls, and more importantly made clear the great respect in which Father Columba was held, because nobody snickered.

This year, although Father Luke got back only just in time from giving the monks at Portsmouth their annual Retreat, we again celebrated Christmas at home and, as the reports were not put in the mail until Christmas morning, in peace. We were, however, having our fair share of illness. Father Luke had no more carbuncles, but Father Timothy had incipient shingles for which Gerry Mudd made his usual prescription of rest, aspirin and liquids which, as usual, worked. Toward the end of the Fall term, many of the boys and some of the monks had bouts of the Asiatic 'flu, and then in the new year, Father Ian was very sick with pneumonia and was sent to Saint Mary's Hospital. While he was recovering there, he had and caused an alarming experience. He was dozing during the day and having some sort of near-nightmare in which he saw a ghost. It so happened that a Lutheran Seminarian from Concordia Seminary, who was also a part-time nurse, had come into Father Ian's room wearing his long white gown. Seeing Father Ian asleep, he had gone into the bathroom to put things straight, and emerged just as Father Ian awoke. Thinking he was seeing the ghost from his dream, Father Ian, who was a good shrieker, shrieked. The Lutheran fled, confirmed in all his worst fears about Catholic priests. Father Ian's many friends said many prayers and the boys collected an enormous spiritual bouquet for him and he recovered (we do not know about the Lutheran) and returned from hospital on 2 April, but it was some time before he was back at full strength. Meanwhile, to fill in for Father Ian, Father Luke returned to the classroom and other faculty members had extra teaching.

As part of our health care for the boys, we required a very comprehensive health report at the beginning of each school year, and during the year offered a patch test for tuberculosis. None of the students was ever diagnosed with TB, though we had a scare or two, but Doctor Gray, who administered the tests, became our friend and in due course several of his grandsons attended the school.

After Christmas, the departure, for academic reasons, of some of our boys, together with the imminence of entrance examinations provoked us to reflect on our procedure for admissions. The entrance examinations still consisted of a standardized IQ test, papers in English, always including a short essay, and Arithmetic. Then there was an interview. We had started with a fair amount of skepticism about IQ tests, but had to admit that our very limited experience so far suggested that the boys we admitted did after all perform more or less according to their IQ, although there were certainly a few bright boys who were also wayward, and a few borderline boys who were very industrious. Sometimes the interview indicated the potential waywardness or industry, so it remained an important item in the testing, but even when there was an indication of potential waywardness, we tended to hope, sometimes rightly and sometimes in vain, that we would be able to bring the best out of the boy. The interview also included asking the candidate to read aloud. This too we considered a good predictor. Each interview was conducted by a board of the faculty. The advantage of having more than one interviewer was that each member of the board had a chance to experience the boy in interaction with himself and to observe him in interaction with the other interviewers. It was also, we believed, a help to the boy himself: if he felt daunted by one member of the board, he might feel more able to reveal himself to another. We thought that American boys of this age were more open than English, and therefore that we were able to form a better impression of them from a ten-minute interview. It was a grueling task for the interviewers, but there were occasional moments of light relief, as when Father Timothy asked one lad what he was reading. He said he was reading a book on Calculus. Incautiously Father Timothy said, "and what do you know about calculus?" "Nothing," replied the lad, "that's why I'm reading the book." He was admitted and surely would have been whatever his grades. After our reflection on admissions, we kept the system as it was.

The most damaging effect of our shortage of experience was on our ability to evaluate the preparation received by the candidates before they came to us. Only gradually did we come to have a feel for the quality of each of our feeder schools, and even when we gained that, it was precarious. This was especially true of parochial grade schools, because so much depended on the principals, who were then almost always religious sisters. Just as we were getting to know them, they would be moved somewhere else.

February brought eleven inches of snow, and Saint Louis was much less prepared for it then than now. It started to fall one day after lunch, and it was soon clear that the urgent problem was to get the boys home. The bus could not come; a few intrepid parents managed to drive here and picked up their sons and others who lived near them. For many we had to walk down to US 40, flag down passing cars, which was quite easy, so slowly were they going, and beg for rides for the boys. The emergency brought the best out of people and almost every driver agreed. All the boys reached home but it took some of them several hours. We would not dare to do such a thing today.

Entrance examinations for the ninth grade were due to be held at Priory on 1 February but the snow made us postpone them for a fortnight. We had a second round much later, on 24 May. There were fifty-five candidates for the first test, but we have no record of those in May. Then this year for the first time we held, on 26 April, examinations for entry into the seventh and eighth grades. These attracted thirty-two and twenty-one candidates respectively. We were hoping to harvest eighteen boys for the seventh grade, thirteen for the eighth (because of the size of the two classrooms) and thirty for the ninth. We achieved eighteen, thirteen and twenty-one respectively. For the Junior House this was quite satisfactory.[106] The ninth grade, however, was much smaller than we had hoped, though the quality was high. Fortunately it was a low point and not a trend, and was due, at least in part, to the economic recession, which had also slowed down The Drive. In subsequent years the numbers picked up again.

We also had to rewrite a label that had already been attached to us of being an eggheadery for Einsteins or a ritzy school for Rockefellers or both; somehow both these phrases were written on the same label, incompatible as they might seem. How opposed these ideas were to our true policy is shown in an article in the Globe-Democrat for 2 September 1956 four days before the school opened, in which Dickson Terry quotes Father Timothy as saying, "We don't aim at getting just geniuses . . . We want boys from all levels of society, who are capable of taking this kind of education. We're very much against the idea that the school is socially exclusive. We want good boys, and if they can't pay, we hope to find someone who can help them financially."

We made every effort to make our policies a reality, but, as so often, the phrases about Einsteins and Rockefellers contained a grain of truth. Some of our boys were bright and even brilliant, and we had no objection to that, but anyone who taught here could bear witness that not all were. And some of our parents both had intelligent sons and were themselves quite wealthy, and we did not object to that either; but we were never a ritzy school, and there was already a generous financial aid program in place to help parents who were not wealthy, and to ensure that we had some economic diversity.

It worried us especially that the idea that ours was a ritzy school seemed not uncommon among the diocesan clergy. Not only were they in a special way our fellow-workers, but because of their influence in their parochial grade schools they could be a great help or a great obstacle to us. We made every effort to cultivate a good

---

[106] We called the seventh grade Form I, the eighth grade Form II, and so on through the twelfth grade, which became the traditional sixth form or Form VI. We referred to Forms I and II together as the Junior House and to the remainder as the Upper School.

relationship with them, and our occasional dinners for the clergy were certainly part of that effort. Later on, it helped us that Father Timothy was elected to the Priests' Council of the Archdiocese and for one year was its secretary, and later again it helped us that we took over Saint Anselm Parish, whose auditorium was used for many Archdiocesan Clergy days.

Nonetheless, it took us years to eradicate these misconceptions from the minds of both clergy and laity, if indeed we ever did, and they were more serious than may have been immediately apparent to us. Members of Inc and others who knew us well had no such misconceptions, but we wanted and, to fill the school, needed to appeal to as much of the Catholic community beyond Inc as we could.

In Europe "elite" was a term of admiration, grudging perhaps, but still genuine admiration; in Saint Louis to cater to an elite was seen by many as undemocratic, and many parents might hesitate to send their sons, and their sons might hesitate to come, to a school perceived as elitist. There were also still traces of anti-intellectual or anti-egghead prejudice (anti-nerd came later), so it was not easy to foster high academic standards without falling foul of this prejudice.

The attitude towards wealth was more complex. There was certainly a class system in Saint Louis when we came, and it was based partly on wealth, but not entirely. There were wealthy families who were not among the socially accepted, and there were also differences in attitude toward those who had themselves made millions and those who had inherited them, as well as toward those who spent their wealth ostentatiously and those who did not. The class system was also based partly on religion, but again not entirely. There were Catholic and Jewish families who were among the socially accepted. This was especially true since in Saint Louis as compared with, say, Boston, the original settlers had been French and Catholic, and so those families had been and still were highly acceptable, had been in fact the ones who accepted or did not accept others.

There were also Catholic, and no doubt Jewish, families who wanted no part of social acceptability, and these may have felt a certain wariness about us and our hopes of preparing boys for entry into any college in the country and, after college, for roles of leadership in the community of Saint Louis or elsewhere. We are speaking here about Saint Louis in the late fifties, and about the many Catholic families who would be deciding whether to send their sons to us or to one of the other Catholic schools.

We were surprised also at the number of parents who left the choice of school to their son. This often meant that the boy went where his friends were going, and that was more likely to be to a larger school. Father Timothy was talking to the parents of a boy whom we had accepted. They said that they would like their son to come to us, but that he wanted to go elsewhere with his friends. Out of his English background Father Timothy assumed this meant that the boy would be coming here as the parents wished, and said so. To his amazement and chagrin they replied that they had acquiesced in their son's choice.

Meanwhile, regardless of our problems with admissions, boys were being boys. The power of the printed word was shown when a group of our sophomores decided to rival Huckleberry Finn by building a raft and floating down the Mississippi. Their parents disapproved, while the monks rather admired the boys' spirit. In the event, the closest they came to being waterborne was when a flood carried away some of the components of the raft.

The Mothers' Club and its exploits will receive special attention later, but we must mention here that on 25 March 1958 they held their first fund-raising event, a House Tour, which they called a March Meander. Their first problem was to explain to Father Timothy what a house tour was, their second to convince him that people would actually pay to see someone else's house (still a mystery to him), their third to get permission for Priory itself to be on the tour and their fourth to get the place cleaned up. With consummate tact they approached Father Luke about dust and scuff-marks and were even allowed to do some redecorating provided that they paid for it and Father Luke chose the colors. For this curious event they sold some 1500 tickets and we, who were last on the visiting list, had perhaps a thousand visitors. The agreed sign was that the US flag would be flown at houses on the Tour. One householder on the route, who was nothing to do with the Tour, happened to fly her flag that day and could not understand why she was deluged with unscheduled visitors. The one thousand or so visitors who came to visit Priory were given a brochure about the school. It is a brief description of the aims, offerings and cost of the school, and concludes with a thumbnail history of the Benedictines, and of our direct ancestors, Westminster Abbey, Dieulouard and Ampleforth. It concludes, "Westminster was noted for its liturgy, Dieulouard for its strict observance, and Ampleforth for its hard, unremitting work. We hope that some heritage from all these three ancestors will pass to Saint Louis Priory."[107]

Soon after this, on 23 April, Inc held a fund-raiser: the world premiere of *South Pacific* as a movie. It was to be preceded by slides of the school, taken by a camera with a special lens so that they could be shown on the wide screen and cover the whole of it. Fred Switzer was discussing with Fathers Columba, Luke and Timothy who should narrate the slides. Father Columba said that as they were mostly slides of the school, the obvious person was Father Timothy. There was a long silence, broken by Fred saying, "Yes, I'm sure he'd do a good job, but I'm afraid he might make some jokes; and we're talking about money." The ensuing gale of monastic laughter was our contribution to Fred's post-professional education.

With May 1958 the end of the school year was approaching, but before it arrived there were excitements to come. The first of these was the visit of Professor Arnold J. Toynbee. He was a long-standing friend of Father Columba and the author of the many volumes of *A Study of History*. He was then working at Chatham House, England's think-tank for international affairs. His correspondence with Father Columba was published under the title *An Historian's Conscience.*[108] He and his wife stayed on our grounds. Besides holding a colloquium with a group of historians from local schools and colleges, he was to talk to the school. Father Timothy was apprehensive on two grounds: he might be well over the boys' heads; and, worse, he was a renegade classicist and given, some scholars thought, to making sweeping and unjustified generalizations. We arranged one period for him, with the possibility of another, if all went well. In the event he held our ninth- and tenth-graders spellbound not only for those two periods but also, after a break, for a third. He was a mediocre lecturer but a wonderful conversationalist and was at his best answering questions. After a short introductory statement he gave the boys their chance, and they took it. He listened to their questions with courteous intentness and answered them, as often as not, out of personal experience. "Can you tell us

---

[107] It is printed in full in Appendix B 5. The earliest extant copy is dated 25 March 1958. It may have been written earlier for prospective parents and then used on this occasion, or possibly was written especially for the house tour and then used for parents.

[108] *An Historian's Conscience: The Correspondence of Arnold J. Toynbee and Columba Cary-Elwes, Monk of Ampleforth*, ed. Christian B. Peper (Boston: Beacon Press, 1986)

about agriculture in Afghanistan?" "Well, when I was there in January . . ." "What about the political situation in Indonesia?" "Well, I happened to be there last year, and . . ." It was like talking to a mixture of the *Encyclopedia Britannica* and the *National Geographic*. The boys listened with equal intentness and were impressed by the extent of his knowledge and no less by the seriousness with which he treated them and their questions. Boys do like to be listened to.[109]

The second excitement was more arduous for those involved: we offered the sophomores a chance to take the tests of the College Entrance Examination Board. These were of two kinds, one designed to measure aptitude for academic success in college and the other to measure achievement in high school, and were named accordingly.[110]

Sixteen took the aptitude tests and thirteen took one or more achievement tests in English, French, Latin, Spanish, Chemistry or Intermediate Mathematics. The scale ran from 200 to 800; our highest score was by Fran Oates with 743 in English and our lowest was 357 in French. Our averages in the two aptitude tests were 524 in the Verbal part and 531 in the Mathematical, and for all the achievement tests together 530. As the aptitude tests were not IQ tests but tests of ability to succeed in college, and as the mean score of 500 was derived from college-bound seniors, we were quite content that the results showed broadly that we were on the right track for American colleges and that many of our sophomores were already academically acceptable to very respectable colleges. In any case, the real purpose was to give these sophomores experience of a type of testing quite different from ours.

It worried us that multiple-choice tests had so much influence on acceptance or rejection by a college and that at one time it was possible for a student to be accepted by even Harvard without ever composing a sentence. Experience seems to have shown, however, that this system works as little injustice as any other, and has the overwhelming advantage of extreme rapidity of scoring. Tests of this kind probably give too much credit to a certain type of quick but rather superficial mind and slightly penalize one that is seriously reflective, but mostly without putting the former in over his head or

---

[109] Professor Toynbee was one of the few who outmatched Larry Spivak and his picadors on the TV program, "*Meet the Press.*"

[110] What was then called simply the Scholastic Aptitude Test or SAT is now called SAT I, and what were then called the College Board Achievement Tests are now called SAT II.

excluding the latter from the place where he should be. When the College Board put out a booklet with a number of sample questions for the aptitude tests, four or five of us, all men with Masters' degrees or Doctorates and with many years of teaching behind us, sat down and recorded our answers. We gave them serious thought. As a result, we would never have completed the test in the allotted time, and our answers, for which each of us could give very adequate justification, were all different. We had thought much too hard.

And so the second school year came to its close. We had examinations on 4, 5 and 6 June and field day on Saturday 7 June, with High Mass at 10.00 a.m. on the lawn behind the Stannard House, Track finals, lunch, prize-giving, a concert by the band, and Father and Son softball.

We then held for the incoming freshmen a two-week summer school, which started on Monday 9 June and offered Math (Father Bede), English (Father Luke) and an Introduction to Language and Study Habits (Father Columba and Father Timothy). There was a summer reading list--we asked the boys to read six books in three months, and one boy complained that we had ruined his summer[111]--and a Diagnostic Reading course. This last was intended to pinpoint difficulties in reading and was not a speed-reading course as such, though these had a brief popularity at about this time. Then we were left more or less on our own until September, when the Mothers' Club had a resale shop for clothes, athletic equipment and textbooks.

When we had caught our breath after this our second school year, we began to take in the amazing generosity of which we had been the target. American generosity is famous all over the world, so in that sense it was no surprise; and because items were given as it were tree by tree, it was only when we had a breathing space that we could stand back and see the whole forest. It was not only Inc's financial generosity; so many parents, friends and even strangers gave things. Books for the library were the most common gift, but others included a monstrance, which we commissioned from the English silversmith, Dunstan Pruden, a mahogany statue of the Madonna and Child by the local sculptor, Richard Duhme, a portrait by Fred Conway of Abbot Herbert--it seems to be a cross between him and Father Columba--a large collection of 78 r.p.m. records, which were being discarded to make room for the then "state of the art" Long-Playing records, valuable items for the science wing, and a very substantial legacy for

[111] He now reads avidly.

scholarships from a man who visited the campus for half an hour, hardly spoke to anyone but must have liked what he saw and heard. Nor was that the limit of the support: countless people gave us their time and labor and friendship, and invitations were more than frequent enough to threaten our monastic simplicity of life.

We took stock also of the buildings, and primarily of the monastery, parts of which were due to be used in September for the expanded school. Its foundations were poured at the end of November 1957 and much of the concrete for the basement in the middle of December, but then there was a sudden cold snap, the new concrete had to be protected with straw and tarpaulins and no more could be poured. Although it was not uncommon to mix anti-freeze with the concrete, HOK would not do so, believing that it was bad for the reinforcing steel. No doubt that was wise, but it made us even more dependent on the weather, and it so happened that, despite our prayers, the winter was especially severe. We have mentioned the snow; there was also a period when the temperature was from 0° F. to 5° below, and we lost the race to have the shell of the building completed before the bad weather so that work could continue inside. Then within a week the temperature rocketed up to 70° and everything turned to slush. Most of the rest of the concrete was poured at the end of March both for the monastery, on which we focused most of our attention, and for the gym. The arguments about the gym roof had been settled in favor of the architects, and work had been proceeding, but whereas we needed the monastery for September, we would not need the gym for basketball until November.

This may have been the winter of a great ice-storm. We have had a number of them, but after this particularly violent one not only every branch and every twig but even every individual blade of grass had its own tiny sheath of ice. Often these storms came during the night and the following morning was sunny and the sun shone on the sheaths. Those going out to say an early Mass for local convents slithered out into a crystal wonderland of sparkles.

There was also work to be done on the kitchen and dining room. The former had to be remodeled and the dining room enlarged to cope with the extra boys. Bids were let and we were happy when John O'Brien came in as the low bidder. Work started the Monday after Field Day, and some of the monks had to migrate from the Stannard to the Singer House. Father Luke found a factory that was giving up its cafeteria and enjoyed acquiring much of the necessary new equipment at bargain rates. Father Luke and Father Timothy were due for a vacation in England, but Father Luke had to postpone his until the end of November. When Father Timothy left in mid-June, the completion of the kitchen and dining room in time for the new school year seemed probable; the completion of the gym by mid-November seemed possible; but there had been further delays for the monastery when the contractor had to wait for frames first for the windows and then for the doors, so the completion of the parts of the monastery needed by the school in September was, at best, doubtful. An outline of what we would do if they were not ready was already in our minds.

At the same time we had been working on the plans for the Science Wing. This was to be placed on the knoll as one of the wings of the biplane to which we have already referred.[112] When we decided to move the high school from the knoll to its present position close to the church, the Science Wing had already been completed and could not be moved, so the boys had to go outside to reach it. They breathed some fresh air between classes and sometimes they got wet. The building codes, apparently, had no objection to that, and no little man and no red notice appeared. Why it should be permissible to get wet on the way to Science but not on the way to the bathroom remains unexplained.

This planning was largely in the hands of Father Thomas. He happened to come from England at a time when British corporations were giving British schools money to improve their teaching of science. To help the schools to spend their money wisely, the corporations produced a pamphlet on the layout, design and equipment of laboratories for high schools. Father Thomas used this pamphlet in planning with HOK, and in this way we were able to build laboratories that were truly "state of the art", or even a little ahead of the art. The final drawings were ready by the end of August 1958 and were then put out to bids. On 12 October the bids came back and the lowest, at around $225,000, was about one thousand dollars below the architects' estimate. Building started on 21 October[113], and our scientists took possession in mid-August 1959.

But it was not enough to design a Science Wing; we also had to be able to pay for it. At the time of the bids we had in cash and pledges a little more than half the amount needed, but we were greatly helped by the federal government which, in the wake of Sputnik, was very much concerned about the teaching of science in the United States. Part of the program to aid schools was the provision of low-interest

---

[112] *See* p.140, *above.*

[113] *The Record* II. 1, p.2.

loans. Father Thomas and his scientific friends, for by now he was well known to the scientists at the universities and in industry, handled all the extensive paperwork to apply for and secure such a loan.

By now Abbot Herbert had decided that Father Bede, who had a heart attack towards the end of the school year--there were indications that he had had one four years previously, which had not been recognized as such--should return to Ampleforth. That was a sad loss. He was a gentle man and the boys had taken advantage of this, but they were also much attached to him, regretted his departure and felt partly responsible for it. He was to be replaced by Father Brendan Smith, also an excellent mathematician, and one who could teach Latin, French and English as well, not to mention German and Italian. He was also a natural athlete. We were delighted to get someone of his caliber.

Abbot Herbert had also decided some time before to send us Father Austin Rennick, an older monk with many years of experience of teaching several subjects, but mostly English. He was also a musician and an athlete. He had gone to Oxford University as an undergraduate and was expected to play soccer and cricket for the University and perhaps to get first class honors in Classics. Instead he became a Catholic, a convert of the great Jesuit, Father Martin D'Arcy[114], and fell in love with music. He seemed to have come to the end of his teaching career at Ampleforth and was about to be sent to one of their parishes. Instead he was sent to us and took on a new lease of life. In due course he completed fifty successive years of high school teaching. So although we lost Father Bede, we acquired two more monks. Father Ian recuperated in Florida at Saint Leo Abbey, and then went to the Bahamas for part of the summer to work in a parish there. He returned in the middle of July looking refreshed. Father Thomas had a month at a parish in Los Angeles. Father Luke postponed until the end of November his visit to England, but in the middle of August fitted in some time in Walloon with the Mudds. Father Columba took his vacation in bits as he could.

At the end of August 1958 Father Austin and Father Brendan arrived, bringing the number of priests to seven. It seemed like a crowd, besides being a number with a long Judaeo-Christian history.

---

[114] A learned Jesuit and a great art-collector; Oxford wits said that when he was Master of Campion Hall, the Jesuits' house of studies at Oxford, it became full of *objets d'Arcy*

We had also in the house Brothers Richard Bauer and Vernon Dockery, postulants for our community, and Brother William Floyd, a postulant in 1958 for Portsmouth Priory, all studying at Saint Louis University. They were soon joined by Brother Matthew Stark, a Junior of Portsmouth who was later their Prior and then their Abbot. This increase of numbers lightened the weight of our Office in choir. We still rose at 4.40 a.m., Matins and Lauds were at 5.00, followed by Masses, meditation, Prime and Terce. Breakfast was at 7.30 and sung Conventual Mass, preceded by Sext, at 8.40. When Mass went to 11.50, Sext went with it. Lunch, followed by None, was at 12.30 p.m., Vespers at 6.15 followed by supper, and Compline at 8.30. We made every effort to put out our lights by 9.30 p.m.

Father Austin's first academic experience in Saint Louis was to attend a high-powered meeting about summer reading lists. It was sponsored by Saint Louis University to harmonize the expectations of college professors with what high school teachers judged to be feasible. The list was nothing if not ambitious: the Epic of Gilgamesh, some of the Old Testament, Homer, Sophocles, Vergil, Dante, the Cid, Corneille and on and on. Father Austin was becoming more and more bewildered and eventually asked, "But will they know all these languages?" "Oh no, they'll read them in translation", whereat Father Austin cried out, "In translation?!" in a tone of voice that included both the question mark and the exclamation point.

CHAPTER 18

The Year of the Sardine

FATHER Timothy prepared the schedule for the first year, Father Bede for the second, and now Father Brendan took it over as his first major task. It was not yet very complex, but what was truly difficult was that we needed four extra classrooms, and the new monastery was not close to being ready. At the beginning of the summer this was already apparent, so we had some warning. By the time Father Timothy came back from England we knew that nothing could be ready before mid-November, which turned out to be when we moved in.

Two of the extra classrooms were needed for the seventh and eighth grades. This was easy: the boys went, as we had always intended, into the Singer House alongside of the temporary science laboratory and those monks who were living upstairs. The real problem was the two extra classrooms needed for the high school. The monks' choir remained in the sun room, but we moved the chapel out of the main drawing room and into the expanded refectory, the only space capable of accommodating the whole school, but even that was not ready for the first week because the painters were still adding the finishing touches, and so for that week we had Mass and lunch in the garden. One classroom took over the drawing-room; the other went into the rathskeller. Neither was ideal: the rathskeller was too secluded and the drawing-room too public. One of our laymen was teaching in the drawing-room just as Father Timothy was coming down the stairs. There must have been some trouble as the master was delivering a considerable harangue and had just reached his peroration, which concluded with the words, "*gaudeamus igitur*."[115] This was followed by two or three seconds of silence and then a round of applause. Father Timothy suggested later that it was certainly the ideal never to lose one's cool in the classroom, but that if one did, the effect should be so awe-inspiring that the silence would last for many minutes or even for the rest of the class, and without applause.

Despite the lack of space, our third school year started on Monday, 8 September 1958 with 28 boys in Form V, 25 in Form IV, only 21 in Form III, 13 in Form II and 18 in Form I, a total of 105. The Juniors

---

[115] Let us therefore rejoice.

resumed their study of History for three periods a week, which meant one less period a week of English, Spanish or French, and Greek or Study Hall. Lay faculty and monks alike taught from twenty-two to twenty-five periods a week, but, because of their other duties, Father Columba taught ten and Father Timothy eighteen. The six monks on the faculty were matched by seven laymen, of whom two were part-time. The seven were Messrs. Edward K. Cook (Latin and Greek), Donald L. Kettelkamp (Mathematics and Athletic Director), Alexander C. Niven (History), James T. O'Neill (English and Spanish), Edward J. Presti (English) with Brent J. Williams and George Hickenlooper part-time for History and French respectively. For the first time we introduced Form Masters, who addressed their forms once a week and were each boy's first recourse in any problem. They wrote a report on each of their boys at the end of each term. Father Brendan had the Juniors, Father Austin the Sophomores, Father Thomas the Freshmen and Father Ian the rest.

The activities were expanded to Mechanical Drawing, Carpentry and Photography (all taught by Reynolds Medart), Art (Mr. Stephen G. Kinsella, with Mr. Rudi Torrini taking over from him towards the end of the year) Music (Father Austin and Ken Scheibal), Speech (Alex Niven & Ed Presti), the Record (Alex Niven) and Chess (Alex Niven). That is an impressive list of activities, but the difficulty was to find time for them. This was and remains one of the disadvantages of not being a boarding school.

The sports remained the same: football and soccer in the fall; basketball and soccer in the winter; baseball, track and tennis in the spring. The fees remained the same too: tuition $750; lunch $108; school bus $110.

It was the year of the sardine: boys were crammed into every nook and cranny; Mass was celebrated and classes were taught in any space that was large enough. It was, therefore, an immense relief when on 13 November, the Feast of All Monks, the boys took up their desks and walked to the ground floor of the newly completed Monastery, two to a desk, as Father Luke insisted, to avoid scuffing the resplendent newness. This gave us four classrooms, one in the northeast corner and three on the south side, and two science labs in the middle of the south side. The northwest corner was occupied by the Faculty Room. The chapel took the center of the north side with the monks' choir at the east end, then the altar and then, west of it, the boys. The sacristy was immediately east of the chapel. The labs, though a great improvement on the kitchen of the Singer House, were still not ideal, but Father Thomas had only the rest of the year to wait before moving into the science wing. Then these labs became regular classrooms. As labs they enabled Father Thomas to impart enough knowledge to his students for them to win recognition both in an examination sponsored by Union Electric and in the Saint Louis Science Fair. The chapel was to remain there until the church was finished in 1962, and the classrooms until our move to the high school in 1970, but we did not yet know this.

The monks had already, on 6 November, moved in upstairs, helped by a troop of undergraduates led by Ed Lanwermeyer.[116] The upper floor was a place of silence, the lower floor was not. On 19 November the Mahaffey Monastery was blessed by the Archbishop, with the Mahaffey descendants in attendance, and then was proudly displayed at an Open House on 23 November, to which six to eight hundred people came. Visitors were also taken to the gym, very nearly complete, and the science wing, just starting.

The monastery was a simple, modular structure. Its only bearing members were columns, it had no bearing walls, and its only frills were a cantilevered overhang down each side, and the flue-tile screens spaced along the overhang. These provided protection against the weather, a balcony outside each room and a covered walk underneath. We knew that the school's occupancy would be temporary, and so wanted something that could easily be remodeled. The monks' floor was somewhere between simple and spartan. The rooms were about eighteen feet by eleven feet. Each had a built-in closet and a basin with running water, which most rooms at Ampleforth did not have, but showers and bathrooms were in the central core. Father Luke acquired beds for fifty cents and desks and chairs from government surplus, and at the age of fifty each monk received an armchair. There was no carpeting in the rooms nor in the corridors. In due course the ground floor was extensively remodeled, and this was made easier by the type of construction. The two big drawbacks were the full-length glass windows of the first floor, which made the classrooms facing south almost unbearably hot on sunny afternoons in the fall, and the flat roof, which gave us endless trouble.

The move into the monastery led to some reshuffling in the Stannard House. Father Columba and Father Luke now slept in the

---

[116] On the north side facing the church were, from West to East, Fathers Austin, Brendan and Ian, postulants, the calefactory, more postulants, and Father Thomas; on the south side Father Luke, spare rooms, Father Columba, the library and three chapels. Father Timothy had a cell next to Father Thomas but still slept behind the bookcase in his office.

monastery, so Father Luke and his secretary moved to the north end of the second floor, and his former office was taken over by Father Brendan. Downstairs, as far as we can reconstruct it, the sun room remained a chapel, the drawing room next to it became the school library, the dining room remained the monks' dining room and Chuck Dattilo moved his office into the breakfast-room. The rathskeller probably became the juniors' form room.

We moved into the gym about 8 December with great pleasure but not with the same sense of relief as into the monastery. We now had our own basketball court, were no longer dependent on others and could host home games. Besides the maple floor, the gym contained locker rooms, a suite for visiting teams, coaches' office, the carpentry shop and a surprisingly elegant boiler room. Bleachers were in preparation, but there was no score board, nor was there any cover for the floor. The scorers had to hold up numerals indicating the score. This was comical, and so we had recourse reluctantly to a magazine subscription drive, for which we sent all parents an apologetic letter explaining the needs and asking them at least to renew subscriptions through us, and if they had any objections to the scheme, to let us know. It took place in March and was successful and through it we acquired a score board and an olive-green cover to protect the floor from the spiked heels of those attending programs arranged by the Mothers' Club. Mr. Bruce B. Selkirk had his company sew together the strips of canvas for the cover, but the canvas was so heavy and oily that it clogged the needles.

On 20 October while we were still in our sardine state, we received an invitation from Mr. and Mrs. Alvey to take over their summer camp. After discussion and after seeing slides of the camp, the community seemed to look on the invitation with cautious favor, and Father Columba wrote to Abbot Herbert along those lines. On 24 November we received a letter from the abbot "damping down the camp scheme" and on 13 December a cable to say it had been turned down, presumably by the Abbot's Council. Their decision was, in all probability, wise--we already had more than enough to do--but the process for making this decision revealed the flaws which were unavoidably built into our situation. It was slow; we could not adequately convey to Ampleforth the impression made on us by a face-to-face presentation with slides; and, at least humanly speaking, men so many thousands of miles away were not in a good position to second-guess men on the spot.[117] On most of the occasions when ratification from Ampleforth was needed for our proposals, such as plans for new buildings, we could see the need coming far enough in advance and could allow for the time Ampleforth would take. But on an occasion like this when an opportunity appeared suddenly and a quick decision was required, the system did not work well.

The academic program went on as before except that public examinations, mostly in the form of standardized, multiple-choice tests, became increasingly frequent and important. As noted, we had our doubts about such tests but concluded that they were here to stay and that colleges were likely to use them more and more. The juniors had three of these tests in quick succession. The first, on 18 October, was the School and College Aptitude Test (SCAT), a standard aptitude test put out by the Educational Testing Service and yielding scores for verbal and numerical aptitude. On 21 October they took the Scholarship Qualifying Test. At that time juniors could take it for practice and then take it in earnest in their senior year. It seemed good to give our boys as much practice as possible. On 25 October they took the Kuder Preference Test, designed to show where their interests lay and what kind of occupation might suit them. This in turn might help them to a wise choice of college. We persevered with this test for a year or two and then decided that it told the boys, their families and us little that we did not already know.

In March 1959 the whole junior class took the College Board Aptitude Tests and some of them took achievement tests too, with Ed Boedeker scoring a perfect 800 and three others scoring over 700, all four in English. At the end of April they took the National Merit Scholarship Qualifying Test and in May the juniors and most of the sophomores took a variety of achievement tests. There were two scores over 700, one in Chemistry and one in Latin. The results in general forecast a very satisfactory degree of acceptability to college, provided that as seniors the boys performed at a correspondingly higher level. This was all the more remarkable considering the very makeshift surroundings in which so much of the teaching, especially that of science, had taken place. Finally, on Friday 29 May the freshmen took a State Aptitude Test, but no results survive.

We had already made an approach to the principals of our feeder grade schools; now we reached out, by way of a "Priory Day", to the boys themselves. The day was 13 December 1958 and by then the

---

[117] Father Columba's diary provides the information given above, but the correspondence with Ampleforth is missing.

new gym was in use. The program started with Mass, after which there was a Spelling Bee, a basketball tournament, lunch and a demonstration of Rugby football. To encourage the idea that it was quite normal to be both bright and athletic, we asked each school to enter a team of five boys for spelling and eight for basketball but no more than ten in all. The day was a success and we received many letters of thanks. Some mentioned one thing and some another, but all mentioned the lunch.

We now had to turn our attention to our own entrance examinations. We had planned to hold them on 20 December but after discussion with the Archdiocesan school office we agreed hesitantly to have them on the same day as the Archdiocesan schools, 31 January 1959.[118] We were hesitant because this arrangement whereby a boy had to choose his school ahead of time and then take the examination at the school of his choice, seemed to work to our disadvantage. Boys who really wanted to come to us might be reluctant to take the risk of being turned down by us, who had only seventeen places left after accepting our own eighth grade, and then finding that their next-choice school had already filled its class. Such boys would tend to apply to schools with more places to fill. As a concession the Archdiocesan Superintendent agreed that we might hold a scholarship examination on 24 January, to which thirty-seven candidates came. In the event, we did fill our class and started the next year with our target number of thirty freshmen.

On 25 April we held examinations for entry into the seventh and eighth grades, attracting thirty-five and nineteen candidates respectively. We drew from them a strong class of twenty-two seventh graders. We had also entertained the idea of doubling the size of the eighth grade if we found enough really strong candidates. We did not, so we urged them to come back next year to try for the ninth grade, which most of them did. Long after the seventh grade was filled, a prominent Jewish lawyer applied to have his son take the test. We warned him that the best we could offer would be a place on the waiting list, but he insisted, and when the boy took the test he turned out to be a very strong candidate, bright, polite, personable, athletic. He was highly acceptable, but the class was full and we had already turned down other boys. It did not seem just to accept him. Father Timothy with sorrow told the parents the decision and explained the

[118] We used the archdiocesan test prepared by Science Research Associates, to which we made brief additions.

reasons, but they remained convinced that the real reason was that they were Jewish. It was a sad moment. We wrote to them later at the time of the examination for entry into the ninth grade, but their son did not come.

At the beginning of April we hosted a meeting of the Modern Language Association of Saint Louis, the first of many times that we hosted various professional organizations of the area. Naturally enough, the Classical Association of Saint Louis was prominent among these.

Meanwhile the sports and activities had been continuing. We had made our peace with and had joined the MSHSAA and now had a Junior Varsity squad and a B team competing with other schools in football, soccer and baseball; in basketball we had also a C team, as well as a Junior House team at least in football. In the spring we had competition scheduled also in Track (JV and B) and Tennis. We permitted boys who had their parents' permission to drive to away games; that was more of a step forward for the monks than for the boys. We held our Father and Son dinner again, in fact, two of them, one at the Bath and Tennis Club for the Upper School and one in our own dining room for the Junior House.

Two individual achievements may be noted: John Cramer, running as a junior against seniors, took fifth place in the State indoor track meet in the 60 yards dash and won the 100 and 220 yards sprints in the Class C Regional meet. Jim Boehm came in third in the 100 yards backstroke at the Catholic High School Invitational Swimming Meet. Another highlight was not in a major sport. We won the Missouri Rugby Football Union's Schools Challenge Cup. For this we played a single game against Whitfield School and won it, and with the game the cup. The athletic powerhouses were unwilling to risk the limbs of their football players. By playing two further games in later years we became State Rugby champions for seventeen straight years, a feat which we have not rivaled in any other sport.[119]

For their spiritual life, the boys had a Retreat at the end of March given by Father Thomas to the Upper School and by Father Luke to

---

[119] Father Timothy's claim to athletic fame at Priory is that he is the only Priory coach in any sport whose teams over seventeen years were never defeated at that sport. The claim is true but not to be taken seriously, as the teams played but a few times in those years. Ironically, when he retired from the position of head rugger coach, he handed his whistle to Father Finbarr, who knows far more about rugger, and we lost the next game. Next year, however, they played five games under Father Finbarr and won them all.

the Junior House. There must have been another pair in the previous Fall, but we have no record of it. For their social life they had a mid-winter dance on 7 February in the refectory[120] and another, for Juniors and Sophomores, in the garden on 8 May--a lovely setting but a rather chilly evening. At the end of May, Father Ian took the Junior House boys for a picnic in Babler Park, an enjoyable experience for them and hair-raising for him.

As our third school year approached its close, we awaited a visit from Abbot Herbert. He arrived on 21 May 1959, and we kept him busy. There was a dinner on 26 May for the clergy. This was to repay the hospitality they showed us, especially at the closing ceremonies of their Forty Hours devotions, which were then held once a year in most parishes. We also wished to maintain our good liaison with them, and to keep them acquainted with the monastic community and the school. We had a number of these dinners, all of them memorable. At one the dessert was spumoni. These had been kept in the deep freeze, and we did not remember to get them out to thaw. Frozen spumoni when attacked with a spoon are almost as slippery as soap in the shower, and flying spumoni are dangerous. At another dinner the dessert was Black Forest cake, delicious and messy. The cake was put on plates, the plates on trays and the trays stacked on a tall trolley, to be wheeled down the dining-room for distribution. One of the monsignori had pushed his chair back into the aisle; the wheel of the trolley caught on his chair leg and there was a graceful cascade of trays, plates and Black Forest cake onto the floor. Only three helpings were rescued intact. Monsignor Curtin commented to the monk who was pushing the trolley, "You have turned a pleasant evening into a memorable one."

30 May was the laity's day with Abbot Herbert: After Mass, he blessed the plaques for the gymnasium, and for various labs and lecture rooms in the new Science Wing.[121] The blessing was followed by our Track finals.[122] There was a luncheon, followed by prize-giving

---

[120] The expenses were: Band, $50; Piano, $15.30; Decorations, $8; Candles, $8.40; Tickets, $7; Food, $4.30; Cokes, $20.70; Priory help, $19. One wonders what the food was. Tickets were $3 double and $2 single.

[121] The plaques, listed in *SLPJ* II. 4, p.1, were for the Mrs. August A. Busch Chemistry Laboratory, the Harry T. Bussmann Advanced Physics Laboratory, the Charles M. Huttig Lecture Theatre, the William McBride Love Physics and Chemistry Laboratory, and the Robert C. Corley Gymnasium.

[122] *The Record* III. 1, p.1

and an address by the Abbot. On 2 June there was a mini-graduation for the eighth grade, with another address by the Abbot.

But the real importance of his visit lay in his four major decisions: the first was that Brothers Vernon Dockery and Richard Bauer were not called to be monks of Saint Louis Priory. They therefore departed. The second was that he would send out Father Augustine and Father Paul to join us in August. That would bring our numbers to nine and also much reduce the average age of the monks, as Father Augustine was in his early thirties and Father Paul in his twenties. Their primary fields were Classics and Math respectively but each was versatile.

The third decision was to call a halt to building. We would for a few years build nothing more after the completion of the Science Wing. The Drive would also cease for a while after the achievement of this year's goal. The *Journal* commented, "This means that the present facilities will be adequate to enable the school to carry out its program for a number of years. This is certainly welcome and wonderful news to all and marks the completion of the job started five years ago to construct the essential buildings of the school."[123] We may interject here that the new buildings were indeed wonderful, but they did bring with them some new problems, especially in their heating systems. In the old days at Ampleforth, if the water went cold, someone went and put some more coal in the furnace. The sophisticated controls of our new buildings were not nearly so simple to correct. At first Father Luke had to summon a technician, but gradually he learnt at least what to look for, and often was able himself to flip the appropriate switch.

This "completion of the job started five years ago" prompts us to quote, from the preceding paragraph in the *Journal*, Father Columba's gracious and well-earned tribute to Inc:

> It is well at times to turn back and examine the way we came. In 1954, five years ago, "Inc." had no land, no community to run the school, no school and they had a paltry sum of money. By 1955 they had acquired over fifty acres, two substantial houses and a cottage, they had interested Ampleforth in the scheme and in the fall of that year three monks from that abbey established themselves in the Stannard house. Three and a half years later, looking around, we find that the community, with novices,

---

[123] *SLPJ* II. 3, p.2

> postulants and all, has increased to twelve. A building (part monastery and part school) has been built and is in use, a gym likewise, while the Science Wing is under construction. The size of the property has tripled, largely a gift of Mr. Joseph Desloge. There are in the school over a hundred students, there are playing fields and tennis courts, plans are afoot for a chapel. This achievement is largely due to the zeal of our supporters . . . But especially this astonishing growth has been the gift of God Himself. His hand is felt at every move, as though He had waited long enough for the people of Saint Louis to undertake this work . . . In humble amazement we thank Him for all His gifts and ask all our friends to join us in this just and necessary response to such goodness.[124]

To this we may add from Inc's report in the next *Journal* [125] that they had by now raised a total in cash of $1,320,000, with further pledges and commitments of about $125,000 plus $65,000 pledged to be paid on the Singer property. Add to this the $500,000 given for the church and Inc had raised $2,000,000. They quickly went on to add that there was still an urgent need for $73,000 to pay debts coming due on 1 January 1960 and after that there were two loans to be repaid, one to the Department of Health, Education and Welfare for $55,000, and the balance of $360,000 still due on the bank's loan of $400,000.

The fourth decision may have been the hardest for Abbot Herbert. He decided to recall Father Timothy to Ampleforth and to have Father Columba undertake for the time being the headmastership of the school. There had been disagreements between Father Columba and Father Timothy about scholarships and about matters of discipline but the real difficulty was the conflict of their personalities. Father Columba was an intellectual but not a scholar and Father Timothy a scholar but not an intellectual. Each was to the other a cause of suffering and an opportunity for forbearance, and each believed that from these two circumstances flowed many of God's blessings on Priory. Their difficulties were not new; in the spring of 1955 when Father Timothy learnt of his appointment as headmaster, and when he was still at Ampleforth, he had said to Abbot Herbert that clashes were likely. Characteristically Abbot Herbert replied, "Yes, you do not overlap much. But if you can establish a *modus vivendi*, think how much of the spectrum you will cover between you." This was borne

[124] ibid.

[125] *SLPJ* II. 4, pp.10-11.

out in the incident of the draft statutes for the Archdiocesan Synod, as will be related below.[126] In other words, their talents were complementary but their temperaments clashed. When the complementarity was uppermost, they were a very strong team; when the clashing was, it was a very strong clash.

A letter embodying Abbot Herbert's decision was sent out on 15 June 1959 and the decision was announced at Ampleforth with the addition that another monk would be sent out to replace Father Timothy. Fred Switzer and the president of the Mothers' Club and others then wrote to Abbot Herbert, trying to dissuade him.

Meanwhile, Father Columba left to give a Retreat to the Benedictine Sisters at Nauvoo. When he returned on about 24 June, he made a transatlantic telephone call--which was still a major and unusual operation--and had the impression, which later proved to be incorrect, that the monk being sent from Ampleforth was to be the new headmaster. Since the monk's experience did not seem to fit the job, Father Columba asked for Father Timothy to be left, and Abbot Herbert agreed. Afterwards Abbot Herbert made it clear that major decisions must never again be made over the transatlantic telephone. The upshot was that Father Timothy was to be left in Saint Louis until the graduation of the first class in May 1960, and that a further decision would be made then.

Shortly after the end of the school year we had our first serious accident to a boy. Jimmy Barnes ('61), riding pillion on a motor scooter, was struck from behind by a car and thrown against its windshield. He suffered a very severe head injury and only the great skill of Doctor Palazzo, his brain surgeon, enabled him to survive. This sad event showed us one of the best traits of our boys, their great concern for anyone who was in serious trouble. We had already seen this when Father Ian was ill, and now Jimmy had so many visitors that we had, at the doctors' request, to send a letter to all parents asking them, for a few days, to restrain their sons from visiting him.

During the rest of the summer, Father Columba, Father Austin and Father Luke went to North Dakota, Minneapolis, New Orleans and elsewhere to give Retreats; Father Austin and Father Thomas worked at a parish in Los Angeles. This paid for their vacations. Henry Hughes took Father Brendan and Father Timothy to visit friends and a variety of academic establishments on the East Coast.

---

[126] *See* pp. *224-25 below.*

Father Luke also worked with HOK on reducing the cost of the church, mainly by using fiberglass windows made by Kalwall. These were less expensive, and would, since they consisted of two layers of fiberglass separated by a gap of about two and a half inches, also provide better insulation than glass. It was Gerry Mudd who first drew our attention and HOK's to Kalwall and insisted that we investigate that possibility, just as later on it was Dayton Mudd who put us on the track of our most successful sound system to date.[127] When Father Luke was not working with HOK, he wrestled with problems of cash-flow and looked after our steers and hogs. All this was making him wonder, with good reason, whether the time had not come to expand his office staff.

In the Fall of 1959, once school had started, he was flown by the president of Kalwall round a number of New England churches which had installed Kalwall. Their private plane ended the day by making a landing in the dark at the same time as a commercial plane was landing on a parallel runway much too close for comfort. After that he flew by regular airlines to New Orleans. Between Retreats there he managed to get away, only to be flown back to the city by a priest friend, who got lost in the clouds and had to come down low over a small town to read the name on its water tower. Father Luke had earned his keep by taking six classes and giving two lectures at Southwest Louisiana Institute, where the chaplain was Father, now Bishop, Jude Speyrer. The bishop had studied Theology at Fribourg, Switzerland and had there become the friend of Cardinal Basil Hume and several Ampleforth monks, who were also studying there.

After much discussion, we decided that we must put up the tuition for our fourth school year from $750 to $850. In the letter announcing this Father Timothy wrote, "I deeply regret the necessity for this, just as you will, but I hope and believe that you will see, equally with us, that it is ineluctable." One of the parents wrote back that it was worth the $100 just to see the word "ineluctable" used in a letter. We also sent the parents of next year's seniors a letter on choosing a college. In it we stated the archdiocesan policy on Catholic colleges, and sent a copy of our letter to the pastors of our seniors. This stood us in good stead later on.

In July our highway opened another stretch of itself, which saved us perhaps ten minutes on every journey downtown, but out by us, although it was a four-lane, divided highway, the lanes were narrower

[127] It was a sad irony that at Dayton's funeral Mass the system, which had been working well until then, behaved badly.

than they are today, which made passing the big trucks an act of faith, greater or less according to who was driving. As the wheels passed over the divisions of the concrete they made a very distinctive sound, another of our memorable sounds, from which you could tell how fast you were going--and no doubt the police could too.[128]

In mid-August the Science Wing was completed, football camp started and Fathers Augustine and Paul arrived from England, so at least the summer ended well.

---

[128] US 40 followed approximately the course of the old road from Clayton to Chesterfield, but a little farther south. Traces of the old road could be seen passing through the middle of our property. As a boy, Joe Blank, Erwin Sellenriek's co-worker, used to leave at 4.00 a.m. from a few miles west of us and take that road to the Soulard market downtown to sell his father's farm produce. It was a day's journey there and back.

CHAPTER 19

We Have Seniors

WE approached the new school year with a mixture of apprehension and excited anticipation. Both the apprehension and the excitement had the same source: we had our first senior class. We were apprehensive about their preparation for college and their acceptance by colleges at the same time as we were excited that soon we would know the answers to many of our questions. The seniors and their parents, and to some extent all the boys, recognized that the moment of truth was approaching. However much the faculty had been impressing on the seniors the imminence of college and the urgent need, therefore, for them to apply themselves to their studies, it was not the same thing as sitting down to fill out a college application nor the same thing as knowing that their transcript would soon lay bare before the college the quality of their achievement.

Having seniors for the first time also entailed making a variety of adjustments. We decided to maintain our ban on driving to school, encouraged by the opinion of at least one local headmaster, who had allowed driving and wished he had not. On the other hand, seniors who had written permission from their parents were allowed to smoke in their common room after lunch. We added, "Nonetheless, it is undoubtedly more prudent not to smoke, and I hope that parents will encourage their sons to aim at this." Today our decision might well have been the other way round, to ban smoking and allow driving.

In the classroom, seniors took Religion, Mathematics, English, Social Studies and one foreign language. To this they could add either a full year of Science or of a second foreign language, or half a year of Science and half of a second foreign language, or half a year of a second foreign language and half of a third foreign language, provided that the schedule could be worked out. We prefaced the announcement of this change with the doleful comment, "To give time for the Seniors to penetrate a little more deeply into certain subjects, it will be necessary to reduce slightly the number of subjects taken." It was a reduction of one full subject. Religion and English were each allotted four periods a week and the rest five. The seniors were therefore occupied on these courses for twenty-eight of the thirty-five periods available. Social Studies included two periods of Elementary

Politics and Economics taught by Father Columba. This was a course on *Rerum Novarum* and the other great Social Encyclicals, but as Father Columba was never one to feel constricted by a syllabus, much else crept in. Francis Oates later described his classes as being "like float trips--calm stretches, sudden riffles of ideas that might shake loose an assumption."[129] The seniors also had one period each of General Knowledge and Choir. That left them with five unscheduled periods each week--not an enormous amount but more than they had before.

The regular faculty now consisted of nine monks and seven laymen. Fathers Augustine and Paul have already been mentioned as the new monks; the new laymen were Messrs. Robert L. Bannister and Herbert J. Schweich. The former came to us from Saint Louis University, the latter from many years of teaching French and German, most recently at the Berlitz School. We should add Mr. Richard R. Weeks who helped Father Columba with the part of his course dealing with Economics. Finally, our seniors had, for the second part of the year, the opportunity of being taught Biology by Doctors J. F. Gerard Mudd and Donald W. Bussmannn. Gerry Mudd volunteered to do this and roped in Don Bussmann to help him. The pair continued through the school year 1970-71. Then Don retired and, through May 1976, Gerry filled his place with a succession of his friends from Saint Louis University. It took several men to replace Don. It was a wonderful contribution to our program.

At this point all form masters and all heads of departments were monks. It says much for the quality of our monastic reinforcements from Ampleforth that the lay members of the faculty felt that this was fair and based on merit.

In our athletic program we greeted our first year of competition at the Varsity level with an enlargement of the coaching staff. Father Ian controlled the main lines of athletic policy and Don Kettelkamp was the head coach and organizer. In charge of Varsity football were Don Kettelkamp and Bob Bannister; in charge of B and C, Jim O'Neill and Father Paul. Soccer was under Father Thomas, who was helped by Fathers Brendan, Timothy and Ian and Ed Presti. Don Kettelkamp coached Varsity basketball with Father Paul as his assistant and Jim O'Neill was helped by Father Brendan and Bob Bannister with B and C. Don Kettelkamp took Varsity baseball and Bob Bannister B and C. Father Augustine was in charge of track, assisted by Fathers Thomas,

---

[129] *LS* p. 57.

Brendan, Timothy and Ian and Jim O'Neill. Finally, Father Paul and Alex Niven coached Tennis. From this it will be seen that Father Paul was the most adventurous of the non-Americans in coaching American sports. His finest hour came when he took one of our basketball squads to play at Saint Thomas Aquinas. In the locker room at half-time the boys suggested that, as we were trailing, we should change to a 1-3-1 zone. Father Paul asked what that was, and when they told him, said, "Well, I don't see why not", so they did and went out to come from behind for a glorious victory. What made it all the sweeter was that the opposing coach was Mr. Martin R. McCabe, who later became our Athletic Director. Was that *propter hoc* or only *post hoc*?[130]

The other big change was that Father Brendan took over full responsibility for the discipline of the Upper School. He was in touch with matters of discipline since he and Father Timothy had, at Father Curtin's invitation, been attending the meetings of a small group of priest-counselors and priest-disciplinarians from various diocesan schools. These meetings were informal. Their chief value to us was that they kept us informed about what others in the trade were saying and writing, and lessened our need to wade through the professional journals for ourselves, except when we learnt of something that sounded interesting. They were also a good link with the diocesan clergy. Through this group we learnt of a new theory of counseling called "non-directive" or "Rogerian" counseling. In it the counselor simply repeated what the boy said. An interview would presumably have gone like this: "I have a problem." "Oh, you have a problem?" "Yes, I can't bear my father." "You can't bear your father?" "Yes, he is always picking on me." "He is always picking on you?" etc. It had the virtue of making the boy express his problem in words rather than leaving a formless sea of discontent inside him, but how much of that could any normal boy endure before he either insulted the counselor or walked out?

It seemed to work better with some parents. Father Timothy once had a mother come to see him. She poured out her troubles for nearly an hour, during which he said "Oh" and "I'm so sorry to hear that" and "That was wise" and similar gems. When she had finished, she got up to go, saying, "Thank you so much, father; you have been such a help." Father Timothy thought she was being sarcastic, but a quick look assured him that she was not. So a form of non-directive counseling worked well with her.

---

130 "Because of this" or only "after this".

Father Brendan was Form Master of the sixth form, Father Augustine of the fifth, Father Thomas of the fourth and Father Paul of the third. Father Ian remained in charge of the Junior House. One of Father Brendan's first actions as Master of Discipline was to establish a monitorial system by which seven selected seniors had "authority over the other boys, [were] responsible for their behavior in many spheres and [had] certain powers of punishment when necessary. In this way, they not only [made] a positive contribution to the school's smooth running, but also [learnt] to wield authority justly and without fear or favor, and [developed] their own character and leadership."[131] They learnt to stand up for what they knew to be right, to persuade others of its rightness, and not to flinch from the embarrassment or unpopularity that this might entail. They learnt the difference between driving and leading. One small example of their authority was to enforce the rule about not walking on the grass. The rule had a practical purpose, to preserve the grass, but also served another function. There is something to be said for having a rule whose observation is seen to be highly prized by authority and yet which can be broken without much moral turpitude. On it boys can work off some of their spirit of rebelliousness (or independence, if you will) but without much loss of moral tone. They certainly lose less moral tone by walking on the grass than by smoking it.

The monitorial system worked smoothly, the *Journal* reports, and was accepted happily by the rest of the school. Lest any think that the writer, Father Brendan, was biased in favor of the system which he himself had introduced, there is in the yearbook this comment written by the boys: "(The monitorial system) is certainly one of the greatest advantages that our school offers to its students, even though at times this is not altogether evident. The monitors learn how to wield their authority, when necessary, among their equals, and the rest of the student body learns how to accept this without resentment. Both these lessons will prove invaluable in life after graduation."[132] Nor was even this a flash in the pan: next year, the yearbook called the system "one of the most liberal forms of self-government entrusted to students at any school,"[133] and even more remarkably, the *Record*, our school newspaper, in its issue for November 1964, published short

---

[131] *SLPJ* II. 4, p.6. The seven were John Cramer, Dewey Dempsey, Bob Dunn, Mike Fox, Peter Igoe, Mike Lardner and Dan Richardson. It is possible that the system was given a trial run toward the end of the previous school year.

[132] *The Shield* 1960, p.73.

[133] *The Shield* 1961, p.50.

biographies of the monitors for that year, and dedicated the issue to them. The headmaster's committee[134] continued in its advisory function but relinquished to the monitors its admittedly rudimentary role in matters of discipline.

The same yearbook, on page 72, says of this committee, "Student opinions, when expressed formally by the committee, have always been given due consideration and have proven to bear some weight in official pronouncements." The Committee discussed student privileges, arranged dances and served as an *ad hoc* committee to meet various needs. Among the hot topics discussed were driving to school and the school jacket. They made little headway with the driving but more with the jacket. The first jacket chosen had felt sleeves, which the boys did not like; the model they preferred had leather sleeves, which Father Timothy referred to as a truck-driver's jacket. In this instance, the boys gradually wore him down.

Besides these serious matters, two trivial incidents stick in the headmaster's memory: one was a discussion of French fries. The committee opined that the French fries were too crisp. When Father Timothy asked if they would truly prefer them to be soggier, their reply was, "Yes." That was undoubtedly their most unexpected request, for soggy French fries. The other incident was when Father Timothy was driving them home after the meeting, as he usually did since the meetings went on after the school day. We had just acquired a Volkswagen bus, which he had never driven. All went well until he had to turn round after delivering a boy in a subdivision. He drove, incorrectly, nose-first into someone's driveway and tried to back out. He could not find reverse, nor could the boys in the car. At that point the owners of the house, whose driveway he was blocking, emerged in their full evening glory and wanted to drive out. Father Timothy explained what he was trying to do and enlisted their help. They could not find reverse either. There was a boy of eleven playing on the other side of the road. In desperation Father Timothy called to him and asked if he knew where reverse was. "Sure," said the lad and showed us. He later applied to the school and was accepted, though not simply for that reason.

The activities available were, alphabetically, Art (Rudi Torrini), Carpentry (Reynolds Medart), Debate (Father Augustine), Library

---

[134] The members for 1959-60 were: Seniors Ed Boedeker, Hank Dilschneider, Bob Dunn, Fran Oates, Dan Richardson and Mike Spearing; Juniors Claude Bakewell, George Convy, Jim Murphy and Jay Weaver; Sophomore Lemoine Skinner and Freshman Fred Sauer.

(Father Brendan), Mechanical Drawing (Reynolds again), Music (Father Austin and Ken Scheibal), *The Record* (Ed Presti) and the yearbook (Alex Niven). There was to have been Photography too under, yet again, Reynolds Medart, but this was the year when the Fire Marshall, just before school opened, banned it from the basement of the Junior House, and even Reynolds could not make ready a new home for it, nor indeed had we yet found a place. Both the *Record* and the *Shield*, as the yearbook was named for our coat of arms, had censors, Father Austin and Father Timothy respectively. Father Augustine was now in charge of the monastic library, which was then still separate from the school library, and of the sports store. Father Paul was in charge of the bookstore.

Now that we had all the buildings that we were going to have until the late sixties, we could establish a nearly permanent layout; nearly, because the church was likely to be completed within a year or two and the chapels, especially that for the school, would no longer need to be in the monastery. There were now six classrooms in the monastery on the ground floor and two at the far end of the science wing; laboratories and lecture hall were in the science wing; the seniors had their common room in the rathskeller of the Stannard House, the juniors and sophomores in one half of the barn and the freshmen in the other half; Father Brendan and his monitors were in the room which had been the faculty room, at the top of the stairs in the Stannard House; Don Kettelkamp operated as Athletic Director from the faculty room, which was now in the northwest corner of the monastery and Father Ian operated from his office in the Junior House; the reception area was a couch in the hall of the Stannard House or the room over the front entrance, provided that there was no guest in it; music and art each used half the barn; carpentry was in the gym in the locker room area, not all of which was needed for lockers; publications and mechanical drawing were in the Junior House (Singer House); the gym served also as an auditorium, when needed, and school assemblies took place in the dining room or in the Science lecture theater.

And so school started on Tuesday 8 September 1959, the day after Labor Day, for the lower three grades and on 9 September for the upper three. The numbers in the various forms were: VI,28; V,23; IV,21; III,30; II,14; I,22 for a total of 138. As usual, the days before and after the opening were hectic, but once everyone settled down, there was a lull of two weeks or so before the phones really began to ring. As the school year picked up speed, we began to be visited by admission people from colleges, coming now not out of curiosity but in a genuine search for candidates. That was followed by the submission of application forms and the inevitable "Would you mind writing a recommendation for me?"

For the seniors we introduced the Thesis, whose purpose was to give them practice both in composing a somewhat extended treatment of a topic and in stringing three thousand or so words together. If they could manage it, we expected them to state a point of view and then support it, for example: *Samuel Clemens: How His Writings are a Result of His Life*. Other theses were narrative, for example: *A History of Dixieland Jazz*. A supervisor suggested sources to each boy, helped with the outline and answered questions. Nobody liked it very much at the time, but when alumni came back from college, many agreed that it had been helpful.

At the same time, that is late in September, we made, in response to suggestions from parents, faculty and students, and in an effort to find more time for our Activities, an attempt to start a Saturday morning club. We offered a choice of music, paper and yearbook, debating, elementary surveying, scientific club and library. Transportation would be provided by the school, and therefore there would be some fee, probably between $25 and $50. A few families were interested, but not enough to warrant our continuing. The effort, however, was not wasted because Father Thomas, whose Lancastrian tenacity was not to be put off by a lukewarm response, quietly went about building enthusiasm for a scientific club which was to meet on Saturday mornings.

After the two-day Retreat by Father John Campbell for the upper school and the one-day Retreat by Father Austin for the Junior House,[135] October saw the beginning of the external tests, mostly College Boards. We had learnt that Ed Boedeker, George Hellmuth and Francis Oates had been named as semi-finalists in the National Merit Scholarship program. In due course they became finalists, but had to be content with that honor and glory. On 20 October all seniors and juniors took the Preliminary Scholastic Aptitude Test (PSAT), designed as a dry run and predictor for the Scholastic Aptitude Test (SAT), which was and is a major factor in college entry. The averages of the senior class in the PSAT were 58.321 in Verbal Aptitude and 58.785 in Mathematical. Usually boys are higher in Mathematical, so we felt that the strength we attributed to our language program was verified. These scores predicted class averages

[135] There was another pair of Retreats in the spring.

in the SAT of 603 and 618 respectively, but in fact the averages in January, including one senior who took the SAT in December and did not repeat it in January, were 581 and 610.[136]

Even so, as 500 was the national mean for college-bound seniors, everyone had good reason to be satisfied. This confirmed our opinion that these objective, multiple-choice tests which could be scored by machines were the only practicable way of dealing with the huge number of candidates and that they were as equitable as any other tests. It remained disturbing, however, that they gave no indication whether the candidate could write a sentence, still less construct a paragraph.

In November three seniors took the American College Testing Program (ACT). This was a rival program to the College Board and was required by some, mostly mid-western, schools. In December four seniors took SATs or Achievement Tests or both, and then in January twenty-five of them took the SATs, with the results given above. In March, twenty-six took the Achievement Tests, designed to test their knowledge in particular subjects. The averages are given here in the following form: the first figure is the average score by our seniors in 1960, the second, the number of seniors who took the test, the third the "recentered" score, i.e. what it would have been in 1994. English 559-26-616; French 490-6-529; Latin 617-7-644; Advanced Math 646-7-616; Intermediate Math 530-17-552; Physics 569-7-599; Spanish 515-4-536; Social Studies 543-6-591. Ed Boedeker and Fran Oates each scored 794 in the English test and Oates 780 in the Latin. All three of these scores would be 800 today, so they deserved their places at Harvard and Yale respectively. Finally, during the week of Monday 16 May, some seniors took the Advanced Placement tests of

---

[136] In 1994, because the median score on the SATs had dropped considerably below the median score when the tests were introduced, the College Board decided to compensate for the drop by "recentering" SAT scores. As a result, a score obtained before the recentering would indicate a higher standard than the same score obtained after it. In the verbal test, a score of 500 before would be converted to a score of 580 after; in the math test 500 would become 520. The tables published by the College Board show that a class-average score of 581 in the verbal would be 651 now, and a class-average math score of 610 would be 616 now. The recentering was applied also to achievement tests. Readers thinking in terms of scores obtained after the recentering should make the necessary adjustments. That for the verbal test is quite significant, but that for the math test hardly, which means that math aptitude had hardly dropped while the verbal had dropped significantly.

the College Board in English, Physics and Chemistry. And that concluded their testing.

Meanwhile the juniors, who had taken the National Merit Scholarship Qualifying Test at the beginning of March, took the SATs later in the month, together with a handful of Achievement Tests. In May they took a battery of Achievement Tests, as did about half the sophomores. Also in May, on the thirteenth, the freshmen and sophomores took the NDEA tests, as required by the federal government in the wake of Sputnik. While all this testing was going on, the seniors had to address themselves to applying to colleges and we had to address ourselves to the problem of conveying to the same colleges information about each boy in a form which colleges would understand. This gave the seniors plenty to do, and because they approached faculty members with requests for a recommendation, it kept the faculty busy too. We encouraged the seniors to keep the list of colleges to which they applied reasonably short, but to include in it one college by which they were sure to be accepted and to which they would be if not overjoyed at least content to go.

We had also to design a college transcript, but before describing that, we need to consider our decision about accreditation. What the schools in New England had told Father Timothy about the difference in outlook between the New England Association and the North Central had been borne out by the limited amount of experience that we had had with the latter. Two or three of the monks had served on accrediting teams at local high schools and had liked the idea of judging each school by its own philosophy, but had been dubious about much else. The North Central was dominated by the public schools, whose outlook and problems were very different from ours. That, after all, was part of the reason why we were here. The main advantage of being accredited was that it would give us a status that state colleges and universities, especially those of other states, would recognize, That would certainly have had its value, even though we did not think that many of our graduates would go to them. In the event, three of our first graduating class did so, but their colleges, the Universities of Michigan and Virginia, were not typical state schools. We might have overcome these hesitations but for one virtually insurmountable problem: teachers in schools to be accredited were required to have a substantial number of college credits in education. This requirement was unknown in England for schools like Ampleforth, and none of the monks had any such credits. It would have required years of part-time schooling to accumulate the required number, and we felt that this was out of the question. We had therefore decided to forgo the status of accreditation, to make ourselves as well-known as we could to the University of Missouri and to deal with other state schools one by one. In due course, we joined the Independent Schools Association of the Central States (ISACS) and received accreditation from them.

We now return to our designing of our college transcript, bearing in mind that we needed, because we were not accredited, to make everything as clear as we possibly could. In our grading system, 80% and above was equivalent to A. We were reluctant to change this system, because we believed, as we said above,[137] that a grade of 80% meant that the boy had mastered 80% of the material, an achievement that was both creditable and possible. This seemed to us a statement that could be true, whereas to give grades in the high nineties, implying that he had mastered virtually all the subject matter of the course, seemed to us to be either untrue or an implicit criticism of the course. A further problem was the class rank. We established a rather complex system of weighting the grades whereby more credit was given for grades in A sets than for those in B sets--we had homogeneous grouping--and more for grades in the harder subjects than in the less hard. Latin and Math were seen as the hardest subjects, followed by French or Spanish, English and Science, which were all equal, then History, and finally Religion and Greek. Greek was rated low because it was usually taken as an extra subject, and we did not want to tip the balance too far in favor of those who took it, whatever the headmaster's predilections.

This produced a rank in class that we could accept as fair, but it did not solve the problem we had with universities, especially State schools, which automatically rejected any out-of-state applicant who was not in the top half of his class. We had to convince them that a student in the lower half of our class could well rank in the top tenth of another school's class. We could in fact point to a boy who flunked out of Priory and next year was on the Dean's list at his new school.

With the transcript we included a description of the courses and a statement by the headmaster about each candidate. To this statement by the headmaster, or later by the college guidance counselor, together with the recommendation of one of the faculty, we attached great importance, because so many of the most valuable characteristics of an applicant--generosity, for example--cannot be directly measured and so cannot be deduced from a transcript. It therefore took some time to write a careful and reliable recommendation. Colleges, too,

---

[137] *See above*, p. 115.

gave them weight, especially when they knew and trusted the school and its officials. We believed that colleges, provided that they read the package with care and believed what they read, could form a very just opinion about our candidates, but not all college admission staffs had the time to do so. That was why we spent so much time in visiting colleges and in explaining ourselves to visiting admissions officers. We gradually built up a personal acquaintance with many of them but, as with the Catholic grade schools, it often happened that just as we got to know them, they moved on, sometimes out of admissions altogether. Such problems as we had were mainly with State colleges, but a letter or phone-call was often enough to set things right. One such school turned down our applicant, but when we explained further, agreed that he could come and take their test. When they saw his results, they not only accepted him but gave him credit for the whole of the first semester.[138]

Not all our energy was directed to colleges. On 5 January 1960 Father Thomas invited students, parents and friends to an Open House in the new Science Wing. The many who came saw the new labs and were able either to be impressed by a variety of experiments, all performed and described by the boys, or to be amazed at the sight of an unconnected faucet hanging in mid-air from a piece of string and pouring forth water. Not all the mothers wished to have a boy with a generator make their hair stand on end like Struwwelpeter's, but other boys did. There were also, and more importantly, experiments catering to the seriously and even expertly scientific. On 20 February Father Thomas followed up the triumph of the Open House with the first meeting of the Science Club, an organization which both brought to Priory top flight scientists from the local universities and industries, and took our boys on tours to corporations of scientific interest. Father Thomas had friends at Saint Louis University and Washington University, and also at McDonnell Aircraft, as it then was, Monsanto, Mallinckrodt, Scullin Steel and others. Father Thomas was persuasive and both Academe and industry were most willing to co-operate by sending speakers and arranging tours.

On 9 January we repeated Priory Day and again struck a blow for the valuable quality of versatility by giving the teams from the eight schools present a quiz on General Knowledge, to which we attached considerable importance, and a basketball tournament. Again we gave them a good lunch preceded by Mass.

---

[138] Tom Cuba at Texas A. & M.

Also in January, we were featured in *Jubilee Magazine*.[139] Their article started with a pleasing reference to Stephen Leacock, who "once said that every educational establishment should be built around a man smoking a pipe."(We had several such) Students, he felt, could be added later, then books, and finally (if the climate insisted) some sort of housing. There are in the article some fine photographs, including one of Father Ian chasing five boys, who are themselves chasing a soccer ball on the site now occupied by the church. Other boys are watching from patio lounge chairs set out on the north side of the old monastery. When the boys were not around, killdeer used to swoop and sweep up and down that area uttering their shrill, exciting cry.

On the last two Saturdays of January we held our entrance examinations for the ninth grade. The first Saturday was for scholarship candidates and others interested and the tests were set by us. The second was the common Archdiocesan entrance examination and was intended for boys for whom we were the first choice. The first day produced exactly one hundred candidates, the second twenty-five, of whom thirteen were from our own eighth grade. The other 112 were therefore competing for just seventeen places, or six and one half boys for each place. From them we culled a class of 35. Then on 30 April we tested fifty-one sixth-graders, along with six seventh- and twelve fifth-graders, the last taking the test as a dry run. From these we were able to draw a class of sixteen for our next seventh grade. This was all we intended, as we still were taking half the class into the seventh grade and the other half into the ninth, two years later. We continued to do this for several more years.

In the various sports, this was the first year in which we competed at the Varsity level, and we soon found that there was a quantum leap in intensity from the C and B and even JV levels. Our football squad won the first home game 26-0 against Lutheran South, but that was its only victory. They often played well for two or three quarters before being worn down by the greater weight and, especially, greater numbers of our opponents. The B team, although coached by Jim O'Neill in a fedora, could not emulate the Dallas Cowboys and went 1-3. The season ended with a football dance in our gymnasium, wonderfully decorated for the occasion.

The soccer season is so discreetly described in the yearbook that it is hard to tell what the results were, but it seems that the Varsity tied

139 Vol.7, no.9, January 1960, pp.8-15.

three games and lost four and that the B team was 2-3. A similar discretion about basketball seems to reveal or conceal that the Varsity won two games, B four and C none. It is hard to tell how many they lost. We had some individual track stars such as John Cramer and Bob Barlow but do not seem to have won any meets. Nonetheless the performances at our own Field Day were impressive. Our tennis team, which had been unbeaten the previous year, went 3-4-1. Our swimmers placed fifth in an eight team meet at Saint Louis University High School, but the records for baseball have fallen into the gap between the yearbook, which went to press too soon for them and next year's *Record*, which did not look back to them. The Father and Son softball games, one for the upper school and one for the junior house, took place again but Lethe has absorbed these results also.

The Father and Son dinner was held after the football season at the Lennox Hotel. This was the occasion on which Judge Nangle "set sail". The other noteworthy feature was our distribution of letters, which revealed yet another difference between American and English customs. At Ampleforth, fifteen boys would make up the First Fifteen (varsity squad) at rugger; they would play the whole game, and if anyone was injured, the remaining fourteen carried on. Of those fifteen perhaps half a dozen would be awarded their "colors". That was an honor over and above the honor of representing the school. We started out on that principle, but were soon apprised that very different customs obtained in Saint Louis: not only would all the starters receive a letter, but so would the substitutes and even the managers. This seemed to be a case where we should bow to local custom, and we did so, but at the time it seemed very odd.

The principal money-raising effort was, of course, The Drive, but there were others. The juniors needed money for their Prom and so organized a car wash, at which they washed a number of cars, some juniors and some other bystanders. The Mothers' Club project for this year was a dialogue on 13 March between Father Walter J. Ong S.J. of Saint Louis University and Father Timothy on *The Ugly American*, which had recently been published[140]. This was to have been at our gym, but because of the severe weather was moved to the Chase-Park Plaza Hotel, which was packed with Father Ong's friends. The Mothers were pleased to make $4000.

That brings us to the eve of graduation, and our account has been largely of the affairs of the school. This is natural enough, since these

---

[140] William J. Lederer & Eugene Burdick, *The Ugly American* (New York: Norton [1958])

affairs occupied so large a part of the monks' time and energy. But there were other events as well. At Christmas our chapel was full for Midnight Mass; and for Holy Week we had eighteen students from Saint Louis University making a Retreat. They slept for the most part on common room floors. For the first part of April we also had two monks from Ampleforth, Father, later Abbot, Patrick Barry and Father, later Cardinal, Basil Hume. This was partly general liaison and partly a sequel to a visit Father Columba had paid to Ampleforth after Christmas. He went because Father Brendan's health was becoming a cause for concern, and there was also the question whether Father Timothy should stay or return to England. Neither letters nor, as we noted, transatlantic telephone conversations were as satisfactory as communication face to face.

Fathers Patrick and Basil saw the monks in action during Holy Week, saw the school in operation, attended a parents' evening and were able to get a feel for their friendly support. They were the excuse for a dinner arranged at the Deer Creek Club by the members of Inc, and were able to experience their friendly support too. They also had long conversations with the individual monks principally concerned. They left on 20 April after a stay of about ten days. By 10 May Abbot Herbert had written to say that Father Brendan was to be recalled to Ampleforth and would be replaced by Father Leonard Jackson.[141] Presumably the same letter from Abbot Herbert would have said that Father Timothy was to stay; anyway, stay he did. It was a severe blow to lose someone of Father Brendan's versatility, but Father Leonard, though not so academic, had many talents and plenty of Lancastrian toughness. The boys would not easily get him down, as a sign in his office later proclaimed.[142]

And so we approached the long-expected day of our first Graduation, but just before its arrival, came a shock. We received a letter signed by Archbishop Ritter commenting on the duty of Catholic parents to ensure the Catholic education of their children, and spelling out in particular their obligations, including written permission from him, if they chose to send them to non-Catholic colleges. The letter included very strong words on the danger of this practice. *Time Magazine* picked this up, with acid comment, and included in the same issue comments by Prior Aelred Graham of

---

[141] JLR Letter, 10 May 1960.

[142] *ab illegitimis non carborundum.* Nonsense Latin for, "Don't let them get you down."

Portsmouth Priory on the benefits of Catholics attending non-Catholic colleges. At the time, Prior Aelred knew nothing of the Archbishop's letter and *Time* did not tell him.

Archbishop Ritter had agreed to come to our Graduation and to speak. When he arrived, Father Columba at once asked him whether he had changed his mind from what he had said to Abbot Herbert and Father Columba back in 1955. The Archbishop, being a straightforward man, made no bones of the fact that he had written a mild letter asking to be informed about who was going to non-Catholic colleges, had left the letter with his staff, instructing them to improve it if necessary, and had then departed to Washington for a meeting of the U.S. Bishops. One of the staff had "improved" the letter and turned it into an attack. The Archbishop said that we should continue as we were. Later Inc gave a dinner in his honor, at which he said the same quite publicly. That was a relief to us, and his straightforwardness made us respect him all the more.[143]

Thus on Monday 6 June at 10.00 a.m., our first graduation took place on the beautiful lawn, as it then was, east of the Stannard House. The weather had for several days been quite uncertain, and we had plans, if the weather were wet, to use the gym. Fortunately the day looked fine, we started putting out the chairs at 6.30 a.m. and the weather was perfect. The sun was warm enough that those who had chosen places in the shade of the four fine elms, were glad that they had done so. About five hundred people came.

Graduation started with a solemn procession of the Archbishop, the faculty and the graduates. They were formally welcomed. Next was the presentation of academic prizes for the seniors, followed by addresses by Fathers Brendan, Timothy and Columba. In the circumstances it was fortunate that Father Timothy highlighted the ten accepted by Georgetown University (eight attended) rather than the five accepted by Yale, three by Harvard and two by M.I.T.

Then the Archbishop spoke with great kindness about the school. People said afterwards they had never heard him speak so enthusiastically about any school.[144] The diplomas were presented and the Archbishop, fortified by coffee and buns, departed. Then we had Mass on the lawn, celebrated by Father Columba, with Father Curtin as

---

[143] See the Chapter on *The Founding of Saint Louis Priory* in an unpublished ms. by Father Columba entitled *To Be a Pilgrim: Memories 1971*, from which much of this material is drawn.

[144] JLR Letter 13 June 1960.

Deacon and Father William J. Lyons as Sub-Deacon. Mass was followed by refreshments.

The practiced attender of graduations may be surprised at the order--Mass after the graduation--and at the absence of addresses by any of the graduates. The former must have been due to the Archbishop's schedule, the latter to our unawareness of American customs, or possibly to the reluctance of the graduates. It has to be remembered that Ampleforth had no equivalent of this ceremony so, although we received much advice on how to do it, the whole thing was to us uncharted territory. Perhaps the real surprise was that what we did resembled a typical graduation as closely as it did. We made another blunder through lack of local knowledge. In England, one common form of ranking was to give outstanding scholars the rank of *summa cum laude*, very good students *magna cum laude*, respectable but in no way outstanding students *cum laude*,[145] and the rest nothing. In the United States, *cum laude* is reserved for outstanding scholars. We inscribed the diplomas in the English way and thereby enrolled a number of the respectable in the ranks of the brilliant.

And so we dispatched our first ambassadors to college. These were the colleges:

Charles F. Bealke, Jr.	Washington U.
Howard Benoist III	Georgetown
David A. Blanton III	Georgetown
Edgar C. Boedeker	Harvard
Daniel J. Burke	Saint Louis U.
John C. Carleton	Spring Hill
Michael L. Carton	Rensselaer
Richard H. Chomeau	Notre Dame
John E. Cramer, Jr.	Georgetown
Dumont G. Dempsey, Jr.	Brown
Henry J. Dilschneider III	U. of Virginia
Robert C. Dunn, Jr.	Yale
Michael H. Fox	Georgetown
George W. Hellmuth	Yale
Peter M. Igoe	Yale
Kevin M. Kelly	Georgetown
William D. Kerckhoff	U. of Virginia
Theodore A. Kienstra	Regis

[145] These categories are: "with the highest praise", "with great praise" and "with praise".

Michael W. Lardner	M.I.T.
Samuel W. Mitchell, Jr.	Westminster
Jack R. Mueller	U. of Michigan
Edwynne C. Murphy	Georgetown
Francis M. Oates	Yale
Joseph G. Pfeffer	Georgetown
John J. Rice	Holy Cross
Daniel E. Richardson	Wesleyan, CT
Richard C. Schmidt	Georgetown
Sean M. Spearing	Saint John's, Collegeville

The Priory Journal comments:

> It is clear, first of all, that what we have expected of the boys in the way of study is, provided that we have the cooperation both of them and of their parents, a perfectly realistic goal. It is far worse for a boy to be underworked than to be fully extended, and there is so much built-in sales resistance that there is little danger of serious strain. The same is true of what we have expected in the way of behavior and discipline, though here the cooperation of the parents is even more important. Boys can be spoilt, and are, in any country of the world, but perhaps there is more opportunity for doing so where the standard of living is high.
>
> It is also clear that our graduates are quite acceptable to representative colleges and universities across the land, though much remains to happen before anything like a final verdict on this can be given, and meanwhile there is no room for complacency.
>
> It is a reasonable claim, then, that the record of the first class has fully justified the supporters of the school in their confidence, but neither they nor the faculty would doubt for a moment that a great deal is yet to be done and as far as the graduates are concerned, their present task is to stay in college.[146]

Were we content? In some ways, supremely. We had completed our first full school cycle from admission to graduation; we felt that our first class had coped amazingly well with the countless difficulties of a new school and had developed remarkably from what they were in September 1956; some of our seniors had won entry into some of the

---

[146] *SLPJ* III. 1. p.9

most famous colleges in the country, and they all had before them the possibility of an excellent college education; we had justified the confidence placed in us by the parents and by Inc and had shown that their dream could be and indeed had been realized; we had done all that we could to ensure that those of our graduates who were not going to Catholic schools were prepared in such a way that, as Catholics, they could benefit from and contribute to the life of those schools.

But we were also in a position like that of a good architect who turns from a traditional style to thin shell concrete. He may be pleased with his first building in the new style, but at the same time may recognize that he still has much to learn and that he can make many improvements to future buildings. But when all is said and done, these seniors and their teachers, especially those who had taught them for all four years, had grown up together in the school and bonded in an unrepeatable way. They had and have a unique place in our hearts. Other classes may have surpassed their achievements, but they can never supplant these men. There can be only one First Graduating Class.

✠

Part 2 Toward Independence: 1960 - 1973

INTRODUCTION

> Like a generation of leaves is a generation of men. One year's leaves the wind scatters on the ground, but then the branches, green with the coming of spring, grow a fresh set. And so with men. (Homer, *Iliad* vi. 146-49)

IN 1956 when we started the school, a generation of boys was four years; in 1958 when we opened our seventh grade but also maintained our ninth grade entry, it could be either four or six years; from September 1963 when we stopped our intake into the ninth grade and took boys only into the seventh, a generation of boys was six years.

So far in this history we have watched our first, four-year generation progress from admission to graduation, but that is not the end of the story even of them. We have kept up with the great majority of them on their way through college and in their later lives. We have already mentioned our Christmastide Day of Recollection for the most recent alumni.[147] As I write, Father Luke is away witnessing the marriage of the daughter of one of the members of that first class, and from that class itself we have married some, buried three,[148] baptized many of their children, and had countless friendly visits. When four of them graduated from Yale, Henry Hughes took Father Brendan and Father Timothy to their graduation. Many of that class and of later classes have given many of the monks hospitality in this and other countries, and even as far away as Japan.

Our first graduation was a milestone, and one that we can mark in this history by a slight change of style. Hitherto we have recounted the events year by year in more or less chronological order and in some detail. Henceforward we shall recount them thematically and in less detail. The first planning of a building, the first fund-raising meeting, the first entrance examination, the first football victory, the first graduation have a built-in excitement simply because they are the first; their repetition does not. Now, therefore, we propose to deal in turn with one topic at a time, and to carry our comments on each topic

---

[147] *See* p. 39 *above*.

[148] As at 31 December 1999.

from 1960 through our achievement in 1973 of independence from Ampleforth--our monastic Fourth of July.

CHAPTER 20

Monastic Life

The Monks

WE start with the monks. Our resident monastic community at the graduation in June 1960 consisted of the following monks, all from Ampleforth: Father Columba, Prior; Father Luke, procurator; Father Timothy, headmaster; Father Brendan, second master; Father Ian, head of the Junior House; Father Austin, who was appointed our first Sub-Prior at some time before October 1961; and Fathers Thomas, Augustine and Paul on the faculty; nine priests in all. Toward the end of June 1960 Father Brendan returned to England and in August Father Leonard Jackson came to replace him. He arrived on one of the hottest days of the summer wearing thick topcoat and hat and carrying an umbrella. As the song says, "There'll always be an England".

Brother Christopher Rush of Saint Louis,[149] had come to us in 1958, and entered the novitiate at Ampleforth in 1959.[150] He made his Simple Profession for three years on 22 September 1960 and his Solemn Profession three years later. Richard Allin of Chicago, after a brief postulancy with us, entered the novitiate at Ampleforth in September 1960 as Brother Benedict, and in due course became Father Benedict. So we started the new school year, 1960-61, with nine priests here in Saint Louis, and at Ampleforth one monk about to be simply professed and one novice.

In September 1962 we sent two men to the novitiate at Ampleforth: one in due course became Father Laurence Kriegshauser, but the other, George H. Morrison, Jr., left during the novitiate. The latter's departure was a particular sorrow to us as he was the first alumnus of our school to enter the novitiate, and our prayers were very much with

---

[149] For tables of monks sent from Ampleforth to Saint Louis and of Americans who tried their vocations as monks with us, see Appendices A 2a and 2b.

[150] A man who wants to join our community normally comes for a short visit or visits. If all goes well, he becomes a Postulant, or one who urgently seeks entry, then is clothed as a Novice and enters the Novitiate for at least a year, at the end of which he makes his Simple Profession of vows for three years. This period may be extended. After three or more years of Simple Vows, he makes his Solemn Profession of vows for life.

him. In 1963 we sent three men to the novitiate. All three were simply professed; all three left before Solemn Profession. One of them, however, went on to become a diocesan priest in Tucson, Arizona. In 1964 we sent two men, one of whom left the novitiate to become a priest of the London Oratory, the other left us in 1969 in a moment of high drama, flinging down the pen with which he was about to sign the renewal of his simple vows and following out of the church the young woman whom he later married.[151] In 1965 we sent Ampleforth two more men, one of whom was our alumnus J. Joseph Horan, Jr., and then one more man in each of the next two years, the man in 1967, Donald W. Bussmann, Jr., being likewise an alumnus. All told, including the three we had sent in 1957, we sent Ampleforth fifteen men, of whom two became and still are monks with us; one made his Solemn Profession with us but was later dispensed from his vows; two became priests elsewhere; the other ten returned to lay life. From September 1968 we were permitted to train our novices here, and between then and our independence in 1973 we had four more novices, none of whom persevered with us, but two became priests elsewhere. Offsetting these disappointments were two very happy events, the priestly ordinations on 23 September 1967 of Father Benedict Allin, who thus became our first American priest, and on 27 September 1969 of Father Laurence Kriegshauser. Nonetheless, the most significant and sobering fact is that after September 1966, although we had numerous candidates, we had no Solemn Professions until 31 August 1981. Our problem was retention, not attraction. This long drought caused the monastic equivalent of a generation gap to be added to the already existing nationality gap.

Any comment on our having sent our candidates to Ampleforth for their novitiate must start by recognizing first that it was at that time required by Canon Law and secondly that it was an act of great generosity on the part of the Ampleforth monks to take them: not only did they house and feed our novices; they also paid for their education while they were in England. That said, we may add that this low yield from the novitiate may well have been the saddest effect of the reduction of the number of founding monks to three from the original hope of nine. Had there been nine, we would surely have sought special permission to have our own novitiate here--even though a newly formed house is not the ideal place for a novitiate--

[151] 1969 was a black year for us. During it, in addition to this departure, Brother Christopher Rush asked to be dispensed from solemn vows, and Father Vincent Marron left the monastery and the priesthood.

and would have appointed at least one of the nine from the beginning to care for guests, postulants and novices. As it was, when our novitiate here opened in September 1969--nobody entered the novitiate in 1968--the duties of the novice master, which were assumed by the Prior, were not something for which we had been budgeting for many years but were added to his existing duties. His Council had reservations about this: it was a major addition to his many burdens, and it is not ideal for the same man both to be in charge of the novices and to have the final decision about them. It is preferable that the novice should have someone above the novice master to whom he can speak. But the advantages seemed to outweigh these reservations. Not until December 1973, when Father Laurence was appointed novice master with Father Vincent Wace as his associate, were we able to relieve Father Luke.

How much the low yield was due to the previously mentioned differences in nationality, temperament, temperature, humor, food and life-style between the Ampleforth monks and our candidates,[152] how much to our inexperience in discerning the spiritual readiness of young Americans, how much to other causes cannot be judged here. What was most distressing to us was that none of our three alumni persevered, and this had a most discouraging effect on those boys in the school who might have been considering a monastic vocation. There was also the Second Vatican Council (1962-65), after which, for whatever reasons, fewer people entered religious life and many who were already in that life departed from it.

Thus it gradually became clear that the attractive scenario proposed to us, that within five or ten years young Americans would be waiting in the wings eager to snatch the management of affairs out of our hands, was not to be realized. As none of us had ever completely believed in such a scenario, we were not unduly disappointed, but we did recognize that this difference between scenario and reality was of crucial relevance to our success and even to our survival. Later, whenever we turned our thoughts to long-range planning, vocations to the monastery were always our first consideration.

But one must also remember that our prospects often appeared to be quite rosy. Thus Father Columba could write with accuracy in our *Journal* for December 1964, "The young Saint Louis Priory monks, American by birth, now number eight," and in December 1965 they were all still there, with the addition of one postulant. Had they all persevered, some snatching of management might well have occurred.

---

[152] *See* pp. 153-54

We recognized, too, that there was a limit to the number of monks we could expect from Ampleforth. Father Nicholas Walford came to us from England in August 1961, but Father Augustine returned there in 1964. One of his last actions was to demolish a greenhouse with a sledgehammer. It may have been his happiest day here. His departure was balanced by the arrival from Ampleforth of Father Colin Havard just in time for the new school year 1964-65. In the summer of 1965 we were sent Father Miles Bellasis, whose abundant energy was welcomed by all of us; in 1967, when Father Luke was appointed Prior, Father Vincent Marron came out to take over the job of procurator, or business manager, but he was somewhat unsettled when he arrived here, and by April 1969 had decided to return to lay life.

Several of the men we were sent seemed to be in need of a change. Sometimes coming to Saint Louis worked wonders and gave them a new lease of life—Father Austin was a prime example of that—but not always. In no way is this to suggest that Ampleforth sent us its misfits; on the contrary, we were most generously treated. But it remains true that some temperaments and talents that do not greatly thrive in English soil may bloom wonderfully in the United States, some that thrive in England may wilt here, and in each case vice versa, and, also in each case, the blooming or wilting is hard to predict.

That same summer of 1969 saw the decision by Brother Christopher Rush, who had spent a year with the ecumenical community of Taizé in Chicago, that he was called to lay life rather than to an apostolate which he saw as the education of the affluent. It was the time when the call to social action and the preferential option for the poor were what appealed to young idealists like him--and they appealed to many older monks too. As part of our response to this we gave 10% of our strictly monastic earnings to various charities and asked Monsignor Slattery, when the parish was established, to use for the same purpose 10% of his rental payment. The Council in September 1969 suggested the undertaking of some small corporate act of denial. This started as the absence of beer from dinner on Mondays, to which later was added the substitution of a bowl of rice for the normal evening meal. The idea in each case was to give to the poor the money saved--the cost of the beer and the difference between the cost of a rice-bowl and that of a normal meal--and at the same time to remind ourselves of the many for whom rice was a normal meal. Not a major deprivation, but a little more than a token, and OXFAM and CAFOD, to whom we sent the money, were grateful.

That summer saw also the departure of Brother John Dahm, who had been assistant procurator to Father Vincent Marron. Then in

October 1969 Father Ian recognized, and we had to agree, that his eleven years in charge of the Junior House had brought him close to exhaustion and that he needed a change. He went away on sabbatical, expecting to return refreshed for the following school year. Father Miles took over the Junior House, with Father Colin, Mr. Wilkes and Mr. Geiss to help him.

But besides the two ordinations, there was another joy to balance the sorrows of 1969, and that was the arrival in October of Father Mark Haidy. He was to be an addition not to the school staff but to the monastic community. After his Ordination to the priesthood, he had been assigned to Ampleforth's parishes in England and Wales and so was able to contribute much to our liaison with Saint Anselm parish. Almost on arrival he had to go to hospital with severe hepatitis—indeed he may have brought it with him—but when he recovered, he was for the next eight years until his death on 21 June 1977 a lift to our spirits in ways that were unique to him. Whether celebrating Mass or partaking in a community meeting or just talking one to one, time and again, by some unexpectedness of diction or pronunciation (for example, "practising" to rhyme with "arising") or some originality of thought he relieved tension or threw light on a situation from an unusual direction.

In the following summer, 1970, Abbot Basil Hume withdrew Father Nicholas and sent us Father Ralph Wright to replace him. Then, early in 1971, Father Finbarr Dowling came out from Ampleforth to take over as disciplinarian from Father Leonard, who was anxious to be nearer his ailing sister and had also been tending to develop carbuncles toward the end of each school year. Father Finbarr had five months of overlap to see how discipline worked in Saint Louis, and then, when in the summer Father Leonard left us, took over that task in the school. At the same time as Father Leonard, we lost also Father Ian, who had been on sabbatical since October 1969. Much of that time he had spent with Father George Kosicki, C.S.B. and a charismatic group in Detroit and then in Dexter, Michigan, which much influenced his later career in England. The plan had been that he would resume his place at the head of the Junior House, but when he came back, we all sadly agreed that it would be better for him if he returned to England. Monks, parents and boys were greatly distressed at losing a monk who had been such a wonderful influence on the boys under his care. He came back for many visits, and specialized in giving Retreats to our alumni.

In the summer of 1972, when, because of our impending independence, all the monks from Ampleforth were asked to make up their minds whether to stay in Saint Louis or to return to Ampleforth,[153] Father Thomas decided to ask to return, after first taking a sabbatical in Alaska, where he had established a happy working relationship with Father Anderson Bakewell at Delta Junction. All the others decided to stay. In January 1973 Father Vincent Wace arrived, and in August was appointed Sub-Prior to relieve Father Austin. Father Vincent was the last monk to come from Ampleforth, because on 25 July 1973 we became a Conventual Priory, that is, an autonomous monastery independent of our founding abbey. This status has since been abolished in the English Benedictine Congregation, so now every monastery of ours must be either a dependent priory or an independent abbey. But at that time the status still existed, and meant that from then on we would be numerically and financially on our own. Inc's wonderful support indicated that finances would probably not be a crippling worry; but we were taking a considerable risk, or, if you will, putting firmly on the line our conviction that the foundation of the Priory was truly God's will, in committing ourselves to attracting enough American candidates to ensure that, without help from Ampleforth, we could indeed survive.

In summary, during the eighteen years of our dependence, 1955-1973, Ampleforth sent us nineteen men, of whom seven stayed here and twelve left us. Of the seven who stayed, Father Mark and Father Austin have since died. Of the twelve who left us, one remained in the United States for a while and then returned to England, two remained in the United States permanently, and the remaining nine went back to Ampleforth. By the end of the millennium, five of those nine had died. For details, see Appendix A 2a.

---

[153] When a dependent monastery becomes independent, the monks from the founding monastery, in this case the monks from Ampleforth, have the constitutional right to make an entirely free choice to stay where they are or to return to the founding monastery.

The Life of the Monks

THESE, then, were the men who were leading their monastic life at Saint Louis Priory. What was the nature of the life they led? In 1960 we were still getting up at 4.40 a.m. In May 1968 this was modified to 5.00 a.m., at which it stayed for the rest of our period. We had twenty minutes to wash, dress and get to choir in chapel or church.[154] There we prayed Matins and Lauds, which lasted about forty minutes. We then had two rounds of Masses, before or after which we made our meditation, or personal prayer, for at least thirty minutes. We then came back to choir for Prime and Terce, two of the Little, or shorter, Hours, and then went to breakfast. There were four class periods, the first of only thirty-five minutes, the others of forty-five, starting at 8.40 a.m. and lasting until 11.40 a.m., with a milk break of ten minutes in the middle. At 11.50 a.m. we had our Conventual Mass, at which the boys were always present, with the Little Hours of Sext before and None after. At 12.25 p.m. we went to lunch, for which we had a good appetite. Classes started again at 1.10 p.m. The Upper School had three classes of forty-five minutes and then athletics; the Junior House one class, athletics, and then the other two classes, the first of which lasted only forty minutes. The buses departed at 5.00 p.m. We prayed Vespers at 6.00 p.m., ate supper at

---

[154] Monks spend a substantial part of their time reciting in choir the Divine Office, which Saint Benedict calls *opus dei* or the work of God. This way of praying, which has ancient Jewish roots, consists of a hymn, psalms, readings, canticles, responsories and prayers and was at this time divided into eight Hours, with the intention that the monk should sanctify his day by turning to God in vocal prayer at a number of fixed points during the day, as the psalmist says, "Seven times a day I praise you" and "At midnight I will praise and thank you" (Psalm 118[119], 164 and 62). This was to lead him towards praying without ceasing (1 Thess. 5,17). The eight Hours were Matins, Lauds, Prime, Terce, Sext, None, Vespers and Compline and were said at times corresponding as nearly as possible to the hours of the Roman day: Prime at the first hour, or about 7.00 a.m., the next three at about 9.00 a.m., noon and 3.00 p.m. respectively, Vespers in the evening and Compline (*completorium*) to complete the day. Prime, Terce, Sext and None are the Little Hours. In Saint Benedict's time, Matins was said between 2.00 and 3.00 a.m. and Lauds at daybreak. Before Vatican II most Benedictine houses had Matins quite early in the morning rather than during the night, and Lauds a little later. After Vatican II the whole schedule was greatly modified.

6.30 p.m. and then sat and talked for as long a time as we could spare. Our last prayer was Compline, the church's night prayer, at 8.30 p.m., after which there was the *summum silentium*, or complete silence in the monastery, and we aimed to put out our lights at 9.30 p.m. There were slight changes on days when we had no school, and larger changes at the weekend, when we got up later.

Supporting this daily round and providing an opportunity to reflect on it was the annual Retreat for the monastic community. Many but not all of those who gave us our Retreat were Benedictines. We also had Jesuits--and once a team of them--other religious priests, and clergy from the Archdiocese.[155] The usual time was late in August, but we experimented also with early June and even with the few days after term before Christmas.

A monk who was not an administrator would be in the classroom for four or five periods a day, and might, in addition, be coaching or in charge of an activity. There was a little unoccupied time between breakfast and the first class, a little after lunch, an hour or so between the end of the school day and Vespers and a little more than that before Compline. There were also the two or three periods during which he was not teaching, and the athletic period, if he was not coaching. Into those spaces had to be squeezed half an hour of *lectio divina*, or divine reading, then preparation of classes, correction of homework and the performance of miscellaneous chores. The first casualty tended to be personal chores such as laundry, sewing on buttons and writing letters to family and friends in England, along with time for recreation. We who had been teaching in a boarding school at Ampleforth and had consequently come to Saint Louis in favor of having a boarding school here, gradually came to see the boy-free, or more or less boy-free, week-ends as almost essential to our sanity and survival.

This load presented us then, and still does now, with problems more serious than unsewn buttons. Every individual needs time off for recreation, but, when there is so much to be done, and especially when the doing involves the needs of people, it is hard to take the time for recreation without feeling guilty. Things and papers can wait, up to a point; people often cannot or will not. This is one of the regular causes of burnout, especially in the caring professions, of which that of monk-educator is one. Besides, the first monks to come from Ampleforth easily saw the need for a special effort at the beginning in order to get the monastery and school going. It was not nearly so easy

---

[155] For a complete list of Retreat Givers through 1999, see Appendix C 1.

to prevent the special level of effort from becoming habitual. This was to some extent a matter of delegation, and neither Father Luke nor Father Timothy was particularly good at that. Consequently each continued to do things which he had had to do at the beginning, because there was no one else, but did not have to continue to do later, when help was available. The Ampleforth monks were, in addition, heirs to an especially Amplefordian tradition of hard work. There has always been a large element of discipline in monastic life: some monks have eaten very little, others have prayed for very long hours; for Ampleforth the traditional discipline was hard work.

At a level more immediate than that of these long-term problems, it was very difficult to put out one's light at 9.30 p.m. The phone did not ring often after Compline—we did also manage to establish a Sunday telephone truce—and so it was possible to do an hour's work in an hour. There was, therefore, a strong temptation to go on working at this time, but if one yielded to it and went on working after 9.30 or even after 9.15, then either one got up for Matins next morning and became increasingly weary, or one did not, and risked becoming increasingly lax.

Besides personal chores and recreation, there was also some difficulty over communication, whether on personal matters or on matters of business. This had been less of a problem so long as there were only a few of us and we had talked at all meals, though even then we seldom talked shop at table. But once there were enough of us to have reading at supper—at lunch we were eating with the boys—all forms of communication became more difficult. Regular meetings of various kinds enabled us to achieve at least the essentials of official communication, but personal communication, which is as necessary in a religious community as in a marriage, demands a certain leisurely spaciousness, which was hard to come by.

We gradually came to see that meetings of the whole monastic community were necessary, however difficult it might be to find time for them. This necessity remained even after the formation in May 1967 of a local Council to advise the Prior and of a local Conventual Chapter[156], at which all the solemnly professed monks transacted monastic business, their decisions being subject to approval by Ampleforth. Our experience showed that we were not skilled in communicating at meetings of all the monks, and gradually the idea of a professional facilitator gained ground. A variant on meetings of the whole community was when we broke up into small groups. But

---

[156] *See above*, p. 18, footnote 11.

there were those who empathized with the joke that was going around at the time, in which at the Last Judgement, the decision was, "Come, you whom my Father has blessed, take for your heritage the kingdom prepared for you since the foundation of the world[157]--and the rest of you go off into small groups." To someone looking back our hesitation may seem strange, but it was a time when some lay sensitivity sessions had had disastrous results, and even in some religious communities seemed to have done more harm than good. So our hesitation was not due simply to Anglo-Saxon reticence or British stiff-upper-lippishness.

There was a discussion by the Council on 16 July 1970 at which the importance of community meetings was stressed, but no decision was made whether they should be voluntary or not. In the Conventual Chapter of 31 August 1970 Father Prior observed that they could be a valuable way of establishing our goals. A year later, at the Conventual Chapter of 28 August 1971 it was agreed "that a professional man might come and talk to the community about this, although the non-secular nature of our community must be kept in mind."[158] Both Council and Chapter also raised the possible dangers of such a procedure. As a result of the discussion in Chapter, Mr. Wally Andrews came out and talked to the community. Several of the monks were interested, and so, on 5 October 1971 the Council discussed the matter again, focusing first on the topics that might be discussed. These, in order of preference, were: "To get to the heart of what God wants of us now; to get to know one another better and to learn to communicate; questions relating to monastic government (Prior's role, co-responsibility); the role of each monk in community responsibility; and questions concerning our prayer, work and recreation."[159]

The Council was against sensitivity sessions, but felt that we had two choices: to invite a professional facilitator to act as a catalyst, or to attempt to facilitate ourselves "with no other help than our own good will and the Holy Spirit".[160]. Later in October, the community met in small groups, also to discuss possible topics for discussion. Substantially they agreed with the council, but added: the role of the *Rule* in our community; vocations; our works--should they be more diverse?--and our relation to those involved; the role of priesthood in

---

[157] Matthew 25:34.

[158] *Minutes*, #3.

[159] *Council Minutes*, 5 October 1971.

[160] *Ibid.*

our lives; the ability to receive love; leisure. This shows what was on our minds in the early seventies. It must be added that, although it did not show up in this context, social justice was a hot topic with many of the monks. Our general policy was to raise consciousness of it as much as we could in the school, but to be watchful that outside work did not absorb so much time and energy as to reduce our effectiveness as teachers.

Other matters on our mind in December 1972 were reflected in a list of problems placed before the members of the Council to be considered and then discussed later: independence as an abbey or as a priory; hiring of teachers to replace monks who might return to England; the need of an operating budget; the position of the novice master; vacation arrangements for the future; public relations; relations with Saint Anselm Parish; a professional financial plan and projection for the future; over-busyness; monastic prayer. As we go on, we shall see how we dealt with these. In matters of this sort we did not move hastily, and it was not until some years later, and after the end of our period, that a professional facilitator did come out. But at least our leisureliness meant that there was something much closer to consensus than if we had made a more impetuous decision. We also tried to foster communication through communal activities. There is an old joke in which the parents are saying to their child, "We brought you to the seaside to enjoy yourself, and enjoy yourself you shall." But one cannot mandate either enjoyment or friendly communication. We were fortunate in discovering on television a program that appealed to the whole community and was on at a time when we could all be there, so we enjoyed together Alfred Hitchcock's half-hour on Saturday evening. We liked the program for its own sake, but it also tickled our funny-bone that a man trained by the Jesuits not that far from Ampleforth in England should be entertaining a group of Ampleforth Benedictines so far from his home and ours. That program kept us going for as long as it lasted, and was then succeeded in our affections by *Get Smart* ; but whatever came after that lost us.

Another instance of communal celebration was our Christmas. It varied slightly over the years, but typically we started with a half-day of recollection on Christmas Eve or a day or two before, celebrated Midnight Mass, with light refreshments after, and then our Conventual Mass in the morning. Until the changes in the liturgy, each priest also fitted in one or two other Masses. After that we visited our friends, especially members of Inc, and then came back, prayed Vespers and went to our Christmas dinner, embellished with Christmas pudding from England. After it we repaired to the calefactory[161], or common room, where we had heavier refreshments and opened presents. Then we might watch a movie or have some other form of entertainment. And so to bed.

Much later, the coming of the VCR enabled us to select communal programs for Saturday or Sunday evenings. But the interlocking problems of overload, communication and recreation are with us still, never insurmountable and never fully resolved. They and our various attempts to solve them will recur in our narrative.

Our monastic life is guided in general by Saint Benedict's *Rule*; more specific guidance is provided by the *Constitutions*, which apply to all the monasteries of the English Benedictine Congregation; the most specific guidance comes from the *Customary*, which is peculiar to each monastery. For most of our period, the customs of Ampleforth were so ingrained in us that there was no need to have our own *Customary*, but toward the end of it the number of men living in the monastery who knew nothing of Ampleforth was growing, and our life itself was diverging from that of Ampleforth. In September 1973 the Monastic Life Committee was given the task of compiling a *Customary*, and in due course carried it out, but after our period.

At about the same time Father Luke proposed that we provide a little hermitage in the woods, where monks could withdraw for the inside of a day for prayer and recollection. The Council welcomed the idea, though with a touch of sorrow that neither church nor monastery could be such a place, and a touch of concern about vandalism. This project, too, was realized, but not until later.

One thinks of monastic life as being lived by monks, and so it is; but almost every monastery attracts a group of lay people who want, if not to live monastic life to the full, at least to have some share in it. This desire may be met by forming groups of non-resident oblates. Another way is to make some of these lay people "*Confratres*", or "brothers with us". To be chosen as a *confrater* one should have shown notable friendship for the monks, connection with and support of the monastery, and appreciation of our way of life. These can be demonstrated in a variety of ways. There is a brief ceremony of induction, and the new *confrater* is urged to share in our life of prayer and in the sacraments in a way consonant with his situation.

---

161 Warming place. In ancient monasteries it was the place with the fire. The scriptorium was next door so that the scribes could come into the calefactory to warm their hands for copying manuscripts.

Women are just as eligible as men, but have never been called "*consorores*", or "sisters with us".[162]

[162] A list of our *confratres* through 1999 may be found in Appendix A 2c.

Archdiocesan Synod

THE new school year opened in September 1960. In October there arose from an entirely unexpected source a major threat to our well-being. Although the immediate threat was to the school, the principle concerned the monastery too, and so we recount it here.

Every ten years or so, each Catholic diocese and archdiocese holds a synod, which meets and deliberates over a draft of the Statutes, which, until the next synod, are to regulate the life of the archdiocese in many areas, including education. These Statutes are normally a useful rather than an exciting document. In October 1960, we duly received copies of the draft statutes and nearly took them as read, but fortunately Father Timothy decided to inspect the section on education and compare it with the previous Statutes, which we had been given on our arrival in 1955. To his dismay, he found a major alteration. Whereas the previous Statutes read,

> "103. Parish and diocesan schools are subject to the supervision of the Archdiocesan School Office in all fundamental regulations regarding, for example, the school calendar, curriculum, textbooks, examinations and certification of teachers"

the new draft read,

> "188. The Archdiocesan Superintendent of Schools will have supervision of all formal Catholic education in the first twelve grades. 189. Elementary and secondary schools within the Archdiocese engaged in the apostolate of education will be subject to the Archdiocesan School Office in academic matters.
>
> Examples of this are such items as curriculum, text-books, examinations, and the certification of teachers."

The simple omission of three words, "parish and diocesan", seemed to place under the control of the Archdiocesan Superintendent not only our school but also those of other religious such as the Jesuits, the Religious of the Sacred Heart, the Christian Brothers, the Marianists and more. It also involved the whole complex and disputed question of the exemption of religious from diocesan control.[163] Under instructions from Father Columba, Father Timothy conducted extensive research in Saint Louis University's library. At the same time we enlisted the expertise of Father Cuthbert Wilson, a canon lawyer from Fort Augustus Abbey in Scotland, who happened to be in Florida for the sake of his health, and of other experts. We kept Abbot Herbert fully informed, and also alerted the Jesuits and others.

Armed with the results of these men's labors, Father Columba, emulating the character in *My Fair Lady*,[164] wrote a masterly letter "oozing charm from every pore" in which he indicated with clarity and firmness the necessary legal points, but without forcing the prickly issue of the exemption of religious.[165] In due course the draft statutes were amended and schools run by religious were left as they had been. This was a good example of the complementary strengths of Father Columba and Father Timothy working together.

---

[163] It was truly a complex question. Our Benedictine advisors in Rome felt that, although the present resolution of it favored exemption, Roman opinion was uncertain on the subject and it would be better to let sleeping dogs lie. We should therefore proceed cautiously and avoid a confrontation.

[164] A. J. Lerner and F. Loewe, *My Fair Lady*, 1956.

[165] For the complete text, *see* Appendix D 1.

The Priory Church

WHILE this was going on, we were also negotiating with the School Office about our entrance examinations, as will be recorded in its place;[166] and while both negotiations were going on we were planning the construction of the Priory church.

The members of the Mudd family, that is, Mrs. Paul F. (Muddie) Fletcher, Mr. Dayton H. Mudd and J. Gerard Mudd, M.D., had offered to give us our church, and had made it a condition of their gift that the whole church would be built at one time. They were, by now, anxious to start construction. Early in 1960, we brought the plans out of cold storage[167], and by March they were nearly ready to be put out for bids. Hellmuth, Obata and Kassabaum's estimate was $500,000. On 30 June we opened the bids: the lowest was from McCarthy Brothers for $538,947,[168] and this was about $100,000 lower than the next lowest.

So great a gap is quite unusual, and there is a story behind it. Mr. John McCarthy, head of the firm, took one look at the specifications and threw them into the trash can. Mr. Paddy McCarthy, John's nephew, pulled them out and, with his brother, Mr. Tim McCarthy, took a quick look. They saw enough to be interested and even excited. They asked for permission to do some figuring and were told that they might, "but not on company time." They did their figuring and concluded that they could use Gunnite, a new process by which the concrete was shot on with a gun. They could then use a single form instead of the double forms which all the other contractors planned to use, and that made their bid so much lower.

Our difficulty was that even that bid was still nearly $40,000 over what the Mudds had promised us, and the cost of the furnishings (choir stalls, pews, etc.) was still to come. By mid-July, the Mudds had raised their promise to $560,000, and we decided to go ahead. On 23 July we held a simple ceremony of ground-breaking with Father Columba officiating in a white cope, Father Luke carrying the cross and Gerry Mudd the spade. On 11 August 1960 construction began.

---

[166] *See below*, pp. 296-97.

[167] *See* pp. 144-47 *above*.

[168] Father Columba's diary has the figure $581,000, but the signed bid contract is on file with the figure given in the text. There is no way of telling how long after the event Father Columba wrote this entry in his diary. It is possible that he mis-remembered 538 as 583 (or 581), but more probably he was including an estimated cost of the furnishings.

The piles for the foundations, in the shape of inverted Vs, had to reach down fifteen or twenty feet to hit bedrock. They were to provide the twenty *points d'appui* on which the whole structure was to rest. This was a type of construction not unlike that of the interesting building we saw at M.I.T.[169] The earth was compacted, the partial crypt built, and by the end of the year we reached the most exciting part: the construction of the parabolic arches. The first element was a massive scaffold to support the forms for the upper and lower arches of five bays, that is, one quarter of the church. It was so designed that each form of the five pairs of forms could be removed independently. The scaffold was then sheathed in heavy plywood bent into parabolic shape, to the outside of which was then attached the reinforcing steel. The concrete was to be shot on with a gun and had to be only just moist enough to flow through the gun, otherwise, even with the support of the reinforcing steel, it would not set on the sloping sides of the forms, which, near ground level, were almost vertical. As the concrete was shot on, men with long, straight-edged boards smoothed it. At the base of each arch the concrete is two feet thick, at the top, only three inches.

McCarthy's men started with the central bay of the five which made up the southwest quadrant, working from ridge to ridge, not from valley to valley. The forms, on the other hand went from valley to valley,[170] and so the builders had to pour not only one complete bay, but also half of each of the bays on either side of it. The nozzle of the gun clogged from time to time and had to be rinsed, but in due course they finished the pouring, or rather shooting, of the first bay and its two adjacent half-bays, and waited for the concrete to set. When it had set, they needed to remove the upper and lower forms of the central bay. They tried, but nothing happened: the forms were firmly stuck to the underside of the concrete. Not until they bored a hole in the concrete and blew in compressed air did the forms come free. After that they copiously greased the upper surface of the forms before starting to shoot the concrete. When they had finally extracted the first pair of forms, they added them on at the right end of the structure, then the next one on the right of that, and so on until eventually they completed the circle.[171] The concrete arches were supported on the

---

[169] *See above*, p. 72.

[170] *See* plate 12.

[171] Memories differ whether they went clockwise or counter-clockwise, but one monk remembers the meeting of the bays occurring in the northwest, in which case they would have gone counter-clockwise.

inside by enormous telephone poles until the arches and the two massive ring beams, one between the two sets of windows and the other between the upper set and the tower, were all complete. There is so much reinforcing steel in these two ring beams that it was hard to force the concrete down into place. The first quarter of the church was poured by 23 March 1961. By the end of April, the pouring was nearly half done and on Friday 23 June it was completed, leaving only the tower still to do. When all the concrete was set, the moment came for the removal of the supporting telephone poles. If the church was going to collapse, that was when it would do so. The poles were removed and the downward movement, if any, was imperceptible.

Meanwhile, in May, we had chosen Mr. Emil Frei, a Saint Louisan and a noted designer of stained glass, as our artistic advisor for the interior of the church. He was to advise us about artists and designs for crucifixes, tabernacle, sanctuary lamp and so on. On 1 September pouring started for the tower and on 6 September it was completed, with Father Luke's hand on the nozzle for the final shots. The church-to-be was turned for a short time into a beer garden in celebration of that milestone. On 22 September 1961 a helicopter hoisted the Cross into position at the top of the tower, bringing the total height of the church to 99 feet. Its diameter is 134 feet. The height of the lower ring of windows is 24 feet, of the upper, 18; the height of the tower, 30 and of the Cross, 24. [172]

It then remained to finish the predella, or platform for the altar, and to install the altar, a massive monolith of Georgia granite. It took the men most of a day to bring it into the church; when it was in place, they put cement around its base, presumably to prevent its removal. Then they had to finish the ducts for the heating, fit the lights, lay the tiled floor, part of which contained pipes for radiant heat, and bring in the choir stalls and several rows of pews. The latter were at first going to be rectilinear, but at the last moment the makers found that they could, after all, make them curved. Rectilinear pews would have looked incongruous in a church with few other straight lines.

At the end of September 1961 we received, through the good offices of Mr. and Mrs. Otto L. Spaeth, the gift, from Mr. and Mrs. James B. Mabon of New York, whom we had never met, of a wooden statue of the Madonna and Child, carved in Burgundy in the Gothic style in the early fourteenth century. Its simplicity fitted in very well with the simplicity of the interior and helped us to solve the problem

---

[172] The missing three feet are accounted for by the upward slope from the windows in towards the center.

of a Lady Chapel in a round church. Somewhat later, in 1963, but appropriately mentioned here, we received from the same Mr. and Mrs. Spaeth the gift of a beautiful Christmas Crib. The figures and ensemble were made in Naples at the end of the sixteenth century and much of the clothing is original, though some has had to be restored. The pillars and steps were designed by the Metropolitan Museum of New York.

Then we heard of a peal of five bells from Saint Mark's Episcopal Church in New Canaan, Connecticut, and after Father Luke and Dayton Mudd had gone there, listened and approved, we obtained them. They were blessed on 10 March 1962 with Mr. Robert Speaight reading the psalms in English while we sang them in Latin. The Kalwall windows had not yet been installed and so the wind sweeping through the church made it bitterly cold inside, and the light pouring in made it dazzling.[173] The hanging of the bells was completed on 10 April. Their names are Benedict, Frederick, Joseph, Jerome and Edward, the last four being for the Switzer brothers. The first and largest is named for Saint Benedict and is, not surprisingly, sometimes called Big Ben. The Kalwall windows[174] were seriously delayed, but arrived in the end. Their absence at least brought home to us that we needed their shelter and opacity to make the inside of the church tolerable.[175]

There were side-altars at the perimeter in most of the bays, as this was before Vatican II and each priest still celebrated his own private Mass each day. When, in 1968, concelebration became normal for us, we thought of removing the side-altars, but the adhesive used to keep them in place was so strong and the labor of removing them so great, as we discovered when we needed to remove the Blessed Sacrament altar from the back of our choir, that we let them remain in place. Not the least advantage of doing so was that the crucifixes remained with them. These were from the hands of an international group of artists: Robert Adams and Leslie Thornton of England; Jean Lambert-Rucki of France; Gerhardt Marcks of Germany; Luis Sanchez of Spain; and Wolfgang Behl, Doris Caesar, Clark Fitzgerald, William Schickel and Rudi Torrini of the United States. Emil Frei designed and his son

---

[173] This increased our appreciation of what Saint Benedict Biscop had done for the monks of Northern England in the seventh century, when he brought glaziers from France to place glass in the church windows.

[174] *See above*, p. 187.

[175] By day, the windows look black and the concrete shell white; by night, if the lights are on in the church, the windows look white and the shell black.

Robert, with Messrs. Lester Syberg and Charles Statts, executed the choir screen, but the crucifixes and the screen came later.

On the outside of the church, after two battles royal between the contractors and Father Luke, won by Father Luke, two coats of waterproofing were applied to the roof,[176] which was then given a series of coats of paint, each of a different color and all applied by hand. After each coat, black, red lead and gray, the church looked so fine that we were sorry to pass on to the next. Similarly the church, now resplendent in white, looks equally fine against blue sky, or white clouds, or the livid and louring background of a thunderstorm. On the inside, the plaster, also applied by hand, was skillfully smoothed with a bathroom sponge, giving an elegant swirl finish.[177] Few churches can have been hand-finished inside and out so many times as ours. An architect called it "a Gothic arch in three dimensions" and Abbot Herbert, "a song in concrete."

Dedication had been set for 7 September, and almost everything was ready. Almost everything, but not quite. There were two last-minute hurdles to leap: the first was that at the eleventh hour, or even later, there arose a contretemps which could occur only in a liturgical context. The rite of consecration calls for the bishop to consecrate the church by anointing with chrism twelve crosses attached to its walls, "But," said the liturgists, "your church has no walls; it is all roof and floor, and therefore cannot be consecrated." The architects came to our rescue by deciding that the main ring beam , by holding up the roof, performed the function of a wall, and the crosses were attached to it. When the bishop said he was certainly not about to clamber up scaffolding to bless crosses, we traced token crosses on the inside of the bays and within reach of the ground. Thus the real crosses were blessed by proxy. The second problem was less a problem than a happy solution. It seemed that the stools for the ministers and servers would not arrive in time, so we had put out in church our best kitchen chairs, which added nothing to the décor. Strong pressure on the factory by the manufacturer's representative seemed to be having no

---

[176] Despite these victories, in the summer of 1965 the roof needed considerable repair. Over the winter it had developed faults. There were many hours of consultation, field inspections and laboratory tests, which led to spot checks all over the roof and in the basement. The areas where the waterproofing had failed were cut out and replaced, and a new coat of waterproofing applied, fortunately all under warranty.

[177] Most of this elegant swirl was lost when the church was refurbished and the interior repainted in the nineties.

effect until at 4.00 p.m. on 6 September, the day before the consecration, we heard that the stools were ready--in Wisconsin. Mr. James C. McKelly, Jr., son of the manufacturer's representative, set off at once to drive to Janesville, Wisconsin. Early next morning as we were saying Matins, Father Luke looked up, and there was Jim's station wagon, very much down at the stern, plowing towards the church. Our chairs were returned to the kitchen and the designer stools put in their place.

Mr. Christian B. Peper and Mr. Henry J. Mohrman, the latter being the future Father Gregory Mohrman's father, had completed a translation into English of the new Rite of Consecration, and had made it into a handsome booklet with the Latin and English texts in parallel columns. This was given to all those present at the consecration, and, together with an unobtrusive live commentary by Father Aloysius F. Wilmes of the Archdiocese, made the lengthy ceremony "user-friendly".

Abbot Herbert arrived from Ampleforth on the morning of Monday 3 September and proceedings started that afternoon with the consecration by Father Columba of the Blessed Sacrament altar at the back of the choir and of the five side-altars on the south side of the church. On Tuesday, Father Richard Wright and Father Robert Coverdale arrived from Ampleforth. They had been the reconnaissance party sent in 1954 by the Ampleforth community to spy out the land before the Chapter at Ampleforth voted on the acceptance or rejection of the invitation to come to Saint Louis.[178] On Wednesday, Abbot Herbert consecrated the five side-altars on the north side of the church.

On Friday 7 September, before some six hundred and fifty laity, one hundred clergy, twenty abbots and many distinguished ecumenical guests, Bishop Glennon P. Flavin, then Auxiliary Bishop of Saint Louis, knocked on the door of the church and was admitted, with his retinue and all the faithful, by the *ad hoc* "custodian of the church", Father, now Monsignor, Robert L. McCarthy, brother of McCarthy Brothers, the contractors. Once inside, the bishop duly consecrated the church and the high altar. This was followed by the first pontifical High Mass in the new church, celebrated by Abbot Herbert , who also preached. Cardinal Ritter was able to be present for it, and spoke at the end, after which all adjourned for luncheon on the lawn. There our guests included Bishop George L. Cadigan of the Episcopal Diocese of Missouri, Doctor Edgar C. Taylor, Honorary

---

[178] *See* p. 23 *above*.

Canon of Christ Church Cathedral, Bishop Eugene M. Frank of the Methodist Church, Rabbi Ephraim Epstein, President of the Rabbinical Association of Saint Louis, Doctor Edwin T. Dahlberg, former President of the World Council of Churches, and Doctor G. Curtis Jones and Doctor O. Walter Wagner of the Metropolitan Church Federation of Saint Louis.[179]

Saturday was the day for some four hundred and fifty religious sisters and Sunday that for the laity. Bishop Leo C. Byrne, by then Coadjutor Bishop of Wichita, preached on Saturday, Bishop Albert R. Zuroweste of Belleville on Sunday. On each of the three days, the Mass was followed by a luncheon in a marquee on the lawn east of the Stannard House. On the Saturday there were twelve Sisters of Mercy sitting at a round table with their bonnets almost meeting in the middle, a memorable sight, especially from above. Finally, on Sunday 16 September there was an Open House for all the men who had worked on the church and for their families. The master gunner of the gunnite gun, who had held the nozzle during the whole of the operation, remarked to Father Luke, "You will have to say a mighty lot of prayers in this church to make up for all the cusses uttered during its construction."

The church won awards both for the design and for the reality. Its design was "commented on very favorably in many national publications including *Liturgical Arts* and *Architectural Forum*," [180] and won awards from *Progressive Architecture Magazine*, the Church Architectural Guild of America and the Unit Masonry Association of Metropolitan Saint Louis. It was one of twenty-six winners, out of seven hundred entries, of a P/A award for projects in architectural design, urban design/planning, and research, from a panel of five that included Messrs. I. M. Pei and Felix Candela. In 1963, after completion, it won the top award in the annual "Design in Steel" competition, and much other acclaim. It was intended to be, and is, the principal architectural attraction on our campus.

Many people had seen the church on television and a high percentage of them came out to see the real thing, especially at weekends. Mostly they were content simply to take photographs and look around by themselves, but monks who happened to be visible

---

[179] At the luncheon, Father Columba welcomed them as O.S.B., meaning by that not "Order of Saint Benedict" but "Our Separated Brethren", a *bon mot* which they enjoyed.

[180] SLPJ III. 1, p. 2-3. Other information was kindly supplied by Ms. Shirley Henn of HOK.

were asked many questions. In May 1963 the local chapter of The American Institute of Architects arranged a visit that brought some four hundred connoisseurs to the church. Father Luke explained all to them.

In 1965 and 1966 there were many meetings among ourselves and many suggestions from others about acoustics, and nearly as many about a screen behind the choir. This would define that space and the general axis of the church, and spare those who entered the church by the east door the embarrassment of seeming to arrive in the midst of the monks at prayer. The screen of translucent stained glass of various shades of green was duly designed, and was installed in 1966.

Dealing with the acoustics was much harder. As our *Journal* for December 1964 prophetically remarked, "Acoustics remain a problem."[181] The church has a resonance of about seven seconds, which enhances instrumental music and singing, but impairs all but the most carefully enunciated reading and preaching. After lengthy consultations between HOK and the leading acoustical firm in the country at that time, Bolt, Beranek and Newman of Boston and M.I.T., a system was installed. It greatly improved the chance of hearing the spoken word in church, but without achieving complete satisfaction. The final adjustment of their system was made in December 1966, but even after that it was never easy to hear, unless the church was full. Acoustics remained a major problem until the nineties. We should add, in fairness to our consultants, that we were unwilling to carpet the floor, which would certainly have helped the acoustics, and hesitant even about cushioning the benches, which would also have helped, though to a lesser extent.

The next major addition to the church was not made until 1967. This was the organ. An outstanding church called for an outstanding organ, but how were we to choose? Even before the building of the church we had made some investigations, and when the church was being planned we made provision, on the east side of the interior, for the largest pipes to be dropped through the floor into the basement. We were blessed in having the wise advice of Doctor Thomas Harmon, himself an organist, who turned our thoughts towards Europe. There we made contact with Herr Gregor Hradetsky, whose firm at Krems-on-the-Danube in Austria built our organ. He was already well known in Austria, but ours was his first instrument in the United States, as well as being one of the first fully baroque organs in our area. It has a mechanical tracker action with low wind-pressure and slider-type

---

[181] SLPJ IV. 1, p. 6.

windchests, all of which give the organist more delicate control.[182] It has over 1400 pipes.

It arrived in an enormous container on 3 August 1967. There came also two *monteurs*, Herr Gerhardt Hradetsky, Gregor's son, and Herr Oswald Wagner to assemble and voice it. This took them six weeks, working often sixteen or seventeen hours a day. It was worth it. The organ was blessed at our Conventual Mass on the morning of Sunday 17 September and was played first by Doctor Thomas Harmon, and then by Doctor Marie Kremer, who also conducted the Saint Louis Chorale. In the evening Doctor Harmon, as was fitting, gave a recital to put the organ through its paces. On 17 November our Mothers' Club organized another magnificent recital, this one by the internationally renowned French organist, Marie-Claire Alain. Ever since, it has given us wonderful service both in daily use and at recitals. It flatters the average player and extends the maestro.

The other important question was air-conditioning. The Mudd family was opposed to it, and we went along with them; and, because of the expense, we did not adopt the suggestion of putting the ducts in place in case we later changed our mind. Much perspiration, combined with strong pressure from the parish from as early as 1972, led us to install air-conditioning in the 1980s. The monks had neither enthusiasm for nor opposition to the project, provided that the parish paid for it, that it did not mar the beauty of the church, and that the parish claimed no equity in it.[183]

---

[182] A more complete description, based on SLPJ V. 1 pp. 8-10 and our pamphlet, *Saint Louis Abbey: A Guide to the Church* pp. 9-10, may be found in Appendix C 2.

[183] *Council Minutes*, 7 March 1972.

The Divine Office

ONE of the disadvantages of dealing with our story topic by topic is the loss of a sense of simultaneity. We have described the dedication of the church; it will be some little time before we reach on paper the beginning of that school year. But for us who lived through that time, the events connected with the new church ended on Sunday 9 September and the boys arrived for the new school year on Thursday 13 September after all the preparation that a new school year entails. Not that this simultaneity is peculiar to monk-schoolmasters; it links their lives to those of mothers, housewives, executives, professionals and workers all over the world. We simply ask the reader to bear it in mind.

Our next monastic excitement was in the area of liturgy. In 1963, Benedictines everywhere had been reciting the Hours of the liturgical day, that is, the Divine Office, in the same form for several centuries, so the idea of change was no small shock.[184] Fortunately there were preliminary rumblings and tremors, warnings of the seismic events to come. For some decades, especially in northern Europe and in the United States, movements for liturgical reform had been gathering momentum. In general they aimed at greater participation by all who attended liturgical actions, especially the Mass, and at greater intelligibility, which in particular meant the use of clearer symbols, and of the vernacular rather than Latin.

There had already been little breakthroughs: a new and more intelligible Latin translation of the Psalms was produced under the aegis of Cardinal Augustine Bea and was authorized for use by those praying their Breviary in private; the requirement that all official translations of the Bible be made from the Vulgate and not from Greek or other versions was cancelled—just after Monsignor Ronald Knox had completed his *tour de force* of translating the Bible single-handed; and the rites of Holy Week were revised. This last set the ball rolling, slowly, it is true, but still rolling. The most spectacular result of this revision of the rites of Holy Week was the changes made to the Easter Vigil, which we experienced for the first time at Ampleforth in 1952. Neither the church in Italy, however, nor most of the officials of the Vatican were in the vanguard of these movements, so enthusiasts elsewhere were not unduly surprised when a document, *Veterum Sapientiae*, came from the Vatican in February 1962 maintaining the position of Latin as the universal language of the church.

---

[184] *See above*, p. 217 and footnote 154.

Then the Second Vatican Council, which, on 25 January 1959 had been unexpectedly announced by Pope John XXIII, opened on 11 October 1962. Its first completed work was the Constitution on the Sacred Liturgy (*Sacrosanctum Concilium*), which was promulgated on 4 December 1963. It called for "full, conscious and active participation in liturgical celebrations" by all the faithful. In other words, liturgy was to be an action by the people of God, not an action performed for them by the liturgical ministers; and conscious participation at least implied that the people understood what was going on, and that in turn implied the use of the vernacular.

In April 1963 Father Hans Küng, who had attended the first Session of the Council as a *peritus,* or expert, came to Saint Louis to give a talk on *The Church and Freedom*, which offered us a preview of what might come. Next, our National Liturgical Conference held its meeting for 1964 in Saint Louis. Some sixteen thousand people attended. It was a showcase for the kinds of change that might be expected as a result of *Sacrosanctum Concilium.* Father Columba wrote in our *Journal* that the conference "triumphantly broke through into the new world of the sharing by all God's People intimately in the action of the Mass . . . Some false starts are sure to be made. The prayer of many is that the period of experimentation be not cut short . . . "[185] This, he pointed out, was not a victory for new ways so much as a return to old ways.

After the Liturgical Conference we introduced into our Masses hymns sung in English, we read the Scripture passages in English, and started the so-called dialogue Mass, in which the whole congregation made certain responses. These first steps, modest as they seem now, were quite radical in the fall of 1964, and some found them unpalatable. One might have expected that monks, vowed as they are to lead a regular life, both in the normal sense of "orderly" and in the technical sense of life according to a *regula*, or rule, in our case the *Rule* of Saint Benedict, would have been more reluctant to accept change than laity, whose lives are compact of change. In practice, it was mostly the other way round.

There were no doubt many reasons for this: these changes came to us more gradually, often first as rumors; the decisions reached in Rome had to trickle down through the normal channels, and we might hear them gurgling as they trickled, whereas the first the laity might

---

[185] SLPJ IV. 1, p. 2.

know of them was that they were taking place in their parish.[186] In addition, monks had more training in liturgy and often had some awareness of both the sources and the aims of these changes; not very many of the laity at that time studied the liturgical literature. But no matter what the reason, it was our experience that it was often the laity who were more seriously upset than the monks over the Mass in English, or the priest facing the people, or Communion in the hand. This meant that we had to be especially aware of the need for careful and gradual catechesis to prepare the ground for any change.

Holy Week 1965 saw the introduction of some changes. The first was the use of some English, but not very much: on Good Friday, the Passion was read in our church in English by three readers, with occasional bursts of song from the crowd. The second was a major change: concelebration, in which we took part for the first time on Maundy Thursday. The boys were present. Concelebration means that the priests of a religious community, or the priests present, say, at a liturgical convention or at a diocesan Retreat, may all celebrate the same Mass at the same time. Almost all of us accepted this, some with some reservations. Later, when it became our daily practice, it had an immediate impact on our schedule, as we no longer needed to allow for two rounds of Masses in the early morning. All we needed was one Conventual Mass at which all the priests could concelebrate. There was still the need for Masses for the school, for the public, for Convents nearby and, in due course, for the parish, but all that the monks needed for themselves was one Mass a day. This meant that it was possible for us to get up a little later and to be less rushed in the early morning before school. Both were welcome.

In the summer of 1965 we started some gentle experimentation with the Divine Office in choir by reciting in English one of the psalms at Matins either on a single note or in a speaking voice. It soon became clear that there were in our monastic community one or two firebrands, who wanted as much change as possible as soon as possible and saw it as a liberation; one or two conservatives who wanted as little change as possible, perhaps even none, and saw it as a disruption; and the main body, composed of those who wanted to proceed, but with care—in other words, we were a miniature bell curve. Neither extreme was typically Benedictine. Although there are occasions when the superior has to decide, and that's that, we like change to be organic

---

[186] The Not In My Back Yard (NIMBY) syndrome is not unknown in modern parishes. It is long pre-dated by the English music-hall song, "Anywhere else, you can do that there, but you can't do that there 'ere."

and consensual. It should have its roots in what is already there, and should be such that all the monks can at least live with it even if they cannot be enthusiastic about it. This way calls for good will from everyone and discretion from the superior. On the whole, we conformed to this paradigm and avoided precipitate change, except perhaps that we threw out too much plainsong too swiftly, and introduced some music that was mediocre at best.[187]

In the summer of 1966--the summer was when we had most time for thinking of these things, and often during the summer it happened that the younger and, on the whole, more experimentalist members of the community were there in greater numbers than the rest—we made further experiments with psalms and hymns and even with where we stood or sat at Mass. But things moved slowly, partly because, as a dependent priory, we were not free to do whatever we decided without reference to the Abbot of Ampleforth.

As late as November 1967 Father Luke was writing to his parents, "We will be changing our Divine Office and almost certainly having it in English. I suspect that the morning office will be somewhat shorter." This came about in May 1968 when we started an interim revised Office, all in English except Vespers, and omitting Terce and None.[188] No monks went on strike, though some were sad about the high quantity of the vernacular, the low quality of the music and the lessening of structure and reverence. Others found Latin meaningless and were glad to see it go. This revision was further revised in August, by which time everything was in English, and a new booklet was prepared, to be brought into use at the annual Retreat in the second half of August. We also started singing the psalms to simple psalm-tones rather than reciting them on a single note, an improvement because we were better able to maintain pitch when singing than when reciting, especially in the early morning. At the Conventual Chapter, which immediately followed the Retreat, although there was some regret that Vespers had not remained in Latin, the community voted strongly in favor of the new Office as being more intelligible and

---

[187] Plainsong, plainchant and Gregorian chant are different names for the same body of church music. Palestrina, Bach, Mozart and many others have written great pieces of church music, but plainsong covers every day and every occasion of the church's year.

[188] Prime was still said on Easter Sunday, 1968, but memory records that it was dropped before Terce and None were. If so, it would have been dropped very soon after Easter; or it may even have been dropped before that and have been said especially for Easter.

more prayerful. This approval was renewed annually in Chapter through August 1972, after which it was apparently no longer an issue.

At the Chapter in 1969 we rejected a motion to subject the monks to a course from a professional voice-trainer but passed one to form a Liturgy Committee[189] which would issue a liturgical questionnaire, collate the feelings of the community, and make recommendations to the Prior. In due course[190] Fathers Colin, Finbarr and Laurence were chosen for this committee. Part of its function was to reduce the number of comments coming from individuals direct to the Prior: Father X would come and say we should have more Latin and then Father Y would come and say we should have none. If X and Y would not talk directly to one another, at least they could each lay their case before the committee, and there could be some discussion and possibly some meeting of minds..

Prompted by the mention of this committee, we may digress and comment on the role of committees in contemporary monastic life. They are not mentioned in Saint Benedict's *Rule*. The closest he comes is the Council of Seniors, which we have called the Prior's Council--in an abbey it is the Abbot's Council--and which has always been a feature of monastic life. From our earliest days here we had occasional *ad hoc* committees, especially in the school and for new buildings, but it was not until the late sixties that they began to proliferate. In monasteries, as everywhere else, there are two kinds of committee: standing and *ad hoc,* each of which has advantages and disadvantages. A good example of *ad hoc* was our committee on the amalgamation of the monastic and school libraries. Its charge was to recommend whether or not they should be amalgamated and if so, how. The committee did this and died. The advantage was that those who were most concerned and most knowledgeable spent the necessary time on the problem, thus saving the time and energy of those who were not. The committee's recommendation was submitted to the Prior and Council, and then, when they approved, to the Conventual Chapter, which also approved. The Prior then said that it should be done, and it was. Examples of standing committees were those on Liturgy and Music, Monastic Life, Vocations, and Donations

---

189 This idea had been raised in the Prior's Council as early as November 1967.

190 At the Conventual Chapter on 30 August 1971. The delay reflects partly our wariness about committees. It was not until the next year's Chapter that we fully accepted committees as one good way of forwarding the community's affairs.

to Charity. In 1972, the Council even discussed a committee "to study and present plans for implementing the committee approach to our community self-evaluation." [191]

Both kinds of committee can be useful for collecting information, for representing a variety of points of view, for making recommendations on major matters and for dealing with small matters or complaints with which the Prior should not be troubled. But, like committees anywhere else, although they can be extremely helpful, they can also become cliques or be dominated by one powerful personality; and in a monastic context, they can usurp powers that properly should be exercised by the Council. In political life, developed countries have been able to establish a system of checks and balances or, in other ways, to set limits to the powers of monarchs and presidents and to make dictators exceptional. Consequently, it is now the departments of government and the lesser bureaucrats who occasionally oppress the people. Similarly, in monastic life over the centuries our Constitutions have set limits to the powers of the superior in many areas, so that now, if any difficulties occur for the rank and file of the monks, it is more likely to be with committees or lesser officials. The Prior and the Council, therefore, proceeded with some caution, but there was no doubt that committees were establishing a foothold in our life. In August 1972 our Conventual Chapter voted unanimously for "pursuing the use of committees as a way of giving all a chance to share responsibility and of opening channels of communication."[192]

We now return to our narrative. In choir, most of the psalms were sung to new and simple tones, some were spoken by one man or by all, and plainsong virtually dropped out. The schedule for Holy Week 1968 will give an impression of where we were by then:

MAUNDY THURSDAY

6.10 a.m.	Rise
6.30	Morning Office
7.30	Breakfast
7.30	Parish Mass
12.15 p.m.	Terce, Sext, None
12.30	Lunch
4.00	Liturgy, Compline
6.30	Dinner

[191] *Council Minutes* for 29 August 1972.

[192] *Conventual Chapter Minutes* for 26-27 August 1972 #8.

GOOD FRIDAY	
6.25 a.m.	Rise
6.45	Morning Office
7.30	Breakfast
12.15 p.m.	Terce, Sext, None
12.30	Lunch
4.00	Liturgy, Compline
6.30	Dinner

HOLY SATURDAY	
6.25 a.m.	Rise
6.45	Morning Office
7.30	Breakfast
12.15 p.m.	Terce, Sext, None
12.30	Lunch
6.15	Vespers
6.30	Dinner
10.45	Easter Vigil and Mass

EASTER SUNDAY	
6.30 a.m.	Parish Mass
7.30	Parish Mass
8.20	Rise
8.40	Prime, Terce
9.00	Concelebrated Conventual Mass
10.00	Brunch
11.00	Parish Mass
2.15 p.m.	Sext, None
2.30	Refreshments - Sun Room
4.45	Vespers, Compline, Benediction
5.30	Dinner

From this it may be seen that Terce and None were still being said, but that at Easter the schedule was more restful than at Christmas. Unless Christmas Day was at the weekend, the parish had the equivalent of two weekends in one week both at Christmas and at the New Year. This meant more work for the monks, too, in the sacristy, the singing and so on. In Holy Week, until Easter Sunday, there was only one Liturgy a day, and that was a joint ceremony with the parish. Also, we got up later than usual.

This was a time of change and experiment, and we were better at experimenting than at keeping records of our experiments. Consequently to reconstruct our daily schedule from May 1968 is always difficult and sometimes impossible. From 1968 until the end of our period we got up at 5.00 a.m. and started Matins at 5.20. After Matins, although most of the monk-priests were now concelebrating, there were still Masses needed for the parish and for the convents that we served. On Saturday, we got up at 6.40 a.m. and on Sunday at 5.25 a.m. until May 1972, by when we got up at 6.10 a.m. on Sunday.

Our Conventual Mass for the weekend was stable throughout our period at 8.45 a.m. on Saturday and 9.00 a.m. on Sunday. On weekdays from 1960 until September 1967 it was at 11.50 a.m. on school days and at 8.45 a.m. on other weekdays. After that there was a period of experimentation for school days: for the next two school years, from September 1967 to June 1969 it was at 10.10 a.m. with the whole school attending on Fridays. In September 1969 it was at 7.45 a.m. on Monday through Wednesday, 5.50 p.m. on Thursday and probably at 7.45 a.m. on Friday. In September 1970 it was the same except that on Friday it was at 8.30 a.m. with the whole school attending. Then in September 1971 we settled into the simpler schedule of 6.00 p.m. every weekday except Saturday, and Mass was combined with Vespers,[193] except that on Fridays in term time Conventual Mass was probably at 8.30 a.m. with the whole school attending, and a solitary monk celebrating Mass at 6.00 p.m. for the people.

In 1968 our revised prayer took advantage of the permission to conflate Matins and Lauds into one office. Then, to compensate for the reduction of the praise, for which Lauds was named, we introduced on Monday through Friday a short Office of Praise, prayed, by those who could be there, at 8.15 a.m. on school days and 8.45 a.m. on other days. Prime had probably dropped out already; now we dropped Terce and None too, and prayed Sext, or Mid-day Prayer, at noon on Monday through Friday and at 12.10 p.m. (by May 1972, 12.15 p.m.) on Saturday and Sunday. Vespers initially were at 6.05 p.m. on Monday through Saturday; on Sunday they were at 5.50 p.m. followed immediately by Benediction. When Mass on Monday through Friday went to 6.00 p.m., Vespers were combined with it, but Saturday and Sunday remained the same. Compline was at 7.45 p.m.

All that sounds, and to some extent was, confusing, but it is more confusing to read about it than it was to live through it. Perhaps as

---

[193] There was no Mass for the whole school in 1969/70.

schoolmasters we were used to a day broken up into discontinuous segments, and on the whole we found the changes of time less disconcerting than the changes in language and music. Latin is a wonderful language for prayer, and the body of plainsong is unique in Catholic church music, and perhaps in any church music, as a complete body of music of sustained excellence. There must have been mediocre or dull pieces written, but over the centuries they dropped out and were replaced. And so one could see why those who knew Latin well or had a deep appreciation of music, or both, would find the changes unpalatable. What was pleasing was that so many with one or both of those qualifications were ready to embrace the new ways, if not out of personal delight, at least for the sake of the common good. What was surprising was that both in the United States and in England so many of those who mourned for the past had neither a great knowledge of Latin nor a deep appreciation of music.

Change of Command

OUR status as a dependent priory of Ampleforth meant, as we have seen, that our major decisions could not be put into effect until they had been ratified by the Abbot of Ampleforth. Because Ampleforth sensibly acknowledged that decisions about American matters would normally be wisest when made by those with some American experience, this need for ratification was as little irksome as was possible. But there was another way in which our dependence had a vast effect on us and one over which we had minimal influence, and that was the election of an abbot. Abbots in the English Benedictine Congregation have an eight-year term of office but may be re-elected as often as the monks choose. Abbot Herbert was first elected in 1939. He was re-elected in 1947 and 1955, but in 1963 he was seventy-eight. He had served us wonderfully well but, after twenty-four years as abbot, he was pleading for a rest. The monks acquiesced and elected as his successor Father Basil Hume, who later became Cardinal-Archbishop of Westminster. He had always been a good friend of Saint Louis Priory and had visited us with Father Patrick in 1960. He made an official Visitation as abbot in October 1963. In the following years Father Columba, Father Luke and Father Timothy were each called to Ampleforth for consultations, and then at the end of March 1967 Abbot Basil came to us again for his second official Visitation,[194] in the course of which he told Father Columba that he was taking him back to England and was appointing Father Luke as Prior in his place. This was to take effect in June, after the end of the school year.

Father Columba's mark on Saint Louis was noted by the *Saint Louis Post-Dispatch* in an editorial which we reprinted, with permission, in our Journal.[195] Part of it reads, "It would hardly be an exaggeration to say that in the relatively few years he has lived in the community Father Columba has become an institution. A wise, witty, urbane and gentle Oxford-educated priest, he insisted on rigorous scholastic standards that brought the Priory school an enviable reputation for excellence. Beyond this, he has participated actively in ecumenical projects in the community, where the weight of his learning in historical, philosophical and theological matters, along with his tolerance and keen sense of humor, made him much sought-

---

[194] The abbot is required to make a formal Visitation of all parishes and dependent houses at least once every four years.

[195] *Saint Louis Post-Dispatch*, 12 June 1967 reproduced in SLPJ V. 1, p. 3.

after as a speaker and moderator of discussions. He has been a prolific reviewer of books on a wide variety of subjects; many of his reviews have appeared in this newspaper." They might have added that he was also a prolific writer of books, one of which, on monastic renewal, was completed shortly before he left.[196]

In the same issue of our *Journal*, which was dedicated to Father Columba, Father Luke, the new prior, wrote, ". . . Fr. Columba has a spirit of dedication to God, the Church and his brethren. In great measure he formed the Priory in that same spirit. From the earliest days, we have prayed the Divine Office, the prayer of the Church, together. All our friends have a part in our prayer; they share in the tribute it renders to God and in the return that God makes to us—a share acknowledged and recognized only by faith. We serve the Church through education, bringing boys to God and God to them; Fr. Columba's gentle but sure manner has left its mark on the school. Maybe the Priory has helped open some windows over the past few years. Fr. Columba certainly had a hand in that. So strongly has he helped show the warmth and vitality of a monastic community that the Priory spirit has arisen, embracing our friends and alumni in a unique bond of love and friendship." Commenting from the point of view of the school, Father Timothy wrote, "In his eleven school years here he taught Religion, French, Spanish and E.P.E. [Elementary Politics and Economics], with a little History here and there. Besides all that, he counselled and encouraged many a student; and the school was constantly in his prayers. Perhaps readers will remember him best . . . for his addresses at parents' evenings, graduations and such. These were brief, thoughtful, vivid and pungent."

And so Father Columba returned to a full life in England preaching, writing and giving Retreats. He was active in the field of ecumenism in England, then went on a preaching and teaching tour in Africa, after which he went to Nigeria to assist in the foundation of Saint Benedict's Priory in Eke and then Ewu. He returned to Ampleforth and in due course became a trouble-shooter for Benedictines around the world. He died at Ampleforth Abbey on 22 January 1994. Father Luke was there soon after Father Columba's death and buried him in the new vault, south of the Abbey church.

In Saint Louis, after Vespers on 23 June 1967, the monks gathered round the high altar and sang the *Veni Creator Spiritus*, (Come Creator Spirit) and then Father Luke took over as prior. His new task

---

[196] Columba Cary-Elwes, O.S.B., *Monastic Renewal* (New York: Herder and Herder 1967)

was complicated by his having to carry on the duties of procurator until the arrival of Father Vincent Marron in mid-September. Father Colin had, since his arrival in 1965, been assisting Father Luke, but only part-time. Father Vincent did arrive, but then Father Luke had to train him, so it is no surprise that Father Luke's letters home at that time were mainly concerned with procuratorial matters such as the installation of the organ. Besides that, when we were permitted by Ampleforth to train our novices here, and when, in September 1969, we had our first novice under this new arrangement, Father Luke was his Novice Master, with Father Benedict to help him. Some of Father Luke's activities, like architectural planning and fund-raising, linked his past as procurator with his present as prior, and some were purely prior's business, like the arranging of the Divine Office. That meant that he filled his days with preparing and delivering sermons—they were not yet called homilies—and other talks, meeting with Inc and the architects, meeting with the monks and listening to their requests, problems and, sometimes, complaints, and coping with the multiple affairs of routine priorial and procuratorial administration.

Although the Priory was not a member of either of the two main American Benedictine Congregations, the American Cassinese and the Swiss-American, Father Luke was by courtesy invited to the meetings of their superiors, and attended regularly. He also attended by right a meeting at Oxford in 1968 of the English Benedictine superiors. They were to discuss the first draft of our Constitutions, revised in the light of Vatican II by a commission set up for the purpose in 1965 by the General Chapter of the English Benedictine Congregation. As a result of the meeting in Oxford, a radical revision was made and, in due course, a new draft was produced and circulated to every monastery to be discussed. A final text was approved in 1969. After all that, the next major monastic decision facing Father Luke was our independence, to which we shall come in its place.

Father Columba's return to England was a serious moment in our history, and marked the end of the beginning. But most serious events include an element of light relief. When Father Timothy was summoned to England by Abbot Basil, he decided to fly on 4 July in the hope that the plane would be less crowded. He was right. The plane's capacity was 130, but there were only about a dozen passengers, mostly English. For dinner, British Airways served *filet mignon*. When Father Timothy had finished the first one, the flight attendant offered him another, which he accepted, and when he had finished that, a third, and no doubt he and his fellow-passengers could have had one hundred or so more. Contentedly replete, he noticed that the man in the seat in front of him was reading *The Times*. Knowing that there was a cricket match in progress between England and Australia, he asked if he might see the paper when its owner had finished with it. The man in front looked round, gave him an icy stare in complete silence and turned back to his front. Father Timothy went sadly to sleep. Next morning, being still curious about the match, he tried again, explaining this time that he was interested in the progress of the Test Match.[197] Now the man in front turned round and said, "Are you English?" Father Timothy agreed, and the man said, "My dear chap, I'm so sorry; I'd have talked to you last night if I'd known."

[197] This is the name for an international cricket match.

The Priory and the Archdiocese.

WE were much blessed in coming to an archdiocese where the archbishop had done part of his priestly studies with the Benedictines at Saint Meinrad and liked Benedictines. He paid us a number of visits, some official, some mainly social, as when he came to dinner with us in 1961 on 21 March, the Feast of Saint Benedict. This meant that there existed between us a margin of good will and tolerance, which was to us a very valuable asset. And so, when the archdiocese turned to us to ask that in April 1965 their Ordinations be held in our church as the Cathedral was being renovated, we were glad to assent. As a result our church, which was designed to hold six hundred and sixty, was packed with the thirty-nine ordinands, about one hundred and twenty priests and some eighteen hundred laity, along with a massive scaffold for the television cameras. All went very well despite torrential rain and muddy access, and many of those ordained look back happily on their experience here.

Then in August 1966 Cardinal Ritter—he had been created a cardinal in 1961--decided to divide the parish of Saint Monica in two, and to make into a new parish, named for Saint Anselm, the half that contained us. We were honored that the archdiocese chose to name the parish for this great Benedictine theologian and philosopher. The new pastor was to be a diocesan priest, Father, later Monsignor, Robert P. Slattery, and the plan was that he would build a parish church a little less than a mile north of our church, on a piece of ground which the archdiocese already owned. After due discussion, Father Columba suggested to Father Slattery that the parish should, until its own church was ready, use ours. Father Slattery agreed, and both parties were originally thinking in terms of a year or two. But as early as January 1967 it became evident that the monks' use of the church for themselves and the school meshed well with the needs of the parish. The heaviest use by the parish was at the weekend, when the boys were away, and on weekdays the monks could finish their early morning prayer before the first parish Mass, and fit in more prayer before the second. To have two large churches within so short a distance of one another would be poor stewardship. There was, therefore, no obvious reason why the arrangement should not become permanent.

Discussion started among the monks and between the monks and Father Slattery, and there emerged the idea of "a continuing but not irrevocable agreement that the Archdiocese and the Priory would cooperate in serving the Saint Anselm's Parish Community." [198] This led to the preparation of a legal agreement for the consideration of both parties, but there was some delay before it was signed. Partly this was due to the combination of the death in April 1967 of Cardinal Ritter, and the return in June of Father Columba to England, partly to our need to have the plan approved by the Abbot of Ampleforth, and partly to some hesitation felt on both sides about the feasibility of such a plan. The doubters on each side believed that friction was inevitable. But the spirit of Vatican II was upon us and we persisted. The agreement forged by Cardinal Ritter and Father Columba was in May 1968 signed by Cardinal John Joseph Carberry, the new Archbishop of Saint Louis, and Father Slattery on behalf of the Archdiocese, and by Abbot Basil and Father Luke on behalf of the Priory.

By the agreement, legal title to all real property remained in the Priory; the integrity of the church's design would be maintained; payment would be made by the parish to the monks for their services to the parish and for operating expenses; a review board would be established; either side could give two years' written notice of termination; and any pastor appointed would be acceptable to both parties. If the parish ceased to be here, what would then happen to parochial buildings on our land was not fully resolved. There was also a letter of intent that "when there is a change of pastors envisaged, the monks might take charge of the parish."[199] The arrangement was not in perpetuity, but renewable every twenty-five years. In the same issue of our *Journal*, Father Luke, responding to questions raised within the Priory family, commented, "For close to six years now we've had this happy arrangement" and went on to enumerate some of the advantages accruing to the parties concerned: by a kind of spiritual osmosis the parishioners absorb something of the Benedictine spirit; the monks become more evidently part of the local community; those who are priests are able to exercise some priestly ministry on the campus and without administrative burden; our links with the Archdiocesan clergy are strengthened; in a small way, the arrangement helps to build up the unity for which Jesus prayed at the Last Supper.

All the monks were to some extent assistants in the parish, but, for administrative simplicity, Father Leonard was appointed to be our

---

[198] *SLPJ* IX. 2, p. 18

[199] *SLPJ* IX. 2, p. 19. We would have preferred more than a "gentleman's agreement", but in the event, the agreement was honored in March 1981.

liaison. He, more than any of the other monks, assisted Father Slattery, who was pastor from the start of the parish in 1966 through 30 March 1981, when the monks took over. By the time of our *Journal* for December 1968 Father Leonard is referred to as Father Slattery's Associate.[200] When Father Leonard returned to England in June 1971 Father Laurence succeeded him. For the rest of us it meant the celebration of Mass for the parishioners from time to time, occasional talks or even a series of talks in Lent or Advent, occasional celebrations of the Sacrament of Reconciliation with the children in the Parish School of Religion. A request for the novices to teach the children was turned down. For its annual picnic, the parish used our grounds, sometimes the lawn behind the Stannard House, sometimes the woods by the gym, and when it started an athletic program, used our fields.

The Parish School of Religion, after starting in classrooms at Maryville College in September 1966, moved to the classrooms in the monastery in September 1967, and then to those of the new Junior House, when it was completed in September 1968. Later, it added the use of some classrooms in the new high school when they were available after September 1970. There was a program at Visitation Academy for parish boys and girls in high school or junior high school. When our seventh and eighth grades moved into their new building, the old Junior House became the home of four Incarnate Word Sisters, of whom Sisters Helen Ann Collier and Annette Pezold worked for the parish. In 1969 the parish agreed to pay $850 a month for the use of the church, the house for the Sisters, and the classrooms, plus a stipend of $250 a month for the monks' services. At the Conventual Chapter on 31 August 1970 we approved in principle the building, somewhere near the church, of a rectory for the pastor,[201] and in 1972 Father Slattery built it on the acre we had acquired from the Nolands in March 1955,[202] and moved in there with his mother. The house included the parish offices, and had space roughed out for

[200] *SLPJ* VI. 1, p. 4.

[201] Our first choice was a site near the old barn down the hill and nine hundred feet north of the church.

[202] *see* p. 32, *above*.

an associate pastor, should there ever be one. The parish had in 1966 about one hundred and fifty families on the books, but grew rapidly.

External Activities

THE Ampleforth that we left in 1955 was self-contained and even isolated more than we recognized when we there. We very soon saw that Saint Louis was going to be quite different, but it took us longer to see in what ways. Part of the difference was geographical: instead of being twenty country miles of country road from the nearest city we were just off a highway on the fringe of a metropolitan area. We soon learnt that the parents were on our doorstep in a way that was unthinkable at Ampleforth, and that the same was true of Inc and its members. We did not take long to adapt to the need to spend on them much more time than we had expected, and this fitted in very well with our general policy of close cooperation with the laity. We took longer to see how closely the whole community of Saint Louis, and even of places much farther afield, would expect us to relate to them. In other words, we adapted ourselves to public relations without recognizing the extent of the public. It did not surprise us to be asked to provide a chaplain for Maryville College (later University) when in April 1961 they became our neighbors, nor to be asked to teach Scripture to the novices of the Good Shepherd Sisters. We were surprised to be asked in January 1967 to host a demonstration of Rugby football to benefit the victims of a tornado, or to provide a chaplain for the Creve Coeur Fire Brigade, and to bless their fire pump.

There were so many calls of so many kinds that it is hard to give any account of them, and yet some attempt must be made in order to indicate the versatility which was expected of us. It will be only a selection, and will be grouped under the headings of *liturgical*, *spiritual*, *intellectual* and *other* activity.

The *liturgical* requests were, in the beginning, mainly for Sunday Masses and came from pastors we knew. We felt a special debt of gratitude to Monsignor Faris and so went often to his parish, but there were others too, including some out in the country. It was on his way to Monsignor Faris that Father Columba missed the turn, found himself in North County and made his celebrated U-turn on Lindbergh Boulevard. As time went on, we became more and more hesitant about these "supplies" because they prevented us from being at our own Sunday Conventual Mass.

We were asked to be chaplains to local Convents, first to the Religious of the Sacred Heart at Maryville, as mentioned, and then to the Visitation Sisters, to the Passionist Sisters, and on occasion to the Sisters of Saint Peter Claver. All of these we accepted, as also requests for Mass or Masses each Sunday at the neighboring parishes of Ascension (Chesterfield) and Incarnate Word. We visited the hospitals--there are three large hospitals within a mile or two of us--and Delmar Gardens Nursing Home. We were very occasionally asked to say Mass for television, and later, as home Masses became permissible, we were asked for those, especially for school families. Our Midnight Mass at Christmas always drew an enormous crowd, with standing room only despite our putting out an annually increasing number of folding chairs. There was never nearly enough room when the chapel was in the monastery; and even when we moved into the church and put out yet more chairs, many people still had to stand.

As well as the requests for Mass, there were many for the sacraments, which might or might not be in the setting of the Mass. These requests normally came from within the Priory family, and so, initially, from parents of present or former students or from members of Inc. The latter, especially, formed ties with us that went far beyond fund-raising, and asked us to baptize their children or, sometimes, grandchildren, or to bury older members of their families. It was quite natural that, when our alumnus Claude Bakewell died, his parents, who were very close to Father Columba, asked him to celebrate the funeral Mass at the Cathedral. We were often asked to visit the sick in hospital and, later, to give them the Sacrament of the Sick, which in our early days was still called Extreme Unction, was reserved to the dying, and so was less common.

Then as we started to have alumni, they would ask us to marry them and then to baptize their children; and later still, when our connection with the parishioners of Saint Anselm Parish became closer, they too would ask us for all the sacramental services. One of the weddings, an ecumenical event in which Father Leonard "concelebrated" with an Episcopalian priest, Reverend Claudius Miller, in marrying our alumnus, Patrick C. Barker, was the first of its kind in the United States and earned two columns in *Time Magazine.*[203]

The saddest of these requests were for us to celebrate or attend the funerals of our friends. They might be of any age from infancy to over a hundred, and might be from school families, Inc, friends, suppliers or employees. We made special efforts to attend the funerals of our faithful retainers. At the funeral of Willie Williams, Chuck Dattilo's right-hand man for twenty-five years,[204] five of the monks were present, out of friendship not duty, and so it was on many

[203] *Time Magazine,* 17 July 1964, p. 56.

[204] Eleven years elsewhere and fourteen at Priory.

occasions. And the larger the Priory family became, the more funerals we attended each year.

The *spiritual* requests were headed by requests for spiritual direction. When we arrived in Saint Louis, Benedictine spirituality was somewhat unfamiliar, and as Benedictine life and lay life are closely related, it was no surprise that Benedictine spirituality appealed to those who came to know us. Some requests came through Inc or other contacts, some came from those who had attended a retreat or a day of recollection given by one of us. Father Columba and Father Luke answered most of these requests.

We were also asked for many retreats and days of recollection, the latter usually in town. We were especially glad to host, in November 1971, a Day of Prayer for the priests of the Archdiocese. We experimented with retreats on campus. One of the most successful was for students from Saint Louis University, and was held during the last three days of Holy Week in 1963. We were hampered by lack of rooms for retreatants, who therefore had to be young and content to sleep in sleeping bags on couches or even on the floor. Nonetheless, in 1964 we repeated this Retreat.

But most of our retreats were out of town. In those days, a retreat was not a matter of six or so conferences, a few Confessions, and then back home. Nineteen was a very normal number of conferences—three a day for six days plus one on the opening evening—and almost every retreatant was likely to come to Confession. There were American Benedictine men and women who thought there might be value in pollination from the English Benedictines, and there were other religious women and, less frequently, men who thought the same. Schools, including our own, were in need of retreats, and so, occasionally, were lay groups. The leaders in this were again Father Columba and Father Luke, but most of the other monks took part, though mainly during the summer, because of their full load of teaching during the school year. In this way we covered the country from California to Vermont and Louisiana to Minnesota, and that in itself was valuable experience. Several local Retreat Houses, such as the Cenacle, had regular schedules of retreats and turned to us for help in filling them. We also entertained groups of graduates and undergraduates from Saint Louis University, members of Inc, and members of the women's auxiliary who wanted to deepen their spiritual lives and came out to us to do so.

Preparing retreats was laborious and so was giving them, but it was not all solemn. When Father Timothy was giving his first retreat in this country, he was anxious that it should go well. In the first conference, he had made a point about talents, that even the lowliest of them should be cultivated, and gave as an example his ability, taught him by his nanny, to make a cord out of a piece of string. At the end of the conference, he said that he would be in his room, should anyone wish to come. Sure enough, there was knock at the door, and he expected that he was about to solve weighty, spiritual problems. The sister came in and chatted of this and that. Eventually Father Timothy asked if there was anything he could do for her. "Oh yes, father," she replied, "I have brought along a piece of string; could you show me how to make a cord out of it?" On another retreat in mid-December, he was sleeping in a very cold room and the wind was whistling through the window, which was not quite closed. He was already in bed before he noticed this, and because he was just getting warm, decided to try to sleep nonetheless. But the whistling kept him awake, he was becoming more and more frustrated, and eventually had to get up, despite the cold, to try to close the window. He discovered that it was jammed and would not close. Once he knew that, he returned to bed and immediately fell fast asleep. Psychosomatic we are.

Some of these lay groups that came to us for retreats became groups that met regularly, most notably our women's auxiliary. They had been active from the beginning, interesting themselves especially in altar linens, vestments and furnishings for the church. They supplemented the liturgical supplies that we brought from England, and then, when the church was being built, gave us the Cross on top of the church and the monks' stalls in choir. On 4 October 1957 they were formally organized as the Friends of the Priory, with officers, by-laws and dues ($5). They met four or five times a year for Mass and homily, coffee and donuts, a meeting and a talk by one of the monks.[205]

Other ongoing groups were one of college graduates who met with Father Columba, and one of undergraduates who read Plato and discussed the idea of the good with Father Augustine; a group of Oblates, formed in October 1962 to learn from Father Columba about Benedictine life; a gospel-study group of older boys in the school led by Father Thomas Loughlin, who, with Father Leonard, also led in Saint Mary Magdalen Parish in Brentwood, a Catholic Family group known by the monks as Happy Families. There were two other groups that met with Father Columba: the "Eggheads" (men), who discussed theology and comparative religion with him,

---

[205] One notice invited them to a meeting of the Fiends of the Priory. Fortunately we could all laugh as there can seldom have been a group less fiendish.

and the "Ostriches" (women), who studied the Bible. Toward the end of Father Columba's tenure, Sister Mary Byles was admitted to the brotherhood of Eggheads; then, when Father Columba returned to England, the Eggheads continued under Father Vincent Marron but ceased when he left. Later they were revived under Father Finbarr, who directed their studies towards the documents of Vatican II. As time went on they again expanded their membership by including clergy and laity of other Christian churches. The Ostriches were taken over by Father Luke, and in due course hatched another group, the Young Ostriches.

In the parish five monks were involved in Post-Vatican II Renewal groups. These met in parishioners' homes and discussed the documents of Vatican II. Finally, for a number of years Father Austin convened an ecumenical group of pastors of neighboring churches, who lunched with us once a month and then discussed the readings for the following Sunday. Most of these groups had an ecumenical tinge and some an explicitly ecumenical intent, so this may be the place to mention that Father Columba was appointed by the Archbishop to be one of the official Catholic observers at the Episcopal Church of America's Convention held in Saint Louis in August 1964.[206]

But the mountain did not always come to Muhammad: on a fair number of occasions Muhammad went to the mountain. In the late sixties, the charismatic movement started to engage the attention of Catholics. Father Ian was the first of us to become interested, learning of it through Father George Kosicki. Father Ian in turn introduced it to our community, and many of the monks became first interested and then involved. One of the most successful of the prayer groups near us met on Saturday evenings, a good time for us, at Visitation Academy, a convent of the Visitation Sisters just down the highway. The leader, charismatic in both senses, was Father Francis S. McNutt, O.P., whose artist-father had given us a collection of books and periodicals when he moved from his fine old house on Vandeventer Place.[207] For several years, many of the monks attended these prayer meetings and profited greatly from the renewed emphasis on the Holy Spirit and the Bible. It took the Anglo-Saxon element in each of us longer to feel at ease with spontaneous prayer, and Father Luke was wisely cautious in introducing it into our monastic prayer. But elements crept in, and it was not long before spontaneous petitions at

---

[206] *SLPJ* IV. 1, p. 2.

[207] The gates of Vandeventer Place are now in Forest Park, near the Jewel Box.

Compline, our night prayer, and at Conventual Mass became routine. Father Luke wrote of this kind of prayer, "Shared prayer bridges the gap between the objective prayer of Christian liturgies and the intensely private prayer of a man alone with God . . . a rhythmic blend of conversational prayer, vocalization of praise, shared silence, Scripture readings, spiritual songs, shared faith experience and shared bidding prayers." The last part he drew, with acknowledgment, from Father Kosicki.[208] In all of this we were ahead of the monasteries in England, and when they were producing a book to present the Benedictine idea in the light of Vatican II, Father Luke was asked to write the section on Charismatic Prayer, and did so.[209]

There were also many *intellectual* demands made. Father Columba taught a course at Kenrick Seminary, and somehow found time to write a book on Monastic Renewal. Father Augustine taught a course at Marillac College, and Father Timothy taught for two summers in the Classical Languages Department at Saint Louis University. The second was a challenging Graduate course in the difficult Roman poet, Lucan, but the first was a course which met three hours a day for six days a week and was intended to cover four years of high school Latin in six weeks. The Jesuit who was due to teach the course wisely died in April, and Father Timothy unwisely accepted the invitation to replace him for the first three weeks. He scored two great successes, of which the first was that the course was never offered again. The second concerned a Sister some thirty-five years old, who had been exposed to two years of Latin in high school but had gone on to study and to teach English, in which she was happy. At the end of the school year, her superior had sent for her to say that she would be teaching Latin the following year, and so she had best go to learn some during the summer. Father Timothy saw that she was not making much progress, learnt that she was spending ten hours a day on homework, and wrote a vehement letter to her superior. Receiving no reply, he thought he had erred once more, but was relieved in the Fall to hear from the Sister that she was happily back to teaching English.

The Mother-General of the Ursuline Sisters, a priest and two laymen from Dallas, a party of Hungarian Cistercians from Dallas and another of Hungarian Benedictines from Portola Valley, California, came at various times to pick our brains about education. Father John Main, an English Benedictine from Ealing Abbey in the

---

[208] *SLPJ* VIII. 2, p. 19.

[209] Daniel Rees et al., *Consider Your Call: A Theology of Monastic Life Today* (London: SPCK 1978) chap. 14, Shared Prayer.

suburbs of London, who was sent to be headmaster of Saint Anselm School in Washington, DC, also came to talk about the problems of being an expatriate educator. He was going to an already well-established school, but the Hungarians were starting from scratch, so they were of particular interest to us because they had to face many of the same problems as we had faced. There was enjoyable interplay between their proposed and our actual solutions to the same problem. For example, they did not initially take to football, nor did we, but we accepted it as part of the American scene and they would not. That kind of problem, calling for a balance between the good in one's own background and the good offered by the new surroundings, faces all immigrants; we hoped that discussing it with us had helped our visitors; and for us, being faced with a view different from our own was a valuable challenge.

Sometimes, rather than visitors coming to us, we went to them. One such expedition took Father Timothy to Chicago for the first time for a brainstorming session on Catholic education. It must have been early in our time here, because he went, in mid-winter, without gloves and knowing the address only as, let us say, 3400 Lawndale. He did not know that there would be a North Lawndale and a South Lawndale, several miles apart. He went by train, and when he reached Chicago there was on the platform a booth of the Citizens' Advice Bureau. Mindful of the procurator's views on expenditure, he sought their advice on getting to Lawndale by streetcar—he probably said "tram". They asked him, "North or South"? Between them they guessed wrong, so Father Timothy took a streetcar to Pulaski, waited for another and then headed south. He had been told, truly, that Lawndale was a few blocks east of Pulaski, and so asked to be put off at the 3400 block of Pulaski. By this time it was night, but he thought he could find a side street and walk to his destination. Unfortunately he was in the middle of an overpass over a railroad and thousands of empty freight cars. So instead of a straight walk of a few blocks, he had to walk all round the perimeter of the enclosure. It was very windy and fifteen degrees below zero, he was carrying a suitcase and had no gloves. When he arrived at the proper address, there was no sign of any institution, only homes. He decided to do what he should have done in the first place, use a telephone. He knocked on a door and asked if he could use their phone and from behind the closed door was refused. At the third attempt he was admitted and, procurator or no procurator, called a taxi and was taken to the north side. The memory of all this, in some detail, is with him still.

Father Columba for the *Post-Dispatch*, Father Timothy for the *Globe-Democrat* and the *Saint Louis University Classical Journal*, and sometimes other monks, wrote book reviews, partly as a way to build up our library. Father Columba mainly and Father Timothy occasionally was in demand to chair meetings, especially if they might be stormy. One such involved the Saint Louis Symphony, another an exhibition under the auspices of the Art Department of Washington University.

We were asked to give talks both within our fields of competence and outside. Father Timothy was to give a talk to the Classical Club of Saint Louis. He had found from experience that there was no point in saying anything serious for a minute or two, because people took that long to understand his accent, and therefore he usually started with a joke. On this occasion, he was going to tell about three men in a railway carriage in England. As the train slowed, one man asked the second whether this w-w-was W-W-Wigan. The man made no reply, so the first man repeated his question. Again, no reply, so the third man, against English etiquette, said, "Yes, sir, this is Wigan." When the train moved on, the third man rebuked the second for his rudeness, to which the second replied, "Y-Y-Yes, I kn-n-now, but d-d-do you think I w-w-wanted a b-b-bloody n-n-nose?" So far, so good, until the chairman for the evening arose and said, "W-w-we are s-s-o happy t-t-o have Father T-T-Timothy here t-t-to t-t-talk to us this evening."

There were *other* demands on our time that were neither liturgical nor spiritual nor intellectual. Father Austin started by playing the 'cello in the Brentwood Orchestra and later was invited to conduct it. He also gathered a group of parents and friends to listen to opera together. He would make a brief introduction and then play a recording of the opera. This was very popular and went on until his health failed.

We made various expeditions in pursuit of books. Father Columba and Father Luke went to Pine Island, Massachusetts, the home of the Welds, to secure Bill's fine collection, which was especially strong on the Catholic recusants in England. Henry Hughes and Father Timothy went to Yellow Springs, Ohio, at the generous invitation of Colonel and Mrs. Stacy B. Rankin, and brought home large quantities of books and three fine paintings, one by the school of Van Dyke. Two very satisfactory windfalls fell into our laps in Saint Louis. We had had dealings with a secondhand bookseller in the city. One day he called us to say that a man had died in South Saint Louis leaving a remarkable collection of books, many of them brand new and wrapped in newspaper. He seemed to have had three main interests:

archaeology, the War between the States, and pornography. We bought the lot at a very good price, put the first two categories into the library and used the pornography to fill in washes and to prevent further erosion on our grounds. The second windfall fell when Saint Stanislaus Jesuit Seminary closed. It occurred to us that they were likely to have had a fine collection of Greek and Latin classics. On enquiry, we found that this was indeed so, and, although the Jesuits had picked it over, what was left was well worth having and Mr. James F. Maginot, father of Peter ('76) bought it for us.

The most interesting of these other demands on our time was the invitation in the summer of 1965 to establish a summer camp at Walloon Lake, Michigan. Gerry Mudd wanted to provide some socializing activities for the children who went to Walloon each summer and was ready to finance the camp, if we would staff it. This was a very different proposition from that of the Alveys in 1958. [210] Not only was there no financial risk, but the clientele was already there on the spot. The range of activities would not need to be great and we would not have to compete with any rivals. We discussed the offer at length and eventually decided that, if we were going to do anything of this kind, the best use of our resources would be to hold a summer program here on our own property and to make it available to children from the inner city, which is what we eventually did in a program called ASSIST. So we declined Gerry's invitation, but he went ahead anyway with the help of Brian Barry and Marty McCabe, two members of our faculty.

Our decisions were interesting too. A few years previously, Father Timothy had made a proposal for a summer program for inner-city children, which was promptly turned down for several reasons, not the least being that priests who had been teaching all the school year preferred, if they were to work during the summer, to do something more overtly related to their priesthood. There was force in that and we acted on it; but the march on Selma had taken place earlier in 1965 and although, as British citizens, we thought it would be

---

[210] *See above*, pp. 179-80.

impertinent for us to march, our consciousness about civil rights had been raised.[211]

---

[211] These four decisions, against the Alveys, against Father Timothy's proposal, against the Walloon proposal and in favor of ASSIST are an interesting study in the democratic process.

Recreation and Vacations

WE noted at the start of the section on the Divine Office that in dealing with topics one by one we ran the risk of losing the sense of simultaneity, of many, diverse things happening at the same time. In dealing with our recreation, however, we run the opposite risk: by recounting in a group the various ways in which the monks refreshed themselves, we may easily give the impression that our life was one long recreation. In truth, for some monks recreation took one form and for others another. None attempted all forms, and even with the forms they did attempt, there were, especially in the early days, long intervals between recreations. Once the school opened, we never went out for dinner except strictly on business, and seldom even for lunch--once a month was our norm, again except on business--so our social life was much restricted by that; and anyway the school kept us too busy for much play.

But one of the pleasant by-products of having a school and living on its grounds is that the school's facilities are at one's doorstep. The school's library, copying machines and now computers are always there, though not always working, and so are the athletic facilities. From the beginning we were able to use the tennis courts, and very soon after the beginning the gym, with the consequent opportunity of shooting baskets, pumping iron and, later, playing squash or racquetball. When this caused strained muscles, there was a whirlpool at hand. Some played golf, Father Finbarr being easily the monastic champion. Some of the English monks used to go for runs, but as the years passed, they settled into jogging. Some entered for the various long runs, usually the ten Kilometer race; Father Luke and Father Ralph ran the eighteen miles to the arch between 2 and 5 a.m. on a morning in June 1979; Father Ralph has run the full Marathon thirteen times. We have mentioned the brief appearance of Father Luke and Father Timothy on the cricket field.

Some of the monks took their exercise by coaching. The English monks could manage cross-country, soccer, swimming, tennis and track, and most of them coached at least some of those. Father Paul was the only one who coached whole seasons of football and basketball, but Father Timothy pitched occasional batting practices, and he and many other monks took part in the Father and Son softball games. In the early sixties Father Timothy undertook to coach a rugby football team that went under the name of Saint Louis University, but in fact contained only six of their students, the rest coming from Washington University, the University of Missouri in

Saint Louis, the Junior College District and from as far away as Southern Illinois University in Edwardsville. The game caught on, and by the end of the season Saint Louis University could field two full squads of its own students. This led to a demonstration of Rugby by Saint Louis University and the Ramblers Rugby Union Football Club before one of the home games of the football Cardinals, the professional football team that had recently moved from Chicago to Saint Louis. The game was at the old Sportsman's Park.[212] Coach Timothy was allowed to stand on the sidelines to coach his team, and remembers looking many inches up at Big Daddy Lipscomb of Pittsburgh as he walked past, a Goliath in full armor. Father Paul and others took groups of boys on Upward Bound courses, float trips and so on.

We had other adventures at Sportsman's Park. When Father Nicholas arrived from England in 1961, Father Timothy took him to watch the baseball Cardinals, the professional team owned then by the Anheuser-Busch Brewery. After a very brief survey containing all he knew about baseball, Father Timothy was telling Father Nicholas that sometimes the ball was hit on the fly into the crowd and if a spectator caught it, he would be given an honorary contract with the Saint Louis Cardinals, signed by Mr. August A. (Gussie) Busch himself. Right on cue a high fly ball came to them, Father Timothy caught it and received his contract. Two of our boys were also at the game in seats nearby. The first came over and said indignantly, "Did you catch that ball?" "Yes." "That's not fair. I've been coming to games all my life and have never had a chance to catch a ball. You have come to a mere handful of games and you get to catch a fly ball." Father Timothy assumed that the boy was kidding, but his indignation was completely genuine. The other boy came over and said, "Did you catch that ball?" "Yes." "Did you have your glove with you?" "No." In shocked tones, "You caught it *with your bare hands*?"

There was also more passive recreation. There was a television set in the monastery, tucked away in the basement. We asked permission if we wanted to watch after 9.00 p.m. Parents and friends have always been more than generous in taking us to or giving us tickets for the Saint Louis Symphony, the "Muny Opera" (musicals), plays, movies and even the ballet. We have watched the baseball Cardinals and the hockey Blues; we have seen the basketball Hawks go, and the football Cardinals (the Cardiac Cards) come and go, and some have watched

---

[212] The Chicago Cardinals moved to Saint Louis in 1960 and played their games in Sportsman's Park before moving to the new Busch Stadium.

the Saint Louis indoor soccer team under its various names. In the very early days we saw an English third division soccer team get a scare from a good Saint Louis team, though the visitors won in the end. In the course of the game a smart shot from one of the English forwards crossed the goal line, struck the metal bar supporting the net and rebounded into the field of play. It all happened so quickly that play continued and nobody protested. We also saw Pele and the Brazilian soccer team, Santos, play at the new Busch Stadium. Again they were given a scare, but won handsomely in the end.

On another occasion in the early sixties, professional golf came to town. Jack Nicklaus was in his heyday, and Father Timothy, who happened to be giving a Retreat at a convent not too far from the course, slipped away during the afternoon to watch him. A press photographer took a pleasing shot of Nicklaus' approach to one of the greens, with, in the foreground, a tree in its fall colors. Under the tree, very recognizable, stood Father Timothy. This was published in the early edition of the Post-Dispatch, which was then an evening paper, and reached the convent before Father Timothy's return, but he knew nothing of this. The Sisters asked him where he had been that afternoon, and fortunately he came clean. Then they showed him the picture.

The most enjoyable of all these visiting troupes, partly because they came for a number of years in a row, were the professional tennis-players. For several of these years the event was put on by the father of a boy in the school, and so we saw a fair amount of the Holton Classic and players like Laver, Rosewall, Hoad, Gonzales, Segura and others at the peak of their form. One year they played on wood in Washington University's fieldhouse, but the rest of the time they played outdoors in Forest Park. One could make a case for this having been the finest array of athletic talent to visit Saint Louis in our time.

Not all the athletic events to which we were invited took place in Saint Louis. There were among our friends some alumni of the University of Notre Dame and many more who were their supporters, so we would be invited to accompany them to a game. This could usefully be combined with a visit to the Admission Office. One of the monks was invited to watch the University of Illinois play at Champagne-Urbana. He was to meet his hosts at Union Station, but had difficulty finding anywhere to park and, despite a valiant sprint down the platform, just failed to catch the train. In a taxi he then made a frenzied dash across town to the Delmar station, which was still in service, and found the train just about to pull out. He located his hosts, and the train set off. It traveled for two or three hours and then stopped, literally, in the middle of a cornfield, where they all, again literally, jumped off and were taken by coach to the game. The monk was, by now, used to football, but the half-time show and the solemn attention with which it was received, were eye-openers to him, especially the solemnity. From all of this it may be seen that the limits to our entertainment in these varied forms were set by monastic restraint and not by any shortage of invitations.

At other times we would make our own recreation: there are many beautiful parks in and around Saint Louis. We would take a couple of sandwiches and a soda and then go for a walk and picnic in one of these parks. Or one might stop in the Busch Wildlife Reservation and see a small flock of goldfinches splashing in a large puddle, or turn a corner of a country lane and come upon a Great Blue Heron fishing in a stream right beside the ford, or have to wait for two adult wild turkeys and six young to cross the road. Farther afield, Johnson's Shut-ins provided a spectacular mixture of boulders and water, the Elephant Rocks were huge masses of red granite, and Taum Sauk Mountain had an ingenious hydro-electric scheme. But we did not always need to leave home to enjoy the beauties of nature. We mentioned earlier the splendid sunsets varying with the season.[213] In the fall, the leaves, like Shelley's, "yellow, and black, and pale, and hectic red", not to mention brilliant gold and even some that remain green, can be as striking on our own campus as anywhere. In the winter, if we have an ice-storm, that too is as enchanting on our grounds as anywhere. In December 1972 we had the worst and most beautiful ice-storm since our arrival: worst because driving, though always perilous in these storms, was unusually perilous in this one, and most beautiful because it surpassed our memories of the great storm in the winter of 1957-58.

Father Austin and Father Timothy once decided on an outing to Jefferson City to see the Capitol and its Benton murals. Within the first few miles, something went wrong with our car. We limped back, had it put right and set off again. Once more we had not gone far when the car in front of us, a Cadillac, swerved off onto the shoulder, the hub cap of one of its rear wheels skittered across the road in front of us and the tire went flat. We stopped and offered to help, inwardly hoping that the driver would decline. Instead he said that, like Father Austin, he had a heart condition and could do no heavy work. Father Timothy jacked up the car, unscrewed the nuts, put on the new wheel and screwed up the nuts. He then had three white walls and one black,

---

[213] *See above*, p. 59

so he unscrewed the nuts, reversed the wheel and screwed them up again. The owner said that was very kind of us and went on his way. We were by now quite late and wanted to make up for lost time, when out of nowhere stepped a trooper of the State Highway Patrol. "Do you know how fast you were going?" he asked, and other such questions. His manner was uncivil. He looked at Father Timothy's license, asked his name and when and where he was born. The last answer was "Quetta". The officer gave Father Timothy a dirty look and said, "How do you spell that?" "Q-u-e-t-t-a, " "Where is that?" It was here that the trouble started. Had the trooper been civil, Father Timothy would have said "In India, officer," but he had been uncivil , and Father Timothy replied, quite truthfully, "In Baluchistan." A second dirty look, "And how do you spell that?" "B-a-l-u-c-h-i-s-t-a-n." "And where is that?" "In Pakistan." A third dirty look, and "How do you spell that?" "Officer, Pakistan is a sovereign state about fifty times the size of the state of Missouri, and you ought to know how to spell it." It cost twenty-five dollars and was worth every penny.

There were also community outings, some of which combined business with recreation, others were sheer recreation. One of the latter type was to the Horans' farm, in delightful country some fifty miles west of Saint Louis. We could sail on their lake, walk in their woods or just do nothing. Shortly before this outing, one of the monks, who loved Brie, had been given a large round of the cheese, and the plan was to make this a feature of our happy hour and evening meal. It so happened that two of the monks had business at the monastery and had to leave later than the rest. As they were leaving, the phone rang. A voice from the farm said that the Brie had been left behind, and could the two monks find it and bring it with them? They said they would, and would the community please keep them some lunch? They arrived with the Brie, but the community forgot to keep them any lunch. There was nothing for it but to make a sandwich from bread and some of the Brie, all the other food being needed for supper. Two things then happened while they were eating: first, the imp entered into them and they decided to hide the Brie, and secondly Father Ralph came by and saw them eating their bread and Brie. It is important that it was he, because of all the monks he is the man most without guile.

Come the happy hour, everyone assembled, eager for Brie, but none could be found. At that point, Father Ralph revealed that he had seen two monks making a late lunch of bread and cheese, and perhaps . . . Everyone knew that Father Ralph would not be playing games, and sadly it was agreed that the two monks, for whom, after all, no lunch had been kept, had some justification for consuming the Brie, and holy resignation took over. The culprits, feeling that justice had been done, then produced the nearly intact Brie, and the hour became much happier.

Perhaps we should include guests under the heading of recreation, because besides being entertained they are also entertaining. Professor and Mrs. Toynbee returned more than once, with similar éclat as before, attracting among other notables, Dr. Kurt von Schuschnigg, former Chancellor of Austria, who was then a professor at Saint Louis University. Mr. and Mrs. William G. Weld moved into our northern cottage around Christmas 1960 and stayed for several months. Father William Price, after retiring from the headmastership at Ampleforth, came to spend time with us and was always available to enliven classes in the school; Father Martin D'Arcy, the famous English Jesuit and author, renewed his friendship with Father Austin; Bishop Christopher Butler, former Abbot of Downside, brought us up-to-date on Vatican II, at which he had been present as a *peritus*, or expert; and Father Bede Griffith told us about his Benedictine *ashram*[214] in South India.

Knowing that Indians still link religious poverty with holiness, he and his fellow-monks decided to have in their rooms a simple bed, a chair, a table, and nothing else. They were not going to perform practical good works such as education or health care, but would simply try to lead a holy life of prayer. They hoped that the holiness of their life would attract visitors, and, behold, the visitors came. It was some little while before they discovered that their visitors were coming to see this life-style from a higher civilization which provided a beautiful bed AND a table AND a chair, things seldom seen all in one room in their village. He told the story on himself, but it was clear that he and his monks had made a lasting impression by what they were doing.

We also had a near miss with Lord Louis Mountbatten when he came to Saint Louis on his way to Westminster College in Fulton, Missouri. There he was to open a memorial to Sir Winston Churchill,[215] and to dedicate a small church originally built in London by Sir Christopher Wren, and then transported stone by numbered stone and re-erected in Fulton. Mr. J. Brian Barry of our faculty had served in one of the ships commanded by Lord Louis in World War II and Father Timothy had been one of his hosts at a small Chinese

---

214 "A religious retreat, especially that of a Hindu sage." Merriam-Webster.
215 Sir Winston had made his "Iron curtain" speech at Westminster College.

dinner in Bangkok just after the end of that war. We invited him to our campus, but all that we could achieve was that Brian was summoned to Lord Louis' hotel in Saint Louis, where, to Lord Louis' pleasure, he paraded himself, his wife and his children in descending order of height.

Vacations were of two kinds: those that occurred between the terms of the school year and the much longer one in the summer. The former were the Christmas and spring breaks. During these, or at least for part of them, the monks slept longer, initially by a system called half-choirs, which meant that only half the community got up for Matins at the usual time while the rest slept until 6.30 a.m. The next morning the other half got up early and the first half slept. This was abolished late in 1967. After that, during these monastic holidays, everyone got up a little later, but not as late as 6.30.

The summer vacation was when most of the monks went away. As almost all of us were teaching in the school, the only time we could take a vacation was while the school was on vacation, which in practice meant during the summer. Most of the monks gave retreats, assisted in parishes nearby or far away, gave talks or days of recollection, and then took as much vacation as those would pay for, or spent some time with friends.

Our four-year rotation of visits to England caused many adventures. Father Columba was an unlucky traveler: the hours after his departure were anxious for us, and almost as often as not would end in a telephone call, "I'm in Iceland, but all is well," or "They diverted us to Luxemburg, but I should be in England tomorrow." Another monk on his way back here, arrived at the airline counter at Heathrow to find that although he had a booked seat and had reconfirmed it, the plane was overbooked. For some reason the clerk was wearing a yachting cap, blue blazer and white flannel pants, which the monk thought pretentious. The clerk went off to see what other airlines could offer, and then came back and apologetically said that all they had was a first class seat on Pan-Am. Impishly the monk averred that, considering his vow of poverty, he was conscientiously dubious about accepting. The clerk almost bent his white-flanneled knee begging the monk to accept, which in due course he did. The monk was duly repaid for his pertness when the plane reached Washington and all the baggage was taken off for the passengers to go through customs. The plane took off again for Saint Louis, but soon circled around and returned to Washington. No one had reloaded the baggage.

Members of Inc, parents and, as time went on, alumni offered us hospitality, especially the Mudds, who had a summer home on Walloon Lake, Michigan, which almost all the monks visited at one time or another. On one of those visits the Mudds took Father Austin to Mackinac Island, where he encountered, by chance, his Repton schoolmate, Bunny Austin, who played tennis for England in the Davis Cup and then became involved in Moral Rearmament. Or they might take their family and a monk on a trail ride in the Rocky Mountains in Montana, where the bluebells and harebells and other wild flowers and some of the wildlife were nostalgically like those in England. They also took monks skiing both on Boyne Mountain, Michigan and in Vail, Colorado. Father Columba and Father Luke were among these, but the best skier was Father Vincent Wace, who appeared splendidly arrayed in the latest European fashions of his youth. But his youth was a while ago and to the eyes of the young in Colorado he looked as if he had skied straight out of a ski museum.

On an adventure of a different kind, Father Augustine and Father Timothy drove up the beautiful Columbia River Valley and found themselves at Pendleton in Oregon. There they learnt that forest fires were breaking out along much of their route to Saint Paul, Minnesota, where Father Augustine was due to give a Retreat. Having heard tales of passing motorists being stopped and pressed into service as fire-fighters and fearing they might be delayed in that way, they decided to drive on through the night, and did so through the eerie glow and occasional bright flames of the fires. That also enabled them to reach friends in Boise, Idaho in time for the Snake River Stampede, their first rodeo.

One variation on this pattern of retreats or visits to England started in 1960 when Father Timothy embarked on a program of visits to colleges to which our boys might apply. In the course of the next decade he visited colleges in each of the forty-eight contiguous states, and in four Canadian provinces. This investment of time and energy paid abundant dividends: it made Priory known to a wide range of colleges and enabled Father Timothy to explain to them our curriculum and grading system and the reasons for them; it enabled him to draw on personal experience in recommending colleges to individual boys or in dissuading them from applying to schools unsuited to their needs; it helped to create confidence and trust between the school and the colleges. It also provided Father Timothy with extensive experience of the American countryside and with vacations that were hard work, but far from unenjoyable. On occasion he used public transportation, but the most practical way of travelling was by car. The problem was to find a car. Sometimes it was one of the monastery's cars; sometimes a car belonging to a friend or a parent; once it was a car on which a bank had foreclosed. These trips led to many adventures but no accidents.

The most interesting was a ten thousand mile expedition to the Northwest. On the way out, Father Timothy stayed with some friends in Colorado. When he asked them what they would like him to bring them from Canada, they requested a salmon. On reaching Vancouver and after visiting the University of British Columbia, to which he later sent a student, he went down to the dock, bought a freshly caught salmon, packed it in dry ice and put it in the trunk of the car. Because it was summer, the dry ice needed to spend each night in a deep-freeze. Campgrounds seldom had such, but he was usually able to find a friendly hotel or hospital that did—he spent one night on the operating table in a disused operating theater, was woken by orderlies in the middle of the night and for a horrifying moment thought they were going to cut him up. Another evening he was just North of Yellowstone Park and was having no luck. At the eleventh hour, a kindly cafe-manager said that the cafe's deep freeze was full, but she had one in her basement at home, which we could use. We (Father Timothy had picked up a priest in Jasper, Alberta and was bringing him home towards Chicago) said that was very kind, but that we would be leaving early next morning. She replied that this was no problem: there were outdoor steps down to her basement and she would leave the door unlocked, so we could slip in, take our fish and depart without disturbing anyone. Next morning, therefore, Father Timothy slipped in, made for the deep freeze and was about to take his fish, when a man's voice said "What are you doing?" "I'm taking my fish." "What fish?" "The one I left here last night." This, the man not the fish, turned out to be the husband, who had returned unexpectedly very late at night, and, not wanting to disturb his wife, had crept down the steps and gone to sleep on a couch in the basement. In due course everything was explained and believed, but it was not how one would choose to start the day. Perhaps the husband felt the same.

Earlier in that same trip and before picking up the priest, Father Timothy had spent an idyllic night at a campground in the Canadian Rocky Mountains on Kicking Horse Creek. There for the princely sum of fifty cents he found a tiny peninsula just large enough to take his car, slept soundly with the lullaby of the rushing creek surrounding him on three sides and awoke in the morning to find towering peaks all around. Rising early he had a hot shower and found an outlet for his razor, all for the same fifty cents, and walked down the creek to the camp store accompanied, but on the far side of the creek, by a mother bear and two cubs. From there, after Banff and Lake Louise, he took the Icefields Parkway past the Columbia Icefield and past straying moose, elk and deer up to Jasper. He had a much gentler encounter in Yellowstone Park with a deer which had a sweet tooth and loved lemon drops. The salmon was eventually cooked in Colorado and was well worth all that effort.

Another trip was memorable for a completely different kind of reason. This was a trip to Oklahoma and Texas in October 1968. Father Timothy had an appointment with the Dean of Admissions at Rice University in Houston, Texas. The World Series was in progress, and as Father Timothy left his car—a monastery car, this time—Detroit was just coming up to bat against the Cardinals. He went in with his usual dossier of materials about the school: a brief history, the curriculum, a summary of what was taught in each course, a specimen transcript and an explanation of our grading system, a table of our results in the College Boards and in the Advanced Placement examinations. In return he received information about Rice. These interviews normally lasted forty to fifty minutes, and this one was no exception. When he came out, Detroit was still batting in the same inning. They scored thirteen runs, but the number was unlucky for the Cardinals, not for Detroit. It was unlucky also for Father Timothy: on the return journey, the headlights of the car kept flickering. The driver of the car in front must have thought Father Timothy was making some kind of signal and suddenly pulled off the highway—a twisty one—and Father Timothy nearly followed into the ditch. It was not an interstate and it took some time to find a garage open late on Sunday night.

On another occasion he was driving with some friends from Atlanta to New Orleans. We stopped for a shrimp lunch in Biloxi. There was a ramshackle hut on an old wooden pier that ran out into the sea. You could see the waves between the floor boards. For $1.75 (this was in 1961) we were each given a large plate heaped with freshly caught shrimps with heads and tails still attached, and a bottle of ketchup was dumped on the table. It took a while, but it was a wonderful lunch. On the way back we tried a fancy restaurant on the other side of the road, where, for the same price, we were given an elegant plate with twelve little compartments with one elegant shrimp in each and *sauce tartare* in the central ring. On yet another occasion Father Timothy was driving through the early morning mist on the Blue Ridge Parkway in the Appalachians, when he rounded a corner and came upon an eagle standing in the middle of the road. As the eagle was almost as tall as his little car, he was content when the magnificent bird flapped lazily away.

All in all, these journeyings took Father Timothy into every state, and he considered them a successful piece of public relations. He visited not only most of what one might call the brand-name schools, but also many schools where well prepared students of good but not outstanding ability could receive a very suitable college education.

CHAPTER 21

The School

Planning and Building

WE have described the building of the monastery and of the church. For the rest of our period most of the planning, building and remodeling concerned the school. This may, therefore, be a suitable place for an account of it, so that the reader may have a picture of the surroundings in which the activities of the school took place. In September 1960 the layout was this: The monks were living on the upper floor of the monastery, and praying in the chapel, which occupied much of the north side of the ground floor, with the sacristy in the small room east of the chapel. Classrooms occupied most of the rest of the ground floor, but the room in the northwest corner was for the faculty. We were taking our meals in the elegant dining-room of the Stannard House. Our library was in steel shelves lining the corridors of the upper floor of the monastery. We had just signed the contract for the church, but did not occupy it for another two years.

The Science laboratories, two classrooms and a lecture theater were in the Science Wing. The procurator and the headmaster were at the north and south ends respectively of the upper floor of the Stannard House, and Father Leonard, the disciplinarian, was between them in the room on the right at the top of the stairs. The Junior House, which had one classroom for the seventh grade and one for the eighth, was quartered in the Singer House. The school library, which was still small enough to be moved easily, had moved from the dining-room to the living-room of the Stannard House. The bookstore was in the basement in the small room next to the rathskeller bar, and the seniors had their form room in the rathskeller; the juniors' form room was a classroom in the monastery, and Forms III and IV shared the barn,[216]

---

216 Since the barn was demolished in March 2000 to make way for the new monastery, readers may need to be reminded that this was the central building of the original "cloister plan" (see p. 52 above). It was still quite serviceable and we thought of moving it, but the cost was disproportionate. Even so, its brutal demolition by an enormous set of mechanical jaws was a saddening sight and

which was also used by the music and art activities. The other activities were accommodated thus: Mechanical Drawing was in the basement of the monastery, Carpentry in the carpentry shop in the unused north end of the locker rooms at the gym. The Yearbook, whose staff members were seniors, worked in their form-room, and the school newspaper upstairs in the room west of Father Leonard's, all in the Stannard House. The Radio club used the radio hut, where the Stannards had kept chickens and which had then become our first carpentry shop. The Junior House debate took place in their new common room, which had been the Singers' garage. Photography, having been ejected by the Fire Marshal from the basement of the Singer House, had in 1960 no home.

The first remodeling had been done in the summer of 1960 in this Singer House. Under Father Luke's guidance and with the help of monks, three alumni and some boys from the Junior House itself, one classroom was enlarged and the garage was converted into a common room. The former kitchen was now a cloak-room and the breezeway housed the boys' lockers. In the following summer, we provided parking at the gymnasium for one hundred cars at a cost of $7,000 and rolled the studio from the Reasor House to the gym to serve as a store for lumber and paint, thus leaving more room for the coaches; the Stannard House was repainted and a bees' nest was removed from the windings of a large electric motor.

After the completion of the church in September 1962 several moves took place. The chapel on the north side of the monastery was no longer required. The school library moved into that space and, at the east end of the space, two small rooms were made, one for the librarian and his assistants, the other for a paper-back bookstore. The faculty took over the living-room in the Stannard House, which had been vacated by the school library. The bookstore proper moved into the small room in the monastery which had been the sacristy; what had been the bookstore in the Stannard House became a darkroom for photography, and what had been the faculty room at the northwest corner of the monastery became a classroom.

In September 1963 we took into the seventh grade two sets (thirty-five boys) instead of one, and the same in 1964. That meant that we needed two extra classrooms for the Junior House. The two upper rooms in the Singer House were turned into classrooms, but that meant evicting Father Ian and his office. He went downstairs into what

---

removed one of our major landmarks – almost like demolishing an ante-bellum structure on a Southern campus.

had been a classroom, so we were still one short. To meet this need and to provide a little more space, Father Luke gave us a modest but pleasing prefabricated building, just west of the Singer House. It gave us two classrooms. At the same time we expanded the boys' dining-room by one half, and moved into its spaciousness in September 1963. John O'Brien was again our contractor for all this for a bid of $42,000. The expansion of the dining-room entailed the removal of the archway building and its greenhouse, the one that Father Augustine took pleasure in sledgehammering. After the demolition of the greenhouse, the archway building, which had considerable grace, was rolled to its present position just east of the boys' dining-room, and through June 1968 was the home of Mechanical Drawing. It was then remodeled into our fund-raising office.

In April 1964 there was a planning discussion of a rather wider kind. Some of our friends were exerting pressure on us to produce a five- or even ten-year plan. In favor of this was that it was the American way to proceed; that if we did not keep the men of Inc busy, they might take their enthusiasm elsewhere; that it would help them in their fund-raising to have such a plan; that we might steer a straighter course if we knew where we were going; that it was better to have a plan, even if we did not stick to it, than not to have a plan at all. Against was our native distrust of *a priori* procedures; our hesitancy about making long-term plans when we were only too well aware of our own ignorance; our wish not to build buildings according to one plan only to find that they obstructed the execution of a better plan later on; Father Luke's preference for building up an endowment before expanding the school.

After discussion we went ahead with the long-range plan. The first decisions needed were: should we become a boarding school, or at least add a boarding section? Should it be full time boarding or five-day boarding? Should we start at the fifth grade? Should we simply enlarge each grade, and if so, by how much? These were matters which would normally be discussed by the superior and his council, but we had as yet no council and so no council minutes. If any written record was made, it has not survived, but memory reports that at this time we were definitely against five-day boarding. We were still favorable in principle to full-time boarding for all boys, but dubious about its feasibility in the Mid-West, and still more dubious about having only a section of boarders. We did not rule out going down to the fifth grade but did not think we were yet ready for it. Of these various possibilities, enlarging the grades we already had was the most appealing, but what we really wanted to do was to take a few years to digest what was on our plate and to settle down. And anyway, there was still debt for Inc to pay off.

Nonetheless, by the late fall, Father Luke was writing home, "Plans for the future include extensions to the gymnasium . . . plans for extensive scholarship and laymaster salary increase; a new football field; new workshops and storage space and long range planning for a 50% increase or more in the school. So it does not look as if we were going to be allowed to stagnate."[217]

Nor did we stagnate. By spring 1965 Father Luke had begun work on a new entrance road, to be paid for by the Fausts and called the Faust Expressway or F1. Until then we had been using the Stannards' driveway, which led to the Stannard House. To drive to the church, one took a dirt road which forked to the left near the top of the hill, went between the monastery and the barn and then turned north. There were a few parking places east of the church. To reach the Science Wing the road went on to the north and then turned to the right onto the knoll, to a parking area where the Parish Center now stands. (*See* plate 9b) The new road was not only greatly superior but also took traffic around the far side of the church and away from the monastery and so increased our peacefulness. Nor was this all. The new road also prompted us to continue the program of tree-planting which we had started back in 1956, after HOK's landscape architect/consultant had made his recommendations.[218] The new trees, too, were underwritten by the Fausts and were luckier than the previous batch, which were still young when we had, in the summer of 1964, a prolonged heatwave--it was 105°F for three days in a row--and then a drought, which necessitated intensive watering. In September 1966 the additions to the gym, mentioned in Father Luke's letter, were in use: two new locker rooms, doubling the previous capacity, and a new room for wrestling and weight-training. Until then wrestlers had wrestled in all sorts of odd places, including the dining-room, and boys had lifted weights where they could. The General Contractor was R. K. & A. Jones with Murphy Company, by now our preferred contractor for plumbing and HVAC, and Schaeffer Electric. The bid was $118,582.

Early in 1965, 27.505 acres of land belonging to the Sellenrieks and lying at the east end of our property became available. Much of it

---

[217] Letter of 15 November 1964.

[218] The contract (for $2,000) for this landscaping by Hideo Sasaki and Associates, which was included in the contract for the site plan, but paid for by us and not by HOK, was signed on 8 August 1956.

was flat land, suitable for playing fields. By February 1966 Joe Desloge had made the first payment and guaranteed the rest. It cost us $4000 an acre, or $110,020. In 1966, however, we were constrained to sell to the Highway Department a strip of 3.186 acres at the Southwest corner of our property along Mason Road. After an extended tussle, we received $15,912.40 for it. We then owned 176.178 acres. That remained our total through 1973, but from the late sixties on we had a number of inquiries from groups wishing to buy or lease some of our land, usually the strip along the north access road of highway 40, for condominiums, an apartment complex, Khoury League baseball fields, or two skating rinks.

The wisdom of selling some or all of that land was discussed at the Conventual Chapters of 1970 (both Inc and our Council advised against it), 1971 (decision postponed), 1972 (left open until a specific offer was made), and 1973, when the American Automobile Association and Blue Cross/Blue Shield expressed definite interest in erecting one- or two-story office buildings on it. Discussion ensued: Joe Desloge had given us this acreage as an investment, so one question was whether the land would appreciate faster or more slowly than stocks; but there were also those who questioned in principle the idea of selling the land. On the other hand, an endowment was an urgent need if we were to maintain the financial stability of the Priory and its works while continuing our policies on fees and financial aid; the sale would not remove the possibility, then being considered, of building condominiums for our friends who wished to live near the monastery; there should be enough money to repay Inc for the original cost of the land and still to establish the endowment. Two motions were then made: the first, that we agreed in principle to realize in cash the investment made in the property along the north access road, passed narrowly; the second, that we should negotiate with the AAA and Blue Cross, passed a little more easily. Finally, at an extraordinary meeting of the Conventual Chapter on 22 March 1974, Father Prior was authorized to negotiate with Mr. Sam Priest of the AAA the sale of the property under discussion. By coincidence, this property, like the Sellenriek property, was of about 27.5 acres, but the two were not the same. Blue Cross, by this time, was uncertain. Six years later we consummated the sale.[219]

[219] The re-zoning was challenged in court. The case and the appeals, which reached the Supreme Court of the State of Missouri, were not resolved until 15 January 1980. This cost us legal fees and six years' interest on our potential endowment.

Late in 1966 the roof of the monastery, which had developed some leaks earlier, needed to be replaced. When the building was being planned, we had expressed doubts about a flat roof but had been told that with modern techniques all would be well. Nonetheless in all later buildings with flattish roofs the roof has been given a slight pitch. In the monastery, the faulty flatness was compounded by equally faulty advice given us by an ex-employee, who had himself been a roofing contractor, and our difficulty in getting the roof replaced was compounded by the bankruptcy declared by the roofing contractor. Even so, in due course Father Luke succeeded in having the roof replaced.

Meanwhile the idea of expansion had been maturing gradually, because it was only gradually that the majority of the monks came to desire it. Ten years previously, in May 1957, Father Columba had written in our *Journal,* "After 1967 it is planned to increase the enrollment of students, as circumstances permit, to 400 or more . . . "[220] but many of the monks of 1967 had not been with us in 1957. The old theological maxim, *bonum est diffusivum sui,* (good wants to spread) encouraged expansion. The school had been founded to benefit Catholic education in Saint Louis, so the benefit should be spread as widely as possible, but there was also some fear that enlargement might bring dilution, and Ampleforth feared we might be pressured into expanding too far too soon. In favor of expansion were many arguments, whose cumulative effect gradually proved decisive: there seemed to be an adequate supply of candidates—in 1967 we had 149 candidates for the seventh grade examination. Over seventy of them were quite acceptable but only thirty-five could be taken. There was some value in diversity, as a school "misses something important if the students are too homogeneous scholastically".[221] Any group of boys tends to divide academically into three--very bright, bright and less bright--rather than two. We would be able to give more consideration to younger brothers, and might be able to find African-American candidates more easily. We could consider a less rigorous stream that would not take Latin, say, in the seventh grade. A larger school could offer a greater variety of courses, teaching methods, activities and sports. In a larger school, there is less pressure on a few outstanding boys to try to lead and excel in everything, since there are more to share the burden. The schools in Saint Louis that were most

---

[220] *SLPJ* I. 3, p. 6.

[221] *SLPJ* V. 1, p. 20. *See also* the *Minutes* of the first Conventual Chapter, 3 May 1967.

like us were larger. We would need four more full-time lay faculty members, but we should be able to attract them and it would urge us to draw them more into the running of the school and to give them more responsibility. The members of the Saint Louis Priory Society, as Inc was by then properly called, who would have to raise the money, were strongly in favor, and in the spirit of Vatican II we should listen to the laity. There was also a non-educational incentive: as the number of monks grew, we became more and more cramped in a building which housed both monks and boys. We therefore wished to move the boys out of the monastery and into a building of their own.

After many meetings of the community and many discussions with our supporters, a consensus emerged, and was expressed unanimously on 3 May 1967 at our first Local Conventual Chapter—that is, the first deliberative meeting of the solemnly professed monks of the Priory. Then "on Thursday 18 May 1967 the Board of Directors of the Saint Louis Priory Society came to a great decision. They approved unanimously a large scale development that will mark a big step forward towards the fulfillment of our Master Plan."[222] This was Father Columba's last major action here. By it he left to his successor the unanimous mandate of both the community and the Priory Society to turn the plan into reality.

At that point, although a school of four to six hundred boys[223] was still a possibility for the future, our intention was to have an average of fifty boys in each year, giving us a school of around three hundred instead of around two hundred. We knew that if we were to have a senior class of fifty, we would need to take more than fifty into the seventh grade. In order, therefore, to start the plan, we needed a new Junior House capable of accommodating at least one hundred and twenty boys. Two years later we would need to have ready a new high school capable of accommodating around two hundred, and at the same time we should provide for possible future expansion beyond two hundred by providing adequate offices, faculty room, rest rooms and similar facilities, so that if further expansion occurred, all that would be needed would be more classrooms. This last decision was prompted by the strong feeling of the Board of the Priory Society that

---

[222] *SLPJ* V. 1, pp. 19-21

[223] We were still open to having eventually 100 boys in each of six grades; or to having 100 in the high school grades and 50 each in the 7th and 8th grades, or even 50 each in the 5th, 6th, 7th and 8th grades.

they would rather launch a drive for $3.5 million over eight to ten years than one for $2 million at once and the rest later.

A few months later, by which time Father Luke had taken over from Father Columba as prior, we were discussing the possibility of extending the use of our facilities. It is hard for any organization to survive if it is generating income for only nine months of the year. We looked first at what we could do during the summer, when school was not in session, and thought of "small lay Retreats, days of recollection for the Diocesan Clergy, study groups for young people at the Universities, a continuation, on a larger scale, of the summer school . . ."[224] At various times we also discussed activities on a larger scale, such as the use of part of our grounds to provide retirement homes for our friends, who might then form an Oblate community; or the construction of some kind of nursing home. Lack of manpower and of capital meant that nothing came of our discussions. However admirable and even necessary these ideas might seem to a financial planner, it remained true that most of the monks were already overloaded to the point where the quality of their monastic life was at risk.

A change of superior is naturally an occasion when new ideas have a better chance of being realized. Coinciding with the decision to expand the school, the change ushered in a time of planning, and therefore of countless meetings. The first building needed was the Junior House. Much work had already been done on that and we were almost at once able to give the architects, HOK again, our needs and then discuss possible layouts with them. After the necessary meetings, the specifications were put out for bids and came back about one third over the estimate, $499,661 rather than $384,000. We then sat down with HOK and McCarthy Brothers, the low bidder, and, with the help of Mr. Watker, recommended to us by Mr. Donald L. Barnes, one of our parents, cut out the fat, but left in the wall-to-wall carpeting and provision for future air-conditioning of the whole building. Some thought the original plans must have verged on extravagance if, even after the cutting, we still had a very serviceable building.

In March 1968 Father Timothy was able to report in a letter that the building was ahead of schedule but that we had plans for "tents, bubbles, classrooms on wheels, wigwams, etc." just in case there was a strike at the last minute.[225] We felt some anxiety because, having decided on the expansion, held the entrance examinations and

[224] Father Luke's Letter of 19 November 1967 to his family.
[225] Letter to his father, 11 March 1968.

accepted an enlarged seventh grade, we would look remarkably foolish if we had nowhere to teach the extra boys. Fortunately all went well and the building, with classrooms, offices and a large common-room-cum-auditorium on the main level, and a substantial basement below, was duly put into service in September 1968 and was duly shown off after our Homecoming football game on 21 September. It was no mean feat for the contractor to have completed a building of fifteen and a half thousand square feet in eight months. At the time, it seemed large and, with ninety-three boys in it, noisy despite the full carpeting. Father Ian was very well satisfied, and another monk remarked that the reality looked surprisingly like the usually rather imaginative "Architect's Impression". But its completion only transferred our anxiety, as it became equally imperative to have a new building for the high school ready by September 1970.

This was a more complex problem, as by now new technologies such as closed circuit television and computers were on the horizon, if not closer, and there was also talk of "undifferentiated space" as a flexible way of providing teaching areas in a time of change. Father Timothy visited a school nearby which had adopted that plan, and had four classes meeting in opposite corners of a large room. He was not impressed. There was also the vexed question of air-conditioning, which was for us at that time far from being a foregone conclusion.[226] Our instinct was not to jump onto band-wagons but to let them roll by. We did not jump onto the one called "Language Labs" and seemed to have been right, and initially we were inclined to let undifferentiated space roll by too. Nonetheless, we did think it worth our while to investigate the use of an educational consultant, and picked the firm of Engelhardt, Engelhardt and Leggett. Perhaps the repetition of the name, in the manner of old-fashioned firms of English Solicitors, reassured us. In the event, it was Mr. Leggett who, on 12 March 1968, came to see us. He convinced us, and Mr. Richard McKinley was appointed to help us. We had two and a half years to plan and complete the building.

There ensued a murmuration of meetings, some of them for two days, with Inc, HOK, and among ourselves, as we gradually worked out, with the aid of our consultant, what we needed and how the various needs should be related to one another. In the course of this,

[226] It was not, apparently, until May 1968 that the monks started to wear, as official monastic summer dress, an open-necked white shirt and black pants instead of the habit. (*Council Minutes* for 14 May 1968) We retained the habit for Matins, Lauds and Conventual Mass.

Richard produced three plans, the third of which won our approval. The culmination of this long process was a meeting on 29 August 1968, with the full faculty, lay and monastic, in the course of which Richard with his eloquence nearly swept us into a futuristic utopia of undifferentiated space and recreational alcoves. It was heady stuff, and we felt we needed to call time-out, so we had lunch. During the lunch interval, the effervescence subsided, and we came back to a more conventional scheme. Richard felt he should push us towards the experimental to see whether we really liked it or not. Later that same day, our local Conventual Chapter unanimously approved the plans for submission to HOK, and, subject to approval by Ampleforth, HOK went ahead.

By December, HOK was going into working drawings and by mid-April 1969 the bids had come in at $756,231.80, a little less than 1% below HOK's estimate. On 1 May Hercules Construction Company, (the general contractor), Murphy Company (plumbing and HVAC) and Ledbetter Electric Company were all set to go, but the Iron Workers Union went on strike and cost us three and a half of the year's best months for building. It was also a time of rapidly rising prices, especially in construction, so every month's delay added seven to nine thousand dollars to our cost. Work eventually started on 18 August, just over a year before we needed the building to be in operation. We had hoped to move in early in the summer so as to have good time for preparation, but the strike made that virtually impossible. It was only by the great efforts of the contractors, cheer-led by Father Luke, that we were able to occupy before the start of school every room except the headmaster's office. School, therefore, opened on time, but the headmaster and his secretary were operating out of cartons in another office. The time of final preparation coincided with some of the year's hottest days, and the air-conditioning was not yet running. Open the windows, and we caught any breeze and all the flies around; shut them, and we sweltered; so we opened the windows until we could not bear the flies, then closed them and swatted the flies until we could not bear the heat, and so on in alternation.

The eventual building was of one story on the west facing the church and two on the east, conforming to the natural slope of the land. It was pleasant enough but, in order to leave the church as the main feature on campus was deliberately not architecturally audacious. The spacious library, designed to house 85,000 volumes, had in the middle an ingenious, multilevel structure made of heavy plywood and carpeting called variously "*massif central*", "lounge and learn", or "play-pen". Its architectural name was "megaform seating". This structure was HOK's suggestion, which we liked and still like. It accommodated forty boys and cost $400. Father Timothy found that when he was showing prospective families around the school and came to the library, the younger members of the family always made a beeline for the *massif*. The classrooms were on the east side on two levels facing the lake. Between one pair on each floor there was a flexible divider so that they could become one double room.[227] Each classroom had a projection screen and many power outlets for audio-visual devices and possible computers. Offices and the faculty room were on the west side facing the church. Connecting with the library was a lecture theater and projection room with the latest equipment and devices, which at that time included record-players for 78s and LPs, movie-projectors, slides and synchronized slide projectors, a few film-strips still and an opaque projector, which had superseded what was probably the most ancient epidiascope west of the Mississippi--it even retained its ancient name. Closed circuit television was provided for but not provided, and VCRs and CDs were still in the future. The boys were enthusiastic about their new school, and the yearbook commented, "Because of the immense care with which this building was planned it's [sic] excellence as a teaching facility will last for many years to come."[228] They specially commended the provision of "all the necessary outlets for a computer terminal". *Plus ça change, plus ça change.*

The dedication of the High School and the Columba Cary-Elwes library took place on 7 November 1970. Cardinal Carberry had accepted our invitation to officiate but was prevented at the last moment,[229] and so Bishop Joseph A. McNicholas celebrated the Mass. Father Columba returned for the occasion and preached the homily, and then the ministers and a select group went in procession to the new building, which the bishop dedicated. Father Columba was present both in person and in paint, in the portrait by his cousin, Simon Elwes, and he and other notables received guests in the library afterwards.

---

[227] Dividers are seldom fully satisfactory, and in due course one was taken out and replaced by a wall.

[228] *The Shield*, 1971, p. 126.

[229] Our memory is that Cardinal Carberry was able to come out for part of the reception, but this is not mentioned in the records. He certainly held Father Columba in high enough respect to have done so.

Meanwhile, at our Conventual Chapter on 29 August 1968 we approved unanimously the preliminary plans for a new football stadium and track. Father Paul was the master mind and Ray Sellenriek the contractor for this. The cost was $128,000. It was in use for the track season of 1970 but was not solemnly opened until the fall. It was named for our good friend, John Valle Janes.[230]

Not so exciting but, because of the enlargement of the Junior House, almost equally necessary was the enlargement of the southern entrance road, which served principally the Junior House, but also the Stannard House and the dining room. The work was donated by Fred Weber, Inc., and was completed in November 1968. It was at this time, too, that we provided additional parking north of the church and in an arc starting north of the north end of the high school and curving down to the gym, but we had to pay for that ourselves.

In the summer of 1971, with the help of the bequest from Mrs. Anna May L. Nussbaum, we remodeled the Music area by turning the ground floor of the barn back into one large room, updating its equipment and converting what had been the locker-room southeast of the music-room into three practice rooms for musicians.

In April, the Council had enthusiastically approved the plans for remodeling the ground floors of the monastery and the Stannard House, for which The Friends of the Priory had given $5,500. We made what had been classrooms on the south side of the monastery into guest rooms and the monastic kitchen. The west end of what had been the library on the north side became the monks' dining-room, and the east end a small chapel, with an even smaller chapel in it for the Blessed Sacrament. The northeast corner of the building became the business offices, the southeast corner a reception room, and the southwest corner room was enlarged and became the monks' common-room or calefactory, complete with fireplace. We tried to make it a little more inviting than its predecessor, even installing paneling. A patio was planned adjacent to it and was built a little later by the monks. The northwest corner became a laundry-room, which later acquired a pool-table, not an ideal combination. A little later we had the chance to install central air-conditioning on the ground floor of the monastery for $18,000 and eagerly grasped it. Not so much was done in the Stannard House, but it was decided in November that when the monks moved their dining-room from the Stannard House to the monastery, the seniors would use that room for their lunch, and from January 1972 they did so. One other change took place right at

[230] He died suddenly on 6 January 1972.

the end of our period: we agreed to a contract with Food Services International to feed our boys, but this did not start until January 1974.

The move of the seniors was to ease the overcrowding in the boys' dining-room--yet another consequence of expansion. The obvious solution would have been to have two sessions, but Father Timothy felt that it was desirable for the whole school to be together in one place once a day, and so in September 1971 Father Finbarr managed to squeeze about 285 bodies into the existing space. When the twenty-five seniors moved, Father Finbarr then designed for the dining-room a new layout which accommodated 21 faculty and 236 boys.

The only other remodeling was to expand the Chemistry laboratory in the Science Wing. This was done by our own maintenance men, with help from monks and lay faculty, for a cost of less than $7,000.

We conclude this section with a table showing a comparison of the cost in dollars per square foot of three somewhat comparable buildings, the monastery being comparable because, when it was built, the ground floor was mostly classrooms:

Building	date of bids	sq. feet	cost	cost per sq. ft.
Monastery	10/1957	18,754	333,871.63	17.80
Junior House	09/1967	15,432	386,000.00	25.01
High School	05/1969	30,847	756,231.80	24.52

The cost per square foot for the high school was less than for the Junior House, which was built two years earlier, so despite inflation and the strike, Richard McKinley saved us money as well as providing good advice. The cost was also less than Richard's estimate.

The Academic Program

OUR second yearbook, dealing with the school year 1960-61, showed at least that our ideals were getting across, as the editors made the following introduction to the section on the administration: [231]

> *Priory* has been most fortunate in securing a most dedicated faculty, both lay and monastic. Aside from their contributions toward the academic achievements of the student and his athletic progress, these erudite and understanding men are ever present to proffer a word of counsel, or to assist in solving any problem which may arise. Whether in the classroom or on the field, their actions are aimed at developing character and instilling a sense of responsibility in the boys.
>
> Each has had a distinguished and interesting life, and his experience and knowledge is passed on to the boys who benefit greatly by it. The graduate of *Priory* represents the unselfish toil and labor of these scholarly educators, and in his character is [*sic*] clearly reflected the firm and adamant principles which have been presented to him during his four years at the school. We would like to take this opportunity to thank the faculty for all their time, effort and perseverance.

It is a fact that for the first few years of our period the Senior Masters in each subject were M.A.s of Oxford, except for Father Thomas, who had a Doctorate from the University of Liverpool.

What follows may show how far our ideals became reality. When our fifth school year started in September 1960 Father Timothy was headmaster, Father Leonard had just taken over from Father Brendan as second master in charge of discipline, and Father Ian was in charge of the Junior House. This continued until October 1969 when Father Ian went on sabbatical leave and Father Miles took over the Junior House, as well as continuing to be school librarian. In the summer of 1971 Father Leonard returned to England and Father Finbarr took over as second master, thereby inheriting from Father Leonard not only the discipline of the school, but also the coordination of Activities and dances, and care for the radio hut, our audio-visual equipment and our summer programs. It is a tribute to Father

---

[231] *The Shield*, 1961, pp. 6-7.

Leonard's versatility that, in addition to what Father Finbarr inherited, Father Paul inherited from him the care of the seniors and the alumni, and arrangements for internal examinations; Father Ralph the retreats for the boys; Mr. Geiss the yearbook and Mr. Pomeroy the lecture series and General Knowledge; and that still left the drama unaccounted for.

After four complete cycles of the school year, a pattern was beginning to emerge, one that was both similar to and different from that of the school year we knew at Ampleforth. We had three terms, as at Ampleforth, but our year started early in September rather than in the middle of the month, and ended at the beginning of June rather than late in July. That meant that the vacations between the terms were much shorter, the vacation in the summer much longer, and the part of the school year after Christmas again much shorter. In practice, if a teacher had not by Christmas covered a good half of the year's material, there was little likelihood of his covering all the material by the end of the year. Not all the monks from Ampleforth acted on this difference.

The student body grew from 139 in September 1960 to 285 in September 1973. This occurred inevitably as we increased the size of the seventh grade from one set of about fifteen in September 1958, to two sets of seventeen or eighteen in September 1963 and to three of about twenty in September 1968. When we had two sets, the A set was intended to be smarter than the B set. When we went to three sets, the A was still intended to be the smartest but the other two, B and Beta, were intended to be equal, but the boys could not be convinced of this.

The daily schedule was, since we were a day school, quite unlike that of Ampleforth. We show here in the left-hand column the daily schedule for the school year 1960-61 and in the right-hand column that for 1972-73. The text will then explain how we went from the former to the latter.

UPPER SCHOOL

1960-61		1972-73	
(Monday through Friday)		(every day except Wednesday)	
8.35 a.m.	buses arrive	8.25 a.m.	buses arrive
8.40 - 9.15	1st period	8.30 - 9.00	at form masters' disposal
9.15 - 10.00	2nd period	9.00 - 9.45	1st period
10.00 -10.10	milk break	9.45 -10.30	2nd period

10.10 -10.55	3rd period	10.30 -10.40	break
10.55 -11.40	4th period	10.40 -11.25	3rd period
11.45	Mass	11.25 -12.10 p.m.	4th period
12.20 p.m.	wash	12.15	lunch
12.25	lunch	1.10 - 1.55	5th period
1.10 - 1.55	5th period	1.55 - 2.40	6th period
1.55 - 2.40	6th period	2.40 - 3.25	7th period
2.40 - 3.25	7th period	3.25 - 4.40	athletics
3.25 - 4.40	athletics	5.00	buses depart
5.00	buses depart		

JUNIOR HOUSE (as Upper School until 1.10 p.m.)

	(M.T.Th.F)		(Wed.)
1.10 - 1.55	5th period	1.10	change for athletics
1.55	change for athletics	2.20	change after athletics
3.05	change after athletics	2.40 – 3.25	5th period
3.25 - 4.05	6th period	3.25 – 4.05	6th period
4.05 - 4.50	7th period	4.05 – 4.50	7th period
5.00	buses depart	5.00	buses depart

In September 1964 a small modification was introduced for the upper school on Wednesdays, to give the form masters twenty minutes of what was normally class time after lunch. The fifth period started at 1.30 p.m., the sixth ended at 3.00, the seventh was cancelled and the athletes picked up an extra twenty-five minutes. In September 1967 there was a major change when we decided to make Mass available each day but no longer required for everyone, except on Fridays:

10.00 - 10.45	Mass/ Study Hall/ Class
10.45 - 10.55	break
10.55 - 11.40	3rd period
11.40 - 12.25	4th period

We eliminated the five minutes allowed for washing and went straight to lunch at 12.25, and the rest was as before. Those who did not choose to assist at Mass might pray, study, be counseled or tutored. Gospel study groups were encouraged, but meetings of other clubs or activities were not, nor was homework nor "practical or theoretical athletics." This lasted for only two years, and then in

September 1969, the period 8.30-9.00 a.m. each day was allotted to form masters. Each form had Mass one day a week in church at 8.30, and on the other days, the form masters transacted whatever business there was or let the boys study. In September 1970 we restored Mass for the whole school at 8.30 a.m. on Friday. The first two class periods then ran from 9.00 to 9.45 and 9.45 to 10.30. There was the ten minute break and then the next two classes until 12.10 p.m. The fifteen minutes saved at 9.00 a.m. were used to lengthen the period of free time after lunch. On Wednesdays, as the form masters no longer needed the period 1.10-1.30 p.m., the fifth period started at 1.10 and the sixth ended at 2.40, and the athletes of the upper school picked up a further twenty minutes. This meant that on Wednesdays the Junior House had their athletics after lunch and their fifth, sixth and seventh periods after athletics.

We kept, in 1960 and for many years after, the parents' evening in early October for the lower three grades. Some faculty complained that they hardly even knew the boys' names by then, but the administration felt that it was essential to make contact with the parents of, especially, boys in these lower three grades as soon as possible so as to guard against the possibility of a boy's wasting half the first term. By a compromise, the grading period tests came after this parents' evening, but before the parents' evening held for the upper three classes. There was a report period but no testing in November. These reports commented on progress, industry, behavior and general attitude when these had been either above or below normal. At the end of the term there were examinations just before Christmas. In the second half of the year, there was a report period in the second week of February and end of term examinations before the spring break. Another parent-faculty evening was held in April, and then, at the end of May, graduation examinations for the seniors and end of the school year examinations for everyone else.

We took the examinations quite seriously and expected the boys to do the same. The Examination Rules, after stating that there should be formality about the examinations and that any boy found cheating must be sent to Father Timothy, continued:

i. Examination rooms are out of bounds at all times on days when examinations are taking place. Boys therefore may not enter the examination room until the master arrives and lets them in.
ii. No books may be taken to a boy's desk in the examination room. Any books needed for review after the examination

may be left at the front of the classroom, or at the back of the gym.

iii. Paper should be distributed by the master. Boys should write on both sides.

iv. There is to be no talking in the examination room before, during or after an examination. A boy who wishes to ask a question simply holds up his hand and waits for the master to come to him.

v. Boys should not leave the examination room. Those who have finished and looked their papers through may hand them in and review for the next examination. Those who need to go to the bathroom may go one at a time. With normal precautions, this should be a rare necessity.

These rules were well kept. When examinations were held in the gym, the boys carried the necessary desks from the classrooms to the gym before the examinations and back again after them.

The climax of the year by now was the Graduation itself. If the weather permitted, this took place on the lawn behind the Stannard House, where the four great elm trees provided shade for some of those present. But often enough the weather was either wet, windy or uncertain. Then we had to go to the gym, which could be quite hot and humid, or to the church, when it was built, which could be equally hot and humid. It was not air-conditioned until the mid-eighties. The lawn was a delightful place for it until the elms succumbed to their Dutch disease, but the church, once it was air-conditioned, was the most appropriate setting. All graduations are memorable and it is invidious to pick and choose, but that of 1966 was the first occasion on which members of the graduating class addressed the assembly. They were Vernon L. Haug, Jr., and Bernard P. O'Meara. Robert D. Crowe and Larry Haug won our first two Scholarships from the National Merit Scholarship Qualifying Test. Members of the class also won five college scholarships, one ROTC scholarship and our first athletic scholarship, Patrick J. Healey for basketball to Benedictine College, Atchison, Kansas.[232] Graduation was also the time when we chose the names to be inscribed on the handsome, mahogany Honor Roll Board, given to us by Henry Hughes.

We also held each year a ceremony for the eighth graders, even though they were going to continue with us. This consisted of Mass

[232] Our first full football scholarship had to wait until 1982, and was won by Paul Constantino to Duke University

and a breakfast, and so was easily accommodated in the church and the boys' dining-room. The best part of the program was Father Ian's address each year, in which he showed his skill in making and illustrating his points in language enjoyed by the boys no less than by their parents. The rest of us improved the shining hour as best we could.

Such was the skeleton of the academic year, but what of the spaces in between, what Samuel Johnson calls the "interstitial vacancies"? [233] The courses taught between the tests were, after all, what the academic year was about as well as what the tests were about.

In 1960 boys coming into the ninth grade had to take four years each of Religious Instruction,[234] English, Math, and one language and three years each of History, Science and a second language. The languages were Latin and either Spanish or French, with German making an occasional appearance in the upper forms when there was sufficient interest; the Sciences were Physics, Chemistry and Biology. Father Thomas started by teaching Chemistry and Physics as a unified course, but eventually yielded to local custom and to practicality, and taught each for one year.[235] Greek could be started in the ninth grade, and could be continued until graduation, but it was an extra course and recommended only for real linguists. Seniors could choose to continue with both Latin and French, or to take one language and Science. Some years later they could opt for one language and half a year of a second language and half a year of Science, which in this case was Biology. They could continue their Greek, if they could fit it in, but very few did. They also had a mini-course of Elementary Politics and Economics from Father Columba, supported by Mr. Richard Weekes and others, and a still minier course of General Knowledge and Current Affairs from Father Leonard. In addition, the Thesis was still required, first as a condition of graduating *cum laude*, and later as a condition of graduating at all. There was also for a while from 1963 a class of spoken French given on Saturday mornings by

---

[233] *The Rambler* 108, p. 7. Appendix E 2a shows the block program of courses for September 1960 and Appendix E 2b that for September 1972.

[234] This course was called at various times Religion, Theology, or Seminar. It provided an introduction to the Bible and to Catholic faith and morals, with some study of other religions. *See* Appendix E 5.

[235] Appendix E 3 contains the breakdown of courses for the year 1964-65 to show what was taught in Math and how Physics and Chemistry were taught in combination in the sophomore and junior years. Appendix E 4 shows how the curriculum was to develop between 1964 and 1968.

Mme. Bulus, and for several years in the sixties there was, also on Saturday mornings, the Novel Seminar, which owed its origin to Mr. Frank L. Schmertz and a group of enthusiastic boys of the class of 1965.[236] They read and discussed a wide range of novels in English. The list for 1968 included Fielding's *Joseph Andrews*, Dickens' *Hard Times*, Joyce's *A Portrait of the Artist . . .*, Camus' *The Stranger*, Evelyn Waugh's *Decline and Fall*, and *A Handful of Dust*, and Tolkien's *The Lord of the Rings* trilogy. The English Department also instituted the Headmaster's Literary Prize, which was the stimulus for a television script and a full length play by David Linzee.

Boys coming into the seventh grade started Latin and French on entry, and in two years covered the equivalent of more than one year of high school language but less than two. In Math they covered the normal grade school Arithmetic and embarked on Algebra and Geometry. To these they added Religious Instruction, English, History plus Geography, one period each of Choir and Musical Appreciation and two periods of Activities, which were in 1960 Music in the Barn, Mechanical Drawing in the monastery basement, Carpentry in the locker room area of the gym, or Debate in the Junior House.

Between 1960 and 1973, the period we are considering, various other courses made occasional appearances: Speech, taught by Mr. Edward G. Marsh, a parent, and others, was offered most years at a variety of levels. Handwriting was offered in the Junior House. This has always been something of a monastic speciality. Father Luke brought the tradition over from Ampleforth, Father Augustine continued it, and Father Miles, whose own formal lettering was both beautiful and swift—his informal writing was amazingly hard to read—brought it to a peak. Spanish was dropped for a time, and then reintroduced. There were lecture series on Art, Music, General Knowledge and Classical Civilization at various levels, but especially in the Junior House. Government was taught in the ninth grade to those who did not learn Greek.

This was what went on in the classroom, but it had to be complemented and reinforced by homework. To this and especially to its careful and prompt correction by the master and prompt return to the student we attached great importance. In September 1963 Father Timothy wrote to the faculty, "There is an almost exact equation between the quality of a boy's homework and his final results at the

---

[236] This class also originated the Glee Club, won three Reserve Officers' Training Corps (ROTC) scholarships and a number of awards in Science. The leading actor in their play, *The Haunted House*, was Kevin Kline.

end of the year." One unit of homework was intended to occupy the average boy for forty-five minutes. This called for a degree of skill and experience on the part of the faculty, and some set too little, others too much. Fortunately the risk of overload was reduced by the innate, or at least ingrained, sales-resistance of the boys. The juniors and seniors had some library periods for which work was assigned but was not tied to a particular period. The purpose of these was "to encourage independent study, to give the boys practice in written exposition, and to train them in budgeting their time. This training . . . will be effective only if enough work is set and its completion by the deadline rigorously required."

Both the teaching in the classroom and the boys' homework were supported by the school library. From our earliest days here, the acquisition of books and their use by faculty and boys were among our highest priorities. Acquisition, in the beginning, was almost always by gift. Public libraries and other monasteries, most notably Portsmouth Priory and Holy Cross Abbey, were most generous to us from their duplicates. Bill Weld and Lemoine Skinner left us books; Mr. James Murray gave us a thousand books; and we made other book-hunting forays.[237] Our Mothers' Club organized a BYOB party, by which they meant Bring Your Own Book; and Messrs Chris Peper and Cliff Greve allowed us the use of their accounts with Blackwell's Bookshop in Oxford, when we were there. Fortunately for them, that was not very often. All this was necessary because until 1967 the budget for the school library was hardly as large as minuscule. In the two previous years, the school library had received gifts and books worth $13,000, but this was exceptional and could not be relied on for the future. We therefore decided to increase its budget from the astonishingly small sum of $250 to an annual sum of $2,000.

Initially we had two libraries, one for the monastery and one for the school. Gradually we moved towards the economy of books, space and personnel attained by having only one library. The question was first formally raised at the Conventual Chapter of 21 December 1967 and the motion to form a committee to look into it was approved unanimously. It was discussed again at the Chapter of 29 August 1968. Finally, at the Chapter of 1 December 1968 after the committee had presented its report, the amalgamation along the lines of the committee's report was unanimously approved.[238] Thus the

---

[237] *See above*, pp. 259-60.

[238] The report is appended to the *Minutes* of the Chapter. The kernel: "that the monastic and school libraries be united, both for reasons of economy and

amalgamation was virtually complete by 1970 when the high school moved into its own separate building. We kept in the monastery only those books that were used mainly for teaching the novices or were of mainly monastic appeal.

So in the summer of 1970 Father Miles, the librarian, organized the moving and reshelving in the school library of some 30,000 books from the two libraries in the monastery. The Anheuser-Busch Brewery provided one necessity for this move, namely 1200 empty cartons. Some of the metal shelves collapsed and needed to be fitted with handsome wooden endpieces, which improved both their looks and their stability. In our *Journal*, Father Miles listed twelve boys in the school and eight alumni who worked indefatigably throughout the summer on the project. Egon Doering, our instructor of carpentry, built, and Henry Hughes and Father Timothy polished sturdy oak shelves for the south wall and mahogany presses for the books of reference.[239]

Fathers Timothy, Brendan and Augustine, and Alex Niven had had charge of the library at various times, but none of them rivaled Father Miles' amazing achievement of increasing the library's holdings by five thousand books in a single year. If he worked at it every day of the year, which is quite possible, he added nearly fourteen books a day. Not that he did quite all of it himself; one of his many achievements was to enlist a company of volunteer mothers. They did invaluable work in the unexciting tasks of getting a book into the library and keeping it, once there, in the right place, and in the more exciting task of creating a Title Index to supplement the Author Catalog. Father Miles trained several generations of boys to act as assistant librarians. He first showed the talents that later made him a successful Director of Development by encouraging parents and friends to give or bequeath books to the library.

A school library has to be a very versatile resource. It has to support the classwork of both faculty and boys; it has to cater to those who read for general interest; it has to provide books that will stimulate interest; it has, in our case, to satisfy the theological and spiritual needs of the monks. It is hard for the librarian to decide what is worth having on the shelves and what not. Father Timothy remembers being very hesitant about recommending for the library

---

monastic frugality, and to make the books and materials available to more people. Certain books of special usefulness to the monks should, however, be kept in the monastic building."

[239] *SLPJ* VIII. 2, p. 13.

Apicius' *Roman Cookery Book*, an esoteric volume, you might have thought, if ever there was one. Two or three years later we had to buy another copy because the first was in pieces.

Support of a kind different from that provided by the library came from the Danforth Foundation, which in 1965 made grants to four independent schools, of which we were one. Their intention was that the funds should be used "primarily for student aid, strengthening of faculty, and improvement of the educational program."[240] We had to write a lengthy proposal, but it was the foundation's initiative, so we were successful. Our grant-writing skills were more severely tested when we applied to the federal government for a grant to develop a series of lectures entitled *The Classical Background*. After initial encouragement, we were told that it was a most interesting and praiseworthy proposal, but they were not going to give us any money for it.

These were the courses taught and the resources supporting them. We now turn to the students who took them. In September 1960 we had in the high school four full classes of about thirty each, and in each of the seventh and eighth grades one half-class of about fifteen. Because in September 1958 we had taken half a class and not a full class into the seventh and eighth grades, when these half-classes reached the ninth grade, we had to hold an examination for boys from outside the school to bring the ninth grade up to what we then considered full strength of thirty plus. Thus in September 1960 our ninth grade consisted of thirteen boys who had been in our eighth grade and twenty-two from outside. In the languages and in Math, this created a problem for our homogeneous grouping. To take Math as an example: from our own eighth grade we had one small group of bright boys with some knowledge of Algebra and Geometry, and a second small group of less bright boys with some of the same knowledge; and from outside we had a small group of bright boys and a small group of less bright boys all lacking any such knowledge. This gave us four, small homogeneous groups, but to have had four sets in a class of thirty-five would have been quite uneconomical. We tried to solve the problem by offering the brighter boys from outside a summer school in Math, Latin or French, or by giving them extra work and tutoring during the school year in the hope that they would be able to catch up with the A set. We had varying success with this, but we never fully solved the problem until we made the seventh grade

[240] *SLPJ* IV. 2, p. 14.

our regular level of entry for all boys, which we did in September 1963.

Taking into the seventh grade thirty-five boys all at one time rather than taking in fifteen or so then and adding another fifteen or so two years later, enabled us to accept a more diverse group, and so in September 1964 we took in our first two African-American boys. One of these, Rodney Maxwell, became a semi-finalist in the National Achievement Scholarship Program, roughly the equivalent of a National Merit Scholarship semi-finalist, was invited by NASA to the launching of Apollo XIII, and in due course graduated from the Massachusetts Institute of Technology. We had this possibility of greater diversity because, when we made the seventh grade our only level of entry, we at once started to attract a much larger number of candidates: just under 100 for 1963 and 1964, and then 130 for 1965. The number increased until we peaked at 168 in 1972 and then, in demonstration of hubris and nemesis, dropped precipitously to 86 in 1973; but there may have been in 1973 some conflict on the first date for the examination, as we had a second round six weeks later, which brought the numbers up. We continued to hold, on the same date, a dry-run for fifth-graders, to give them an idea of how they might fare in the following year. When we found that some ingenious parents were using us as a free testing agency and had no intention of sending their son here, we made it a condition of releasing the results that the parents had filed an application form with us.

We had been hesitant about making the seventh grade our only normal level of entry because a proportion of our parents found it a burden to pay the fees for the four years of high school, and would have found it even more of a burden to pay them for six years. We had found also that some parents thought that two years in our Junior House would be a good preparation for high school elsewhere. That, no doubt, was true, but from our point of view highly regrettable, as it meant that we were left with empty places, which it was possible to fill only if we had a regular entry into the ninth grade. It was only after some years of experience that we became convinced that the overall academic gain of having all the boys start in the seventh grade did indeed outweigh these disadvantages.

There was another reason for taking all our students into the seventh grade. All the Archdiocesan schools and most of the Catholic independent schools held an examination for entrance into the ninth grade, and many tried to choose a day on which theirs would be the only test. This led to a series of examinations and a candidate might find several successive Saturdays occupied by them. In a very understandable desire to simplify the procedure, the Archdiocesan School Office wished to establish a single date on which all applicants for the ninth grade would take the Archdiocesan standardized test at their preferred school. If they were not accepted there, they could then apply to another school. We felt that this would penalize those boys who really wanted to come to us but might be afraid to take our test when we had so few places to offer. This would be especially true if they needed a scholarship. In both cases we would suffer. In 1961, when we still hosted our own entrance examination as well as the Archdiocesan common examination, only twelve boys from other grade schools took the Archdiocesan test at Priory. Had we not held our own test on the following Saturday, we would have been in a poor way. This seemed to justify our opinion that we might find ourselves looking to the rejects of other schools to fill our class. In a way there was nothing wrong with that, but it did not seem to be what the Archdiocese had invited us to Saint Louis to do. We also felt that the Archdiocesan test gave us less accurate information than our own test.

After much discussion and correspondence[241]--for this was a matter which seemed to threaten the well-being of our school and possibly even its survival—we were permitted to hold our own scholarship examination for boys needing financial aid, which helped us somewhat but did not fully solve the problem. So when we started for other reasons to consider making the seventh grade our regular level of entry, we thought that we could kill this bird too with the same stone. We did, however, continue to require our eighth-graders to take the Archdiocesan test, so that they would have something to show if they ever needed to transfer to another school. In the rare case of a boy in our eighth grade whose acceptance into our ninth grade seemed doubtful, we recommended that he take the test at another school.

By 1960 we had slightly reduced the amount of in-house testing partly to give more time to teaching and less to testing, and partly because of the amount of outside testing to which the boys had to submit. There too a pattern was emerging. The two main agencies whose tests were an important factor in admission to college were the College Entrance Examination Board, or C-E-E-B, and the American College Testing Program, or A-C-T. Also important for financial aid was the National Merit Scholarship Qualifying Test, or N-M-S-Q-T, on whose results large numbers of corporations based their financial aid to college students. This was a separate test, held in February or

---

[241] *See* Appendix D 2 for a sample.

March until 1971, when the National Merit Corporation decided to use the College Board's Preliminary Scholastic Aptitude Test (PSAT), administered in October of the Junior year. This reduced by one the number of tests a student had to take, since our juniors took take the PSAT anyway.

Our policy on testing, as stated in October 1961,[242] was that in May sophomores in the A set should, and those in the B set might, take the College Board Achievement Tests (CBATs). One of the tests should be English; each boy should decide with the senior master for each subject what other achievement tests he should take, and the headmaster would approve their choice, or not. The limit, set by CEEB, was three tests on any one date.

Juniors should all take the PSAT in October, the Scholastic Aptitude Test (SAT) in March, and, again after discussion, the appropriate Achievement Tests in May. Other things being equal, they were encouraged to take in May the subjects they would be dropping in their senior year. This meant that they had to choose their senior year electives before applying for the CBATs, and that in turn meant that we could prepare the program for next year's seniors in good time and assign and inform the teachers.

Seniors should take the PSAT in October, the SAT and writing sample[243] normally in December or January, and the CBATs in January or March, but some colleges had special requirements such as taking all tests by December. Later on, some seniors chose to take both the SAT and the CBATs in November. If they were applying to colleges which required the ACT, they took that in November, February or April. Again, the choice of CBATs was discussed with senior masters and the headmaster, and was subject to the specific requirements of various colleges. In addition, qualified seniors, and in due course juniors, might take the College Board's Advanced Placement examinations (AP), a program which started, opportunely for us, in 1956. These were tests given in the middle of May and were designed to enable very good students, who had been doing college level work in high school, to show colleges that they deserved college

---

[242] File, *Organization 1961-62*, document, "College Board Policy" dated 9 October 1961.

[243] The Writing Sample was introduced by CEEB in December 1960 to meet the criticism that one could get into college without being able to write a sentence, all the other tests being multiple-choice. As was to be expected, it produced a few very good samples, a few very bad samples and an enormous pile in between. It did not last long.

credit or advanced standing, or both. In this way they could satisfy some distributional requirements, have a wider choice of elective courses in college, take a semester or sometimes a year abroad, or even graduate earlier. This last entailed a notable saving of expense.

We have seen above that we required Religion in every grade. The course led to no outside examination but was its own reward. English and, initially, Math were likewise required in every grade, and most boys took the CBATs in them and, if they were competent and they and their parents were willing, the AP tests as well. Latin and French were offered in every grade and one of them had to be continued through the senior year. Many took the CBATs in them and, starting in 1963, a smaller number took the AP Latin. None of our students took the AP French until 1972. Spanish was offered as an alternative to French while we took boys only into the ninth grade, but was phased out when we started taking boys into the lower grades. Later it crept back in and we had a few candidates for the CBAT in Spanish. We offered History in all six years, and it was required in the Junior House (with Geography) and in the high school, except that boys taking Greek in the ninth grade could not also take History. In the senior year, History took the form of an introduction to Catholic social thought by Father Columba, and Economics from a variety of teachers. A few boys took the CBATs in American History and two in Social Studies. Starting in 1966, a few each year took the AP in American History.

An introduction to Science was given to boys in the Junior House for one period a week in alternate years. In the high school, Science started by not being offered in the ninth grade, then was required for half a year and finally for the whole year. It was required in the tenth and eleventh grades, and was offered in the twelfth. Initially, in the twelfth grade, those who chose to continue two foreign languages had to drop Science, but later it was possible to take half a year of their second foreign language and half a year of Science. We came to recognize the excellence of the Biology course offered to seniors by Doctors Bussmann and Mudd, and in 1965 we made it a requirement for all seniors. During the period under review, boys took the CBATs in Chemistry and Physics, with a few taking Biology. In the AP, more took Chemistry (93) than took Physics (52), and none took Biology.

In September 1962 the senior class included, for the first time, boys from the Junior House. These were the ten survivors of the thirteen who had started with us in the eighth grade. The balance of the class came from outside. We made no change in the schedule that year nor in September 1963, when the senior class included, also for the first time, boys who had started with us in the seventh grade. The requirements remained the same but much more material was covered, and not only did the number of AP tests taken rise from thirteen to thirty-nine, but our scores rose too. In September 1965 we added an AP course in American History as an alternative to Science or a second foreign language.

The next big change was in September 1968 when, for the first time, the whole senior class had started in the seventh grade. From this year on, with very few exceptions, all boys entering the senior year would be in their sixth year with us. This prompted us to reconsider the layout of the junior and senior years. Our decision did not reduce the amount of learning but did give each student more choice. Juniors had to take Religion, English, Math and Science, and chose two out of Latin, French, Greek and History, but Latin or French had to be one. Seniors had to take Religion, English, Biology and EPE, and chose three of Latin, French, Greek, American History, Math, Chemistry and Physics. We added riders that a choice either of Latin, French and Greek or of Math, Chemistry and Physics was unbalanced and in general undesirable, but that each case would be decided on its merits; they should take Physics and History in at least one of the two years, and could take them in both as the History was European in the junior year and American in the senior; anyone taking a foreign language in the senior year must have taken that language in the junior year. There was also a series of lectures once a week on topics such as Space, Appreciation of Movies, Music, etc.

On 28 April 1969 there was a joint meeting for heads of departments and members of the headmaster's committee to discuss the curriculum. This occurred annually for the remainder of the period under review. This first meeting produced the most practical idea of any, that we should replace Religion and EPE in the senior year by a course that came to be called the Senior Seminar. It started in September 1969 and focused in its first year on the Nature of Man but widened its purview as time went by.

This remained the arrangement for the rest of the period under review. In summary, what this meant was that everyone studied Religion, English and Math all six years. They studied one language for at least five years and usually six, and another for at least four. They took Chemistry, Physics and the Doctors' half year of Biology. They had four years of History, unless they started Greek in the ninth grade instead of History. Those were the minimum requirements in the subjects mentioned, and to them each boy added his own electives. It was a very strong language requirement, but, as it seemed to us, very fairly balanced by the strength of the requirements in Math and Science. If there was a weakness, it was in History, but this area we tried to reinforce as we went on.

These were the courses taught, and to validate our teaching we relied most of all on our own testing and reporting. These satisfied the boys, their parents and us, satisfied, that is, in the sense of providing good information, but they did not give colleges a firm basis for comparing our boys with others. For this they relied on the various tests of the CEEB, or sometimes the ACT, and so, perforce, did we. In addition, for some years after 1962 ninth-graders took the ninety-five minute test of Math and English set under the National Defense Education Act.

To take them in the order in which a student would encounter them, the significant programs of the College Board were, for us, the Preliminary Scholastic Aptitude Test (PSAT), the Scholastic Aptitude Test (SAT, now SAT I), the Achievement Tests (CBATs, now SAT II) and the Advanced Placement Tests (AP). We regarded the first of these as a dry run for the SAT and even after 1971, when the National Merit Corporation decided to base its awards on this test, we never summarized its results. For the SAT, whose scores ran from 200 to 800,[244] we did calculate class averages, using the best score if the boy took the test more than once. The average for the class of 1960 was 583 in the Verbal test and 612 in the Mathematical. For the class of 1973 the averages were 600 and 654 respectively. It is not surprising that these scores show much less increase than either our AP results or those in the CBATs, because they measure aptitude for learning rather than the actual amount of learning. There is little reason to suppose that the class of 1960 was much less apt for learning than that of 1973. The reader will remember also what we said above[245] about the gradual inflation of grades and the consequent " " applied by the College Board.

For the College Board Achievement Tests (CBATs) also, the scores ran from 200 to 800, and ours showed a marked increase from 1960 to 1973, though not, as we shall see, so gigantic an increase as those for the Advanced Placement tests. The table below shows the class averages for the classes of 1960 and 1973, and the best class average

---

[244] Father Austin found it hilarious that a boy received 200 points simply for turning up for the test.

[245] P. 196, note 136.

for any year in between. The figures in parentheses show the number of students (minimum, after 1960, 10) who took the test.[246]

Class of	No.in class	Eng. Comp.	Mathematics Intermed.	Adv.	Latin	French	Chem.	Physics
1960	28	573(28)	554(23)	674(3)	576(11)	497(10)	511(25)	569(7)
1973	29	586(28)	584(12)	711(16)	655(12)	623(14)	673(16)	637(12)
best average		634(33)	616(12)	738(16)	660(13)	634(23)	680(12)	654(12)
by class of		'70	'70	'72	'72	'70	'70	'71

Some boys took Greek, Spanish, the French or Spanish listening tests, Social Studies, European History, American History or Biology, but the numbers were too small to be representative. Likewise, three boys of the class of '65 took Physics for an average of 678, but this again is too small a group to represent a whole class.

The complete table shows steady upward progress, with some dips, but the dips were not in the same years in all subjects. 1966, for example, saw a dip in Latin and Chemistry but the continuation of a surge in Level 2 Mathematics. We made no attempt to "teach to the test"; it would hardly be possible either to do so, or, in another sense, to avoid doing so. The tests were based on the content of normal high school courses in the subject, and the best preparation was a normal or better high school course.

A similar upward progress may be seen in the results of the National Merit Scholarship Test: in 1960 we had three semi-finalists and no Letters of Commendation in a class of twenty-eight. In 1966 Bob Crowe and Larry Haug became our first recipients of Merit Scholarships. By 1971 we had had several years when about half the class either became semi-finalists or received a Letter of Commendation, and in 1971 fifteen out of twenty-nine did so. In the spring of 1973 we had eight semi-finalists and eleven Letters of Commendation in a class of forty-three.[247] As this was the first class of

---

[246] These figures are taken from a document compiled in 1973 by Father Paul. The complete document may be found in Appendix E 6.

[247] *The Record*, vol. 3, No. 2, p. 1. 10 October 1973.

the enlarged entry into the seventh grade, it was reassuring to us that we did not seem to have diluted the quality by increasing the quantity.

The National Merit Scholarship Corporation was very firm in insisting that their test measured ability to learn rather than achievement in learning and therefore should not be used (as it nonetheless has been) to compare schools. School A's having more merit scholars than school B does not mean that it is a better school, nor that it has better teachers, but it does suggest that school A has more of the smartest students.

The Advanced Placement Tests were designed, as we have said, as a way to give boys who, in their senior year or even earlier, were taking college-level courses, a chance to earn college credit or placement or both. The College Board started this program cautiously with a few subjects and with conservative grading, because they were anxious that colleges should accept the idea of advanced placement cheerfully and give credit generously. They also knew that colleges were likely to be at least a little reluctant to do so "because no-one teaches Freshman Chemistry like our Professor X."

We entered the program even more cautiously in 1960 with eleven of our first seniors taking a total of fifteen tests in English (9), Chemistry (1) and Physics (5). In 1961 we had candidates in English, Math and Chemistry, and in 1962 the same. Next year we added Latin; two years later we had a candidate again in Physics, and the year after that some in American History. In 1969, the College Board offered Calculus AB and BC, and Physics B and C, the latter being in each case the more advanced, and in 1973 added Physics E&M. Latin had already been divided into two levels, and we were teaching Vergil (Latin 4) in the junior year, and Latin Comedy (or Prose) and Lyric Poetry (Latin 5) in the senior year. In September 1972 Father Austin started tutoring Stephen H. Lockhart for the AP Music, which he took as a junior in May 1974 and scored 3. In 1973 we had seventeen seniors taking fifty-two tests in English, Calculus AB and BC, Chemistry, Latin 5, French Language, Physics B, C and E&M, and American History. We also had twenty-three juniors taking thirty-one tests in Latin 4, European History, Chemistry and Physics B.

The College Board grades these tests on a scale from 5 to 1. 5 is intended to mean that the candidate is "extremely well qualified" for college credit; 4 is "well qualified"; 3 is "qualified"; 2 is "possibly qualified"; 1 is (diplomatically) "no recommendation". That was the interpretation published in the College Board's literature. At a workshop a spokesman said less guardedly that 5 demonstrates unusual competence or mastery; 4 demonstrates competence; 3

suggests competence; 2 suggests incompetence and 1 demonstrates incompetence.

In 1960 20% of our candidates were "qualified" or better, that is, they scored 3,4 or 5; in 1973 that percentage had risen to 87 for both seniors and juniors.[248] Moreover, in 1960 eleven out of twenty-eight boys, or 39.3%, took the tests, but in 1973 eighteen out of twenty-nine, or 62.1%, did so. The percentage of seniors taking the AP tests is significant since a school could, in theory, by advising only its most brilliant students to take the tests, achieve a very high average score; but the percentage taking the test would reveal how this high score was achieved.

There were several causes of our giant's stride forward: the first was our growing familiarity with the tests. Although several of us had had experience at Ampleforth of teaching the Higher Certificate courses, which were roughly equivalent to Advanced Placement courses here and certainly of no lower standard, all we knew in 1960 of the AP courses was what the slim pamphlets put out by the College Board told us. Neither then nor later did we "teach to the test", but our increasing familiarity with the style of the tests was obviously an advantage. The College Board held AP workshops in various parts of the country, and those of our faculty who were teaching AP courses attended them.

Father Timothy served a three-year term from 1970 to 1973 on the College Board's National Advanced Placement Committee, which was a valuable experience both for him and for the school, and involved one meeting a year in New York and occasional appearances at AP workshops elsewhere. The meetings lasted several days, during which members of the committee were put up at a hotel nearby. One year, when he checked out, Father Timothy asked the clerk how he should indicate that the College Board would pay. He did what the clerk told him and thought no more of it. A month later, the hotel sent him a bill, which he threw away. Another month, another bill, so he made copies of all the relevant correspondence and dispatched them to the hotel. The bills kept coming until the sixth month, when they were accompanied by a letter threatening prosecution unless the bill were paid. Father Timothy consulted Mr. Fred M. Switzer III, our lawyer and son of the founding father, and found that he had been subjected

[248] The juniors edged out the seniors by a whisker, 87.097% to 86.538%. In 1995 the figure for the seniors was 87.368%. For the whole period 1960-1973 nearly two thirds (62.769%) of our candidates scored 3 or better. For fuller information *see* Appendix E 7.

to "malicious harassment". He wrote and told the hotel as much, enclosing once more copies of the correspondence, noting that this had been sent to them some months before, and saying that, so far from their suing him, he would sue them. By return mail he received a reply saying that they were so sorry he had been troubled.

Next summer, he was driving to New York for the annual meeting and unfortunately coincided with hurricane Agnes, which shed sixteen inches of rain in two days. When he reached Lewisburg, Pennsylvania, where he was planning to visit Bucknell University, the city was flooded, martial law was in force, and he learnt that two people had drowned there that morning. Nonetheless, he managed to wriggle around by back streets despite members of the National Guard at every intersection, and reached Bucknell, to their surprise. Understandably, they were not at their best. He regained Interstate 80, but after a few miles found the road under four feet of water and closed by the police. He made his way by country lanes, themselves under water up to two feet in places. At one point he met a torrent coming down a hill, but the car valiantly breasted the waves and he reached New York only a few minutes late for the opening session. After all that, it was a real anti-climax that his sleeping-bag was stolen from the car in the hotel's garage.[249]

A second cause of our better scores was that since September 1963 our regular intake had been into the seventh grade, and so we had all our students, with only occasional exceptions, for six years. As they studied Latin, French, Algebra and Geometry in the seventh and eighth grades, they were able, by their senior year, either to go considerably further in those subjects or to study them more deeply or to study more subjects.[250] A third, but lesser, cause may have been that whereas in 1959-60 our textbooks were roughly 55% from England and 45% from the United States, in 1972-73 they were roughly 30% from England and 70% from the United States. Those setting the tests would assume that the candidates had been using American texts. A fourth cause was the acquisition for the library of a large number of books related to the A.P. courses. This was made possible for us by the Fathers' Club. A fifth cause was the simple

---

[249] In 1992 Father Paul became a regular reader, that is a member of the grading team, for Mathematics, and in 1995, 1998 and 2000 Father Laurence for English, appointments which were even more valuable for them and for the school.

[250] Boys at the lower end of the class, even if they did not take the AP tests, had still covered more ground than those who started in the ninth grade.

truth that, as each year passed, both boys and faculty were more settled and the physical surroundings more stable; a degree of serenity is conducive to learning.

The Advanced Placement Program fitted in very well with our thinking in three ways: first, unlike the other tests of the College Board, which (apart from the Writing Sample) consisted entirely of multiple-choice questions, most of its questions demanded answers in sentences and paragraphs; secondly it gave our boys the opportunity to gain college credit for subjects that we would have been teaching them anyway; thirdly, the AP syllabus was flexible enough not to crush the initiative of the teacher. Nonetheless, in April 1973 we hosted, at the suggestion of Dr. O. William Perlmutter, Academic Vice-President of Saint John's University, Collegeville, MN, a meeting of the headmasters of Saint John's Prep School, Saint Anselm in Washington, DC, Portsmouth, RI, and Delbarton, NJ, to consider the possibility of starting a Benedictine Advanced Placement Program, and of seeking support by a Foundation. Dr. Perlmutter came with great experience of the College Board, which lent more weight to the scheme, and by it we would have great freedom in our curricula, but the practical difficulties, the labor involved, the uncertainty of its acceptance by colleges and an instinct against fragmentation led us to drop the idea.

We found that, as years passed, colleges became increasingly aware of the AP program and increasingly willing to grant credit for its tests. On the whole, the better the college, the more generous it was in granting credit. Those schools that acquired a reputation for being stingy with credit tended to receive fewer applications from our students.

The American College Testing Program, although sometimes a whole class took it, was never integral to our program. We had far fewer candidates for it, and its tests—English and Math Aptitude, and Reading and Comprehension in Social Studies and Natural Sciences--did not tell us anything new nor validate our courses in any new way. So, although we recorded the results, we never tabulated nor analyzed them as we did those of the College Board.

We experimented with a few other tests, mostly at lower levels, but none endured except a reading test in the Junior House. Our teachers could say easily enough that a student did not read well, but the test was often able to point to a physical or other problem and enable us to recommend the right kind of special help. There were also national contests in various subjects, of which the most interesting was the National Math Contest, in which we took part for the first time in

1962. It was the most interesting because it enabled us to compete both within the United States and also with Ampleforth. But such competition immediately raised the question of the level at which we should compete so as to make it a fair contest. Ampleforth's best mathematicians at any particular age would be well ahead of ours of the same age. To explain why this was so we must make a brief digression on English education at that time.

The primary reason for the difference in level was that serious learning for boys who entered Ampleforth started earlier than in the United States—in France and Germany it started earlier still—and so a bright boy entering Ampleforth for high school might well have been learning French and Latin for six or seven years. Of course he would have been making slower progress in a year than an older boy, but he would still arrive at Ampleforth with a good knowledge of the grammar, vocabulary and basic syntax of the languages. He might have had a year or two of Greek as well. He would have been learning Algebra and Geometry, as well as Arithmetic, and might have mastered Algebra through quadratic equations and most of plane geometry. Another year or two of high school and he would have reached in these subjects a level adequate to carry him through life, unless he wanted to specialize in one of them. Thus he would be free either to drop Math or to specialize in it. If he dropped it, he would not be able to take part in this Math Competition, but if he specialized, he would, age for age, be well ahead of our students.

It is also relevant that, unlike us, Ampleforth was not a strictly college preparatory school. This was largely because at that time only between one fifth and one quarter of English youth went on to college, a much smaller proportion than in the United States. Even from Ampleforth, where the percentage going on to college was higher than the national percentage, boys were quite likely to go straight from school into business or the Armed Forces or into medical or legal training, which for the most part did not mean going to college. The upper school at Ampleforth was also about four times the size of ours, which allowed a far greater flexibility of curriculum for the various groups in the school.

All this meant that a boy who wished to specialize in Math, or in any other subject, could do so sooner and more intensely than was possible here. Between us, therefore, we agreed that our best mathematicians should compete against their boys about a year younger. Even so, their boys came out ahead more often than ours, but one could not argue from this that their math teaching was better than ours, nor even that their boys were brighter, nor vice versa when we came out ahead. What was much more indicative of a good standard was that in 1972 our team had the highest score in Missouri, and in the following year the highest score not only in our state but in our seven-state region. As a result Roger Schlafly and Steve McKenna were among the one hundred students invited to the National Math Olympiad.

So far we have been describing what took place during the regular school year, September through early June. In the summer, when the dust had settled after Graduation, we held in June and part of July a summer school for up to six weeks. It had to finish in time for any monks teaching in it to get away for their holiday and still be back in time for the monks' Retreat and the preparations for the next school year. We offered various kinds of courses: some were remedial and were taken by students from our school or from other schools who had failed in one or more subjects at the end of the regular year; some were accelerated courses to enable good students, who had come into our ninth grade without a background in Algebra and Geometry, Latin or French, to cover what our boys had covered in the Junior House; some were courses of general interest, such as handwriting. In 1972 we offered strengthening courses in English and Math for incoming seventh graders who, though acceptable, seemed to need further preparation. Our own faculty, lay and monastic, taught most of the courses. We found that in the accelerated courses a good student could make up the gap in two summers and be fit to enter A sets in his sophomore year.

In June 1967 we started a new kind of summer school, one for African-American boys who were about to enter high school and who had been recommended by the principals of their grade schools. This first year Father Leonard took charge of twenty boys. To assist him he had Father Thomas, Mr. Walter Ambrose, Athletic Director and Counselor at Vashon High School and a man not to be trifled with, four more monks and another layman, and ten of our boys as junior counselors. This program continued all through the period under review and beyond. It was able to make the proud claim that no boy who had attended failed to complete high school. The summer of 1969, when forty-five boys from Vashon and Central High School districts attended, was notable for two events: Mr. Bob Gibson, the Saint Louis Cardinals' Hall of Fame pitcher, came out for an afternoon; and one of the boys, Sam Greene, missed the bus, walked from Grand Boulevard to Brentwood Boulevard, got a ride from there to I 270, walked the rest of the way and arrived here at 11.30 a.m having walked about ten miles. The program also, though this was not part of our plan, included an eighth-grader who later became a distinguished priest of the Archdiocese of Saint Louis. Father Finbarr took over when Father Leonard returned to England in 1971 and, with Walter Ambrose, ran it for the rest of the period under review. Funding was always difficult. Some came from our parents, some from the Danforth Foundation, some from business, some from the Human Development Corporation, some from our own resources.

For advanced students there was in Clayton from 1958 a summer school of a different kind, the Mark Twain Summer Institute, with which we were involved through Brian Barry, who taught in it and was later its Director for ten years. This provided intense courses of a standard comparable to that of the Advanced Placement Program but in a diversity of less standard topics, such as Dance, Chinese Language and Civilization, or International Studies. A fair number of our students attended.

For all our students we had always required some summer reading: in 1961 two books for those entering the seventh grade, three for those entering the eighth or ninth grade and five for the upper classmen. They had to mail in reports on some books during the summer, be tested on the rest in September and had to learn some lines by heart. We provided a longish list of books from which to choose, and which we hoped would be both challenging and attractive. Summer reading persisted for many years; it was probably a greater burden on the teachers who had to administer and grade it than on the boys. Sometimes we simply gave the boys a list to choose from; sometimes we arranged the books in pairs. An example of the latter arrangement was the program in summer 1963 for the following year's seniors:

(	EITHER	Marlowe, Dr. Faustus and Anouilh, Antigone
(	OR	Vergil, The Aeneid, trans. Day Lewis
(	EITHER	Browning, Selected Poems
(	OR	Frost, Pocket Book . . .
(	EITHER	Greene, The Power and the Glory
(	OR	Hawthorne, The House of Seven Gables
(	EITHER	Catton, This Hallowed Ground
(	OR	Xenophon, The Persian Expedition

(EITHER Adams, Mont Saint Michel and Chartres
(OR Newton, European Painting and Sculpture

Once or twice, and always with hesitation, we offered summer courses in what was first called Speed Reading and later Developmental Reading. These were run for profit by outside agencies.

The Spiritual Program

FOR close on fifteen centuries, Benedictine monks have been involved in the education of boys. Sometimes the intention has been to train them for monastic life and death, sometimes for lay life and death. Today, the majority of the boys in schools such as Ampleforth, Portsmouth and our own are going to be laymen, though we naturally hope that some will become monks, and so their education aims to help to prepare them to be good laymen.

As we said above,[251] education is the responsibility of parents, and others are called in to help them when, for a variety of reasons, the parents cannot do it all themselves. This is particularly true of academic education, but applies also to religious, social, cultural and athletic education. Many a father has time and skill to play catch with his son, but not, perhaps, to spend whole afternoons coaching him in football or baseball. So too parents form their children in goodness, but can still welcome the school's cooperation both in imparting information to their children—study of the Bible and of church history, and instruction in theology—and in forming them to live their faith. Schools like ours attempt this cooperation in both formation and information.

We have seen that we required the boys to take the religion course each year. That was intended to impart the necessary information. A sample syllabus and explanation may be found in Appendix E 5a and b. Being Benedictines, we set great store by the formative effect of the Liturgy and of its crown, the Mass. At the beginning of our period, the whole school came to Mass every school day. Few, if any, resented this: it was generally regarded as "the way things are." Some prayed, some were bored and some oscillated between prayer and boredom. When we started to admit non-Catholic boys to the school, they were not required to attend Mass, though they often did, but they were required to attend Religion classes. This was explained to their parents ahead of their admission, with the comment already mentioned[252] that, although we would make no attempt to proselytize, it could happen that their son might wish to become a Catholic, and if they would regard that as distressing, they should not send him to us.[253]

---

251 *See above*, p. 109.

252 *See above*, p. 84.

253 Through 1967 non-Catholic boys were never more than 3% of the student body.

After the second Vatican Council, it seemed opportune to review our policy on attendance at Mass, especially as we started to hear that at the weekend boys were saying to their parents that they had taken part in the Mass five times that week and saw no need to do so on Sunday as well. Committees were coming into fashion, so we appointed a committee, which met and met and reached no conclusion, but did lay the groundwork for a decision. As mentioned above,[254] we decided in 1967 that there would be a period in the middle of each morning which on Fridays would be a school Mass, and on other days would be allocated on a sliding scale by which seniors and juniors had class one day and the option of Mass or study on the other three days; sophomores had Mass one day, class one day and the option on the other two days; freshmen had Mass on two days, class one day and the option on one day. The Junior House had the option one day and Mass the rest of the week. Theirs was a simplified Mass in the pastoral spirit of Vatican II. When Father Benedict came onto the faculty in 1967, he helped to plan the form Masses and their music. Thus Mass was available and any one who wanted could take part every school day.

After another committee had deliberated and again had reached no consensus, this arrangement was modified in September 1969 by moving the mid-morning period back to 8.30 a.m. and reducing it to thirty minutes. There was no Mass for the whole school that year, but each form had Mass in church once a week, and members of other forms could attend with their form master's permission. Form masters were free to arrange Mass on other days in their form room. In September 1970 this was again revised and Mass for the whole school reinstated on Fridays at 8.30 a.m.

Whatever the general schedule of Masses, there were always special Masses or services for special occasions. Thus there was Mass for President Kennedy after classes on the day of his assassination. It was remarkable that earlier in the day, as the first uncertain reports were followed, during the break after lunch, by definite information, the boys moved unprompted towards the church. It was impressive and at the same time somewhat eerie. There was a shadow over the day, and their instinctive feeling seemed to be that they were facing something with which they could cope only before God and in prayer. The faculty, lay and monastic, felt the same.

There was a Mass of thanksgiving for peace in Vietnam, a Mass in the Byzantine rite—many of the boys had no idea that there were

---

254 *See above*, p. 288.

Catholic priests who could celebrate Mass in that rite as well as in the Roman rite—a service to mark the holiday for Dr. Martin Luther King, for whom we had some kind of program every year. Every now and then there was a Mass for vocations to the priesthood and religious life with a sermon on the same theme, but on the whole we were rather reticent about ourselves, believing that an indirect approach was more effective. Sometimes it was so indirect as to pass unnoticed.

We also encouraged the normal good works, collecting cans of food at Thanksgiving and bundles of clothing at Christmas. One year an award was promised to the class that collected the greatest number of cans. An ingenious class discovered a source of mini-cans about the size of an airline serving, procured hundreds of them and won in a canter. That was the end of that competition. Another way of bringing home both respect for life and the reality of poverty was the poverty lunch. It came in various forms: sometimes everyone simply had a bowl of rice, but a more advanced form provided some with nothing, others with a bowl of rice and others again with a full meal. That caused a stir, almost a riot.

The most interesting of these projects was the challenge to build a school in Molapowabojang, Botswana. The Paramount Prince of Basutoland, as it then was, had been a student at Ampleforth just before we came to Saint Louis, so when we heard in the late sixties that a school was needed at Molapowabojang, we pricked up our ears. If we could raise $1000, they would buy the building materials and put up the school. We divided up the sum between the various forms and left them free to raise the money as best they could. What with car-washes, magazine subscriptions, mission fairs and maybe direct approaches to their parents, they raised the $1000 and we sent it off.[255] In return we received photographs of construction in progress and, finally, of the completed school. In the Junior House, Father Ian and Father Miles kept up their efforts after the completion of the school. They sent money to buy school supplies, and collected stocks of our unworn but outmoded tee-shirts, and once more received photographs, this time of Botswanian boys proudly wearing Priory tee-shirts in the Kalahari Desert.

The boys of the Junior House held, with the help of many parents, an annual Mission Fair with a variety of side-shows, and when they did not send the money to Molapowabojang, responded to an appeal by representatives of the Christian Appalachian Project or sent the money

---

[255] To be exact, the school raised $992.33.

to the foreign missions. They had their own Mass, tailored to their needs; and on Maundy Thursday, when that was a school day, attended the Chrism Mass at the Cathedral.

In 1960 we were still having two Retreats a year, lasting two days for the Upper School and one day for the Junior House. We experimented with various formats, always, in an attempt to get away from the "speaking head" in the direction of more discussions and of more visitors to lead them. To help the boys to make good use of the times of silence, we provided suitable books to read. The Retreats were on campus, but in 1962 the seniors' Retreat before their graduation was at one of the Retreat houses in Saint Louis, and so it continued to be for this period.

In 1964 for the Upper School the number of conferences each day was reduced from four to three, and in 1966 to five over the two days. The schedule then differed for each form; for the sixth form it was:

	first day	
a.m	9.10	assembly
	9.30	first discourse
	10.15	Form Mass
	10.45	meeting with Retreat giver
	11.30	reading
p.m.	12.25	lunch
	1.15	second discourse
	2.00	discussion period with Father Austin
	3.30	third discourse
	4.15	buses depart

	second day	
a.m.	9.10	assembly
	9.30	fourth discourse
	10.15	singing practice
	10.45	Confessions
	11.15	discussion period with J. Guarneschelli
p.m.	12.25	lunch
	12.45	manual labor
	1.30	discussion period with Robert C. Dunn, Jr., alumnus in medical school
	2.45	fifth discourse
	3.30	Votive Mass for youth (concelebrated)
	4.15	Buses depart

The books provided for the seniors were Leo Trese's *Vessel of Clay* for the A set and C. S. Lewis' *Mere Christianity* for the B set. In 1968 the Retreat for the Upper School became, as that for the Junior House had always been, a one-day exercise, and from 1972 we held only one Retreat a year instead of two.

In a school, as in the rest of the world, there is a spectrum of goodness and piety, at one end of which is a group of the genuinely good and at the other a group of the indifferent. The majority moves up and down between the ends, more pious on some days and less on others. The pious, using the word in an entirely good sense, tend to want more unscheduled time in which to read, reflect and pray, and would use it well. Those at the other end might also like more unscheduled time but would not use it well. Hence arises the first dilemma in arranging a Retreat schedule: how to provide for the one group, guard against the other, and at the same time care for the majority. At Ampleforth in 1955 the whole school had a single schedule for the Retreats, and we started in that way. Our first step forward was to have a separate schedule for each form. This took more of the faculty's time, but proved to be time well spent.

By March 1970, partly as the result of the responses to a questionnaire given to the boys, we had gone much farther in the direction of unscheduled time: Assembly at 8.30 a.m. was followed by a movie.[256] After that each form in turn met for an hour with the Retreat-giver. That, with a break for lunch,[257] took until 2.30 p.m., and during that period the two forms not meeting the Retreat-giver had nothing scheduled. At 2.30 there were discussion meetings. The boys chose which one to attend. The topics were: drugs, sex and marriage, the dating game, and coping with student problems. There were also two which were less overtly spiritual or moral: "Crisis in the Inner-City Schools" and "Life under Chinese Communism". At 4.00 there was Mass in church and the buses left at 5.00. The monastery, which then still contained the classrooms, was a silent zone, but talking was allowed elsewhere. The seniors made their Retreat just before graduation and so did not attend this one.

The other question was where to hold the Retreats. A Retreat is a break from the daily routine and for our boys our campus was inextricably associated with the daily routine. That points to a place off campus. But, for a Retreat one needs an atmosphere of serenity, which completely unfamiliar surroundings do not provide, at least not for inquisitive male adolescents. In the spring of 1973 we experimented with sending the juniors off campus for their Retreat. The results were mixed. The ideal, we thought, would be our own Retreat House off campus, but there was then little prospect of that.

---

[256] It was the era when religious educators were discerning powerful spiritual themes in movies.

[257] The music at lunch in 1968 was by Simon and Garfunkel.

Besides the Mass and the Retreats there were other formative influences. Form masters, monastic and lay, addressed their forms not less frequently than once a week, and piety from a layman, or latterly laywoman, sometimes made more impression on the boys and always was a more direct model for them than piety from the monks. From the beginning of Lent 1962, the first year of Vatican II, we were requested by the Apostolic Delegate and directed by the Archbishop both to pray for the Council and to take time in Religion classes to instruct the boys about the achievements of past councils and the prospects for Vatican II. As the Council went on, we were to keep them informed, and did so.

Discipline

WE had come a long way from the early days. That is not to say that there were no disciplinary problems—that would be incredible in any school—but it did mean that discipline was no longer *the* problem. The monitors were now part of school life and remained so for the sixties. In September 1970 they were replaced by a Disciplinary Committee consisting of three elected members and three appointed by Father Leonard. They were to allot to appropriate seniors the various monitorial tasks, such as supervising the library or the labor squad. They took part in presiding over examinations. There were also custodians of the rathskeller, which was the seniors' common room, assistants in the bookstore, the sports store and the library, and official raisers and lowerers of the flag. The English monks, to their surprise, had to show the boys how to fold the American flag correctly. Father Leonard still needed to promulgate rules for conduct on the school buses, and it should not be forgotten that new faculty members had to be instructed in what kind of behavior to require of the boys, so discipline still took up some of our time.

The headmaster's committee continued to meet and continued its function of liaison. Some of its Minutes have been preserved. A complete summary would be tedious, so we list here, as typical, the principal topics for the first half of the school year 1968-69: driving to school; colored shirts rather than plain white; girl cheerleaders; a dance to raise money for the Prom; the formation of an athletic committee; permission to wear khakis in winter as well as summer; permission to bring a brown bag lunch rather than eat the school's lunch; student input into the summer reading list; inter-school committee for social work, charity drives, activities, speakers, finance, school problems etc.; behavior at Mass; plans for the Singer House. A little more than half of these discussions eventually led to action of the kind desired by the committee.

Driving was perennially the committee's top priority. A poll in 1969 revealed that the parents were in favor of our rule against driving by the surprising margin of more than five to one. The rule then was that driving was allowed only with permission requested by the parents ahead of time, and only in an emergency or to some athletic events away from Priory. In November 1971 the thin end of the wedge was driven in a little deeper, largely because of the difficulty of providing buses for an increasingly scattered school population. Some boys were spending up to three hours a day on a bus. The rule did not change that year, but the number of "emergencies" increased. It was clear that the dam was weakening, and in September 1973 it finally collapsed and driving was permitted.

In the summer of 1957 we had joined a group called the Inter-School Parents' Committee, on which each of the leading independent schools was represented.[258] Every year it produced a Social Code for Teen-age Conduct, which was designed more as a guide for parents than as rules for teen-agers, and was intended to strengthen parents' hands and encourage if not uniformity, at least a measure of agreement among them. It covered mostly parties off campus but included some suggestions about school dances. Some examples of the contents of the code for 1963 are:

2. " . . . No one should assume that he has the right, even in his own home, to allow alcoholic beverages to be served to other people's children."

4. Invitations should be made personally. "This . . . will control crashing, which is in bad taste."

9. " . . . that the following be considered as closing hours for private parties:

Grade 7	10.00 P.M.
Grade 8	10.30 P.M.
Grade 9	11.00 P.M.
Grade 10	11.30 P.M.
Grade 11	12 Midnight
Grade 12	12.30 A.M.

11. "Dating hours . . . Boys should be willing to accept and keep hours which should be set by girls' parents on all occasions. Young people should be expected to notify their parents of any unusual delay or change of plans. "

12. "That telephoning on school nights be limited as to length and number of calls."

Since laws are normally retrospective, reflecting what has been happening that the legislators want to stop, they often serve as a

---

[258] *See* p. 151 *above*.

commentary on the mores of the time. The code was gently worded and by and large it was followed; it certainly strengthened parents' hands, and we tried to do the same. Early one year, reports began to reach us about our freshmen's behavior at parties. We called a meeting of their parents to clear the air. In other years we had similar meetings about other forms and about the Junior House, including in 1970 our first discovery of drugs on campus. No doubt, as almost always in such matters, there was more than the authorities knew of, but we were blessed to have as little trouble as we did. These meetings with parents dealt with the matter in hand, and also fostered the liaison between home and school, to which we attached much importance, and which was especially valuable if anything went wrong. Then, a cushion of mutual trust often made all the difference in helping the boys concerned. We tried to keep the families informed about what was happening on campus, and also about helpful agencies such as the County's Youth Task Force on Drugs, and at the same time to remind them of the right that each boy has to his good name.

Besides official links between the students and the administration, there is in schools also a need for individual counseling. At Ampleforth the primary responsibility rested with the housemasters, but any boy was free to approach any member of the faculty. This worked well in a boarding school, where the boys and the faculty were there all the time, and in a larger school, where there was a wider range of personalities on the faculty and most boys could find someone congenial. When Father Timothy visited American schools in the winter of 1955-56, he found that there was often a full-time counselor or counselors who did no teaching, and who had regularly scheduled meetings with the boys. We felt that counseling was part of teaching and did not readily take to the idea of separating the two. We felt also uneasy about the idea of scheduling counseling for a particular time. Come 10.15 a.m. on Tuesday, a boy might not feel like being counseled; and conversely problems might arise that would not satisfactorily wait until then.

We started by leaving counseling primarily to the form masters, with each boy being free to approach any other member of the faculty, and this worked reasonably well. But sometimes the form master was not available when needed, or he might even be the problem. We therefore formed a committee headed by Marty McCabe and having Father Benedict and Mr. Stephen S. Pomeroy as members. After wisely saying that they were aiming at "a system which reaches all the boys, but does not . . . make them feel that they *must* have problems"[259] they recommended drawing up a list of monastic and lay counselors and asking each boy to choose three in order of preference. This was done. Most boys were given their first choice, and no faculty man had more than fifteen boys to counsel.

We never had a school uniform but there was a dress code, which, in the period under review, moved slowly in the direction of less formality but still remained somewhat formal: jacket, dress shirt and tie, or a true turtle-neck sweater, dress pants, dress socks and shoes ("work shoes, tennis shoes, sneakers, `boondockers', moccasins are not acceptable"). The originally required blue tie became first a sober tie and then just a tie, and the original white shirt lasted a little longer before becoming a dress shirt. In 1965 the code contained the paragraph, "Every now and then there arise special occasions on which a boy who does not possess a dark suit may be painfully conspicuous. On such occasions it would be a sartorial solecism not to wear black lace up shoes," but that too dropped out, perhaps because people could not translate it.

Hair gave us more headaches than dress. In our early days, flat-tops and crew cuts were fashionable, and the occasional duck-tail met with little admiration from the boys themselves. The members of one early class started to let their hair grow unduly long. They were warned, and duly went to the barber, except for three boys, to whom Father Timothy unskillfully applied electric clippers. Not until the late sixties did we have problems, but then hair became a symbol of protest. Once hair becomes symbolic, it becomes troublesome. In itself, long hair on a man can be quite becoming, and many past ages have thought it so, but when it is a symbol, authority may feel it has to take up the challenge. Certainly some parents thought that the school authorities should do so, even when they failed to take it up themselves. One difficulty is to decide how long is too long. To make a rule that sideburns may be no longer than the bottom of the ear is to invite boys to test that limit. We did and they did. Eventually "too long" was left to the decision of the Dean of Discipline, with the right of appeal to a disciplinary committee. After a while hair ceased to be symbolic, we became more relaxed, and the problem went away.

Hair was but one instance of protest, and protest was sufficiently in the air by 1967 for both Prior Luke and Father Timothy to take "Responsibility in Protest" as their topic at the Father and Son dinner in November. Major protest occurred at colleges, and our students were aware of what was going on. Boys are always critical, but there

---

[259] Their report of 26 September 1972 is in the Organization file for 1972-73.

was at the end of the sixties more of an edge to their criticisms as expressed, say, in the school newspaper. For the most part, however, our boys showed remarkable responsibility in their protesting. Four examples, all from the school year 1969-70 when protest was at its height --the spring of 1970 saw the shooting at Kent State University-- will bear this out. The first is the final paragraph of *The Record's* report of a meeting between the headmaster's committee and the heads of Departments:

> The discussion was peaceful and open. In an age of communication on high school and college campuses by violence, it was encouraging to see intelligent discussion without resort to rocks and tear gas.[260]

In these peaceful days it may be surprising that such a comment would enter an editor's head, and the language may seem exaggerated, but those who lived through the late sixties and early seventies may not be so surprised.

The second example is from an editorial in the same issue of *The Record*. After commenting on the slight relaxation of the rules for dress and about driving to school, and on the abuse of these relaxations by some students, they conclude:

> The danger here is that the school will decide—perhaps rightly so—that the students have demonstrated themselves to be unworthy of this trust and will reinstitute the older, stricter regulations. To do this would be a mistake. Whenever rules are first relaxed, the immediate response is to abuse new freedoms. If the school wants to achieve its goal of producing responsible students it must be prepared to allow abuses for the first year and possibly the second. Perhaps a tightening and then a gradual relaxation of the rules would now be in order.

The third example was the rise of an interest in the environment. This was certainly a legitimate and laudable area of interest. It was sad that it could also be seen as a way of vilifying the members of the older generation, who were presumed to have been willfully negligent.

The fourth example is the Valedictorian's address to the class of 1970, delivered by David D. Chaplin, now a physician on the faculty

---

[260] *The Record*, XIV. 8, p. 2.

of Washington University and a research professor of the Howard Hughes Medical Institute there.[261] He said, in part:

> In the beginning God made the world. God created man to have dominion over the world. Then God was made flesh to teach man of his commitment to make and remake the world . . .
>
> The youth of America does not see love in our world: rather it sees war, poverty, racism, and violence. Students have no desire to participate in a politically corrupt and culturally insane society which kills a million Vietnamese, pretends not to notice starvation, oppresses black people in filthy ghettoes, destroys the environment, and punishes as a capital offense dissent at Kent State and Jackson State . . .
>
> We cannot see that our world is progressing towards the ideal that Jesus set up for us. We cannot take part in such a society. Instead we will pursue a society in which service is the measure of success.

To some he sounded like the Pope, to others more like Karl Marx; the parts of his speech that sounded like the Pope have lasted the better. Considering the times, it was a fairly moderate presentation, which would have been strengthened, especially in that context, by a recognition of what his class owed to some of the successes of previous generations. But who can fit everything into ten minutes? Father Timothy, who, perhaps providentially, was suffering from temporary, partial but quite genuine and not diplomatic deafness, and so did not hear all of it, commented that this was what happened if you tried to take Jesus' teaching seriously, and went on to the next part of the program.

Many schools suffer from senior pranks, in which the graduating seniors play some kind of practical joke on the school. In any context a practical joke is one of the hardest forms of humor to bring off in such a way that both the joker and the victim agree that the joke can be seen as amusing, just as it is difficult to draw a cartoon that amuses both artist and victim.[262] The difficulty is aggravated in the context of a school, where the victim has disciplinary powers. Nonetheless there have been occasions when both boys and members of the faculty were amused, as well as other occasions when at least the members of the

---

[261] The full text may be found in Appendix E 8.

[262] We did have in the school a boy, John R. Keene, Jr., '83, who had this rare talent.

faculty were not. We were fortunate enough to escape pranks for nearly our first decade, but then they went on until one was seriously destructive, after which they were outlawed. Sometimes the faculty had the better of it and sometimes the seniors. We give three examples.

For the first one, before there was any permission to drive to school, many seniors drove to school and parked their cars down by the gym, far from the classrooms and farther still from the headmaster's office. After lunch, news of this reached Father Luke and Father Timothy, who decided to go to have a look. They then removed the rotor arm from each car's distributor, one of the army's ways in World War II of immobilizing a vehicle, and put each rotor arm in an envelope inscribed with the engine number from the engine block. No more was said, but when the seniors tried to drive home, the cars so treated would not start. Then it came out that two monks had been seen in the parking lot earlier in the afternoon, so the seniors walked the half mile or so up to the headmaster's office and asked if he knew why their cars would not start. When he explained, they asked for their rotor arms back and were told that they could have them, but for safety's sake it was necessary to put the right arm in the right distributor, and would they please state their engine number. That meant a walk back to the gym, then back to the headmaster's office and then back to the gym again. One of them that evening indignantly told his parents what had happened, ending with the comment that the monks had no sense of humor. He was surprised at his parents' reaction.

On another occasion the boys had the better of it. When Villa Duchesne was searching for a new headmaster and Father Timothy was a member of the search committee, the seniors composed, allegedly in Father Timothy's style, a letter typed on school letterhead and announcing the merger of Villa with Priory and appointing Father Timothy headmaster of the new amalgam. The letter was mailed to the parents, many of whom believed it, and started to call us to discover more. By coincidence, Father Timothy was just leaving for a meeting of the search committee when the first call came in congratulating him on becoming headmaster of Villa. Knowing nothing of the letter, Father Timothy assured the caller that he was not headmaster of Villa but simply helping them to search for one. He then left and his secretary had to face the deluge.

A third occasion might be called a tie. We had a VW Beetle. During the night the boys managed to push this from the carport into the school library, which was then in the monastery building. There with a heavy chain they chained it to a structural column and padlocked the chain. When we came down to Matins the next morning, we happened to notice it and Father Vincent Marron, the procurator at the time, spent some of Matins filing through the chain, and then drove the VW back to the carport. When the seniors arrived for school, they got hold of Father Leonard and asked if he had seen what was in the library. He said, "What?" and so they led him to the library and flung open the door. There was no VW. One may concede, however, that a VW in the school library would have been incongruous.

On yet another occasion an unidentified group—we like to think it improbable that boys with local knowledge would have chosen such an exposed spot for such an illicit activity—started to hold an evening party on what was then the parking lot for the Science Wing. Father Thomas emerged from the Science Wing and the group fled, leaving behind them a bottle of bourbon and an abundance of beer, which were never reclaimed.

Admissions

OUR first problem was to publicize our school, the date of the entrance examination and the grade-levels concerned. We have already mentioned[263] "Priory Day", our day of academic and athletic competition for sixth graders. This continued for several years into our period and was part of our publicity. We also mailed to principals of parochial, independent and some public schools announcements of our examination, choosing in each case those whom we thought most likely to send us students, and sent a similar notice to the pastors concerned, and sometimes to the teachers of the sixth grades. For several years, we also sent pastors a summary report of how the boys from their parish were getting on, and, again for several years, held our Saturday afternoon program for grade school principals.

As long as we were taking boys into the ninth grade, we held both the common Archdiocesan test and, on the following Saturday, our own scholarship test. These were at the end of January and the beginning of February. At the end of April, we held our own entrance examination for the seventh grade. When we stopped our regular entry into the ninth grade, and consequently did not need to hold those tests, except for our own eighth-graders, we were able to move the test for sixth-graders back to February. As we became better known, the number of candidates increased, peaking at 168 in February 1972. Initially all the candidates were white boys. Our first African-American applicants appeared in 1964--two of them entered the seventh grade--and a few years after that, an African-American girl came to take the entrance examination. We explained that this was a school only for boys, but her mother insisted that it would be discriminatory to send her away, so after further, fruitless explanation, Father Timothy decided that it could do no harm to let her take the test, and found her a place to sit and write. By that time the girl, showing better sense than her mother, had decided to go home.

An important part of the process of admission was an interview. Initially, we interviewed every candidate, but as the numbers increased, we interviewed only those with some chance of admission. After the interview, we assembled all the data from the tests and the interviews, compiled a document called "the field" which listed the boys in order of merit in each section of the entrance examination, and held our admission meeting, in which we went through the list boy by boy.

---

263 P. 180 *above*

We then sent out the letters to winners of scholarships, to those to whom we could offer financial aid, to those we accepted, to those on the waiting list and, always the saddest letters to write, to those whom we could not accept. There was also a special letter to families who asked for financial aid and whose son, though acceptable for entrance, did not qualify for aid. Each year some of these decided to send their son even without aid. Another feature of the entrance examination was the chicken lunch provided by Mr. Charles M. (Chuck) Dattilo for the candidates, who paid fifty cents for it until 1962, when the price went up to seventy-five cents. Some boys said later in their school career that it was the best lunch they ever had at Priory.

Chuck was in charge of the boys' dining room and their lunch for thirty-four years, and fed us well. It is normal for boys to complain about school food, and they did about Chuck's, but there was no question of the esteem in which both they and the faculty held him. He would get up at a pre-monastic hour to be at Produce Row at opening time to pick the day's bargains. During the vacations, he would pick up the mail, mow the grass, and during the winter might stay up at night to watch the boilers when the temperature went down to 0° F. When the faculty was discussing how to arrange help for Chuck after the school lunch and there was a question of bringing in outside help, the faculty felt that the volunteer system[264] should continue, because "there was a real value in a fairly wide range of boys becoming better acquainted with Chuck."[265] This view was shared by the boys, who, as alumni, made Chuck an Honorary Alumnus. Chuck did not do it all by himself. There were also Gean Wilson, whose full figure was proof of the pudding and who mothered both the boys and the monks; Robert Davis, who cooked for many years and found more peace here than at home; Willie Williams, who worked for us for fourteen years, until his untimely death, and answered the boys' many requests with unfailing cheerfulness;

[264] Some of the boys in this system did indeed volunteer; others were miscreants assigned to kitchen duty.
[265] Memo from the headmaster to Mr. Kubiak, dated 22 September 1971, in *Organization File, June 71-June 72.*

Margarie Dean, who cooked for both boys and monks. And there were others.

Entrance into College

HAVING described the boys' entry into our school, we now turn to their exit from it and entry into college. For any school that calls itself "college preparatory" the success of its graduates in gaining entry into college is of great importance, and it is a sad fact that parents and alumni so easily take success in this as *the* criterion of the quality of a school. But the real criterion is the quality of the education in the broadest sense that the school imparts. Fortunately there is a good correlation between the two, and boys who have been well educated usually get into good colleges. There is, however, always a temptation for people in college guidance to nudge bright students towards prestigious colleges, when they may prefer, or may be better suited by, some other college. It is a matter of integrity to resist this temptation.

How did we try to guide our seniors towards the most appropriate colleges? We have already referred to the starting point: the visits of Father Timothy and others to a wide range of colleges across the country. This was all the more important for us who had so recently arrived in the country and had no first-hand knowledge of its institutions of higher learning. The total of colleges visited in our period reached over one hundred and thirty. To list them all would be unbearable, but we must give a selection to indicate both the scope of the task and high priority we gave to it.

In the East, we started with Harvard, Yale, Princeton, Brown, Cornell, Dartmouth, West Point and M.I.T., and later added Columbia, the University of Pennsylvania, Villanova, Williams, Amherst, the University of Massachusetts, Bowdoin, Bates, Colby, Middlebury, Saint Michael's in Winooski, VT, and others. **In and around Washington, DC**, we visited Georgetown, Catholic University, American University, Annapolis, Johns Hopkins and Villanova; **in the South**: the University of Virginia, William and Mary, Washington and Lee, Fisk and Randolph-Macon--the latter two were, for different reasons, surprised at the visit--Vanderbilt, Davidson, Duke, Emory, the Universities of Georgia, North Carolina and Alabama, Spring Hill, Tulane, Loyola of New Orleans, and others. **In the Mid-West** (besides all the schools in and around Saint Louis) we went, often more than once, to the University of Chicago, Northwestern, the Universities of Notre Dame, Illinois and Wisconsin, Beloit, Carleton, and Saint John's, Collegeville; Purdue, Oberlin, Gambier and Denison, and others; **in the plains**, Saint Ambrose and Loras Colleges, Grinnell, Coe, the Universities of Kansas, Iowa and Colorado, Iowa State, Creighton, Colorado College, the Air

Force Academy, Regis, the University of Denver, and others; **in Texas**, the University of Dallas, Texas Christian University and Southern Methodist University, Rice, the University of Texas and Texas A. & M.; **on the West Coast**, Cal. Tech., the University of California at Los Angeles and at Berkeley, the University of Southern California, Stanford, the University of San Francisco, Reed College, Gonzaga of Spokane, the Universities of Oregon and Washington, and others; and finally **in Canada**, the University of Vancouver in the West and that of Toronto in the East, with St. Michael's College in Toronto, McGill in Montreal, and Laval University in Quebec. These colleges, and those visited but not mentioned, gave our seniors a broad field of choice since they included Catholic and non-Catholic, independent and public, local and distant, even some in another country, large and small—some of our boys, having attended a small prep school, wanted to go to a small college; others wanted anything except a small college—liberal arts schools and those concentrating on the sciences. In this way Father Timothy visited two thirds of the "most competitive" schools, over two fifths of the "highly competitive", one seventh of the "very competitive" and a handful of the rest.[266]

Sometimes these visits were at the invitation of the college. In November 1961 M.I.T. invited groups of high schools to send a representative to a workshop at which they let the evident excellence of their programs in Math and the Sciences be seen, while also pointing out that it was possible to major there in the liberal arts. It was appropriate that Father Timothy's first journey by jet should be to this Institute of Technology. Tulane held a similar workshop stressing the strength of their courses in Communications and their unrivalled archive of the early history of jazz. Dartmouth, at another workshop, told us the story of the Math professor who spent two years working out all the equations that needed to be solved in order to decipher his problem, took his work to the computer and in due course was handed an envelope containing a blank sheet. When he expostulated, he was asked by the supervisor to read out the last command he had given to the computer: "Solve these equations." "Yes," said the supervisor, "and you did not add 'and print out the answer'." The humblest secretary, though unable to solve the equations, would have known that the professor wanted the answer printed out, so the story is a great comfort to all who have any fear of computers. It may have been this comfort that led Father Timothy to

---

[266] These categories are taken from Barron's *Profiles of American Colleges*, 21st ed. (Hauppauge: Barron's Educational Series 1996) pp. 219-30.

attend in Saint Louis in June 1969 a two-week course on computers, organized by National Cash Register. Although at that time a computer filled a room, if not more, the course convinced him that computers were here to stay, and that the school should somehow include them in the curriculum. We moved slowly, not least because computers, besides being enormous, were also enormously expensive. Our first was a gift from Mr. A. Roberts Naunheim. It had been used in his bank in posting savings accounts, so with us its use was limited, but it gave the boys some idea of what computers were, and as it was vast and its cost ran well into six figures, it was an object of awe. It was followed by a similarly enormous computer, given us by the local branch of National Cash Register. These whetted our appetite, and with money from Xanadu for 1971 the Mothers' Club acquired for us a Hewlett Packard 9100 computer, which, when installed, occupied a substantial part of one of the classrooms in the Science Wing. It became an instant center of attention and was put to constant and varied use.[267]

Soon after the end of each school year Father Timothy's mailing to the parents for the next school year included his *Notes on College Entrance*, based on the knowledge acquired from his visits. It was sent to the parents of sophomores, juniors and seniors. It started as a single page, grew first into an unassuming little leaflet and finally into a document of six pages. The salient points were: "Fortunately it is with college as it is with marriage, and most students are very well suited by any one of a fair number of institutions." It went on to suggest ways of reducing the field to a short list of about three, and repeated the advice that "one of these must be a college to which your son's admission is certain, and to which he would be at least content to go." It warned against the rose-tinted spectacles of elderly alumni "whose information is often quite out of date, but whose enthusiasm increases with the years."[268] It gave a short list of helpful books and concluded with two organizations which tried to match candidates who had not been accepted by any college with colleges which still had vacancies, a safety-net whose efficacy we never had to test. What the document said about college alumni was no doubt true, but it was also true that alumni in those days did have some influence on admissions. One of

---

[267] When the original two were superseded and had no longer any practical use and not yet any historical value, they were hard to dispose of. Eventually one was bought at our Xanadu auction by a student and moved to his basement. His parents were not well pleased with us.

[268] The document is printed in full in Appendix E 9.

our parents took his son and another of our seniors to an interview with a representative of the University of Michigan. A local alumnus of the university, who had no connection with our school, was present and recommended the two boys from Priory saying, "Priory is way ahead of all the other schools in Saint Louis," and the two were admitted. That was a nice compliment, which at least shows what the alumnus' perception was and what power it had.[269]

On 4 October 1967 we initiated a series of panel discussions on admission to college. To these we invited sophomores, juniors and seniors along with their parents. The panelists were the Deans of Admission of Notre Dame, the University of Missouri at Saint Louis and Westminster College, and the Director of Financial Aid at Washington University. These men represented a large Catholic and a large non-Catholic university, a large State university and a small liberal arts college. The program stated, "The purpose is to provide information and guidance for students and parents in making a sensible choice of college. The purpose is not to 'sell' this or that college." We arranged these panel discussions for four years and after that recommended that families should attend the Greater Saint Louis College Day or the All-County College Day organized by the public schools. Those days served much the same purpose.

The next contact was often the visits to the school of members of the colleges' admission staffs. Any boys interested in applying could have an interview, and as this often occurred in class time, the boys were not averse. In the summer after their junior year, or before, or at Thanksgiving or even Christmas of their senior year, boys often went, with their parents or without, to visit selected schools. During the junior year the boy and his parents were invited to come for a visit with Father Paul or Father Augustine or Father Timothy. This worked best when both parents came, as otherwise the absent one might, and often did, disagree with the decisions reached, and the time was wasted.

At the beginning of his senior year each senior received a detailed schedule, prepared by Father Paul, which showed all the dates and deadlines for tests, applications and so on. Next came the application forms. The senior was responsible for getting, completing and returning these. He also gave us the parts for the school to fill out. We then sent a transcript, an explanation of the courses, a profile of our

---

[269] We often felt, too, that any good effect we had on other Catholic schools in Saint Louis was due as much to perception as to reality, but in such matters perception can be an effective stimulus to action.

school,[270] which showed how the two or three previous classes had fared in the College Board's SAT and AP tests, and an explanation of our grading system. This explanation converted our numerical grades to A, B and C, and included the sentences, "In view of the importance often attached to rank in class, it may be noted that the last junior who failed his courses with us went directly into his senior year in public school and was on the Honor Roll. After all due allowances for psychological factors, this is a thought-provoking event." We also included a list of all the sixty-two colleges to which we had by 1967 sent our seniors.[271] Of these sixty-two we had visited fifty-two.

Our package to the college included a recommendation from our college counselor or the headmaster, and the boy's package a recommendation from one or more teachers. To do this several times for each senior was time-consuming, especially as it had to be done with great care, and we wished that the United States had a system like that of England's University Central Committee for Admissions, (UCCA) whereby the school and the candidate sent one package to UCCA, which UCCA duplicated and sent to the colleges requested by the candidate.

Our transcripts provided good communication with those colleges whose admission people knew us and had the time to read the information we sent them, but some schools programmed their computers to reject anyone from out of state who was below the middle of the class. Mostly, if we wrote to explain the situation, they took a second look and all was well.

Near the beginning of each school year, Father Timothy sent our college freshmen a letter combining news of the school with avuncular suggestions, which he hoped would be acceptable at a time of possible bewilderment and would be at least less patronizing than those of Polonius in *Hamlet*. Before graduation we had impressed on our seniors attending non-Catholic colleges the importance of making contact with the Newman Chaplaincy; now we sent letters to the Newman chaplains giving them the names of their Catholic freshmen from Priory. A little later in the term, Father Leonard wrote our alumni a more chatty letter and collected and then distributed their addresses. This went on for a number of years, until most of these functions were taken over by the Alumni Society.

To conclude this section we give an alphabetized running total of the colleges entered by our seniors through the class of 1973:

---

270 Our profile for 1967 is reproduced in Appendix E 10.

271 Through June 1971.

Amherst College	2
University of Arkansas	1
Babson College	1
Boston College	3
Bowdoin College	1
Brown University	3
University of California at Los Angeles	1
California Institute of Technology	2
Carleton College	1
Catholic University	1
University of Chicago	3
Claremont Men's College	1
Coe College	2
Colorado College	2
University of Colorado	3
Columbia University	1
Cornell University	5
Dartmouth University	3
DePauw University	2
University of Denver	3
University of Detroit	1
Drury College	1
Duke University	7
Emory University	1
Fairfield University	3
Florida Institute of Technology	1
Florissant Novitiate S.J.	1
Georgetown University	36
Gonzaga University	1
Hamilton College	1
Hanover College	1
Harvard University	9
Harvey Mudd College	1
College of the Holy Cross	9
Indiana University	1
John Carroll University	2
Johns Hopkins University	4
Kalamazoo College	1
Kansas State University	1
McGill University	1
University of Miami	1
University of Michigan	2
Michigan State University	2
Middlebury College	2
University of MO, Columbia	17
University of MO, Rolla	2
University of MO, Saint Louis	3
United States Naval Academy	1
New York University	1
Northwestern University	7
University of Notre Dame	27
Oakland University	1
University of Pennsylvania	8
Princeton University	13
Purdue University	1
Reed College	1
Regis College	11
Rensselaer Polytechnic Institute	2
Rice University	1
Rockhurst College	2
Rollins College	1
Saint Benedict's College	1
Saint John's University, Collegeville	2
Saint Joseph's College Rensselaer	1
Saint Louis University	26
St. Michael's College, Toronto	2
University of San Francisco	2
University of Santa Clara	5
Spring Hill College	1
Stanford University	11
Texas A. and M.	1
Texas Christian University	2
University of Toronto	2
Trinity College	1
Trinity University	1
Tufts University	2
Tulane University	3

Kenrick Seminary	2	Vanderbilt University	1
Kent State University	1	Villanova University	2
Knox College	1	University of Virginia	8
Lawrence University	4	Washington University	25
Lawrenceville	1	Washington & Lee University	1
Loyola University of Chicago	1	Wesleyan University, CT	5
Loyola University of New Orleans	2	Westminster College	4
University of Manitoba	1	University of Wisconsin	3
Marquette University	5	Worcester Polytechnic Institute	1
Massachusetts Institute of Technology	6	University of Wyoming	1
		Yale University	18

This gives a total of 386 seniors sent to 97 colleges and one post-graduate year at Lawrenceville. Of these 98 schools we had visited 76. Through 1973 Georgetown led the pack, and perhaps that is why they asked Father Timothy to be toastmaster when they held their annual John Carroll dinner in Saint Louis in June 1967. The next largest group went to Notre Dame and the third largest to Saint Louis University. The fourth largest group, and the first to a non-Catholic school, went to Washington University in Saint Louis.

This list of colleges to which our seniors won acceptance is impressive, but we must repeat our warning that this is not the main criterion of a good school, and we must add that the results of one era cannot satisfactorily be compared with those of another. Competition is stiffer today, tuition and airfare are much higher, more students are going to colleges closer to home, and there are other variables.

Alumni

IT does not fall within our scope to enumerate the many and varied achievements of our alumni, but we must make some mention of their continuing relationship with the school. Some instances of this we have already recorded: the letter sent to freshmen in college, the notice sent to their Newman chaplain if they went to a non-Catholic college, the chatty follow-ups sent by Father Leonard, Father Columba's Days of Recollection around Christmas concluding with a bull session in which the alumni could tell us how to improve the school.

The first death of an alumnus occurred on 31 March 1962 when Claude I. Bakewell, Jr., a freshman at Yale, was back for the spring break and fell asleep driving home one night. Father Columba celebrated the funeral Mass at the Cathedral with many monks and many of his classmates present. It was our first such tragedy and so was especially tragic.

Alumni came back from college to relate their experiences to our seniors. As time went on and they became gainfully employed, they came back to advise current students on their choice of a career; and Father Leonard made use of them in various capacities in the new-look Retreats. In athletics, too, they helped us both with coaching during the times when we were in school and colleges had not yet started, or during the Christmas and spring breaks, and there were unofficial but nonetheless challenging scrimmages with the alumni in soccer, basketball and sometimes football.

On 1 September 1966 the Saint Louis Priory Alumni Association was formed. This had been discussed at several meetings during the previous year, and Francis M. Oates ('60) had been commissioned to draw up a constitution. It was approved (as amended), and the association was chartered as a non-profit corporation of the State of Missouri. Its first activity was a luncheon at the Cheshire Inn on 29 December at which over one hundred alumni were present. They elected as directors Messrs. Robert C. Dunn, Jr., ('60) president; Francis M. Oates ('60) secretary; Daniel E. Richardson ('60) vice-president-treasurer; and as board members Messrs George C. Convy ('61), Maurice L. Sullivan ('62) and Calvin F. Gatch, Jr., ('61). They appointed class representatives through the class of 1967, established an Alumni Prize for a student who had "brought into reality an especially creative idea", and the Columba Cary-Elwes scholarship. They then heard addresses from Mr. George H. Capps, Dr. John W. Higgins and Mr. Frederick M. Switzer. Over the years they were addressed by men of the caliber of Senator John C. Danforth, Mr. Lawrence K. Roos, Saint Louis County Supervisor, Messrs. Dan Dierdorf, Bob Costas, and others no less notable.

The purposes of the association are "to preserve and foster in the alumni of the Saint Louis Priory School the Benedictine spirit of Christian community and to further the interests of the Saint Louis Priory," and "to provide means whereby the alumni may maintain contact with one another, to keep the alumni informed about the progress of the school, to provide liaison between the school and the colleges attended by the alumni, and to channel the alumni contributions to the Priory into those areas which the alumni as a whole regard as most important."[272]

The association was definitely up and running, and showed this by holding at Priory on 7 June 1968 a picnic and barbecue for the alumni and their wives and children. It was so popular that it became an annual event. That year the Christmas luncheon became a reception at Priory 4.30-7.00 p.m. on Friday 27 December and the Day of Recollection was abandoned, but the Christmas event was difficult for many, and in the period under review oscillated between morning and evening. More often than not it was a luncheon, but eventually it took another form at another time of year. It had also become evident that some kind of publication was needed and around December 1968 the Saint Louis Priory Alumni Bulletin was born.[273] It continued under various names—there is more than one "Vol. I, No. 1."—until it was taken over by the Development Office.

---

[272] *SLPJ* V. 1, p. 18 and IV. 3, p. 17.

[273] The first issue traced is dated 1 August 1969 but it seems probable that there was an issue in December 1968 or thereabouts.

Faculty

IN September 1956 the academic faculty was composed entirely of monks except for one layman who taught one course. By 1960 eight of the full-time faculty were monks and seven were laymen; in 1966 it was twelve and twelve, but by 1972 ten and seventeen. In 1960 there was one lay Head of a Department but no lay Form-master; the same was true in 1966, but by 1972 there were two lay Heads of a Department, two lay Form-masters and four lay Assistant Form-masters.[274] All members of the faculty were men and were white. We had interviewed some women and some African-Americans, but although some were very suitable, none of them accepted our offer.

The initial balance between laymen and monks reflected, both in numbers and in types of job, our experience at Ampleforth, but we had, even before we came to Saint Louis, resolved to aim at having a faculty without subdivisions. We had a Faculty Room rather than a Laymasters' Common Room, as it was called at Ampleforth, and it was for monks as well as for laymen. We welcomed lay faculty rather than acquiescing in them as a necessity. We recognized that most of our boys would as adults be lay and American, that we were neither, and that we needed to have some role models who were both. Also in the beginning, it was taken for granted rather than overtly decided that members of the lay faculty would be men. In line with these ideas, when, on 17 February 1965 a committee met to consider "faculty tenure and related matters", it was composed of three lay members of our faculty and one lay advisor, who were to advise Father Luke and Father Timothy. But old habits died hard, and when, for the school year 1966-67, some small steps were taken towards delegation of the headmaster's tasks, Father Leonard dealt with college admission people and the arrangements for all our own examinations except the entrance examinations; Father Nicholas took over the summer school, the calendar and the prizes; and Father Paul became responsible for the College Boards and other external tests. It was some years before laymen had any considerable responsibility in those matters. Nonetheless, in 1970-71, the three major standing committees, on Discipline, Dress and Curriculum, were fifty-fifty laymen and monks.

There is no record of the conclusions of the committee on tenure; possibly they did not satisfy the monks' feeling that there should be

---

[274] A complete listing of faculty members through June 1973 may be found in Appendix E 1.

some quid pro quo, some undertaking by the faculty member to continue with the school in return for the school's undertaking to continue with him. What the "other related matters" were is not recorded either, but the committee may have discussed sabbaticals and salaries, because in May 1966 we introduced a policy allowing a sabbatical semester on full pay after six and one half years of service, with the school being willing to pay for up to twelve semester hours of college courses, later amended to $500. The faculty man would then remain on our faculty for at least three years after the end of his sabbatical. The first two beneficiaries were Ed Cook and Brian Barry, and others followed. Then in January 1967 we decided that we needed again to grant the senior members of the faculty more than their normal annual increase. This was necessary because each time we offered incoming faculty a starting salary higher than that of their predecessors, this reduced the gap that should exist between them and their seniors, to the disgust of their seniors. This in turn meant that we had to raise the fees for 1967-68 from $850 to $1000, the first raise, incredible as it may seem today, for eight years.

The first layman on our faculty[275] was Jack Peters, who was also interested in becoming a monk, and most of the early applicants either were familiar with monastic ways or wanted to become familiar. This, and the smallness of their numbers, meant that we did not immediately need either to face the problem of how to impart the Benedictine spirit to the faculty or to decide whether we could accept lay faculty who were not Catholic. Ampleforth at that time made little effort to "benedictinize" lay faculty and did employ non-Catholics. It was, however, some time before they appointed a lay housemaster, and even the appointment in 1964 of a lay coach of the First XV (Rugby football), the equivalent of the Varsity football coach, provoked an outcry from both alumni and monks ("The boys will never play for a layman in the same way as they do for a monk;" "it will be the end of rugger at Ampleforth;" and so on). The outcry was redoubled later in the sixties when the same man was appointed Games Master (Athletic Director). History shows that the rugger improved and that the appointment was an unqualified success.

Our early lay faculty seemed to pick up the Benedictine spirit simply by associating with the monks, by hearing the talks at parents' evenings, graduations and so on, and by taking part in the discussions at Faculty Meetings. By the mid-sixties we were beginning to feel that the laymen should be more actively involved in the discussions that

---

[275] The first from our alumni was Mr. J. Tracey Leiweke in September 1967.

led to the formation of policy. The whole faculty had always been present at the full faculty meetings at the beginning and end of each term, but between those meetings it had been our custom for the monks to meet once every two weeks to discuss matters of routine as they cropped up. This started as a continuation of Ampleforth's weekly meetings of the housemasters with the headmaster, where all were monks; and since here too in the early years all the officials in the school, apart from the head coaches, were monks, only monks attended these fortnightly meetings. They were held at 7.30 p.m., so it would in any case have been slightly inconvenient for laymen to be there. As laymen became both more numerous and more important in the school, they were invited to attend, but as the time of the meetings remained the same, few came. On 30 October 1967 we experimented with a meeting from 5.10 to 6.30 p.m. From then until June 1973 meetings varied between this time and 7.30 p.m. Our impression was that the members of the lay faculty were glad to have been invited, but when they attended, did so with little enthusiasm.

In November 1961 we learnt that Mr. Alexander C. Niven of our department of History had become Chairman Elect of the Social Studies section of the Teachers' Council of the Independent Schools Association of the Central States (ISACS). This was our first contact with an organization to which, in the mid-seventies, we turned for accreditation. In 1961 it had 112 member schools in fourteen central states. It was for independent schools what the North Central Association was for all public and many parochial schools. Like the North Central, it conducted periodical visitations of its members, and provided them with a stamp of outside approval to display to colleges and parents.[276]

Since the raison d'être, though not the only task, of faculty is to instruct, we include in this section on the faculty a note on others who had instructional contact with the boys. The most numerous visitors were members of college admission staffs, each with his own axe to grind—one with her own axe to grind was a rarity then—and the boys were eager to see the men on whom their future might depend. In the fall of 1960 we recorded visits from representatives of Harvard, Yale, Princeton, the University of Chicago and many others.

We also had professionals and businessmen coming to describe what life as a lawyer or physician, businessman or banker was like.

---

[276] As with the visitations by the North Central Association, much of the value lay in the extensive self-examination required of the school as a pre-requisite of the visitation.

They too were welcome, and as time went on, tended more and more often to be alumni. In addition to them we had prominent people who came and talked about topics of the day. Arnold Toynbee, with his unparalleled knowledge of world affairs, paid us several more visits, but perhaps the most remarkable occasion was when, on 13 October 1969 Phyllis (Mrs. John F.) Schlafly, Mr. Leonard Tinker, a member of the American Friends Service Committee who had been an observer at the peace talks which had recently been held in Paris, and Father Leonard took part in a panel discussion on continuing the war in Vietnam. (National Moratorium Day was on 15 October). Father Leonard gave the historical background, and then both speakers turned out to be in favor of a speedy end to the war, Mrs. Schlafly by a major military effort on our part, leading to a quick victory, and Mr. Tinker by the withdrawal of our troops. Their presentations occupied two periods before lunch, and after lunch the panelists answered written questions. Questions and answers were thoughtful, sometimes provocative, and always impressive. Although no votes were taken, it appeared that before the panel the student body strongly supported continuing the war, but that Mr. Tinker's gentle and persuasive arguments for peace won over many of his hearers. Two days later, we celebrated a school Mass for peace (though in a sense every Mass is a Mass for peace).

Among the other speakers the largest group was of politicians, never averse from wooing potential voters, and of diplomats. President Nixon addressed the seniors and juniors of Saint Louis in Kiel Auditorium, but Mr. Whatley came to our campus to campaign for Mr. McGovern. Mr. Nicholas Nyaradi, ex-Finance Minister of Hungary and Mr. Donald Cape, First Secretary of the British Embassy in Washington, DC, and an Old Boy (alumnus) of Ampleforth did what diplomats should do for their respective countries; Dr. Anima Bose spoke on Gandhi, and MM. Maurice Druon[277] of the Académie Française and Reginald de Warren of the French Embassy on King Saint Louis IX at our program to celebrate the seventh centenary of the death of the eponymous patron of our city. Our alumnus, Mr. Nicholas M. Hellmuth, lectured on Archaeology as a career, using slides from his recent excavations at Tikal in Yucatan, and

[277] M. Druon was described in *The Times Literary Supplement*, 23 June 2000, p. 36, as "until very recently Secrétaire Perpétuel" to the Académie Française, a surprisingly illogical state of affairs for a body dedicated to guarding the purity and logicality of the French language. Nonetheless, he is the most distinguished Frenchman to have visited our campus.

Ampleforth's alumnus, Desmond Leslie, lectured, without slides, on Flying Saucers. Sir Arnold Lunn, the international skier and Catholic apologist, advanced an interesting and rather two-edged argument in support of international sports, saying that countries tend to treat one another in politics in the same way as they treat one another in sports. Mr. Howard Griffin spoke of his experiences collecting material for his book, *Black Like Me*. As long ago as 1970 Dr. Barry Commoner lectured on the environment, which was already a lively issue, and others of equal distinction spoke on equally fascinating topics.

Contact between faculty and boys was not limited to teaching or coaching. We have mentioned occasional "Allcomers" games of soccer between faculty and boys.[278] There were also occasional scrimmages at basketball and, more rarely, football, and games of softball and, more rarely, baseball in which faculty took part. On one notable evening in February 1966, surely to benefit some good cause, our faculty basketball team, coached by Ed Cook, (Is Saul too among the prophets?) [279] took on a team sponsored by radio station WIL and composed of members of the Cardinals football team. It was memorable to see our ex-state-champion shot-putter Gerry Wilkes, hefty himself, come charging down the court into Cardinals guard Ernie McMillan and simply bounce off. To redress the balance for Gerry, we may mention another incident. He and Tom Geiss were teaching in adjacent classrooms and each was finding a pupil troublesome. Finally Tom guided his troublemaker towards the door and urged him into the passage. At the same moment the door of Gerry's classroom opened. Gerry came out carrying the boy sitting at his desk, and deposited boy and desk in the passage. Father Ian happened to be passing and said to the students, "Perhaps you had better come to my office."

This is an appropriate place to say something about our secretaries, who were often, if not quasi-faculty, certainly quasi-counselors. In part I, we noted the arrival of secretaries for Father Luke and Father Timothy. Miss Mary Bennace was Father Luke's secretary and accountant all through our period and for long after it. There is no longevity without fidelity, and Mary personified both longevity and fidelity. She was also scrupulously exact with the accounts. She was no less reluctant about our spending money than was Father Luke, so our Golden Fleece was guarded by two dragons, not one. The school's

---

[278] *See above* p. 162.

[279] *See* 1 Samuel 10,11.

first secretary was, as already mentioned, Miss Christine M. Little.[280] After her came the secretarial equivalent of our cook, Genevieve: she assumed that there would be sundry help to run the machines and do the filing. She left at the end of her first day, and for several days we ran our own machines and did our own filing, and then we secured as a replacement Nancy (Mrs. James J.) Dougherty, whose mother had just died. She thought the job would be an anodyne, but she arrived on a hectic day when the reports were going out. It was a frustrating day, and at the end of it, to relieve her feelings, she waited until Father Timothy went to see the buses depart and then hurled her ruler at the place where he had been sitting. Returning home exhausted, she poured herself a stiff drink and went out into the garden to relax. Feeling better, she thought of something to eat, but found the back door locked, the front door equally locked, her keys inside on the kitchen table and her husband in Nebraska. Then she saw that one of the front windows was slightly open, was able to open it farther, and started to climb in, at which point, inevitably, the police arrived with lights flashing and asked her what she thought she was doing.

She was also, but unwittingly, the cause of some alarm at Priory. In due course we all became good friends, and after her husband returned from Nebraska, Father Timothy was visiting their house when a friend of theirs, Mr. Frank L. (Pete) Key, who later sent a son to our school, stopped by on his way home from a duck-hunt. He asked whether the monks would like some ducks and gave some to Father Timothy, who returned to the monastery and put the ducks into the deep freeze in the basement. He did not notice that the ducks were moist and bloody, and went insouciant to bed. In the morning, Father Luke was the first one down to Matins, passed the steps to the basement and, to his horror, saw a trail of blood. Fearing the worst, he rushed down the steps. He was relieved to find that the trail ended at the deep freeze.

Nancy was with us for six months and then was replaced by Virginia (Mrs. Joseph F.) Mazy, whose special but not only gift was her accuracy with figures. That was especially valuable with the marksheets, which, if they were not accurate could cause anguish and even injustice. Unfortunately for us, her husband, a colonel in the Air Force, was moved to Georgia, and she moved with him. She was succeeded by Joyce (Mrs. Edward S.) La Pointe, who stayed for ten years. Both she and her successor, Jeannette (Mrs. Ben) Karp--"age 57 but quite spry and very mature" Father Timothy wrote home

---

[280] *See above*, p. 81.

about her—were dependable, discreet, gracious and calm. Jeannette said of her initial interview with Father Timothy that towards the end of it she thought she should mention that she was Jewish, and did that bother him? Father Timothy remarked in return that she would be working in a Catholic institution, and would that bother her? When she said it would not, Father Timothy continued, "Well, if the one does not bother you, the other does not bother me." Jeannette arrived towards the end of August 1970 as we moved into the new high school and stayed for a number of years after the end of our period. Jane Geislinger came in temporarily to bridge the gap between Joyce and Jeannette. Two of these school secretaries were Catholic, one Protestant, one Jewish and one a Latter Day Saint. In addition to all their hard work they gave us their friendship. It is so easy to take for granted what they and the receptionists do for us: let this be a small tribute of grateful recognition.

Athletics

IN the period we are considering, 1960-73, we emerged in athletics from having an embryonic, almost pre-embryonic, program to being able to field, in most sports, Varsity, B and C teams which sometimes struck terror into their opponents and were always worthy competition.[281] There was, during the period, rather constant pressure on the headmaster from the coaches to allow more time for practice, but on the whole we succeeded in preventing the athletic tail from wagging the academic dog. We applied for admission to the ABC League, a group of schools whose athletic policies were harmonious with our own, and in due course were admitted. We started the period with two freshly graded fields south of the gym on the newly acquired Singer property, one mainly for baseball, the other mainly for football. Then on 10 October 1970 we dedicated the John Valle Janes bowl, farther down the slope to the east, which provided us with a Varsity football field, a track, jumping and pole-vaulting pits, a press box and all the appurtenances, in very pleasing surroundings, especially when the leaves were turning in the autumn.

In September 1960 Father Ian was still in charge of athletic policy, but Mr. Walter J. Ruesch replaced Don Kettelkamp as Father Ian's right-hand man in athletics and arranged the schedules, officials and so on. He and Marty McCabe were both inducted later into the Saint Louis Baseball Hall of Fame. The coaches in 1960 were: Varsity football: Gerry Wilkes with Bob Bannister; B football: Wally Ruesch with Father Paul. Varsity basketball: Wally Ruesch with Gerry Wilkes; B: Bob Bannister; C: Father Paul. Varsity soccer: Father Thomas, B: Father Ian with Father Austin. Wally Ruesch took care of the Varsity baseball and Bob Bannister of B. Various monks coached individuals in track, and Father Paul and Alex Niven coached Varsity and B tennis respectively. In September 1961 Father Paul, who had shown great resourcefulness in coaching American sports, took over from Father Ian the direction of athletic policy. In 1964 he relinquished the post to Marty McCabe, and since then our Athletic Director was always an American. There is no record of the coaches in the Junior House, but as the same men shared the coaching there as coached the high school, the continuity was a great benefit to our program and the results in the Junior House were usually excellent.

---

[281] For tables of our athletic results as far as we can ascertain them *see* Appendix F 1.

The Junior House, which had from its first year been a member of the parochial leagues of the Catholic Youth Council (CYC) and was a charter member of their football league, hosted league games in football and basketball, but it took a little while for the results to be recorded. One consequence of our hosting these football games was that Father Ian frequently had to mark out the field. This he did on Saturday afternoon for Sunday's game. As often as not, or so it seemed, this provoked a thunderstorm on Saturday night and the obliteration of the lines. On one such occasion the lines were visible but faint. A visiting parent complained bitterly after the game, saying that these boys should be treated just as well as the Saint Louis Cardinals. "In that case," we asked as gently as we could manage, "what will they have to look forward to as they grow up?"

Another and far more pleasant consequence was the following cameo: after a game between two sixth grade teams an obvious bench-warmer, who perhaps had been put in for a play or two, came running—in reality in all that armor he could only waddle—across the parking lot to greet his mother. "Hey, Mom; guess what." "What?" "We lost." And he had a broad grin. "What was the score?" Still the same grin, "Fifty to nothing." He must be having a very happy life.

Gerry Wilkes was to be our Varsity football coach, with one interval, through 1973. On taking over, he announced that to our single-wing offense he would add the T formation "and possibly the Spread," as well as a new series of defenses "fairly revolutionary to high school football in this part of the country," which should "therefore prove extremely confusing to the opposition." [282] Much of our own confusion was eradicated at football camp, but even so, as one might expect with such novelties, it was not always only the members of opposing teams who were confused.

This is not the place to give an account of each game, but we must record some of the milestones and highlights. In the spring of 1961 we suffered from our ignorance of the rules of the Missouri State High School Activities Association and had our introduction to whistle-blowers in other schools, when Claude Bakewell, our tennis star, was barred from playing because he had competed, during the spring break, in a tournament in Florida.

---

[282] letter dated July, 1960, in file *Organization 1960-61.*

In the fall of 1961 our B team in football played five games and won them all, our first unbeaten and untied team.[283] In May 1962 our Varsity baseball team, despite a record of 4-9, reached the semi-finals of the District tournament. and our B team (2-5) achieved a victory over Country Day by the score of 18-17. History in its mercy does not record the names of the pitchers. That fall, the Varsity football team had what the yearbook described as "the best season any Priory football team has had." It is a measure of the strength of our opponents that the record was 3-5 and yet the comment was fair. That same winter, our varsity basketball squad reached the final of the Fort Zumwalt tournament, and thereby won our first varsity trophy in a major sport.

The next school year, 1963-64, started with our varsity football team losing its first three games. They then came back and won the next five, giving us our first winning season. Jim Holton rushed for 245 yards in one game and for 13 touchdowns in the season. For five weeks he was the area's leading scorer. Our quarterback, Dan Sexton, completed (tidily) 49 of 98 passes, and our defense held one school to minus 22 yards. The coaches were Gerry Wilkes and Al Salsich. The varsity basketball also had a winning season (16-5), won the Fort Zumwalt tournament and was second in the District. The spring term passed without much athletic distinction. In the fall of 1964 the varsity football had the superb record of 6-1-1, the single loss being to Country Day. The results of football games at this level are less predictable than at most levels: it is quite possible for team A to beat team B; team B to beat team C; and then for team C to beat team A, and for all the victories to be quite decisive. In addition, psychology plays a large part. Our teams were always particularly eager to defeat Country Day, where many of their friends went to school, but even when we seemed to have a better team and a better record, we failed, and it was not until 1973 that we defeated them. After the successful season of 1964, Gerry Wilkes decided to rest on his laurels, and did so until the fall of 1968, when he resumed his position as head coach of the varsity. In the meantime he was coach of the B team or assistant coach of the varsity.

In the winter of 1964-65 our B basketball completed its first winning season. It was also the first time we had a winning season for both Varsity and B teams. Naturally enough, given our small numbers,

---

[283] In our first year, our soccer team won both the games it played, but two games hardly constitute a season. In 1958 our tennis team was undefeated, but yielded one tie.

we were more likely to be able to produce strong teams in sports with fewer boys on the team, such as basketball and tennis.

Celebrating his second year as Athletic Director, Marty McCabe introduced in September 1965 a physical fitness program for all students, but especially for those in the intra-mural program. This was in response to the President's Council on Physical Fitness, and consisted of a series of exercises of increasing difficulty, to be performed more and more rapidly as the student progressed. It was a time when surveys were repeatedly indicating that the young of other nations ran faster, jumped farther, and were generally fitter than ours. That winter—though who can say whether there was any causal connection?--our basketball squad, although only 11-11 in the regular season, was second in the John Burroughs tournament, won Fort Zumwalt's, won the District but was defeated in the State play-offs by Owensville, the eventual winner. This was the first time we reached that level in basketball. This was also the year when, through the generosity of Mr. William F. James, we inaugurated four cups, one each for the best athlete and the best sportsman in the upper school and in the Junior House.

In the mid-sixties, we used to participate in the Archdiocesan Sports Festival, held at the old Public Schools' Stadium on North Kingshighway, not far from McBride High School. It was a track meet for all the Catholic schools, most of which were far larger than ours. As we were in the ABC League, we played against Catholic schools only when we were playing outside the league, so this meet extended our acquaintance with students at the Archdiocesan schools.

At the football camp in the summer of 1966, our first boarding camp at $65, one of our key players, co-Captain Lou Kahle, started to bleed from his ear. He was promptly sent to the doctor, and although no cause could be found, he was told not to play that season. Towards the end of the season, he was in the doctor's office when a senior partner came in, heard the sad story, and suspected he knew what was wrong. With an otoscope he looked into the boy's ear. Then he took a forceps and pulled out an earwig, whose bite had caused the bleeding. When asked what made him think of that, he replied that in earlier days, when it was still safe to do such things, people used, on hot summer nights, to sleep out in Forest Park. From time to time they were visited by earwigs, which crawled into their ear and bit, causing bleeding from the ear. The boy could have played all season, and old-fashioned medicine would have enabled him to do so.

That same fall, we were admitted to the ABC League. That had long been our goal because the other member schools were independent schools like us, and shared our philosophy: athletics are important but are not all that schools are about, and winning is important but not all that sports are about. We also liked the ABC system whereby qualification to play on varsity, B or C teams depended on the boy's age, height, weight and semester in school.

We had applied earlier for membership but, being a Catholic school, had been turned down. We were advised to bide our time. Messrs Tom O'Connell and Russ Stickney of Saint Louis Country Day School did some lobbying on our behalf. In the State baseball tournament we were drawn to play the school that voted against us and beat them amicably. The President of the Board of Trustees of that school heard so many comments—"This is the middle of the twentieth century, you know," and the like—that the decision was reconsidered and that school's headmaster was given the unenviable task of seeking an interview with Father Timothy to check him out. Fortunately, the other headmaster had been at Cambridge and had played Rugby football for both Cambridge and England, and Father Timothy had been at Oxford and had been an Authentic,[284] so the two saw eye to eye. The necessary recommendation was made, we applied again and in October 1966 were admitted. We started league competition in September 1967 but had been playing several of the member schools for some years before that. In our first year, our varsity football squad was 4-4; B, 7-0 and league champions; C, 5-1 and league co-champions. Also in September 1967 we introduced Wrestling, which was one the ABC League's sports. Two meets can be traced, both of which we lost. It was never our forte, though we did have some fine individual wrestlers.

In addition to the inter-scholastic change brought about by entering the league, we experimented intramurally by dividing the school into four "houses", after the pattern of Ampleforth, but it never caught on and we did not persevere. At Ampleforth, the athletic rivalry between houses, or dormitories, was as keen as, or keener than, rivalry with other schools, but there it was reinforced by geography: the boys did indeed live in the different houses, fifty or so to a house. In a day school, that was not so.

In the winter of 1966-67 we held our "first annual" crusader boys' basketball tournament for boys in the sixth grade in various parochial schools. We had two motives: coọperation with the Archdiocese and public relations. Our varsity squad that year was 14-

[284] Roughly equivalent, if English readers will forgive me, of being a member of the varsity cricket squad, if there were such a thing.

9 with the help of a sophomore, Bill Daake, who scored 40 points in one game and, like Milton's Lycidas, "flame[d] in the forehead of the morning sky."

In the following winter, 1967-68, our V basketball was 24-3 and won the tournaments at Priory and John Burroughs, but, to our disappointment, was beaten in the semi-final of the District tournament. Bill Daake was the super-star, but it was by no means a one-man team. In one game when Bill was injured, Pete Ramey scored 43 points, a new school record.

In the school year 1968-69 our basketball was again distinguished. The Varsity (18-7) won the ABC League championship and the District tournament, but lost in the State playoffs. Bill Daake recaptured the school record by scoring 47 points against John Burroughs, was chosen by the Post-Dispatch as the Scholar-Athlete to represent our area, won the Globe-Democrat's trophy for the "Basketball Player of the Year", and was picked for *Scholastic Magazine*'s All-American Squad. He then went off to Princeton looking like another Bill Bradley.[285]

By the beginning of the next school year, 1969-70, schools were beginning to feel trickle-down effects from what was happening on college campuses, and phrases like "owning decisions" were beginning to be heard. This was what led us to form an Athletic Committee. It consisted of two members of each class in the upper school and a member from the varsity squad of each of the sports in season plus a member from the intramurals. It was to the athletic director what the Headmaster's Committee was to the headmaster. One item on their agenda was the nickname of our teams. At first it had been "Saints" but that did not last long; then it became "Rebels". This, combined with the use of the Confederate flag, was thought to be possibly offensive to African-Americans. The committee opined that it would be civil to cease waving the Confederate flag but were keen to retain the name, thinking, perhaps, partly of the 1770s as well as of the 1860s. A year or two later another committee was formed to supervise the care and maintenance of athletic facilities. This too was under Marty McCabe.

The intramural program took care of those who were not on the squad of any of the sports in season. In the early days of the school, everyone or almost everyone was needed to man the squads, but as the school grew and we had more than enough boys for the teams and their attendant benches, the problem of providing exercise for the rest

[285] He died suddenly of an aneurysm on 20 July 1984.

became more urgent. When the weather was reasonable, they could go outside and play soccer, touch football, volleyball, softball etc. What taxed the ingenuity of the coaches was when the weather was bad and the school's representative squads needed the gym. Among other solutions was the idea of switching the intramurals with study-halls, thus giving them a time when the rest of the school was in class and the athletic facilities unoccupied.

During this school year, and even starting a little earlier, we watched the preparation of our new stadium and track. The track itself had a surface of rubberized asphalt called Reslite, which was at that time "state of the art". Thanks to great industry by Father Paul and his helpers, it was close enough to completion to be put into use in the spring, but the solemn dedication of the John Valle Janes Memorial Stadium and Track was not held until 10 October 1970 in the following school year, during our football game with Country Day. The name marked the generosity of the Janeses to the school and the track talent of their son John. The facility itself was a great leap forward for us. Until then, our field had been just adequate and our track makeshift. We now became, in this respect, the cynosure of every eye with what the yearbook called "the finest field and track in the area".[286] The Varsity football team greeted the new field with a record of 5-2 and was second in the league; the B team was 3-3, unremarkable except that they achieved it with a squad of only fourteen players, and C was 5-0-1 and league champion. At the end of this same school year, two seniors graduated whose fathers, Mr. Thomas J. Tobin, II, and George A. Mahe, M.D., had in quite different ways been mainstays of our athletics. The yearbook said of them, "Mr. Tobin's vociferous cheers can rouse a team to performance, while Dr. Mahe's quiet encouragement can ease the sorrow of an athlete."[287] The recognition of these two men was just, and they can stand for innumerable other fathers and mothers, students and friends who have supported our teams in sunshine, wind and rain, and on hard and sometimes splintery bleachers.

The 1971-72 school year passed with little athletic glory or shame, but the fall of 1972 brought us our first undefeated Varsity football team, with a record of 7-0-1. The tie was with Country Day, with whom we shared the league championship. We scored an average of 27 points a game and allowed only 3.5. We opened the season against Francis Howell, then a new public school west of the Missouri River.

---

[286] *The Shield*, 1971, p. 123.

[287] *Ibid.* p. 17.

We were reminded of our size when, for the half-time entertainment, they put onto the field in their marching band more students than we had in our upper school. In the course of the game we fumbled seven times, but won glory when Francis Howell had a first down on our three yard line but advanced only two yards and thirty-four inches. We then marched from our two inch line for a touchdown, which must have been at least close to our longest drive ever. After the next game, a headline in the press read, "Awesome Priory Bombs Waynesville." The English teacher in Gerry Wilkes disapproved of the misuse of "awesome" while the coach in him was purring. The B team was 7-1 and second in the league, auguring well for the future. Our Varsity soccer was 9-0-1 in the league and won the league championship; our basketball 18-9, was second in the league and reached the semi-finals of the District tournament. To encourage them, what *The Record* hailed as Priory's first Pep Rally ever was held during the 8.30 period on Friday 19 January 1973. Paul Beuttenmuller was named to all-state first team in soccer, and also took first place in the ABC cross-country meet. The Junior House produced in Steve Larson and Joe Tobias the table tennis champion and runner-up in the CYC's city tournament, and our Rugby football team was 5-0 and state champion once more. Even in baseball, where we had rarely shone, we won the Regional play-offs and reached the state semi-final. Two bus-loads of students traveled to Springfield, where we were soundly beaten by the eventual winners. Tim Brady, whose law-abiding fast ball was superbly accurate, proved that for a pitcher in high school accuracy is more important than speed, and, with a good defense behind him, had a record of 5-0. There was a wealth of talented athletes up and down the school, and because many of them were to return next year, our prospects looked very bright.

In Cross-country we had a winning season in 1965-66 but did not show the sustained excellence that we achieved in later years; in Tennis we had three winning seasons, but during our period never recaptured the luster of our earliest years; in Swimming, Wrestling and Track, we had brilliant individuals--Scott McBride and Bob Bender in swimming; Joe Hadzima[288] and Caldwell Gaffney in wrestling, John Riley and Tom Ellinwood in track, for example; but in these sports an individual can do no more than win his event or his bout. In the team sports a skilled coach can build a very respectable team around two or

---

[288] At the beginning of one season Joe sprained his wrist. Astutely he put the bandage on the other wrist. His opponents concentrated against what they assumed was the weak wrist and were duly pinned.

three talented athletes. Paradoxically, the outstanding individual is more valuable in team than in individualistic sports.

We must mention, too, some of the highlights of our athletic program in the Junior House.[289] As in the high school, a principal feature was the very high percentage of boys who represented the school against another school. This was achieved sometimes by having as many as three teams in one sport. In the major sports we played in the leagues organized by the CYC. In the thirteen years under review, we won our divisional title in basketball at least eight times and were city champions, at our grade level, at least twice.[290] In football we won our division at least four times and were city champions at least once. In soccer we had at least five winning seasons. In baseball, track and tennis we did not take part in CYC competition but arranged our own, with results that were creditable rather than spectacular. By a natural development, the seventh grade wanted to have a team of its own,[291] and so the Rinky-dinks were born.

One of the many benefits of providing a strong athletic program in the Junior House, and of having the same coaches as for the high school, was that the boys arrived in the high school knowing what these coaches expected and knowing many of the plays. It may well be also that in the Junior House the level of enjoyment was greater and the pressure less. It was a highly satisfactory program and was pursued with much enthusiasm even by the less athletically inclined. The less satisfactory part of it was that the schedule necessitated having two classes after athletics, which on a warm spring or fall day was hard on both boys and teachers, but at least the boys were returned to their parents with some of their surplus energy released.

That brings us to the close of the school year in June 1973, but the athletic events of that fall provide so fitting a climax to our account that we include them here. Only two sports completed their season by the end of 1973: cross-country and football. Our team in the former looked as if they should be world-beaters, since all the previous year's team returned except one, and Paul Beuttenmuller had already shown that he was the best runner in the ABC league. But "there's many a slip . . ." and Paul suffered an ankle injury and was unable to run,

---

[289] *See* Appendix F 1, b.

[290] We say "at least" because the earliest records are not to be found and the extant records are incomplete.

[291] In the fall of 1967 a football team "under 110 pounds" and led by a seventh grader, Rocky Kistner defeated Chaminade. By 1970-71, if not before, there was a seventh grade team in basketball, and the following year in soccer.

and four of the previous year's lettermen opted not to run. The remainder worked hard and improved greatly but did not beat the world.

In Varsity football it was another story. The yearbook claims that in our area we were the smallest school playing football; half the previous year's team had graduated; and we had only 26 players on the squad. Nonetheless, in ten games we scored 297 points and gained 3148 yards while allowing our opponents an average of only 8.4 points a game. Jim Merenda, with 279 yards against Waynesville, set a new school single-game record for rushing. Our only loss was against Francis Howell, when, after leading 20-6 at half-time, we were overcome by heat, humidity and much greater numbers. The highlight of the regular season was our first victory over Country Day. It was too long coming, but the score, 32-0, was decisive and Country Day never crossed our forty-yard line. By the end of the season we were, for the first time, alone in first place in football in the ABC league. Whether or not we qualified for the State AA playoffs—AA was the second smallest classification—depended on the results of games to be played the next weekend, so we had an anxious week until we learnt that we had indeed qualified and would play Brookfield High School in the semi-final round. The most exciting moment of that game occurred at the start of the second half, when Priory was leading 9-0. Brookfield marched to our 9-yard line, where our defense, as it had done so often in previous games, held them. We went on to win 23-0. The final was played on 1 December at Kansas City's Arrowhead Stadium, the home of their professional team. Our opponents were from West Platte High School in the suburbs of Kansas City, and were reputed to have a demon quarter-back. We scored a touchdown on each of our first three possessions, but then Platte came back and scored twice, making it 21-14. By the half, it was 40-14, but even then, given their demon, who had already shown that he could indeed add points quickly, we could not feel secure. We did not relax, and the final score was 60-26, the highest in the six-year history of the playoffs, and the first time a team from Saint Louis had won the AA title. We set a fashion, as the ABC league has won the title many times since then. George Ahlering, Bob Ciapciak, Dave Dooley, Ron Ervin, Jim Hyde, Dave McMahon, Jim Merenda, John Morrissey and Bill Sciortino were named to the ABC All-Star team; McMahon, Merenda and Sciortino to the Class AA All-State team; McMahon to the All-County team, which included all county schools, independent and public. The whole coaching staff—Gerry Wilkes, Dave Beckner, Jim Wortham, Bart Margiotta and Joe Genoni—was recognized at the

Quarterback Club banquet of the Sporting News. Finally, after fifteen years of Varsity football, we had overall won more games than we had lost.

Plato, in *The Republic*,[292] provides a fitting conclusion on the role of academics and athletics in education:

Socrates:	Don't you see how it affects one's outlook if one has a lifelong devotion to athletics to the exclusion of academics, or vice versa?
Glaucon:	I'm not sure what you are referring to.
Socrates:	I'm referring to wildness and hardness on the one hand, and to softness and mildness on the other
Glaucon:	Oh yes. I see that those who devote themselves exclusively to athletics turn out wilder than they should be, and those who devote themselves exclusively to academics become softer than is good for them.
Socrates:	And yet, the wildness might provide the spirited part of a character and, if rightly nurtured, might turn into bravery; but if exaggerated, would, I suppose, become hard and troublesome.
Glaucon:	I think so.
Socrates:	But would not the academic character contain some mildness which, if exaggerated, would be softer than it should be, but if rightly nurtured would be gentle and orderly?
Glaucon:	Yes.
Socrates:	Then presumably we say that our Guardians should have something of both these characters

292 III, 410 c - e.

Activities

UNDER this heading come Art, Carpentry, Music, Chess and the like. They all have their own intrinsic value as manly pastimes which may add usefulness, enjoyment, fullness or even profit to life—it is one of the great advantages of a boarding school that it is possible to devote more time to them and to offer a wider range—but they have beneficial by-products too. It may happen that a boy who is achieving little success in the classroom finds that he has a natural talent for and enjoyment of woodworking. This raises his self-esteem and sometimes encourages him to go on to consider that if he can do well in the carpentry shop, he may be able to do well also in the classroom—sometimes, but not always. In a monastic school, many of the activities are moderated by monks and so give the monks and the boys a chance to meet and know one another in an informal setting. For these and other reasons, we went to great lengths to provide time, space and instructors for as many activities as we could. Each of these three was hard: time was not easy to find in an already well-filled schedule; space was difficult because no planner likes spaces that are used for only a small percentage of the time, and many activities demand specialized space, which cannot be "multipurped";[293] and, thirdly, not by any means all competent instructors are able or willing to come in for, say, parts of two afternoons a week. For availability, the best instructors are either faculty or volunteers, faculty because they are already on the spot and volunteers because their time is usually more flexible; and the prince of our volunteers was Mr. Reynolds Medart, whom we have already mentioned.[294]

One of the most important qualities, then, for any of these instructors was adaptability. Mechanical Drawing, for example, started in the breezeway of the Junior House, migrated to the basement of the monastery and thence to the "archway" building across from the boys' dining room, and ended up in the basement of the new Junior House, when that was completed. The archway building itself was a flexible building which had started life as a potting-shed, served as the green room for our first play, was then moved on rollers to make room for the extension of the dining room and became first the home

---

[293] Sadly we record that this odious word was a favorite of one of the monks. Here he meant that you cannot do much in a carpentry shop except carpentry, whereas a classroom can be used for many purposes beyond teaching.

[294] *See* p. 159 *above*.

of Mechanical Drawing, then the fund-raising office, and then much later, headquarters of the maintenance service. After that it was the headquarters of the team of mothers working on the Xanadu auction, and later still it became the vocations office. Many of the other activities were similarly nomadic. Initially the charge for the activities was included in the tuition; then we thought it fairer to charge only those boys who took them; then in 1972, as they became more popular, we again included them in tuition, making a charge only for materials, where applicable. Naturally enough, noticeably more boys signed up for them when the charge was included than when it was separate.

The activities offered for all or part of the period 1960-73 were: Art, the Barry Project, the Bridge Club[295], Carpentry, Chess club, Debate, Drama, Driver Education, European Travel, French Club, Investment Club, Library, May Projects, Mechanical Drawing, Music (which fathered also a Glee Club and a Guitar Group), Outings, Photography, Proms and Football Dances, Radio Club, *The Record* (school newspaper), Rifle Club, Science Club, Surveying, Tutoring, Typing and our yearbook, *The Shield.* We shall comment briefly on each of these.

Of all our activities, *Art* suffered most from not having a fixed and specialized abode, and therefore most taxed the ingenuity of the instructors, of whom in our period there were six. In the beginning it was taught in a classroom in the barn, and then, for a while, in the Science Wing's lecture theater, which ruled out the use of paint, and an Art course without paint is unavoidably jejune. The boys could and did draw indoors and out, they learnt a fair amount of Art History, they could model in plasticene, cut paper and study the design of our coinage, but an art class needs to be able to make a mess, and we had no suitable space for that until, in 1970, the school library moved out of the monastery and left an ideal space with light from the north. This gave us a place for painting and mess. In September 1972 we acquired potters' wheels and a kiln and more good mess. Despite the handicaps, we had a number of quite talented artists and took part both in the Archdiocesan Festivals of the Arts and in the West County Fine Arts Festivals. The boys produced animated cartoons, one of which started with an egg, whose top came off; a head emerged, looked around and saw in the distance a mushroom cloud. The head

---

[295] Bridge Club: there was certainly one later under Brother Antony. Its earlier existence has left faint traces in the memory of some of us, but apparently no other record.

withdrew and the top came back on the egg: a powerful fifteen seconds' worth from Keith Naunheim. Once we started to produce works of distinction, we used the split level in the new high school as a display area. Only at the end of our period did this activity get into full swing.

In the *Barry Project*, chosen boys had the opportunity to work with Brian Barry on the solution of some scientific problem. The first was the desalination of sea-water. Their research showed that the application of an electro-magnetic field was effective but, with the technology of the 1960s, uneconomical. Although Monsanto showed interest in patenting the process, the real value lay in what the boys learnt. In a similar vein but later on, boys experimented with the delivery of solar energy to the Stannard House. Solar panels were installed on the roof of the dining room and energy was produced, but not under Brian's auspices.

Carpentry, which had been practiced by Henry Hughes and some of the monks in the Stannards' chicken-shed even before the opening of school, was by 1960 established in the northern locker-room at the gymnasium, under the care of Reynolds Medart. He set up and equipped eight work-benches, each with its own color-coded set of hand-tools. All sorts of artefacts emerged from the shop, including a boat, which traveled at speed on Lake Michigan, but then needed to be taken into dry dock. One item that failed to emerge was a doghouse which, when completed, was too big to get out of the door. In 1964, Reynolds had to give up this activity because of the sawdust, and at once we found how invaluable he had been. Professional carpenters were not attracted by the awkward hours. After Reynolds, our most successful instructors were Brother John Dahm, Father Finbarr and Father Vincent Wace, who, as monks, did not find the hours awkward, and Mr. Egon Doering, a retired expert from Bank Building Corporation, and Mr. Bernhardt Voss, also retired. In the summer of 1971 the carpentry shop moved from the gymnasium to the basement of the Junior House, and the Sports Store moved, initially, into where the carpentry shop had been.

The *Chess Club* was yet another of Father Thomas' activities. As some of the boys were able to beat some of their instructors, one should speak rather of moderators. Brother James succeeded Father Thomas in 1968 and handed over to Mr. James L. Wortham in 1971.

The Debate was the preserve of the Junior House. There they sharpened their wits and sometimes their claws, but the latter sharpening was discouraged by Father Nicholas, and by Brother Christopher Rush, who succeeded him.

Drama was one of the major activities. The first full-length play was *My Three Angels*, produced on 10 May 1961 by Father Leonard and Bob Bannister. The stage building was the archway building in its original site between the dining room and the barn. The audience sat north of the stage. The female parts were played by girls from Nerinx High School, one of whom later married one of our actors. After that the plays were (one a year, unless otherwise noted): Steinbeck's *The Moon Is Down*; Gogol's *The Inspector General*; Molière's *L'Avare*; Plautus' *Mostellaria* (*The Haunted House*); *Twelfth Night*; Ustinov's *Romanoff and Juliet*; Rattigan's *The Winslow Boy*; Shaw's *Arms and the Man*; Ira Wallach's *The Absence of a Cello*; McLeish's *JB*; *A Dramatization of Mark Twain* and Masters' *Spoon River Anthology*, both in the school year 1972-73. There seems to have been no play in 1970, but in that year David Linzee's play *O'Finnegan's Wake* was performed at the West County Drama Festival at Saint Louis Country Day School. He was a senior that year.

The production of plays at any level is always eventful, and our productions were no exception. In 1962 we were invited to use Villa Duchesne's brand new stage for *The Moon is Down*. In the course of the play a shotgun has to be discharged. We gave a boy a shotgun and a large barrel to shoot into. He managed to miss the barrel and blew a sizable hole in Villa's brand new stage. We were never asked back. Thereafter plays were staged either at Visitation Academy or west of the Stannard House or on the lawn east of the house, a lovely setting, especially before the great elms died. In 1965 on that lawn we produced Plautus' play, *The Haunted House*. Since all our students were boys, we preferred plays that had few or no female roles, and such plays were not easy to find. Father Leonard was at a loss one year, but some seniors were reading Plautus' *Mostellaria*, (*The Haunted House*) in the Advanced Placement Latin course, so this play was chosen. Unfortunately, the manuscripts are defective and the play lacks an ending. The seniors, therefore, each wrote a suggested ending, and from them Father Leonard concocted a script of which Plautus might well have been proud. *The Shield* commented, "It was said that this was the most professional play put on at Priory. It was certainly the funniest."[296] That it was the funniest was largely due to Tranio, the clever slave whose cunning keeps the plot going. He was played by Kevin D. Kline.

---

[296] *The Shield*, 1966, p. 95.

In response to parental requests, *Driver Education* was introduced in 1969 under Mr. Robert Boehlow, but so much was already available that it did not last.

European travel was planned by Father Paul and executed by him, sometimes under the wing of the Foreign Study League, and with help on various trips from Father Ian, Steve Pomeroy and Bill Daake. On one of the trips, by the kindness of a parent, Mr. George H. Capps, he picked up in Zurich a Volkswagen minibus, in which the group toured Switzerland, Italy, France and England. He then dispatched the bus by sea to the United States. Eight boys spent over five weeks with him, saw the Pope in Rome, the Palio in Siena, not to mention Mr. Churchill and Sophia Loren elsewhere. One boy lost his passport and another lost himself, but Father Paul was unperturbed. The planning was always meticulous.

The *French Club* was organized by Ed Cook, who once impressed a Parisian waiter by being able not only to converse but also to curse in French like a Frenchman. The members of the club conversed, without cursing, in French of things French and played French music of many kinds. Their most tangible product was an edition of *Le Journal du Prieuré*, Mai 1964.

The *Investment Club* was moderated by Mr. Robert McGloughlin of A. G. Edwards. Four juniors started the club to discuss stocks and bonds. It met for two years, 1967-69, but whether it went from theory to practice and, if so, with what results, is not recorded.

From the very beginning our school librarians recruited boys to act as *Assistant Librarians*. Starting with such humble jobs as returning books to their shelves—to do this accurately is not so easy as it sounds, and a misplaced book is almost as good as lost—or keeping the periodicals in order, they would move up into the process of the accession of books to the library and perhaps even to full cataloging. Not all boys want to do this kind of job, and of those who want to not all can, but by 1970 Father Miles had a group of seven assistants, the culmination of a process fostered in turn by Father Timothy, Alex Niven, Father Laurence and Father Augustine. As Priory Day became established, so did exhibits on that day in the library. The librarian decided what would be exhibited, the boys arranged it, and in so doing became acquainted with some of the library's treasures. But boys were not the only volunteers. Over the years, a number of mothers have provided indispensable assistance. Mrs. Samuel S. Pomeroy and Mrs. John F. Wilkinson, a splendid pair, were able to talk continuously and work continuously (and accurately) all at the same time. They achieved local fame when Father Nicholas, who happened to be walking by their office, heard the tantalizing fragment, "And do you know, of her own volition . . ." and then, a tribute to his willpower, passed out of earshot. We also had a volunteer from outside, Mr. Lawrence E. Tanner, who stayed in the monastery for a while and helped Father Columba to catalog the growing monastic collection.

The *May Projects* were an effort to kill two birds with one stone: to introduce upperclassmen to the practice of community service or at least to interaction with the community, and to maintain seniors' interest in the last month or two before graduation. The program was introduced in 1969, was voluntary and took a while to catch on. Two seniors took part the first year, seven the next, after which it ceased to be news. Two worked with the Ladue Police; three tutored at Sophia House and one at Bishop Healy High School; one worked with our architects, HOK; and one composed music on his own, and others did other things. It was a flexible program. The boys did some service to others and some to themselves.

Mechanical Drawing was taught from 1960 to 1964 by Brian Barry,[297] but after that, for the rest of our period, it was the domain of Reynolds Medart and the activity with which he was principally linked. One of the first tasks of the class was to make a diagram of the stage of the Muny Opera in Forest Park to be sent to New York, presumably for the information of visiting performers. Countless boys took with Brian and then with Reynolds the first steps towards neatness and accuracy. Reynolds loved notices such as

PLAN AHEA
D

Music had always been made in the Barn,[298] but in September 1961 it formally took over one half of the building, with Forms III and IV sharing the other half as their form room. Then in September 1971 it took over the whole building. In our period, it was always the domain of Father Austin. Already in December 1960 the musicians were able

---

[297] *The Record* V. 6, pp. 1-2 quotes "the facetious words of Mr. Barry" that the purpose of Mechanical Drawing is "to lift the heavy hand of Aristotle from the minds of the students, and practise them in the great, liberal, material sciences." With friends like that in one's midst . . .

[298] Demolished in March 2000. *See above*, p. 273, footnote 216.

to give a concert which included pieces by Purcell, Haydn, Chopin and Dvorak for violin, 'cello, clarinet, flute and piano. Father Austin himself played another 'cello, which he took with him on holiday, partly to play and partly as a means of transporting spare clothing, which was stuffed inside.[299] By 1963 they had added Beethoven, William Handy, Lecuona, Mozart and Schubert; and in 1972 gave us a world première of a Symphonietta composed by a sophomore and a junior, Steve Lockhart and Steve McKenna. The former also played second violin in the Saint Louis Symphony Youth Orchestra. Father Austin built up a catholic collection of records, helped by a windfall from the music department of Washington University which, when LP records came in, gave us its superseded 78s. He found these more suitable for illustrating his sessions of Musical Appreciation, and with them he also provided short concerts after lunch, which were well attended. The records were played and amplified on a hi-fi sound system and a huge speaker constructed by Mr. Geoffrey Kimball, with occasional help from Henry Hughes, Reynolds Medart and Father Timothy.

In September 1964 John Leavitt, then a senior, persuaded Father Austin to form a *Glee Club*, which sang for two years, sometimes at Mass. After a boy's voice breaks and he becomes a tenor or bass, there may be some years of uncertainty before it sounds settled again, and those are the years of high school. We have been unable to rival the striking success of Ampleforth in training not only a large choir of boys but also the whole school to sing well in church and out of it. There was also a *Guitar Group*, moderated by Father Colin.

On occasion we hosted outside groups such as the Graham Road Rock Group, consisting mostly of boys from De Smet Jesuit High School, but playing hits by Pat McLaughlin of our class of 1970. By far the most distinguished of these visiting groups was the Saint Louis Symphony Orchestra itself, which, on 19 October 1966, gave a one-hour concert in our gymnasium "to illustrate the musical principle of variation. It was a lively program embracing both the familiar and the *outré*, and was well received."[300] This was arranged for us by some of our mothers. There have been many organ recitals in our church, including two by the renowned Marie-Claire Alain, who came at the

---

[299] The trick was to get the clothing out again. One of Father Austin's well-remembered remarks was, "I can never understand why people think musicians are odd."

[300] *SLPJ* IV. 3, p. 12

behest of the Mothers' Club.[301] The church, with its seven-second resonance, is beloved not only of instrumentalists but also of choirs. The Saint Louis Choral Society and countless others have sung here. Finally the very substantial bequest of Mrs. Anna May L. Nussbaum, which enabled us to renovate the barn, was also used for musical scholarships and has ensured a constant flow of musical talent into the school.

The *Outings*, which occurred mainly on school holidays, were intended to provide the boys with information on which to base their choice of a career. They were arranged by Father Leonard, often in cooperation with Father Thomas, who arranged similar outings for the Science Club. A visit to Monsanto might be relevant to a boy both as a student of science and as a possible future scientist. Father Leonard arranged excursions to the Lumaghi coal mine, Bank Building Corporation, the *Post-Dispatch*, the Fausts' farm, Union Electric, KSD Radio and Television Station, the U.S. Coast Guard Station, Saint Louis Union Trust and many others. A memorable outing to Jefferson City included a visit to a session of the State Supreme Court sitting *en banc.* The case being heard at the time of our visit concerned a truck, which had struck the abutment of a bridge and scattered its cargo of soda across the road. Just as torpor seemed to be settling on both the boys and the *banc*, one of the justices, who had seemed to be dozing, sat up and said, "Oh my goodness! All that sody-pop all over the road!" These outings were truly impressive both in themselves and for the generous hospitality of the places we visited. Often the boys ended up in the Board Room.

Photography does not readily lend itself to description. The first instructor was Reynolds Medart (who else?), from whom Mr. Robert C. Dunn took over in 1965. He was followed by Mr. Robert C. Corley in 1972. The boys had the opportunity of learning how to use a camera and its attachments, how to compose a picture, how to develop and print their film. The chief problem was a place. After the stern edict of the Fire Marshal banning them from the basement of the Junior House, they went to the basement of the Stannard House, and thence in 1970 to the north end of the new high school, but not until long after our period did they find a home comparable to the one that was planned and banned. Boys in the Junior House were included from September 1966.

Proms and Football Dances absorbed much of the energy of the juniors and seniors, or at least of their dance committees. Many were

---

[301] *See above* p. 234.

held in the gym, which presented the major problem of making a large, bare space look cozy. In 1967 the football dance was held in the boys' dining room, in 1969 in the Junior House with orange fluorescent goalposts at each end and the field marked out with blue fluorescent tape, and in 1970 and 1971 in the new high school. In 1970 by the kindness of the late Mr. August A. Busch, Jr., the Prom was held at Grant's Farm and was enlivened by a variety of animals, including an elephant painted pink. In 1973 by the kindness of Mr. William T. Dooley, Jr., it was held in the old Melody Museum downtown.

The Radio Club was founded in 1960 by Father Leonard, with three projects in mind: to run a phone line from the Stannard House to the Science Wing; to put an amateur radio station on the air; and to produce on tape a periodical commentary on school news. These were all achieved. The line ran; it is uncertain how often it was used or usable. The station WA∅JMT, complete with FCC license, came on the air in 1964 in the old chicken shed. With the help of a huge mast and antenna, it made its first contact by reaching a station in Norfolk, Virginia, at 12.20 p.m. on 17 October. Four years later, its signal was picked up in England, but we never managed to establish a regular link with Ampleforth. The club undertook other projects such as providing sound for a Mothers' Club book review on the lawn; installing new speakers in the boys' dining room, so that the announcements after lunch could be more easily heard; recording on tape the dedication of the church. They sold 53 copies of this. The commentary on school life was called "Anything Goes" and was popular with the boys. As the name suggests, it was a blend of news, commentary, humor and anything else that came into the mind of the man with the microphone. Father Leonard was always the mainspring, but he was helped for two years by Mr. Walter Rishoi and for ten by Mr. Charles Scott, who became a well-loved figure on campus.

The Record was the name of the school paper. Because so little time was available, the production of anything at all was an arduous task both for the staff of the paper and for its moderators, of whom there were eight in thirteen years. At its start, the moderator's chief difficulty was to prevent athletic news from monopolizing all the space, that being the part of school life that the reporters found easiest to report. Another difficulty was that the writing and reproducing took so long that anything properly called news had long become stale by the time the paper appeared. Nonetheless, as *The Record* matured, it began to take on topics of wider interest and, especially in the early seventies, of greater provocation, such as Central America, or the pollution of the environment. One happy by-product was that *Prom Magazine* used to arrange occasional interviews with celebrities as various as NATO chiefs and the Liverpool Five, and invited school reporters to them.

When we first discussed with HOK the requirements of the school, one that we had mentioned as a possibility was a rifle range. Ampleforth had one under the auspices of their ROTC, and we were open to the idea. Consequently, when in 1965 Mr. Donald L. Barnes, Jr., offered us the use of a rifle and skeet range on his property on Kehrs Mill Road, Father Leonard and he immediately entered into negotiations. The *Rifle Club* was born and for two or three years boys were given tuition by police experts. *The Record*[302] reports renewed interest in 1972 and a proposal was made for a range on campus, but because of the cost, and because it was a time of financial stringency, the range was not built.

The Science Club was, of course, moderated by Father Thomas. It had three areas of activity: meetings, visits and projects. The success of all three was due to the respect that the scientific community of Saint Louis, both academic and industrial, had for Father Thomas. For the meetings, therefore, he was always able to persuade one of his scientific friends to be honorary president and deliver a presidential address on his favorite topic. In this way the boys heard Professor William A. Barker (Physics) and Father William V. Stauder, S.J. (Seismology) from Saint Louis University, Professors Barry Commoner (Biology and environment) and Alexander Calandra (Math and Physics) from Washington University, Mr. Mike Witunski and Dr. J. David Keating from industry, and many others. To the non-scientist, and perhaps to the scientist as well, Dr. Keating's presentation of the hologram was the most startling. To see the front view of an aircraft in a hologram, and then by bending down to be able to see under its wings was nearly incredible. At these meetings, too, the boys had the opportunity to speak of their own projects.

McDonnell Aircraft was probably the favorite visit because of its connection with the space program and the building of fighter aircraft—who, in the immediate presence of space capsules and Phantom jets, could be uninterested?—but hardly less fascinating visits were paid to Monsanto, Mallinckrodt Inc., Granite City Steel, Owens Glass Works, etc. On occasion, instead of our visiting them, they came to us. Late in 1972 the Spacemobile came to Priory with a preview of some of NASA's projected missions: skylab, space shuttle and the

---

[302] *The Record*, 18 February 1972 I. 5, p. 1.

SCRAMLACE engine, which "can be converted in flight from a fanjet, to a turbojet, to a ramjet, and finally to a rocket engine, depending on the altitude of the aircraft."[303]

The two main projects of the club were the annual Saint Louis Post-Dispatch Science Fair and our own nearly-annual Science Open House. In the Science Fair in 1962 Bob Landy won a four year scholarship to Washington University, and in the following year his brother, Dick, was chosen to represent Saint Louis at the International Science Fair. So were Jim Moran and John Schier in 1970, when they took first place in two separate divisions, an amazing and perhaps unique achievement for one school, and a small one at that. In our period, our students won two first prizes in the Post-Dispatch Special Division and ten in the Senior Regular Division, along with four second prizes, four special awards and an alternate.

The Science Open House was an opportunity for all the boys, not just the brightest, to assemble a variety of demonstrations and then explain them to the visitors, some of whom were potentates in the scientific community. This could not be done until the Science Department had moved to its final home in the Science Wing. The demonstrations varied in complexity, so that both beginning students and advanced scholars had something to show, and often enough the simplest were the most eye-catching.

Surveying was offered in response to the interest of Ed Thomas and Roger Wells, seniors in 1962, but did not survive them.

Two kinds of *Tutoring* were available: tutoring students from Sophia House, which started in 1969, and tutoring by upperclassmen of boys in our Junior House, which started in 1968. Sophia House, which *The Record* for October 1969 describes as "a study-center located downtown in the area of the Pruitt-Igoe Housing Project", offered selected students from that area an environment favorable to learning. We explored, with the Danforth Foundation, the possibility of more extensive cooperation, but the program of tutoring seemed to be as much as was feasible.[304] Members of Sophia House also cooperated in our summer school in 1969. The program for the Junior House was originally designed as an introduction to the study of Science, but was expanded to include boys who needed help in any

[303] *Ibid.* 19 December 1972 p. 1.

[304] We tried to find out what the students concerned wanted and to provide that rather than what we thought they wanted or ought to want, and this proved difficult.

academic subject. Brian Barry inaugurated the program and in 1972 handed it over to Steve Pomeroy.

Typing was offered as an activity from after the football season of 1969, was taught by Mrs. Elaine Winn and lasted for the rest of our period.

The yearbook, which was called *The Shield*, after our coat of arms, was another activity that demanded far more time than could be officially allocated to it, so the staff had to put in much of their own time. The first was produced in 1960 by members of the first graduating class, and it has come out annually ever since. In the early days it was more or less punctual, but the events of the spring term were left until the yearbook of the following year. Later, the staff tried to include all the events of the school year, but that meant that the yearbook appeared later and later. Deadlines and punctuality are an ongoing, unsolved and, perhaps, insoluble, problem. Compared with *The Record*, the yearbook has been blessed in having in our period only three moderators: Alex Niven, Father Leonard and Tom Geiss. Mr. Harry Swain, our representative from Josten Yearbook Company from 1960 through 1971, earned the gratitude of successive yearbook staffs by being an invaluable advisor and doing far more than he had to. With George Thompson[305] he has a special place in our hearts. The yearbook is the best summary of the school year written from the boys' point of view. Though not wholly free from inaccuracy, it has been an immense help in the compilation of this history. It is also a vehicle for the expression of sentiments and judgements that penetrate deeper into the spirit of the school than the simple recording of events. Two quotations, both from the yearbook for 1964, the first class of whom half started in the seventh grade, may illustrate this. The first is from the letter of the headmaster to the class of 1964:

> . . . But there is more to you than this: a general level-headedness and a cheerful tolerance of minor adversities; the absence of fanaticism and hysteria, and of that overdeveloped capacity for indignation that can turn a class sour. Consequently you have been more than usually teachable; in fact there is in the classroom and other areas you inhabit a not infrequent spark of enthusiasm and perception that may draw the best out of your masters, coaches and other mentors. This art of classmanship is a valuable art to possess.

---

[305] *See* p. 95 *above*.

The title-page of the same yearbook has an unusual paragraph at the top:

> The Priory is primarily a monastery for the praise of God. It is also, though not separately, a school. The monks, all devoted and excellently educated, have taught us both religiously and scholastically, This yearbook is the work of the seniors; we have all spent much of our life at the Priory and have become quite attached to it. In a way all of us are sorry to leave the school for it is here that we have spent our most formative years. We take this opportunity then, to express our profound gratitude by presenting
>
> THE SHIELD

The editor of this yearbook was Steve Higgins, later United States Attorney for Eastern Missouri.

Members of the Junior House participated in most of these activities and had a few of their own, some of them short-lived, such as the First Aid course in 1966. They attended the highly organized Fleur de Lis, Fortnightly and Service Bureau Dances; they had, under Father Miles, their own newspaper, *The Hooter*, in which they tooted their own horn; they practiced *calligraphy* , of which someone on the cocktail circuit remarked in shocked tones, "Have you heard about those monks? They practice calligraphy", as though it were some strange medieval sin; Brian Barry organized contests in applied engineering such as the construction of paper airplanes or of bridges made from popsicle sticks; they raised money for the foreign missions by holding an annual Mission Fair with a variety of sideshows and by running a candy store. They took a special interest in the school in Molapowabojang, Botswana.

Public Relations

AT this point one may well ask, "If all these good things were going on, what was being done to publicize them?" and we must answer that at the beginning we were very amateurish in anything involving public relations. Ampleforth up to 1955 did virtually nothing in this line apart from maintaining some contact with its alumni, and yet managed to have a constant supply both of novices for the monastery and of students for the school. We recognized from the start that our situation was different, not least when we heard the title "great educator" given to people whose prowess was not in teaching but in public relations and fund-raising. From the start we recognized that we were bound not merely to communicate with Inc but also to support them in whatever they did to raise funds for us. We also recognized that communication with parents and the rest of the Priory Family was a high priority, but, apart from mailings and our *Journal,* parents' meetings and the Mothers' Club, we did not go very far. Although we were pleased enough when the media, and especially the newspapers, were kind to us, we would not, in the early days have accorded any very high priority to seeking publicity for its own sake. In general, the whole concept of "image", especially if contrasted with reality, was distasteful to us and even embryonic in society at large, compared with what it is today.

In cooperation with Inc we produced several fund-raising brochures, which involved two rather painful processes: tooting our own horn and being photographed. We were also accomplices in the production of a filmstrip and several videos, which was even more painful. These were all primarily for fund-raising, but served also as a means of informing prospective parents about the school, and were useful when we went on visits to grade schools.

For the school we soon found that we needed to compose a factual brochure. The earliest extant copy is dated 25 March 1958 and was distributed to visitors on the Mothers' Club's first house tour; it may have been written a little earlier, but not before the beginning of 1958. A revised version appeared in September 1962.[306] This evolved as the years passed and in the late sixties was the occasion of our choosing as our logo the silhouette of the church, which we still use, and for which we are still grateful to the late Lemoine Skinner.

The *Globe-Democrat* and the *Post-Dispatch* were both generous to us, starting even before our arrival with good coverage of our plans,

---

306 *See* Appendix B 5.

continuing with comments on our arrival, and then covering special events such as the activities of the Mothers' Club and, especially, the construction of the church and its dedication. The weekly newspaper of the Archdiocese, the *Saint Louis Review*, was no less generous, which helped especially with Catholic families, from whom we drew most of our students. The media also covered the activities of the students. In academics, the National Merit Scholarship Program and the Post-Dispatch Science Fair received the most space but not nearly so much as that devoted to athletics, where Bill Daake as scholar athlete and our football team of 1973 as state champions, but also very many others, kept our name before those who studied the sports pages.

In October 1965 when the Archdiocese started to hold an Open House for all Catholic high schools, we took part, though by that time our whole intake was into the seventh grade and few parents came to visit. Our own Priory Day, in its original form as a combination of quiz and basketball for sixth graders, was more effective with the schools concerned. We were invited from time to time to speak at grade schools about vocations, and that sometimes led to an invitation to speak about our school. In due course Father Miles developed a slide show, which could be taken on the road at a moment's notice and often was.

Many of our other activities, though not overtly aimed at public relations nor done with that purpose, did have the effect of bringing us before the public eye. When Father Columba taught at Webster College, as it then was, or Father Luke gave a Retreat at the Cenacle, or Father Timothy spoke at the Archdiocesan Teachers Institute, all of these made us known to people outside the Priory family; and on the less frequent occasions when we appeared on television or radio, we reached an even wider audience. Our summer school for boys from the inner city helped to make us known there, at least to the officials of the participating schools.

It is hard to estimate, and perhaps hard to overestimate, the effect of word of mouth communication on the cocktail and hair-dryer circuits. What is certain is that the mothers and fathers of boys in the school were our most influential communicators, and especially the mothers. The Mothers' Club and the Fathers' Club were also two of our principal means of keeping our parents informed. To them we now turn.

The Mothers' Club

THE foundation of the Mothers' Club has already been described,[307] but it may be relevant here to repeat that English boarding schools have no such organization—distance from home to school precludes it—and that several American schools, as well local friends, had advised us at least to be cautious about founding one. They may well have had in mind Parent Teachers Associations rather than Mothers' clubs. We approached the idea, therefore, with suitable caution, but have never had cause to regret what we did.

Our purpose in starting a Mothers' Club was to help the boys by establishing an atmosphere of friendly cooperation between the home and the school, but we soon saw that the first need was to establish understanding. Linguistic difficulties were not too hard to overcome, but there were also considerable, unexpected and unpredictable differences of outlook. One small example, in which the American-English gap was widened by the male-female gap, must suffice. Father Timothy came to one early meeting with chalk on his monastic habit. He was greeted with what seemed like a shocked comment, "Father, you have chalk on your habit." He replied that he had been teaching, and thought that was the end of the affair. He was surprised when they persisted in commenting on the chalk on his habit, and he persisted in his explanation that he had been writing on the chalk board and that tended to cause a deposit of chalk on the habit. No doubt he eventually saw that the meeting would not start satisfactorily until he rubbed off the chalk, and did so.

The meetings enabled the mothers to get to know the faculty, which initially was almost all monks, and to get to know one another. We started by discussing various aspects of school life, discussions which often took the form of the monks giving reasons for their unaccustomed ways of action; but soon it became apparent that one of the best ways of getting to know people is to work with them. Thus the mothers embarked on a series of projects, starting, as we have said, with house tours and book reviews or panel discussions, and starting with two a year. In the school year 1960-61, for example, in October Father Austin reviewed Evelyn Waugh's biography of Monsignor Ronald Knox and next April the mothers organized another successful House Tour. For one of their house tours they wished to persuade the noted home-designer, Mr. Burton Duenke, to let his

[307] On p. 122 *above*.

home be on the tour. They had been unable to make contact with him until one of them was driving by and, providentially, ran out of gas and came to a stop right outside his house. She had to go in and ask to use his telephone. Once inside, she oohed and aahed so effectively about the beauty of the interior that he agreed to her request. That was her story and she stuck to it.

A typical panel discussion was the one held in the gym on 1 April 1962 under the title, "*In Pace with Space*." Our *Journal* reports, "The panelists were Dr. Carl Kisslinger, Messrs. Charles A. Schweighauser, Joseph J. Simeone and Michael Witunski. This highly articulate group was moderated by Father Columba. The result was a skillful blend of learning and lightness, which neither scared the unscientific nor left the pundits without matter for reflection." [308] This was a success and, carrying out the military dictum, "Don't reinforce failure but exploit success", they held two more, one of which included Dr. Barry Commoner, a biologist and environmentalist from Washington University and Mother Kernaghan, a physicist from Maryville College of the Sacred Heart (now Maryville University). There was some apprehension about this as Dr. Commoner was liberal and Mother Kernaghan was no less known for her summer Workshops on the Sacred Heart than for her courses in Physics. What would be the outcome? In the event, Mother Kernaghan nobly held her own, and there were even those who thought she stole the show. Not knowing what to do for an encore, the mothers reverted to house tours. They had also discovered that the burden of organizing two events a year was excessive, and so decided to concentrate all their efforts on one event and make it major. They were always looking for new ideas.

One year they arranged a program with the distinguished artists, Siegfried and Harriet Reinhardt. There was a showing of some of Siegfried's paintings, including some of his early work, and a panel discussion on art in general. Next year they arranged a demonstration of Cricket and Rugby Football, inveigling four teams to come out and play, and Fathers Austin and Timothy to comment. For this they also arranged a fine fall afternoon. The crowd found Rugby the easier to follow. In 1967 the mothers, besides getting Marie-Claire Alain to inaugurate our organ, mounted a travelogue on England and Wales, accompanied by an English tea that was worthy of a royal garden party--except that the refreshments were innocuous--and the following year a travelogue to Greece, with Greek food and music.

---

[308] *SLPJ* III, 3, p. 12

For the third year they went to Spain, but then they must have been travelogued out, because in 1970 they broke entirely new ground. One or two city-wide organizations had raised funds by holding auctions. At a board-meeting of the Mothers' Club the question was raised whether we could do the same. After discussion and a fair amount of cold water, the mothers decided to go ahead, despite the smallness of their numbers. Exotic names such as *Camelot* and *Khorassan* were in the wind, so Claire (Mrs. Glennon J.) Travis christened it *Xanadu*.[309]

This revolutionized their projects. No previous event had reached $4500; in its first year *Xanadu* made over $10,000. Since then they have never looked back, and there has been an auction every year. By 1973 they were up to nearly $50,000 and had, besides the main auction, a silent auction and a gift bazaar. It has been an almost unbelievable success both as a fund-raiser and as a social event, and many other schools have followed suit. Our alumnus, the late Bruce B. Selkirk, Jr., was the auctioneer for all the years of our period, and for many more. To start so ambitious an event was an act of true bravery, which also demanded endless hours of skill, diplomacy and sheer hard work. No less remarkable was the harmony in which it was all carried out. From the earliest days of the Mothers' Club we established as a slogan, "NO UMBRAGE"; it was well realized, year by year, in the preparations for *Xanadu*.

But these projects were far from being the only way in which the mothers helped the school. They held monthly meetings in the early afternoon—easier then as comparatively few mothers worked—of which the first in each school year included Mass and a luncheon to welcome the new mothers. In 1968 this meeting also included a new kind of house tour, namely one of the new Junior House. They contributed to our scholarship fund, and after some hesitation agreed to make the annual contribution $1,000. They organized a "resellit" shop for textbooks, clothing and equipment. They helped with the early Priory Days when we entertained other schools, and in general helped when we entertained anybody. They assisted Larry Tanner in cataloguing the monastic library and Father Miles in compiling a subject index for the school library. The latter would have cost us $10,000 had we bought the cards. They enabled Father Timothy to take his mother on a trip to Ireland.

Out of their knowledge of local customs, they advised the school about such matters as dress, on which they tended to be more

---

[309] There are other claimants, but without a tape-recorder, who can say?

conservative than the school authorities, and about food and dances. The headmaster's directive of 6 October 1963 to the Parents' Dance Committee shows the degree of trustful cooperation between the Mothers' Club and the school:

1. The purpose of the committee is to advise Father Leonard on the general conduct of the school dances.
2. The committee may be divided into executive sub-committees to carry out particular tasks.
3. The committee should use its discretion on what to leave to the boys and what to do itself, but should remember that it is good for the boys to have as much scope for genuine initiative and responsibility as possible.
4. The final decision about the band and entertainment rests with the committee or its delegate, but suggestions from and discussion with the boys concerned should be encouraged.
5. The main topics seem to be:
   a. Decoration and lighting;
   b. Band and entertainment;
   c. Catering and table service;
   d. Reception;
   e. Behavior and etiquette;
   f. Chaperones;
   g. Disciplinary arrangements.

   But this list is not intended to prevent the committee from considering other relevant matters.
6. The committee is empowered to take any other action or deliberation suggested by Father Leonard.

Lest all this seem to be too idyllic to be true, let it be recorded that there was one great row. The details have become misty, but the gist of it was that some mothers wanted the annual project to be an excursion on one of the river boats and others thought this was below the dignity of the Mothers' Club. It was a storm in a teacup, no doubt, but the meeting did end stormily. Fortunately, by the next meeting enough people had said enough prayers and Father Timothy had, in the interval, had his unfortunate encounter with a state trooper,[310] which he recounted at the beginning of the meeting. Guided by the Holy Spirit and distracted by the story, we reached an amicable resolution of the problem.

---

[310] *See* p. 266 *above*.

All of these were splendid achievements, but the greatest of all was the friendship that was established between the families and the school. This made all our dealings so much easier and more pleasant, and if anything went wrong, there was, as a result, a margin of good will and tolerance on both sides. Thank God we overcame our initial hesitation about the club's existence.

The Fathers' Club

IT has often been said, sometimes even by women, that when women meet they have other agenda than the official agenda, but that with men this is not so. Perhaps it was for this reason that the Mothers' Club was formed within a few months of the school's opening, but the Fathers' Club not until February 1959, when Father Timothy invited all fathers to a meeting at Priory to set up the club. This meeting and subsequent meetings of the fathers appear to have left no trace in the records until April 1961, when a dinner was held at the University Club. Father Ian, carrying his Athletic Director's hat in his hand, presented his needs, which included the first set of bleachers, mats and a parking lot for the new Corley Gymnasium. He raised $5600 on the spot. This paid for the dinner and for most of what he wanted. After the dinner the fathers wisely elected as President Fred Switzer, who, not so wisely, was absent from the dinner, with Mr. Bernard J. Huger as Vice-President and Mr. J. Joseph Horan as Secretary-Treasurer.

Even before the formation of the Fathers' Club, the fathers had been attending the Father and Son annual dinner and taking part in the annual softball games, and these continued. In our period, the dinner was held first at the Lennox Hotel and then at Le Château.

In the summer of 1964 a committee of the Fathers' Club met to consider further needs. They reported that "among the items urgently needed are: Additional spectator seats for the gym, outdoor bleachers on the visitors' side of the football field, a time clock for the field, further photographic and dark room equipment, the provision of a rifle range, and the development of track and field facilities."[311] They went on to ask for an annual gift of around $100, the start of annual giving by parents. The results must have been satisfactory, because in the fall we were able to equip the football field east of the McCabes' house with a very legible scoreboard, which is pictured in the *Journal* in healthy condition after our home game against Lutheran Central. It read Visitor: 0; Home: 40; Time: 0.00. That was the year when our Varsity was 6-1-1. At the same time we could buy bleachers for the North side of the gym, so visitors could sit together and home supporters together. Photography also benefited but riflery and the track had to wait.

The next burst of activity was in May 1965 when the club met under the chairmanship of Joe Horan and formed committees for

---

[311] Letter of 8 July 1964 in Organization file 1964-65

Library, Activities, Athletics, Grounds, Speakers, Public Relations, Scholarships, and Summer Jobs. These were to assist Father Timothy, Father Leonard, Mr. McCabe and Father Luke (Grounds) in their various areas, and did so. The most notable result was that the Library Committee decided to concentrate on books needed for our Advanced Placement courses. The faculty promptly produced an extensive list of the books required, the fathers raised the money, and we acquired all the books that we could lay hands on. This was part of the reason for the dramatic increase in our Advanced Placement scores, to which we have alluded above.[312] It also did justice to the fathers by showing them taking an interest in something other than athletics. At a follow-up meeting in November, the various committees made their reports and Don Barnes offered the use of his rifle and skeet range, as noted above.[313] These committees acted when there was a special need, and much of their best work was done by a single member in cooperation with the faculty man concerned, as happened between Don Barnes and Father Leonard over riflery.

In the fall of 1966, the fathers arranged a brunch at Busch's Grove before the games against Country Day and John Burroughs. They could hardly be called pep rallies, as no students were present, but they certainly included an element of encouragement and ensured that a considerable group of supporters arrived at the games in an upbeat mood. This successful event was repeated a number of times.

In one program the fathers were the receivers not the givers of benefit: Marty McCabe started the 7.30 Club, by which the gym was available at 7.30 a.m. to fathers or alumni who wished to work out before going to work. This started in November 1967 and evidently met a need.

The Fathers' Club was a different kind of organization from the Mothers' Club. Although it contributed to the liaison between home and school, that was not a priority. It did not in this period hold monthly meetings, but was summoned when some action was needed. Then, as can be seen from this account, it was very effective.

---

[312] *See* pp. 304-6 *above.*

[313] *See* p. 364 *above.*

Other Schools

OUR membership of the ABC League brought our students and, to a lesser degree, our faculty into contact with the other member schools. This led to occasional exchanges for a day or less of both students and faculty with schools in the ABC League, and also with quite diverse schools such as Vashon High School in the city and the Jesuits' Saint Louis University High School. These were brief, stimulating and, in the jargon of the day, "consciousness-raising", and we did learn from one another.

In January 1973 we launched a program called "Impact 73", whose aim was to increase understanding among boys of very different life-styles. Ten boys from the inner city spent a day of prayer, discussion, movies and basketball with us. It seemed to be well received on both sides, but there is no record of any continuation. Later we exchanged faculty rather than students, and have long entertained the hope, as yet unfulfilled, of such exchanges with Ampleforth.

Beyond this, Father Timothy was from 1963 to 1977 a member of the Higher Education Council of Metropolitan Saint Louis (HEC)[314], on which he represented the independent schools. Almost at once, HEC turned its attention to the question of Advanced Placement, which was of immediate interest to his constituents. The first concern of the schools was the extent of the recognition given by colleges to students who did well in the Advanced Placement examinations, and their particular hope was to persuade local universities to be more generous. In due course, the committee of HEC and the College Entrance Examination Board did sponsor a meeting in Saint Louis of colleges and secondary schools to describe the Advanced Placement program, which was then in its infancy, and to discuss the appropriate reaction of colleges to it. Father Timothy was chairman of the meeting, which was successful in making the Advanced Placement Program more widely and more accurately known but was marred by the absence of one local university whose presence was especially desired.

In May 1964 at the behest of HEC, Father Timothy explored the possibility of some kind of joint purchasing or joint insurance by the independent schools. Eight schools expressed interest and attended a

---

[314] In 1963 it was still called the Higher Education Coordinating Council, but for fear of looking like a super-board, HECC later dropped its first C and became HEC.

meeting in the fall, but the purchasing agents of the various schools felt that their present arrangements were satisfactory and that the possible small gain did not outweigh the possible complications. At a meeting of heads of school at Priory in January 1965 it was confirmed that Advanced Placement was a topic of real concern to them, and that they hoped that the University of Missouri would come to accept College Board results as well as those of the American College Testing program. They also expressed considerable enthusiasm for the idea of an annual meeting of the heads of the independent and Catholic schools, but the idea lay dormant until 1968. At a meeting of the Prior's Council in June, Father Timothy reported that he had met with the principals of Country Day, Mary Institute, Principia, John Burroughs and Sherwood Day School, who wished to form a group to organize cooperation among the schools and the dissemination of information of common concern. A rather cumbersome and expensive structure was rejected, and the heads of school started to meet in an informal and beneficial way.

In September 1969 one item on the agenda for our faculty meeting was the Missouri Association for Non-Public Schools.[315] Later in that school year, or at the beginning of the next school year, a meeting was convened, perhaps at Missouri Military Academy in Mexico, Missouri. Father Timothy, who should have known better, spoke enthusiastically of the idea and so was asked to be its president. At that point he recalled that he was due to depart for a sabbatical in the fall, and so was able to decline. Thus the Missouri Independent Schools Association (MISA, to be pronounced Meeza) was born.

Many of us served other schools as members of teams evaluating their schools. Father Timothy served on the teams for McBride High School, Saint Louis University High School and Visitation Academy. At the first of these he had a curious experience: headmasters tended to be put on the committee dealing with the school's Philosophy and Objectives. Father Timothy duly wrote the report for this committee, handed it in for typing and departed. Next morning he arrived and found his committee already in session and reading a document. When asked if he approved, he said that it seemed to him quite sensible as far as he could understand the jargon. The members of the committee laughed and said, "Well, you should like it; you wrote it." When he denied this, they said, "Of course, we had to translate it into

---

[315] What follows is based on Father Timothy's memory. No other record seems to exist.

proper educational terminology, or nobody would have taken any notice of it."

For some while we had a tutoring program for students from Sophia House.[316] We provided the appropriate facilities for a leadership conference for the Banneker-Vashon School District, a Retreat for De Andreis High School, the track meet of the CYC and many of the games of their football and basketball leagues, for the County Softball Association, and Missouri Baptist College's basketball.

Sometimes the schools served were farther afield, as when Father Timothy was invited to Atlantic City to speak to a section of the annual convention of the National Association of Secondary School Principals on *Strategies for the Education of the Gifted.* He shocked them by saying that often enough the best thing to do was to step back and let the Holy Spirit carry on. That was before the days of political correctness—and yet it was spiritually correct.

---

316 *See above*, p. 365.

CHAPTER 22

The Business Office

APART, perhaps, from prayer, nothing of all that we have described so far could have taken place without the business office. After the abbot, Saint Benedict's *Rule* makes the procurator or business manager the most favored official in the monastery. Saint Benedict casts him in the same mold as the abbot--"he must be like a father to the whole community"[317]--and has none of the misgivings about him that he has about the prior. Occupying this position at the start of our period was Father Luke, with Mary Bennace at his right hand. By 1960 he had built several buildings on campus and remodeled others; he had established communication and often friendship with many suppliers, contractors and the staff of our architects. He had learnt about boilers and machinery of many types, butchering, seeding and sodding, accounts and insurance and the like, not to mention occasional visits from the F.B.I., a pleasure that he shared with Father Timothy. Father Luke's visits were about employees, Father Timothy's about boys or their families.

In a letter home dated 11 October 1961 Father Luke gives an account of how he spent a typical day: "Got most of my Office [i.e. breviary] said in choir; went to Maryville for 7.0 a.m. Mass; then set off in the Morris [Morris Minor car] to look over some surplus material in an Army camp. It is 135 miles away on one of the main roads, mostly divided highway. Was back by 3.0 p.m. After phoning around about the equipment I had seen, I decided it would not do for us. I managed to beg from a friend a coating of liquid asphalt for applying over a parking lot we are making for ourselves near the monastery. We just could not afford to have it done professionally after the fancy one we had done at the gym . . . When I was in the [auditor's] new office, I met his secretary who told me she was interested in the Catholic Faith and had been for five years but had never met a priest before. The net result is that I am now giving her instruction, complicated by the fact that her husband is violently opposed. I am to meet him to explain things to him and hope that he will join in the instructions."[318] A variegated day.

---

[317] *The Rule of Saint Benedict* 31, 2.

[318] He did for a while but then stopped.

Early in 1962 Father Luke started to look for someone to supervise our maintenance. Up to then he had done it himself, helped by Fred Deal, the Stannards' invaluable yardman and factotum, by faculty and boys during the summer, and all year round by Erwin Sellenriek, who took care of the fields and crops and was himself helped as needed by Mr. Joseph Blank, a man of solid physique and unfailing cheerfulness. Joe once fell some distance out of a tree, landed on his back and jumped up as though nothing had happened. Most of us would have had a broken back. Next day Father Luke asked him how he was, and Joe said, "I'm fine. I got myself some horse liniment and that did the trick." On another occasion he cut himself quite badly, and when Marty McCabe, who was working with him, wanted to take him to the hospital, said, "I can't go to the hospital. I shall miss my pinochle game." Fred, Erwin and Joe were much more than employees. At the very least they were our friends and members of the Priory Family. Fred retired at the end of February 1971. We inherited him from the Stannards, one of their best gifts to us. He cared for the grounds, tended the irises and the grapes, looked after the furnace and other machinery in the Stannard House, and could cook a fine meal, if needed. His head, like Father Austin's, had a fine bone structure. He was courteous and, when talking to women, often used that, to our ears, strange phrase, "Yes sir, Ma'm". When Joe Blank died on 19 July 1969 it was a personal loss to us. We attended his funeral, and an appreciative obituary of him appeared in our Journal.[319] On a happier note, when Erwin married his well-named Pearl, we attended with joy, and when at the end of May 1973 he retired, our sorrow was palliated only by his willingness to be still available for special jobs, but "not for heights". He had been employed by Inc before our arrival, so he had been around here for nearly twenty years. His departure was noted not only by our *Journal*, but also by the school's *Record*[320]. He and Fred died after our period.

Since in the preceding paragraph we have mentioned the names of three of our most faithful retainers, this may be the moment to digress about them and others. Every monastery seems to attract both faithful retainers and a lunatic fringe; the former remain and the latter drop away, though sometimes with reluctance. How does one become a faithful retainer? Length of service, friendship, willingness to go beyond the call of duty are essential qualities, and all of these men qualified *cum laude*. When in due course Fred and Joe retired and in

---

[319] *SLPJ* VII. 1, p. 14.

[320] *SLPJ* X. 2, pp. 18-19 and *The Record*, 24 May 1973 p. 1.

further due course died, the monks who attended their funerals were truly in sorrow. When Erwin retired and married, we were there and truly happy, and when Erwin died we were again present and in sorrow. And so it was with many another.

Starting on 1 April 1962 Mr. Raymond Adams became our supervisor of maintenance, but he left us in the middle of March 1963 as the result of a heart attack. It was not until mid-January 1964 that Father Luke could find a replacement, Mr. Estul Wooten, with whom came his son Norman. He served us faithfully and well through October 1969 when he too fell ill and had to retire, but Norm remained and is with us still. Father Luke and Erwin between them carried on until September 1971, when Mr. John Bohn took over and finished out our period. In January 1973 Father Vincent Wace arrived from Ampleforth and took over supervision of the upkeep of the grounds.

In the business office, too, changes were occurring. In August 1964 Father Colin Havard arrived from Ampleforth partly to teach in the school and partly to be the assistant procurator. He continued as assistant procurator until the summer of 1968 when Brother John Dahm returned from Ampleforth and relieved him. But Brother John lasted only one year before deciding not to renew his simple vows. Father Luke took over as Prior on 23 June 1967 but had to continue to carry out the duties of procurator until the arrival from Ampleforth of Father Vincent Marron (not to be confused with Father Vincent Wace) at the beginning of September 1967. Even after his arrival Father Luke had to spend some time instructing him. Then by April 1969 Father Vincent decided that monastic life was no longer his vocation and left us. As there was some warning of this, Father Luke was able to get Mr. John C. Tobin, brother of Tom Tobin, of whom we have written,[321] to come to us as business manager, starting in mid-June 1969. Father Thomas, who had had long experience in the procurator's office at Ampleforth, was appointed to be procurator, but, as he was also to continue with some teaching, he could not make it a full-time job. This could not be a permanent arrangement but Father Thomas was asked to continue at least until the completion of the new high school in 1970. Then, as no monk either here or at Ampleforth could be spared for the job, we consulted Dean Stephen W. Vasquez of the Business School of Saint Louis University. He recommended that we look for a layman, on the grounds that monks were more valuable in the classroom than in an office (which is true,

---

[321] *See above*, p. 350.

provided that they can teach) and that the Prior should be freed of routine responsibilities in the business office (which too is true). The financial crisis being experienced then by so many independent schools was nudging us in the same direction by indicating that in the business office we needed to replace talented amateurs by expert professionals. We decided to bite the bullet and search for a lay procurator.

We had been discussing this possibility since at least March 1969, but initially Abbot Basil would not approve—it was not envisioned by our *Constitutions*--and we ourselves were reluctant. The reason for our reluctance was that, as may be inferred from what Saint Benedict writes about him in the *Rule*, the procurator stands in a very close relationship to the monks as monks, and Saint Benedict never conceives of his being anyone but a monk. But we also believed that Saint Benedict would have been astounded and perhaps appalled at the work-load of a modern procurator, and might well have agreed that much of it was not the most monastic way for a monk to spend his time. In August 1969 General Chapter approved new Constitutions for the English Benedictine Congregation.[322] Influenced in part by our experience, General Chapter accepted the possibility of a lay business manager. We were free to search and did so, sending out as part of the job description Chapter 31 of *The Rule of Saint Benedict*, the chapter dealing with the Procurator. Our long search came to an end when Mr. Robert L. San Soucie, Vice-President of Emerson Electric, recommended a fellow employee, and we became the first monastery of the English Benedictines to have a layman in this position. In mid-January 1971 Mr. Edmund E. Kubiak became our Director of Finance. He was that and much more for many a year. Had he been a monk, he would have been very like Saint Benedict's procurator, "a father to the whole community". Initially, Father Mark Haidy was appointed Monastic Cellarer to be our liaison with Ed in looking after the immediate personal needs of the monks.

When Ed Kubiak took over, Father Thomas returned to the classroom, Brother John Dahm had left, and Ed and John Tobin were in charge of our business. This did not work out, and in mid-August 1971 we sadly parted company with John, who was not only our business manager but also our friend. Thereafter Ed and Mary Bennace were on their own in the office, but the outside staff was

---

[322] Once they have been approved by General Chapter, the quadriennial meeting of superiors and representatives of the member monasteries, and by Rome, the *Constitutions* guide the life of all the monasteries of the Congregation.

strengthened by the colorful addition of a Southerner, Mr. James Coleman, at the beginning of April 1972.

Besides banker's blood, Father Luke must have had farming genes in him, as he always took a keen interest in our grounds, crops and livestock. Early in 1964 we held a dinner to celebrate the bank's accepting a note of hand in place of our mortgage--we had reduced our debt to the bank from $400,000 to less than $100,000--and invited those who had most helped us in reaching this stage. The guests included Mary and Leicester Faust. The main course was strip steak. On the way home Mary upbraided Leicester for not having provided the beef for the feast, so Leicester offered Father Luke a couple of steers, and ended by sending him five Aberdeen Angus weighing about nine hundred pounds each. Whether this says more for Leicester's generosity or Father Luke's persuasiveness is moot.

Another of Father Luke's interests was vehicles. At various times, and for about fifty dollars each, he acquired an ammunition truck, a jeep and a bulldozer. Nothing pleased him better than a bargain, unless it was getting something free. These vehicles all served us well. Father Luke was driving the truck, late in its career, to Jefferson City for a raid on the Government Surplus Depot, when it broke a piston shaft, which wrecked the cylinder block. Some Brothers of Mary gave him a ride back to Saint Louis and a friend towed back the truck, and in due course gave us another second-hand truck, which he had bought and found he did not need. Tractors for the maintenance of the grounds came at a higher price and with varied attachments. They always had an angle-blade for snow, and when there was snow, Father Luke was often out before daybreak making it possible for the boys to reach our parking lots.

His bargains were not limited to vehicles. He is proud that a large Hobart mixer, bought from Government Surplus for $30 in the sixties is still in use in the next millennium; and much of the furniture for the monastery and even some for the school, especially filing cabinets and office equipment, came from the same source and for similar prices.

The vehicles he provided for the use of the monks were more orthodox. We made an attempt, early on, to be simple, to save gasoline and at the same time to buy British, by getting a Morris Minor. It did well, but it was extremely difficult to find spare parts for it. We switched to Volkswagen Beetles, of which one of our parents was a supplier. These, too, did well, and we added a Volkswagen mini-bus for hauling small numbers of boys, like teams for tennis, cross-country, swimming and even basketball. But eventually geography won. We always had some American cars: Chevrolet, Ford, Dodge etc.

Now all our vehicles have American names, though who can tell where their parts were made or where they were assembled?

Our man of many talents also climbed a precarious scaffolding, forty feet above the high altar in church, to inspect, oil and grease the fan motors. This was no mean act of courage for one who suffers from vertigo, and was necessary because none of our maintenance men had the head or the stomach for it. On another occasion, the flow from our water fountains was becoming so slight that the boys were drinking almost from the outlet itself--insanitarily. Father Luke dismantled the works, found an encrusted diaphragm, decrusted it and reassembled the works. The result was so good with the first fountain that he did the same with another, and perhaps more. Another instance of "don't reinforce failure but exploit success" was that, having successfully rolled the archway building a hundred feet to a point east of the boys' dining-room, he decided to move a much larger bungalow from the site where the new high school was due to be built, nearly half a mile to a site on the gym road, where concrete foundations and a basement had been prepared.

In 1966, after seeking advice from a carpenter friend, he built a three-car carport to protect our cars from winter's chill and summer's sun. It still stands. Did nothing ever go wrong? Of course it did. On one occasion, he and Erwin Sellenriek and others needed to remove some surplus dirt and had no vehicle. Erwin volunteered to fetch Oscar Sellenriek's brand new dump truck. Unfortunately the driver left the truck with the break off and the gear lever in neutral. When they tipped the first load of dirt into the truck, it took off by itself and cut a swath about fifty feet into the woods at the bottom of the hill. It was almost unscathed, but Oscar may well have had a comment or two nonetheless. We could record more exploits but these must suffice. It takes nothing away either from Father Luke's skill or from his virtue that, for the most part, he thoroughly enjoyed himself while performing them.

In March 1970 we were making a preliminary investigation of the legal requirements for a cemetery on our own property. The idea was approved in principle by the Conventual Chapter of 31 August, but the requirements turned out to be literally extensive, a minimum of five acres, and a motion to abandon the idea was passed by a narrow majority. Instead we bought a plot in Calvary Cemetery in North Saint Louis. The archdiocesan cemetery in Ellisville did not then exist.

In three areas affecting the school: faculty salaries, scholarships and tuition, any procurator and any headmaster have very different points of view. The procurator wishes to pay the bills and still remain solvent;

the headmaster hopes to make salaries and scholarships as high as possible, and to keep tuition as low as possible. Their wishes are not wholly incompatible, but they are antithetical, and the difficulty is that both are right. In our case, the urgency of solvency was somewhat reduced because Inc was still subsidizing the school as late as the late sixties. By then, however, we had all seen that our policy of setting tuition at about two thirds of the real cost of a student[323] could not go on for ever, and had agreed on the urgent need either to establish an endowment or to produce income during the summer or to find some source of income other than the school, such as a summer camp, or orange groves, as two of the monasteries that we knew did, or a combination of all these.

A school which aims at excellence must have a good faculty, and to get a good faculty one must pay good salaries.

Scholarships were no less important to us because such a school must have good students as well as good faculty, in fact needs good students partly in order to retain good faculty. Many good students cannot come without a scholarship. We were also anxious to give no justification for anyone to call us a ritzy school--some still did so but we believed it was unjustified.

Our reason for wishing to keep the tuition low was twofold: again we did not want even to seem ritzy; but there was also a more complex issue. Our class size and other characteristics made our expenses comparable to those of, say, Saint Louis Country Day School. But most Catholic parents were choosing not between us and Country Day, but between us and Saint Louis University High School or one of the other Catholic independent schools, whose classes were larger, and whose expenses (per boy) and tuition were therefore lower. Especially in the early days, before there was, in the shape of alumni, any proof of our pudding, this was a major concern, and our failure to get Ampleforth to see this, a major failure.

There were two further elements in our financial situation, one common to most religious schools, the other unique to us. The first was the contributed services of the monks[324] and the second the debt to Ampleforth.

---

[323] *Minutes* of the Conventual Chapter of 29 August 1968 #9.

[324] This is a term for the difference between the actual cost of keeping a monk (food, clothing, etc) and the normal salary for a lay teacher doing the same job. In the budget, the market value of the monk teachers and administrators is charged to the school, their expenses are deducted, and the balance is returned to the school as "contributed services".

The reason why Catholic education has often been such a bargain is the contributed services of religious men and women teaching in Catholic schools. This was especially true of the heroic Sisters who forged the Catholic school system in the United States (and elsewhere) and was also true of us. When our school started, we wanted to keep the tuition as low as we could, so as not to start by pricing ourselves out of the market when we were still unknown. Only because of our contributed services were we able to keep our tuition anywhere near the tuition of our actual competition. In addition, we came from England already educated and reasonably fit, so our monastic overheads were minimal. As time went by, we had young men coming to be monks and needing training and education; and the English monks grew older and needed more medical care. Our overheads increased and had to become part of our budget. Our living expenses increased 55% during the first fifteen years of the school's existence--6.2% in 1969-70 alone--and faculty salaries more than that. The result was that for the fiscal years ending in July 1967 and July 1968 we showed a substantial deficit. It was less in 1968, but even so this could not continue. It was also pointed out to us that unless our budget showed the monastic salaries as an expense, then if, for whatever reason, a monk stopped teaching, the salary of his lay replacement would upset our budgeting.

In addition--and this took us longer to appreciate--some of our supporters, including some parents, did not like the idea that each boy was in effect receiving a partial scholarship from the monks, paid for by their contributed services. They wanted those who could afford it to pay the true cost, and they wanted to pay it themselves, when that applied. We were hesitant on two counts: first, Saint Benedict, in chapter 57 of his *Rule*, writes, "The evil of avarice must have no part in establishing prices, which should, therefore, always be a little lower than people outside the monastery are able to set, so that in all things God may be glorified". We believed that through our contributed services, we were following this. Secondly, we were concerned not so much about boys on full scholarship as about those whose parents could afford to pay some fees but not the full "true cost". Economic diversity meant having boys on full scholarship, boys whose parents paid the full fees, and in between, boys whose parents could pay something but not the full fees. Our experience showed that it was this last group that most felt the pinch when fees were raised, and therefore we were especially solicitous for them. Not all our supporters shared this solicitude; not all even sympathized with our desire for economic diversity. These differences of point of view were not fully resolved then, and perhaps never can be.

The second element was the debt to Ampleforth. When the deputation from Inc visited Ampleforth in 1954, one of the difficulties pointed out by Ampleforth was that any monks who had been teaching there but were then sent to Saint Louis would have to be replaced at Ampleforth by laymen, and that would cost money. Inc, rather euphorically, undertook to pay their salaries for a maximum of ten years, according to Fred Switzer, and indefinitely, according to Abbot Herbert.[325] This payment was made for several years, by when it was becoming obvious that it was turning into a millstone round Inc's and our necks. In March 1960 Fred suggested to Father Columba that Inc should pay off the current balance of nearly $17,000 and that thereafter the matter should be settled between the Priory and Ampleforth. Father Columba agreed to this arrangement, which left Inc free but us still obligated. We kept this debt on our books, though not in our annual budget, and made few, if any, payments. The debt gradually accumulated. This went on throughout the sixties, with Ampleforth from time to time pressing for what they saw as their money, and us thinking both that the time-limit had passed, and that, practically, no school could pay two sets of salaries and survive. In this case, the very success of Inc worked against them by giving Ampleforth the impression that in Saint Louis money was easy to come by. By December 1971, however, Father William Price of Ampleforth, who had visited us in 1964, had proposed an ingenious solution, which, it was hoped, would ease our burden and at the same time mollify those at Ampleforth who claimed the payment of their alleged due. The proposal was to convert the debt into our "stable patrimony". This is an inalienable portion of its property which, by our *Constitutions,* every independent monastery must possess. We were about to become independent, and so we would need one. It was a notional transaction because the debt was never covered by a specific fund but was set off against part of the value ($4.6 million) of our property and equipment. That meant that if we ever had to convert the patrimony into hard cash, we would have to sell some of our property and equipment. Later, it was pointed out to us that this

---

[325] *See above*, pp. 22-23. Fred understood that there were young monks in training, who would, in a few years, fill the gaps left by men sent to Saint Louis, and that then the payments would cease. This was quite reasonable in itself, but did not coincide with the memories of authorities at Ampleforth.

was not a legally satisfactory arrangement, and we did specify part of our property as our stable patrimony.

By the time of our audit of the fiscal year ending 31 July 1972 the last in our period, Ampleforth claimed that $192,932.87 was due to them. Finally, by January 1973, "the erasing of the debt to Ampleforth [had been] dealt with by a Capital Adjustment."[326] By this capital adjustment, about which the secretary of the Council was excited enough to give it capital letters, Ampleforth generously enabled us to face independence without that encumbrance.

We can now show a table of the fees through the end of our period, and the reader may understand both why, amazingly, the fees stayed at the same level for no fewer than eight years, and why this happy state of affairs could not continue.

Date	$
September 1956	750
September 1957	750
September 1958	750
September 1959	850
September 1960	850
September 1961	850
September 1962	850
September 1963	850
September 1964	850
September 1965	850
September 1966	850
September 1967	1000
September 1968	1000
September 1969	1250
September 1970	1250
September 1971	1400
September 1972	1600
September 1973	1675

This table shows that Ed Kubiak, who came in January 1971, convinced us that our fees had to become still more realistic, and

---

[326] *Minutes* of the local Council 7 December 1971: . . . we may soon be able to remove from our books . . . ; 25 January 1972: Since we can eliminate the "Debt to Ampleforth" figure from our books . . . ; 30 January 1973: (as quoted in the text).

increased the speed at which they did so. Opinions differed whether we had until then been generous or quixotic, but even $1675, about which we agonized then, seems utopian today. We showed a deficit of $45,500 for the fiscal year ending July 1967, a smaller but still significant deficit for 1968, a surplus of under $1000 for 1969 and a workable surplus for 1970. After that we oscillated between surplus and deficit, but our new business and budget procedures gave us both greater control and a greater sense of control. Our annual operating budget in 1973 was around half a million dollars and the value of our plant nearly five million.

Another area of procuratorial contact with the school was school equipment. Here strict economy was seldom the most economical way of proceeding, particularly for items such as desks, with which boys came into physical contact. Our first desks were economical but unsatisfactory; our second batch sturdy but far from the cheapest available. They lasted well. We then tried some for the Junior House which were too small for our more substantial seventh graders. They too were unsatisfactory and, before long, had to be discarded. We gradually reached a compromise whereby the school kept our equipment from being flimsy and the business office kept it from being extravagant.

Ed Kubiak arrived fresh from the business world and full of the business world's ideas. This was why we hired him. Within two months he produced a Business Office Manual, which immediately brought to his notice that there was by no means total overlap between the business world and the monastic world. There is also a difference between a large operation and a small one, and our operation had started with three members. Ed came from a large operation, and we still thought of ourselves as a small one, although we were in fact becoming medium-sized. It was hard for the monks to adjust, but very necessary, not only because we needed to operate in a business-like way, but also because we had to recognize that our numbers and our annual turnover were no longer those of a small operation which could be run largely in people's heads.

The Business Office Manual was not a success: both its ideas and its phraseology were foreign to monks and lay faculty alike. But Ed was a sensitive man and a quick learner, and adjusted well to an environment that was just as strange to him as his ideas were to us. He was soon active in other areas. Telephone systems are a perennial problem for any monastery, because there is an inherent conflict between the intrusiveness of the telephone and a monastery's natural and proper desire for peace and quiet; and yet schoolmasters must be at least somewhat accessible. We started with a boy operator for the evening hours after school. Then we acquired a switchboard. Now Ed recommended a larger number of external lines and no switchboard. This was cheaper and more efficient, and provided voice-mail for the prior and headmaster, but we did not achieve full efficiency until everyone had voice-mail. Voice-mail was an enormous boon for the headmaster on days when the weather was poor but school was still possible. With it, he could leave a single message on the school phone; previously, it had been necessary for someone, in practice the headmaster, to be in the office from about 5.00 a.m. to answer each call in person.

Then in March 1972 Ed laid before the Prior's Council his proposal for a budget procedure which would involve all, such as heads of departments, who spent money. Fears were expressed that it might involve much work at busy times of the year, and then simply become a formality. We were reluctant to recognize that we were passing from being a small and, as it were, family-type business, which could be run informally, to the equivalent of a small or even medium-sized corporation, which needed systematic management and accountability. It was a struggle, especially for those most involved in the school, both laymen and monks, to accept this discipline, but we had help and encouragement, and some firm insistence, from our lay friends. The proposal was refined and made easier for the participants, and was ready to go for the next fiscal year.

By the summer of 1972 it was apparent that providing buses to bring the boys to school was more and more difficult and less and less satisfactory. Instead of living tidily in the East-West corridor along Highway 40, our families were scattered all over the city and county. Some boys were spending three hours a day on the bus, and the cost was rapidly increasing. Father Finbarr wrote a cautious letter indicating that in hard cases boys might be given permission to drive to school. It was used as the thin end of the wedge, and before too long, the door was wide open, and the Headmaster's Committee was bereft of one of its staple topics.

The final procuratorial achievement of our period, initiated by Father Luke, was the resuscitation in September 1972 of the Priory Society's Finance Committee, not now to raise funds but to advise Father Luke and Ed Kubiak on Priory's finances. The first three lay members were Mr. Dolor P. Murray, Mr. Edward L. O'Neill and Mr. Daniel E. Richardson, an alumnus from our first class and President of Shure Manufacturing Company. Father Paul and Father Finbarr were the monastic members. Father Timothy was called in when appropriate.

CHAPTER 23

Inc Becomes the Priory Society

"THE function of the Board is not just raising money, but to join with the monks in perpetuating the founding purpose of the school--preparing leaders for the future," said Fred Switzer at the meeting of the Board of Directors of Inc on 31 March 1970 at which he presided.

In the early days of Inc both these functions were clearly in evidence, but during the sixties, partly because fund-raising was then Inc's most observable function, and partly because its difficulty had meant that most of Inc's effort had to be put into it, the second function had been less prominent, so the reminder was timely. It is also true that the second function is less measurable. It is performed in innumerable and often small acts of friendship and availability, some account of which has been woven into our narrative.

By way of continuing education for its own members, Inc brought to its meetings educators such as Father Paul C. Reinert, S.J., then President of Saint Louis University, and Arnold Toynbee, as well as Father William Price, ex-headmaster of Ampleforth, and Abbot Herbert Byrne and Abbot, later Cardinal, Basil Hume. In support of culture in general, Inc provided us with portraits of Father Columba and Father Timothy, both by Father Columba's cousin, Simon Elwes, and both shown in the Royal Academy's summer show in different years, and also a with a collection of fifty of Frederick Frank's pen and ink sketches of the Second Vatican Council and its leading participants. He was the only artist allowed at the first session.

Money, however, can be counted and tabulated, and so, despite Fred's wise words, it may be informative to start with a summary of Inc's fund-raising achievement from May 1954 through 15 May 1960[327] and then to say what they did after that. By 15 May 1960 they had raised $1,440,104.62. Their expenditures were $165,830.32, which included payments on bank and other loans of $52,000 and fund-raising expenses of $82,000. With the sum raised, and loans of $400,000 from Mercantile Bank[328] and of $55,000 from the

---

[327] *See* Statement of "Funds Received and Disbursed" as in footnote 330, *below*.

[328] The loan, at 5%, was dated 29 May 1958. The first payment was due on 1 January 1960.

Department of Health, Education and Welfare,[329] they had given us the following sums for the following purposes:[330]

	$
Stannard property and improvements to the house	228,000
Gallagher property	138,000
The Noland acre	3,000
Singer properties	147,000
Reasor property	101,000
Monastery building	344,000
Gymnasium	291,000
Science Wing	237,000
Total	1,489,000

In addition, they had contributed just under $50,000 to the school's scholarship fund and just over $50,000 to Priory's operating expenses. In 1960, they still had to pay $360,000 plus interest on the bank loan, the whole of the HEW loan plus interest, and $27,000 on the second Singer property, but the $27,000 had been guaranteed by Joe Desloge. The two loans and their interest added up to just over $470,000.[331]

That was the situation in May 1960 when, since we now had graduates, it was decided to expand Inc to include alumni, faculty and friends, and to rename it the Saint Louis Priory Society. Amended by-laws were approved. We now give some account of its meetings. They always included reports on the monastery, school and business affairs,

---

329 It was a ten-year loan at 4 1/8%. The total amount of interest was $10,209.40.

330 *Funds Received and Disbursed from May 1954 through 15 May 1960.* This document is in the Inc Minutes Book before the *Minutes* of the Board Meeting of 23 May 1960. The sums shown are not the exact costs of the buildings . Inc was always generous to Father Luke. The two Singer properties cost $169,187.50, but the table shows $147,000 with $27,000 still owing.

331 Title to the Stannard property was conveyed to us on 11 July 1956; to the Gallagher property, the first part of the Singer property and the Noland acre on 19 May 1958; to the Reasor property on 23 May 1960. The second part of the Singer property was acquired nearly two years after the first, presumably early in 1958, and title handed to us after that. *See above*, Chapter 8: especially pp. 56-57.

but in this account we omit matters that have been adequately dealt with elsewhere.

At the inaugural meeting of the renamed body on 15 September 1960 at the Deer Creek Club, Father Columba was elected Chairman, Fred Switzer President, Henry Hughes Secretary and Dewey Dempsey Treasurer. Clarkson Carpenter, Joe Desloge and Gerry Mudd were elected Vice-Presidents and Leicester Faust Substitute Vice-President. Fred remained President until November 1966 when Mr. William T. Dooley, Jr. succeeded him and Fred became Chairman of the Board.[332] Bill presided at the meeting of the Board of Directors on 18 May 1967 but thereafter, although the minutes are not perfectly clear, it seems that Fred presided. Dewey Dempsey was Treasurer for the whole of our period, but Mr. Wilton L. Manewal, Jr. succeeded Henry Hughes as Secretary in 1966, and Henry became a Vice-President. Also in 1966, Mr. Dayton H. Mudd was elected Assistant Treasurer.

At this inaugural meeting, Fred appointed first an Education Committee of eight lay members plus monks with Mr. Christian B. Peper as chairman, and secondly, as our fund-raising arm, a Finance Committee of no fewer than fourteen lay members with Mr. George H. Capps as chairman. At the dinner at the end of this meeting Archbishop Ritter made his gracious explanation of his letter about Catholic boys attending non-Catholic colleges.[333]

The fund-raising Drive had several heads. In the beginning, naturally enough, the head was Fred, but in 1957, a year of slight recession, Mr. Fristoe Mullins took over from him.[334] In 1958 it seems that the drive was reorganized into separate divisions: for Founders under Mr. Edward J. Walsh, Jr., for New Gifts under Dayton Mudd, and for Corporations under Fred. There was also to be a division for Parents, but it is uncertain whether this became a reality as soon as this. In 1960 when Inc was converted into the Priory Society, fund-raising became the special domain of the Finance Committee.

In 1967 with the cabinet reshuffle, Mr. J. Joseph Horan took over as chairman of the Drive, to be followed in 1969 by Mr. F. Lee Hawes, who in turn was followed in 1971 by Mr. A. Roberts Naunheim, and in 1972 by Fred Switzer himself. In 1968 when Mechanical Drawing

---

[332] At this point we seemed to have two chairmen, but in fact Father Columba never sat in the chair.

[333] *See above*, p. 203.

[334] His co-chairmen were Dr. Bussmann, Messrs. Dempsey, Faust and Hughes, Dayton and Dr. Gerard Mudd, Messrs. Fred Switzer and Ed Walsh and Mrs. David Q. Wells.

vacated the archway building east of the boys' dining-room, the fund-raising office moved in. This was the first step toward our taking over from Inc the responsibility for fund-raising, and so we mention here the fund-raising staff so far. All the leading members of Inc were, of course, deeply involved. Lemoine Skinner we have mentioned above (pp. 14 and 28-29). In the very beginning there was Miss Barbara Chrisler. She had an astonishing memory for people and their names and was invaluable not only to Inc in fund-raising but also to Father Timothy during entrance examinations--a gold-mine of information about the candidates, which made up for our lack of local knowledge. She died suddenly in 1967. In 1957 she was joined by Mary Ann (Mrs. Daniel G.) Croghan, still happily part of the operation and no less valuable. Before her but going into her time was Miss Patricia Yeldell, who became Mrs. Jones and left not long after. She was the only one of various helpers and volunteers who stayed any length of time, except that Mrs. Roda Munro filled in for eighteen months or so while Mary Ann was on maternity leave. Inc also employed, in our period, two consultants, Messrs. Bud Jennings and Frank Rose. All of these reported to Dewey Dempsey and his secretary, Miss Joanna Clavenna.

How did we go about fund-raising? In April 1958 Father Columba wrote[335] that, in view of our change of plan,[336] instead of trying to raise $2.5 million, we should raise $1.1 million now and the rest after 1967, which was when we expected, with remarkable prescience, that the second phase would begin. "We should, so we all agreed, make a bid to get the money needed for the first phase right away and then give our supporters a rest. . . . This plan has another advantage, it gives other Drives for very worthy causes a chance to receive help from our friends, once our needs have been met. Thus, for instance, we would be happy to get ourselves out of the way--having collected our objective--before Saint Louis University launches its mammoth and most important Drive." Father Columba's punch line was, "We shall not be back every year, so give more now."

It is hard to comment on those altruistic sentiments without sounding cynical. They were indeed our feelings at the time, we did all agree to them and, no doubt, they reflect our innocence and inexperience. To give one's supporters a rest is certainly to fly in the face of fund-raising orthodoxy, and to get ourselves out of the way of other drives shows that we had not yet accepted multiple drives as a

---

[335] *SLPJ* II, 1, pp. 3 and 5.

[336] *See above* pp. 143-44.

way of life. And yet, for the year ending 31 July 1959 Inc raised $340,700. For the following fiscal year the figure was $158,357 and for the year ending 31 July 1961 $112, 313. Between then and 1 March 1963 they raised $210,745.[337] This seems to show first that Father Columba's words acted as a stimulus and, secondly, that even when resting, Inc could raise a little over $100,000 a year.

At the first meeting of the Priory Society, Father Luke reported that "for the first two years the school barely broke even, but that since that time it has been on a firm financial foundation, but from tuition alone the school could not finance any major capital expenditure nor maintain a number of scholarships. Funds are now needed from the Saint Louis Priory Society in part for scholarships and in part for capital improvements."[338] This meant that subsidies to us would be minor, since we were not planning any major buildings, and that the Society's main financial task would be to pay off the debts.

In 1962 there was no meeting of the Priory Society, a fact that is significant in itself, but on 9 October 1963 there was a meeting whose main purpose was to meet the newly elected Abbot of Ampleforth, Abbot Basil Hume. On 23 October 1964 there was a meeting, called in the Minutes Book "Priory Meeting", at which Fathers Columba, Luke and Timothy, Messrs. Fred Switzer, Dewey Dempsey, Henry Hughes and Dayton Mudd, an inner ring of the directors of the Priory Society, were present. At it Father Luke reported that our needs were for more locker rooms in the gymnasium, a two-lane entrance road, a Varsity playing field with stands and a track, which entailed acquiring land, probably at the east end of our property, faculty housing, county water, and central storage for maintenance. Father Timothy then outlined the need for an increase in the scale of faculty compensation, to the tune of around $25,000 a year, and the need for more scholarship funds. All these needs had accumulated gradually over several years. In response to some previous pressure from Inc, Father Columba explained the need for future expansion of both monastery and school, to start, probably, in 1968. Dewey Dempsey reported that $100,000 was due to the bank on 1 January 1965 and $27,500 to the government over the next five years. Cash in hand was $13,299 and

---

[337] These figures are from the Treasurer's Report attached to the *Minutes* of the Saint Louis Priory Society, held on 19 March 1963.

[338] *Minutes* of the special meeting of the Board of Directors, 15 September 1960 p. 3.

pledges about $30,000. Father Columba reported that the Auguste B. Ewing bequest of about $150,000 would not be available for a year.[339]

After discussion, those present concluded that Father Columba should sign a letter asking for contributions to pay off the bank; Father Luke should prepare a plan for his projects; Father Timothy and others should prepare a plan for faculty compensation; Father Columba should initiate "as soon as convenient" planning for the expansion. The faculty compensation should be funded by donations in 1965--it was hoped that the bank debt would have been paid off by then--and interim needs should be financed "by anticipating the Ewing bequest". A drive to pay for the expansion should not be started until construction was imminent; there should be a meeting of the Priory Society to hear Father William Price, headmaster emeritus of Ampleforth, and to discuss these plans "to [the] extent deemed advisable". The letter was duly written, but was signed by Fred, Henry and Dewey rather than by Father Columba, the Ewing bequest being diplomatically reduced to "some $125,000 or more".

The annual meeting of the membership of the Society was held at the Deer Creek Club on 8 December 1964, followed by a meeting of the Board of Directors, and a dinner. There were four monks and sixty-seven laymen present. At the general meeting, after the elections to the Board of Directors, which included one member of our faculty, Mr. Edward K. Cook, and one member from each graduating class, Dewey reported that we had in hand $62,000 to pay off the bank and therefore needed $38,000 by 31 December. The Directors then heard reports from the monks, from Fred, who announced that a "working meeting" of the Board would be held in January, and from Chris Peper, chairman of the Education Committee, which had been considering the report on salary scales. Extensive discussion was not deemed advisable. At the dinner there was an address by Father William.

On 13 January 1965 the working meeting was duly held. By then the debt to the bank had been reduced to $30,000; Father Luke outlined his plans for the improvements already mentioned and Father Timothy presented his proposals for faculty salaries. The gist of them was:

---

[339] Mr. Ewing was a relative of Mrs. Faust, which was, no doubt, the reason for this handsome bequest.

a. to establish two scales, A and B. A man--and it was then all men--would be eligible for B after three years. This would not be automatic, but would be decided by a committee;
b. to establish the position of Head of Department and to establish Chairs of subjects (e.g. Physics) as appropriate;
c. to give a sabbatical of one semester on full pay after six and a half years of service
d. to increase the remuneration for coaching;
e. to leave the fringe benefits as they were.

The new salaries would be:[340]

Scale A	B.A.	5200	x	200	to	7200
	M.A.	5500	x	200	to	7700
Scale B	B.A.	6100	x	250	to	9100
	M.A.	6350	x	250	to	9600
Department Head		9000	x	250	to	11000
Chair		8000	x	250	to	10000

The average base salary at the time was $4982. The new proposals would cost $21,000 to 24,000 a year. Scholarship aid amounted at that time to $21,625, or roughly $3500 a class, of which about $2500 a class came out of the school's budget and $1000 from gifts. This aid should be increased by $1000 a class ($6000 in all).

The only action recorded in the Minutes is that the Society voted 20-2 to recommend that the Priory consider an increase in tuition from $850, noting that at Saint Louis Country Day School it was $1200.[341] But as the salaries were increased in September 1965 at a cost of about $15,000 and as 23% of the boys were then receiving aid from the school, the proposals were evidently put into effect.[342]

---

[340] In 1967 these scales were increased again for senior faculty.

[341] As noted, the principal reason for this difference was the contributed services of the monks, estimated for September 1965 at $85,000.

[342] This high percentage (23) was our policy, to ensure some economic diversity; it was made possible partly by specific gifts such as that by Mrs. Faust of a full tuition scholarship in memory of Father Luke's mother, to be awarded preferably to an African-American boy.

At the end of the meeting, Father Columba commented on the relationship between Inc--the name persisted in speech--and the monks. "We have talked much about the unique relationship of cooperation between the monks and Inc. We have had much. We want to continue. This requires two things; i, information provided by the monks to Inc. or its committees, so that the advice of Inc. may be INFORMED advice, ii, understanding by Inc.--and in this there has never been any difficulty in the past--that their relationship to the monks is one of advisors to them, and no more; this is an inevitable limitation, the result of the nature of the monastic institution to which the monks belong. There should be no reason to fear the breakdown of the splendid relationship now existing, provided both sides loyally play their parts. It is a matter of mutual confidence, and an excellent opportunity to put into practice the integrating of the laity into the life of the church."

In practice, there was often a preliminary discussion or a series of discussions between Fred and Father Columba, and with any other monks concerned, at which either general agreement was reached or the areas of difference were clarified. A meeting of the appropriate group then ratified or modified the plans and action was taken. The first key to the success of this procedure was that there was real consultation, that is, what Inc said had a real effect; and the second was that Fred in his own person provided continuity of policy from the beginning of our story and was accorded by all of us unique respect and prestige.

Father Columba went on to suggest that the time had come to separate the three elements of the Society: original founders, parents of boys and of alumni, and the alumni themselves. "Each have different functions to perform; each should perhaps have a separate existence--though linked with one another."[343]

His comments on Inc show that this unique relationship not only existed but was recognized at the time; those on the three elements throw light on the way the relationship worked. His comments were based on conversations among the monks, especially himself, and Fred, in which Fred indicated that he thought the time had come for a younger generation to take over. We were unenthusiastic. The matter was brought up and discussed at the meeting in January 1965 but not until the next meeting, in March 1966, was anything decided, and then, "[a]fter a general discussion it was concluded: that persons who were interested in the school should be elected to the Board; and that

[343] *Minutes* of the Saint Louis Priory Society, 13 January 1965.

parents should be a part of the Society with separate meetings for parents on subjects of special interest to them".[344]

Although we were capable, when necessary, of rapid action, major decisions, and especially changes, tended to mature gradually. But they did mature, and one of the reasons for this was that when there was disagreement, neither side was intransigent. Thus it was possible to reach a solution with which everybody could live without unhappiness, even though no group got exactly what it wanted. But in truth, disagreements were usually defused in conversations well before the meeting. At this meeting, Dewey Dempsey reported that the school debt had been "retired or provided for". There was great rejoicing, but although there had been at one point a plan to hold a public burning of the mortgage, this was never done.

The annual General Meeting on 8 November 1966 and the meeting of the Board of Directors on 18 May 1967 were two of the most memorable of our meetings. At the first, Dewey Dempsey reported that the Society was free of debt and had met all the commitments made to the Priory in 1965 (for salaries, scholarships, etc.). Fred Switzer then said that "the initial phase of the Priory Society had been accomplished".[345] Emulating Chairman Mao, President Switzer announced a New Leap Forward, but not before reminding the members of the Board that whereas he had suggested that they leave this task to a new generation, they themselves had insisted on retaining the reins.

Father Luke then presented a summary of the income and expenses for the school year 1965-66:

INCOME	$	EXPENSES	$
Tuition & other student activities	225,500	Administration	17,900
Contributions	24,500	Educational	165,100
Interest & misc.	3,000	Maintenance & Operation	78,500
Monastic activities	40,000	Monastic	40,000
TOTAL	293,000	TOTAL	301,500

These totals, showing a deficit of $8500, are less than one twenty-fifth of the operating budget at the end of the century. Capital assets

---

[344] *Ibid.* 28 March 1966.

[345] *Ibid.* 8 November 1966.

in the plant fund had increased by $250,000, the largest items being the additions to the gym ($106,000) paid from the Ewing bequest, the Faust Expressway ($42,000), land to our East ($34,000) and improvements to the church ($42,000). Most of the cost of the last three items had been donated. Father Luke requested $14,500 for salaries, $11,500 for scholarships, $9000 for operations and $29,000 for the track and stadium. These were granted, except for the $9000, but the total was brought up from $55,000 to $80,000 so that a payment of $20,000 might be made to Ampleforth for their expenses in housing and training our young monks. At the very end of this meeting it was resolved to merge the meetings of the Directors with the annual general meeting. Thereafter there was only one type of meeting.[346]

The next meeting was on 18 May 1967 at Fred Switzer's home. The purpose was to consider an expansion of the school. Father Columba reported that, on his recent visit, Abbot Basil Hume of Ampleforth had set in motion our move towards independence and in particular had asked for the establishment of a Prior's Council, to advise the Prior, and of a local Chapter, or meeting of the solemnly professed monks of the Priory, to frame recommendations, which, until independence, would need Abbot Basil's approval. The Chapter had met and had unanimously agreed to the expansion. Father Timothy repeated the reasons already given[347] and concluded that "an expansion of the student body [from one hundred and ninety-five] to three hundred would be very beneficial and that a further expansion of the student body in the future was indicated." This future expansion might be in 1977 or thereafter.[348]

Father Luke then presented, with an abundance of charts, an outline of how the expansion might go. The essence was that the particular needs such as classrooms should be built for the present expansion, but the general needs, such as the library, administrative and faculty offices, dining-room, and so on should be able to accommodate the later expansion too.[349] Quite apart from any expansion, there were two reasons for needing more space: the present Junior House was too

---

[346] The first meeting was "of Catholic men interested . . ."; then there were meetings of the Board of Directors or of the membership of Catholic Preparatory School for Boys, Inc.; then of the Saint Louis Priory Society, and in due course of the Saint Louis Abbey Society.

[347] *See* pp. 278-79 *above*.

[348] *Minutes* of the Saint Louis Priory Society, 18 May 1967.

[349] Details may be found in Appendix D 3.

small; and the number of monks was growing, making it more and more urgent to remove the classrooms from the monastery. The total cost, he estimated, would be $3.5 million, of which $1.5 million would be needed for the first phase.

Chairman Switzer stated that he and President Dooley had met several times with Fathers Columba, Luke and Timothy and had recommended the presentation to the Board of these preliminary plans. They called for the completion of the original idea for the school, and though the task of raising that much money was formidable, it was much less formidable than the task undertaken in 1954 "when we had no school, no property, no money, no Community or faculty, and when we had to start from scratch to create the fine school that is now in existence."[350] There had been no organized Drive for the past three years.

After considerable discussion it was unanimously resolved that the long-term project for $3.5 million be approved, that the First Priority building program for $1.5 million be started as soon as practical and that the Board take responsibility for raising this $1.5 million. Fred then announced that he and Bill Dooley would make plans for raising the money and report back, and that Father Luke should go ahead with the plans, in consultation with HOK and other experts. And so funding was unanimously approved for the plans which the monks too had unanimously approved.

By the next meeting, held on 17 June 1968 Joe Horan, who was now chairman of the Drive, was able to tell the membership that we had received $267,865 in cash and pledges and that Father Luke had "received indications" of another $130,000, a total of $397,865. When they were summoned again on 30 September, they were able to meet in the Common Room of the newly completed Junior House to hear Gyo Obata, the "O" of HOK, explain the plans for the High School building. Joe Horan announced that the total received from the various divisions, present parents, alumni parents, founders, alumni, friends and corporations, now amounted to $450,968.

In 1969 the meeting was held on 22 September to coincide with Abbot Basil's visit to us. Father Luke reported that Priory had spent $610,150 and had $1642 in hand. $160,000 was a loan from the bank, and $56,500 an internal loan; the rest must have come from Inc. Projected needs were now $1,232,000, with an auditorium and a maintenance building as the next priority, at a cost of $600,000. Fred Switzer then announced that Mr. F. Lee Hawes had agreed to become

---

[350] *Minutes*, 18 May 1967.

the head of the fund-raising, representing the younger generation. Lee then proposed a new name, "Facilities Completion Program", and a new organization, of which the most interesting feature was the Library Club under Dayton Mudd. To become a member you contributed $25,000 to the Columba Cary-Elwes Library. What could be simpler? He collected nine members. There would be a concentrated drive from 15 October to 15 December, a review period, a spring program of about six weeks, then planning in August for another October-December campaign. He wished also to discuss annual giving. At the meeting on 8 December 1969 Lee was able to report a total in cash and pledges of $450,000.

We recognized partially at the time and more fully as we went on that this meeting was a milestone. The Council *Minutes* for 4 November 1969 comment, "Lee Hawes is putting in many hours with a business-like approach and contagious enthusiasm . . . The character of Inc. is changing with new men taking over the work and alumni now available for responsible positions. Lee Hawes would like to see a Director of Development responsible to Priory, not to Inc."[351]

When the Board next met, on 31 March 1970 Mr. Stephen W. Vasquez, Dean of Saint Louis University's Business School, recommended that we should seek a lay Business Manager.[352] There was no motion, but in due course we acted on his recommendation. On 7 October when the Board met again, Father Luke observed that two main reasons for his visit to Ampleforth had been to seek advice on vocations and to seek new monks. In response, Abbot Basil had sent Father Ralph Wright and was to send Father Finbarr Dowling after Christmas. We should be most grateful for that. Lee Hawes reported that $262,555.12 was raised last year, and the goal for this year was $288,810.63. The secretary did not record the reason for the precision of the figure. About $1,000,000 had still to be raised, but Lee was receiving wonderful support in general, and in particular Bill Dooley was producing a fact book about Priory's achievements. This should be a great help to all his fellow fund-raisers.[353] The meeting on 8 December was given over to reports and a talk by Father Columba, who had returned for the dedication of the High School and its Columba Cary-Elwes Library.

---

351 The Council's *Minutes* for 6 September 1973 show that we were by then seeking such a full-time person.

352 *See above*, p. 382.

353 It has also been a great help to the historian.

It may be noted that at the last few meetings two new concerns had been heard, both of which were causing us much anxiety: the shortage of vocations to the monastery and to religious life in general, and the threat all across the country to the independent schools. Our concern about vocations was not so much that men were not coming to the Priory as that they were not staying, and we were asking Inc both to pray and to spread the good word about monks and monasteries, especially about Saint Louis Priory. The concern about independent schools was simply that, mainly for financial reasons, so many across the country were closing. In our area, the casualties were Western Military Academy in Alton, Illinois, a member of the ABC League, with whom we were consequently in frequent contact, and the Taylor School in Clayton, which closed when Dr. Taylor retired. One of our reactions to this crisis, for such it had to be considered, was to discuss among ourselves our need for a greater involvement of our lay friends in the running of the school, so that we could draw more regularly on their experience and expertise, especially but not solely in areas such as finance where we ourselves did not have them. It was a time when colleges run by religious were moving towards greater involvement of laity--Webster College for example under Sister Jacqueline Grennan, S.L. had in 1967 formed a largely lay Board of Trustees--and we had been talking of it informally for some time. The first recorded discussion of this seems to have been on the second day of our Conventual Chapter of August 1971 and as with the idea of a professional facilitator for monastic discussions, we moved slowly. Father Timothy was probably typical of the majority in thinking that we should certainly seek much advice but should be very cautious about setting up any kind of formal board with constitutional powers. No motion was made. The group called "Advisors" did not come into being until long after our period.

In the Fall of 1972[354] we launched a three-year drive to celebrate our approaching independence by paying off all our debts. Our chairman, Mr. A. Roberts Naunheim set the goal at $725,000, from which it may be inferred that about $275,000 had been raised since October 1970. In the first year he and his team raised $362,000 in cash and pledges, and in the second $158,000. The precise total for the two years was $519,384, leaving an apparent total of $205,616 to be raised. Unfortunately both the interest rates on the bank loan and the cost of fund raising had increased by nearly $85,000 between

[354] The Priory Society's Minute Book starting in 1971 is missing. What we print comes from other, often incomplete, sources.

them, and so in July 1974 we had to report that there was still $290,000 to raise, and that was the state of the debt at the end of our period. To conclude, as Inc deserves, on a high note: our Journal for July 1975 reports that at the conclusion of the three years we had received more than $730,000 in cash since the effort began in 1972. Of this $80,000 came from the Mothers' Club's *Xanadu*, very much the shape of things to come. So the goal of $725,000 was achieved.[355]

[355] It only adds luster to their achievement to report that in January 1973 Ed Kubiak was pondering the purchase from Maryville College of an automatic letter-writer, to save our fund-raisers much time. Until then all personal and "thank you" letters were individually typed or hand-written.

CHAPTER 24

Independence

WHEN a Benedictine abbey makes a foundation, as Ampleforth did in 1955, the foundation starts by being dependent on the founding abbey, which will nurture the foundation and provide for its growth. There are then two possible outcomes for the foundation: independence or closure. If it appears to be becoming numerically and financially viable, it can expect independence; if not, closure. It should not remain dependent indefinitely.

By the time that Father Luke was appointed Prior in 1967, it was clear that, with Inc's help, we were financially viable, and it seemed that the school was firmly established and was attracting students each year. What was in question was the numerical viability of the monastic community. So when Abbot Basil came for an official Visitation late in September 1969, his first concern was about vocations to our monastery. We had then thirteen priests, of whom only two were American. Brother Christopher Rush had just asked for dispensation from his solemn vows, and Brother John Dahm had decided not to renew his simple vows. We had one American novice. We had had a considerable number of young men trying their vocation, often for several years, only to depart before Solemn Profession. This made us wonder whether part of the reason for their departure was the discrepancy between their life in the novitiate and their life as monks teaching in the school, and that in turn led us to consider having the novices during their novitiate get some minimal experience of teaching.[356] After being raised in the Prior's Council, the matter was discussed at a community meeting, but no record of a decision has survived either on paper or in men's memories. It seems likely that we made the experiment, though, because the Council in December 1973 opined that "a more closed novitiate program than last year's seems to be called for". We also, at least by June 1973, discussed the advisability of some kind of psychological testing for candidates.

These departures of young monks before Solemn Profession were baneful in two ways: first, our numbers did not increase, and secondly, the presence of novices in the novitiate and of simply professed

[356] Council *Minutes*, 28 April 1972.

monks in the juniorate made our situation look deceptively hopeful. Abbot Basil pointed out that he could not go on indefinitely sending us monks and that the time for the fateful decision was drawing near. It was a critical moment, but none of us was as frightened as we should have been. It did not seem possible to believe that all the work of the past fourteen years could simply be wiped away.

Abbot Basil's diagnosis of our situation was this: we were, like virtually every other religious house, in some disagreement over the way in which the changes made by the Second Vatican Council should be put into practice, especially in our liturgy; the monks who had been here from the beginning or nearly so were growing weary and older; if we became independent, it was uncertain how many of the Ampleforth monks would choose to become members of the independent Saint Louis Priory. He said that he would, as soon as he could, send us two monks under thirty-five, but these would be the last to come from Ampleforth; he might recall one or two of the older monks; we must attract and retain candidates; independence would be possible if we could recruit six novices, if some of the monks from Ampleforth decided to stay here--to transfer their stability is the technical term --and if the two young men due to come to us from Ampleforth stayed here; finally, he recommended that we should go straight to the status of abbey, rather than first becoming an independent priory.

This gave us more than enough to pray and think about and was, especially, a stimulus for us to discuss what more besides prayer and fasting we could do to attract young men to our way of life. This became the focus of our community discussions. One conclusion that we drew from our experience was that seniors in high school were seldom ready to make a mature commitment to monastic life and that therefore we should look to university rather than to high school. This was especially distressing to us because Ampleforth had, in our time, drawn a substantial proportion of its monks from the equivalent of seniors graduating from their school. We had hoped similarly to attract novices from among our alumni, and in our first decade here, it had looked as if we would succeed, but there had been none recently. We now decided to try to attract young men from the local colleges and universities to come to spend some time here as guests. They could live in Chuck Dattilo's old house or we could remodel part of the Stannard House. This idea entailed visits by monks to the universities and cooperation with the university chaplains. We did attract some visitors but no permanent vocations. Another suggestion, which had been made some years previously, came to the surface again: it was to have young monks from Ampleforth come out here at the beginning of, or at least early in their teaching career, to broaden their experience. There would be evident gain for both Ampleforth and us, but it has never yet happened. At the Conventual Chapter in August 1970 the suggestion was made that we should appoint a Director of Vocations, so presumably, strange though it may seem now, we had not had one previously.

The next step forward was taken by the prior and his Council in 1971. At the Council's meeting on 12 May Father Luke reported on his recent visit to Ampleforth. Here we must interject that at some time a brief but very important verbal exchange took place between Father Luke and Abbot Basil, who in April 1971 had been re-elected as abbot. Abbot Basil commented on our lack of novices and said that he would have to close the priory, but would leave us for five years so that we could hand over the school. Father Luke banged the table with his fist and said, "You can't do that to us; we have too much invested. Rather than that, we'll go independent." Abbot Basil replied, "It's a deal." And that was that. It is certain that this exchange took place, but uncertain when and where.[357] This visit is a possible time, and it is quite believable that Abbot Basil, when he had pondered this, would have been much in favor of independence. Be that as it may, Father Luke reported to the Council that Abbot Basil was much more in favor of our independence than he, Luke, had expected, and that he had heard that Abbot Victor Farwell, Abbot President of the English Benedictine Congregation, who, as it happened, was due to come to us in June for our quadriennial Visitation, was also warmly in favor. When Abbot Victor came and advised the Council, from his own experience as head of a dependent monastery which became independent, that there was a real difference between the two states, and that the advantages were definitely with independence, our Council strongly urged Father Luke to put the matter before our Conventual Chapter on 28 August.

This he did, giving as reasons in favor of independence that commitment to an independent community would be a boost both to our morale and to that of the priory family, whose members would see that we were here to stay; that we were virtually on our own anyway, since Ampleforth would send us no more monks; and that it would lead to our more deeply rooted integration into the area and into the

---

[357] There is no written record even in the relevant correspondence. Father Luke is certain of the fact, but not of the date or place. He believes that it was in Missouri rather than at Ampleforth.

archdiocese. If we were slightly short of the canonical number of monks, dispensation could be sought. Against this it could be said that Ampleforth might relent and send us some more monks; the final break would be painful; that some of us might decide to return to Ampleforth. There was a fair amount of discussion, followed by a unanimous vote "that the community wishes to initiate the movement of seeking independence and accepts the necessary steps involved in pursuing the subject to a final decision."[358] Thus the wheels started to turn. Abbot Basil was informed, a list of our reasons for seeking independence was sent to the other English Benedictine monasteries, which would have to give their approval, and we held further discussions on how this would affect us. But the wheels turned with no immoderate haste, and it was not until the following April that our council recommended unanimously to Father Luke that we should, at our Local Conventual Chapter in August 1972 vote on whether we should ask Abbot Basil to ask the General Chapter of the Congregation, due to meet in 1973, to grant us independence. This would presuppose the agreement of Abbot Basil and his Council, but we had heard by the time of our Chapter that the Council at Ampleforth, at its meeting in May 1972 was unanimously and enthusiastically in our favor, and that Abbot Basil was now a strong advocate. It would also entail seeking the approval of the other English Benedictine monasteries, which was not expected to be a problem either.

And so, at our Chapter held on 26-27 August 1972 the motion was made that "the community of Saint Louis Priory should formally request Father Abbot that he take the steps necessary under Canon Law and the Constitutions of the English Benedictine Congregation for the granting of independent status to Saint Louis Priory; that, further, Father Abbot take such steps, if he so agrees, so that the request may be placed before the General Chapter of the English Benedictine Congregation to be held in July 1973."[359] We had then nine monks committed to staying, three more who might stay, and three novices. As there had been extensive discussion during the year, there was little at the Chapter, and the vote was unanimous in favor. The only surprise was that the next proposal, that we should ask to be an abbey, not a priory, was narrowly defeated. It was a time when "triumphalism" was a very dirty word, and there were those who saw abbeys and abbots as "something much larger, more prelatical, and

[358] *Minutes* of the Local Conventual Chapter, 28-30 August 1971 #3.

[359] *Minutes* of the Local Conventual Chapter, 26-27 August 1972 #3.

more restricted by structures of the past than we would like our community to be."[360] Although others pointed out that the abbot is an essential feature both of the *Rule* and of Benedictine monachism, the anti-prelatical view prevailed.

These votes meant that we had done what was required of us, and now had to wait for the necessary approvals from outside. It is a measure of our confidence in those approvals that we spent two days in the Christmas vacation at the Walshes' lovely house on the bluffs overlooking the Missouri. There we discussed the implications of independence and the complicated question of vocations to our priory. In September 1970 the Council had discussed the appointment of a Director of Vocations, and suggested Father Benedict, who seems to have been appointed soon after. In June 1971 the Council heard a report from Father Luke on his meeting with the seniors in the school: they showed interest in dining in the monastery from time to time, but little in a more extended stay. They knew very little about monastic life, but preferred informal to formal discussion about it. The next issue of our *Journal*[361] mentions that we started an advertising campaign--there was some reluctance about this, but we thought we would never find out whether it was effective unless we tried it--and started a Vocations Committee of monks and laity, presumably as a result of these discussions. We spent about $7,500 on the advertisements and had over 500 replies, of which about twenty could be called serious. One of the others started, "I am married, with several children, and am not a Christian." We also recognized that, under God, attracting vocations is a task for all the monks and not only for the committee.

Independence also raised the question of naturalization. As long as there was the possibility, however remote, of being taken back to Ampleforth, it was unwise for the English monks to change their citizenship. After independence such a possibility was almost eliminated. Most of the English monks duly passed the test and took the oath and became citizens of the United States. Father Mark expressed much indignation over some of the questions he was asked and felt that his interviewer had rather woodenly stuck to the questions in the document, regardless of whether they applied to monks. But on the day of the oath, his interviewer approached him with a wink and said, "When it comes to the part about bearing arms, you just keep silent". One monk became naturalized a few years later when he

---

[360] *Ibid.* #4

[361] *SLPJ* X. 2, pp. 5-6.

learnt that it would be cheaper than renewing his "green card", or so monastic legend has it.

In this interval of waiting for approval, we learnt that all our monks from Ampleforth were planning to transfer their stability to Saint Louis except Father Thomas Loughlin. This was announced at our Family Day at the Priory in May 1973 and was greeted with a five-minute standing ovation for Father Thomas. It was a major loss. Apart from his extraordinary dependability in monastic observance, his extensive pastoral work with the Sacred Heart Sisters of Maryville College and with the "happy families" of Brentwood, and his coaching of Soccer in the school, he had been the first and only head of our Science department. He "nursed it through a rather precarious infancy and brought it to maturity. He designed the Science Wing, built up the faculty, molded the syllabus and taught the students . . . it will be a long time before our school (or any other) takes two first places in different sections of the International Science Fair in the same year."[362] The achievements of his students in the Saint Louis Science Fair were no less distinguished. For many years he was on the board of the Saint Louis Planetarium. In 1970 he was chosen as the outstanding high school science teacher in Missouri, and in 1972 he received from the American Chemistry Society its first ever Mid-West Region Award for high school teachers of Chemistry. His students won awards at the city, state, regional and national levels; NASA would hardly launch a rocket without his or their presence, and it almost seemed as if even the sun would not suffer eclipse unless he were there, and sure enough he was present in Alaska for the total eclipse in 1972. The experiments of two of our boys were nearly carried out on Skylab, the long space flight. In the end they were not, because they duplicated experiments submitted by others. Some of his students appeared on television to describe their projects in the Saint Louis Science Fair, or their impressions of the launching of Apollo XII; they traveled to London, Washington, DC, Baltimore, Albuquerque, Huntsville and elsewhere to read papers or attend conferences; one especially illuminating trip was to Chicago in June and July 1966 to attend a summer program run by the University of Chicago. Father Thomas and our four boys were the only representatives of an independent school; all the rest were from public schools, such as the Bronx School of Science, which specialized in Science. Our boys found the competition "rugged, but they held their own, and rather

---

[362] *SLPJ* X. 2, p. 7.

more."[363] In fairness to other departments it must be said that in the wake of Sputnik, more money was put into encouraging science than into any other subject, but even so, Father Thomas' record was astonishing.[364] As a sample of achievements in other subjects, we mention here that in 1969 our freshmen had an average score of 97 out of 120 in the Association for the Promotion of Latin Studies' contest, compared with the national average of 43; that they won a trophy in the *auxilium latinum* for two successive years at the end of our period; that our mathematicians came in first in the Central (seven state) Region of the National High School Mathematics Contest, also for two straight years, and won their match on the side with Ampleforth; and John Schier took first place in the prize essay contest of the *Alliance Française*. But when all is said and done, the achievements in Science were the most triumphant.

In due course, the other monasteries all approved of our independence, it was passed by General Chapter, and on 25 July 1973 the *Decree of the Founding Abbot erecting the Priory of St. Mary and St. Louis, King and Confessor, in the County of Saint Louis, Missouri in the United States of America into an independent Conventual Priory* was signed by Abbot Basil Hume, O.S.B. of Ampleforth and Father Barnabas Sandeman, O.S.B., secretary of the Abbot's Council. On 4 August 1973 Father Luke was elected prior, and so, after almost eighteen years and for the first time in their history, the monks of Saint Louis Priory were living under a superior whom they had themselves elected, had a Conventual Chapter and a Council which existed in their own right, and whose decisions no longer needed ratification by Ampleforth.[365] Just before this great step, Father Luke wrote:

> When we become an independent monastery, we will be given the full responsibility under God for our own life and future. A monk commits himself to stability in one monastic family, not to a province or Congregation. Independence includes the radical step

---

[363] *SLPJ* IV. 3, p. 12.

[364] On 3 June 1994 he was going in procession into his diocesan cathedral in England, when he collapsed. The priest next to him happened to be carrying the Holy Oils in his pocket, which is quite unusual. Father Thomas was anointed, and so died. He presumably went straight to heaven. That part of the news gladdened us.

[365] *Minutes* of the Council meeting on 6 September 1973 are entitled just that, and no longer *Minutes of the* Local *Council.*

> of changing our stability from Ampleforth to Saint Louis Priory -- it will mean that we choose the Priory definitively as our home, that Ampleforth has no claim upon us, that we no longer ultimately belong there. The monks here will, through independence, sign and seal the commitment they have already made and lived for a varying number of years, and such an act will, we believe, bring God's blessing and life in a renewed and rich way.

Making the point that there was no question of severing all connection with Ampleforth, he went on to say that our ties of tradition, loyalty and love to Ampleforth would remain strong, and that the tradition of our Congregation was to leave to each monastery its own jurisdiction and administration while enabling the houses to support one another if needed.[366] Elsewhere Father Luke wrote the best summary of the state of affairs immediately after the granting of independence:

> I pray that it is grounds for deep thankfulness to God for what He has achieved through us and grounds too for trust in Him that He will provide us with men to continue our mission and to be responsive to His call to us. We deeply believe this call makes a lot of sense these days, the call to prayer in community and to the service of His people, especially youth, by witness and teaching in the widest sense.[367]

All that remained then was to celebrate, and this we did when Abbot Basil came to visit us in the fall. On 1 November 1973 the Solemnity of All Saints, Abbot Basil celebrated Mass and preached; Cardinal Carberry was present along with Monsignor Curtin, who had come to Ampleforth with the original ambassadors, and Monsignor Slattery, the pastor of Saint Anselm, and Father (later Abbot) Patrick Barry, who, with Abbot Basil, had made the important visit in April 1960.[368] Abbot Basil told us to become a house of prayer, learning and compassion . At the end of the Mass, Cardinal Carberry said it was a joy to have the Priory "solidified with the Archdiocese of Saint Louis", and added kind words about the educational and pastoral

---

[366] *From The Calefactory*, October 1972, pp. 2-3. This was an occasional newsletter to the Priory Family.

[367] *SLPJ* X. 2, p. 6.

[368] *See above*, p. 202.

work of the monks. A reception followed. Next day there was a reception for sisters and for clergy of many denominations; on Saturday 3 November many of our alumni attended our homecoming football game, in which we defeated John Burroughs 29-0 and became the first ABC team since 1951 to beat Burroughs and Country Day in the same season. On Monday we reverted to normal.

What it all meant was that we were here to stay, to sink or swim in Saint Louis. Before independence the monks from Ampleforth were still monks of Ampleforth Abbey; now they, no less than the American monks,[369] were monks of Saint Louis Priory, to live here and to die here. Some have done one, some the other.

This brought to conclusion a period of our history for which it is hard at this close range to find a good expression. It was more than an introduction, more than an overture, more than the foundations, because by 1973 the monastery and school, which it was our mission to found, had come into existence and were thriving. Perhaps it was more like the first model of a new aircraft. It flies and meets the specifications, but further experience will lead to development, refinement and improvement. But the story of that development from 1973 onward another tongue must tell.

---

[369] Legally, our American novices and juniors at Ampleforth had been monks of Ampleforth, but always with the understanding (*see* p. 153 *above*) that they would return and lead their monastic lives in Saint Louis.

EPILOGUE

WE did stay, and we did swim; in fact, we swam rather robustly. On 31 March 1981 we took over Saint Anselm Parish, thus adding another dimension to our apostolate, and in 1989 we were granted the status of an abbey. This meant, among other things, that we had to elect an abbot. Over an extended period the monks of Saint Louis Priory prepared in various ways, individually, in small groups and as a community, for this their first abbatial election. Then on Tuesday 13 June the solemnly professed monks met at what is called a *tractatus*, or handling (that is, mental handling) to discuss the possible candidates. At it many people say many things, and before, during and after it many people pray many prayers in which, no doubt, the thought "Lord . . . show us which . . . you have chosen" [370] predominates. This *tractatus* ends when it ends, and then, by a wise regulation, a night must intervene before the election itself. Consequently it was on the next day, Wednesday 14 June that, with Abbot Francis Rossiter, Abbot President of the English Benedictine Congregation, presiding, Prior Luke was elected as the first abbot of our monastery.

He had been appointed prior in 1967 by Abbot, later Cardinal, Basil Hume, then abbot of Ampleforth Abbey; had been elected in 1973 by the solemnly professed monks of the newly independent Priory to continue as prior, and had been re-elected in 1981. The monks had had twenty-two years in which to assess his quality as superior, and so it was no upset when he was elected abbot. Both the monastic community and the numerous members of the Abbey Family were well pleased by the outcome.

On the evening of Saturday 16 September 1989 sixteen years after independence and nearly thirty-four years after our arrival in Saint Louis, the Very Reverend Luke Rigby, Prior of the Priory of Saint Mary and Saint Louis, received from Archbishop John L. May, Archbishop of Saint Louis, the abbatial blessing and so was confirmed as the first abbot of the Abbey of Saint Mary and Saint Louis. "Twelve abbots, two archabbots, dozens of priests and nuns and a gathering of

---

[370] *Acts* 1.24.

eleven hundred friends from across the country were in attendance at the 5 p.m. Mass."[371]

Our founding abbey of Ampleforth had already marked the elevation of its daughter house to the rank of abbey by enabling us to commission from the local sculptor, Wiktor Szostalo, a stainless steel statue of Saint Benedict. This was unveiled and blessed by Cardinal Basil Hume during his visit in July 1992.

In January 2000 we moved out of our monastery into trailers, tore down the old monastery and started to build a larger one because the old could no longer accommodate the new monks. It was a wonderful, though slightly uncomfortable, way to start the new millennium. On 6 August 2001 we moved into our new monastery.

Quod bonum faustum felix fortunatumque sit![372]

✠

[371] *SLAJ*. Summer 1990, p. 8.

[372] An old Roman wish meaning, "May this be good, blessed, happy and fortunate!"

LIST OF APPENDICES

Appendix A 1: Early Supporters.

a. Signatories of the Articles of Incorporation for Catholic Preparatory School for Boys. (See *p.13*):

Frederick M. Switzer
William G. Weld
Henry C. Hughes
John L. Gilmore
J. Gerard Mudd
Christian B. Peper
Eugene L. De Penaloza
Paul H. Goessling
James D. Switzer
Thomas J. Tobin II
Dumont G. Dempsey
Herbert D. Condie, Jr.
Clarkson Carpenter, Jr.
Samuel W. Mitchell
Daniel F. Sheehan
Edward S. Hock
Henry G. Keeler, Jr.
Oliver L. Parks
Charles F. Bealke
Philip Platt Smith
Frank J. Pollnow, Jr.
Joseph W. White
J. J. Mullen, Jr.
A. W. Manley
Edward J. Walsh, Jr.
Fred M. Switzer III
John K. Switzer
Ward Fickie
Jerome A. Switzer

These names may be found in the Minutes Book of the Corporation just before the Minutes for 13 May 1954.

b. The Names of Directors, 18 October 1954. (See *p.19*):

Claude I. Bakewell
Donald L. Barnes, Jr.
Frank C. Blumeyer
Clarkson Carpenter, Jr.
Herbert D. Condie, Jr.
Jim Conzelman
Dumont G. Dempsey
William T. Dooley, Jr.
Curtis Ford
Paul M. George
Paul H. Goessling
Newton S. Gorman
Joseph E. Griesedieck
Henry C. Hughes
John V. Janes
Henry G. Keeler, Jr.
D. S. Kelley
William G. Lytton, M.D.
Glennon McDonald
Samuel W. Mitchell
Richard I. C. Muckerman, M.D.
J Gerard Mudd, M.D.
James J. Mullen, Jr.
Oliver L. Parks
Christian B. Peper
F. Joseph Pfeffer
Daniel Schlafly
Arthur B. Schneithorst
Lemoine Skinner, Jr.
Philip Platt Smith
Frederick M. Switzer
John K. Switzer
Glenn Travis
Joseph H. Vatterott
Edward J. Walsh, Jr.
William G. Weld

Robert D. Mattis, M.D.
Joseph W. White

They were unanimously elected, but Messrs Barnes, Conzelman, Griesedieck, Kelley and Schlafly later declined.

*c. Directors Added 14 March 1955. (*See *p.19):*

Paul Bakewell III
Charles F. Bates II
Frank E. Brennan
John J. Cole
John C. Corley
John L. Gillis
Joseph A. Glynn, Jr.
William H. Harrison
F. Lee Hawes
Thomas A. Hennigan, Jr.
Edward Simmons Hock
Joseph F. Imbs II
William F. James
John E. McCadden, Jr.
Dean Sauer, M.D.
John L. Stocker

The minutes do not record that they were elected, but as they were all either present at the next meeting or recorded as absent, one may assume that they were.

d. Counselors of the Priory, 21 January 1957, as listed in our golden brochure, To Praise God and Serve Man, p. 20. *(See p.143):*

Paul Bakewell III
Frank Blumeyer
Donald W. Bussmann, M.D. %
Clarkson Carpenter, Jr.
Dumont G. Dempsey %
Joseph Desloge*
William T. Dooley, Jr.
Leicester B. Faust %
Joseph Gander*
Norman George
Alvin Griesedieck, Jr.
Henry C. Hughes %
Theodore A. Kienstra
Samuel Mitchell
Dayton H. Mudd %
J. Gerard Mudd, M.D. % *
James J. Mullen, Jr.
Fristoe Mullins #
Lemoine Skinner, Jr.
Fred M. Switzer % *
Jerome Switzer
Edward J. Walsh, Jr. % *
William G. Weld
David Q. Wells*
Joseph Werner
Leo J. Wieck
William McBride Love

\# campaign chairman
% campaign co-chairman. Note that Mrs. David Q. Wells was a co-chairman of the campaign, but was presumably deemed to be represented on the counselors by her husband.
* member of the Building Committee.

Appendix A 2: Monks and Confratres through 31 December 1999.

a. Monks Sent from Ampleforth to Saint Louis. (See *p.211*):

NAME	ARR.	DEP.	COMMENTS
Fr. Columba Cary-Elwes	10/55	7/8/67	prior 55-67; + 1/22/94
Fr. Luke Rigby	10/55		procurator 55-67; prior 67-89; abbot 89-95
Fr. Timothy Horner	10/55		headmaster 55-74; sub-prior 78-81* pastor 81-95
Fr. Ian Petit	8/56	6/71	head of JH 58-69 +11/4/96
Fr Bede Burge	7/57	summer 58	+ 11/22/60
Fr. Thomas Loughlin	7/57	summer 73	+ 6/3/94
Fr. Austin Rennick	8/58		sub-prior 61-73;* + 3/6/92 at Priory
Fr. Brendan Smith	8/58	6/19/60	
Fr. Augustine Measures	8/59	summer 64	
Fr. Paul Kidner	8/59		headmaster 74-83; sub-prior 81-89*; prior 89-
Fr. Leonard Jackson	8/60	6/71	+ 2/23/99
Fr. Nicholas Walford	8/61	summer 70	+ 6/3/00
Fr. Colin Havard	8/64	6/9/74	dispensed from vows and priesthood
Fr. Miles Bellasis	9/65	7/11/94	head of JH 69-82 dispensed from vows and priesthood
Fr. Vincent Marron	9/67	4/69	procurator 67-69
Fr. Mark Haidy	10/69		+ 6/21/77 at Priory
Fr. Ralph Wright	8/70		
Fr. Finbarr Dowling	1/71		headmaster 83-92
Fr. Vincent Wace	1/73	6/21/78	sub-prior 73-78*; + 4/27/01

* While we were a priory, the superior was the prior and the second official the sub-prior. When we became an abbey, they were abbot and prior. + = died.

b. North American Monks through December 1999 (All US except Br. Antony Hookham and Brother Hamish Currie, who were Canadian) listed by date of clothing as novices or, if not so clothed, by date of postulancy. (POST = Postulant; NOV= Novice; SIM= Simply Professed; SOL= Solemnly Professed). (See *p.211*):

NAME	POST	NOV	SIM	SOL	COMMENTS
John Brod Peters (Br. Gregory)	2/10/57	9/22/57	9/23/58		Confrater; + 8/28/82
Paul Bryant (Br. James)	2/57	9/22/57			Left 11/57
Joseph Hanon (Br. Joseph)	5/57	9/22/57			Left 11/57
Richard Bauer	/57				Left 5/59
David Farrelly	/57				
Richard Garger	/57				
Vernon Dockery	/58				Left 5/59
Charles Rush (Br. Christopher)	/58	9/21/59	9/22/60	9/22/63	Dispensed from vows /69
Fr. R. Benedict Allin	1/60	9/22/60	9/19/61	9/19/64	Ordained priest 9/23/67; administrator, St. Anselm 95-96
Fr. Laurence Kriegshauser	8/61	9/21/62	9/23/63	9/23/66	Ordained priest 9/27/69; sub-prior 81-89* (see A 2 a above)
George Morrison (Br. Francis)	6/62	9/21/62			Alumnus; + 10/5/69
Robert Voss (Br. Louis)		9/22/63	9/23/64		Left 4/66; now priest in Tucson, AZ
Jack Winkler (Br. James)	4/63	9/22/63	9/23/64 9/23/67		Left summer 70; 3 one-year renewals in 67,68 & 69; + /90
August Imholtz (Br. Michael)		9/22/63	9/23/64		Left 1/67
Robert Martin	3/63				Recorded only in CCE's diary
John Dahm (Br. John)	9/63	1/19/64	7/15/65		Renewed SIM for one year 7/68; left summer 69 before 2nd renewal
Ronald Jobe (Br. Augustine)		9/20/64			Now priest of London Oratory
John Lucido	4/65				Left after a week
William Hochmuth	4/65				Left 8/65
J.Joseph Horan (Br. Joseph)		9/21/65			Alumnus; left 2/66
George Schoelkopf (Br. George)	4/65	9/21/65			Left before Christmas 65

NAME	POST	NOV	SIM	SOL	COMMENTS
Michael Metzger (Br. Hugh)	9/15/66	9/14/67			
Donald W. Bussmann, Jr. (Br. Anthony)		9/14/67			Alumnus; left 10/68; + 1/18/00

N.B. Hereafter the Novitiate was at Saint Louis Priory

NAME	POST	NOV	SIM	SOL	COMMENTS
Van Moomjian (Br. Gregory)	/68	9/9/69			Left 1/1/70
Richard Murphy (Br. Noel)		7/22/72			Left 3/23/73
David Cowden (Br. Andrew)		7/22/72			Left 6/18/73. Now priest in Oklahoma City
Carl Pieber (Br. Jerome)		7/22/72			Left 12/19/72. Now Vincentian priest
Charles McWilliam (Br. David)		1/11/74	1/12/75		Left 8/9/75
James Currie (Br. Hamish)		1/11/74			Left 5/13/74. Now priest in Sault Ste Marie
Fr. William Driscoll		7/10/74			Left 4/11/75
Fr. Michael Boutton	/75				
Robert Gallagher (Br. Terence)		9/10/75			Left 5/25/76
Lawrence Larkin	/75				
Br. John Hotchkiss		9/5/77	9/7/78		+ 10/22/81 studying at St. Meinrad
John Graczak (Br. Mark)		9/5/77			Left 1/5/78
Warren Andrew Wimmer (Br. Andrew)	5/77	9/5/77	9/7/78	8/31/81	Ordained priest 12/17/83; leave of absence 6/85
Br. Antony Hookham		5/5/78			Oblate; + 11/11/91
Br. Symeon Gillette (Br. Michael)	11/77	9/4/78	9/5/79	9/5/82	Br. Michael became Br. Symeon w.e.f. 3/12/82
Edward Martin (Br. Basil)		9/3/79			Left 12/2/79

NAME	POST	NOV	SIM	SOL	COMMENTS
Fr. Gregory Mohrman	8/30/79	9/3/79	9/4/80	8/30/83	Ordained priest 6/21/86; headmaster 95-
Sean M. Collins (Br. Patrick)		9/3/79	9/4/80		Took vows for 1 year; renewed 9/4/81 & 82. Left 9/10/83
Abbot Thomas Frerking	/79	9/1/80	9/2/81	9/2/84	Ordained priest 6/12/86; headmaster 92-95; abbot 95-
Fr. Joseph Weber	/80				Was and is priest of St. Louis
Fr. Gerard Garrigan	3/80	9/1/80	9/2/81	9/2/84	Ordained priest 6/24/89; pastor 96-
Fr. Joseph Marino		9/1/80			Clothed as oblate novice;
		9/7/86	9/8/87	9/8/91	Clothed as novice; ordained priest 6/11/94; left 7/11/98
Br. Martin Brown		1/4/82			Left 3/5/83
		8/17/84	5/11/85	4/23/88	+ 5/3/01 at Priory
Patrick Ambler	/82				
Br. Edward Dahlheimer		10/13/82			Oblate
Louis Magdaleno	8/83	11/27/83			Left 2/22/84
Br. Stephen Chappell		(2/1/84	2/2/85	1/9/88)	Joined us 6/7/92 from St. Pius X; left about 9/93
Robert Irish	/84				Priest in Lansing, MI
Michael Gunn (Br. Michael)		9/1/85	9/2/86		Left 9/1/89
Br. Mark Kammerer	5/87	9/4/88	9/4/89	8/27/94	Renewed vows for 1 year 9/4/92 & 9/4/93
Daniel Reese	6/87	9/4/88			Left 2/14/89
(Br. Aelred)	4/90	9/2/90			Left 3/22/91
Fr. Christopher Hanson	6/87	9/4/88	9/4/89	8/15/92	Ordained priest 9/1/96
Robert Zacher	Early 88				Left before 6/88
Fr. Placid Hamblen	4/88	9/3/89	9/3/90	8/21/93	Ordained priest 7/8/95; left w.e.f. 7/23/96; now C. of E. priest
Kenneth C. Jones	6/88				

NAME	POST	NOV	SIM	SOL	COMMENTS
Fr. Dominic Lenk	1/90	9/2/90	9/2/91	8/27/94	Ordained priest 7/4/98
Fr. Bede Price	12/8/90	9/1/91	9/7/92	6/24/95	Ordained priest 9/1/96
Louis Stiller	1/92				
Gregory Cochran (Br. Kieran)	9/92	9/5/93			Left 7/24/94
Richard Sherman	4/94				
Abdullah Abdur	12/94				Left 2/95
Rashid	9/95				Left 7/96
(Br. Michael)		8/24/97	8/29/98	9/1/01	
Br. Augustine Wetta	8/95	1/8/96	12/30/96	1/1/00	
Joseph Damukaitis (Br. Basil)	2/1/96	8/25/96	9/6/97		Left 6/8/00
Paublo Guzman					Long term guest, never postulant; left 2/97
Br. Ambrose Bennett	10/4/97	1/3/98	1/9/99		Was A. Aufill
Fr. Bernard Persson	7/98				Former monk/priest of St. Leo Abbey; left 4/00
Joseph E. Neske	6/99				Left 6/99
Br. Aidan McDermott	1/7/99	8/28/99	8/26/00		
Fr. Peter Kessler	6/5?/99	8/28/99	8/26/00		Was priest of Columbus, OH
Br. Philip Gutweiler	7/1/99	8/28/99	8/26/00		Left 8/01

c. Confratres through December 1999. (See *pp.222-23*):

M/M. John Bryan Allin
M/M. Joseph L. Aubuchon
Mr. Paul Bakewell III
Mrs Mona Bellasis
M/M. Peter F. Benoist
Mrs. Mary Blackden
D/M. Donald W. Bussmann
D/M. Eliot C. Casey
Fr. Edwin Cole
M/M. Frank J. Jostrand
M/M. Gene E. Kalhorn
Mrs. M. C. Kidner
D/M. Edward D. Kinsella
M/M. Edmund E. Kubiak
M/M. Charles S. Lamy
M/M. Joseph S. Lenk
M/M. Wilton L. Manewal
Mrs. Mary Marino

D/M. John M. Collins
M/M. Herbert D. Condie
M/M. Michael C. Convy
Mrs. Robert C. Corley
M/M. John E. Cramer
M/M. Dumont G. Dempsey
M/M. Louis F. Desloge, Jr.
M/M. William T. Dooley, Jr.
M/M. Patrick J. Dowling
Mr. Joseph D. Dubuque
D/M. William R. Fair
Mr. Paul S. Falcey
Msgr. Charleville B. Faris
M/M. Leicester B. Faust
Mrs. Paul F. Fletcher
M/M. Emil Frei
M/M. Louis F. Lanwermeyer
Mr. Anthony T. Garnett
Mrs. Harold W. Garrigan
Mrs. Mary Gillette
M/M. Frank J. Guyol, Jr.
M/M. Edward V. Hamilton
M/M. John C. Hanson
M/M. Charles C. Harvey
M/M. F. Lee Hawes
M/M. J. Joseph Horan
Mrs. Bernard J. Huger
M/M. Henry C. Hughes
M/M. John V. Janes
M/M. Matthew F. Mayer
M/M. James K. McAtee
M/M. Henry J. Mohrman
M/M. Dayton H. Mudd
D/M. J. Gerard Mudd
M/M. James J. Murphy
M/M. A. Roberts Naunheim
M/M. R. Michael O'Brien, Jr
M/M. Edward L. O'Neill.
M/M. Christian B. Peper
M/M. J. Gerard Quinn
M/M. Daniel E. Richardson
M/M. Fred N. Sauer
M/M. J. Joseph Schlafly III
M/M. Bruce B. Selkirk, Jr.
Msgr. Robert P. Slattery
M/M. Frederick M. Switzer, Jr.
M/M. James D. Switzer
Mrs. John C. Tobin
Mr. Thomas J. Tobin II
M/M. Larry D. Umlauf
M/M. Edward J. Walsh
M/M. Will F. Warner
Fr. Joseph A. Weber
Mr. William G. Weld
M/M. John F. Wight
Mr. Brent J. Williams
Mrs. Gean Wilson
D/M. Warren J. Wimmer
M/M. Andrew R. Zinsmeyer

Appendix B 1: Principles, Philosophy and Objectives.

a. *Statement of Principles, 21 June 1954 (revised 26 October 1954). (See p.14):*

CATHOLIC PREPARATORY SCHOOL FOR BOYS, INC.
STATEMENT OF PRINCIPLES

I. General.

It is the purpose of this corporation to establish and support a Catholic secondary school for boys in St. Louis County.

The objective is to provide Catholic preparatory education of the highest excellence. By "Catholic education" we mean thorough training in the knowledge and practice of the Roman Catholic faith and a school experience that puts awareness of religious truth in the central place. By "preparatory education of the highest excellence" we mean a thorough and effective program of studies in the subject matter offered by recognized leaders among established schools and required or recommended by outstanding American universities. Our aim is an intellectual discipline that will fit young men for admission to the colleges, universities and technical schools of their choice and enable them to undertake their continuing studies with success.

It is intended that, within the limits of scholarship funds to be available, the school shall be open on the basis of merit to boys from the entire archdiocese.

We dedicate this undertaking to the Immaculate Heart of Mary.

II The School and Its Program.

Scope.

The immediate need is for the establishment of a school to offer class work equivalent to that covered in the last four years in the best preparatory schools. As soon as practical, provisions should be made for the fifth through eighth grades. Whether the school should attempt to include lower grades should be left to developments and further study. It should grow from small beginnings and be allowed to develop. We recognize it cannot be the function of this corporation to define the curriculum or fix a definite form for the program of the school—these being properly the responsibility of the headmaster and the faculty. We are, however, in agreement on certain fundamentals. It will be our purpose to seek an administrator, whether lay or religious, and teachers who will share our conviction as to the importance of these fundamentals set forth below:

Religious Character.

1. The Catholic influence we seek in the life of students appears to require that ultimately the school shall be a part of a religious foundation under the direction of a religious order, and that there shall be full observance of the liturgical and monastic life in accordance with the rule of the order. However, this ideal should not be permitted to interfere with the establishment and maintenance of the highest scholastic standards. In the event it is not possible, at the outset, to place the direction of the school in the hands of a religious order qualified by educational practice, tradition and accomplishment to conduct the sort of school here contemplated, and approved as such by His Excellency, the Archbishop, we are prepared to go forward initially with the establishment of the school under lay direction. This should not be permitted to modify, however, the religious character of the school.

Educational Character.

2. The educational program of the school should provide the foundation for a Christian education in the Liberal Arts tradition. It should be preparatory in the fullest sense of the word. It should give boys mastery of the basic intellectual skills that underlie the development of a mature, educated man.

The school should stress mathematics and language. It should lay the groundwork for enjoyment of literature, understanding of history, appreciation of art, achievement in natural science—in short, it should be preparation for later studies, whatever their direction.

We conceive of a formal curriculum—similar to that of the Portsmouth Priory School—made up of a limited number of courses in the following basic fields: Christian Doctrine, Latin and Greek, Mathematics, English History, Modern Languages and introductory work in General Science, Physics, Biology and Chemistry.

The Faculty.

3. The faculty should be picked and formed in the spirit of these principles. The faculty should be picked not only for academic records but for sound intellectual capacity, a sense of the teaching vocation, ability to lead and influence boys, and devotion to God.

Recognizing that the character of a school is largely formed and developed by the headmaster, the greatest care should be taken to secure for this position the services of the finest man available who is in accord with the principles stated herein and qualified to put them into practice. Recognizing, also, that the school can be no better than its teachers and that the best lay teachers can be secured only by paying attractive salaries adequate to support them and their families in respectable and dignified circumstances, special attention should be given to the establishment of a salary range designed to achieve this result.

Standards.

4. Levels of performance and testing should be related to national criteria like those of the College Entrance Examination Board. It is intended that standards be such as to require diligent work by boys of normal intelligence aiming at mastery of subject matter and study habits that will fit them not only for admission to college, but for success in college studies.

Small Classes.

5. The number of teachers in relation to students should be as great as financial circumstances permit, and emphasis should constantly be put on thorough, exacting instruction of small classes. The curriculum should be flexible enough to permit boys of unusual ability to progress faster than their classmates and to accomplish more. The pace for all students should be more rapid and intensive than is customary in high school education generally.

Affiliation.

6. The school should not be designed or controlled to guide or influence students to enter any particular university nor should it be associated directly or indirectly with any particular university or system of universities. Its goal should be to prepare boys to enter the finest universities thoroughly grounded in their religion and qualified scholastically.

Methods.

7. The school should always be alert to new developments in education and new techniques in teaching methods. It should not, however, be an experimental school. Its aim should always be to impart mastery of the traditional and fundamental tools of scholarship as noted in the sketch of the curriculum under (2) above. Emphasis should be on what is taught and on teaching the subject matter in the best way. Substance should never be sacrificed to methods.

Athletics.

8. The school should provide a well-rounded program of athletic and extra-curricular activity. These should never be permitted, however, to interfere with its main business of education.

General Character.

9. Moral probity, intellectual development, physical well-being, good discipline and good manners each should have the place in the total scheme of the school which its relative importance requires.

Physical Plant.

10. The physical properties should be in keeping with the character of the school which would depend somewhat upon whether it will include a monastery, or whether it will be operated by a religious order or by a lay board.

The location should be spacious, beautiful, and located in St. Louis County, readily available to West St. Louis, Clayton and adjoining territory.

The buildings should be simple and adequate but all ostentation and heavy investment in monumental edifices should be avoided. It should always be kept in mind that the principal investment should be in teachers and pupils, and in establishing the proper environment and atmosphere for the educational objectives described herein.

Catholic Tradition.

11. Finally, and in summary, the school should exemplify the Western Catholic tradition in the full intellectual and religious richness of that tradition through many centuries. It should graduate young men who will be a credit to their tradition as students in the universities of the nation and as citizens of the St. Louis community.

III. Immediate Policy.

We recognize that action should be taken to establish the school in the immediate future. Interest in the project is now very great. This is the time to go ahead after careful study and planning.

As we plan, however, for the acquisition of property, the participation of a religious order, and the other steps that must be taken, we should, at the same time, carry forward a program of study and evaluation of the ideal program of a secondary school. In particular, we should seek guidance from leading secondary schools and from universities such as Notre Dame, which in cooperation with the Ford Foundation has recently completed a revision of its Liberal Arts program—a revision based on a thorough re-examination of the methods of Liberal Arts education. The results of this study should be of the greatest value to the headmaster and faculty when the time comes for them to make final decisions on the school's curriculum.

We are concerned with liberal education. It is for this we wish our school to prepare boys. The liberally educated man, we believe, should be a complete man, intellectually and morally fit for the life of individual responsibility—the life enriched by faith—the life broader than the limits of self-interest or occupation—the life of the good man and the good citizen.

b. Supplementary Statement, November 1955 [i.e. after the arrival of the first three monks]. (See *p.14*):

THE ST. LOUIS PRIORY AND SCHOOL
SUPPLEMENTARY STATEMENT
OF THE PROGRAM

Our Goal - $1,500,000

St. Louis Priory will need physical facilities to accommodate a growing monastery and a country day school of some 400 boys within a very few years. Present building plans must be designed to that end. While emphasis will be upon quality of spirit, faculty and teaching, rather than upon monumental buildings, nevertheless the buildings must be adequate and attractive. Minimum requirements include:

The School

Class rooms, library, study space, dining facilities and assembly room, gym, showers and locker space, playing fields and the necessary equipment.

The Monastery

Simple living quarters, library and assembly room for the monks. Not only must we house the monks who will be sent here to teach, but adequate quarters must be provided for the young men who will be called to join the community and to carry on the high teaching vocation of the monks of the Priory of St. Mary and St. Louis. Remember that the monastery will be their permanent home. Certainly it must be adequate. A properly staffed monastery should have a minimum of 20 monks to carry out all the monastic duties of prayer and divine office.

The Chapel

The monastic church is, of course, the heart and soul of the foundation. While a beautiful church will ultimately be needed as the appropriate place for the masses and prayer of the community and the daily singing of the divine office in common—which is the true work of the monastery—it will be necessary to start with a decent chapel adequate to accommodate the boys and the faculty. An attractive feature of Benedictine education is the fact that the boys are deeply conscious that their education is God-centered and that, while they are important in the scheme of things, the inner vital life of the institution is directed toward an even more important thing—the worship of Almighty God.

The Land

An attractive site with several useful buildings has been selected and purchased. It must be paid for. The approximately 95 acres are a minimum requirement to provide adequate space for the school and its activities and some atmosphere of isolation and remoteness so essential to the proper spirit of a great monastery. Total land cost: approximately $400,000.

$1,500,000 From Where?

The primary appeal must be made to Catholic people who are interested in higher education and in the fullest development of future Catholic leadership. By its very nature, this appeal must be somewhat restricted. It is limited to generous people who have an appreciation of the great need for setting the very highest standards of traditional Catholic education.

It must not be overlooked, however, that there is a great and broad appeal here to every person interested in being identified with the establishment of a great Benedictine monastery in our community—and that should include practically every Catholic in a position to make a donation to this great cause. Every donor will be considered as one of the founders of the monastery and, as pointed out in the brochure, along with his descendants, will be the object of the prayers and masses of the community as a benefactor of the monastery as long as it shall exist in this world. At the close of the campaign, all the donors will be listed in a Founders' Book that will be preserved in the monastery church as a reminder of the generosity of those who participated in this great enterprise and as an historical document

Traditionally, Benedictine monasteries are associated with particular cities or towns—as Westminster has been with London and St. Denis with Paris. This is the monastery of St. Louis. The monks will, in particular, pray for all the people of our city and community. It should be considered a real privilege to be associated in a substantial way with the establishment of such a monastery here through the transplanting of the seed of the great Abbey of Ampleforth.

How much should an individual give?

In every campaign to raise money, this is a vital question. In many cases those in charge of the campaign attempt to answer this question by suggesting in dollars the amount each donor should give. Cards are rated, and solicitors are asked to try to get that amount. The success of workers and teams is judged by the degree to which they approach that standard.

We have no wish to try to tell anyone how much he should give. That is a matter of personal ability, interest, judgment and conscience. We do not presume to be able to decide these things. But the success of our efforts will depend chiefly on two things:

(1) The ability of the solicitor to inform prospective donors, to give them an adequate understanding of this great project and to create a desire to help.
(2) Giving the prospective donor a true appreciation of the extent to which the success of our project depends upon his responding in a substantial way, according to his means, to this appeal.

All the solicitor can do is to present the facts—help the prospect to have a real understanding of the true significance of this project in the field of Catholic education and religious life and its relation to the prospect and his family—and to show him in a general way his position and responsibility among those to whom this appeal is made. Roughly, we may assume there are approximately 1,000 Catholic families who could give from $1,000 to $10,000 (and more, in not a few cases). There are many thousand more who could afford to give from several hundred dollars up to $1,000.

We have a strong and dedicated corps of some 300 workers, men and women, to carry the message and inspire those Catholic families to provide the means to achieve the great goal.But the workers are human and so are the prospects. We know you cannot interest and inspire all these people to do the utmost every one of them could so as to realize all the potential. One thing is clear, however. We must secure substantial gifts from as many as possible of these prospective founders of the Priory of St. Mary and St. Louis, that is, substantial in view of the means of each donor.

From the beginning this enterprise has been dedicated to the Immaculate Heart of Mary and has been almost providentially successful.

Most Catholic men and women can properly evaluate their ability to give in relation to the Catholic community. Given a true understanding of this cause, a realization of the goal and the available resources, we can confidently rely upon them to be moved to give according to their means, in the light of the need.

An important point, of course, is that this is a capital investment for the future, not an annual plan for maintenance. Another thing that should be emphasized is the desire to provide scholarships to qualified and deserving Catholic boys. Of course, the solicitor should be prepared promptly to show that there is involved no aspect of giving to provide a school for the sons of rich men. Unfortunately (or, perhaps, fortunately) there are very few such men among us and they (certainly those whose children or grandchildren may be expected to attend the St. Louis Priory School) may be relied upon, we hope, to do their share. But practically, the great majority of parents whose children will attend the school will be making a substantial sacrifice to send them. A substantial number of students, we hope, will be boys who, but for the generosity of the founders, would not be able to pay the cost of an education of equal quality and excellence. So having given the facts, and a picture of the need and the resources available, the solicitor can only indicate that we will need a substantial number of gifts of $10,000 and more, a great many gifts of $1,000 and more, and an even greater number of gifts up to $1,000. Primarily we must depend upon the degree to which the donor is moved to generous sacrifice.

The Catholic community of St. Louis has long felt the need of such a school as is planned. The great teaching community of St. Benedict at Ampleforth has been asked to fill this need and has responded in a most generous and wholehearted way. It is an inspiring privilege and opportunity for us. It is also a great challenge. We must meet it in the same spirit with which the invitation was accepted. We must work and pray for success and we have the comfort of knowing that daily masses and the divine office are being offered for our success at the Priory of St. Mary and St. Louis.

c. Philosophy and Objectives, 1992. (See *p.14*):

[We composed this document in preparation for our visitation in 1992 by a team from the *Independent Schools Association of the Central States (ISACS)]*

The mission of Saint Louis Priory School is to provide
Catholic college preparatory education
of the highest excellence in the Benedictine tradition
for qualified boys of the Saint Louis area.

By *college preparatory education of the highest excellence*, we mean a thorough and effective secondary educational program in the liberal arts tradition, which prepares young men for admission to distinguished colleges and universities and enables them to undertake their continuing studies with success. Through a broadly based curriculum in the fundamental arts and sciences, such a program imparts the intellectual skills and the habits of inquiry, study, and reflection which characterize the educated man. It challenges each boy to discover and develop his unique set of talents and stimulates in him an intellectual curiosity and independence of thought. This program is of the highest standard, proceeds at an accelerated pace in relation to secondary education generally, and prepares its students to perform with distinction in relation to nationally recognized criteria. The aim is an educational program which makes the School outstanding in the Saint Louis area and one of the best schools of its kind in the country. Essential for the program are a faculty of the highest caliber, small class sizes, and wise and careful attention to each boy.

By *Catholic education*, we mean a thorough formation in the knowledge, understanding, and practice of the Catholic faith, which seeks to give a Catholic boy the basis for a free and mature dedication of himself to that faith. In the environment of a school community centered on the Eucharist and the Word of God, this education sees the harmony of all knowledge with religious truth. By its Catholic nature, it welcomes boys and families of other Churches and religious traditions and joins with them in a common search for God. Its aim for each of its boys is his development into a complete man, intellectually and morally fit for a life of responsibility, for the life of a wise and good citizen and a wise and good man.

By *education in the Benedictine tradition*, we mean an education marked by the values and tone of Benedictine spirituality. A community of Benedictine monks is a spiritual family centered in God and open to the world through hospitality and service. The students and families, faculty and staff, alumni and friends of a Benedictine school are part of the extended family of the monastery and share deeply in its values. Among the most important of these are care, concern, and support for every member of the family, links with the monastery and its family which perdure and deepen beyond a boy's time in the School, a sense for the contemplative dimension of life and learning, and rootedness in that wise and balanced Christian humanism which marks our English Benedictine heritage. Such Benedictine education invites a boy to become aware of the goodness of God and of himself, to grow in confidence in his developing talents, and to see his future life and career as an opportunity for the service of others and of God.

By *qualified boys*, we mean boys who have the aptitudes and motivation needed to succeed in the School's program. Admission to the School is necessarily quite competitive, yet not only exceptionally gifted boys are accepted. Motivation and industry are as important as native ability for success in the program, which requires diligent work by all boys and challenges those of unusual ability to more rapid progress. In response to the call of the Church, the School seeks and values a student body composed of boys of diverse socioeconomic, racial, and ethnic backgrounds.

We, the members of the Saint Louis Priory School community, dedicate ourselves to this educational mission for the service of our boys and their families that in all things God may be glorified.

Laus Tibi Domine

Appendix B 2: Report on the Reconnaissance. (*See* p.24):

PRIVATE AND CONFIDENTIAL

A REPORT ON THE PROSPECTS OF FOUNDING A MONASTERY AND SCHOOL IN SAINT LOUIS, MISSOURI, U.S.A.

INTRODUCTION.

. . . The purpose of the report is to give an objective picture of how the invitation looks at St. Louis against its indigenous American background. It is not an advocacy or a plea for rejection, nor is it exhaustive. It is the fruit of some talking and a great deal more listening, observation and, may we add, much travelling. Finally, it does not claim infallibility. It has not been too easy to maintain complete objectivity in the face of great kindness, consideration and generosity on the part of the St. Louis Group who were our hosts during the greater part of our stay in the united States. . . .

ECCLESIASTICAL CONSIDERATIONS.

In company with Fr. Curtin we had a most cordial interview with Archbishop Ritter of St. Louis. He said he had been aware of the great need for an independent Preparatory School of high scholastic quality for some time and had given his full approval to this project because it was sponsored by laymen whom he knew to be solid and sound Catholics and substantial citizens. He stated that it was he who insisted that Ampleforth must be left entirely free to conduct the school and its policy as we thought fit. There must be no "strings".

He envisaged a "domus formata" in the usual Canonical form and ultimately an abbey, but fully realized we might have to start with very few Monks assisted by American lay staff. On our acceptance, he would issue his "Bene Placitum" in the widest terms, binding his Successor not to turn us out, but leaving us free to go. For Rome, he said with a twinkle, always had " two strikes on a Bishop." The force of this reference to baseball was only partly comprehended by your investigators . . .

The Archbishop said he thought we should get Vocations from the St. Louis area and seemed confident on this point. This was confirmed by all the ecclesiastics we met. Their training was a matter for our judgment; he approved of them being sent overseas, as being the "natural" thing to do. There was a good theological faculty at St. Louis University, if that was found convenient for part of Juniors' studies.

After the interview Fr. Curtin said that the Archbishop was a very shrewd man of affairs and had made independent inquiries about Ampleforth's standing and capacity to do the work long before our American friends visited us, and that once he had accepted us, he would never "let us down", even financially, hence his careful assessment of the Sponsors of Catholic Preparatory School for Boys

Inc. We certainly formed the view that his Excellency was a shrewd, kindly and very accessible person, that he would prove a staunch friend and discreet counselor. His second Auxiliary, Bishop Byrne, met us in company with about twenty leading Secular Clergy and invited us to a private lunch. No one could have been more courteous and encouraging. We should have a very good friend in him too.

One of the features of our ecclesiastical contacts that frankly surprised us was the enthusiastic support of the Jesuit Fathers, who practically control education in the U.S.A. and indeed, very many parishes. The choicest intellects we came across were Dean Bender of Harvard and the Rector of St. Louis University, Fr. Rheinert [Reinert], S.J., both very outstanding men. Fr. Reinert gave us an hour of his valuable time. The gist of his observations was that the need of such a school in St. Louis was desperate. The Heads of the Universities of good standing were extremely worried about the decline in general educational standards and that Catholic education lagged behind even that in adequate Preparatory Schools (High Schools or Secondary Education). He said "We here have been talking about the problem for a long time, if only you would come and *do* something about it, the repercussions would reach far beyond St. Louis." This was also expressed by the various Jesuit Fathers who talked to us during breakfast (we said Mass at the Jesuit University Church) where there were strange liturgical "goings on".[373] One said "You must come out, it is an apostolic work for the Church of God". The others nodded assent. This was also said on many other occasions by many different people.

It may seem strange that the Society is unable to undertake this work, but Fr. Reinert explained that they are fully stretched, and indeed, sometimes wonder if they have not "bitten off more than they could chew". The Headmaster of a distinguished S.J. Preparatory School near Washington promised us every help. We understood he (and other Jesuits) were infiltrating various official Boards. Fr. Reinert and he promised every assistance it was in their power to give. Fr. Reinert said that he spoke for Fr. Provincial, though not officially. It appears that not only will the Society be not opposed to the project, but its most active and enthusiastic backers. This means something anywhere, especially in U.S.A.

We found the Secular Clergy most friendly, although not all equally aware of the need for higher education, being pre-occupied with parochial schools. One of the most influential and respected figures in the Archdiocese is Msgr. Farris [Faris], the Archbishop's official representative on the Board [i.e. Inc], who do nothing without consulting him. It was he who arranged the meeting with the Secular Clergy at his Rectory. It is hardly necessary to add that he is solidly behind the project. There may be such, but we heard no dissentient voice . . .

As about forty per cent of St. Louis is Catholic, it looks as if there would be ample room for them [The Brothers of Mary] and us. At any rate, they showed no apprehension at our possible advent into the educational field, but went out of their way to provide information and advice. They [Chaminade] are not a large

[373] We print what they wrote, but it seems more likely that the strange goings on went on in church not at breakfast.

school and their site would preclude much enlargement. We understand their Father General in Rome (who was at Chaminade in the past) would greatly appreciate the St. Louis project becoming actual. He had expressed this view to Mr. Switzer in the hearing of Abbot Aidan Williams. Mr. Switzer wrote to Fr. Abbot on this subject.

We found both E.B.C. Houses in the States very enthusiastic about the project. There is no doubt they would be extremely disappointed if we turned down the projected foundation. They have a strong congregational sense; and indeed an affection for it. They think it has a real mission in the U.S.A. and we agree with this opinion. We received the greatest kindness, fraternal hospitality and co-operation from both Portsmouth and Washington Priories. In the interests of veracity, it must be recorded that they await our decision as something deeply affecting themselves.

It would be in place to record the views of a Fr. Manning, an American priest returning to San Francisco whom we met outward bound. He was a man of considerable culture and great charm, close to the Archbishop of San Francisco as we understood from another priest in the party, and known well by Fr. Hilary of Portsmouth. He said there was no better milieu in the whole of the States than the St. Louis area for us to start a monastic school. The most stable and solid Catholics were to be found there. They had real Catholic traditions, and would find liturgical Catholicism congenial - unlike the Boston Catholics. He deplored the trends of much American education, such courses as basket weaving contributing to a B.A., or a Ph. D. on a thesis of the different methods of washing up, to take two extreme cases. Catholic education was even lagging behind secular education in some respects instead of giving a lead (see a comment in "Time" Magazine). Those who knew were greatly disturbed. The Archbishop of San Francisco would watch the foundation with great interest if it materialised. We hastily explained that any St. Louis effort would represent an outside edge.

When we put the alternative of an English Foundation, he said at once that the St. Louis project would help it by paying for it in a few years. This opinion was voiced by many others also. He was emphatic about St. Louis being an excellent field for Vocations.

Finally a courtesy call on the Apostolic Delegate to U.S.A. was made in company with Fr. Anselm [Alban] Boultwood, Prior of Washington. Archbishop Cigognani [Cicognani] made three points. There was a dearth of Catholic Preparatory Schools of high standing. St. Louis was an area of solid and fine Catholics who would provide Vocation material. He personally would welcome the E.B.C. to the States very cordially.

THE AMERICAN EDUCATIONAL SYSTEM.

We began our visit in the U.S.A. with a stay of some days at Portsmouth Priory School where we were greatly helped by Fr. Prior and the school staff. We were able to visit preparatory schools (equivalent to our public schools) at Milton Academy and Roxbury Latin School in the Boston area as well as St.

Louis Country Day School (the type of school envisaged by the Group but to be specifically Catholic, whereas St. Louis C.D. is Episcopalian or less), Chaminade School run by the Brothers of Mary, and Georgetown Preparatory School run by the Fathers of the Society of Jesus. The remarks which follow are based on what was learned at all of these schools. In many, in fact most, cases there was agreement between all these authorities on the questions dealt with here.

The main difference between our system and that followed in the United States is that our last or VI Form year corresponds almost exactly to the Freshman year in a U.S. University. Thus a preparatory school, or "high school", as it may be called, carries out the work of four years up to the end of the English V Form, but does not attempt any of the specialisation familiar to us in the VI Form years. Some exceptions to the rule are to be found in a few schools of unusually high standard, but they are very definitely regarded as exceptions and treated as "special tuition". The Universities make allowances in some cases for such boys to skip part of their freshman year. Thus we should be expected to take boys to good fifth form standards (School Certificate) and this would be adequate to ensure entry by way of College Board Exams to any university. This opinion was endorsed by all schoolmasters who had had contact with the English system and included Mr. Acheson of Portsmouth and the Headmaster of Milton Academy.

The second great difference between our two systems is that what we know as Preparatory Schools, [grade schools, usually boarding] do not, with one or two exceptions only, exist. High Schools, Grades 9, 10, 11 and 12, (i.e. the last four years before College viz. University) have to depend upon the Grade Schools, (Grades 5, 6, 7 and 8) run by the State or often by Nuns, for their intake. It was generally agreed that the preparation given in these Grade Schools was inadequate or of low standard.

In order to cope to some extent with this situation it was often suggested, and it seemed obvious to us, that any school started in St. Louis should include, besides the four grades, 9, 10, 11, 12, of a normal High School, the last two grades 7 and 8 of a normal Grade School. This was always regarded as desirable as well as possible. In that case the full school would range from age 12 + to 17+. This will again be referred to under the next heading.

It would also seem desirable and was often recommended that candidates for admission should be carefully, indeed rigorously, selected. This seemed to be expected on all sides, even by prospective parents who hoped we would exclude those who had no chance of graduation from our school, but that their own son might not fall within this category! In this matter of selection the U.S. makes much greater use of "objective" testing - what we suppose would be called psychological testing [multiple choice] in England. Modern methods of testing have evolved a way of evaluating 'teachability'. An entrance exam, corresponding to the Common Entrance, (but of the "objective" type) is set by the Secondary Education Board and is widely used, which many apparently honest "educators" including Dean Bender of Harvard say shows a remarkable correspondence to the eventual result of a boy's school and even university career. Tests of achievement are not nearly so seriously regarded as here, but they could certainly be combined with objective tests should we so desire. Roxbury Latin School selects only 40% of its applicants each year - some schools only admit a boy on a "probationary" basis for the first term. They can always refill the place of an unsuccessful candidate such is the demand for better education. This system is universally accepted.

English educational standards are very greatly admired and on all sides we were urged to insist on high standards at all stages, and to apply them most rigorously.

The American Grade system, so far as the names of forms is concerned, need not be used. In fact, many schools use English form names for "prestige" purposes. But the marking system which is more elaborate than ours would need to be adopted since the Colleges (Universities) set great store by the school record of a boy in granting admissions. The Colleges watch carefully a school's standard of marking to give credit to a school which has a high standard. This was confirmed by all the University people we met, including Dean Bender, Dean of Admissions at Harvard, Fr. Reinert S.J. Rector of St. Louis University, and Dr. de Ferrari, Registrar of the Catholic University at Washington D.C.

This American marking system is much more elaborate than anything we use and applies at all four grades of High School. "Credits", which count towards college (university) entrance, are taken in all four grades as from the time of entrance to High School.

It would probably be necessary to engage an experienced American lay master to act as School Registrar and operate this system which would probably be beyond the competence of an Englishman in the first years.

Sixteen "credits" are normally required for University entrance and so at least four 'courses' must be taken successfully in each year of High School (i.e. in the last four years at school). It is abnormal for a boy to take more than five 'courses' at any one time, but a 'course' need not last for a full year. In some subjects 'continuation courses' are taken, as in Maths, Latin, Languages, English, which may last two, three or more years, or all through a boy's schooling.

With reference once more to 'standards' we had thought of bringing back text books used in various grades to illustrate these, but it proved impractical except in one or two cases. We were satisfied after seeing work in a large number of High Schools, that good fifth form standards of achievement would get a boy through the College Board exams. These give entrance to any University including the best of the Eastern ones. This statement was confirmed by Dean Bender of Harvard, by Mr. Henry Keeler, representative for admissions of Princeton for the Mid-West and St. Louis (and a member of the Board of Catholic Preparatory School for Boys Inc.), Dr. de Ferrari of Catholic University, Washington D.C., Mr. Lemoine Skinner, representing Rhodes Scholarship Board in St. Louis area, and many others closely connected with education.

METHOD OF STARTING. (to be computed)

. . . It seemed to us that the school would best be started with one or possibly two grades only. These should be the 7th (12 to 13 Years), or 8th (13 to 14 years) or 7th and 8th grades together. This would allow the School to grow gradually one grade being added each year as the foundation members moved upwards. To begin with a full High School is obviously out of the question; to take the lowest grades ensures that even foundation members get a full run through the school and benefit from five years, if it began with 8th grade, or six years, if it began with 7th grade, of our sort of schooling.

This method of starting was regarded as the right one by all those to whom we talked on this subject including many parents, even those whose children, by reason of age, would be excluded from the School. All were emphatic on the subject.

It was our opinion that for the first two or even possibly three years, the Stannard house (photographs and blueprints may be seen) could provide nine classrooms to hold ten or more each. In the first year there might be one grade of 30 boys in three sets - in the second year two grades of 30 each in six sets and in the third year three grades of 30 each in nine sets - obviously these figures would be contingent - or in the first year there could be two grades of up to 30 boys each in three sets each, six sets in all.

While these numbers obtained the Stannard house would be sufficient for Class purposes and meanwhile the School building could be under construction. During the same period the larger Gallagher house could comfortably house four members of the Community and the smaller Gallagher house an unmarried layman. The Reasor house, if it is obtained, would also be available for lay staff - this has been referred to under "Buildings". Such a start would not be envisaged before September 1956 - there would be much to be done before that date by a Superior and/or Headmaster . . .

Fees at other comparable schools are:-

	per year
Portsmouth	\$ 725 + \$50 Games Fund
Georgetown Prep.	\$ 700 + extras
Milton Academy	\$ 750
Groton	\$ 1750 (boarders only)
Lawrenceville	\$ 775
Andover	No details given
Kent	Sliding Scale

The Headmaster of Roxbury Latin School said a boy cost \$650. Fr. Peter Sidler, Procurator at Portsmouth, advises an all inclusive fee per annum.

UNIVERSITY ENTRANCE.

As regards the Catholic v non-Catholic University question, it must be realised that the Catholic Universities just could not absorb all the Catholic students. There is tacit recognition of this by the provision of Newman Chaplains and groups at non-Catholic Universities by the hierarchy. It is ultimately the parent who decides which university his boy is to attend. We could advise parents when a boy was unsuitable for a Secular University on scholastic or religious grounds. The general opinion amongst informed Clerics was that the State Universities are more pagan, than the independent ones. The aim of the St. Louis foundation would be to prepare a boy in such fashion that he would be able to enter any university. We are certain the Board would not regard it as a preparatory school for Harvard, Yale or Princeton only.

Dean Bender told us that 15% of Harvard Students were Catholics, but that he would fall over backwards to get a greater percentage; however, with the exception of Portsmouth and one or two others their scholastic training was inadequate. Most of their Catholic students came from non-Catholic establishments. The explanation of this ardent wish for more Catholics is that the few great eastern Universities are very sensitive about any charge of being an enclosed enclave of wealthy eastern families. They wish their students to present a cross section of American life and to come from all parts of the States.

As has been stated, the school record of a boy throughout the high school grades is of great importance. Entrance into a University is determined by this record and College Board examinations which are largely of the multiple choice type. There are also Scholarships to the Universities, but less store appears to be set by them than on this side of the Atlantic.

We came to the firm conclusion that a liberal education up to good fifth form standards would secure entrance to any American University. A boy who reached this standard with any sort of distinction would normally be duplicating some of the work as a freshman, but there is movement to obviate this at the better Universities, Catholic and non- denominational.

FINANCIAL ASPECT.

When the school starts, the Group envisages that the site and existing buildings will have cost $300,000 and will be free of debt. They propose to provide $500,000 over the first two years for purposes of alterations to existing buildings and possible construction of new school buildings, e.g. classrooms, dining hall, etc., and also to provide a trust fund producing $10,000 per annum to cover running expenses, repairs, etc. (This would be handed over in toto to the Community under the new Incorporation - see below). This is confirmed in a letter from Mr. Switzer:

> "The group thoroughly approved and enthusiastically agreed to recommend to the Board the building and financial program which we have discussed and which I believe is satisfactory to you. The plan is, of course, to acquire the Stan[n]ard property as well as the Gallagher property and the Reasor property if possible and putting this property in shape to provide a

school starting with several classes and building on up to a full schedule, including the fifth grade to the last year of high school. You would, of course, decide what additions and changes would have to be made to the present buildings on the property, which I believe would include dining room, kitchen, chapel, equipment, library, driveways, playing fields, etc. This would be the first phase of the building program and would enable the school to have an early start. We would also pay the expense incident to bringing personnel from England to St. Louis to operate the school, and we would cover the operating deficit of the school during the first five or so years, when the school could not be expected to operate at a profit. It was also recognised that Ampleforth might find it necessary, temporarily at least, to hire teachers to replace men coming to St. Louis. In that case it is recognised that reasonable compensation to Ampleforth for such expense would be a proper item of the St. Louis budget. " . . .

. . . "We would pay all the expenses of this first phase of the operation. We will raise $500,000.00, which we estimate is a reasonable sum for this purpose. After the school is in operation for several years, it will be necessary to provide additional buildings and facilities. A definite building and financial program would be adopted by the school in the light of the circumstances at the time. We will cooperate fully in carrying out this purpose."

Note: At St. Anselm's Priory [now Abbey], Washington, a school building is at present being erected for eighty-five day boys. It comprises five senior and three junior classrooms, a library for 4,000 books, a lecture room with raised seating, a Physics and Biology Laboratory, a Chemistry Laboratory, an Auditorium to seat two hundred with green room, store, studio, etc., a Headmaster's Study, Secretary's room, book room, Lavatories for seniors, for juniors, for guests, a Masters' Common room and Cafeteria for mid-day meals. The whole has been contracted for at $310,000. Their gymnasium (already built) with one basketball court would nowadays probably cost $200,000.

It is envisaged by the Group that compensation would be paid to Ampleforth for the loss of members of the staff. Details of how this compensation should be evaluated and paid were not discussed at the present stage.

The sums of money mentioned, representing a capital of about $1,000,000 are not at present held by the C.P.S.B. Inc. in hard cash. But Mr. Switzer's letter, backed by the Board of Directors of about forty members, all people of considerable standing and position, allied to the assurance of His Excellency the Archbishop, is considered by us to be ample guarantee.

The Board has not yet launched its main appeal for funds as it is considered that to do so when the scheme has not yet been accepted by the Ampleforth Community would considerably reduce its chances of success. To ask people to give considerable sums of money for a possible future scheme is thought to be unsound. When the project is accepted the Board will immediately go forward with a fund-raising campaign which will have the advantage of a concrete object in view.

The Board is confident that the target they envisage will be attained. The enthusiasm we saw on all hands, and among people of substance, gives us every reason to agree with their opinion. The present tax situation in the U.S.A. makes this confidence still more sure . . .

FORMATION OF TRUST CORPORATION.

On the project being started all the funds and title deeds to the property at that time held by Catholic Preparatory School for Boys Inc. would be handed over by a deed of gift to a new Corporation formed of the members or some members of the Community at St. Louis and including probably the Abbot President, and/or members of the Ampleforth Community. It will be necessary to form this American Corporation which will become exempt for tax purposes. This is expressed in the Articles of Incorporation of C.P.S.B. Inc.

It is not necessary that all or any of the members of the Corporation be American citizens provided the Corporation itself be properly set up and Incorporated under American law. Much excellent professional advice is available in this matter among the members of the Board of C.P.S.B. Inc. There is no objection to the sending of money out of the country to England. The new Corporation, in this respect, would be in the same position as Lever Bros., or Royal Dutch Shell, in the opinion of Mr. Frank Belcke, [Bealke] a Vice-President of the Mercantile Trust Co., and of members of the Board.

STAFFING.

Mr. Switzer said that since his visit to Ampleforth he had come to realise much more that the heart of the school was the Monastery; without it the School would be quite a different institution. This was said at the Board Meeting we attended and seemed to have general assent. However, everyone realised that competent American lay-staff are an essential adjunct. It was emphasised that it was essential to pay good salaries to get the right men. The balance of opinion was that well-qualified men were not too easy to find. Fr. Manning thought that St. Louis with its two independent, as opposed to State, Universities, would provide some staff. Fr. Glynn, Newman Chaplain to Washington University, thought there were so very few Catholic schools of good scholastic attainment, that with a little searching around and contacts with University authorities, good men could be found. The Board pointed out that the very attractive residences available already on the site would be of great assistance. England is not the only country with a housing problem. It might be necessary to give them from $3,000 to $7,000. One well qualified R.C. layman teaching at Andover, a very good non-Catholic school, had made a tentative approach after hearing about the project. We also heard casually of two others. At a later stage it would certainly be possible to "import" some British lay-staff (though not from Ampleforth!!). The Sports Coach, a very important member of the Faculty, would of course have to be an American.

The important qualification for the members of the Faculty is that of being a good teacher and an allround one. American boys leave at 17 (graduate) and the best reach what we could call a good fifth form standard. VI Form Specialization is unknown. Highly qualified specialists are not required either amongst Monastic or lay-staff. It would be a mistake, however, to make a poor investment in staff. In the initial stage of starting with one or two grades, a Superior, Procurator (he would have a full-time job) and two other Monastic staff would be ample along with an American School Registrar and a Coach, at least from the School angle. It might be necessary to have a trained Nurse, combined perhaps with catering duties, to deal with minor injuries at games, etc.

SITE.

. . . This area is situated about eight miles from Clayton, the centre of the area of population to be served by the proposed school and about 12 miles from the centre of the city of St. Louis. It has a frontage of 345 yards on Conway Road with a driveway leading to the two Gallagher houses and a frontage of 492 yards on Mason Road with a driveway leading to the Stannard House. A private road over which there is an easement leads from Mason Road along the south and east boundaries of the Stannard property on to the Reasor property. The whole area lies about half a mile to the north of a double carriageway. (The site can be reached in about twenty minutes from St.Louis City or twelve minutes from Clayton, express highway from St. Louis.)

The site is undulating and partly wooded, There is a stream on the Stannard property which provides an ornamental pond and another on the Gallagher property which could provide more ornamental water. To the South of the Gallagher property and adjoining the Stannard property the ground rises to a plateau which could provide a fine site for a Church and monastic buildings. An engineer's site plan may be inspected.

The site, lying to the west of the city of St. Louis, is in an area which is now being developed by the building of dwelling houses each on about two to three acres. These are substantial middle class homes and belong to the sort of families which the proposed school would serve. A map of the city and environs is available.

Public Utilities. [Electricity and telephone are there. City water could be available for about $7,000.] . . . Water is available to each property from wells below the houses and it is pumped electrically, yielding in the case of the Stannard property, about 40 gals. per minute. This flow could be increased by installation of a more modern type of pump. The well is some 600 ft. deep and has never failed even in the most severe droughts.

Sewage disposal is by septic tank, the effluent being discharged into the stream on the Stannard property and over a seepage bed in the case of the Gallagher property. This is normal practice. The development of the area suggests that public sewage disposal will be available in the course of a few years. A sewage disposal plant for 400 persons would cost between $5,000 and $6,000. . .

Buildings. On the Gallagher property are two single storey houses, and some outbuildings. The larger house comprises entrance hall, large living room, four bedrooms with baths, smoking room, kitchen and pantry, basement (heating and pump). The smaller comprises entrance porch, small hall, two bedrooms with baths, kitchen and pantry, large attic, basement (heating and pump). Both these are timber frame built houses and are in excellent condition inside and out. Both are at present occupied by reliable tenants. Outbuildings include a barn and stockyard and a brick built hen house.

The Stannard property includes a ferro-concrete built dwelling house on two floors. Five sizeable rooms, kitchen and pantry, and garage for two cars on the ground floor, and four large and two small rooms on the first floor. A large basement with bath and toilet and cooking facilities could perhaps provide quarters for servants. This building is also in excellent state of maintenance both inside and out. It was built in 1936. Blueprints are available for inspection.

All buildings are centrally heated on the hot-air duct principle. This is readily adaptable for cooling in summer at a relatively small outlay. This would be advisable in view of the hot summer climate. In this area temperatures are stated to average 10 degrees less in summer than in the city, but in the city they can rise as high as 110 degrees F. The average is about 90 degrees F in the city and so about 80 degrees F on the site.

On the Stannard property there is a large and well-built timber frame barn which would convert into a chapel capable of seating about one hundred and fifty and a separate garage for four cars which could be adapted to many purposes. At present it houses farm implements, including a tractor, which go with the property.

We consider that the Stannard house could be used for teaching purposes in the first few years, providing nine classrooms and dining hall. Later it would divide very easily into two very adequate houses for lay staff. The larger Gallagher house could at first house a Community of up to four with private chapel. The smaller house could provide accommodation for school staff.

RELATION OF PARENTS TO SCHOOL.

General advice was do not have a formal Parent-School association. Formal resolutions pushed through by an ambitious and loquacious parent can be embarrassing. But informal contacts between the Faculty and parents at "bun-fights" etc., are admirable, and to be encouraged. There is a great respect for Priests and Religious in the States (Nuns can control boys of 16 and 17). The relationship of teacher-parent would present no greater difficulties than it does in England; possibly less.

COLOUR QUESTION.

Archbishop Ritter was a pioneer in the matter of non-segregation - even to the point of excommunicating those who publicly attacked the policy of racial integration. The matter is regarded as settled in St. Louis, so it would be imprudent to make an issue of this question.

ENGLISH AND AMERICAN CATHOLICISM.

It has been asked how "English and American Catholicism"' would get on together. As America is not yet entirely integrated as a nation, though the American national character is rapidly developing, so there are many types of Catholicism according to racial ethos. There is the Irish type of the East and the Spanish flavoured type of the West. The Catholic roots of St. Louis are of French and German origin, which has given birth to a singularly solid and stable type, free from some of the exotic or Jansenist-tinged manifestations of other areas. Our E.B.C. traditions would fit in well at St. Louis. There is a feeling for a central, sane and liturgical type of religious spirituality. An English Benedictine House forms a focus for these aspirations and, we believe, exerts a surprisingly powerful influence. It is attractive to many Americans, we were told. We see no problem here.

THE NEED FOR A FOUNDATION OF THIS KIND.

In speaking of the need of a foundation of this kind we shall instance especially the scholastic side of things. That this is to be a monastic school and [that] therefore a monastic foundation, first a Priory and later probably growing to an Abbey, is taken as axiomatic. This is the view of all members of the St. Louis Group. They consider they have in the English Benedictine Congregation exactly what is needed. They are admirers of the work of the Portsmouth Community (they have for obvious reasons no contact with the Washington one as it runs a day school) and hope for a school in St. Louis, a day school at first but possibly a boarding school later, which has the same ideal and object and also the method of achieving these.

There is, so far as we can see, nothing in the whole of the United States which can compare with Portsmouth other than the well-known non-Catholic Prep. Schools of the Eastern States such as Groton, Exeter, Andover, Kent, etc. One single exception may perhaps be made for Canterbury School run by laymen for Catholic boys. Portsmouth has a high reputation, among non-Catholics and laymen, such as Dean Bender of Harvard who said that he was glad to get Portsmouth boys, and many others. The prestige of the English Benedictine Congregation in education is very high in the United States. The American Swiss Congregation is reported as saying that the work they themselves are doing is but a pale imitation of what is being done at Ampleforth and Downside. There is a real need for the raising of the American educational standard. This is quite clear and is an opinion expressed an all sides by "educators" and by everyone else at the same time. This is all the more true of the standards of American Catholic education, and we can quote Archbishop

Ritter, Bishop Byrne, Mgr. Faris, Fr. Reinert, S.J. and a host of others on this point. The group who formed C.P.S.B. Inc. feel strongly enough about this to make a sacrifice to bring about a scheme which will go towards this improvement, and it can fairly be regarded as a real work for the Church.

This is a real challenge to us. America has everything except the men with the European educational tradition behind them, and as we know in our own State schools, it is the teachers who are the crux of the problem. This foundation could produce men to carry on a true educational tradition and men to demand it for their own sons and so the whole course of American education can and would be influenced for the better.

A foundation of this kind could and would produce Catholic leaders, and these are needed desperately in the United States. St. Louis is a splendid source of such men. With a 40% Catholic population and an unusually large percentage of these descended from the old French settlers, reinforced with more French from Maryland and by Irish and South German Catholics, now in the higher income groups, there is an exceptional opportunity for a work of this nature. We might add as a footnote at this point that Portsmouth is 1,000 miles from St. Louis, as far as Ampleforth from ? Rome.

There is a need too in the world today for better Anglo-American relations. Americans certainly are looking to Europe and England especially for help in their educational problem and we should be doing a real work for our own country by taking on this foundation. The Foreign Office have spoken in this sense in a letter to Fr. Abbot. Again we might add a personal note, that though neither of us was anti-American at the start, we return from the United States in far greater sympathy with their problems, hopes, aspirations and fears.

There is a need for discipline in American education. In the past, discipline has been lacking to the Americans in large degree, but we frequently heard the opinion expressed that more discipline was needed and that parents are now realising this need. It may be an effect of this last war. The fact is that they feel this need and so look to us and our methods to supply it. This we feel sure we could do.

We think on careful reflexion that in the United States there is a very real need of saving Catholic boys from non-Catholic schools and that this applies in the particular case of St. Louis. The object of a foundation there would be the same as ours at Ampleforth, in the often repeated words of Abbot Edmund Matthews, i.e. to provide a Catholic School of such standing that no parent should ever have any excuse for sending his son to a non-Catholic School.

We think that the Community should not reject this opportunity to play a part in American education without very serious consideration. The offer by the St. Louis Group is all that it seemed to be and indeed more. It is made in the most generous terms possible, and if we may at this final point express a personal opinion, we would urge that if it is at all possible, the Community should go forward in this enterprise.

R. R. WRIGHT
12th January 1955. F. R. COVERDALE.

Appendix B 3: Basic Ideas for the Architect. (*See* pp.93 and 132):

BASIC IDEAS FOR THE ARCHITECT WHEN PLANNING THE BUILDINGS OF SAINT LOUIS PRIORY AND SCHOOL
(Preliminary statement)

[NOTE: Paragraph 2 below must have been written before the end of January 1956 because by then we had abandoned the Cloister scheme, but paragraph 5, with its more advanced thinking about style, suggests a rather later date. The document may have been put together over a period of time and not been fully harmonized with itself. We have not edited the idiosyncratic style of the original]

This is being handed to architects who we hope will be ready to give a preliminary sketch - without any commitment either way - of how they would deal with the problem of planning the development of St. Louis Priory and School.

1. Existing Buildings.
   a. The Stannard house, facing Mason Rd, towards the south of the property, "Georgian" style, luxury residence.
   b. The Gallagher house, frame building with 2 spacious halls, 4 bed rooms, a sitting room and kitchen.
   c. A brick cottage near b.
   d. A number of wooden farm buildings.
   e. <u>In four years' time</u> on the Reasor property a frame building comparable to b. Another frame house smaller than b, removable.
2. <u>The Cloister Building</u>. This is a brick building to be erected in the immediate future, in line with the Stannard house and in the same style. It will be 4-sided with a cloister garth, have c. 11,000 sq. ft. Its immediate use: to house monks and provide classrooms. Its ultimate use: either a boarding house for 50 boys, or classrooms, or workshops, administration, top boys' studies, etc.

3. THE PROJECT is the planning of a monastery and school with their associated areas and services on the Stannard, Reasor and Gallagher properties. It should be borne in mind throughout that we do not want the buildings all to be erected at once, nor even necessarily the whole of each particular building. The growth of the monastery and school will take years and depends on many factors (rate of supply of boys, of novices, of funds etc.) which are unpredictable.
   In general, the buildings liable to expand - church, monastery, school classroom block, refectories etc. - should have plenty of elbow room for enlargement or for the erection of additional buildings. The plan must have a certain spaciousness and elasticity from the start.
4. THE COST of the building and the drive for funds are closely related, though neither entirely determines the other.

5. THE STYLE. We wish the architect to use contemporary methods and style and yet keep in mind the traditional character of a monastic foundation. The spirit needs to be emphasized in both monastery and school. The materials should be lasting but not lavish.
6. THE BUILDINGS.
a. THE CHURCH should be geographically and psychologically central to the whole plan. The monastery should be one side and the school another side of the church. The floor of the church should be approximately level with the cloister, monks' refectory, calefactory and monks' library. The high altar should be central to the church, so that the monks and all the boys should be as near the altar as is fitting. If possible the church should be orientated east and west. It will probably prove to be an advantage to have the monks' choir behind the altar. In time the number of monks may reach 100 and more.
This may take 20,30,100 years. We might eventually need 35 side altars. It is useful for a church to have a crypt. There should be two sacristies, one for the monks, entered from the cloister; one also for the boys, near the first. The organ should be a real one.
b. THE MONASTERY should ultimately be able to house 100 monks or more. It should have a broad down-stairs passage or cloister, it should have a calefactory or common room capable of holding 60 monks comfortably; cells for the monks, i.e. small bed-studies; a number of sick rooms on the ground floor; some guest bed-rooms; parlours and a dining room just outside the enclosure, i.e. approached from the outside; three lecture rooms to hold 25; novices' common room - the usual bath rooms etc.

The monastery REFECTORY might be in such a position that its kitchen could serve the boys' refectory. The monks' refectory is likely to need enlarging in time.

LIBRARY - part of the monastery - might be a combined monks' and boys' library with linked book stacks and separate reading rooms on either side. This room must be close to the monastery - approachable under cover from it.

LAY-BROTHERS' QUARTERS. These should be in the monastic area and would include cells and common room, toilets etc for 10 - 20 lay-brothers.

NOTE. 1. In planning the whole layout, some area should be allotted for monks to walk, play, garden etc.

2. It is axiomatic that the monastery should be away from the highway and preferably its windows should look onto its own property and not straight at school buildings in close proximity, all this in order to give a sense of seclusion and quiet. It seems likely that land not acquired by us will fairly soon be heavily built over.

3. For procurator - who should be near at hand - cf. 6.c.1

c. THE SCHOOL. Initially a day school but in all probability the time will come (5, 10 or more years) when there will be a boarding element. The possibility must be borne in mind. In 1956 there will be 30 boys. The likely growth is 30 a year up to 120. After that (and even before that) it is hard to estimate, it is probable that a separate Junior School (grades 5-8 or 7-8) will be started, possibly before 4 years elapse. It might well be up to 120 strong and the Upper School up to 400.

The buildings and areas should include:

i. Administrative building. Central to the school.
Contents: Headmaster's office, waiting room, etc.
Secretariat (admissions, office of studies, etc.)
Procurator's department. cf. 6.b.note 3.

The Procurator should be near his stores and central yard and these should be near the refectories. This area is usually unsightly and needs to be screened both from the school and from the headmaster's office. The Procurator should be easily accessible both to the monastery and to outside (tradesmen).

ii. Class rooms: as close together as possible, except for the science labs which could be a little apart (smell) but not too far. Somewhere, each boy should have a desk or locker in which to keep his books.

iii. Library reading room (assuming stacks are shared with the monks' library. cf. above 6.b. LIBRARY.

iv. Gym etc. including sprays, drying room, lockers (full length); coaches' rooms, stores, massage etc. It might be possible to include squash courts, wrestling and boxing rooms, soda fountains etc. It might be possible to combine the gym with other activities on other floors, or to use the outside walls as common with other buildings, or both.

v. The refectory or cafeteria might be alongside the gym. It might be linked to the kitchen of the monks' refectory. It should certainly be capable of expansion. It should be divisible into small units suited for seating 40-50 persons.
N.B. St. Vincent's, Latrobe, has used the outside walls of the gym as walls of other buildings.

vi. There should be play rooms not one vast one.

vii. At some later time, a boarding house, i.e. accommodation for 30-50 boys, housemaster, refectory, chapel, common-room, baths, lockers etc.

viii. Auditorium - stage, cinema, etc. Another expanding building.

ix. Playing fields: football, soccer, baseball, track; tennis; shooting range; perhaps squash racquets. All boys will be expected to play some game.

x. Car parks.

xi. Arts and Crafts rooms, music rooms, carpentry shop, dark rooms.

xii. School store, book room, tuck shop, storage space for paper, etc.

xiii. Wash places, W.C.s, hanging space for clothes.

d. A JUNIOR SCHOOL, self-contained - separate from the Upper School, but fairly near the monastery. It should have its own entrance from the road, class rooms, playing fields etc. Its size would probably not exceed 120.

e. GUEST ACCOMMODATION - dining room and bed rooms.

Final remarks. Although the monastery is the private living quarters of the monks, the building should not be very far from that part of the school where many of the monks will be teaching every day - the class rooms. It will be seen that there are a number of buildings or parts of buildings that need to be co-related more or less closely: the church and monastery and school; the monastery and the class rooms; the administration with the headmaster, with the monastery, with the stores; the refectory with the kitchen and the monastery and boys' refectory; the library with school and the monastery (almost part of the monastery block, as also its refectory). These are some of the more obvious co-relations that need to be kept in mind.

Appendix B 4: Names of the Members of our First Ninth Grade, with their Previous Schools. (*See* p.84):

Charles F. Bealke, Jr.	Saint Joseph, Manchester
Howard Benoist III	Barat Hall
David A. Blanton III	Barat Hall
Edgar C. Boedeker	Saint Joseph, Clayton
Daniel J. Burke	Barat Hall
John C. Carleton	Our Lady of Lourdes
Michael L. Carton	Our Lady of Lourdes
Richard H. Chomeau	Saint Peter, Kirkwood
John E. Cramer, Jr.	Our Lady of Lourdes
Dumont G. Dempsey, Jr.	Barat Hall
Henry J. Dilschneider, III	Horton Watkins Jr. High
Robert C. Dunn, Jr.	Barat Hall
Joseph E. Flynn, Jr.	Saint Joseph, Clayton
Michael H. Fox	Fern Ridge
William J. Gilmore	Barat Hall
George W. Hellmuth	Barat Hall
Peter M. Igoe	Hixon Jr. High
Kevin M. Kelly	Chaminade
William D. Kerckhoff	Admiral Farragut Academy
Theodore A. Kienstra, Jr.	Barat Hall
Michael W. Lardner	Saint Peter, Kirkwood
Robin H. Mattis	Whitfield
Jack R. Mueller	Saint Gabriel
Edwynne C. Murphy	Barat Hall
Francis M. Oates	Saint Roch
Christian B. Peper	Saint Louis Country Day School
Joseph G. Pfeffer	Chaminade
John J. Rice	Little Flower
Daniel E. Richardson	Chaminade
Robert L. Sain	American Community School, Buenos Aires
S. Michael Spearing	Our Lady of Lourdes

N.B. Barat Hall was an independent Catholic grade school of the Religious of the Sacred Heart of Jesus and Chaminade is a grade school and high school of the Brothers of Mary. They sent us nine and three boys respectively. Twelve came from Parochial grade schools, four from non-Catholic independent schools and three from public schools. Bob Sain's family moved out of town before school started. We started, therefore, with thirty boys, if one includes Chris Peper, who joined us a week or two after school started but proved to be too old and too advanced and left us during the first year. In the course of four years, three others departed and two, Samuel W. Mitchell, Jr. and Richard C. Schmidt, arrived, and so twenty-eight graduated.

Appendix B 5: Brochure on the School. (*See* pp.168-69):

SAINT LOUIS PRIORY SCHOOL
Mason & Conway Roads
Creve Coeur, Missouri

Saint Louis Priory School is a day school for boys run by Monks of the English Congregation of the Benedictine Order. For your convenience there follows a summary of information about the school.

1. THE PRIORY AND SCHOOL are located on the former Stannard, Gallagher and Singer properties, amounting to about 140 acres. The Reasor property, of 10 acres, is due to pass into the possession of the Priory in January 1960. The main house used to belong to Mr. A. C. Stannard, ex-president of Bell Telephone Co. It was built by Mr. Raymond Maritz.

2. AIMS. The first aim of the monks is to seek God by living as faithfully as they can to the rule of their Order, in this case the Rule written by St. Benedict for his monks near the beginning of the Sixth Century. In following the Rule monks normally perform some practical work, which in this case is the school. In this they draw on the traditions and experience of 15 centuries. The school has a double aim, to train boys to become good citizens of Heaven and to give them the best possible moral and intellectual training for the rest of their current life. This entails training their wills as well as their intellects, and fostering the qualities of character which make a fine Catholic leader. Examples of what this means in practice are: the boys attend the Conventual High Mass of the Community and sing the Ordinary; the courses offered stress solid learning in Mathematics, Latin, English, Science and foreign languages; some of the boys are chosen to help the Headmaster in running the school; any signs of extravagance or ostentation are firmly discouraged.

3. GRADES. In September 1956 we took thirty boys into the ninth grade. In September 1957 we took in another thirty, while the previous year's boys entered the tenth grade. This September we plan both to take another thirty into the ninth grade, and to open seventh and eighth grades of about ten boys each. This will give us the seventh and eighth grades, and ninth through eleventh. In September 1959 we shall have a full house, seventh through twelfth. The boys are divided for teaching into sets of about 15.

4. COURSES. In the High School, four years of Religion, English,

Mathematics and Latin; currently three of Science and History. The boys start French or Spanish in the ninth grade, and those who wish start Greek then. One of these languages can be continued for four years. They have about 2 - 2 1/2 hours of homework a night. They also have opportunities for taking Art, Music and Carpentry. In the seventh and eighth grades the boys will start Latin and Spanish, besides their normal grade school subjects, and will get as far with Algebra and perhaps Geometry as they can.

5. SCHEDULE. The school bus arrives at 8.35 a.m. Classes start at 8.40 a.m. and continue, with suitable pauses, until 3.15 p.m. High Mass is sung by monks and boys just before lunch each day. At 3.15 p.m. the boys change for athletics, which last till 4.40 p.m. The bus departs at 5:00 p.m.

6. ATHLETICS. The games played so far have been Football and Soccer in the winter; Baseball, Tennis and Track in the spring. Our gym is to be completed by September 1958. We have been playing B & C team games with such schools as CBC, Chaminade, St. Louis U. High, John Burroughs, St. Louis Country Day, Ladue, Lutheran and others.

7. COST. Tuition is $750 a year. Extras include lunch, school bus (if used), books and athletic equipment. The bus is $110 a year and lunch $108 a year. The rest depends on what the boy purchases.

8. SCHOLARSHIPS. We offer each year three scholarships of a nominal value of $100, which may be increased up to full tuition, according to the financial circumstances in each case. There is also available a certain amount of additional assistance, which varies from year to year.

9. ENTRANCE. Entrance is by an examination, held in February or thereabouts each year for the High School and for the lower grades, later. It includes papers in English and Math, an aptitude test and an interview. Account is taken of all these and of the boy's past school record.

10. BUILDINGS. The first buildings of the overall program are already well under way. We have been fortunate in getting as our architects the noted firm of Hellmuth, Obata and Kassabaum, the firm which created the Saint Louis Airport building.

11. THE BENEDICTINES. The Order was founded by St. Benedict early in the Sixth Century. In 1215 Pope Innocent III ordered the Benedictine Abbeys to form themselves into Congregations by countries. The English Abbeys were the first to complete

this organization, and the English Congregation is consequently the oldest. The various Benedictine Congregations form the Benedictine Order, and all follow the same Rule.

St. Louis Priory is a foundation (1955) from Ampleforth Abbey, in Yorkshire, England. The Ampleforth Community was first established at Westminster, a hundred years or more before the Norman invasion of England in 1066. Here the monks of this royal abbey witnessed the coronation of the Kings of England until, at the dissolution of the monasteries under Henry VIII in the Sixteenth Century, the monks of Westminster were dispersed. After a brief restoration under Queen Mary (1555-58) the Abbey was again dissolved, and it was only by the slenderest thread that the continuity of the Community was preserved until their transplantation to Dieulouard in Eastern France. Here they survived, running both a school and a brewery, until the French Revolution. Expelled from France, they returned to England where, after some wandering, they found their eventual home at Ampleforth in 1802. There, for over 150 years, they have been running a school, but no brewery.

Westminster was noted for its liturgy, Dieulouard for its strict observance, and Ampleforth for its hard, unremitting work. We hope that some heritage from all these three ancestors will pass to Saint Louis Priory.

[Comment: Father Timothy was initially lukewarm about basketball and seems, by a Freudian slip, to have omitted it from #6. We did play it from the beginning.]

Appendix B 6: List of Spaces Required. (*See* p.136):

This list appears to derive from the lists we took to the meeting and will serve to show more or less what was in our minds at that time. It deals only with the school.

Space	9/57	9/58	9/59	9/60-9/70	remarks
Chapel	1	1	1	1	The numbers are totals: in 60-70 we need 1 chapel, not 4, etc.
Classrooms	5	7	9	13	
Science rooms	2				[9/59 on, in Science Wing]
Form rooms	1	1	2	3	
Dining room	1	1	1	1	
Gymnasium	-	1	1	1	
Auditorium	-	1	1	1	use gym
Assembly	1	1	1	1	
Changing room	1	1	1	1	
Sports store	1	1	1	1	
Library	1	1	1	1	
Music area	1	1	1	1	
Art area	1	1	1	1	
Dark room	1	1	1	1	plus one in Science Wing when built
School paper	-	1	1	1	
Multi-purpose room	-	1	1	1	
Shops area	1	1	1	1	
Headmaster's area	1	1	1	1	Hm, Dean, Sec, conf. rooms, Reception, telephone exchange, etc.
General Office area	1	1	1	1	
Reception area	1	1	1	1	
Gamesmaster's room	-	1	1	1	= Athletic Director
Faculty room	-	1	1	1	with toilet
Book store and school clerk	1	1	1	1	near headmaster, include duplicating room
Health room	-	1	1	1	
Boys' locker area	-	1	1	1	NOT those in gym
Storage space	as much as possible				
Masters' lockers					1 per master for handing in homework
Public telephone	-	1	2	2	
P.A. system	-		1?	1	
Toilets					as needed

Appendix C 1: List of Retreat Givers through 1999. (*See* p.218):

1955 (at Ampleforth)
1956 (privately)
1957 Prior Aelred Graham, O.S.B.
1958 Father Christian Martin
1959 Father Benedict Brosnahan, O.S.B.
1960 Father Robert Coerver, C.M.
1961 Father Illtud Evans, O.P.
1962 Monsignor Martin Hellriegel
1963 Abbot Hilary Dreaper, O.S.B.
1964 Father Urban Schnaus, O.S.B.
1965 Abbot Columban Thuis, O.S.B.
1966 Father Hilary Martin, O.S.B.
1967 Father Augustine Schmitz, O.S.B.
1968 Abbot Alban Boultwood, O.S.B.
1969 Father Kevin Seasoltz, O.S.B.
1970 Prior Wilfrid Tunink, O.S.B.
1971 Prior Martin Boler, O.S.B.
1972 Abbot Martin Burne, O.S.B.
1973 Father David Fleming, S.J.
Father Dennis Hamm, S.J.
Father Edward Kinerk, S.J.
Father Martin Palmer, S.J.
1974 Fathers Austin, Timothy, Laurence, Miles, Ralph
Brother David
1975 Father Ambrose Wathen, O.S.B. and Priory monks.
1976 Father David Turner, O.S.B.
1977 Father Sebastian Moore,O.S.B.
1978 Prior Luke and Priory monks
1979 Abbot Jerome Hanus, O.S.B.
1980 Father John Main, O.S.B.
1981 Father Aidan Shea, O.S.B.
1982 Father Demetrius Dumm, O.S.B.
1983 Prior James Jones, O.S.B.
1984 Father Benedict Viviano, O.P.
1985 Abbot Matthew Stark, O.S.B.
1986 Father Claude Buchanan, s.P.
1987 Abbot Thomas Keating, O.C.S.O.
1988 Father Michael A. Jamail
1989 Father John Padberg, S.J.
1990 Sister Donald Corcoran,O.S.B.
1991 Father Timothy Kelly, O.S.B.
1992 Father Gerry Weber, O.M.I.
1993 Father Luke Dysinger, O.S.B.
Doctor Jane Goerss
1994 Abbot Bernard Johnson, O.C.S.O
1995 Father Thomas Ward
1996 Abbot Marcel Rooney, O.S.B.
1997 Abbot Patrick Barry, O.S.B.
1998 Abbot Francis Kline,O.C.S.O.
1999 Abbot Gregory Polan, O.S.B.

Appendix C: 2 Description of the Organ. (*See* pp.233-34):

Our twenty-eight rank, tracker-action, pipe organ was built and tested by Gregor Hradetsky Orgelbau at Krems-Donau, Austria in 1967. It is a fully baroque organ. It adopts the basic elements of the classical organs built in Europe in the seventeenth and eighteenth centuries, but combines them with the use of modern materials and technology. It is free-standing and self-contained.

It is built according to the "Werk" principle, used in those centuries but forgotten or discarded in the nineteenth and early twentieth. It has therefore a mechanical or tracker, rather than an electro-pneumatic action, being thus more durable and giving the organist more control over the speech of the pipes. The divisions of the organ—Great, Swell and Pedal—are completely separate, and no extension is used. The fourteen hundred pipes, made of tin and mahogany, are placed on slider wind chests, are unnicked and operate on a low wind-pressure. Hradetsky and Gyo Obata cooperated closely in the design of the solid oak organ case, which is beautiful in itself, acts as a soundboard, and is an integral part of the instrument. So too is the console of two manuals and pedal. It is made of oak, cherry, ebony, mahogany and ivory.

These features give the organ a clear, free-flowing and unforced tone, and because it follows the traditions of southern rather than northern Germany, its tone is warmer and less strident, and well suited to the resonance of the church.

The organ was assembled *in situ* in three weeks and voiced in another three during August and September 1967. It was dedicated by Father Columba on Sunday, 17 September at our community Mass.

The specification is:

GREAT	SWELL	PEDAL
Prinzipal 8′	Gedeckt 8′	Subbass 16′
Rohrflöte 8′	Kleingedeckt 4′	Oktavbass 8′
Oktave 4′	Prinzipal 2′	Gedecktbass 8′
Waldflöte 2′	Quint 1 1/3′	Choralbass 4′
Sesquialtera 2 ranks	Scharff 2/3, 4 ranks	Nachthorn 2′
Mixture 1 1/3, 4-6 ranks	Krummhorn 8′	Fagott 16′
Trompete 8′	Tremulant	

Appendix D 1: Father Columba's Letter to Bishop Leo C. Byrne about the Draft Statutes for the Archdiocesan Synod of 1960. (*See* p.225):

18 October 1960

Your Excellency,

You have asked me to comment, should I wish, on the new proposed Statutes for the Archdiocese of Saint Louis.

I would like to comment upon #188 and #189. If I seem to go against your wishes please forgive my doing so. It is out of a sense of duty that I do so.

In the first place these statutes show a change from the statute in force now on the same subject. The evident implication of the change is that a new policy is intended, namely to bring all Catholic schools within the Archdiocese, and not only parochial ones, under the immediate supervision and direction of the Superintendent; and not only in matters of faith and morals or in matters of general policy but in the minutiae of school management: curriculum, books, faculty qualifications and the like.

This new policy has many aspects and I respectfully submit my thoughts under the following heads.

(1) Legal aspect. As this is a law it must be considered so. It is unwise for all concerned to say "oh! no one would dream of interfering". I am quite sure that our Archbishop - who has shown such interest in us and in our Benedictine approach to education - would not, nor would Father Curtin who took so leading a part in introducing us to Saint Louis. He knows the dangers of regimentation, the deadening hand of officialdom. One might even go further and say that the American temper is against socialistic approaches. But a law is a law and a time might come when the King in Egypt no longer knew Joseph. A law must be just and workable as it stands. If we were told there would of course be no interference in detail, the fact remains that the statute does get right down to detail. This is no broad approach.

(2) From the point of view of privilege. We must remember that exempt Religious claim not only personal exemption from the jurisdiction of the Ordinary of the place but also for their schools. This question was thoroughly gone into in the last century and given in favour of the Religious. Are we to go over that battlefield again?

These statutes undoubtedly will be resisted at the highest level. In other words it is considered a usurpation of powers. Of course it may not be, but that is how I see it. Nor am I alone. Abbot Herbert K. Byrne, President of the English Benedictine Congregation, after consultation with his canonists, holds this view and hopes that a clash may be averted.

(3) From a practical point of view. Father Timothy has loyally responded to a multitude of minute enquiries in school matters from the diocesan office, out of respect not out of obligation. He would say that much of it was unnecessary and a waste of time. Would it not be wiser to admit the status quo ante and have a small body, who would act as representatives of the independent schools and meet with the Superintendent at regular intervals; there he and they would discuss matters of common interest; he point out his desires and they theirs. But this should in no way be a place of dictation but one of mutual respect and understanding, of give and take.

(4) From a human point of view. Whilst it is possible by legal enactment to have one's way against a person or group, it would be infinitely preferable to come to an understanding not by the harsh techniques of law but by the more Christian method of close human understanding.

My suggestion, therefore, dear Bishop Byrne, is that the legal approach to this thorny question be dropped and a more human one taken up. Otherwise, I foresee a great worsening in human relations between the Seculars and Regulars over this question, which is bound to rouse ire, suspicion, distaste, no matter who "wins".

If the Archbishop wishes some closer cooperation between the 'private schools and the parochial schools', let us hear what the points are and discuss them in a friendly way. Let us go to law only when no agreement can be reached. These new statutes if adhered to are the equivalent of "going to law", because they go clean contrary to an ancient privilege and one upheld by Leo XIII himself, by which the schools of Regulars are not under the immediate jurisdiction of the Ordinary of the place.

I am,
Your Excellency,
Yours humbly and obediently in Christ,

Columba Cary-Elwes, O.S.B.

Appendix D 2: Father Timothy's Letter on High School Entrance. (*See* p.297):

A submission by Father Timothy to the Archdiocesan Committee on the topic.

1. In the Bad Old Days a candidate for high school might have to take as many as five examinations with all their attendant strain, wear and tear, disruption, and so on. The present system is certainly a vast improvement on that.

   It may be, however, that the pendulum has swung too far and that the present system, in achieving simplicity, has become monolithic and has lost the necessary flexibility.
2. In particular, it appears to be vulnerable at the following points:
   a. Some schools are still reluctant to rely solely on 'objective' multiple choice tests.
   b. In practice, the parents' and students' choice among the private schools is restricted to one. From personal experience, I can say that many parents and students deprecate this, and that a good deal of tension and sense of injustice is caused thereby. This has repercussions in both the High Schools and the grade schools.
   c. This restriction also operates, in fact, especially against our school (and perhaps other very small schools) because -
      i. Prospective scholarship candidates who want to go to a private school are put off applying to us when failure to win a scholarship here (which for any individual is quite likely with so small a number of scholarships available) would mean that they forfeited their chance of a private school education. They would not be able to afford the tuition here and would not have a second chance to apply for a scholarship at any other private school.
      ii. Regular candidates are also discouraged by the small number (twenty or less) of places available. For them, too, failure to qualify means their forfeiture of a chance of private school education.
   d. It is hard that the scheme works so much to the disadvantage of a school not represented on the committee, especially when the committee is, in fact, a policy-making body.
3. The Ampleforth Community was invited by the Most Reverend Archbishop to set up a school in Saint Louis with a specialized and very clearly defined purpose. The *Statement of Principles* presented to the Ampleforth Community by the Saint Louis delegation, on which Fr. Curtin served as the Archbishop's representative, says inter alia, "it is intended that, within the limits of scholarship funds to be available, the school shall be open on the basis of merit to boys from the entire archdiocese". This, and the other purposes for which the Archbishop invited the school to his archdiocese will

be frustrated unless we have a fair chance, on level terms, of attracting suitable students. I predicted last year that the new scheme would effect this frustration. The facts subsequently showed that, had we gone along strictly with the scheme, such would indeed have been the result.

4. The following possibilities are, therefore, put forward:
   a. That there should be TWO administrations of the S.R.A. test and that any candidate should be free to take both.

or b. That candidates submit a list of three schools in order of preference and that their scores, together with their order of preference, be released simultaneously to each of the three schools.

or c. That the S.R.A. test be administered on the stated date, and that any school that wishes should be free to set its own private test on one, and only one, other stated date. e.g. the S.R.A. test on January 28 and the private tests on January 21st; or, the S.R.A. test on January 28 and the private tests on February 4th.

5. 4a meets objections 2b and 2c above, but would greatly increase the administrative burden.
   4b also meets objections 2b and 2c but would complicate the admission problem of individual schools.
   4c seems to meet all the objections and still confines the testing program to two days. It is a great improvement on the Bad Old Days, and yet retains a degree of flexibility.
   4c is, therefore, recommended.
6. It is hard to see any alternative solution for us which would not in practice substitute financial for intellectual criteria of admission. Were we to yield to this temptation, we should certainly be guilty of 'selling the pass'. I should also be failing in my duty to my own superiors if I concealed from the committee their view that under the existing arrangements, unless some modification can be made, the Archbishop's hopes and wishes for this school cannot be realized. Fr. Abbot has written to me on this matter that "its gravity could scarcely be overestimated".
7. I hope that the committee will be able to give this sympathetic and favorable consideration

Salvis praescriptis canonum quorumlibet C.J.C.
Respectfully submitted

21 November 1960

Timothy Horner O.S.B.

Appendix D 3: Father Luke's Plans for Expansion. (*See* p.402):

On 18 May 1967 Father Luke presented the following plans to the Directors of the Saint Louis Priory Society:

First; The Priory needs a number of buildings; these will upgrade the present facilities that are in part temporary and inadequate, and will serve all the boys in the school; they will also provide space for the extra boys we plan to take.

Secondly; a number of buildings will be highly desirable once the school reaches the 300 mark. The sooner the Priory has these facilities, the better the program the school can offer.

Thirdly; Priory will always have an eye to the future, as well as to excellence here and now. When the essentials are a reality in the mid-seventies, we envisage reaching the optimum in facilities. This will give us a plant of outstanding quality and provide practically all but classrooms when the time comes for yet further increase in student enrollment.

Chart A—First Priority

Step One 1967-1968

New Junior House	$350,000	
Varsity Fields	50,000	
Subtotal	$400,000	

Step Two 1969-1970

Upper School Classrooms	$250,000	
Administration, Faculty, Miscellaneous	350,000	
Library	500,000	
Subtotal	$1,100,000	
Total		$1,500,000

Chart B—Second Priority

1971-1973

Auditorium	$500,000	
Multi-purpose Activities	250,000	
Maintenance Building	100,000	
Roads, Parking	75,000	
Total		$925,000

Chart C -- Third Priority

Refectory	$400,000	
General Student Activities	350,000	
General Administration	200,000	
Roads, Parking	75,000	
Total		$1,025,000

Grand Total		$3,450,000

Appendix E 1: List of Faculty September 1956 - June 1973, starting in September each year. (*See* p.337):

	56	57	58	59	60	61	62	63	64	65	66	67	68	69	70	71	72
Father Columba (Prior 1955-67)	x	x	x	x	x	x	x	x	x	x	x						
Father Luke* (Prior 1967-89)	x	x	x	x													
Father Timothy (Headmaster 1955-74)	x	x	x	x	x	x	x	x	x	x	x	x	x	x	x	x	x
Father Augustine				x	x	x	x	x									
Father Austin			x	x	x	x	x	x	x	x	x	x	x	x	x	x	x
Father Bede		x															
Father Benedict												x	x	x	x	x	x
Father Brendan			x	x													
Brother Christopher Rush											x						
Father Colin									x	x	x	x	x	x	x	x	x
Father Finbarr (from Jan. 71)															x	x	x
Father Ian (until Oct. 69)	x	x	x	x	x	x	x	x	x	x	x	x	x	x			
Brother James Winkler											x	x	x	x			
Brother John Dahm*													x				
Father Laurence						x								x	x	x	x
Father Leonard					x	x	x	x	x	x	x	x	x	x	x		
Father Miles										x	x	x	x	x	x	x	x
Father Nicholas						x	x	x	x	x	x	x	x	x			
Brother Noel (from Jan. 72 and see Richard Murphy, below)*																x	x
Father Paul				x	x	x	x	x	x	x	x	x	x	x	x	x	x
Father Ralph															x	x	x
Father Thomas		x	x	x	x	x	x	x	x	x	x	x	x	x	x	x	x
Father Vincent Wace*																	x

	56	57	58	59	60	61	62	63	64	65	66	67	68	69	70	71	72
Rev. Michael Azkoul															x		
Yvon Baber							x	x									
Robert L. Bannister				x	x	x	x	x									
J. Brian Barry					x	x	x	x	x	x	x	x	x	x	x	x	x
David E. Beckner								x	x	x	x	x	x	x	x	x	x
James C. Bowman											x						
Donald W. Bussmann M.D.*					x	x	x	x	x	x	x	x	x				
James Caffery (from Jan. 71)															x	x	x
Dr. Harry J. Cargas*																	x
Richard V. Cavanaugh																x	x
William T. Collins									x								
Edward K. Cook			x	x	x	x	x	x	x	x	x	x	x	x	x	x	x
Daniel G. Croghan		x															
Egon Doering*															x	x	x
Rev. David Dooley*								x									
Robert C. Dunn*								x	x	x	x	x	x	x	x		
James R. Ellington															x		
Paul J. Fingerhut															x	x	x
David J. Fraser									x								
James W. Fullinwider																x	x
Calvin F. Gatch													x	x	x		
Thomas N. Geiss									x	x	x	x	x	x	x	x	x
Joseph A. Genoni																x	x
Henry G. Gilland (Part time in 69)										x	x	x	x	x			
Austin M. Gomez																x	x
George Hereford*															x		
S. Richard Heyman*														x			
George Hickenlooper*			x														
Rudolph Imm*											x						
Clinton P. Jakeman								x									
Paul M. Jurkowitz																	x
Donald L. Kettelkamp			x	x													
Stephen R. Kinsella							x	x	x								
Ervin T. Leimer	x																

	56	57	58	59	60	61	62	63	64	65	66	67	68	69	70	71	72
J. Tracey Leiweke												x					
Bart J. Margiotta															x	x	x
Paul M. Marquis*											x	x					
Edward G. Marsh*					x	x	x	x	x	x	x	x	x	x	x		
Martin R. McCabe							x	x	x	x	x	x	x	x	x	x	x
Joseph P. McKenna*																x	
J. Reynolds Medart*		x	x	x	x	x	x	x	x	x	x	x	x	x	x	x	x
Michael D. Metzger (Br. Hugh)										x		x		x			
Jerome J. Miller									x	x	x	x	x	x	x	x	x
Larry Miller*		x															
Van Moomjian														x			
James F. Moran (from Jan. 61)					x												
Richard C. Murphy (see Br. Noel, above) (from Jan. 72)*																x	x
J. Gerard Mudd, M.D.*					x	x	x	x	x	x	x	x	x	x	x	x	x
Alexander C. Niven			x	x	x	x											
James T. O'Neill			x	x													
John B. Peters*	x																
S. Samuel Pomeroy																x	x
Edward J. Presti			x	x													
William H. Quayle										x	x						
Harriet Reinhardt*													x	x			
Roy C. Rishoi*						x	x										
Walter J. Ruesch					x	x	x										
Albert J. Salsich								x									
Edward Sarmiento		x															
W. Curtis Schade															x		
Kenneth J. Scheibal*	x	x	x	x													
Frank L. Schmertz									x	x	x	x	x	x	x		
Robert E. Schnorf*											x	x	x				
Herbert J. Schweich				x	x												
Charles Scott*									x	x	x	x	x	x	x	x	x
Mrs. Singer*	x																
Thaddeus Strobach							x										
Mrs. Edwin S. Taylor*		x															
Rudolph Torrini*		x	x	x													
Anthony R. Treweek*						x											

	56	57	58	59	60	61	62	63	64	65	66	67	68	69	70	71	72
Bernhardt Voss*									x	x							
Mr. Walker*	x																
Mrs. Frank E. Walleman*																x	x
Richard Weekes*				x	x												
Stephen Weinress											x	x					
Gerald L. Wilkes					x	x	x	x	x	x	x	x	x	x	x	x	x
Brent J. Williams*		x	x														
Joseph Winkelmann*										x							
James J. Wochner													x	x	x		
James L. Wortham																x	x
David L. Yarian														x			

N.B.

1. * signifies "part-time", often but not always in one of our Activities. We recognize that men like Reynolds Medart often put in full time.
2. Professor McKenna gave four lectures on Economics in 1972.
3. Drs. Avioli, Boldt, Horan (our alumnus of '63), Kinsella, Lindeman, Monafo, Pernoud and Tucker joined Dr. Mudd in 1972 in lecturing to the seniors on Biology.

Appendix E 2: Block Program of Courses. (*See* p.291):

a. *September 1960*

FORM	I	II	III	III	IV	IV	V	V	VI	VI
SET			B	A	B	A	B	A	B	A
Religion	3	3	4	4	3	3	3	3	4	4
Latin	5	5	5	5	5	5	5	5	5	5
Math	5	5	5	5	5	5	5	5	5	5
English	5	5	5	5	4	4	4	4	4	4
History	3	3	5	-	3	3	3	3	3	3
Science	*	*	-	-	5	5	5	5	6	6
French	5	5	5	5	-	5	-	5	-	5
Spanish	-	-	-	-	5	-	5	-	5	-
EPE	-	-	-	-	-	-	-	-	2	2
Greek	-	-	-	5	-	4	-	4	-	?
Study Hall	5	4	3	3	4	-	4	-	-	-
Gen. Knowledge	-	-	1	1	-	-	-	-	1	1
Choir	1	1	-	-	-	-	-	-	1	1
Music	1	1	-	-	-	-	-	-	-	-
Speech	-	1	1	1	-	-	-	-	-	-
Form masters	-	-	1	1	1	1	1	1	1	1
Activities	2	2	-	-	-	-	-	-	-	-

*= one period in alternate years, taken from Study Hall

NOTES:

1. VI Form must take Religion, Math., English, History and EPE, one language, Choir and General Knowledge. They add five periods:
   EITHER a whole year of Science or of a second language;
   OR a half year of Science and a half year of a second language;
   OR a half year of a second language and a half year of a third language.
   N.B. Biology will run for three periods a week right through the year, as will the half year of languages.
2. After this year History will not be taken in Form VI.
3. In Form III, Greek and History are alternatives.
4. All three periods of speech should be scheduled consecutively on the same afternoon.
5. French supersedes Spanish year by year.
6. EPE = Elementary Politics and Economics.

b. *September 1972*

FORM	I			II			III		
SET	a	b	β	a	b	β	a	b	c
Religion	5	5	5	4	4	4	3	3	3
Latin	5	5	5	5	5	5	5	5	5
Math	5	5	5	5	5	5	5	5	5
English	5	5	5	5	5	5	5	5	5
History	4	4	4	4	4	4			
Chemistry							3	3	3
Biology				3	3	3			
French	5	5	5	5	5	5	5	5	5
Greek							5		
Government								4	4
Speech				1	1	1			
Lecture Series	1	1	1	1	1	1	1	1	1
Handwriting	1	1	1						
Study Hall	2	2	2						
Reading Period							2	3	3
Activities	2	2	2	2	2	2			

FORM	IV			V			VI	
SET	a	b	c	a	b	c	a	b
Religion	3	3	3	3	3	3		
Seminar							3	3
Latin	5	5		5			5	
Classical Background			3					
Math	5	5	5	5	5	5	5	5
English	4	4	4	5	5	5	5	5
History	3	3	5	5	5	5	5	5
Physics				5	5	5	4	
Chemistry	3	3	3					4
Biology	2	2	2				3	3
French	5	5	5	5	5		5	5
Spanish						5		5
Greek	4							
Lecture Series				1	1	1	1	1
Study Hall				1	5	5	2	2
Intramural							1	1
Reading Period		4	4					

N.B. In forms V and VI students did not take all the subjects shown.

Appendix E 3: Breakdown of Courses 1964-65. (*See* p.291):

[This is a summary, by grades, of what was covered in the various courses. It may be taken as true, by and large, for all years up to 1964-65. But in June 1964, we graduated the first class to contain some who had started in the seventh grade. As we reflected on their achievement, we thought we should reorganize the curriculum so as to offer in the eleventh and twelfth grades fewer subjects but in greater depth. Our first steps in this direction are shown in Appendix E.4. The following was the state of affairs in September 1964:]

Religious Instruction — In the seventh and eighth grades the focus was on the New Testament and the new Catholic Catechism; in the ninth grade, on the Old Testament; in the tenth on Church History; in the eleventh on Moral Theology,and in the twelfth on the existence of God and the application of reason to Theology.

Latin — In grades seven through nine, English textbooks were used to give an introduction to the grammar and syntax from Hillard and Botting, North and Hillard, Kennedy's *Latin Grammar*, [names familiar to every English schoolboy of those days]. In the eighth grade they started to read Caesar; in the ninth, Ovid; in the tenth, Cicero and Virgil; in the eleventh more of the same, and in the twelfth, Plautus and Terence, Catullus and Horace for the Advanced Placement Examinations. The B set, and those who entered in the ninth grade followed a similar course at a slower pace and did not get so far.

Greek — The course started in the ninth grade. Again, English textbooks were used for the foundations, leading to the reading of Plato's *Apology* in the eleventh grade, and Euripides' *Medea* in the twelfth, if any ventured that far.

English — In the seventh and eighth grades there was a mixture of grammar (based on Warriner's *Handbook of English*) composition and reading, which included Shakespeare's *Julius Caesar*, Brother Raphael's *A Book of Stories* and Sister Theresa Clare's *A Book of Poetry*. In the ninth grade, they added Browne's *A Book of Non-fiction* and the old-fashioned but invaluable Clay's *Certificate English Practice*, which contained practice in précis-writing and other such. They also read Shakespeare's *Richard the Third*. In the tenth grade they used Engels and Engels' *Writing Technique* and read Shakespeare's *Macbeth* and Shaw's *Arms and the Man* . In the eleventh grade they read Shakespeare's *Hamlet* and Shaw's *Caesar and Cleopatra* , and extracts from West and Stallmann's *The Art of Modern*

Fiction and Williams' *Immortal Poems*. In the twelfth grade the emphasis was on the theatre, ancient and modern, with the addition of Milton's *Paradise Lost*. Again, the B set and those who entered in the ninth grade did a similar but reduced course.

Mathematics The seventh and eighth grades used Durell's *General Arithmetic for Schools* which they completed, and Weeks and Adkins' *First course in Algebra* and *A Course in Geometry*, in both of which they went as far as they could. In the ninth and tenth grades both sets pursued algebra and plane geometry, with the A set starting solid geometry and elementary trigonometry in the tenth. In the eleventh grade the A set took algebra, trigonometry, analytic geometry and elementary calculus, and the B set went on with algebra and started elementary trigonometry and a little solid geometry. In the twelfth grade the A set took the Advanced Placement course in calculus and analytic geometry and the B set took algebra, trigonometry, analytic geometry and an introduction to calculus.

French The basic text was Micks and Longi's *Fundamental French* with the various levels of Mauger's *Langue et Civilisation Françaises* coming in at the ninth grade. By the twelfth grade they were reading Molière, Rostand, Pascal's *Pensées*, etc.

Spanish was not offered this year.

History In the seventh and eighth grades, the focus was on geography. The ninth graders studied Ancient World History to the Middle Ages; tenth graders American History; eleventh graders World History from the Middle Ages on; twelfth graders had an introduction to Politics and Economics, including the social encyclicals.

Science This was started in the tenth grade. In this and in the eleventh grade the text was Hogg, Bickel and Little's *Physics and Chemistry - A Unified Approach*, books I and II. In the tenth grade in Physics, the text covered mensuration, properties of matter and the mechanics of liquids and gases; in Chemistry, a thorough grounding. In the eleventh grade they covered in Physics statics, dynamics, optics, electricity and magnetism, sound and heat. In Chemistry they covered the rest of a normal high school course. In the twelfth grade, the A set's text was Sisler, Vander Werf and Davidson's *College Chemistry*, leading to the Advanced Placement examination. The B set took, in the first semester, a normal introductory course in Biology, followed by a semester of Human Biology from Drs. Mudd and Bussmann.

Appendix E 4: Notes on the Curriculum (July 1964). (*See* p.291):

[N.B. This was a planning document, a basis for discussion. It shows what was in our minds at the time. This is a slightly simplified version.]

1. In Sept. 65. Science could receive three periods a week in Form III [ninth grade] taken from study halls. With these, one semester of Biology, i.e. the botany and zoology, could be fitted in before the senior year (perhaps in the junior year).

   Then in the senior year the whole class could have the human biology from Drs. Mudd and Bussmann either two or three periods a week.

   Art Lecture and Classical Background or General Knowledge, or all three, could be put back into the junior year, but boys who take Greek would then miss them.

   OR if the History curriculum were reorganized, possibly Elementary Politics and Economics could go back into Form V, and these three periods be given to seniors' Biology. For details, see 2. below.

2. Science - September 1964

Form III 1 semester of Biology after Christmas
IV Physics/Chemistry
V Physics/Chemistry
VI A Chemistry
B Biology - Botany & Zoology before Christmas
- Mudd & Bussmann after Christmas

September 1965

Form III 3 periods of Physics/Chemistry throughout year
IV Physics/Chemistry
V A Physics/Chemistry before Christmas
Biology after Christmas
B Biology before Christmas
Physics/Chemistry after Christmas
VI Chemistry A.P.
Physics A.P.
Whole senior class: 2/3 periods of Biology from M/B
N.B. This class would not get botany and zoology, but all would get human biology.

September 1966

Form III 3 periods of Physics/Chemistry throughout the year
IV Physics/Chemistry
V Physics/Chemistry (these boys had Biology in Form III)
VI Chemistry A.P.
Physics A.P.

Whole senior class 2/3 periods of Biology from M/B

N.B. This class would have had botany & zoology in Form V in 1965.

September 1967

Form III as 1966

IV as 1966

V as 1965

VI as 1966 and thus in subsequent years.

3. History See para 1. above. We should try to offer American History as an A.P. subject in the senior year, as an alternative. Seniors would then choose any TWO of Latin, French, Science and History. A possible arrangement:

Grade	*1964/65*	*1965/66*	*1966/67*	*1967/68 and after*
7	Geography	Ancient History	Ancient History	Ancient History
8	Geography	American History	American History	American History
9	(Anct. Hist.)	(Anct. Hist.)	(?)	(?Geography?)
10	Amer. Hist.	World History	World History	World History
11	World Hist.	EPE	EPE	EPE..
12	EPE	EPE.	A.P. Amer. Hist.	A.P. Amer. Hist.

N.B. In grade 9, the subjects are alternatives to Greek. In grades 11 and 12, EPE = Elementary Politics and Economics.

4. This whole scheme is a first step toward the pursuit of fewer subjects in greater depth in the senior and perhaps junior years. This seems possible and desirable now that all boys enter in the seventh grade, so that the class as a whole may be expected to reach the minimum acceptable level in a broad range of subjects rather earlier than now.

Appendix E 5: Religious Instruction. (*See* p.291):

a. Syllabus

[In response to Vatican II, the program was reorganized by Father Miles as follows:]

Seventh Grade: Textbooks were The Bible, Confraternity edition, and Grollenberg"s *Shorter Atlas of the Bible*. The theme was a thorough survey of the history of Israel from Abraham to Solomon, showing God's love for his chosen people and the continuance of that love for us.

Eighth Grade: Textbooks were the Bible as before, and Novak, *The Lord of History*. The theme was a continuation of the survey from after Solomon to the eve of the coming of Christ, and an acquaintance with the message of the prophets; all this seen as revelation of God's dealing with us. Creation, the Fall, Cain and Abel and Noah were introduced.

Ninth Grade: Textbooks were *The Shorter Knox Bible*, *The Illustrated New Testament*, and *Hi-Time*, a series of pamphlets on topics such as happiness, forgiveness, peer pressure, racism, etc. The theme was getting to know Jesus Christ, our Redeemer, and so love him more easily and follow him in service more effectively. This was based on selected chapters of the Gospels and 1 Corinthians.

Tenth Grade: The same textbooks and theme, with a further selection of chapters.

Eleventh Grade: Textbooks were *The Shorter Knox Bible* and the complete Knox *New Testament*, with Sheed, *God and the Human Condition*, vol. 1. The aim was to give the boys a taste and aptitude for theological thinking, talking and writing, and to lead them to a more mature understanding of the nature and demands of Christian morality.

Twelfth Grade: The textbooks and aim were the same. In this year the emphasis was more on dogmatic theology and less on morals. The particular topics were left very much to the teachers.

b. Underlying theory

[This interpretation of Vatican II was written by Father Finbarr about eight years later than Father Miles' syllabus:]

The religious education program at Priory aims to be a strong formative element in helping people to develop a strong sense of their relationship with one another before God. The persons primarily in view are the students in their growth from the seventh through the twelfth grades. Also involved are the faculty, both monastic and lay. Around and with these elements are the parents and families of the students and the friends of the Priory.

The basic starting point is the life of each person as experienced on and away from the School campus. This life is in the context of a complex contemporary society. Here a person encounters an array of positive and negative values. There are strong currents of opinion fostering a desire for social justice, peace and brotherhood, a meaning in life which transcends the limits of our experience, a bewildering sense of technological advances. Clear also is a confidence that man has the almost unlimited ability to progress as he desires. On the other hand there is widespread fear, social and cultural disintegration, violence and injustice, poverty and prejudice. Thus there is a confusion of hope and despair.

Young Christians have a desire to see truly human values prevail in society and they have the energy to achieve this. The older Christians have the experience gained in triumphing over previous obstacles. The young are drawn on by visions of building peace founded on justice and love. The elders have the wisdom nurtured by a life in the midst of a pluralistic and merciless society. It is through the interaction of these varied elements that the Christian community is formed and in turn the community forms the individual Christian.

The Priory school has a predominantly academic character. It is inevitable that religious studies in the school will be approached in this light. This allows for a certain scriptural and historical knowledge to be acquired in the early years. Such learning provides a basis for the moral and philosophical explorations of the later years. Thus the studies are intended to make a boy's faith become living, conscious and active, through the light of instruction (Vat II Bps, 14). These formal religious studies should foster a real conviction of the reasonableness of the Christian faith.

The family and, to a lesser extent, the school communities are the context within which the young Christian first experiences the vitality of the Christian way of life. The religious and social values reflected in these communities form the living tradition within which his own faith must mature. This process is favoured by a perceivable harmony between the asserted values and the experienced way of life. A boy can perceive this harmony more easily when the values are simply expressed and clearly and unashamedly followed.

A prominent value in our time is the freedom of each person to follow his or her own lights. The Vatican Council II declared that this freedom means that all men are to be immune from coercion on the part of individuals or of social groups or of any human power, in such wise that in matters religious no one is to be forced to act in a manner contrary to his or her own beliefs. This freedom has its foundation in the very dignity of the human person.

Jesus prayed that all might be one, united in the peace that He alone could give. Today, in many parts of the world, under the inspiring grace of the Holy Spirit, multiple efforts are being made through prayer, word and action to attain that fulness of unity which Jesus desires. The concern to realize unity is a matter for all Christians. It should be true of the young in a special way, because they will have to carry the burdens which such a process of reunification will undoubtedly entail. Hence the ecumenical dimension of the Christian life and education is of utmost contemporary importance.

The religious studies at Priory are thus conceived as an integral part of the formation of persons mature in spirit and with the courage and the competence to respond to the call, which the Father of all addresses to each person, to be guided by the Spirit in the following of His son Jesus.

Appendix E 6: Table of Scores in Achievement Tests. (*See* p.302):

Scores are the average of the best score by each student in each subject. The number taking each subject is shown in parentheses.

Class of	Number in class	English Comp.	Mathematics Intermediate	Mathematics Advanced	Latin	French
1960	28	573 (28)	554 (23)	674 (3)	576 (11)	497 (10)
1961	22	515 (22)	553 (16)	682 (6)	509 (8)	480 (4)
1962	17	534 (17)	556 (11)	706 (6)	568 (4)	575 (3)
1963	28	546 (28)	526 (11)	650 (17)	600 (11)	426 (4)
1964	29	548 (28)	559 (17)	676 (11)	625 (10)	491 (21)
			Level 1			
1965	35	590 (34)	574 (16)	723 (19)	642 (15)	510 (16)
			Level 1	Level 2		
1966	31	571 (31)	583 (20)	725 (11)	556 (17)	536 (14)
1967	28	600 (28)	593 (14)	682 (14)	618 (5)	542 (24)
1968	31	586 (30)	610 (16)	720 (14)	598 (8)	595 (16)
1969	25	608 (25)	589 (9)	724 (16)	634 (7)	631 (15)
1970	33	634 (33)	616 (12)	731 (20)	570 (9)	634 (23)
1971	29	626 (28)	611 (14)	708 (14)	584 (1)	626 (24)
1972	25	602 (25)	616 (9)	738 (16)	660 (13)	613 (15)
1973	29	586 (28)	584 (12)	711 (16)	655 (12)	623 (14)

Class of	No. in class	Spanish	Social Studies	American History	Chemistry	Physics	Biology
1960	28	526 (7)	543 (6)	- -	511 (25)	569 (7)	- -
1961	22	447 (5)	469 (4)	- -	462 (13)	433 (19)	- -
1962	17	494 (6)	503 (2)	- -	563 (13)	592 (1)	- -
1963	28	477 (10)	- -	615 (1)	623 (27)	- -	529 (2)
1964	29	- -	614 (1)	496 (13)	600 (21)	- -	606 (1)
			European History				
1965	35	- -	629 (5)	- -	609 (27)	678 (3)	- -
1966	31	- -	485 (2)	534 (2)	571 (24)	610 (4)	- -
1967	28	- -	- -	563 (7)	580 (20)	- -	503 (1)
1968	31	- -	573 (5)	510 (2)	582 (19)	580 (22)	508 (2)
1969	25	Literature	- -	689 (2)	685 (8)	599 (17)	733 (1)
1970	33	664 (7)	- -	488 (3)	680 (12)	599 (25)	435 (1)
1971	29	587 (6)	- -	- -	607 (17)	654 (12)	- -
1972	25	710 (1)	537 (3)	- -	676 (17)	615 (15)	- -
1973	29	- -	560 (3)	- -	673 (16)	637 (12)	- -

N.B. In view of what we said about "recentering" (p. 196, note 136) it is reasonable to suppose that any score in 1960 was worth a little more than the same score in 1973. For the subjects listed above, a score of 600 on the old scale would, on average, be worth 631 in 1994, when the recentered scale was introduced.

Appendix E 7: Summary of Seniors' Scores in Advanced Placement Tests through 1973. (*See* p.304):

	ENGLISH					MATHEMATICS											CHEMISTRY					LATIN 5				
	5	4	3	2	1	5	4	3	2	1		5	4	3	2	1	5	4	3	2	1	5	4	3	2	1
1960	-	-	2	6	1												-	-	1	-	-					
1961	-	-	1	5	1	-	-	2	-	-							-	-	1	3	-					
1962	-	-	-	5	1	-	-	1	-	-							-	-	2	3	1					
1963	-	1	-	8	2	-	2	1	2	3							1	1	4	5	1	-	1	2	4	1
1964	-	-	7	7	-	-	1	4	2	-							-	-	5	4	2	-	4	3	3	-
1965	1	-	7	11	-	1	3	5	8	-							-	5	5	-	-	1	5	4	1	-
1966	-	2	4	7	1	-	4	1	4	1							1	-	2	1	-	-	-	4	2	2
1967	1	1	2	8	1	-	-	3	3	1							-	3	4	1	-	-	-	1	2	3
1968	-	1	8	6	2	-	1	4	4	1							-	-	4	1	-	-	1	3	3	1
						CALCULUS BC						CALCULUS AB														
1969	-	2	11	1	-	1	2	3	1	-		-	3	-	3	1	-	4	1	2	1	1	3	1	-	-
1970	5	3	4	5	1	2	2	5	2	-			1	1	3	1	2	2	5	-	2					
1971	2	4	6	5	-	-	2	3	2	-		-	1	1	2	-	-	1	4	2	-					
1972	2	1	8	2	1	2	-	1	-	-		-	5	3	1	-	1	-	3	2	-	1	5	4	-	-
1973	2	3	10	-	-	4	-	2	-	-		-	1	3	1	-	1	3	6	1	2	1	1	-	-	-
TOTALS	13	18	70	76	11	<	<	<	10	28	43	38	8	>	>	>	6	19	47	25	9	4	20	22	15	7

(continued)

	FRENCH LANGUAGE					P H Y S I C S										AMERICAN HISTORY					ALL SUBJECTS				
	5	4	3	2	1	5	4	3	2	1	5	4	3	2	1	5	4	3	2	1	5	4	3	2	1
1960						-	-	-	2	3											-	-	3	8	4
1961																					-	-	4	8	1
1962																					-	-	3	8	2
1963																					1	5	7	19	7
1964																					-	5	19	16	2
1965						-	-	-	1	-											3	13	21	21	-
1966						-	-	2	1	6						-	-	1	2	2	1	6	14	17	12
1967																1	-	-	2	1	2	4	10	16	6
1968						-	1	1	3	2						-	2	5	-	-	-	6	25	17	6

	(French Lang.)					PHYSICS C						PHYSICS B					(Amer. Hist)					(All subjects)				
1969												-	2	4	-	-	-	3	5	-	-	2	19	25	7	2
1970						1	-	-	-	-		3	1	-	1	1	2	3	9	6	-	15	12	24	17	5
1971						-	1	1	-	-		-	-	5	2	-	-	2	6	1	-	2	11	26	14	-
1972	-	-	1	4	-	1	1	-	-	-		-	2	3	1	-	-	4	4	-	-	7	18	27	10	1
1973	-	-	-	1	-	1	-	-	1	-		-	-	-	1	-	-	3	2	1	-	9	11	23	6	2
TOTALS	-	-	1	5	-	>	>	>	6	8	16	13	12	<	<	<	3	17	32	12	3	42	110	231	184	50

N.B. 1. Two or more digits shown vertically in the same column should be read as if they were side by side: e.g. the totals for All Subjects are 42, 110, 231, 184 and 50.

2. The totals for Mathematics and Physics are, in each case, combined totals for both levels of test.

Appendix E 8: David Chaplin's Address to the Class of 1970. (*See* pp.321-22):

Fr. Austin, Fr. Timothy, faculty members, parents, alumni, and friends:

I wish to address you concerning the future of this graduating class. But before I begin, I would like to ask for a few moments of silence in respect for those who have died in Vietnam and for those of us who will end our lives there.

In the beginning, God made the world. God created man to have dominion over the world. Then God was made flesh to teach man of his commitment to make and remake this world. God made man the only creature with a purpose outside of himself. This purpose is to cultivate and perfect a world of justice for all men. Each generation must approach this goal in a different manner. The challenge lies in evaluating the foundations or principles upon which the society is built and, if necessary, changing them. In particular, the challenge that faces the class of 1970 is this: what roles are we to assume in our economic and political structure? A decade ago, Bob Dylan first sang these words:

Come gather round people wherever you roam
And admit that the waters around you have grown,
And accept that soon you'll be drenched to the bone.
If your time to you is worth savin'
Then you'd better start swimmin' or you'll sink like a stone.
For the times, they are a-changing.

The nature and quality of life are changing, and unless we become involved in the world, it will just pass us by. We must commit ourselves to a person or a cause. Commitment means involvement, trust, selflessness, in other words --- love.

The youth of America does not see love in our world: rather it sees war, poverty, racism, and violence. Students have no desire to participate in a politically corrupt and culturally insane society which kills a million Vietnamese, pretends not to notice starvation, oppresses black people in filthy ghettoes, destroys the environment, and punishes as a capital offense dissent at Kent State and Jackson State. This is not our dream and it cannot be yours.

In three months, this class is going to be confronted with the reality which is America today, for universities merely reflect the American reality. At college, we will continue our education, not only through traditional courses of study but by making use of the full potential of the campus and student body. We will educate our consciences and formulate our ideals. We will search for the truth.

We will search for the truth by trying new ways of conducting our lives. We wish to break away from the traditions that force us to drink beverages from aluminum cans which cannot be disposed of. They and other pollutants make our world ugly. Soon our world will be so ugly and cluttered that our sensitivity to art will be dulled to the point that beauty is meaningless. We wish to break away from the traditions that force us to transport ourselves in vehicles that make the air unbreathable. We no longer wish to allow the murder that takes place in Vietnam and is commonplace in our cities. We will not exhaust ourselves in the pursuit of wealth that we have found is only an opiate for the soul. Our material goods do not bring us joy. We will not be content with taking up a position as a cogwheel in our economic machine that measures its success in growth. Growth implies the accumulation of wealth. This wealth comes from nature. This wealth comes from those who do not have the power to protect their meager possessions. This wealth is not paid back.

We fear that to assume the traditional position of bright college graduates in this machine would mean that we would be perpetuating the selfishness that dehumanizes man. We cannot see that our world is progressing towards the ideal that Jesus set up for us. We cannot take part in such a society. Instead we will pursue a society in which service is the measure of success. We will attempt to build relationships with our brothers to help dispel the loneliness that fills this world We will try to help each other in our searching, we will have breakthroughs and we will have failures. We will be praised and we will be condemned We will rejoice and we will despair We ask only that you support our search for the good life . We ask for your help and advice. But most of all, we ask for your involvement in the world. We ask that you share your knowledge and happiness with others. Give your time to others. Finally, we ask that you have faith in us. Pray for the courage to sustain the truth and to reject that which breeds inhumanity. Pray that we may have patience. And pray for wisdom and stamina. In the words of folk singers Crosby, Stills, Nash and Young, "Carry on. Love is coming. Love is coming to us all."

Appendix E 9: Notes on College Entrance (revised 1972). (*See* p.330):

1. PREFACE — There are well over 2000 accredited universities and colleges in the U.S. How can one set about making a sensible choice? Fortunately it is with college as it is with marriage, and most students are very well suited by any one of a fair number of institutions. It is a great mistake to think that "one particular college is the only one for me."

The following are a few brief hints for parents and their sons.

2. BIBLIOGRAPHY — These are very useful books:

The College Handbook. College Entrance Examination Board, Box 592, Princeton, N.J. 08540 $4.75
Gives invaluable information, but only about C.E.E.B. member colleges.

Comparative Guide to American Colleges. Harper & Row $3.95
by Cass and Birnbaum
The discriminating reader can glean a good deal of information between the lines of this rather "subjective" guide.

College Ahead by Eugene S. Wilson & Charles A. Bucher	Harcourt	$4.50
Who Gets into College & Why by Charles H. Doebler	McFadden Books (paperback)	$ .75
How to Prepare for College by A.H. Lass	Pocket Books Inc. (GC 954)	$ .95
The College Student's Handbook by A.H. Lass & Eugene Wilson	David White Co. (paperback)	$1.95
Catalogues of various colleges	Many are available in school library, or in Fr. Paul's office.	

There are many other reputable works too.

3. WHY GO TO COLLEGE? — It is becoming more and more important that your son should have a reasonably clear idea why he is going to college, and should not do so just because everyone else does. This is a matter well worth discussing at home.

4. WHO CHOOSES?	Almost universally the student chooses, which seems right. But he would be foolish indeed not to seek advice and hold discussion with his parents and the school.
5. HOW TO CHOOSE	The following considerations may help your son to reduce the field to a group of manageable size, from which the final "short list" will be chosen:

<u>Can I get in?</u>	Be realistic, but not at this stage pessimistic. Bear in mind that state universities have higher standards for admission of non-residents.
<u>Can I stay in without undue pressure?</u>	On the whole, private schools, once they admit you, have fewer drop-outs than state schools; you do need *some* time for non-academic pursuits.
<u>Catholic or non-Catholic</u>	
<u>Cost</u>	
<u>Size</u>	Important, especially after attending a small school.
<u>University or College</u>	Do you know the difference?
<u>Location</u>	There is much to be said for going away to school but don't go East just for snob value. Also consider whether the college is in a city or in the country. Availability of ski slopes etc. is NOT necessarily an advantage.
<u>All men or co-ed</u>	
<u>Position of fraternities on campus</u>	Varies all the way from tyranny to non-existence.
<u>Course offerings, strengths and requirements.</u>	As related to your own requirements, abilities, interests and personality. Note also the "year abroad" programs. If you are uncertain about your

	ultimate field, two years of liberal arts are a fairly safe start.
Colleges attended by your parents	Alumni's sons are still given a little extra consideration, though not very much.
Recommendations about various colleges.	Those from students currently in the school are often very helpful, but beware of alumni and especially elderly alumni whose information is often quite out of date, but whose enthusiasm increases with the years.
Computers.	These are entering the field of college-selection. Most of the present programs seem quite unreliable; but there is some gain from answering the elaborate questionnaire that the candidate has to submit. Being forced to make this mental effort is possibly worth the fee charged. The College Locater Service of the C.E.E.B. is promised for this September.

The following considerations may safely be ignored:

Prestige.	There are many good reasons for wanting to go to, say, Harvard but ivy is not one of them.
Nearest girls' school	Irrelevant, and anyway never seems to be a problem.
The Group.	"All my friends are going to . . . "

6. WHAT ARE COLLEGES LOOKING FOR? Colleges vary in the relative importance they attach to these items, but their decision usually takes into account:

High School Record.	Grades and rank in class. Most colleges recognize that the rank in a Priory class is not comparable to the rank at a public school.
Recommendation.	For your comfort, this is not just Father Paul's opinion. He consults

	the other relevant faculty men. But clearly this has to be the truth, as seen here. Your son can help us by letting us know early in his senior year of any specialized, or out of school interests.
Test Scores.	Especially S.A.T. Verbal.
Activities & Interests.	Colleges are more interested in depth of interest and of participation than in multiplicity. It is better to do a few things thoroughly than many cursorily.
Interviews.	Especially with visiting admissions officers, and to some extent with local alumni (e.g. by members of the Notre Dame club of St. Louis)
Geography	Many schools seek a diverse student body, but not many have, and hardly any admit to having, quotas.
Sons of Alumni	At least they are turned down with greater regret.

Many colleges construct a graph showing "academic rating" and "personality rating" thus:

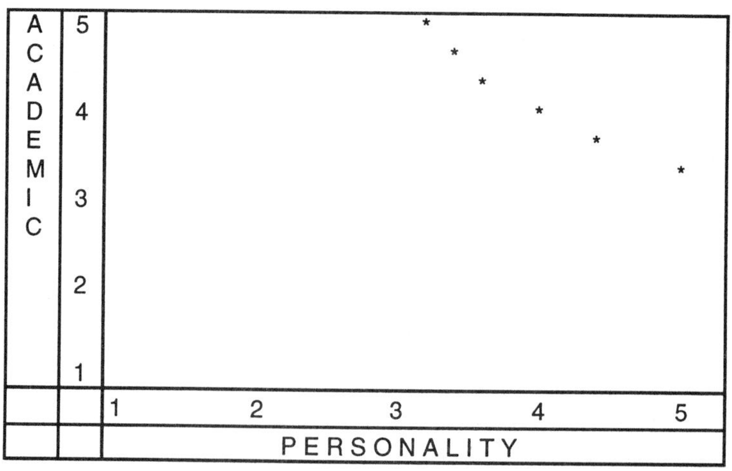

The ideal candidate is in the top right hand corner. Those accepted tend to fall inside the dotted arc. The radius of the arc depends on how competitive entry is. Colleges are asking increasingly "What can you do for the college?"

7. PROCEDURE — Your son should write to the Admissions Office of the colleges in which he is interested saying that he is a (junior) at St. Louis Priory School, expecting to graduate in . . . and wishes to apply for admission (and financial aid) in (Sept. 73), in the department of (engineering, modern languages, etc., as appropriate). Please send relevant catalogues, information, and application forms. If he is a candidate for "early decision" (8), he should say so.

This can be done late in the junior year, or in the following summer, or early in the senior year. After studying the catalogues and requirements you should be able to draw up a SHORT LIST of about three schools, *but one of these must be a college to which your son's admission is certain, and to which he would be at least content to go.*

8. EARLY DECISION — Some colleges have an "early decision" program whereby they will let a candidate have their decision well ahead of the normal date. In return the candidate, if accepted, must actually attend the college. The candidate gains by being freed from worry about college entry and the college gains by knowing that this student will, in fact, be there next September. A student can apply for E.D. at only one college and must go there if accepted by them. Some colleges even forbid other applications until they have made their decision.

9. VISITS — It is very helpful to visit colleges. This can be done at any time, but most usefully in the summer after the junior year, or at Thanksgiving or even Christmas. You will be much more welcome if you write or call for an appointment, and anyway this is only civil. The candidate should take a record of his grades, rank in class, and test scores. It is best if he is interviewed alone, and he, not his parents, should be evidently carrying the ball.

10. INTERVIEWS — The interviews with college admissions people (here or at the college) or with local alumni are an important part of tbe general impression the college forms of a candidate. It

is worth giving some thought to the obvious questions ("why do you want to go to college? Why to this college? What are your interests, hobbies, reading habits? What can you contribute?" etc.)

It is hard to advise your son beyond his telling the truth (harder than it sounds) and remembering that he is not the interviewer but the interviewed. On the other hand he should not be a doormat to be trampled on, nor should he sell himself short. His appearance will increasingly, I expect, be regarded as significant and prognostic.

11. APPLICATION FORMS

Your son is responsible for sending in his own application form in time and for letting us have the school's application form in time. Sometimes both are on the same form, in which case he fills out his part and hands it to Fr. Paul for completion and despatch. We send the colleges a complete record of your son's high-school grades, tests and activities to date, and automatically send supplementary transcripts at Christmas, Easter and the end of the school year to all colleges in which your son is still interested, and which are still interested in him.

12. TESTS

Your son is responsible for signing up for and taking the tests required by his colleges, but the school will advise him and will publicize the dates of the tests, and the dates on which entries are due.

There are two types of entrance test, those run by the College Entrance Examination Board (C.E.E.B.) and referred to as "College Boards", and those run by the American College Testing Program. (A.C.T.)

The College Board runs:

PSAT / NMSQT A test taken by Juniors.

S.A.T. Scholastic Aptitude Test. This produces a verbal score (V) and a numerical score (M), and tests ability rather than achievement.

C.B.A.T. College Board Achievement Tests. These test actual achievement in various subjects.

[N.B. These are now called S.A.T. I and S.A.T. II.]

Provided that your son uses *exactly* the same name, initials, etc. on each testing, the C.E.E.B. will send colleges all his test scores to date. The C.E.E.B. also administers the Advanced Placement program in May.

A.C.T. consists of one test with four sub-headings: English, Math, Social Studies reading, and Natural Sciences reading. It is designed to test both ability and achievement. Most colleges use the "composite" score, an average of the other four.

Special coaching has little value for the aptitude tests, and nervousness has little effect on the results, but a study of chapters 5, 6 & 8 of "*How to Prepare for College Entrance Examinations*" can be useful; so can the use of vocabulary flash-cards. Above all, a good night's rest before the examination is essential. To be feeling sleepy or costive makes clear thought very difficult.

13. CANDIDATES REPLY DATE

Although some colleges still require a reply from accepted candidates within a stated time, most use the candidates' reply date, normally in the first week of May. If a senior finds himself due to reply to one college before he will have heard from all the others, he should let Fr. Paul know at once.

14. FINANCES

Costs have risen, are rising and will continue to rise. The main headings are:

Room and board
Tuition and fees
extras
Traveling
Personal expenses

Besides the parents, there are various ways of meeting these costs.

Scholarships: are available, the basis being a mixture of ability and need. To assess the need, most colleges use the elaborate and detailed form produced by the College Scholarship Service. Those that do so will all offer your son the same (or very similar) total amount of assistance, but the proportions of gift, loan and job may vary. Note also the ROTC scholarship programs.

Jobs: are available at most colleges as well as during the summer holidays, though the latter are scarcer each year.

Loans: Many colleges have their own loan programs. There are also loans available under N.D.E.A. for up to $1000 a year and $5000 in all. Repayment at 3% starts nine months after the end of education and must be completed in ten years. Up to half may be forgiven to those who teach in public or nonprofit (that's us) schools. There are also insurance policies, loans through banks, etc. Tuition Plan has a college plan.

Cooperative programs. Some schools in some fields have programs whereby the student can spend e.g. two semesters in school and one in industry, being paid for the latter.

15. CONFERENCES Your son will receive a certain amount of guidance from us in the normal course of events, but in addition Fr. Paul is always glad to meet with families to discuss colleges. It is most productive if the family has done a certain amount of homework on this document and on college catalogues, before the meeting, and then if parents and son all come out at the same time.

16. S.O.S. Two organizations, Catholic College Admissions and Information Center, 3805 McKinley St. N.W., Washington, D.C. 20015, and College Admissions Center, 610 Church Street, Evanston, Illinois 60201, attempt to pair off students who have not been accepted, and colleges with vacancies. I understand that they have had considerable success.

17. TRANSFERS It is preferable to spend the four undergraduate years in the same school, and deliberately to plan otherwise is to choose a second-best. There may, however, be compelling reasons for this. Before considering a transfer one should find out what, if any, loss of credit it will entail, and whether the courses will fit in with what he has already taken.

18. CONCLUSION As college entry, especially into the best known schools,

becomes increasingly competitive, it is important for parents and sons to look to an ever wider range of colleges. It is especially unwise (and also untrue) to let your son believe that his happiness for the next four years depends on entry into one particular college. Many schools which may have been of little account twenty years ago are now excellent. Time spent on surveying the field is normally time well spent.

TH:jk
June 1972

Appendix E 10: School Profile for 1967. (*See* p.332):

SAINT LOUIS PRIORY SCHOOL
500 South Mason Road
Creve Coeur, Missouri
Telephone: 314-434-3690

1. <u>HISTORY</u> The school was founded in 1955, at the invitation of a group of Saint Louis citizens, by the English Benedictine Abbey of Ampleforth, which has conducted a school, Ampleforth College, in Yorkshire, England since 1802, and in other places, starting with Westminster Abbey, since an unrecorded date before the Norman Conquest in 1066. The faculty consists of English and American monks and laymen. The English members of the faculty are mostly graduates of Oxford University.

2. <u>ADMISSION</u> Entrance into the school is based on competitive examination, interview and previous record. Last year we had just over 4 1/2 candidates for each place.

3. <u>S.A.T. PROFILE FOR SENIORS</u>

	Dec. 1964		Dec. 1965		Dec. 1966	
	V.	M.	V.	M.	V.	M.
750-800	0	3	1	0	1	3
700-749	2	8	1	5	3	5
650-699	6	5	1	4	2	3
600-649	10	6	7	6	6	2
550-599	4	7	5	9	5	10
500-549	6	2	8	3	5	1
450-499	0	0	2	1	3	1
400-449	3	1	3	0	0	0
Below 400	1	0	1	1	0	0
N	32	32	29	29	25	25
Median	605	646	551	608	593	617
Mean	586	647	543	612	598	639

4. <u>C.E.E.B.</u> <u>A.P.Tests</u> In May 1965, 23 seniors out of 34 took 58 tests in Latin 5 (11), English (19), Math (17), Chemistry (10) and Physics (1), for an average score of 2.97. In May 1966, 22 seniors out of 31 took 50 tests in Latin 5 (8), English (14), Math (10), Chemistry (4), Physics (9) and American History (5) for an average score of 2.34. In May 1967, 19 seniors out of 28 took 38 tests in Latin 5 (6), English (13), Math (7), Chemistry (8) and American History (4), for an average score of 2.47.

5. GRADES Our grading system is explained on the transcript. Each class is divided into sets by merit. Grades in A sets are worth more than those in B sets. The rank in class is worked out on a weighted system, but the average is a simple average of all grades regardless of set. A grade in the 90s is quite unusual. 70 is steady, respectable work. We have 3 terms in the school year. Seniors' grades are automatically reported to the colleges concerned in late December, late March and June. In view of the importance often attached to rank in class, it may be noted that the last junior who failed his courses with us went direct into his senior year in public school and was on the Honor Roll. After all due allowance for psychological factors, this is a thought-provoking event

6. COLLEGE ENTRANCE So far all graduates have entered four year Colleges. The list is:

Amherst College
University of Arkansas
Boston College
Bowdoin College
Brown University
California Institute of Technology
University of Chicago
Coe College
Colorado College
University of Colorado
Cornell University
University of Detroit
Drury College
Duke University
Fairfield University
Florissant Novitiate S.J.
Georgetown University
Gonzaga University
Hamilton College
Harvard University
College of the Holy Cross
Indiana University
John Carroll University
University of Kansas
Kenrick Seminary (Diocesan)
Lawrence University
Loyola University of New Orleans
University of Manitoba
Marquette University
Massachusetts Institute of Technology
University of Miami
University of Michigan
Middlebury College
University of Missouri, Columbia
Missouri School of Mines, Rolla
Northwestern University
University of Notre Dame
Oakland University
Parks Aeronautical College
University of Pennsylvania
Princeton University
Regis College
Rensselaer Polytechnic Institute
Saint Benedict's College
Saint John's University, Collegeville
Saint Joseph's College, Rensselaer
Saint Louis University
Saint Michael's, University of Toronto
University of San Francisco
University of Santa Clara
Spring Hill College
Stanford University
Tufts University
Villanova University
University of Virginia

Washington and Lee University
Washington University
Wesleyan University
Westminster College
University of Wisconsin
Worcester Polytechnic Institute
Yale University

7. OTHER INFORMATION

We shall be glad to answer any further questions and would welcome your suggestions of other information that would be useful to colleges.

TH.jl
30 October 1967

Timothy Horner, O.S.B.
Headmaster

Appendix F 1: Table of Results by Sport and Season. (*See* p.344):

[N.B. 1. These tables are incomplete because our records are incomplete. Perhaps participants may be able, from accurate memories, to supplement these data.

2. 1956-57 means Sept. 1956 – June 1957, but for football and cross-country, 1973 means Sept. – Dec. 1973.]

a. For the High School:

Football

	V			B			C		
	W	L	T	W	L	T	W	L	T
1956-57							2	3	
57-58				2	4		0	5	
*58-59	2	1		2	2	1			
59-60	1	6	1	1	3				
60-61	3	5		1	3				
61-62	1	7		5	0				
62-63	3	5		0	4	1			
63-64	5	3		3	2				
64-65	6	1	1	2	2				
65-66	1	7		3	2				
66-67	1	7		3	1	1			
67-68	4	4		7	0		5	1	
68-69	3	4	1	7	0		4	1	1
69-70	6	1	1	2	2	3	4	2	
70-71	5	2		3	3		5	0	1
71-72	4	3	1	4	1	1	3	2	1
72-73	7	0	1	7	1		4	3	
1973	9	1		3	3	1	4	2	1

* = This year our team was JV in all sports.

Soccer

	V			B			C		
	W	L	T	W	L	T	W	L	T
1956-57							2	0	
57-58				0	3	1	0	1	
58-59	2	7	1	1	0				
59-60	0	4	3	2	3				
60-61	4	4		1	3				
61-62	3	3	1	0	4				
62-63	3	4	2	?	?				
63-64	4	4	1	4	5	2			
64-65	3	5	2	5	4	1			
65-66	2	7	4	5	2	3			
66-67	4	8	2	4	7	5			
67-68	3	12	3	2	8	3	4	3	1
68-69	5	10	6	5	6	4	4	2	1
69-70	9	10	1	3	6	1	0	6	4
70-71	7	10	4	7	3	4	3	7	1
71-72	7	7	1	8	2	2	3	4	3
* 72-73	14	0	1	9	6	5	4	4	3

* A reliable alumnus remembers the record for 72-73 as 13-13 3. It seems probable that he is including the results of the soccer summer camp. For the season, our yearbook records 14-0-1 as above.

Cross-Country

	V		B	
	W	L	W	L
62-63	0	3		
63-64	1	5		
64-65	2	4		
65-66	5	3	1	1
66-67	2	10		
67-68	2	10		
68-69	1	9		
69-70	3	9		
70-71	2	8		
71-72	1	3		
72-73	3	6		
1973	1	6		

Basketball

	V		B		C	
	W	L	W	L	W	L
1956-57					2	11
57-58			2	5	1	6
58-59			2	4	0	2
59-60	2	?	4	?	0	?
60-61	6	11	6	9	3	3
61-62	1	16	0	9	0	?
62-63	7	15	8	8	0	8
63-64	16	5	2	12		
64-65	10	9	10	6		
65-66	11	13	2	11		
66-67	14	9	7	11		
67-68	24	3	5	12	6	7
68-69	18	7	10	10	13	0
69-70	10	10	8	12	10	2
70-71	7	15	7	9	8	6
71-72	14	11	10	10	3	7
72-73	18	9	6	13	0	10

Wrestling

	V	
	W	L
66-67	0	2
67-68	0	4
68-69	0	5
69-70	1	5
70-71		
71-72	0	3
72-73	1	0

Baseball

	V			B		C	
	W	L	T	W	L	W	L
1956-57						0	2
57-58				0	3		
58-59	?	3		?	2		
59-60	0	5		2	2		
60-61	4	9		2	5		
61-62	1	1					
62-63	1	6					
63-64	2	6					
64-65	1	11	1				
65-66	2	6		1	2		
66-67	3	12		0	12		
67-68	6	8		3	6		
68-69	4	8		3	8		
69-70	6	10					
70-71	2	2					
71-72*	0	3					
72-73	12	10		4	5		

* = incomplete

Track

	V		B		C	
	W	L	W	L	W	L
1956-57					1	0
57-58			3	1		
58-59	0	1				
59-60	0	4				
60-61						
61-62						
62-63	0	1				
63-64	1	2				
64-65						
65-66						
66-67	1	7				
67-68	2	5				
68-69	1	5	5*	0		
69-70	3	5				
70-71						
71-72	1	1				
72-73	5	5				

* = won ABC meet

Tennis

	V			B		
	W	L	T	W	L	T
1956-57						
57-58				5	0	1
58-59	5	2	1			
59-60	3	4	1	1	4	1
60-61	2	5	1			
61-62	4	3		1	2	
62-63	2	6		1	4	1
63-64	3	5	1			
64-65	3	6				
65-66	5	7		4	3	
66-67	11	6		4	7	
67-68	4	4		3	3	
68-69	5	9		5	7	
69-70	4	8		8	4	
70-71	5	4		3	7	
71-72	?	?		?	?	
72-73	6	7		4	4	

Swimming

	V	
	W	L
1959-60	3	4
66-67	1	2
67-68	1	3
68-69	-	-
69-70	3	3
70-71	1	4
71-72	?	?
72-73	-	-

Rugby Football

	V	
	W	L
1958-59	1	0
59-60		
60-61	1	0
61-62		
62-63		
63-64		
64-65		
65-66		
66-67		
67-68		
68-69	1	0
69-70		
70-71		
71-72	0	1
72-73	5	0

b. For the Junior House. (See *p.352*):

School	Football			Soccer			Basketball		Baseball		Track		Rugby	
Year	W	L	T	W	L	T	W	L	W	L	W	L	W	L
58 - 59	4	1	0											
59 – 60	1	1	0				0	9						
60 – 61														
61 - 62	0	8	0											
62 - 63														
63 - 64	1	4	0											
64 - 65	2	5	1				22	3						
65 - 66	5	1	1				20	6						
66 - 67	6	1	0	6	1	2	14	8	2	0	1	1		
67 - 68	6	2	1	5	0	2	20	4			1	0		
68 - 69	7	1	0											
69 - 70	6	0	0	5	3	1	16	2	2	1	1	2		
70 - 71	4	3	0	6	2	2								
71 - 72	5	2	0	5	1	1	3*	2*					2	0
72 - 73	3	3	0	4	2	0	1	8	0	2	2	0		

* = incomplete

INDEX

Note: People are listed as they were usually known: Fr. Curtin is listed under "Curtin", but Fr. Columba under "Columba". They are given the rank that they held at the time, e.g. *Abbot* Basil, though he later became Cardinal.